W9-BUP-464

Fodor's 2012

CANCÚN AND THE

RIVIERA MAYA

Fodor's Travel Publications   New York, Toronto, London, Sydney, Auckland
www.fodors.com

Eugene Fodor:
The Spy Who Loved Travel

As Fodor's celebrates our 75th anniversary, we are honoring the colorful and adventurous life of Eugene Fodor, who revolutionized guidebook publishing in 1936 with his first book, *On the Continent, The Entertaining Travel Annual.*

Eugene Fodor's life seemed to leap off the pages of a great spy novel. Born in Hungary, he spoke six languages and graduated from the Sorbonne and the London School of Economics. During World War II he joined the Office of Strategic Services, the budding spy agency for the United States. He commanded the team that went behind enemy lines to liberate Prague, and recommended to Generals Eisenhower, Bradley, and Patton that Allied troops move to the capital city. After the war, Fodor worked as a spy in Austria, posing as a U.S. diplomat.

In 1949 Eugene Fodor—with the help of the CIA—established Fodor's Modern Guides. He was passionate about travel and wanted to bring his insider's knowledge of Europe to a new generation of sophisticated Americans who wanted to explore and seek out experiences beyond their borders. Among his innovations were annual updates, consulting local experts, and including cultural and historical perspectives and an emphasis on people—not just sites. As Fodor described it, "The main interest and enjoyment of foreign travel lies not only in 'the sites,' . . . but in contact with people whose customs, habits, and general outlook are different from your own."

Eugene Fodor died in 1991, but his legacy, Fodor's Travel, continues. It is now one of the world's largest and most trusted brands in travel information, covering more than 600 destinations worldwide in guidebooks, on Fodors.com, and in ebooks and iPhone apps. Technology and the accessibility of travel may be changing, but Eugene Fodor's unique storytelling skills and reporting style are behind every word of today's Fodor's guides.

Our editors and writers continue to embrace Eugene Fodor's vision of building personal relationships through travel. We invite you to join the Fodor's community at fodors.com/community and share your experiences with like-minded travelers. Tell us when we're right. Tell us when we're wrong. And share fantastic travel secrets that aren't yet in Fodor's. Together, we will continue to deepen our understanding of our world.

Happy 75th Anniversary, Fodor's! Here's to many more.

Tim Jarrell, Publisher

FODOR'S CANCÚN AND THE RIVIERA MAYA 2012

Editor: Margaret Kelly

Writers: Marlise Kast, Steven McCutcheon-Rubio

Production Editors: Evangelos Vasilakis, Emily Cogburn

Maps & Illustrations: David Lindroth, *cartographers;* Bob Blake, Rebecca Baer, *map editors;* William Wu, *information graphics*

Design: Fabrizio La Rocca, *creative director;* Guido Caroti, Siobhan O'Hare, *art directors;* Tina Malaney, Nora Rosansky, Chie Ushio, *designers;* Melanie Marin, *senior picture editor*

Cover Photo: (The Nunnery, Chichén Itzá): José Fuste Raga/age fotostock

Production Manager: Angela L. McLean

ISBN 978-0-679-00964-1

SPECIAL SALES

This book is available at special discounts for bulk purchases for sales promotions or premiums. Special editions, including personalized covers, excerpts of existing books, and corporate imprints, can be created in large quantities for special needs. For more information, write to Special Markets/Premium Sales, 1745 Broadway, MD 3-1, New York, NY 10019, or e-mail specialmarkets@randomhouse.com.

AN IMPORTANT TIP & AN INVITATION

Although all prices, opening times, and other details in this book are based on information supplied to us at press time, changes occur all the time in the travel world, and Fodor's cannot accept responsibility for facts that become outdated or for inadvertent errors or omissions. So **always confirm information when it matters,** especially if you're making a detour to visit a specific place. Your experiences—positive and negative—matter to us. If we have missed or misstated something, **please write to us.** Share your opinion instantly through our online feedback center at fodors.com/contact-us.

PRINTED IN CHINA

10 9 8 7 6 5 4 3 2 1

CONTENTS

Fodor's Features

MAPS

ABOUT THIS BOOK

Our Ratings

At Fodor's, we spend considerable time choosing the best places in a destination so you don't have to. By default, anything we recommend in this book is worth visiting. But some sights, properties, and experiences are so great that we've recognized them with additional accolades. Orange **Fodor's Choice** stars indicate our top recommendations; black stars highlight places we deem **Highly Recommended**; and **Best Bets** call attention to top properties in various categories. Disagree with any of our choices? Care to nominate a new place? Visit our feedback center at www.fodors.com/feedback.

TripAdvisor ⊙⊙

Fodor's partnership with TripAdvisor helps to ensure that our hotel selections are timely and relevant, taking into account the latest customer feedback about each property. Our team of expert writers selects what we believe will be the top choices for lodging in a destination. Then, those choices are reinforced by TripAdvisor reviews, so only the best properties make the cut.

Hotels

Hotels have private bath, phone, TV, and air-conditioning, and do not offer meals unless we specify that in the review. We always list facilities but not whether you'll be charged an extra fee to use them.

> For expanded hotel reviews, visit **Fodors.com**

Restaurants

Unless we state otherwise, restaurants are open for lunch and dinner daily. We mention dress only when there's a specific requirement and reservations only when they're essential or not accepted—it's always best to book ahead.

Credit Cards

We assume that restaurants and hotels accept credit cards. If not, we'll note it in the review.

Budget Well

Hotel and restaurant price categories from ¢ to $$$$ are defined in the opening pages of the respective chapters. For attractions, we always give standard adult admission fees; reductions are usually available for children, students, and senior citizens.

Listings
★ Fodor's Choice
★ Highly recommended
⊠ Physical address
✢ Directions or Map coordinates
⌂ Mailing address
☎ Telephone
🖷 Fax
⊕ On the Web
✍ E-mail
🎟 Admission fee
⊘ Open/closed times
Ⓜ Metro stations
▭ No credit cards

Hotels & Restaurants
🛏 Hotel
🛏 Number of rooms
♨ Facilities
🍽 Meal plans
✕ Restaurant
🍷 Reservations
🎩 Dress code
↘ Smoking

Outdoors
🏌 Golf
⛺ Camping

Other
👪 Family-friendly
⇨ See also
⊠ Branch address
☞ Take note

Experience
Cancún

WHAT'S WHERE

Numbers refer to chapters

2 Cancún. As the gateway to Riviera Maya, this thriving beach city is Mexico's most popular tourist destination, with a nightlife that has made it the Spring Break capital of the world. In the beach-front area known as "Zona Hotelera," high-rise resorts offer creature comforts. Hotels inland at Cancún's downtown "El Centro" are reasonably priced and will give a more authentic Mexican experience.

3 The Caribbean Coast. The dazzling white sands and glittering blue waters of the Riviera Maya beckon everyone from snorkelers and sunbathers to spa goers and bird-watchers. Although most travelers visit for the sugary beaches, this region also offers the seaside ruins of Tulum, the jungle-clad pyramids of Cobá, and the sidewalk cafés of Playa del Carmen. Catering to families are the numerous theme parks, dolphin programs, and hidden cenotes. Some of the best spas in the world are located here.

4 Isla Mujeres. A 30-minute jaunt across the water from Cancún, Isla Mujeres is light years away in temperament. This quaint fishing village is made up of dirt roads gener-ally traveled by golf cart, scooter, or bike. It's more laid-back, less crowded, and cheaper than almost any-where on the mainland.

5 Cozumel. The island is hugely popular with scuba divers and cruise-ship pas-sengers. Ever since Jacques Cousteau first made Cozu-mel's interconnected series of coral reefs famous in the 1970s, divers and snorkelers have flocked here. Giant ships ferry day-trippers to Cozumel. Avoid the crowds by visiting the island's windward side in search of crumbled monu-ments to the goddess Ixchel.

6 Yucatán and Campeche States. Mérida, the capital city of Yucatán State, is the cultural hub of the entire pen-insula. Known for its weekend festivals, Mérida's restaurants, hotels, shops, and museums bring visitors back year after year. Near the remote north coast, you'll find shell-strewn beaches and charming vil-lages. The state's major claim to fame, however, is its spec-tacular Mayan architecture, including sites at Chichén Itzá and Uxmal.

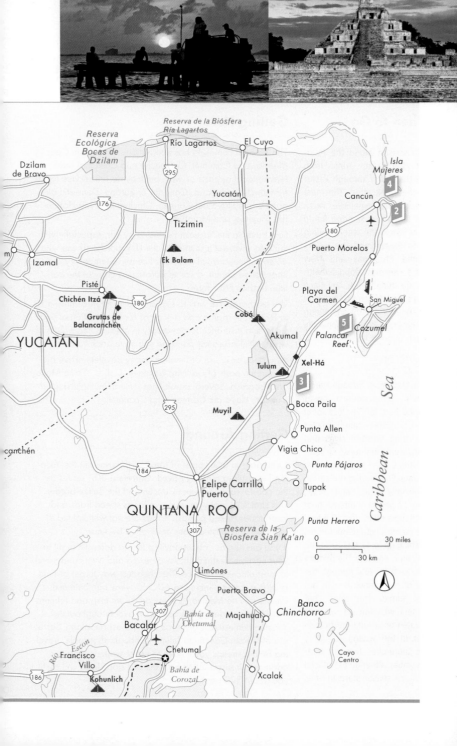

THE YUCATÁN PENINSULA PLANNER

When to Go

High season along the Mexican Caribbean runs from mid-December through Easter (or the week after). The most popular (and expensive) vacation times are *Semana Santa* (Holy Week, the week leading up to Easter) and the weeks around Christmas and New Year's. Resorts popular with college students (i.e., any place with a beach) tend to fill up in the summer months and during Spring Break season (generally March through April).

CLIMATE

From November through March, winter temperatures hover around 27°C (80°F). Occasional winter storms called *nortes* can bring blustery skies and sharp winds that make air temperatures drop and swimming unappealing. During the spring (especially April and May), there's a period of intense heat that tapers off in June. The hottest months, with temperatures reaching up to 43°C (110°F), are May, June, and July. The primary rainy season, July through the end of September, is also hot and humid. The rains that farmers welcome in summer threaten occasional hurricanes later in the season, primarily mid-September through mid-November, although the official hurricane season starts in June.

Getting Here

The Yucatán Peninsula has international airports in Cancún, Mérida, and Cozumel. Campeche and Chetumal have international airports as well, but they do not service flights from the United States, Canada, or Europe. Domestic airports are in Playa del Carmen, Chichén Itzá, Isla Holbox, Isla Mujeres, and Majahual.

Few travel to the Yucatán Peninsula by car, especially with the risks involved just south of the U.S. border. Those who do so will need a valid driver's license, a temporary car-importation permit, a car registration, a copy of the car title, and an FM-T form.

The most practical way to explore the Yucatán Peninsula is to fly to your region and rent a car for the duration of your stay. Auto insurance is mandatory in Mexico, regardless of what travel-insurance package you have back home.

As a popular cruise destination, many travelers arrive by ship at the ports of Cancún, Cozumel, Calica, Costa Maya, and Progreso. Several cruise lines include multiple stops in Cancún, Playa del Carmen, and Cozumel.

Getting Around

Compared to other parts of Mexico, the roads in the Yucatán Peninsula are nicely paved. Carretera 307 serves as the coastal route between Cancún and the Belize border. This stretch of highway is known for its speed traps and large *topes* (speed bumps). Roads are not well lighted at night, so aim to be at your destination by sunset.

If you are nervous about driving, take a domestic flight to your ultimate destination; Aeroméxico and Mexicana travel to most places in Mexico. The cheapest way to get around is by bus. Luxury liners like ADO (⊕ *www.ado.com.mx*), Omnibuses de Mexico (⊕ *www.odm.com.mx*), and Primera Plus (⊕ *www.primeraplus.com.mx*) travel throughout the Yucatán Peninsula. *Colectivos* (mini-buses) run along Carretera 307 from Cancún to Tulum. Although affordable, traveling by bus means you'll have to either walk or organize additional transportation from the bus stop. Taxis will cost you about $20 per hour.

Festivals and Celebrations

Fiesta de la Concepción Inmaculada *(Feast of the Immaculate Conception)* is observed for six days in the villages across the Yucatán, with processions, dances, fireworks, and bullfights culminating on the feast day itself, December 8. Among the many Navidad (Christmas) events are *posadas,* during which families gather to eat and sing, and lively parades with colorful floats and brass bands, culminating December 24, on **Nochebuena** *(Holy Night).*

Carnaval festivities take place the week before Lent, with parades, floats, outdoor dancing, music, and fireworks; they're especially spirited in Mérida, Cozumel, Isla Mujeres, Campeche, and Chetumal.

Semana Santa is the most important holiday in Mexico. Reenactments of the Passion, family parties and meals, and religious services are held during this week leading up to Easter Sunday.

Cinco de Mayo, May 5, is the Mexican national holiday commemorating Mexico's defeat of the French army at Puebla in 1862. Since 1991, the **Cancún Jazz Festival,** held the last weekend in May, has featured such top musicians as Wynton Marsalis and Gato Barbieri.

Founder's Day, August 17, celebrates the founding of Isla Mujeres with six days of races, folk dances, music, and regional cuisine. **Día de Independencia** *(Independence Day)* is celebrated throughout Mexico with fireworks and parties beginning at 11 pm on September 15, and continuing on the 16th. **Fiesta del Cristo de las Ampollas** *(Feast of the Christ of the Blisters)* is an important religious event that takes place September 17 to 27, with daily mass and processions during which people dress in typical clothing; dances, bullfights, and fireworks take place in Ticul and other small villages.

Ten days of festivities and a solemn parade mark the **Fiesta del Cristo de Sitilpech,** during which the Christ image of Sitilpech village is carried to Izamal. The biggest dances (with fireworks) are toward the culmination of the festivities on October 28.

Día de los Muertos *(Day of the Dead),* called Hanal Pixan in Mayan, is a joyful holiday during which graves are refurbished and symbolic meals are prepared to lure the spirits of family members back to earth for the day. Deceased children are associated with All Saints Day, November 1, while adults are feted on All Souls Day, November 2.

Money Matters

Mexican currency, the peso, comes in denominations of 20, 50, 100, 200, and 500. When you arrive, it's a good idea to have smaller bills and some *centavos* (change) to pay for tips, bus fare, or taxis. Avoid having anything larger than a $50, since change is sometimes difficult to find. Do not accept damaged pesos, which are of no value to merchants or banks.

Banks are open Monday through Friday from 9 to 4, and will accept traveler's checks for a small processing fee. Make sure you bring your passport to the bank, since you'll need it even when exchanging U.S. dollars.

ATMs are the most convenient ways to get cash, are readily available, and charge the official exchange rate. Before you leave home, make sure your PIN has only four numbers, and inquire about foreign transaction fees processed by your U.S. bank. Larger resorts have ATMs on the premises, and most hotels will exchange dollars for pesos.

Most businesses accept major credit cards, but may add a surcharge to compensate for their own hefty processing fee. In Mexico, American Express, Discover, and Diner's Club are not as readily accepted as Visa or MasterCard. If you are traveling south of Felipe Carrillo Puerto toward Belize, make sure you have enough cash, since the coastal towns have neither banks nor ATMs.

IF YOU LIKE

Spas

There are dozens of spa resorts scattered throughout the Yucatán Peninsula, primarily along the coast. Here decadent body treatments are offered in luxurious seaside settings. Some incorporate indigenous healing techniques into their services, using *temazcal* (an ancient Mayan sweat-lodge ritual), and plant extracts in aromatherapy facials. Others feature seawater and marine algae in mineral-rich thalassotherapy treatments; still others go the high-tech route with cutting-edge flotarium tanks, seven-jet Vichy massage tables, and Kinesis fitness machines. You won't have any trouble getting your pampering fix here—especially in the areas around Playa del Carmen and the rest of the Riviera Maya—but you'll likely pay top dollar for it.

The spas that get the most consistent raves include Punta Tanchacté's **Zoëtry Paraíso de la Bonita Resort and Thalasso.** Here you can soak away stress in specially built saltwater pools. **Mandarin Oriental** in Punta Maroma has relaxing, womblike flotation tanks and **Banyan Tree,** in Mayakoba, has a 12-step Rainforest Experience that combines hydrotherapy with infrared light to revitalize the body. The **Spa at JW Marriott,** Cancún, is justifiably famous for its Mayan-inspired treatments like the chocolate massage, ground-corn exfoliation, and chaya detoxification. At **The Tides,** in Punta Bete, it's hard to imagine a sweeter way to end the day than a honey massage.

Diving and Snorkeling

The turquoise waters of the Mexican Caribbean Coast are strewn with stunning coral reefs, underwater canyons, and sunken shipwrecks—all teeming with marine life. The visibility can reach 100 feet, so even on the surface you'll be amazed by what you can see.

Made famous decades ago by Jacques Cousteau, Cozumel is still considered one of the world's premier diving destinations. The **Maya Reef,** just off the western coast, stretches some 32 km (20 mi)—and more than 100 dive operators on the island offer deep dives, drift dives, wall dives, night dives, wreck dives, and dives focusing on ecology and underwater photography.

Farther south, the town of Tankah is known for its **Gorgonian Gardens,** a profusion of soft corals and sponges that has created an underwater Eden. Near the Belize border, Mexico's largest coral atoll, **Banco Chinchorro,** is a graveyard of vessels that have foundered on the corals over the centuries. Experienced divers won't want to miss Isla Contoy's **Cave of the Sleeping Sharks.** Here, at 150 feet, you can see the otherwise dangerous creatures "dozing" in a state of relaxed nonaggression.

The freshwater cenotes (sinkholes) that punctuate Quintana Roo, Yucatán, and Campeche states are also favorites with divers and snorkelers. Many of these are private and secluded, even though they lie right off the highways; others are so popular that they've become tourist destinations. At **Hidden Worlds Cenote Park** (on the highway between Xel-Há and Tankah), for example, you can float through cavernous sinkholes filled with stalactites, stalagmites, and rock formations.

Mayan Ruins

The ruins of ancient Mayan cities are magical; and they're scattered all across the Yucatán. Although **Chichén Itzá**, featuring the enormous and oft-photographed Castillo pyramid, is the most famous of the region's sites, **Uxmal** is the most graceful. Here the perfectly proportioned buildings of the Cuadrángulo de las Monjas (Nun's Quadrangle) make a beautiful "canvas" for facades carved with snakes and the fierce visages of Mayan gods. At the more easterly **Ek Balam**, workers on makeshift scaffolding brush away centuries of accumulated grime from huge monster masks that protect the mausoleum of a Mayan king. On the amazing friezes, winged figures dressed in full royal regalia gaze down.

At **Cobá**, the impressive temples and palaces—including a 79-foot-high pyramid—are surrounded by thick jungle, and only sparsely visited by tourists. In contrast, nearby **Tulum** is the peninsula's most-visited archaeological site. Although the ruins here aren't as architecturally arresting, their location—on a cliff overlooking the blue-green Caribbean—makes Tulum unique among major Mayan sites.

Farther afield, in Campeche State, the elaborate stone mural of **Balamkú** is hidden deep within another temple, sheltered from the elements for more than a millennium. Thousands of structures lie buried under the profuse greenery of Mexico's largest eco-corridor at the **Reserva de la Biosfera Calakmul**, where songbirds trill and curious monkeys hang from trees. These and other intriguing cities have been extensively excavated for your viewing pleasure.

Exotic Cuisine

Pickled onions tinged a luminous pink, blackened habanero chiles floating seductively in vinaigrette, lemonade spiked with the local plant called *chaya*—Yucatecan cuisine is different from that of any other region in Mexico. In recent years, traditional dishes made with local fruits, chiles, and spices have also embraced the influence of immigrants from Lebanon, France, Cuba, and New Orleans. The results are deliciously sublime.

Among the best-known regional specialties are *cochinita pibíl* and *pollo pibíl* (pork or chicken pit-baked in banana leaves). Both are done beautifully at **Hacienda Teya**, an elegant restaurant outside Mérida that was once a henequen hacienda. The *poc chuc* (marinated pork served with pickled onions and a plateful of other condiments) is delicious at **El Príncipe Tutul-Xiu**, an off-the-beaten-path and very authentic restaurant in the ancient Yucatán town of Maní. *Papadzules*—crumbled hard-boiled eggs rolled inside tortillas and drenched in a sauce of pumpkin seed and fried tomatoes—are a specialty at **Labná**, in Cancún's El Centro district.

In Campeche, a signature dish is *pan de cazón*, a casserole of shredded shark meat layered with tortillas, black beans, and tomato sauce; the best place to order it is at **La Pigua**, in Campeche City. The dish known as *tixin-xic* (fish marinated in orange juice and chiles and cooked over an open flame) is the dish of choice at Isla Mujeres' **Playa Lancheros Restaurant**.

Some of the Yucatán's tastiest treats come in liquid form. *Xtabentún*, a thick liqueur of fermented honey and anise, can be sipped at room temperature, poured over ice, or mixed with a splash of sparkling water.

CANCÚN AND THE RIVIERA MAYA TOP ATTRACTIONS

Tulum

(A) Although the Yucatán has plenty of ruins to choose from, none are quite as spectacular as those in Tulum. Skirting the ancient architecture is a powdery stretch of coastline that fades into four shades of turquoise water. South of the ruins are dozens of eco-lodges that operate on solar power, wind turbines, and recycled rainwater.

Cenotes

(B) For an underwater adventure, plunge into one of Mexico's sacred cenotes. These limestone pools are fed by subterranean springs that flow throughout the Yucatán. Rays of light illuminate these refreshing sinkholes; swim with the tiny fish that dart between the crevices. Experienced divers can explore the underwater tunnels that connect these hidden gems.

Isla Mujeres

(C) Find a shady spot under the arching palms of Playa Norte, a sugary beach on Isla Mujeres where time is nonexistent. Those who come here fall victim to the mañana mentality, spending days admiring tangerine sunsets while island life sweeps them away. Calm, warm waters make this aquatic paradise ideal for swimming, snorkeling, diving, or fishing.

Celestun Biosphere Reserve

(D) Located on a pristine beach west of Mérida, this 100,000-acre wildlife reserve has one of the largest colonies of flamingoes in North America, and more than 300 other species of birds. Flat-bottom boats float through the mangroves in search of turtles, crocodiles, cormorants, egrets, and herons. Nature lovers can take a break from bird-watching to enjoy the area's beaches, cenotes, or the sweetwater springs of Baldiosera.

Chichén Itzá

(E) Considered one of the Seven Wonders of the World, this archaeological city is best known for its ancient Temple of Kukulcán Also referred to as "El Castillo," the Mayan ruin stands a staggering 78 feet high and features a towering pyramid with four stairways. This surrounding area offers dozens of other archaeological sites as well as the famed Cenote Sagrado (Sacred Cenote).

Majahual and Xcalak

(F) Although a bit of a haul to get here, the colorful towns of Majahual and Xcalak are well worth the journey. This coastal paradise offers incredible offshore diving at Banco Chinchorro and the Mesoamerican Barrier Reef, the second longest in the world. Serious anglers will enjoy fly-fishing in the nearby saltwater flats of the peninsula.

Grutas de Loltun

(G) Roughly one hour southeast of Uxmal, these natural caverns show signs of man dating back to 800 BC. Illuminated pathways meander past stalactites, stalagmites, and limestone formations. Here you can admire the spectacular rays of light shining down on "musical" columns that are formed by the union of stalactites and stalagmites.

Playa del Carmen

(H) Located in the heart of Riviera Maya, Playa del Carmen has all the makings of a great vacation destination. Once a quiet fishing village, the town is booming with boutique hotels and open-air restaurants, making it one of the fastest-growing communities in Latin America. For a day of pampering, relax at one of the nearby luxury spas, or try zip-lining at Xcaret, a 250-acre ecological theme park.

FAQS

Do I need any special documents to get into the country?

Although you can enter Mexico without a passport, you must have a passport to reenter the United States. This means that you'll have to take your passport with you to Mexico if you're returning to the States. Before landing in Mexico, you'll be given an FMT form (tourist card) to be stamped at immigration. Keep this card safe, since you'll need to present it when you leave the country.

How difficult is it to travel around the country?

It's relatively easy, thanks to improved roadways and domestic airlines offering daily flights to 10 destinations in the Yucatán. Mexico's bus system is an excellent way to travel around the country. Deluxe buses are more expensive, but have air-conditioning, reclining seats, movies, and fewer stops. Intercity transportation (used mainly by locals) is extremely reliable, and a great way to experience Mexican culture.

Are the roads as bad as they say?

Compared to other parts of Mexico, the roads in the Yucatán Peninsula are safe, flat, and well maintained. The main highway between Cancún and Belize, known as Carretera 307, is clearly marked and freshly paved. Even most secondary roads like those near Majahual are in decent shape. Only in remote areas like Punta Allen will you find major potholes. Throughout the peninsula, beware of unmarked *topes* (speed bumps) that can leave you airborne. Also, be on the lookout for flooding during rainy season. Although road conditions have improved tremendously, avoid driving at night, since most areas lack street lighting. When you pick up a rental car, double check to make sure the windshield wipers are in working condition and that the tires are

in good shape. Hot summer roads tend to cause blowouts.

What should I do when a police officer pulls me over?

Although not overly common in Riviera Maya, there are some police officers who expect bribes from drivers. When renting a car, ask the agency for a "Tourist Traffic Card," which can be handed to police upon receiving a traffic violation. This voucher allows you to pay the ticket at the car-rental agency when you return the car rather than having to spend several hours at the police station. It also helps eliminate corruption.

Should I get insurance on the rental car?

Yes! Regardless of what coverage you have from your credit card or travel insurance, you must (by law) have additional Mexican auto insurance to rent a car. This mandatory cost is around $12 per day, which is sometimes more than the daily rental fee if you happened to find a good deal online. When renting a car, make sure that your insurance coverage includes an attorney and claims adjusters who will come to the scene of an accident.

Should I consider a package tour?

The Yucatán Peninsula is an easy place to get around, so there really is no need to travel with a tour group. Plus, you'll miss out on spontaneous exploration that comes with traveling at your own pace. However, if planning a trip is not your thing and you prefer to travel with a group, a package tour is always a good option. Most tour companies cover a lot of ground in a few days, and you won't have to worry about getting lost, speaking Spanish, or being ripped off along the way. If you are set on a package tour,

select one with a specific focus like Mayan history or bird-watching.

Do I need a local guide?

Guides are helpful if you're visiting a wildlife area or an archaeological site where local knowledge or history is needed. Most wildlife guides will bring a telescope or binoculars and can locate hidden animals and identify various species that the average traveler might overlook. If you do hire a guide, be sure to tip accordingly, since some (especially in rural areas) depend on tips as their main source of income.

Will I have trouble if I don't speak Spanish?

Si y no. If you stay within the main tourist areas, nearly everyone will speak English, and if they don't, someone nearby certainly will. In remote towns and areas less visited by travelers, you'll have to speak "Spanglish" or rely on a dictionary or phrase book.

Can I drink the water?

Tap water in Mexico is not potable. Most resorts and restaurants have purified water, but if you are concerned about a piece of contaminated ice ruining your vacation, then opt for bottled water.

Are there any worries about the food?

Most restaurants are clean and cater to fussy travelers. If you are sensitive to spicy food, you may have a difficult time at some of the more authentic Mexican restaurants. High-trafficked tourist areas will always have plenty of dining options, and coastal towns serve fresh-caught fish. If you visit a roadside market, unpeeled fruit or crunchy pork rinds are safe road-trip snacks. Unless you are in a nice restaurant, it's best to avoid uncooked vegetables, salads, rare meat, and milk products.

Make sure that food is thoroughly cooked and hasn't been sitting under a heat lamp.

Do I need to get any shots?

Travelers visiting the Yucatán Peninsula do not need to get vaccinations or take any special medications. According to the U.S. Centers for Disease Control and Prevention, there's some concern about malaria along the Guatemala and Belize borders in the state of Quintana Roo.

Should I bring any medications?

Mosquitoes can be a problem, especially along the coast near mangroves and jungle areas. To prevent bug bites, use insect repellent containing 10%–25% DEET. If you can bear the heat, wear long pants when you go out at night. It's a good idea to bring along antihistamine cream to keep you from scratching. Mild cases of diarrhea respond best to Imodium (known generically as Loperamide or Lomotil) or Pepto-Bismol. To avoid problems at customs, any prescription drugs you bring with you should be in their original pill bottle listed with printed identification.

Can I use my ATM card?

Yes. Most ATMs operate on the Cirrus and Plus networks, meaning they accept debit and credit cards issued by U.S. banks. Before your trip, make sure your PIN only has four numbers, since ATMs in Mexico do not recognize more digits. Foreign transaction fees can be high, as much as $10 per withdrawal.

Do most places take credit cards?

Outside of remote areas like Xcalak and Majahual, nearly all tourist-oriented businesses accept Visa and MasterCard. Many businesses that don't cater to travelers won't accept them because of high processing fees charged by their banks.

YUCATÁN PENINSULA TODAY

Government

Yucatán is one of the 31 states (plus one federal district) that comprise Mexico's federal republic. The government consists of three branches: the executive, the legislative, and the judicial. The president of Mexico is elected to a one-time, six-year term by popular vote, and holds such extensive control that the position has been coined "the six-year monarchy." For more than 70 years, the country was ruled by the powerful PRI party (Institutional Revolutionary Party). The party abused its powers, including illegal landholding, charging the public for free services, bribery, and other forms of corruption. For the last half century, the opposition party, PAN (Partido de Acciòn Nacional) organized and slowly rose to power, making Vincente Fox the new president in 2000. Despite his efforts to reduce drug trafficking and corruption, a third political party, PRD (Partido de la Revolución Democrática) began to gain momentum as a voice for the poor. In 2006, the presence of three active political parties led to a hotly contested election and a marginal victory for PAN's Felipe Calderón, who began his presidential term amid widespread protests.

Like each of Mexico's 31 states, Yucatán is headed by a governor who serves a single, six-year term. Currently serving as governor until 2013 is Ivonne Pacheco, who previously served as the mayor of Dzemul and as a state senator. Though elected by a simple majority of the populace, the actual selection of state governors has historically been largely controlled by Mexico's presidents.

Much of Yucatán's revenue (like those of the other states) actually comes from the federal government. Such funding is then channeled to the mayors for distribution to their respective municipalities.

Economy

Before 1970, the Yucatán Peninsula relied solely on agriculture to support its economy, but in the '80s, the region was successfully marketed as a travel destination, especially Cancún and the Riviera Maya. What were once small fishing villages are now bustling beach towns lined with luxury resorts. Each year millions of tourists are drawn to the area's beach resorts and archaeological sites; these attractions inject a steady cash flow into the economy. This influx of mass tourism created more jobs and a higher standard of living. Travelers have also shown more interest in local culture, and spurred the development of historical museums and exquisite Yucatán crafts, which have long been known for their quality workmanship. The Yucatán's economy is also helped by exports of up to 1,500 henequen products such as twine, rugs, and wall hangings. In the past, Yucatán's henequen had a global reputation of being "green gold." Sadly, the advent of similar man-made fibers destroyed the international market for henequen. Recently though, innovative entrepreneurs are using the plants to make other products, like alcohol and honey.

Tourism

In the late 1960s the Mexican government created a strategy to increase tourism in the Yucatán Peninsula, with Cancún selected as the primary destination. As a result, the city's population increased from 18,000 in 1976 to more than 500,000 in 2010. Growth has since expanded to neighboring regions, creating a solid infrastructure that has made the Yucatán Peninsula the most-visited destination in Mexico.

Today the country faces the challenge of protecting its natural resources while allowing development to continue. Cancún's beaches alone are lined with more than 150 towering hotels, many of which have contributed to coastal erosion. Fortunately, building restrictions are now in place in neighboring communities such as Playa del Carmen. Ecotourism in Tulum and most of Costa Maya has helped protect area wildlife and the natural surroundings.

Temporarily decreasing tourism were Hurricane Gilbert in 1988, Hurricane Wilma in 2005, and the state of the U.S. economy in 2010. Fortunately, these setbacks have not permanently affected tourism as the peninsula's driving force of economic development.

Religion

Although Mexico has no official religion, 89% of the population consider themselves Roman Catholic. Second only to Brazil, Mexico has more Catholics than anywhere else in the world, even though less than half attend church. Very few Maya people in the Yucatán Peninsula still practice traditional rituals of offerings and sacrifices of small animals. Central to the Maya religion is the idea of the duality of the soul, one part eternal, and the other supernatural. Only 7% of the population consider themselves Protestant, followed by Eastern Orthodox, Seventh-Day Adventists, Jehovah's Witnesses, and Mormons.

Sports

Soccer (or fútbol as they say in Spanish) is the most popular sport in Mexico. Locals have taken the game very seriously ever since it became a professional sport there in 1900. The country's most successful teams are Club Deportivo Guadalajara, Club América, Toluca, Cruz Azul, and Chivas.

Second to soccer is boxing, with Mexico's biggest knockout rival being Puerto Rico. Other than the United States, Mexico has produced the most boxing world champions. For over 100 years, baseball has been popular in Mexico. There are 16 teams competing in the *Liga Mexicana de Béisbol* (Mexican Baseball League).

With more than 150 fairways dotting the country, golfing has gained notoriety among the locals, and has helped promote tourism with five professional tournaments, including the Mayakoba Golf Classic.

More traditional sports include bullfighting, Mexican wrestling (also known as *lucha libre*), and *charrería*, based on a series of Mexican equestrian events.

Cash Crops

Although tourism is the peninsula's main source of income, both agriculture and fishing are also great economic contributors. Before the tourism boom, production was limited to salt, mahogany, red cedar, and chicle (traditionally used for chewing gum). Until 1960 the main crop was henequen, an indigenous plant that produces sisal fiber used to make rope. Although not as lucrative as it once was, henequen is still manufactured in the north-central region. The peninsula's eastern area raises 65% of the state's livestock, while the southern region, near Peto and Tzucacab, is known for corn, citrus, sugarcane, and cattle. Today the Yucatán Peninsula exports more than 1,500 products, ranging from sponges and oranges to furniture and chocolates.

WEDDINGS AND HONEYMOONS

Imagine yourself exchanging vows on a white sandy beach against a backdrop of swaying palms and the turquoise waters of the Caribbean. Your dream wedding can become a reality as long as you know the necessary steps to take when saying "I do" in Mexico.

Unfortunately, you'll need a lot more than just the wedding rings when organizing your tropical nuptials. Couples will need to bring passports, original birth certificates, tourist cards, and results of blood tests taken in Mexico two days before the wedding. Most clinics charge $150 per person for the required tests of RPR and HIV, and Thorax X-rays.

You also must have four witnesses at the ceremony, all of whom must be over 18 and have passports. If either the bride or groom was previously married, it's mandatory to wait a full year from the date that the divorce was final. Divorce papers must be translated into Spanish and notarized. In the case of a deceased spouse, you have to present a certified copy of the death certificate.

In Mexico the only marriages that are legally recognized are those that are conducted at the Oficina del Registro Civil (Civil Registers Office). The fee can be as much as $250, and you'll find that most people there don't speak English, so plan accordingly. Regulations vary from state to state in Mexico, so contact the Mexican Tourism Board for specifics about your desired wedding location.

Beautiful Backdrops

With so much to offer, the Yucatán Peninsula is one of the most sought-after spots for destination weddings. In fact, this growing trend in beachside nuptials has increased by 200% in the last decade. It's no wonder: the Caribbean coastline not only makes for an incredible backdrop, but it's also a great way to combine a wedding and honeymoon.

Surprisingly, exchanging vows in Mexico can be considerably cheaper than a traditional wedding back home. Some smaller hotels can organize beautiful ceremonies, including food and music, for under $5,000. If you book your entire wedding party at the hotel, special rates and upgrades are generally available, and you can have the entire place to yourselves. Between May and November, rates are at their lowest, but you might end up with a soggy ceremony, especially during hurricane months of August and September.

There are dozens of wedding planners and professional photographers in Cancún, Cozumel, Isla Mujeres, Mérida, and Playa del Carmen. Whether you choose a white sandy beach in Cozumel or a colorful hacienda in Mérida, there's no shortage of ceremony settings for your big day.

Honeymoons

The peninsula's countless treasures, ranging from Mayan ruins to fishing villages, make it a haven for honeymooners. Beach-bound newlyweds have plenty of resort options along Riviera Maya, many of which have luxury spas with treatments for two. Ideal for both weddings and honeymoons, Tulum offers ancient ruins, beautiful beaches, and dozens of eco-lodges willing to host simple weddings with vegetarian buffets and yoga classes between events. Other popular honeymoon spots are Isla Mujeres, where you can swim with nurse sharks, and Cozumel, with its excellent snorkeling and diving.

KIDS AND FAMILIES

Riddled with natural wonders, the Yuca-tán Peninsula has plenty of activities that the whole family can enjoy. The warm Caribbean waters are ideal for water sports such as swimming, snorkeling, and kayaking, and some areas even have roped-off sections designated for children. If you're vacationing in Cancún, beaches facing Bahía de Mujeres tend to have calmer waters and softer sand than those facing the Caribbean. Farther out, there may be undertows or riptides, so take note of warning signs and colored flags posted daily.

Kid-Friendly Activities

For teens, there are adrenaline-pumping water activities like Jet Skiing, banana boat rides, parasailing, and diving. Smaller children may prefer interactive programs like those available at Dolphin Discovery. There are locations in Cancún, Isla Mujeres, Cozumel, and Puerto Aven-turas, and the tour includes encounters with manatees and sea lions, and a chance to swim with the dolphins.

For parents wanting to introduce their children to history, combine a tour of the Tulum ruins with a day at the beach, or opt for the Cobá ruins, where your entire family can explore jungle trails by mountain bike. Cancún's all-inclusive resorts have plenty to keep the kids busy, including swimming pools, children's programs, and on-site water sports. The nearby Isla Shopping Village has an interactive aquarium. Also located in Zona Hotelera is Plaza Kukulcán, an upscale mall with a bowling alley, game arcade, and play area.

Isla Mujeres is home to El Garrafon National Park, where you can go snor-keling, swimming, hiking, or zip-lining. To blend nature and education, visit the island's turtle farm, where you can see res-cued turtle hatchlings and visit an on-site museum.

Choosing a Destination

Just 16 km (10 mi) south of Tulum, the Reserva de la Biosfera Sian Ka'an has hundreds of species of wildlife in their freshwater lagoons, mangrove swamps, and tropical forests. The beaches here are excellent for swimming, snorkeling, and camping.

The colorful city of Mérida has folkloric shows, free concerts, and open-air mar-kets where local crafts are sold. South of Mérida are the impressive Grutas de Lol-tun, one of the largest cave systems on the Yucatán Peninsula.

The quaint fishing villages of Puerto Morelos and Puerto Aventuras are excel-lent for families and close to the 250-acre ecological theme park, Xcaret. Here fam-ilies can experience a butterfly pavilion, bird aviary, bat cave, and dozens of water activities. Catering to adventure-seekers, the neighboring Xplor lets you swim in a stalactite river, ride in an amphibian-vehicle, or soar across the park on the lon-gest zip-line in Mexico. At the entrance to Puerto Morelos is Croco-Cun, an animal farm where you can feed monkeys and hold baby crocodiles.

To escape the heat, families can take a dip in one of the hundreds of cenotes that dot the peninsula. These freshwater pools are ideal for snorkeling and swimming. For a day of horseback riding, Rancho Loma Bonita has tours along the beach or on the jungle trails near Playa del Carmen. Although known for its snorkeling and diving, Cozumel also offers horseback riding, mini-golf, and fishing expeditions.

GREAT ITINERARIES

CANCÚN AND DAY TRIPS

Cancún is the place where you'll likely start your visit. If sunbathing, water sports, and parties that last until the wee hours of the morn are what you're after, you won't need to set foot outside the Zona Hotelera (or even your resort). If you're staying for a week or so, though, you should definitely check out some of the attractions that are an easy day-tripping distance from Cancún.

■ TIP➔ Driving is the best way to see the peninsula, especially if your time is limited. However, there's nothing in this itinerary that can't be accessed by either bus or taxi.

Days 1 and 2: Arrival and Cancún

After arriving at your hotel, spend your first day or two doing what comes naturally: lounging at the hotel pool, playing in the waves, parasailing, and going out for dinner and drinks. If you start to feel restless your second day, you can head to the Ruinas del Rey, go tequila tasting at La Destileria, or take a ride into El Centro (downtown Cancún) to browse the shops and open-air markets along Avenida Tulum and grab some authentic and delicious Mexican food.

Day 3: Cozumel or Isla Mujeres

Spend the day visiting one of the islands off Mexico's Caribbean Coast. If beach-combing and a laid-back meal of fresh seafood under a *palapa* (thatched roof) sound appealing, take a ferry from Puerto Juárez and head for Isla Mujeres. If you like underwater sea life, drive or take a bus south from Cancún to Puerto Morelos, where you can catch a boat over to Cozumel. There are more than 100 scuba and snorkeling outfits on the island, all of which run trips out to the spectacular Maya Reef.

Day 4: Playa del Carmen and Xcaret

In the morning, pack your bathing suit and towel, take a taxi to the Xcaret bus station near Playa Caracol, and catch a 9:45 bus to this magical nature park. You can easily spend an entire day here snorkeling through underwater caves, visiting the butterfly pavilion, sea-turtle nursery, and reef aquarium, and (if you reserve a spot early) bonding with dolphins. Alternatively, get up early and take a rental car south along Carretera 307 toward Playa del Carmen, about an hour and a half away. Once you arrive, head to Avenida 5 along the waterfront where you can choose from dozens of places to lunch. If you want to splurge, try the ceviche or the namesake specialty at Blue Lobster. Then spend the afternoon either wandering among the shops and cafés and watching the street performers, or else jump in the car and head 10 minutes south of town to Xcaret.

Days 5 and 6: Tulum and Cobá

If you have the time, it's worth spending a day at each of these beautiful Mayan-ruin sites near Playa del Carmen; each is entirely different from the other. Cobá, which is about a half-hour's drive west of Tulum, is a less-visited but spectacular ancient city that's completely surrounded by jungle. Tulum, the only major Mayan site built right on the water, has less-stunning architecture, but a dazzling location overlooking the Caribbean. After picking through the ruins, you can take a path down from the cliffs and laze for awhile on the fabulous beach below. Be warned, though: since Tulum is just a 45-minute drive south from Playa, it's the Yucatán's most popular Mayan site.

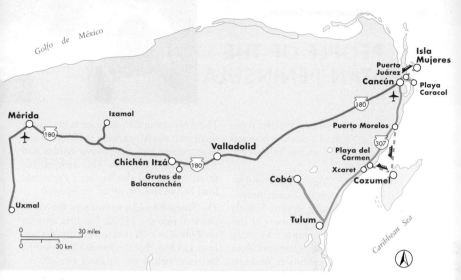

Golfo de México

Izamal

Mérida

180

Chichén Itzá

180

Grutas de
Balancanchén

Uxmal

0   30 miles

0   30 km

Valladolid

Cobá

Tulum

Isla
Mujeres

Puerto
Juárez

Cancún

180

Playa
Caracol

Puerto Morelos

307

Playa del
Carmen

Xcaret

Cozumel

Caribbean Sea

YUCATÁN AND THE MAYAN INTERIOR

If you have more than a week to spend on the peninsula, you're in luck. You'll have time to visit some of the most beautiful—and famous—ruin sites in the country, and to explore some authentic-Mexican inland communities that feel worlds away from the more touristy coast.

For Days 1 to 6, follow the itinerary outlined above in **Cancún and Day Trips.**

Day 7: Valladolid and Chichén Itzá

Get up early, check out of your hotel, and make the drive inland along Carretera 180 toward the world-renowned Chichén Itzá ruins. Stop en route for a late breakfast or early lunch in Valladolid, about 2½ hours from Cancún. One of the best places to go is the casual eatery at Cenote Zaci, where you can also swim in the lovely jade-green sinkhole. Continue another half hour to Chichén Itzá and check into one of the area hotels (the Hacienda Chichén is a terrific choice). Then spend the afternoon exploring the site before it closes at 5 pm. Climb El Castillo; check out the former marketplace, steam bath, observatory, and temples honoring formidable Mayan gods. Chill for an hour or two before the light-and-sound show, then turn in after dinner at your hotel.

Days 8 and 9: West to Mérida

Either take an easterly detour for an on-the-hour tour at the limestone caverns of Grutas de Balancanchén, or head immediately west on Carretera 180 for the hour-long drive to Mérida. After checking into a hotel in the city (Villa Mercedes is an especially delightful choice), wander the zócalo and surrounding streets. Spend the next day shopping, visiting museums, and enjoying Mérida's vibrant city scene.

Days 10 and 11: East to Cancún and Departure

The drive from Mérida or Uxmal back to Cancún will take you some five or six hours on Carretera 180, so if you're flying out of Cancún airport the same day, get an early start. Otherwise, if you can afford to take your time, stop at the lovely town of Izamal on the way back. You can take a horse-drawn carriage tour of artisans' shops, visit the stately cathedral, or climb to the top of crumbling Kinich Kakmó pyramid. Arrive in Cancún in the afternoon, take a last swim on the sugar-sand beach before dinner, and get a good night's sleep at your hotel before your departure the next day.

THE PEOPLE OF THE YUCATÁN PENINSULA

The Maya people, whose ancient ruins have made the Yucatán a world-renowned attraction, also make up the bulk of the area's population.

The Maya are the single largest indigenous group on the entire North American continent. Although predominantly located on the Yucatán, members of this group have also settled in other Mexican states such as Campeche, Quintana Roo, Tabasco, and Chiapas. Outside of Mexico, the Maya can be found in Guatemala, Belize, Honduras, and El Salvador. Their total population is estimated at about 7 million, with 1.2 million living on the Yucatán Peninsula.

The Maya are rightfully proud of their history, which dates back to a period immediately following the rise of the Olmec culture. After the fall of the Olmecs, the Maya rose to power and settled in the Yucatán Peninsula, where they developed several city-states including that of Chichén Itzá.

Mayan architecture, much of it ceremonial in nature, has been archaeologically classified as dating back some 3,000 years. Well-preserved hieroglyphics found in the Yucatán trace the presence of the Maya to 200 BC or before. More than 100 ancient Maya ruins still exist today, many of them drawing travelers from around the world to the Yucatán each year.

These ancient and mysterious ruins clearly show that the Maya were once a regional superpower, and that Maya nobles had widespread influence. This remarkable group inhabited the Yucatán Peninsula long before the arrival of the Spanish.

The Spanish fought to colonize the Yucatán well into the 1500s. The first attempt took place in 1527, but it was only 20 years later, in 1546, that the Spanish saw victory. But long before the Spanish arrived, the once-powerful Mayan civilization was in decline, and no one really knows why—possibly disease, war, or famine.

Linguists have associated 24 distinct indigenous languages among the Maya. Many of the Maya in this area speak "Yucatec Maya" and use Spanish only as a second language.

The Maya continue to blend the elements of their ancient worship practices and rituals (minus the human sacrifice) with more-contemporary religious practices. Many still wear traditional clothing, and construct the oblong, thatch-roof houses of their forebears. The Mayan passion to preserve their long history can be seen in the highly valued handicrafts that they create with the same skill and artistry as their ancestors.

Cancún

WORD OF MOUTH

"Cancun was a perfect getaway for relaxing and great food. I wasn't in the mood to go partying or clubbing, but there's plenty of that for those so inclined. The water is beautiful, the seafood is fresh and delicious and the Mexican people are lovely. Watch out for a few tourist scams and avoid the timeshare agents."

— LLindaC

WELCOME TO CANCÚN

TOP REASONS TO GO

★ **Dancing the night away:** Salsa, cumbia, reggae, mariachi, hip-hop, and electronic music dizzy the air of the Zona Hotelera's many nightclubs.

★ **Exploring the nearby Mayan ruins:** Trips to remarkable sites like Tulum, Cobá, and Chichén Itzá can easily be accomplished in a day.

★ **Getting wild on the water:** Rent Jet Skis, a Windsurfer, or a kayak, and skim across the sea or Laguna Nichupté.

★ **Browsing for Mexican crafts:** The colorful stalls of Mercado Veintiocho will certainly hold something that catches your eye.

★ **Indulging in local flavor:** Dishes like *poc chuc* (a pork dish with achiote and onions) and lime soup, and drinks like tamarind margaritas pay respect to traditional cuisine.

1 El Centro. Cancún's mainland commercial center, known as El Centro, provides an authentic glimpse into modern-day Mexico and a colorful alternative to the Zona Hotelera. Many of the restaurants scattered throughout this downtown area offer surprising bursts of culture and Mexican flavor. With more than 800,000 permanent residents living here, the shops, cafés, and open-air markets cater mainly to locals. Although the majority of tourists choose to bask on the beaches of Cancún, those who venture into the heart of El Centro will be glad they did—prices are much more reasonable and the food is outstanding.

2 The Zona Hotelera Norte. A separate northern strip called Punta Sam, north of Puerto Juárez, is sometimes referred to as the Zona Hotelera Norte (Northern Hotel Zone). This area is quieter than the main Zona, but there are some smaller hotels, marinas, and restaurants. This is also a good launching point for those heading to the nearby Isla Mujeres.

3 The Zona Hotelera. Ideal for those wanting to stay local, the Hotel Zone is structured along a 22½-km (14-mi) stretch known as Kukulcán Boulevard. On the Caribbean side, dozens of resorts and condominiums tightly line the beachfront like a row of Legos. On the inland side, Laguna Nichupté is home to water sports, shopping malls, seafood restaurants, and golf courses. At the northern tip of this main thoroughfare, near Punta Cancún, is a pack of nightclubs, discos, and bars—a nighttime favorite for Spring Breakers.

GETTING ORIENTED

Cancún is a great place to experience 21st-century Mexico. Over the past three decades it has turned into the Miami of the south, with international investors pouring money into property development. The main attractions for most travelers to Cancún lie along the Zona Hotelera—a 22½-km (14-mi) barrier island shaped roughly like the numeral 7. Off the eastern side is the Caribbean; to the west is a system of lagoons, the largest being Laguna Nichupté. Downtown Cancún—El Centro—is 4 km (2½ mi) west of the Zona Hotelera on the mainland.

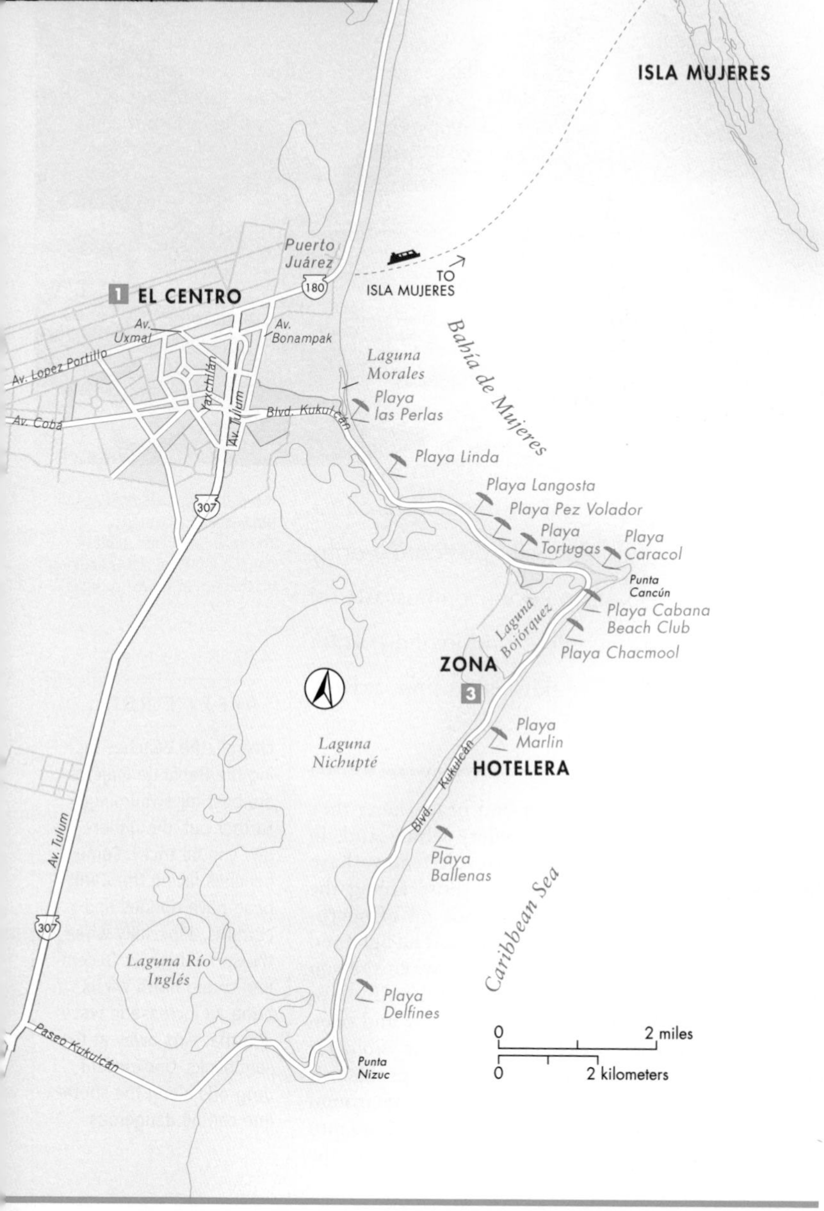

HOTELERA NORTE

Punta Sam

ISLA MUJERES

Puerto Juárez

1 **EL CENTRO**

TO
ISLA MUJERES

Av. Uxmal

Av. Bonampak

Av. López Portillo

Yaxchilán

Av. Cobá

Blvd. Kukulcán

Laguna Morales

Playa las Perlas

Bahía de Mujeres

Av. Tulum

Playa Linda

Playa Langosta

Playa Pez Volador

Playa Tortugas

Playa Caracol

Punta Cancún

Playa Cabaña Beach Club

Laguna Bojórquez

Playa Chacmool

ZONA

3

Playa Marlin

HOTELERA

Laguna Nichupté

Blvd. Kukulcán

Playa Ballenas

Caribbean Sea

Av. Tulum

Laguna Río Inglés

Playa Delfines

Paseo Kukulcán

Punta Nizuc

0   2 miles

0   2 kilometers

CANCÚN'S BEST BEACHES

Offering 22½ km (14 mi) of accessible coast-line, Cancún is riddled with postcard-worthy beaches that beckon outdoor enthusiasts of every ilk. The warm weather and inviting water make it ideal for those seeking sunshine, adventure, and relaxation.

(Above) Palapa-side service on Playa Gaviota Azul. (Top right) The powdery white sand of Cancún. (Bottom right) Soaking up the sun at Playa Tortugas.

It's virtually impossible to find a bad beach here; they all have turquoise waters and powdery white sand. In general, beaches on the northwestern side tend to have calmer waters and softer sand than those facing the Caribbean. The sand in Cancún is made up of microscopic star-shape fossils called discoasters. The light and fluffy texture stays cool underfoot, even when the sun is beating down during prime tanning hours. By law, the entire coast of Mexico is federal property and open to the public. Everyone is welcome as long as you enter and exit from one of the public points—the problem is that these points are often miles apart. One way around the situation is to find a hotel open to the public, go into the lobby bar for a drink or snack, and then head to the beach for a swim.

SAFETY FIRST

Overall, the beaches facing the Bahía de Mujeres are best for swimming. Farther out, the undertow can be tricky. Some beaches facing the Caribbean have riptides and currents, especially when the surf is high. In December, strong north winds bring an increase in wave size that eats away at the sandbanks. Unexpected drop-offs along the shoreline can be dangerous.

2

FAVORITE BEACHES

Playa Langosta (Lobster Beach)

The calm waters and designated swimming area make this Cancún's most child-friendly beach. Facing Bahía de Mujeres at the top of the "7," this stretch of sand is protected from high winds and is less crowded than those on the Caribbean side. Families can take a break from the sun and head to the neighboring ice-cream shop or Dolphin Discovery Center.

Playa Tortugas (Turtle Beach)

Snorkeling, sailing, kayaking, swimming—this beach is an aquatic playground for active travelers. The deep waters and wide sandbanks also make it an ideal launching point for paragliding and Jet Skiing. If water sports are not your thing, purchase a blow-up raft from one of the beach vendors, and float the day away. There are also plenty of snack shops to keep your tummy happy.

Playa Gaviota Azul (Blue Seagull Beach)

As the northernmost beach on the Caribbean side, the waves here pick up wind swell, making it one of the few spots in Cancún where surfing is possible. During hurricane season waves can reach up to 6 feet; all other times of year the waters are great for a playful day in the surf. Adding to the lure of this beach is its proximity to shops, restaurants, and

Playa Cabana Beach Club, where you can rent a beach bed and eat fresh sushi.

Playa Delfines (Dolphin Beach)

This beach is easy to locate, since it is the only one that has yet to be blocked by resorts. The white sand and four shades of turquoise often bring cars to a halt on Boulevard Kukulcán. Families and locals are drawn to this wide-open stretch of sand, where kites and beach supplies are sold. The strong currents and high winds make this a better place to catch some rays than snorkel or swim. Playa Delfines is the only beach in Cancún with its own parking lot.

Playa Punta Nizuc

Located at the southern tip of Boulevard Kukulcán, this beach is so secluded that you may think you're on a deserted island. Since there are no amenities, few travelers visit this stretch of pristine coastline. The water is placid, and the beaches are well manicured by the neighboring Camino Real Hotel. Parking, crowds, and noise are never an issue, and it's most likely the only Cancún beach you'll have entirely to yourself.

MEXICAN FOOD PRIMER

The varied culinary characteristics of each region make it difficult to define "Mexican food" as a whole. Its complexity and diversity is a direct result of the ingredients that are available within each region.

There are, however, overlapping ingredients that are used by the majority of areas throughout Mexico. The most frequently used spices are chile powder, cumin, oregano, cilantro, epazote, cinnamon, and cocoa. Chipotle, a smoke-dried jalapeño chile, is common, as are tomatoes, garlic, onions, and peppers. Rice is the most common grain, but corn, beans, and chiles are considered the cornerstones of Mexican cuisine.

The Spanish introduced rice, wheat, olive oil, nuts, cinnamon, wine, and parsley, and a variety of animals including cattle, chickens, goats, sheep, and pigs. These ingredients were incorporated with indigenous corn-based dishes, beans, turkey, fish, vanilla, chocolate, and fruits such as guava, pineapple, and papaya, giving us what we now know as Mexican food.

JUST DESSERTS

Locally grown fruits—like mango, mamey, cherimoya, pomegranate, tuna (cactus apple), and strawberries—are delicious alone or served with a dollop of cream and sugar. Stewed peaches and guavas are refreshing on a hot summer day, especially with a side of *nieves* (sherbet or sorbet). Among Mexico's most common desserts are *tres leches* (sponge cake soaked in three types of milk), churros (fried-dough pastry), and *arroz con leche* (rice cooked in milk with sugar and cinnamon). Traditionally eaten during Lent, *capirotada* (Mexican bread pudding) is made from French bread soaked in syrup, sugar, cheese, raisins, and walnuts.

REGIONAL CUISINES

Our generalizations of Mexican food have led us to believe that the bill of fare consists primarily of burritos, tacos, and rice and beans. In reality, traditional recipes reach far beyond these stereotypical dishes, varying by region as a result of the climate, geography, local ingredients, and cultural differences among the inhabitants.

Yucatán Peninsula. Characterized by its Mayan heritage, the Yucatán Peninsula has a strong European influence due to its connection with the continent and its geographical distance from Mexico City. Specialties of this region include *cochinita pibil* (seasoned pork colored with annatto seed and wrapped in banana leaves), turkey with black stuffing, and *papadzules* (tortillas filled with hard-boiled eggs and topped with a pumpkin seed sauce). Setting Yucatán's cooking style apart from other regions is the earthen pit oven where meats are slowly cooked with *recado negro* or *chilmole* (a blend of dried chiles that are set aflame and ground with spices to create a paste).

Mexico City and Environs (including Puebla). Largely influenced by the rest of the country, Mexico City still has original dishes such as *carnitas* (braised or roasted pork), *menudos* (tripe stew), and *pozole* (pork and hominy soup). Mexico City is also known for its

incredible cheeses, tamales, and yellow-corn tortillas. The favored *mixiote* (mutton wrapped in maguey leaves) is slowly steam baked in a pit oven. Puebla produces various species of cacti including maguey and nopal, which can be eaten as a vegetable or used to make juices and sorbets. Puebla is best known for *mole poblano* (thick, chocolate-tinged sauce) and *chiles en Nogada* (stuffed chiles topped with a walnut cream sauce).

Oaxaca. With a strong pre-Hispanic influence, the state of Oaxaca has one of the greatest indigenous populations of any state in Mexico. *Gusanos de maguey* (worms) and chapulines (grasshoppers), which were originally indigenous foods, are fried and eaten like roasted peanuts or sprinkled onto tacos. Oaxaca takes pride in its assortment of chiles, including yellow and black *chilhuacles, costenos* and the large, light green *chiles de agua*.

Veracruz. Spanning the coast of the Gulf of Mexico, the cuisine here is characterized geographically by fish and seafood. It is also one of the most versatile agricultural regions of Mexico. Nut- and seed-based sauces are very popular here, as are spicy chicken and vegetable dishes. Spanish influence is evident in the *pescado a la Veracruzana,* fish made with tomato sauce, capers, and olives.

Updated by
Marlise Kast

Cancún is a great place to experience 21st-century Mexico since it has everything you'd want in a vacation, including shopping, sports, spas, and beaches. Here you'll find five-star resorts, exceptional food, Mexican culture, and natural beauty within minutes of the world-famous Mayan ruins. There isn't, however, much that's quaint or historic in this distinctively modern city, many of whose residents have embraced the accoutrements of urban middle-class life—cell phones, cable TV—that are found all over the world.

Most locals live on the mainland, in the part of the city known as El Centro, and work in the posh Zona Hotelera. Boulevard Kukulcán is the main drag in the Zona Hotelera. Kilometer markers alongside Boulevard Kukulcán indicate where you are, starting from Km 1 near El Centro to Km 20 at the southern tip of Punta Nizuc. The area in between consists entirely of hotels, restaurants, shopping complexes, marinas, and time-share condominiums. Most travelers are based within this 22½-km (14-mi) stretch of paradise, unless the charm of El Centro's city life trumps the beach.

The party atmosphere of Zone Hotelera has inevitably earned it the title "Spring Break Capital" of the world. Catering to college students are dozens of bars and nightclubs just south of Punta Cancún at Km 9. Fortunately, this late-night/early-morning scene is contained within a small area, far from the larger resorts. Although Cancún is a magnet for youth on the loose, families are drawn to the island for the limitless water sports, pristine beaches, and children's activities including theme parks, live entertainment, and dolphin programs.

For authentic Mexican food at some of the best hole-in-the-wall cantinas, travel west of Avenida Tulum (El Centro's main street) to Yaxchilán. The more upscale area of El Centro is east of Tulum to Avenida Bonampak. Although El Centro is less visited by travelers than Zona

Hotelera, the downtown area holds cultural gems that will remind you that you really are in Mexico.

PLANNING

WHEN TO GO

The sun shines an average of 253 days a year in Cancún. The months between December and April have nearly perfect weather; temperatures hover at around 84°F during the day and 64°F at night. May through September are much hotter and more humid; temperatures can reach upwards of 97°F.

The rainy season starts mid-September and lasts until mid-November—which means afternoon downpours that can last anywhere from 30 minutes to two hours. El Centro street often get flooded during these storms, and traffic can grind to a halt.

High season for Cancún starts at the end of November and lasts until the first week in April. Between December 15 and January 5, however, hotel prices are at their highest, and may rise as much as 30% to 50% above regular rates. Although costs drop from August to October, travelers might return home waterlogged rather than tanned. For those who are not limited to peak-season travel, lower prices and pleasant weather are available from October 1 to December 15. Keep in mind that winter's strong north winds tend to eat away at the beaches, uprooting surface sea kelp. Less sand and choppy waters may result in overcrowded swimming pools.

If you plan to visit during Christmas, Spring Break, or Easter, you should book at least three months in advance.

TIMING

There's a lot to see and do in Cancún—if you can force yourself away from the beach, that is. Understandably, many visitors stay here a week, or even longer, without ever leaving the silky sands and seductive comforts of their resorts. If you're game to do some exploring, though, it's a good idea to allow an extra two or three days, so you can day-trip to nearby eco-parks and archaeological sites.

GETTING HERE AND AROUND

The Aeropuerto Internacional Cancún is 16 km (9 mi) southwest of the heart of Cancún and 10 km (6 mi) from the Zona Hotelera's southernmost point. There are direct flights from some major U.S. cities, but most flights transfer in Mexico City.

It's simple to get to or from the airport; buses leave every hour from Cancún Airport to downtown Cancún, or you can take taxis or *colectivos* (mini-buses).

Taxi rides within the Zona Hotelera cost $6 to $10; between the Zona Hotelera and El Centro they run $8 and up; and to the ferries at Punta Sam or Puerto Juárez, fares are $15 to $20 or more. You can always find a taxi in Cancún, but make sure you check the fare before accepting a ride. A list of rates can be found in the lobby of most hotels or you can ask the concierge. Keep in mind it's also easy and cheap to get around Cancún by bus.

For farther-flung destinations, buses leave El Centro's terminal for all parts of Mexico. *Autobuses del Oriente,* or ADO, is one of the oldest

bus lines in Mexico and offers regular service to Puerto Morelos and Playa del Carmen every 15 minutes from 4 am until midnight. Tickets, available outside Terminal 2 Baggage Claim, are less than $10 one-way. Playa Express has express buses that leave from a small terminal across from the main bus station every 10 minutes for Puerto Morelos and Playa del Carmen. Mayab Bus Lines has first- and second-class buses leaving for destinations along the Riviera Maya every hour.

Cancún is not the sort of place you can get to know on foot, although there's a bicycle-walking path that starts downtown at the beginning of the Zona Hotelera and continues through to Punta Nizuc. The beginning of the path parallels a grassy strip of Boulevard Kukulcán decorated with reproductions of ancient Mexican art.

MONEY MATTERS

In September 2010, Mexican authorities passed a law stating that foreign travelers may not exchange more than $1,500 U.S. dollars (cash) per person, per month into Mexican pesos. Mexican travelers are also limited to $1,500 U.S.D. cash per person, per month, with the added restriction of no more than $300 U.S.D. cash per day. Other methods of payment including credit cards, traveler's checks, and non-American foreign currencies are not affected by this new law.

When exchanging foreign currency at banks and hotels in Mexico, you must show your passport. Most banks have ATMs where you can withdraw local currency, or you can pay for services with a debit or credit card without restrictions. There's no limit on the number of purchases or the amount of each individual transaction. It is recommended to have Mexican pesos on hand shortly after you arrive in Cancún, especially if you intend to use public transportation or pay cash during your trip.

HOTELS

A growing number of Cancún hotels are now encouraging people to make their reservations online. Some allow you to book rooms on their Web sites; even hotels without their own sites usually offer reservations via online booking agencies, such as ⊕ *www.docancun.com* and ⊕ *www.cancuntoday.net*. Since hotels customarily work with several different agencies, it's a good idea to shop around online for the best rates before booking.

Besides being convenient, booking online can often get you a 10% to 20% discount on room rates. The downside, however, is that there are occasional breakdowns in communication between booking agencies and hotels. You may arrive at your hotel to discover that your Spanish-speaking front-desk clerk has no record of your Internet reservation or has reserved a room that's different from the one you specified. To prevent such mishaps from ruining your vacation, be sure to print out copies of all your Internet transactions, including receipts and confirmations, and take them with you.

When booking a hotel online, be sure to ask if the hotel is currently undergoing renovation. Early-morning construction can be a painful wake-up call for Cancún party animals.

DINING AND LODGING PRICES

	WHAT IT COSTS IN DOLLARS				
	¢	$	$$	$$$	$$$$
Restaurants	under $5	$5–$10	$10–$15	$15–$25	over $25
Hotels	under $50	$50–$75	$75–$150	$150–$250	over $250

Restaurant prices are based on the median entrée price at dinner. Hotel prices are for a standard double room in high season.

SAFETY

Cancún is one of the safest cities in Mexico. Reported violence generally takes place 2,090 km (1,300 mi) from Cancún on the northern border of Mexico (the same distance from New York to Texas). Don't be surprised to see Tourist Police patrolling the Hotel Zone, especially during the holidays and high season when security is increased. The C4 Surveillance and Rescue Center monitors the tourist area through video cameras that have been installed in strategic points throughout the city, and an emergency 911 Call Center is now in place. Visitors are, however, encouraged to exercise caution and use common sense while traveling.

TOURS

GENERAL TOURS

Mayaland Tours (⊠ *Calle Robalo 30, Sm 3* ☎ *998/887–2495, 800/235–4079 in U.S.* ⊕ *www.mayaland.com*) runs tours to Mérida, the Uxmal ruins, and the flamingo park at Celestún. Self-guided tours to Tulum and Cobá can also be arranged; the agency provides a car, maps, and an itinerary.

Olympus Tours (⊠ *Av. Yaxchilán, Lote 13, Sm 17, Mza 2* ☎ *998/881–9030, 786/338–9358 in U.S.* ⊕ *www.olympus-tours.com*) specializes in tours around Cancún, and can book your reservations to Xcaret, Xel-Há, and other local adventure parks.

BOAT TOURS

Kolumbus Tours (⊠ *Punta Conoco 36, Sm 24* ☎ *998/884–5333 or 800/715–3375* ⊕ *www.kolumbustours.com*) has excursions to Isla Mujeres and Isla Contoy on replica boats of the *Pinta,* the *Niña,* and the Bermudian sloop of war *Cosario.*

Sea Passion Catamaran (⊠ *El Embarcadero, next to Museo del Arte Popular Mexicano, Blvd. Kukulcán, Km 4.5, Zona Hotelera* ☎ *998/849–5573* ⊕ *www.seapassion.net*) offers day trips (which includes a buffet lunch, open bar, and snorkel equipment) to Isla Mujeres.

BREATHING BUBBLE TOURS

B.O.B. (Breathing Observation Bubble) Cancún (⊠ *El Embarcadero, Blvd. Kukulcán, Km 4.5, Loc E-3, Zona Hotelera* ☎ *998/849–4440 or 998/849–7284*) lets you sit on a machine resembling an underwater motor scooter, and steer your way through the reef while wearing a pressurized helmet that lets you breathe normally ($75).

SUBMARINE TOURS

AquaWorld's Sub See Explorer (⊠ *Blvd. Kukulcán, Km 15.1, Zona Hotelera* ☎ *998/848–8327, 877/730–4054 in U.S.* ⊕ *www.aquaworld.com.mx*) is a "floating submarine"—a glass-bottom boat that submerges halfway into the water.

VISITOR INFORMATION

The **Cancún Convention and Visitors Bureau** (*CVB* ⊠ *Blvd. Kukulcán, Km 9, Zona Hotelera* ☎ *998/881–2745* ⊕ *www.cancun.info*) has lots of information about area accommodations, restaurants, and attractions.

The **Mexican Association of Travel Agencies** (*AMAV* ⊠ *Av. Tulum No. 200, Plaza Mexico Loc 303, Sm 4, El Centro* ☎ *998/887–1670 or 998/887–4992* ⊕ *www.amavqroo.org*) can refer you to local travel agents who'll help plan your visit to Cancún.

ESSENTIALS

Bus Contacts Autobuses del Oriente (ADO) (☎ *998/884–5542*). **Mayab Bus Lines** (☎ *998/884–5542*). **Playa Express** (☎ *998/887–6782*). **Terminal de Autobuses** (⊠ *Avs. Tulum and Uxmal, Sm 23* ☎ *998/884–5542*).

Currency Exchange Banamex (⊠ *Av. Tulum 19, next to City Hall, Sm 5* ☎ *998/881–6403*). **Banorte** (⊠ *Av. Tulum 21, Sm 2* ☎ *998/887–6815* ⊠ *Plaza Flamingos, Blvd. Kukulcán, Km 11, Zona Hotelera* ☎ *998/883–1653*). **HSBC** (⊠ *Plaza Caracol, Blvd. Kukulcán, Km 8.5, Zona Hotelera* ☎ *998/883–4652*).

InternetInternet B@r (⊠ *Forum-by-the-Sea, Blvd. Kukulcán, Km 9.5, Zona*

Mail and Shipping Correos (Post Office) (⊠ *Avs. Sunyaxchén and Xel-Há, Sm 26* ☎ *998/884–1418*). **DHL** (⊠ *Av. Tulum 29, Sm 5* ☎ *998/892–8449*). **Federal Express** (⊠ *Av. Tulum 31, Sm 23* ☎ *998/887–4003*). **Mas Mail Center Inc.** (⊠ *Av. Xpuhil 3, behind Mercado 28, Sm 27* ☎ *998/887–4918*).

Medical Assistance Green Angels (for highway breakdowns) (☎ *078*). **Hospital Amat (emergency hospital)** (⊠ *Av. Náder 13, Sm 2* ☎ *998/887–4422*). **Hospital Americano** (⊠ *Retorno Viento 15, Sm 4* ☎ *998/884–6133*). **Hospital de las Americas** (⊠ *Avs. Bonampak and Nichupté, next to Plaza las Américas, Sm 7* ☎ *998/881–3400, 998/881–3434 for emergencies*). **Municipal Police** (☎ *998/884–1913*). **Red Cross** (⊠ *Avs. Xcaret and Labná, Sm 21* ☎ *998/884–1616*). **Tourist Assistance Office** (☎ *998/884–8073*).

Rental Cars **Adocar Rental** (⊠ *Plaza Nautilus, Blvd. Kukulcán, Km 3.5, Zona Hotelera* ☎ *998/849-4233* ⊕ *www.adocarrental.com*). **Avis** (⊠ *Aeropuerto Internacional Benito Juárez, Zona Hotelera* ☎ *998/886-0221 or 0222* ⊕ *www.avis.com*). **Buster Renta Car** (⊠ *Hotel Holiday Inn Arenas, Blvd. Kukulcán, Km 2.5, Zona Hotelera* ☎ *998/882-2800* ⊕ *www.busterrentacar.com*). **Caribetur Rent a Car** (⊠ *Plaza Tropical, Av. Tulum 192, Loc 16, Sm 4* ☎ *998/880-9167 or 01800/821-8854* ⊕ *www.caribetur.com*). **Mónaco Rent a Car** (⊠ *Av. Yaxchilán 65, Lote 5, Sm 25* ☎ *998/884-7843* ⊕ *www.monacorentacar.com*).

EXPLORING

The best way to explore Cancún is by hopping on one of the public buses that run between Zona Hotelera and El Centro. The cost is 75¢ no matter the distance you travel. If you intend to travel to El Centro, taxis will cost anywhere between 150 pesos ($12) and 250 ($20) pesos each way. A more affordable alternative is to catch a north-bound bus to the Kukulcán –Bonampak intersection, which marks the beginning of El Centro. From here, you can explore by foot or flag down a taxi to your area of choice. A taxi to nearly every destination within El Centro will cost you around 25 pesos ($2). If you want to get a taste of downtown culture, start at the colorful Mercado Veintiocho or Parque de las Palapas. To return to the Hotel Zone, take a taxi to the Chedraui on Avenida Tulum and then catch a bus that passes every few minutes toward the Hotel Zone. Don't be alarmed if a man in a clown suit roams the aisle in search of money. At night the buses come alive with all sorts of amateur performers, from accordionists to jugglers, hoping to earn a few pesos.

South of Punta Cancún, Boulevard Kukulcán becomes a busy road and is difficult for pedestrians to cross. It's also punctuated by steeply inclined driveways that turn into the hotels, most of which are set back at least 100 yards from the road. The lagoon side of the boulevard consists of scrubby stretches of land alternating with marinas, shopping centers, and restaurants. ■TIP→ Because there are so few sights, there are no orientation tours of Cancún: just do the local bus circuit to get a feel for the island's layout. The buses run 24 hours a day, and you'll rarely have to wait more than five minutes.

When you first visit El Centro, the downtown layout might not be self-evident. It's not based on a grid but rather on a circular pattern. The whole city is divided into districts called Super Manzanas (abbreviated Sm in this book), each with its own central square or park. In general, walks through downtown are somewhat unpleasant, with whizzing cars, corroding pathways, and overgrown weeds. Sidewalks disappear for brief moments, forcing pedestrians to cross grassy inlets and thin strips of land separating four lanes of traffic. Few people seem to know exactly where anything is, even the locals who live in El Centro. When exploring on foot, expect to get lost at least once and enjoy it—you may just find yourself stumbling upon a courtyard café or a lively cantina.

Numbers in the text correspond to numbers in the margin and on the Cancún map.

TOP ATTRACTIONS

Cancún Underwater Museum. Combining art and nature, Sculptor Jason de Caires Taylor has created underwater museums off the shores of Punta Cancún, Punta Nizuc, and Manchones Reef in Isla Mujeres. His main work features more than 400 lifelike statues that serve as artificial reefs to attract marine life. The displays have conveniently been placed in shallow areas for viewing by divers, snorkelers, and glass-bottom boats. Acting as a restoration project, this new artificial habitat also helps restore the natural reefs that have suffered damage over the years. ⊠ *Punta Cancún, Punta Nizuc, and Manchones Reef in Isla Mujeres, Cancún and Isla Mujeres* 🕿 *998/192–1189* ⊕ *www. underwatersculpture.com* 🖃 *Free*

El Centro. Nearly two decades ago, downtown Cancún was the place to be after a day at the beach. The once-barren Hotel Zone had very limited dining options, so tourists strolled the active streets of Avenida Tulum, Xachilan, and Parque de las Palapas. With the emergence of luxury resorts and mass tourism, a major shift brought the focus back to the Hotel Zone. Today many tourists are unaware that the downtown area even exists, while others consider "downtown" to be the string of flea markets near the convention center. In reality, El Centro's malls and markets offer a glimpse of Mexico's urban lifestyle. Avenida Tulum, the main street, is marked by a huge sculpture of shells and starfish in the middle of a traffic circle. This iconic Cancún sculpture, which many locals refer to as "el ceviche," is particularly dramatic at night when the lights are turned on. El Centro is also home to many restaurants and bars, as well as **Mercado Veintiocho** (Market 28)—an enormous crafts market just off Avenidas Yaxchilán and Sunyaxchén. For bargain shopping, hit the stores and small strip malls along Avenida Tulum. While the Hotel Zone becomes increasingly dense and overcrowded, El Centro is booming with the development of Puerto Cancún. Construction of this downtown subset has been carefully designed to focus on the resident rather than the tourist. Shopping centers, marinas, golf courses, and more than 2,500 condos are taking shape, making El Centro's bustling Avenida Bonampak the next "Boulevard Kukulcán."

Ruinas del Rey. Large signs on the Zona Hotelera's lagoon side, roughly opposite Playa Delfines, point out the small Ruins of the King. Although much smaller than famous archaeological sites like Tulum and Chichén Itzá, this site, commonly called El Rey, is worth a visit, and makes for an interesting juxtaposition of Mexico's past and present.

First entered into Western chronicles in a 16th-century travelogue, then sighted in 1842 by American explorer John Lloyd Stephens and his draftsman, Frederick Catherwood, the ruins were finally explored by archaeologists in 1910, though excavations didn't begin until 1954. In 1975 archaeologists, along with the Mexican government, began restoration work on the 47 structures.

Dating from the 3rd to 2nd century BC, El Rey is notable for having two main plazas bounded by two streets—most other Mayan cities contain only one plaza. The pyramid here is topped by a platform, and inside its vault are paintings on stucco. Skeletons interred both at

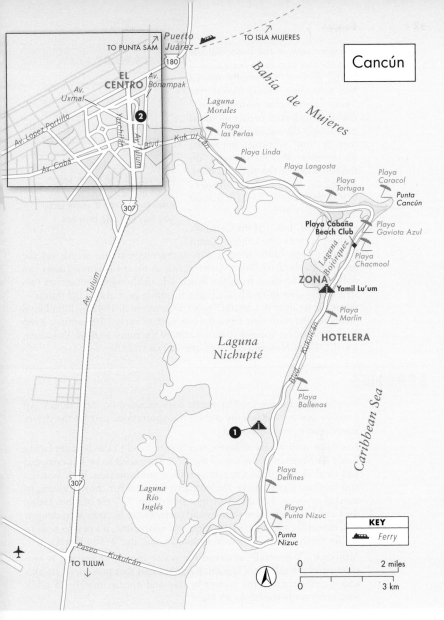

Cancún

TO PUNTA SAM

Puerto
Juárez

TO ISLA MUJERES

180

EL
CENTRO

Av.
Uxmal

Av.
Bonampak

Av. López Portillo

2

Av. Cobá

Blvd.

Av. Tulum

Kukulcán

Laguna
Morales

Playa
las Perlas

Bahía
de
Mujeres

Playa Linda

Playa Langosta

Playa
Tortugas

Playa
Caracol

Punta
Cancún

307

Playa Cabaña
Beach Club

Playa
Gaviota Azul

Laguna
Bojórquez

Playa
Chacmool

Av. Tulum

ZONA

Yamil Lu'um

Playa
Marlin

HOTELERA

Laguna
Nichupté

Blvd.
Kukulcán

Playa
Ballenas

Caribbean Sea

1

Playa
Delfines

Laguna
Río
Inglés

Playa
Punta Nizuc

Punta
Nizuc

307

Paseo
Kukulcán

TO TULUM

KEY
Ferry

0   2 miles

0   3 km

the apex and at the base indicate that the site may have been a royal burial ground. Originally named Kin Ich Ahau Bonil, Mayan for "king of the solar countenance," the site was linked to astronomical practices in the ancient Mayan culture. In 2006, workmen unearthed an ancient Mayan skeleton on the outskirts of the park. ⊠ *Blvd. Kukulcán, Km 17, Zona Hotelera* ☎ *998/849–2880* 🖅 *$3.50; free on Sun.* ☉ *Daily 8–5.*

BUSES MADE EASY

In conjunction with the Cancún tourist board, Autocar and Publi-car have published an excellent pocket guide called "TheMAP" that shows all the bus routes to points of interest in Cancún and the surrounding area. TheMap is free and is easiest to find at the airport. Some of the mid-range hotels carry copies, and if you're lucky you may find one on a bus.

 Yamil Lu'um. Located on Cancún's highest point (the name Yamil Lu'um means "hilly land"), this archaeological site stands on the grounds of the Park Royal Cancún, which means that nonguests can only access the ruins from the beach side. Although it comprises two structures—one probably a temple, the other probably a lighthouse—this is the smallest of Cancún's ruins. Discovered in 1842 by John Lloyd Stephens, the ruins date from the late 13th or early 14th century. Keep your eyes out for iguanas roaming around the ruins. ⊠ *Blvd. Kukulcán, Km 12, Zona Hotelera* ☎ *No phone* 🖅 *Free* ☉ *Daily 9–5.*

BEACHES

Beaches that are not used by hotels have seaweed on their shores. All beaches can be reached by public transportation; just let the driver know where you are headed.

For those with young children, it is best to head to the beaches facing Bahía de Mujeres at the top of the "7." They tend to be less crowded and more sheltered than beaches on the Caribbean side. Wide beaches and shallow waters make the northern tip ideal for those wanting to snorkel or swim. Forming the right side of the "7" are beaches facing the Caribbean Sea. Here riptides and currents can be somewhat dangerous, especially when the surf is high. For snorkeling, it's best to head to the southern end of Boulevard Kukulcán near the Westin Hotel.

Although it's generally reserved for water sports, swimming is also allowed in the saltwater lagoon. Keep in mind that motorized Jet Skis and speedboats rule the waters by day and approximately 25 adult crocodiles wade the banks by night.

The beaches listed here are organized by location, beginning on the northwest side of the "7" facing Bahía de Mujeres, and continuing down along the Caribbean side toward Punta Nizuc.

■ TIP→ Don't swim when the red or black danger flags fly; yellow flags indicate that you should proceed with caution, and green or blue flags mean the waters are calm.

Playa las Perlas (Pearl Beach) is the first beach on the drive heading east from El Centro along Boulevard Kukulcán. Located at Km 2.5, between

ECOTOURS

The 500,000-acre Reserva Ecológica El Edén, 48 km (30 mi) northwest of Cancún, is in the area known as Yalahau. The reserve was established by one of Mexico's leading naturalists, Arturo Gómez-Pompa, and his nephew, Marco Lazcano-Barrero, and is dedicated to research and conservation. It offers excursions for people interested in exploring wetlands, mangrove swamps, sand dunes, savannas, and tropical forests. Activities include bird-watching, animal-tracking, stargazing, and archaeology. You must call to make an appointment before you visit the site; rates are $75 per person for a full-day visit. If you're not into roughing it, these trips aren't for you.

Eco Colors runs adventure tours to the wildlife reserves at Isla Holbox and Sian Ka'an, El Edén, and to remote Mayan ruin sites. The company also offers bird-watching, kayaking, camping, and biking excursions around the peninsula. They operate day trips (from $48 to $205), three-day trips ($336 to $400), and seven-day trips ($780 to $1,500).

MayaSites Travel Services offers educational ecotours for families to a variety of Mayan ruins—including five-day trips to Chichén Itzá during the spring equinox (rates start at $1,100 per person). The outfit also operates custom tours for small groups to ruins throughout the Maya Riviera. Naturama runs ecological tours to 20 different areas, including Isla Contoy, Xcaret, and Xel-Há. Rates range from $54 per person for a jungle tour to $200 per person for the SeaTrek excursion that includes swimming with dolphins.

Eco Colors (✉ *Calle Camarón 32, Sm 27* ☎ *998/884–9580* ⊕ *www. ecotravelmexico.com*). **MayaSites Travel Services** (✉ *1217 Truman Av. SE, Albuquerque, NM* ☎ *505/255– 2279 or 877/620–8715* ⊕ *www. mayasites.com*). **Naturama** (✉ *Blvd. Kukulcán, Km 9, Zona Hotelera* ☎ *998/883–3357* ⊕ *www.naturama. com.mx*) **Reserva Ecológica El Edén** (✉ *Teocaltiche 207, Sm 45, M4 L3, El Centro* ☎ *998/880–5032* ⊕ *www.reservaeleden.org.mx*).

the Cancún mainland and the bridge, it's a relatively small beach on the protected waters of the Bahía de Mujeres and is popular with locals. There are several restaurants lining the beach; however, most of the water-sports activities are available only to those staying at the nearby resorts, such as Imperial las Perlas, Holiday Inn Cancún Arenas, or the Blue Bay Getaway. **Best For:** families with small children, accessibility to Isla Mujeres, swimming. **Amenities:** food concessions, lifeguard (in front of Holiday Inn Cancún).

Small, placid **Playa Langosta** (Lobster Beach), which has an entrance at Boulevard Kukulcán's Km 5, has calm waters that make it an excellent place for a swim. There's a dock (mainly used by Dolphin Discovery) that juts out in the middle of the water, but swimming areas are marked off with ropes and buoys. The safe waters and gentle waves make this a popular beach with families as well as Spring Breakers. Next to the beach is a small building with a restaurant, an ice-cream shop, and an ATM. **Best For:** families with small children, swimming. **Amenities:** food concessions, ATM.

At Km 4 on Boulevard Kukulcán, **Playa Linda** (Pretty Beach) is where the ocean meets the freshwater of Laguna Nichupté to create the Nichupté Channel. Restaurants and changing rooms are available near the Playa Linda launching dock. There's lots of boat activity along the channel, and the ferry to Isla Mujeres leaves from the adjoining Embarcadero marina, so the area isn't safe for swimming—although it's a great place to people-watch and there's a 300-foot rotating scenic tower nearby that offers a 360-degree view. **Best For:** boating, people-watching, trips to Isla Mujeres. **Amenities:** parking, restaurants, toilets (all located at El Embarcadero).

The calm surf and relaxing shallows of **Playa Pez Volador** make it an aquatic playground for families with young children. Marked by a huge Mexican flag at Km 5.5, the wide beach is popular with locals, as many tourists tend to head to the more active Playa Langosta. Occasionally sea grass washes ashore here, but by early morning it has already been cleared away by the staff of the neighboring Casa Maya Hotel. **Best For:** swimming, sunbathing. **Amenities:** none.

Playa Tortugas (Turtle Beach) eroded greatly after Hurricane Wilma. There's now a restored sandbank at the entrance located around Km 6.5 (next to Fat Tuesday) on Boulevard Kukulcán. The water is deep and the swimming is excellent; many people come here to sail, snorkel, kayak, paraglide, and use Wave Runners. The nicest section of this beach is on the far right, just past the rocks. Don't be fooled by the name—this spot is seldom frequented by *tortugas* (turtles). **Best For:** snorkeling, sailing, singles scene. **Amenities:** restaurants, toilets at Fat Tuesday.

Playa Caracol (Snail Beach), the last "real" beach along the east–west stretch of the Zona Hotelera, is near Plaza Caracol and the Xcaret dock. Located at Km 8.5, the whole area has been eaten up by development—in particular the high-rise condominium complex next to the entrance. This beach is also hindered by the rocks that jut out from the water marking the beginning of Punta Cancún, where Boulevard Kukulcán turns south. There are several hotels along here and a few sports rental outfits. This is also the launching point for trips to Contoy Island. **Best For:** water sports, proximity to Contoy Island, sunbathing. **Amenities:** none.

Heading down from Punta Cancún onto the long, southerly stretch of the island, **Playa Gaviota Azul** (Blue Seagull Beach but also commonly called City Beach) is the first beach on the Caribbean's open waters. Here the waves break up to 6 feet during the winter months, making it one of the few surfing spots in Cancún. If you need a break from the waves and want to be pampered in the sand, head right up a short flight of steps to **Playa Cabaña Beach Club**. Located at Km 9.5 behind the City Discotheque, this is a place where travelers can enjoy the full resort experience without booking into a hotel. Facilities include 32 beach cabanas, each equipped with misting machines and a personalized sound system. The $10 entrance fee also includes access to the multilevel swimming pool, sundeck, restaurant, and sushi bar. Chances are, you'll never want to leave your cabana. **Best For:** singles scene, sunbathing, playing in surf. **Amenities:** restaurant, toilets and changing rooms at Playa Cabaña Beach Club; paid parking at

Plaza Forum or minimal street parking in front of NH Krystal Hotel. ⊠ *Blvd. Kukulcán, Km 9.5, Zona Hotelera* ☎ *998/848–8380* ⊕ *www.playacabana.com* ☎ *$10* ⊙ *Daily 9–5:30.*

Located at Km 10 on Boulevard Kukulcán, **Playa Chacmool** can be accessed through the beach entrance directly across the street from Señor Frog's. As at Playa Caracol, development has greatly encroached on Chacmool's shores. There are a lot of rocks, but the water is a stunning shade of turquoise and the beach is close to shopping centers and the party zone, so there are plenty of restaurants nearby. The short strand to the south has gentler waters and fewer rocks. Changing rooms are also available to the public. The shallow clear water makes it tempting to walk far out into the ocean, but be careful—there's a strong current and undertow. **Best For:** singles scene, proximity to shops and restaurants, color of the water. **Amenities:** restaurants, water-sport rentals on the west side of the beach, toilets, changing rooms.

Playa Marlin (Marlin Beach), at Km 13 along Boulevard Kukulcán, is a seductive beach in the heart of the Zona Hotelera, accessible via a road next to Kukulcán Plaza. Despite its turquoise waters and silky sands, the waves are strong and the currents are dangerous. If this beach is crowded, you can walk in either direction to find quieter spots. Sun umbrellas and beach chairs are available for $5 per day. There's also a small tent where you can rent boogie boards, snorkel equipment, and motorized sports equipment. Although there are currently no public facilities, you can always walk over to Kukulcán Plaza if you need a restroom. **Best For:** boogie boarding, Jet Skiing, amenities. **Amenities:** beach umbrellas, chaise lounges, restrooms at Kukulcán Plaza.

Playa Ballenas (Whale Beach) is located at Km 14.5 between Le Meridien Cancún Resort & Spa and Cancún Palace. This stretch of sand and crystal water between the two hotels is open to the public. There are often Jet Skiers zooming through the water here, and the strong wind makes the surf rough. Parking and beach access are available at Calle Ballenas. **Best For:** banana-boat rides, parasailing, Jet Skiing. **Amenities:** parking at Calle Ballenas, water-sports rentals.

Located near Ruinas del Rey at Km 18, where Boulevard Kukulcán curves into a hill, **Playa Delfines** (Dolphin Beach) is one of the last beaches before Punta Nizuc. Hotels have yet to dominate this small section of coastline, and there's an incredible lookout over the ocean; on a clear day you can see at least four shades of blue in the water, though swimming is treacherous unless one of the green flags is posted. Devoid of resorts, this area has plenty of sand and surfers. It's one of the few places in Cancún where you can take surfing lessons. Although decent waves roll in during hurricane season, seldom do they hit "epic" status. At best, you might find choppy, inconsistent surf at Playa Delfines, Playa Chacmool, and City Beach. Those seeking more than just a ripple should avoid the placid northern beaches, where Isla Mujeres lies just offshore. **Best For:** surfing, playing in the waves, flying a kite, isolation from resorts. **Amenities:** parking on Boulevard Kukulcán directly in front of the beach.

On the southern tip of the peninsula at Km 24, **Playa Punta Nizuc** is the most isolated and deserted beach in Cancún. Far from the crowds and party scene, this area has no amenities to speak of, other than what is offered to guests who visit the nearby Wet 'n Wild Waterpark (Km 25). The lack of beach-traffic helps keep the white sands clean and the waters sparkling, except when sea grass is washed onto the shores. This is a great place to swim, since waves only crash here on stormy days. There's plenty of street parking on Boulevard Kukulcán, but make sure you bring water, snacks, sunscreen, and an umbrella for shade, since this beach is about as barren as they come. Bordered by jungle to the south, Playa Punta Nizuc can be accessed directly from Boulevard Kukulcán. **Best For:** solitude, swimming, couples. **Amenities:** street parking.

WHERE TO EAT

Be aware that restaurants that line Avenidas Tulum and Yaxchilán are often noisy and crowded, and gas fumes make it hard to enjoy alfresco meals. Many of the finer restaurants and boutiques are on Avenida Bonampak, making it the continuation of Boulevard Kukulcán. The restaurants in the Parque de las Palapas, just off Avenida Tulum, serve expertly prepared Mexican food. Famous for its taco scene, El Centro's Avenida Yaxchilán caters mainly to large groups and budget travelers. Deeper into the city center, you can find fresh seafood and traditional fare at Mercado Veintiocho (Market 28). Dress is casual in Cancún, but many restaurants do not allow bare feet, short shorts, bathing suits, or no shirt. At upscale restaurants, pants, skirts, or dresses are required. Large breakfast and brunch buffets are among the most popular meals in the Zona Hotelera, with prices ranging from $10 to $25 per person. Most restaurants in Cancún open for lunch around 2 pm and generally stay open until midnight.

⚠ Most upscale resorts in Zona Hotelera purify their tap water, however, ask in advance whether it's safe to drink.

ZONA HOTELERA

$$$$ ✕ **Le Basilic.** If heaven had a restaurant, this would be it. Arched bay
MEDITERRANEAN windows, checkered marble floors, live jazz, and exquisite garden views
Fodor'sChoice create the backdrop for this ideal spot for couples. The 14 chestnut
★ tables surround a sunken gazebo where long-stemmed orchids bloom under glass. The restaurant doubles as a gallery where paintings by local artists are propped on easels. Each week, a profiled artist paints while you dine. The dishes here—created by French chef Henri Charvet—are served beneath silver domes by pleasant tuxedoed waiters. The

Cancún's History

CLOSE UP

The first known settlers of the area, the Maya, arrived in what is now Cancún centuries ago, and their descendants remain in the area to this day. During the golden age of the Mayan civilization (also referred to as the Classic Period), when other areas on the peninsula were developing trade routes and building enormous temples and pyramids, this part of the coast remained sparsely populated. Consequently, Cancún never developed into a major Mayan center; excavations have been done at El Rey ruins (in what is now the Zona Hotelera), showing that the Maya communities that lived here around AD 1200 simply used this area for burial sites. Even the name given to the area was not inspiring: In Mayan, Cancún means "nest of snakes."

When Spanish conquistadores began to arrive in the early 1500s, much of the Mayan culture was already in decline. Over the next three centuries the Spanish largely ignored coastal areas like Cancún—which consisted mainly of low-lying scrub, mangroves, and swarms of mosquitoes—and focused on settling inland where there was more economic promise.

Although it received a few refugees from the War of the Castes, which engulfed the entire region in the mid-1800s, Cancún remained more or less undeveloped until the middle of the 20th century. By the 1950s, Acapulco had become the number-one tourist attraction in the country—and had given the Mexican government its first taste of tourism dollars. When Acapulco's star began to fade in the late '60s, the government hired a market-research company to determine the perfect location for developing Mexico's next big tourist destination—and the company picked Cancún.

In April 1971, Mexico's president, Luis Echeverria Alvarez, authorized the Ministry of Foreign Relations to buy the island and surrounding region. With a $22 million development loan from the World Bank and the Inter-American Development Bank, the transformation of Cancún began. At the time there were just 120 residents in the area, most of whom worked at a coconut plantation; by 1979 Cancún had become a resort of 40,000, attracting more than 2 million tourists a year. That was only the beginning: today, more than 800,000 people live in Cancún, and the city has become the most lucrative source of tourist income in Mexico.

---

menu changes every four months, but it is always comprised of French-Mediterranean cuisine, from fresh tuna and sea scallops to seared duck and roasted lamb. As a keepsake, guests are presented with a box of French truffles and elegant recipe cards recapping the bill of fare. The dress code is elegant, reservations are recommended, and children are not allowed. ⊠ *Fiesta Americana Grand Coral Beach, Blvd. Kukulcán, Km 9.5, Zona Hotelera* ☎ *998/881–3200 Ext. 4220* ☉ *Closed Sun. No lunch* ⊕ *1:D1.*

$$$–$$$$ ✕ **Cambalache.** This Argentinean steak house is rustic yet elegant, with
ARGENTINE   its dark wooden tables and arched brick ceilings. The house cocktail, *clericot*, made from red wine, sparkling cider, and fresh fruit, is prepared at your table. For starters, try the traditional *empanadas* (turnovers

Spend a romantic evening at La Basilic.

stuffed with spinach and cheese). Although tenderloin steak is the most popular choice here, the lamb threaded on skewers and grilled over a brick fire is also delicious. Be sure to leave room for *alfajor* (a crisp pastry dessert layered with caramel and pecans). The tango music coupled with views of Coral Negro Market give this restaurant an international flair, and help you forget that you're inside a shopping mall. With enough room for 350 people, the dining room tends to get rather loud at night, and there's no outdoor seating. ⊠ *Blvd. Kukulcán, Km 9 at Plaza Forum, Zona Hotelera* ☎ 998/883–0902 ⊕ *www. cambalacherestaurantes.com* ✛ *1:D2.*

$$$–$$$$ ╳ **La Capilla.** Nestled in the belly of a brick cavern, this Argentine steak
STEAK house is dimly lighted with wrought-iron chandeliers dramatically suspended from wooden beams. The flavorful menu features Kobe beef carpaccio, lobster tail, *arrachera* steak, and herb-crusted rack of lamb. Centering the circular dining area is Cancún's most extensive salad bar, with exotic cheeses, grilled vegetables, Italian prosciutto, and seven types of olive oil. The creations of Chef Javier Carcamo are served on iron skillets with skewered vegetables and roasted garlic that spreads like butter. Be sure to check out the international wine cave, home to more than 200 types of wine. Vegetarians may want to look elsewhere; you can smell the grill from the moment you walk in the door. Reservations recommended. ⊠ *CasaMagna Marriott, Blvd. Kukulcán, Km 14.5, Zona Hotelera* ☎ 998/881–2000 Ext. 16 ⊕ *www.lacapillaargentina. marriottcancunrestaurants.com* ✛ *1:C3.*

$$$$ ╳ **Casa Rolandi.** The secret to this restaurant's success is its creative han-
ITALIAN dling of Swiss and Italian cuisine. Be sure to try the *carpaccio di pesce* (thin slices of fresh raw fish), the cheese fondue, or the mesquite-grilled

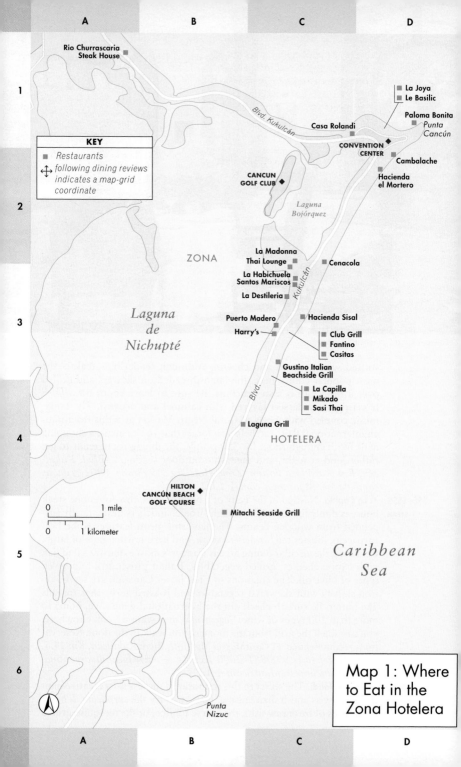

Map 1: Where to Eat in the Zona Hotelera

rib eye. Appetizers are also tempting: there's puff bread from a wood-burning oven and a huge salad and antipasto bar. For something with a bit more local flavor, try the restaurant's specialty *Gamberoni dei Re Maya*—jumbo shrimp baked in banana leaves and topped with a special Mayan sauce. The beautiful dining room and attentive service might make you want to stay for hours, and there are pleas-

ant lagoon views from the spacious terrace. ⊠ *Plaza Caracol, Blvd. Kukulcán, Km 8.5, Zona Hotelera* ☎ *998/883–2557* ⊕ *www.rolandi. com* ✛ *1:C1.*

$$$$ ✕ **Casitas.** Sink your toes into the sand at Cancún's only on-the-beach
SEAFOOD restaurant. The romantic setting caters to couples, and many of the seafood dishes are created for two. Silk curtains drape *palapas* (open-air huts), each centered with an illuminated table adorned with seashells. For a delicious sampling, try the seafood platter of shrimp, oysters, tuna tartar, king crab, and lobster tail. Also available are a variety of steaks and salads. For a little taste of everything, request the tasting menu. The Mayan chocolate cake with Yucatán citrus compote is the perfect way to extend your dinner-with-a-view. Call ahead, since the restaurant operates depending on weather conditions. ⊠ *Ritz-Carlton Cancún, Blvd. Kukulcán, Km 13.5, Retorno del Rey 36, Zona Hotelera* ☎ *998/881–0808* ☉ *No lunch* ✛ *1:C3.*

$$$–$$$$ ✕ **Cenacolo.** Reliably good pizza and pasta, handmade in full view of
ITALIAN patrons, have made this fine Italian restaurant a favorite. Appetizers include beef or octopus carpaccio that practically melts in your mouth and a light calamari. There are more than 15 pasta dishes to choose from, including a delicious lobster ravioli filled with ricotta cheese and served in a white-wine sauce. One of the restaurant's best features is its extensive wine cellar. Although it's inside a mall, the restaurant's main dining room is elegant, with stained-glass panels on the ceiling and live piano music. ⊠ *Kukulcán Plaza, Blvd. Kukulcán, Km 13, Zona Hotelera* ☎ *998/885–3603* ⊕ *www.cenacolo.com.mx* ✛ *1:C2.*

$$$$ ✕ **Club Grill.** The Club Grill has re-created the upscale ambience of the
INTERNATIONAL swank 1960s with such details as a martini lounge, tuxedoed waiters, and live jazz complete with a double bass. A five-course tasting menu, paired with boutique wines, changes monthly. The dining room here is romantic and quietly elegant, with rich wood, fresh flowers, crisp linens, and courtyard views. The contemporary menu changes every three months, but might include starters like caramelized scallops and truffle corn soup, or main courses like tequila duck. Like a waiters' ballet, the delivery of domed platters is synchronized among the servers, making the entire dining experience an unforgettable one. Reservations are recommended. ⊠ *Ritz-Carlton Cancún, Blvd. Kukulcán, Km 13.5, Retorno del Rey 36, Zona Hotelera* ☎ *998/881–0822* ☉ *Closed Mon. No lunch* ✛ *1:C3.*

Fantino's inventive cuisine is known as some of the best in the country.

$$$ ✕ **La Destileria.** Be prepared to have your perceptions of tequila changed
MEXICAN   forever. In what looks like a Mexican hacienda complete with an *alam-bique* (tequila distillery), you can sample from a list of 100 varieties—in shots or superb margaritas—and also visit the on-site tequila museum and store. The traditional Mexican menu focuses on fresh fish and seafood; other highlights include the *molcajete de arrachera* (a thick beef stew served piping hot in a mortar), and the Talla-style fish fillet that follows a traditional recipe from Acapulco. Midday (1 to 6 pm) diners can enjoy tequila tasting, appetizers, and a house cocktail for just $6. Be sure to leave room for the caramel crepes—a signature Mexican dessert. Reservations are recommended. ⌂ *Blvd. Kukulcán, Km 12.65, across from Plaza Kukulcán, Zona Hotelera* ☎ *998/885–1086 or 998/885–1087* ⊕ *www.ladestileria.com.mx/cancun* ✛ *1:C3.*

$$$$ ✕ **Fantino.** Reflecting Mexico's rich Spanish heritage, this Mediterra-
MEDITERRANEAN   nean restaurant lives up to its reputation as one of the country's finest.
Fodor's Choice   Grandeur is at its peak in this ballroom setting, with long-stemmed
★   roses and hand-painted ceiling frescoes that subtly match the fine English china. Each guest, referred to by name, is treated to the melodious sounds of live piano music. Velvet walls mounted with candelabras are only overshadowed by the red satin curtains and ocean views. Each course is paired with its own wine. Designed to play with the senses, appetizers moisten the palate in preparation for the seven-course tasting menu. Divine dishes include watermelon salad with buffalo mozzarella, sautéed foie gras with berries, and herb-crusted lamb with bell peppers and kalamata olive sauce. All ingredients are hand selected from local farms or air-freighted to the hotel. Just when you think you've seen it all, the waiter wheels over a candy cart, featuring 10 glass towers

of handmade sweets. Reservations are recommended. ✉ *Ritz-Carlton Cancún, Blvd. Kukulcán, Km 13.5, Zona Hotelera* ☎ *998/881–0822* ⊗ *Closed Sun. No lunch* ✛ *1:C3.*

$$$–$$$$
ITALIAN
✕ **Gustino Italian Beachside Grill.** From the moment you walk down the dramatic staircase to enter this restaurant, you know you're in for a memorable dining experience.

The circular dining room has artistic lighting and views of the wine cellar and open-air kitchen. The *gamberetti al aglio* (sautéed shrimp with garlic) appetizer is a standout, as are the tagliatelle in truffle sauce and seafood risotto entrées. The service here is impeccable; the saxophone music adds a dash of romance. A private dinning area can hold up to 14 guests. ✉ *JW Marriott Resort, Blvd. Kukulcán, Km 14.5, Zona Hotelera* ☎ *998/848–9600 Ext. 6849 or 6851* ⌂ *Reservations essential* ⊗ *No lunch* ✛ *1:C3.*

$$–$$$
CARIBBEAN
Fodor'sChoice
★
✕ **La Habichuela Sunset.** Following the 30-year success of El Centro location, this lagoon-side eatery is the newest restaurant to join Zona Hotelera. The multilevel dining area features a dramatic staircase leading down to an archaeological dig covered by a glass floor. Blending modern and Mayan designs, the restaurant has a romantic patio with a small stream and illuminated trees. Popular appetizers include the lime soup or Caesar salad prepared table-side. The soft-shell crab tacos and garlic shrimp are delicious as is the amaranth-breaded fish served with tamarind and mango sauce. Dessert lovers will enjoy the butterscotch crepes and Mayan coffee. ✉ *Blvd. Kukulcán, Km 12.6, Zona Hotelera* ☎ *988/840–6240* ⊕ *www.lahabichuela.com* ▭ *AE, MC, V.* ✛ *1:C3.*

$$$$
MEXICAN
✕ **Hacienda el Mortero.** As one of Cancún's first restaurants, the main draw at this restaurant is the setting: a replica of a 17th-century traditional hacienda, complete with courtyard fountain, flowering garden, and a strolling mariachi band. Although there's nothing outstanding on the traditional Mexican menu, the tortilla soup is very good and the chicken fajitas and rib-eye steaks are tasty. Fish lovers may also like the *pescado Veracruzana* (fresh grouper prepared Veracruz-style with olives, garlic, and fresh tomatoes). Sunday brunch ($18) is served from 9 to 2. This is a popular restaurant for large groups, so be warned: it can get boisterous, especially once guests begin sampling the 110 types of tequila. ✉ *NH Krystal Cancún, Blvd. Kukulcán, Km 9, Zona Hotelera* ☎ *998/848–9800 Ext. 778* ⊗ *No lunch* ✛ *1:D2.*

$$$
MEXICAN
✕ **Hacienda Sisal.** Constructed to resemble a sprawling hacienda, this restaurant is warm and intimate, with comfortable high-backed chairs and Mexican paintings. Menu highlights include the goat-cheese and mango salad, Tampico chicken breast, New York steak with stuffed pepper, and annatto-seasoned grilled pork chops. Traditional dances from Mexico and various regions of the Caribbean are performed here several nights a week in the restaurant's Patio section. Children eat free on Tuesday nights. There's a breakfast buffet from 8 to 2 on Sunday, which is the only day on which Hacienda Sisal opens early. ✉ *Royal*

Sands Resort, Blvd. Kukulcán, Km 13.5, Zona Hotelera ☎ *998/848–8220* ⊘ *No lunch* ✥ *1:C3.*

$$$$
STEAK

✕ **Harry's**. Situated on the lagoon across from the Ritz-Carlton, this steak house is easy to spot by the line of luxury cars at valet parking. High-profile locals and visitors alike are drawn to the Vegas–meets–Beverly Hills style of this

WORD OF MOUTH

"There are a handful of restaurants at La Isla Mall that overlook the large lagoon. It looks great during sunset, since the sun sets behind the lagoon."— CancunWithMe

flashy and contemporary establishment. Dominated by onyx and marble, the interior is dimly lighted; cedar beams and railings add a touch of warmth. For two years, the creators traveled the world in search of the best trends in culinary art. The result is a spectacular menu featuring glazed duck, king salmon, Maine lobster, and USDA Kobe beef served with aged Vermont cheddar cheese. If you can get past the glass meat cooler in the lobby, the concept is impressive—all steaks are aged in-house for 21 to 28 days, and then grilled and broiled to perfection. Be sure to save room for Mini Indulgences, six tasty desserts served in shot glasses. The waitstaff deliver a tower of cotton candy with the check. All the stone indoors creates echoes; the outdoor seating is recommended. ✉ *Blvd. Kukulcán, Km 14.2 across from Ritz-Carlton, Zona Hotelera* ☎ *998/840–6550* ⊕ *www.harrys.com.mx* ✥ *1:C3.*

$$$$
MEXICAN

✕ **La Joya**. The dramatic interior of this restaurant has three levels of stained-glass windows, a fountain, artwork, and beautiful furniture from central Mexico. The food is traditional but creative: the grilled beef prepared Tampíqueña-style is especially popular, as is the catch of the day wrapped in maguey leaves. Those with lighter appetites will want to try the tortilla soup or seafood appetizer of shrimp, scallops, and squid. Performances by folkloric dancers and a mariachi band add to the ambience. There's a designated cocktail lounge where you can have a drink before dinner. ✉ *Fiesta Americana Grand Coral Beach, Blvd. Kukulcán, Km 9.5, Zona Hotelera* ☎ *998/881–3200 Ext. 4201* ⊘ *Closed Mon. No lunch* ✥ *1:D1.*

$$$–$$$$
ECLECTIC

✕ **Laguna Grill**. Intricate tile work adorns this restaurant's floors and walls, and a natural stream divides the open-air dining room, which overlooks the lagoon. Delectable menu options such as a mojito shrimp entrée and fettuccine with lobster *satay* match the beautiful setting. The risotto, prepared with coconut milk and Thai curry, is sinfully creamy and mixed with vegetables, shrimp, chicken, and beef. Grill favorites range from lamb and duck to chicken and beef. Blending Mexican and Caribbean flavors, most dishes are prepared with cilantro or tropical fruits like pineapple and grapefruit. For dessert there's a Bailey's crème brûlée and coconut tempura ice cream with ginger and vanilla sauce. ✉ *Blvd. Kukulcán, Km 15.6, Zona Hotelera* ☎ *998/885–0267* ⊕ *www.lagunagrill.com.mx* ⊘ *No lunch* ✥ *1:B4.*

$$$–$$$$
ITALIAN

✕ **La Madonna**. This dramatic-looking restaurant is a great place to enjoy a selection of 180 martinis and cigars, as well as Italian food "with a creative Swiss twist." Guests are dwarfed by a massive reproduction of the *Mona Lisa* and towering Greek sculptures that frame

Nothing beats the seafood—and the view—at Mitachi Seaside Grill.

the three-story restaurant. For starters, try the pan-seared mozzarella wrapped in prosciutto. You can also enjoy classics like fettuccine with shrimp in a grappa sauce, mussels in white wine with saffron cream, and veal parmigiana served on a bed of homemade basil pasta. The lychee martini is a tad expensive but worth it. ⊠ *La Isla Shopping Village, Blvd. Kukulcán, Km 12.5, Zona Hotelera* ☎ *998/883–4837* ⊕ *www. lamadonna.com.mx* ✛ *1:C2.*

$$$–$$$$
JAPANESE
╳ **Mikado.** Sit around the teppanyaki tables and watch the utensils fly as the showmen chefs here prepare steaks, seafood, and vegetables. The menu includes Japanese specialties such as *futo-maki* (large sushi rolls) and panfried sea bass. The sushi, tempura, grilled salmon, and beef teriyaki are feasts fit for a shogun. For added flavor, several dishes are infused with sake or braised with Sapporo beer, like the oriental short ribs served with crispy onions. Unlike most restaurants in Cancún, however, there's no outdoor seating or scenic view. ⊠ *CasaMagna Marriott, Blvd. Kukulcán, Km 14.5, Zona Hotelera* ☎ *998/881–2036* ⊗ *No lunch* ✛ *1:C3.*

$$$$
SEAFOOD
★
╳ **Mitachi Seaside Grill.** The moonlight on the water, the sounds of the surf, and the superbly attentive staff all serve to make this restaurant feel like a sanctuary. The beachfront setting is the star attraction here, but the menu includes a good variety, ranging from salmon tartar to grouper fillet. The simple lunch menu of panini and salads transforms by night into delectable dishes like mahimahi with sun-dried tomatoes on a bed of crab risotto. The basil-lychee sherbet is a delightful cure for the Cancún heat. With 24-hour notice, couples can enjoy the fixed "Romantic Menu," which includes three courses, a bottle of wine, and a private table in the sand. Live Latin jazz can be heard Tuesday

through Sunday from December to July. Make sure you eat on a calm night—high winds may leave you with sandy sushi. ⊠ *Hilton Cancún, Blvd. Kukulcán, Km 17, Retorno Lacandones, Zona Hotelera* ☎ *998/881–8047* ✛ *1:B5.*

$$$$
MEXICAN
✕ **Paloma Bonita.** Replicating three regions of Mexico, this vibrant setting features stone fountains, handcrafted furniture, and colorful linens imported from the western state of Michoacan. Waiters dressed in sombreros dance between the tables while women in traditional costumes serve olive bread from wicker baskets. This is one of the best places in the Hotel Zone to get authentic Mexican cuisine—so be adventurous! Traditional fare like *moles enchiladas* (stuffed corn tortillas covered with thick chocolate and chile sauce) is fabulous here—and if you're unsure about what to order, the waiter explains the different chiles used in many of the dishes. Treat your palate to *queso fundido Oaxaca* (a specialty of bubbling cheese dripping from a stone pot onto handmade tortillas). The glass-enclosed patio with its water view is a great place to linger over tequila—or to try the *tamarindo margaritas.* The live music here is Norteño style. Unlike the neighboring nightclubs, this lively atmosphere will remind you that you are in Mexico. Meals are on the heavy side though, so come with an appetite. ⊠ *Dreams Cancún Resort & Spa, Punta Cancún, Blvd. Kukulcán, Km 9, Zona Hotelera* ☎ *998/848–7082 Ext. 7965* ⊗ *No lunch* ✛ *1:D1.*

$$$–$$$$
STEAK
Fodor'sChoice
★
✕ **Puerto Madero.** Modeled after the dock warehouses that have been converted into modern restaurants in the famed Argentine port city Puerto Madero, this steak-and-seafood house gets rave reviews from locals. It's the small touches—like fresh bread served in leather baskets, or martini reserves chilled in miniature ice buckets—that make this an unforgettable dining experience. The grilled octopus bathed in olive oil is exceptional, and the Big Rib Eye generously serves two people. The Alaskan halibut steak, also a crowd pleaser, is prepared with white wine, shallots, and fresh pepper. No matter what you order, be sure to request a side of *papas infladas* (potatoes fried until they're puffed)—bite down and they crackle on your tongue. Adding to the cosmopolitan ambience is a fun-loving staff, most of whom have been there longer than 15 years. If the restaurant is too loud inside, ask for a table outside on the patio overlooking the lagoon. Reservations are recommended on weekends. ⊠ *Blvd. Kukulcán, Km 14.1, Zona Hotelera* ☎ *998/885–2829* ⊕ *www.puertomaderorestaurantes.com* ✛ *1:C3.*

$$$$
STEAK
✕ **Rio Churrascaría Steak House.** It's easy to overlook this Brazilian restaurant because of its generic, unimpressive exterior—but make no mistake, it's one of the best steak houses in the Zona Hotelera. The waiters here walk among the tables carrying different mouthwatering meats that have been slow-cooked over charcoal on skewers. Besides Angus beef, there are also cuts of pork and chicken, as well as crocodile, ostrich, buffalo, and quail. Simply point out what you'd like; the waiters slice it directly onto your plate. If you are not a true carnivore, there's an all-you-can-eat salad bar and refreshing caipirinhas (made

with Brazilian rum and lime) to keep you happy. ⊠ *Blvd. Kukulcán, Km 3.5, Zona Hotelera* ☎ *998/849–9040* ✛ *1:A1.*

$ ✕ **Santos Mariscos.** A tribute to masked wrestling champion El Santo,
MEXICAN this Mexican cantina is colorfully decorated with retro furnishings like rainbow lawn chairs and sculptures of the Virgin Mary holding plastic roses. A bright red bar dominates the downstairs, and there's an upstairs dining area and a small outdoor patio where guests can watch nature videos on the Discovery Channel as cars cruise Boulevard Kukulcán. Frequented by locals who live in the Hotel Zone, this eatery serves great shrimp tacos with seven types of sauces. For those who want an alternative to the traditional flour tortilla, try the fried cheese taco. The *tamarindo* margaritas are also very refreshing. Located just south of La Isla Shopping Village, this cantina is marked by a string of Christmas lights dangling over the patio. This is not a fine-dining restaurant, so don't be surprised if the one waiter on staff serves your table in stages. ⊠ *Blvd. Kukulcán, Km 12.7, Zona Hotelera* ☎ *998/840–6300* ✛ *1:C3.*

$$$ ✕ **Sasi Thai.** Despite the street-facing views, this open-air restaurant has
THAI one of the most pleasant settings in Cancún. Six thatch-roof cabanas— each housing four tables—are staggered on a hill and dimly lighted with cubed candles and marble lanterns. Plank floors lead to a bamboo bar where fruity mojitos and martinis are prepared. The menu features traditional Thai cuisine such as spring rolls, pork dumplings, red duck curry, and pad thai with chicken or shrimp. The mango crème brûlée with ginger sorbet makes it worth a special visit to this outdoor eatery. ⊠ *Casa Magna Marriott, Blvd. Kukulcán, Km 14.5, Zona Hotelera* ☎ *998/881–2000 Ext. 16* ⊕ *www.sasi-thai.com* ☾ *No lunch* ✛ *1:C3.*

$$$–$$$$ ✕ **Thai Lounge.** Expect a truly unique dining experience from the moment
THAI you walk into this garden oasis. After all, not many restaurants have a dolphin aquarium in the bar area. The individual huts with thatch roofs provide an intimate setting to sample spicy Thai dishes like roasted duck in coconut red curry, and the house favorite, a deep-fried fish fillet prepared with ginger, garlic, and a tamarind chile sauce. The bill of fare also features such traditional dishes as shrimp curry, Thai salad, and spicy chicken soup. Reservations are recommended. ⊠ *Plaza la Isla shopping center, Blvd. Kukulcán, Km 12.5, Zona Hotelera* ☎ *998/176– 8070* ⊕ *www.thai.com.mx* ☾ *No lunch* ✛ *1:C3.*

EL CENTRO

$–$$ ✕ **100% Natural.** You'll be surrounded by plants and modern Mayan
ECLECTIC sculptures when you eat at this open-air restaurant. Start the day with one of their signature omelets and a *bebida inteligente* ("intelligent drink") which combines fruit juice with ginseng. The lunch menu has soups, salads, pastas, and other vegetarian items. Sandwiches, soy burgers, and stuffed pitas are prepared with fresh-baked breads, or for those craving meat, there's grilled chicken, fish, and beef prepared fajita-style. Mexican and Italian specialties are also available. The neighboring 100% Integral shop sells whole-wheat breads and other goodies. ⊠ *Av. Sunyaxchén 62, Sm 25, El Centro* ☎ *998/884–0102* ⊕ *www.100natural.com* ✛ *2:A3.*

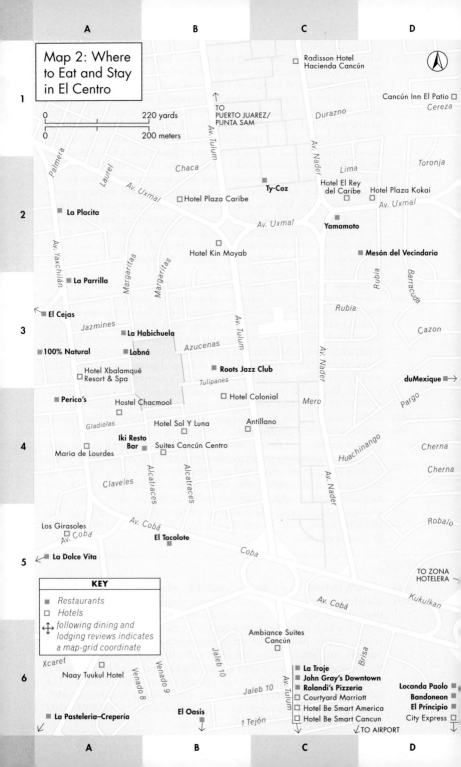

Map 2: Where to Eat and Stay in El Centro

0   220 yards
0   200 meters

TO PUERTO JUAREZ/ PUNTA SAM

Radisson Hotel Hacienda Cancún

Cancún Inn El Patio
Cereza

Durazno

Toronja

Palmera
Laurel
Av. Uxmal
Chaca

Av. Nader

Lima

Ty-Coz

Hotel El Rey del Caribe

Hotel Plaza Kokai

Hotel Plaza Caribe

Av. Uxmal

La Placita

Av. Uxmal

Yamamoto

Av. Yaxchilán

Margaritas
Margaritas

Hotel Kin Mayab

Mesón del Vecindario

Rubia

Barracuda

La Parrilla

Rubia

Cazon

El Cejas

Jazmines

Av. Tulum

Azucenas

La Habichuela

Roots Jazz Club

Av. Nader

duMexique →

100% Natural
Labná

Hotel Xbalamqué Resort & Spa

Tulipanes

Hotel Colonial

Mero

Pargo

Perico's

Hostel Chacmool

Gladiolas

Hotel Sol Y Luna

Antillano

Iki Resto Bar

Suites Cancún Centro

Maria de Lourdes

Huachinango

Cherna

Claveles

Alcatraces
Alcatraces

Av. Nader

Cherna

Los Girasoles
Av. Cobá

El Tacolote

Robalo

La Dolce Vita

Coba

TO ZONA HOTELERA

Kukulkan

KEY

■   Restaurants
□   Hotels
↔   following dining and lodging reviews indicates a map-grid coordinate

Av. Cobá

Ambiance Suites Cancún

Brisa

Xcaret

Naay Tuukul Hotel

Venado 8
Venado 9
Venado

Jaleb 10

La Troje
John Gray's Downtown
Rolandi's Pizzeria
Courtyard Marriott
Hotel Be Smart America
Hotel Be Smart Cancun

Locanda Paolo
Bandoneon
El Principio
City Express

Jaleb 10

Av. Tulum

La Pasteleria–Creperia

El Oasis

1 Tejón

TO AIRPORT

2

$$$–$$$$
ARGENTINE

✕ **Bandoneon**. From the moment you enter the restaurant, you might think you've taken a "right" turn and ended up in Buenos Aires. Every detail replicates the streets of Argentina, right down to the cobblestone floors, the dramatic tango music, and the indoor market that offers wine and pasta. The walls are adorned with antique *bandoneons* (concertinas, similar to the accordion) and paintings of tango dancers. In the center of the restaurant are two enormous lighthouse structures, guarding more than 100 Argentinean wines. The overwhelming menu includes starters like smoked marlin and charcoal-grilled provolone cheese. In addition to beef, Bandoneon also serves salads, pasta, fish, and chicken. The sizzling rib-eye steak is extremely tender and succulent, but if you're health-conscious, ask for a leaner cut. If you still have room for dessert, try the brandy-soaked cake roll with caramel filling and dark chocolate sauce. With 160 seats, this place can get a bit chaotic at times, and reservations are recommended. ⊠ *Av. Bonampak at Nichupté, El Centro* ☎ 998/889–9500 ⊕ *www.bandoneonrestaurantes.com* ✛ 2:D6.

$$–$$$
SEAFOOD

✕ **El Cejas**. The seafood is fresh at this open-air eatery, and the clientele is lively—often joining in song with the musicians who stroll among the tables. If you've had a wild night, try the *vuelva a la vida,* or "return to life" (conch, oysters, shrimp, octopus, calamari, and fish with a hot tomato sauce). The kitchen serves crab (stuffed, steamed, or fried) and whole-fried fish that is crispy on the outside and moist on the inside. The ceviche and the spicy shrimp soup are also good, though the quality can be inconsistent. A favorite with El Centro locals, this no-frills eatery is casual and easy on the wallet, so don't expect to be pampered. ⊠ *Mercado Veintiocho, on southwest end, Loc 90–100, Sm 26, El Centro* ☎ 998/887–1080 ✛ 2:A3.

$$$–$$$$
ITALIAN
Fodor's Choice
★

✕ **La Dolce Vita**. This grande dame of Cancún restaurants delivers on the promise of its name (which means "the sweet life" in Italian). In business since 1983, this local favorite has candlelit tables and discreet waiters who will make you feel as if you've been transported to Italy. The Italian fare includes homemade pizzas and pastas such as Bolognese-style lasagna, veal ravioli, and calamari steak in shrimp and lobster sauce. The wine list is excellent, and the dessert truffle is a must for chocolate lovers. Live jazz is offered from 7 to 11 pm every day except Sunday. Be patient when waiting for your order, though, as good food takes time to prepare. ⊠ *Av. Cobá No. 87, El Centro* ☎ 998/884–3393 ⊕ *www.ladolcevitacancun.com* ✛ 2:A5.

$$$
FRENCH

✕ **duMexique**. Discreetly located on the bustling Avenida Bonampak, this hidden gem shows no resemblance to a restaurant. Chef Alain Grimond and his wife Sonya have converted their home into an intimate dinner-party setting to create a dining experience unlike any other. Doubling as a gallery, the dining room features modern art, a grand piano, and a crystal chandelier that casts spectrums of light onto the pristine ceiling. Accommodating only 20 guests per evening, the restaurant begins the ritual with martinis in the tropical garden, decorated with tiki torches, dark rattan furniture, glass lanterns, and microsuede cushions. The French menu (featuring five appetizers, five entrées, and four desserts) changes daily and is never repeated.

Selections might include duckling with risotto or entrecôte with wine sauce. By calling ahead, you can request *soufflé de huitlacoche,* a delicacy made from mushrooms that grow on cornstalks. A fusion for the eye and palate, each course is a masterpiece of presentation. Be sure to visit the kitchen, where the awards of master chef Grimond are on display. ⊠ *Av. Bonampak 109, Sm 3, El Centro* ☎ *998/884–5919* ⌨ *Reservations essential* ☉ *Closed Sun. No lunch* ✢ *2:D3.*

WORD OF MOUTH

"For good eats you will have to venture into downtown. Fairly easy to do via bus. Once outside the Hotel Zone, use taxis to get around. In downtown, you pretty much pay 20 to 30 pesos for the places you would want to go."
— CancunWithMe

$$$–$$$$
CARIBBEAN
★

✕ **La Habichuela.** Elegant yet cozy, the much-loved Green Bean has an indoor dining room, as well as an outdoor area full of Mayan sculptures and local trees and flowers. Don't miss the famous *crema de habichuela* (a rich, cream-based vegetable soup) or the *cocobichuela* (lobster and shrimp in a light curry sauce served inside a coconut). Seafood lovers will get their fix with Caribbean lobster tail or giant shrimp prepared ten different ways. The menu also features chicken, pasta, and shish kebab flambé. Finish off your meal with Xtabentun, a Mayan liqueur made with honey and anise. ⊠ *Av. Margaritas 25, Sm 22, El Centro* ☎ *998/884–3158* ⊕ *www.lahabichuela.com* ✢ *2:B3.*

$$–$$$
ASIAN
Fodor'sChoice
★

✕ **Iki Resto Bar.** Framing the town square of Parque de las Palapas, this chic, Zen-like utopia dares to go where few restaurants have gone before. The thatched temple beckons you into its velvet sanctuary, discreetly lighted with beaded lamps, candles shaped like Buddha, and teardrop crystal globes. The main lounge features a tropical tributary, a glowing cobalt bar, antique Victorian furniture, and a wine wall complete with a sliding ladder. Slow-spinning palm fans twirl overhead while the sounds of chill music ties together this eclectic setting. Those seeking a bit more privacy can hide away in the Balinese cabana adorned with overstuffed pillows and bamboo flooring. Blending styles in both decor and cuisine, Iki showcases contemporary Asian-infused dishes like oriental pot stickers and coconut cream soup, all with a pinch of Latin flavor. The shrimp "siva" wrap, rolled in spinach and topped with red curry, is deliciously exotic. The young, hip staff also serves sweet conclusions like chocolate cake with green-tea ice cream. ⊠ *Alcatraces 39, Sm 22, in front of Parque de las Palapas, El Centro* ☎ *998/884–7024* ☉ *Closed Sun. No lunch.* ✢ *2:A4.*

$$$–$$$$
ECLECTIC
★

✕ **John Gray's Downtown.** This urban bistro, chef John Gray's fourth and newest eatery, brings a touch of New York into the heart of El Centro. Warehouse meets Zen in the informal yet sophisticated dining room, which has hardwood floors, exposed air ducts, dim light from dangling light bulbs, red velvet cushions, and a chicle tree enclosed in glass. Lack of detail on the chalkboard menu might deliver a pleasant surprise: the nondescript "duck" could come on a bed of sweet potatoes, topped with chile, chipotle, and tequila sauce. The goat-cheese pizza and duck pâté with red onion marmalade are excellent starters—follow with pork loin with Roquefort crust. You can watch the chefs at work in the open

2

kitchen; there's also a lounge area with chilled-out music and powerful martinis. ✉ *Av. Xpuhil, Sm 19, Mza 2, Lote 24, El Centro* ☎ 998/883–9800 ⊕ *www. johngrayrestaurantgroup.com.* ✛ *2:C6*.

$ ✕ **Labná.** Yucatecan cuisine reaches new and exotic heights at this
MEXICAN   Mayan-themed restaurant, with fabulous dishes prepared by chef
★   Elviro Pol. The *papadzules* (tortillas stuffed with eggs and covered with pumpkin sauce) are a delicious starter; for an entrée, try the *poc chuc* (tender pork loin in a sour orange sauce) or *longaniza de Valladolid* (traditional sausage from the village of Valladolid). Finish off your meal with some *maja blanco* (white pudding), and Xtabentun-infused Mayan coffee. You may want to linger and enjoy the trio that performs traditional Mexican music Friday through Sunday evenings. ✉ *Av. Margaritas 29, Sm 22, El Centro* ☎ 998/892–3056 ⊕ *www. labna.com* ✛ *2:B3*.

$$$ ✕ **Locanda Paolo.** Flowers and artwork lend warmth to this sophisti-
ITALIAN   cated restaurant, and the staff is attentive without being fussy. The Italian cuisine includes linguine with lobster and angel hair pasta with seafood. The chicken, stuffed with Serrano ham, spinach, and mushrooms, is also delicious. Despite the formal setting, the staff is laid-back and seems to know everyone who walks in the door, most of whom are locals who have been dining at the restaurant for over 20 years. On any given night, many of Chef Paolo Ceravolo's dishes are specials that do not appear on the menu; most are colorful and innovative, such as hot, coiled bread rolls interlaced with piquant mushrooms and eggplant. The international wines are a major draw for locals, as are the specialty lasagnas, which are revised every four months. ✉ *Av. Bonampak 145, on corner of Calle Jurel, Sm 3, El Centro* ☎ 998/887–2627 ⊕ *www. locandapaolo.com* ✛ *2:D6*.

$$ ✕ **Mesón del Vecindario.** This sweet little restaurant, tucked away from
ECLECTIC   the street, resembles a Swiss A-frame house. The menu has all kinds of cheese and beef fondues along with terrific salads, crepes, lasagna, vegetarian empanadas, and baked goods. Homemade desserts include flan, brownies, and a flaky apple strudel. Popular with El Centro locals is the daily buffet offered from 1 to 5. This is one of the few restaurants in El Centro that has patio seating with a view of trees. ✉ *Av. Uxmal 23, Sm 3, El Centro* ☎ 998/884–8900 ☉ *Closed Sun. No dinner* ✛ *2:D2*.

$$ ✕ **El Oasis.** This appropriately named eatery offers a welcome escape
SEAFOOD   from El Centro's busy streets. A small wooden bridge leads the way into a palapa, which is colorfully decorated with turquoise chairs, mosaic flooring, seashell lamps, and a bamboo bar. Diners can relax to the sounds of a cascading waterfall, skirted by palm trees and tropical plants. House specials include grilled seafood with rice; fish fillet with coconut cream; and shrimp with mango, tamarind, and guava salsa. This spot is popular with the locals; menus are in Spanish, and the staff doesn't speak much English. ✉ *Prol. Yaxchilan, Sm 17, Mza 2, Lote 3, El Centro* ☎ 998/884–4106 ✛ *2:B6*.

$$$–$$$$ ✕ **La Parrilla.** With its flamboyant live mariachi music and energetic
MEXICAN   waiters, this place is a Cancún classic. The menu isn't fancy, but it offers good, basic Mexican food. Two reliably tasty choices are the mixed grill (chicken, steak, shrimp) and the grilled Tampiqueña-style

steak. Combining entertainment and cuisine, waiters flame broil lobster, salmon, shrimp, and filet mignon directly at your table. Offered are 30 different taco dishes as well as sizzling fajitas and thick burritos. Choose from a wide selection of tequilas to accompany your meal. Reservations are recommended. ⊠ *Av. Yaxchilán 51, Sm 22, El Centro* ☎ 998/287–8118 ⊕ *www.laparrilla.com.mx* ✛ *2:A3.*

$–$$ ✕ **La Pasteleteria-Crepería.** This cheery café and bakery has comfortable
CAFÉ *equipales* (rustic Mexican chairs) to plop into as you sample terrific soups, salads, and pizzas. The crepes are what keep the locals coming back for more (the turkey-breast crepe makes a perfect lunch), as well as a variety of sumptuous pastries baked on-site. For travelers with a sweet tooth, this is the best place to buy a delectable dessert. The strawberry shortcake is exceptional. Somewhat difficult to find, this downtown gem is on the bustling Avenida Cobá near Walmart. ⊠ *Av. Cobá 7, past Av. Labna, Sm 25, El Centro* ☎ 998/884–3420 ✛ *2:A6.*

$$$–$$$$ ✕ **Perico's.** Okay—it's a tourist trap. But it's really fun. Bar stools here
MEXICAN are topped with saddles, and waiters dressed as revolutionaries serve flaming drinks and desserts while mariachi and marimba bands play (loudly). Every so often everyone jumps up to join the conga line; your reward for galloping through the restaurant and nearby streets is a free shot of tequila. With 370 seats, this place brings in vacationers by the busload. The Mexican menu (tacos, seafood, fajitas, kebabs) is passable, but the real reason to come is the nonstop party. For a photo op, stop in the lobby, where you can try on authentic Mexican clothing and pose with props like sombreros and ponchos. ⊠ *Av. Yaxchilán 61, Sm 25, El Centro* ☎ 998/884–3152 ⊕ *www.pericos.com.mx* ✛ *2:A4.*

$$–$$$ ✕ **La Placita.** The menu is simple but tasty at this brightly decorated
MEXICAN downtown fixture, where plastic tables and chairs are scattered around an outdoor grill. For those who want a more formal setting, the same menu is served indoors with colorful linens and Mexican music to match. The mixed grill of sausage, steak, and pork chops is a standout, as are the glorious barbecued ribs and the tequila shrimp. A local favorite since 1988 is the *arrachera* (flank steak) served with a basket of warm tortillas. A selection of tasty pastas and salads is also available. A cold beer makes a perfect accompaniment, and the banana flambé is the ideal way to complete a meal. ⊠ *Av. Yaxchilán 12, Sm 22, El Centro* ☎ 998/884–0407 ✛ *2:A2.*

$ ✕ **El Principio.** Despite its rather simple decor, this small and rustic bistro
ITALIAN restaurant, a lunch-hour favorite among Cancún execs, is arguably the
★ best place in town for pasta. The owner, José Campos Frias, is a thirty-something cooking genius. His dishes fuse traditional Italian cuisine with his grandmother's Mexican recipes. The salmon and mango salad with cilantro dressing is a meal in itself. Those with hearty appetites should try the exotic oriental spaghetti or the meatball panini in chipotle sauce. The portions here are enormous (two people often share one entrée). There are only eight tables, so it gets crowded at times; takeout is also available. Lunch is served beginning at 1 pm. ⊠ *Av. Bonampak 227, Sm 4, El Centro* ☎ 998/892–8499 ⊙ *Closed Mon* ✛ *2:B6.*

$–$$ ✕ **Rolandi's Pizzeria.** A Cancún landmark for more than 30 years,
PIZZA Rolandi's continues to draw crowds with its scrumptious wood-fired

2

pizzas. There are 20 varieties to choose from—if you can't make up your mind, try the one with Roquefort cheese, or the "Pizza Popeye" piled with spinach, tomato, basil, and fresh mozzarella. The calzones are smothered with olive oil and packed with fresh ingredients like asparagus, mushrooms, and ham. Homemade pasta dishes like the veal-stuffed ravioli or vegetable lasagna are also very good. Check their Web site for discounts on your next visit. ⊠ *Av. Cobá 12, Sm 5, El Centro* ☎ *998/884–4047* ⊕ *www.rolandi.com* ✛ *2:C6.*

$$–$$$
CAFÉ

✕ **Roots Jazz Club.** Locals and tourists mingle here to enjoy contemporary jazz and flamenco music (piped in during the afternoon but live at night). The performances are the main attraction, but there's also an eclectic, international menu of salads, soups, sandwiches, and pastas. The tables nearest the window, along the quaint pedestrianized Avenida Tulipanes, are the best place to tuck into your *chíchí* (chicken breast stuffed with ham and veggies) or German sausage, since the stage area tends to get crowded. This candlelit venue also frequently hosts local art events. ⊠ *Av. Tulipanes 26, Sm 22, El Centro* ☎ *998/884–2437* ☉ *Closed Sun.–Wed. No lunch* ✛ *2:B3.*

$–$$
MEXICAN

✕ **El Tacolote.** A great place to stop for lunch, this popular *taquería* (taco stand) sells delicious fajitas, grilled kebabs, burritos, and all kinds of tacos. The salsa, which comes with every meal, is fresh and *muy picante* (very hot). Ask for the two-person *parrillada,* a hearty sampler of barbecued meat, served with all the beer you can guzzle in one hour. Portions are large and far from "light," so come with an appetite, especially if you order the stuffed chiles smothered with cheese, salsa, and beans. A mariachi band plays nightly at 8. ⊠ *Av. Cobá 19, Sm 22, El Centro* ☎ *998/887–3045* ⊕ *www.eltacolote.com* ✛ *2:B5.*

$–$$
ECLECTIC
Fodor's Choice
★

✕ **La Troje.** From the moment you enter the garden patio, you'll feel as if you've tapped into a local hideaway. Potted ferns hang from wooden beams in this charming setting that's fashioned around oak trees that pierce through the bamboo roof. A brick staircase leads into the main dining area, where Chef Ana Cano and her two daughters prepare homemade pastas, pizzas, baguettes, and crepes. The colorful menu features 21 different salads, all with the distinctive flavors of fruits, nuts, cheeses, and tangy dressings. For a local favorite, try the grilled chicken stuffed with spinach, apricots, and cream cheese. Early birds can enjoy the full breakfast menu, which includes blended smoothies and fresh-squeezed juices. Although the prices are unbeatable, the service tends to be somewhat brisk. ⊠ *Av. Acanceh, Sm 15, El Centro* ☎ *998/887–9556* ☉ *Closed Sun.* ✛ *2:C6.*

¢–$
CAFÉ

✕ **Ty-Coz.** Tucked behind the Comercial Mexicana grocery store and across from the bus station on Avenida Tulum, this inexpensive restaurant serves croissants and freshly brewed coffee that make for a delicious breakfast. At lunchtime, stop in for a huge sandwich stuffed with all the deli classics. The ham-and-cheese baguette is as good as anything you'll find in Paris, and the coffee—available as early as 6 am—is brewed with bottled water. Pictures of France adorn the walls of the small dining room. ⊠ *Av. Tulum, Sm 2, El Centro* ☎ *998/884–6060* ▭ *No credit cards* ☉ *Closed Sun.* ✛ *2:C2.*

$$–$$$
JAPANESE
✕ **Yamamoto.** As the oldest Japanese restaurant in Cancún, Yamamoto has some of the best sushi in the area. In addition to sashimi, there's a menu of traditional Japanese dishes (like chicken teriyaki and tempura) for those who prefer their food cooked. Large groups can order combination platters of sushi, sashimi, *kushikatsu,* and *gyoza.* The dining room is tranquil, with Japanese art and bamboo accents, but you can also call for delivery to your hotel room. ⊠ *Av. Uxmal 31, Sm 3, El Centro* ☎ *998/887–3366, 998/860–0269 for delivery service* ⊕ *www. yamamoto-cancun.com* ✛ *2:C2.*

WHERE TO STAY

For expanded hotel reviews, visit Fodors.com.

You might find it bewildering to choose among Cancún's many hotels, not least because brochures and Web sites make them sound—and look—almost exactly alike. For luxury and amenities, the Zona Hotelera is the place to stay. In the modest Centro, local color outweighs facilities. The hotels there are more basic and much less expensive than those in the Zona. If you are looking to be in the heart of the action, northern hotels near Punta Cancún are within walking distance of the nightclubs. Quieter properties are located at the southern end of Boulevard Kukulcán and in the residential streets between El Centro and the Hotel Zone at Laguna Nichupté near the Pok-Ta-Pok Golf Course.

PRICES

Many hotels have all-inclusive packages, as well as theme-night parties complete with food, beverages, activities, and games. Mexican, Italian, and Caribbean themes seem to be the most popular. Take note, however, that the larger the all-inclusive resort, the blander the food. For more-memorable dining, you may need to leave the grounds (and essentially pay for food you're not eating). Expect high prices for food and drink in most hotels. Many of the more exclusive hotels are starting to enforce a "no outside food or drink" policy—so discretion is advised.

Many of the larger and more popular all-inclusives will no longer guarantee an ocean-view room when you book your reservation. If this is important to you, then check that all rooms have ocean views at your chosen hotel, or book only at places that will guarantee a view. Be sure to bring your confirmation information with you to prove you paid for an ocean-view room. Also be careful with towel charges, since many of the resorts have started charging up to $25 for towels not returned. Be sure your returns are duly noted by the pool staff. When checking out, make sure the hotel hasn't tacked on excessive phone or minibar expenses, as some tend to do.

PUNTA SAM

The area north of Cancún is slowly being developed into an alternative hotel zone, known informally as Zona Hotelera Norte. This is an ideal area for a tranquil beach vacation, since the shops, restaurants, and nightlife of Cancún are about 45 minutes away by cab.

$$$$ **Excellence Playa Mujeres.** North of mainland Cancún, this adults-only resort has redefined the all-inclusive concept. **Pros:** beautifully sculpted grounds; relaxation spa. **Cons:** repetitive restaurant menus; far removed from activity outside resort. **TripAdvisor:** "loved everything this hotel had to offer," "overwhelmed by the superior quality of the service," "wish we were still there." ⊠ *Prolongacíon Bonampak s/n, Punta Sam, Lote Terrenos 001, Mza 001, Sm 003, Zona Continental de Isla Mujeres* ☎ *998/872–8600* ⊕ *www.excellence-resorts.com* ⇆ *450 rooms* ⚬ *In-room: Wi-Fi. In-hotel: restaurants, bars, golf course, pools, tennis courts, gym, spa, beach, water sports, laundry facilities, parking, some age restrictions* ¶◎¶ *All-inclusive* ✛ *3:C1.*

ZONA HOTELERA

$$–$$$ **Aquamarina Beach Hotel Cancún.** This family-friendly hotel is just a 10-minute walk from El Embarcadero marina and the casino. **Pros:** all-inclusive plan available; many recreational activities for kids and adults; affordable. **Cons:** small beach; no Internet in rooms; at this writing, west-facing rooms had construction views. **TripAdvisor:** "half a step up from motel accommodations," "great location, good price," "food was excellent as you had so much to choose from." ⊠ *Blvd. Kukulcán, Km 4.5, Zona Hotelera* ☎ *998/849–4606* ⊕ *www.aquamarinabeach.com* ⇆ *172 rooms* ⚬ *In-hotel: restaurants, bars, pools, beach, water sports, business center, parking* ¶◎¶ *Multiple meal plans* ✛ *3:B1.*

$$$–$$$$ **Avalon Baccara Cancún.** Amid the towering resorts with sleek, modern interiors that line the Zona Hotelera, the Avalon Baccara stands out for its small size and rustic Mexican design. **Pros:** refreshing home-like setting unlike all-inclusive–resort style; artistically unique. **Cons:** hard beds; small pool and patios; some rooms lack Internet access. **TripAdvisor:** "would definitely stay here again," "can walk to shopping and good restaurants," "roomy quiet and the price was fair." ⊠ *Blvd. Kukulcán, Km 11.5, Zona Hotelera* ☎ *998/881–3900* ⊕ *www.avalonvacations.com* ⇆ *8 rooms, 19 suites* ⚬ *In-room: kitchen (some). In-hotel: restaurants, pool, beach, parking* ¶◎¶ *No meals* ✛ *3:C2.*

$$$–$$$$ **Avalon Grand Cancún.** Formerly a time-share property, the Avalon Grand Cancún now operates as a traditional hotel. **Pros:** guests have access to facilities at nearby sister resort Avalon Baccara. **Cons:** Wi-Fi costs extra; understaffed. **TripAdvisor:** "pool bar was great," "take advantage of the room service," "stay was fantastic." ⊠ *Blvd. Kukulcán, Km 11.5, Zona Hotelera* ☎ *998/848–9300* ⊕ *www.avalonvacations.com* ⇆ *39 rooms, 80 suites* ⚬ *In-room: kitchen (some), Wi-Fi. In-hotel: restaurants, bars, pools, gym, spa, beach, children's programs, parking* ¶◎¶ *No meals* ✛ *3:C3.*

$$$$ **Barceló Costa Cancún.** Ferries to Isla Mujeres are just steps away from this resort, as it neighbors one of Cancún's main piers, El Embarcadero.

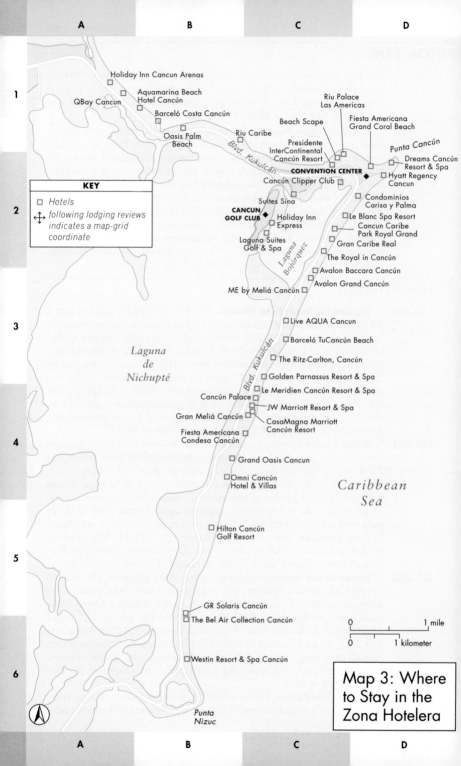

Map 3: Where to Stay in the Zona Hotelera

2

Pros: great for kids; close to Embarcadero; good water-sports center. **Cons:** no air-conditioning in lobby; small beach area; check-in/out times are chaotic in the lobby area. **TripAdvisor:** "we enjoyed the food," "best meal of the day is breakfast," "customer service is not their top priority." ⌧ *Blvd. Kukulcán, Km 4.5, Zona Hotelera* ☎ *998/849–7100* ⊕ *www.barcelo.com* ↩ *258 rooms, 5 suites* ⌂ *In-room: Wi-Fi. In-hotel: restaurants, bars, pool, gym, spa, beach, water sports, children's programs, laundry facilities, parking* ⍾ *All-inclusive.* ✢ *3:B1.*

$$$$ ▦ **Barceló TuCancún Beach.** Just behind the massive Kukulcán Plaza and about a half mile down the road from La Isla, this resort is an ideal location for mall addicts. **Pros:** near two of Cancún's biggest malls; wide range of activities for children and adults. **Cons:** main pool area can get noisy; tennis costs $15. **TripAdvisor:** "would certainly return here again," "found the service to be fantastic," "a bit rundown." ⌧ *Blvd. Kukulcán, Km 13.5, Zona Hotelera* ☎ *998/891–5900* ⊕ *www.barcelo. com* ↩ *316 rooms, 16 villas* ⌂ *In-hotel: restaurants, bars, pools, tennis courts, spa, beach, water sports, business center, parking* ⍾ *All-inclusive* ✢ *3:C3.*

$$ ▦ **Beach Scapes.** This condo hotel is a wonderful place for families thanks to its tranquil beach and relaxed atmosphere. **Pros:** all rooms have balconies. **Cons:** small beach; no children's programs. ⌧ *Blvd. Kukulcán, Km 8.5, Zona Hotelera* ☎ *998/891–5400* ⊕ *www.kinhabeach. com* ↩ *80 rooms, 50 suites* ⌂ *In-room: kitchen (some). In-hotel: restaurants, pool, gym, beach, laundry facilities, business center, parking* ⍾ *Breakfast.* ✢ *3:C1.*

$$$–$$$$ ▦ **The Bel Air Collection Cancún.** The design scheme at this strikingly chic and tranquil resort is unlike that of any other hotel along Boulevard Kukulcán. **Pros:** luxurious spa; all-inclusive plan available; aesthetically pleasing hotel. **Cons:** no kids under 12; far from party zone; open-air lobby can be very wet and windy during rainy season. **TripAdvisor:** "front desk staff was very helpful in arranging transportation," "be careful about the hidden extra costs," "beds were comfortable but a little hard." ⌧ *Blvd. Kukulcán, Km 20.5, Zona Hotelera* ☎ *998/193–1770* ⊕ *www.belaircollection.com* ↩ *136 rooms, 19 suites* ⌂ *In-room: Wi-Fi. In-hotel: restaurants, bars, pool, gym, spa, beach, parking, some age restrictions* ⍾ *Multiple meal plans* ✢ *3:B5.*

$$$$ ▦ **Le Blanc Spa Resort.** An airy and modern hotel with white and beige refined minimalist decor and lots of windows, Le Blanc Spa is the most upscale of the Palace Resorts properties in Cancún. **Pros:** aesthetically pleasing design; excellent spa; butler service. **Cons:** no kids; pricey. **TripAdvisor:** "quiet Zen like feel," "service there was great," "unbelievable tranquility and beauty." ⌧ *Blvd. Kukulcán, Km 10, Zona Hotelera* ☎ *998/881–4740* ⊕ *www.leblancsparesort.com* ↩ *246 rooms, 14 suites* ⌂ *In-room: Wi-Fi. In-hotel: restaurants, bars, pools, gym, spa, beach, water sports, parking, some age restrictions* ⍾ *All-inclusive* ✢ *3:C2.*

Fodor'sChoice ★

$$$$ ▦ **Cancún Caribe Park Royal Grand.** There's a wide variety of accommodations at the Cancún Caribe, and most have ocean views. **Pros:** most rooms face ocean; excellent pool areas. **Cons:** Internet costs extra; poor customer service. **TripAdvisor:** "extremely clean lovely updated

room gorgeous beach," "lots of food options," "can't wait to go back." ✉ *Blvd. Kukulcán, Km 10.5, Zona Hotelera* ☎ 998/848–7800 ⊕ *www. park-royalhotels.com* ⤳ *263 rooms, 23 suites* ⚅ *In-room: Internet. In-hotel: restaurants, bars, pools, gym, spa, beach, water sports, children's programs, business center, parking* ⬦❘ *All-inclusive* ✛ *3:C2.*

$$$ ⛱ **Cancún Clipper Club.** Right next to the Zona Hotelera's main hub of shops and clubs, this hotel still manages to feel secluded because it's set back from Boulevard Kukulcán. **Pros:** close proximity to lots of activities. **Cons:** no beach. **TripAdvisor:** "hidden gem," "good value in good location," "wasn't anything fancy but they had the necessities." ✉ *Blvd. Kukulcán, Km 9, Zona Hotelera* ☎ 998/891–5999 ⊕ *www.clipper.com. mx* ⤳ *71 rooms, 71 suites* ⚅ *In-room: kitchen (some). In-hotel: restaurant, bar, pool, tennis court, business center, parking* ⬦❘ *Multiple meal plans* ✛ *3:C2.*

$$$$ ⛱ **Cancún Palace.** The soothing sound of running water coupled with the creamy hues and light-color walls and floors will put you immediately at ease when you enter this sophisticated minimalist hotel. **Pros:** kids' and teens' center; two tennis courts; access to Palace Resorts' sister properties. **Cons:** some rooms lack ocean views; no water sports; at this writing, north-facing rooms had construction views. **TripAdvisor:** "all the staff was friendly and helpful," "loved the sunsets at night on the lagoon," "pool was the best." ✉ *Blvd. Kukulcán, Km 14.5, Zona Hotelera* ☎ 998/881–3600 ⊕ *www.palaceresorts.com* ⤳ *601 rooms, 24 suites* ⚅ *In-room: Wi-Fi. In-hotel: restaurants, bars, pool, tennis courts, gym, spa, beach, children's program, parking* ⬦❘ *All-inclusive* ✛ *3:B4.*

$$$$ ⛱ **CasaMagna Marriott Cancún Resort.** Sweeping grounds and arched
     ☾   walkways that lead up to the six-story building will make you forget you're at a Marriott. **Pros:** more culturally traditional than most Marriotts; excellent Thai restaurant; on-site wedding planner and car rental. **Cons:** geared to groups and conventions, which account for 60% of the hotel's business. **TripAdvisor:** "hotel is very expensive," "the beach is nice," "bed was very comfortable and the room was spacious." ✉ *Blvd. Kukulcán, Km 14.5, Zona Hotelera* ☎ 998/881–2000 or 800/900–8800 ⊕ *www.casamagnacancun.com* ⤳ *415 rooms, 38 suites* ⚅ *In-room: kitchen (some), Wi-Fi. In-hotel: restaurants, bars, pool, tennis courts, gym, spa, beach, water sports, children's programs, business center, parking* ⬦❘ *Multiple meal plans* ✛ *3:B4.*

$$ ⛱ **Condominios Carisa y Palma.** Unlike many resorts in the area, this budget-price condo hotel is over 30 years old. **Pros:** beachfront location; five-minute walk from nightclubs and markets. **Cons:** street-side rooms with lagoon views are noisy; no restuarant. ✉ *Blvd. Kukulcán, Km 9.5, Zona Hotelera* ☎ 998/883–0211 or 998/883–0287 ⊕ *www. carisaypalma.com* ⤳ *122 rooms* ⚅ *In-room: kitchen. In-hotel: pool, tennis court, gym, beach, business center, parking* ⬦❘ *No meals* ✛ *3:D2.*

$$$$ ⛱ **Dreams Cancún Resort & Spa.** Surrounded on three sides by ocean,
     ☾   this resort provides stunning panoramic views of the Caribbean. **Pros:** dolphin aquarium; excellent beach access; family theme nights. **Cons:** swimming with dolphins costs extra; lobby extremely crowded during check-in hours. **TripAdvisor:** "energetic entertainment staff," "room

service was the best," "don't think there could be a bad room." ⊠ *Blvd. Kukulcán, Km 9.5, Punta Cancún, Zona Hotelera* ☎ *998/ 848–7000* ⊕ *www.dreamsresorts. com* ⊋ *345 rooms, 34 suites* ♿ *In-room: Wi-Fi. In-hotel: restaurants, bars, pools, tennis court, gym, spa, beach, water sports, children's programs, parking* ⫯⊘ *All-inclusive* ⊹ *3:D2.*

$$$$ 🏨 **Fiesta Americana Condesa Cancún.**
☺ This hotel is easily recognized by the 118-foot-tall palapa that covers its lobby. **Pros:** friendly staff; centrally located; smaller pools designated for children. **Cons:** time-share pitch; popular with tour groups. **TripAdvisor:** "would definitely return and bring my kids," "would highly recommend," "great food choices casual atmosphere." ⊠ *Blvd. Kukulcán, Km 16.5, Zona Hotelera* ☎ *998/881–4200* ⊕ *www.fiestaamericana.com* ⊋ *476 rooms, 26 suites* ♿ *In-room: Wi-Fi. In-hotel: restaurants, bars, pools, gym, spa, beach, water sports, children's programs, parking* ⫯⊘ *All-inclusive* ⊹ *3:B4.*

$$$$ 🏨 **Fiesta Americana Grand Coral Beach.** If luxury's your bag, you'll feel
★ right at home at this distinctive all-suites hotel. **Pros:** enormous pool with three swim-up bars; complimentary kids' club; business center has private offices. **Cons:** main lobby feels cold; too big for some; Wi-Fi costs extra. **TripAdvisor:** "hotel itself was beautiful," "would highly recommend," "they go out of their way to make your stay top notch." ⊠ *Blvd. Kukulcán, Km 9.5, Zona Hotelera* ☎ *998/881–3200* ⊕ *www. fiestaamericanagrand.com* ⊋ *602 suites* ♿ *In-room: Wi-Fi. In-hotel: restaurants, bars, pool, gym, spa, beach, water sports, children's programs, business center, parking* ⫯⊘ *No meals* ⊹ *3:D2.*

$$$–$$$$ 🏨 **Golden Parnassus Resort & Spa.** The rooms at this all-inclusive, adults-only resort are warmly decorated with sunset colors, fruit baskets, and rich wood furnishings; some rooms even have private hot tubs. **Pros:** free shuttle to sister property Great Parnassus Resort & Spa; evening entertainment. **Cons:** no kids under 15; no Internet; slightly dated decor. **TripAdvisor:** "huge thank you to the entertainment staff," "room service is sometimes slow but you still get a great meal," "a great time." ⊠ *Blvd. Kukulcán, Km 14.5, Retorno San Miguelito Lote 37, Zona Hotelera* ☎ *998/848–7550* ⊕ *www.parnassusresorts. com* ⊋ *214 rooms* ♿ *In-hotel: restaurants, bars, pools, tennis courts, gym, spa, beach, water sports, parking, some age restrictions* ⫯⊘ *All-inclusive* ⊹ *3:B3.*

$$$–$$$$ ☷ **GR Solaris Cancún**. More upscale than its Royal Solaris sister property in Cancún, this resort is somewhat focused on adults. **Pros:** lighted tennis court; water-sports marina across from sister property; fully equipped free gym. **Cons:** pool area can get noisy; loud Mexican music in the lobby; rooms are nothing extraordinary. **TripAdvisor:** "loved 24 hour room service and a stocked fridge," "were pleasantly surprised with everything," "resort is small but great." ⊠ *Blvd. Kukulcán, Km 18.5, Zona Hotelera* ☎ *998/848–8400* ⊕ *www.hotelessolaris.com* ↩ *306 rooms* ⚬ *In-hotel: restaurants, bars, pools, tennis court, gym, spa, beach, water sports, children's programs, parking* ⏀ *All-inclusive* ✛ *3:B5.*

$$$–$$$$ ☷ **Gran Caribe Real**. There's no such thing as a standard room at this
☺   resort: the most basic option is a spacious junior suite with a sofa bed, sitting area, flat-screen TV, and balcony. **Pros:** wide array of land and water sports; gym has yoga and tai chi lessons. **Cons:** room decor uninspired; mediocre restaurants. **TripAdvisor:** "amenities were all great," "well worth the money," "would love to go back." ⊠ *Blvd. Kukulcán, Km 11.5, Zona Hotelera* ☎ *998/881–7300* ⊕ *www.realresorts.com* ↩ *487 suites* ⚬ *In-room: Wi-Fi (some). In-hotel: restaurants, bars, pools, tennis court, gym, spa, beach, water sports, children's programs, parking* ⏀ *All-inclusive* ✛ *3:C2.*

$$$–$$$$ ☷ **Gran Meliá Cancún**. This enormous beachfront hotel has been built to resemble a modern Mayan temple; its various atriums even have pyramid-shape roof skylights. **Pros:** all-inclusive plan available; privacy of Royal Service Tower; golf course. **Cons:** lacks intimacy due to size; Internet costs extra. **TripAdvisor:** "good location for downtown Cancun," "beautiful views, very clean rooms," "great place to end your evening." ⊠ *Blvd. Kukulcán, Km 16.5, Zona Hotelera* ☎ *998/881–1100* ⊕ *www.solmelia.com* ↩ *678 rooms, 53 suites* ⚬ *In-room: Internet. In-hotel: restaurants, bars, golf course, pools, tennis court, gym, spa, beach, water sports, children's programs, parking* ⏀ *Multiple meal plans* ✛ *3:B4.*

$$$$ ☷ **Grand Oasis Cancun**. This multi-structure hotel, comprised of a main building simply called Pyramid and two side buildings (Palmar I and Palmar II), is right next door to sister property and Spring Break mecca Be Live Cancún. **Pros:** enormous pool area; lively atmosphere. **Cons:** $4 charge for use of room safe; large grounds require fair amount of walking; too boisterous for some. **TripAdvisor:** "decor was beautiful," "buffet was very limited," "service within the hotel is brilliant." ⊠ *Blvd. Kukulcán, Km 16.5, Zona Hotelera* ☎ *998/881–7000* ⊕ *www. belivehotels.com* ↩ *736 rooms* ⚬ *In-hotel: restaurants, bars, golf course, pool, tennis courts, gym, spa, beach, water sports, children's programs, business center, parking* ⏀ *All-inclusive* ✛ *3:B4.*

$$$–$$$$ ☷ **Hilton Cancún Golf & Spa Resort**. The Caribbean plays a central role at
★   this resort, with ocean views from all standard guest rooms and junior suites. **Pros:** outstanding beachfront villas; tasteful decor; angled pool area gets all-day sunshine. **Cons:** only one heated pool; food quality is inconsistent; poor lighting in rooms. **TripAdvisor:** "room service was prompt and accommodating," "an amazing property with the best beach," "hotel and the grounds are beautiful." ⊠ *Blvd. Kukulcán, Km 17, Zona Hotelera* ☎ *998/881–8000* ⊕ *www.hiltoncancun.com* ↩ *426*

2

rooms, 23 suites, 82 villas △ In-room: Internet (some), Wi-Fi (some). In-hotel: restaurants, bars, golf course, pools, tennis courts, gym, spa, beach, water sports, children's programs, business center, parking ⏐◎⏐ *No meals ✥ 3:B5.*

$$–$$$ 🏨 **Holiday Inn Cancún Arenas.** Inside this white, sugar-cube-like struc-
ture are plenty of activities to keep your family satisfied. **Pros:** children under 12 years stay free; on-site lifeguard; free kids' club. **Cons:**
small beach; mosquitoes in common areas; mediocre food. **TripAdvisor:** "friendly and helpful staff," "hotel was very clean," "nice room."
✉ *Blvd. Kukulcán, Km 2.5, Zona Hotelera* ☎ *998/287–0500* ⊕ *www.
holidayinn.com/cancun-arenas* ⤴ *211 rooms, 3 suites △ In-room:
Wi-Fi. In-hotel: restaurants, bars, pools, gym, beach, water sports,
children's programs, laundry facilities, business center, parking, some
pets allowed* ⏐◎⏐ *Multiple meal plans ✥ 3:A1.*

$$–$$$ 🏨 **Holiday Inn Express.** Within walking distance of the Cancún Golf Club,
this hotel caters to business travelers and tourists seeking an affordable
alternative to the pricey resorts. **Pros:** price; good location; free shuttle
to beach. **Cons:** simple rooms; no elevator; not on beach. **TripAdvisor:**
"was disappointed by the rooms," "not on the main boulevard but
very near in a quieter neighborhood," "overall a very good value."
✉ *Paseo Pok-Ta-Pok, Lotes 21 and 22, off Blvd. Kukulcán, Km 7.5,
Zona Hotelera* ☎ *998/883–2200* ⊕ *www.hiexpress.com/cancunmex*
⤴ *119 rooms △ In-room: Wi-Fi, no safe. In-hotel: bar, restaurant, pool,
spa, parking* ⏐◎⏐ *Breakfast ✥ 3:C2.*

$$$$ 🏨 **Hyatt Regency Cancún.** Situated on the tip of Punta Cancún, this
14-story hotel offers the best views in Zona Hotelera. **Pros:** every room
has a water view; on-site beauty salon and car rental; entire property
remodeled in 2008; great restaurants. **Cons:** no children's programs;
bathrooms have showers only. **TripAdvisor:** "rooms were clean and
the service was above and beyond," "great location great service great
people and great beach," "nightlife is nearby." ✉ *Blvd. Kukulcán, Km
8.5, Zona Hotelera* ☎ *998/891–5555* ⊕ *www.cancun.regency.hyatt.
com* ⤴ *287 rooms, 8 suites △ In-room: Wi-Fi. In-hotel: restaurants,
bar, pool, gym, spa, beach, water sports, parking* ⏐◎⏐ *Breakfast ✥ 3:D2.*

$$$$ 🏨 **JW Marriott Cancún Resort & Spa.** This is the best hotel for experienc-
Fodor's Choice ing luxury, Cancún style, and good service. **Pros:** top-notch service;
★ huge spa; iPod docks; artificial reef. **Cons:** lacks the festive mood of
other hotels along the strip; breakfast buffet costs $25. **TripAdvisor:**
"front desk staff less than attentive," "good but not impressed," "caters
well to average American tourist." ✉ *Blvd. Kukulcán, Km 14.5, Zona
Hotelera* ☎ *998/848–9600 or 888/813–2776* ⊕ *www.marriott.com*
⤴ *448 rooms, 74 suites △ In-room: kitchen (some), Wi-Fi. In-hotel:
restaurants, bars, pools, tennis courts, gym, spa, beach, water sports,
children's programs, business center, parking* ⏐◎⏐ *No meals ✥ 3:B4.*

$$$$ 🏨 **Laguna Suites Golf & Spa.** Framing the fairway of Pok-Ta-Pok Golf
Course, this tranquil resort is comprised of 12 white-stucco buildings,
each housing four spacious suites. **Pros:** free shuttle to the beach every
hour; quiet location; access to golf course; all-inclusive plan available.
Cons: at the time of writing, west-facing rooms have construction views;
no children's activities; bathrooms have showers only. **TripAdvisor:**

"meals were high quality," "well worth the price," "quiet and peaceful atmosphere." ✉ *Paseo Pok Ta Pok #3, Zona Hotelera* ☎ *998/891–5252* ⊕ *www.lagunasuites.com.mx* ⇨ *48 suites* ⚿ *In-room: kitchen (some), Wi-Fi. In-hotel: restaurant, bar, golf course, pool, gym, spa, parking* ⏷ *Multiple meal plans* ✣ *3:C2.*

$$$$
Fodor's Choice
★
🛏 **Live AQUA Cancún.** You won't find raucous Spring Breakers or screaming kids at this Mexican-owned Hotelera Posadas property, which mostly attracts luxury-minded thirtysomething sun worshippers. **Pros:** huge suites; all rooms have oceanfront views; extensive spa services. **Cons:** aromatherapy scents in public spaces can be strong; sliding glass patio doors don't have screens; south-facing rooms had construction views at this writing. **TripAdvisor:** "design features were just right," "hotel is well kept," "resort is nice and we loved it." ✉ *Blvd. Kukulcán, Km 12.5, Zona Hotelera* ☎ *998/881–7600 or 888/782–9722* ⊕ *www. feel-aqua.com* ⇨ *335 rooms, 36 suites* ⚿ *In-room: Wi-Fi. In-hotel: restaurants, bars, pools, gym, spa, beach, parking* ⏷ *All-inclusive* ✣ *3:C3.*

$$$$
🛏 **Le Meridien Cancún Resort & Spa.** High on a hill and tucked away from the main boulevard, this refined yet relaxed hotel is an artful blend of art deco and Mayan styles; there's lots of wood, glass, and mirrors. **Pros:** near one of Cancún's best malls; large fitness center; all rooms with ocean or lagoon views; tastefully decorated. **Cons:** expensive considering that it's not all-inclusive; Wi-Fi costs extra; at this writing, south-facing rooms had construction views. **TripAdvisor:** "has the best gym," "low key but luxurious," "a great place to stay." ✉ *Blvd. Kukulcán, Km 14, Retorno del Rey, Lote 37, Zona Hotelera* ☎ *998/881–2200 or 800/543–4300* ⊕ *www.cancun.lemeridien.com* ⇨ *213 rooms, 26 suites* ⚿ *In-room: Wi-Fi. In-hotel: restaurants, bar, pools, tennis courts, gym, spa, beach, children's programs, parking* ⏷ *Multiple meal plans* ✣ *3:B4.*

$$$$
Fodor's Choice
★
🛏 **ME by Meliá Cancún.** The ME takes the chic flavor of a trendy boutique hotel and blows it up to the grand scale of a large resort. **Pros:** great for young couples; amazing contemporary design; pet-friendly. **Cons:** not ideal for kids; lacks traditional Mexican flavor. **TripAdvisor:** "restaurants were top notch and the service was even better," "enjoyed all our meals," "were able to walk to the mall." ✉ *Blvd. Kukulcán, Km 12, Zona Hotelera* ☎ *998/881–2500 or 998/881–2506* ⊕ *www.me-by-melia.com* ⇨ *348 rooms, 71 suites* ⚿ *In-room: Internet, Wi-Fi. In-hotel: restaurants, bars, pools, gym, spa, beach, business center, parking, some pets allowed* ⏷ *All-inclusive* ✣ *3:C3.*

$$$–$$$$
☾
🛏 **Oasis Palm Beach.** Within walking distance of El Embarcadero, this all-inclusive family resort sits in prime location if you're looking to take a boat to Isla Mujeres. **Pros:** great location; access to Grand Oasis Cancún golf course; good for families; Wi-Fi hotspot. **Cons:** no in-room Internet; only Jacuzzi is at the spa and costs extra. **TripAdvisor:** "rooms were fine and clean," "room had bugs," "restaurants are all very good except the seafood place." ✉ *Blvd. Kukulcán, Km 4.5, Zona Hotelera* ☎ *998/848–7500* ⊕ *www.hotelesoasis.com* ⇨ *468 rooms, 2 suites* ⚿ *In-hotel: restaurants, bars, pool, spa, beach, children's programs, parking* ⏷ *All-inclusive* ✣ *3:B1.*

$$$–$$$$
🛏 **Omni Cancún Hotel & Villas.** After undergoing a $17 million renovation in 2007, this 12-story hotel has definitely moved up a notch or

Live AQUA Cancún

two in Cancún's hotel hierarchy. **Pros:** all-inclusive plan available; tons of scheduled activities; educational programs at Kid's Club; on-site ATM. **Cons:** crowded pool area; time-share sales pitches in the lobby. **TripAdvisor:** "as well worth the price," "would highly recommend it," "service and ambiance were very good." ✉ *Blvd. Kukulcán, Km 16.5, Zona Hotelera* ☎ *998/881–0600* 🌐 *www.omnihotels.com* *259 rooms, 19 suites, 23 villas* *In-room: kitchen (some), Wi-Fi. In-hotel: restaurants, bars, pools, tennis courts, gym, spa, beach, children's programs, business center, parking* *Multiple meal plans* ✣ *3:B4.*

WORD OF MOUTH

"LeBlanc is my favorite adult-only all inclusive resort. We have stayed three times so far and had consistently very good experiences. Great food and wine for an all inclusive."

— kfusto

$$$–$$$$ **Presidente InterContinental Cancún Resort.** This landmark hotel boasts one of the best beaches in Cancún. **Pros:** short walk to shops and restaurants; virtually currentless beach is great for families; tower rooms renovated in 2010. **Cons:** focus on business travelers and conventions; Wi-Fi costs extra. **TripAdvisor:** "portions were enormous and the food was well prepared," "gorgeous view of the best beach in Cancun," "very clean and comfortable." ✉ *Blvd. Kukulcán, Km 7.5, Zona Hotelera* ☎ *998/848–8700* 🌐 *www.intercontinental.com/cancun* *274 rooms, 15 suites* *In-room: Wi-Fi. In-hotel: restaurants, bars, pools, gym, beach, water sports, children's programs, parking* *Multiple meal plans* ✣ *3:C2.*

$$ **QBay Cancún Hotel.** Located 5 km (3 mi) down the road from the Zona Hotelera's main hub of bars and clubs, this small hotel is best for people who want to avoid Cancún's famous party environment. **Pros:** friendly staff; very quiet place; Wi-Fi hotspot. **Cons:** musty rooms; small beach. **TripAdvisor:** "fantastic," "covered the basic needs," "price is excellent and rooms spacious." ✉ *Blvd. Kukulcán, Km 3.5 Zona Hotelera* ☎ *998/849–5776* 🌐 *www.qbay-cancun.com* *95 rooms* *In-room: kitchen (some), no safe. In-hotel: restaurants, bar, pool, tennis court, beach, parking* *No meals* ✣ *1:A1.*

$$$$ Fodor's Choice ★ **The Ritz-Carlton, Cancún.** Outfitted with crystal chandeliers, beautiful antiques, and elegant oil paintings, this hotel's style is so European that you may well forget you're in Mexico. **Pros:** progressive dinner plans ($225) allows guests to sample three restaurants in one night; tennis center offers private lessons; hotel hosts Luna Lounge Saturdays with bonfire and music on the beach. **Cons:** conservative atmosphere for the Hotel Zone; expensive; parking costs extra. **TripAdvisor:** "great kids' menu with flexibility for changes," "a refined luxury resort," "best hotel in the world." ✉ *Blvd. Kukulcán, Km 13.5, Retorno del Rey 36, Zona Hotelera* ☎ *998/881–0808* 🌐 *www.ritzcarlton.com* *365 rooms, 50 suites* *In-room: Wi-Fi. In-hotel: restaurants, bar, pools, tennis courts, gym, spa, beach, water sports, children's programs, business center, parking* *No meals* ✣ *3:B3.*

JW Marriott Cancún

The Ritz-Carlton, Cancún

$$$-$$$$ ⬚ **Riu Caribe.** The predominant Mayan theme in this hotel leaps out at you in the main lobby, where you'll see pyramid-shape architectural plans, striking stained-glass Mayan calendars on the high ceiling, and lots of tropical vegetation. **Pros:** tennis courts; large beach and pools; outdoor theater. **Cons:** no Internet in rooms; beach and pool areas can get crowded; no room service. **TripAdvisor:** "beach was breathtaking," "friendly and helpful but not smothering," "good selection of healthy food." ⊠ *Blvd. Kukulcán, Km 5.5, Zona Hotelera* ☎ *998/848–7850* ⊕ *www.riu.com* 🛏 *445 rooms, 61 suites* ⚿ *In-hotel: restaurants, bars, pools, tennis courts, gym, spa, beach, water sports, children's programs, business center, parking* ⎪○⎪ *All-inclusive* ✛ *3:B1.*

> **COOKING CLASSES**
>
> **The Ritz-Carlton Culinary Center** (⊠ *Blvd. Kukulcán, Km 13.5, Retorno del Rey 36, Zona Hotelera* ☎ *998/881–0822* ⊕ *www.ritzcarlton.com* 🍽 *$115* ⏰ *Mon.–Sat. 11–3 pm; wine and tequila tasting at 6:30*) offers two-hour cooking classes led by Chef Rory Dunaway. You can choose from six themed sessions, including Mexican grilling and Tuscan dinner parties. Courses are open to everyone but must be booked in advance.

$$$-$$$$ ⬚ **Riu Palace Las Américas.** A colossal eight-story property at the north end of the Zona, the Palace is visually stunning and different from the modern, minimalist resorts that dot the Zona Hotelera. **Pros:** spacious suites; access to sister properties Riu Cancún and Riu Caribe. **Cons:** small pools and tiny beach; not much sun by the pool or beach by late afternoon. **TripAdvisor:** "hotel is magnificent," "food was very good with plenty of options for every taste," "entire staff is friendly and willing to do whatever they need." ⊠ *Blvd. Kukulcán, Km 8.5, Zona Hotelera* ☎ *998/891–4300* ⊕ *www.riu.com* 🛏 *372 junior suites* ⚿ *In-hotel: restaurants, bars, pools, gym, spa, beach, water sports, children's programs* ⎪○⎪ *All-inclusive* ✛ *3:C1.*

$$$$ ⬚ **The Royal in Cancún.** Luxury is the focus at this high-end, adults-only resort (age 16+), where all 288 suites have mahogany furniture, Jacuzzis, ocean views, balconies with hammocks, and "magic boxes" that allow room service to be delivered without ever opening the door. **Pros:** two-person Jacuzzis in suites; ocean view from all suites and spa. **Cons:** adults only. **TripAdvisor:** "room service was excellent and always on time," "everything was top notch," "best hotel in Cancun." ⊠ *Blvd. Kukulcán, Km 11.5, Zona Hotelera* ☎ *998/881–5600* ⊕ *www.realresorts.com.mx* 🛏 *288 suites* ⚿ *In-room: Internet, Wi-Fi (some). In-hotel: restaurants, bars, golf course, pools, tennis court, gym, spa, beach, water sports, business center, parking, some age restrictions* ⎪○⎪ *All-inclusive* ✛ *3:C2.*

$$$$ ⬚ **The Westin Resort & Spa Cancún.** On the southern end of the Zona
★ Hotelera, this hotel is quite secluded; you'll get privacy, but have to drive to get to shops and restaurants. **Pros:** two beaches; all-inclusive plan available. **Cons:** extra charge for the use of amenities like Internet, gym, and spa. **TripAdvisor:** "beautiful oceanfront property," "great job taking care of individual needs," "one of the best stays in my life." ⊠ *Blvd. Kukulcán, Km 20, Zona Hotelera* ☎ *998/848–7400* ⊕ *www.*

westin.com/cancun ⌁ *362 rooms,
17 suites* ♨ *In-room: Internet,
Wi-Fi. In-hotel: restaurants, bars,
pools, tennis courts, gym, spa,
beach, water sports, children's programs, parking, some pets allowed*
|○| *Multiple meal plans* ⊹ *3:B6.*

EL CENTRO

$$ **Ambiance Suites Cancún.** Branding itself as "your home and office," this modern hotel caters mostly to business executives. **Pros:** convenient location within El Centro; good value. **Cons:** unfriendly staff; no restaurant; Wi-Fi on first and second floors only. ⊠ *Av. Tulum 227, Sm 20, El Centro* ☎ *998/892–0392* ⊕ *www.ambiancecancun. com* ⌁ *48 rooms* ♨ *In-room: Wi-Fi (some). In-hotel: bar, pool, gym* |○| *No meals* ⊹ *2:B6.*

$ **Antillano.** This small, well-kept hotel has a decent-size pool surrounded by wrought-iron patio furniture, and a cozy lobby bar where you can hang with locals. **Pros:** near bus terminal and main avenues. **Cons:** nothing fancy; rooms facing street can be noisy; no elevator. ⊠ *Av. Tulum and Calle Claveles 1, Sm 22, El Centro* ☎ *998/884–1532* ⊕ *www.hotelantillano.com* ⌁ *48 rooms* ♨ *In-room: Wi-Fi (some), no safe. In-hotel: bar, pool, parking* |○| *Breakfast* ⊹ *2:B4.*

¢–$ ★   **Cancún Inn El Patio.** This traditional, Mexican-style inn has been converted into a charming 15-room guesthouse. **Pros:** clean and safe; great value; art gallery and Café d'Art promote a creative, cultural environment. **Cons:** high processing fee if you pay by credit card; major construction project across the street at this writing. ⊠ *Av. Bonampak 51, El Centro* ☎ *998/884–3500* ⊕ *www.cancuninn.com* ⌁ *15 rooms* ♨ *In-hotel: business center, parking* |○| *Breakfast* ⊹ *2:D1.*

$–$$ **City Express.** Across the street from Plaza las Américas, this bright-yellow hotel is mostly geared toward business travelers and those passing through Cancún. **Pros:** great value; clean rooms; children under 12 years stay free. **Cons:** neighboring shopping mall creates street traffic; 15-minute drive to the beach; bland decor. ⊠ *Av. Nichupté, Sm 8, Mza 1, Lote 4, El Centro* ☎ *998/881–1930* ⊕ *www.cityexpress.com.mx* ⌁ *124 rooms, 4 suites* ♨ *In-room: kitchen (some), Wi-Fi. In-hotel: pool, gym, laundry facilities, business center, parking* |○| *Breakfast* ⊹ *2:D6.*

$$–$$$ **Courtyard Marriott.** The draw of this deluxe property is that it's five minutes from the international airport with free round-trip airport shuttle service. **Pros:** access to beach club at Omni Cancún Hotel in the Hotel Zone; complimentary shuttle service to and from airport; quiet area; ATM in hotel. **Cons:** astronomical phone charges; far from Cancún center and beaches. **TripAdvisor:** "bed was amazing," "good airport hotel," "pretty good deal given its location." ⊠ *Blvd. Luis Donaldo Colosio, Km 12.5, Sm 301, Carretera Cancún-Aeropuerto* ☎ *998/287–2200* ⊕ *www.marriott.com/cuncy* ⌁ *195 rooms, 6 suites*

⚒ *In-room: Wi-Fi. In-hotel: room service, restaurant, bar, pool, gym, laundry facilities, business center, parking* ✛ *2:C6.*

¢ 🏨 **Los Girasoles.** Set back on one of El Centro's few quiet streets, this pleasant hotel is within walking distance of the city's main avenues and shopping centers. **Pros:** very affordable; blackout curtains block sunlight; laundry facilities. **Cons:** no decent views or balconies; no elevator. ✉ *Calle Pina 20, Sm 25, El Centro* ☎ *998/887–3990* ⊕ *www. losgirasolescancun.com.mx* ✒ *17 rooms* ⚒ *In-room: no safe, kitchen (some), Wi-Fi. In-hotel: parking* ⦿ *No meals* ✛ *2:A5.*

¢ 🏨 **Hostel Chacmool.** One of the cheapest and hippest places to stay in downtown Cancún, this family-run hostel offers clean rooms, a complimentary continental breakfast, a trendy lobby bar, and a terrace with a pool table. **Pros:** excellent location; no curfew; free Wi-Fi in the lobby. **Cons:** not much privacy in dorms; young crowd. ✉ *Gladiolas 18, Sm 22, in front of Parque de las Palapas, El Centro* ☎ *998/887– 5873* ⊕ *www.chacmool.com.mx* ✒ *40 beds* ⚒ *In-room: no safe, no TV. In-hotel: restaurant, bar, laundry facilities, business center, parking* ⦿ *Breakfast* ✛ *2:A4.*

$$–$$$ 🏨 **Hotel Be Smart América.** With 119 rooms, Hotel Be Smart América (formerly Oasis América) is one of the largest hotels downtown. **Pros:** peaceful atmosphere; walking distance from main avenues; free shuttle to sister properties in Zona Hotelera. **Cons:** small bathrooms; sushi bar is seldom open; seemingly safe but old elevators. ✉ *Av. Tulum and Calle Brisa, Lote 113, Sm 4, El Centro* ☎ *998/848–8600* ⊕ *www.belivehotels. com* ✒ *119 rooms* ⚒ *In-room: Wi-Fi (some). In-hotel: restaurant, bars, pool, spa, parking* ⦿ *Multiple meal plans* ✛ *2:C6.*

$$ 🏨 **Hotel Be Smart Cancún.** This chic hotel plays with the senses by combin-
Fodor's Choice ing textures, colors, aromas, sounds, and flavors. **Pros:** one of the most
★ contemporary hotels in El Centro; comfortable beds; reasonably priced drinks. **Cons:** no Internet in rooms; top-floor rooms lack balconies; street noise. ✉ *Ave Tulum esq Brisa, Sm 4, El Centro* ☎ *998/848–8600* ⊕ *www.belivehotels.com* ✒ *59 rooms* ⚒ *In-hotel: restaurants, bars, pool, gym, spa, parking, some age restrictions* ⦿ *Breakfast* ✛ *2:C6.*

¢–$ 🏨 **Hotel Colonial.** A charming fountain and garden are at the center of this hotel's colonial-style buildings. **Pros:** good location; friendly staff. **Cons:** no meals served; no pool; no elevator. ✉ *Av. Tulipanes 22, Sm 22, El Centro* ☎ *998/884–1535* ⊕ *www.hotelcolonialcancun.com* ✒ *46 rooms* ⚒ *In-room: no safe, Wi-Fi. In-hotel: business center* ⦿ *Breakfast* ✛ *2:B4.*

$–$$ 🏨 **Hotel El Rey del Caribe.** Thanks to the use of solar energy, a water-
★ recycling system, and composting toilets, this unique hotel has very little impact on the environment—and its luxuriant garden blocks the heat and noise of downtown. **Pros:** tranquil atmosphere; eco-friendly; affordable spa; airport transportation ($35). **Cons:** simple and musty rooms; no elevator. **TripAdvisor:** "beautiful interior garden," "peace and quiet in the midst of busy downtown," "options to please all." ✉ *Av. Uxmal 24 at Náder, Sm 2A, El Centro* ☎ *998/884–2028* ⊕ *www. elreydelcaribe.com* ✒ *31 rooms* ⚒ *In-room: kitchen, Wi-Fi. In-hotel: restaurant, pool, spa, parking* ⦿ *Breakfast* ✛ *2:C2.*

2

$–$$ ☷ **Hotel Kin Mayab.** This small, two-building budget hotel is on downtown's main street, Avenida Tulum, and right down the block from the bus station. **Pros:** location; pleasant lobby; clean rooms. **Cons:** fairly simple; on busy street; restaurant serves breakfast only ($6). ⊠ *Av. Tulum 75, Sm 22, El Centro* ☎ *998/884–2999* ⊕ *www.hotelkinmayab. com* ⥌ *45 rooms* ⚐ *In-room: Wi-Fi. In-hotel: restaurant, pool, business center, parking* ⦿ *No meals* ✛ *2:B2.*

$$ ☷ **Hotel Plaza Caribe.** Although directly across from the bus station, this large economy hotel doesn't absorb much street noise. **Pros:** affordable; some thoughtful touches; new snack bar. **Cons:** tiny bathrooms; king-size beds are actually two twins pushed together; no elevator. **TripAdvisor:** "good value," "service was terrible," "moldy, dirty rooms." ⊠ *Avs. Tulum and Uxmal, Lote 19, Sm 23, El Centro* ☎ *998/884–1377* ⊕ *www.hotelplazacaribe.com* ⥌ *127 rooms, 6 suites* ⚐ *In-room: Wi-Fi. In-hotel: restaurants, bar, pool, gym, business center, parking* ⦿ *Multiple meal plans* ✛ *2:B2.*

$$ ☷ **Hotel Plaza Kokai.** With a nautical-themed bar that has live music on weekends and a large penthouse suite that can accommodate up to 10 guests, this place offers amenities that go above and beyond the typical budget hotel. **Pros:** many perks for the price; penthouse suite. **Cons:** rooms near street can be somewhat noisy; no parking. ⊠ *Av. Uxmal 26, Sm 2a, El Centro* ☎ *998/193–3170* ⊕ *www.hotelkokai.com* ⥌ *48 rooms, 1 suite* ⚐ *In-room: Wi-Fi. In-hotel: restaurant, bars, pool,* ⦿ *Breakfast* ✛ *2:D2.*

$$ ☷ **Hotel Sol y Luna.** Reminiscent of a European flat, this four-story hotel with tangerine shutters and signature cupolas is one of the jewels of Parque de las Palapas. **Pros:** creative details for a modest price. **Cons:** no elevator; loud and creaky wooden staircase might mean restless nights if you're on a lower floor; no restaurant. ⊠ *Calle Alcatraces 33, Mza 9, Sm 22, in front of Parque de las Palapas, El Centro* ☎ *998/252–1467* ⥌ *9 rooms, 2 suites* ⚐ *In-room: Wi-Fi. In-hotel: pool, parking* ⦿ *No meals* ✛ *2:B4.*

$$ ☷ **Hotel Xbalamqué Resort & Spa.** A refreshing retreat from the bustling streets of El Centro, this hotel has a lobby adorned with a palapa roof, waterfalls, tropical birds, and stone flooring. **Pros:** only downtown hotel with (small) spa, beauty salon, and yoga studio on-site. **Cons:** street noise audible from front rooms; thin room doors offer limited security. **TripAdvisor:** "rooms are very dark," "inexpensive clean beautiful artwork," "basic but very pleasant hotel." ⊠ *Av. Yaxchilan 31, Sm 22, Mza 18, El Centro* ☎ *998/884–9690* ⊕ *www.xbalamque.com* ⥌ *80 rooms, 11 suites* ⚐ *In-room: Wi-Fi, no safe. In-hotel: restaurants, bar, pool, spa, parking* ⦿ *Breakfast* ✛ *2:A3.*

Fodor'sChoice ★

¢–$ ☷ **María de Lourdes.** A great pool, clean and basic rooms, and bargain prices are the draws at this downtown hotel. **Pros:** two double beds in each room; decent pool area; clean rooms. **Cons:** street noise can lead to sleepless nights; musty rooms. ⊠ *Av. Yaxchilán 80, Sm 22, El Centro* ☎ *998/884–4744* ⊕ *www.hotelmariadelourdes.com* ⥌ *57 rooms* ⚐ *In-room: Wi-Fi, no safe. In-hotel: restaurant, pool, parking* ⦿ *Breakfast* ✛ *2:A4.*

$–$$ **Naay Tuukul Hotel.** This modern budget hotel, meaning "sweet
Fodor'sChoice dreams" in the Mayan language, offers pleasant rooms, each with a
★ flat-screen TV, wireless Internet, iPod dock station, minibar, microwave, and private bath. **Pros:** best budget hotel in Cancún; newly renovated. **Cons:** street noise; no restaurant. ✉ *Av. Yaxchilán 154, Sm
20, across street from Red Cross, El Centro* ☎ *998/193–3580* ⊕ *www.
hotelnaaytuukul.com* ↝ *18 rooms* ⚴ *In-room: kitchen, Wi-Fi. In-hotel:
parking* ❣ *Breakfast* ✛ *2:A6.*

$$ **Radisson Hotel Hacienda Cancún.** A stimulating change from the street
on which it lies, this hacienda-style building is strikingly hip and sleek.
Pros: prices do not increase in high season; state-of-the-art gym equip-
ment; business center with Internet access. **Cons:** east-facing rooms tend
to have street noise. **TripAdvisor:** "pretty rundown place," "service was
unparalleled," "food is good and the hotel is clean." ✉ *Av. Náder 1, El
Centro* ☎ *998/881–6500* ⊕ *www.radissoncancun.com* ↝ *237 rooms,
11 suites* ⚴ *In-room: Wi-Fi. In-hotel: restaurants, bar, pool, tennis
court, gym, children's programs, business center, parking* ❣ *Multiple
meal plans* ✛ *2:C1.*

¢–$ **Suites Cancún Centro.** You can rent suites or rooms by the day, week,
or month at this quiet hotel. **Pros:** in the heart of downtown Cancún;
near many restaurants and bars; clean and affordable. **Cons:** no eleva-
tor; not much of a social scene at hotel. ✉ *Calle Alcatraces 32, Sm 22,
next to Parque de las Palapas, El Centro* ☎ *998/887–5833 or 998/887–
5655* ⊕ *www.suitescancun.com.mx* ↝ *42 rooms, 27 suites* ⚴ *In-room:
no safe, kitchen (some), Wi-Fi. In-hotel: pool, parking* ❣ *No meals*
✛ *2:B4.*

NIGHTLIFE

We're not here to judge: we know that most people come to Cancún to
party. Sure, if you want fine dining and dancing under the stars, you'll
find it here. But if your tastes run more toward bikini contests, all-
night chug-a-thons, or cross-dressing Cher impersonators, rest assured:
Cancún delivers.

■ TIP➙ **If you want to avoid rowdy Spring Breakers, stay clear of "open-bar"
establishments and chain restaurants like Carlos 'n Charlie's, Margaritaville,
Señor Frogs, and Planet Hollywood. You're likely to find them packed with
party animals on the loose.**

BARS

ALL-PURPOSE BARS

Many of these spots daylight as restaurants, but when the sun goes
down, the party kicks up with pulsating music and waiters who don't
so much encourage crowd participation as demand it. Just remember
that it's all in good fun.

At **Carlos 'n Charlie's** (✉ *Blvd. Kukulcán, Km 9, Forum by the Sea
Mall, Zona Hotelera* ☎ *998/883–4468* ⊕ *www.carlosandcharlies.com/
cancun*) waiters will occasionally abandon their posts to start singing
or performing comical skits. It's not unusual for them to roust everyone

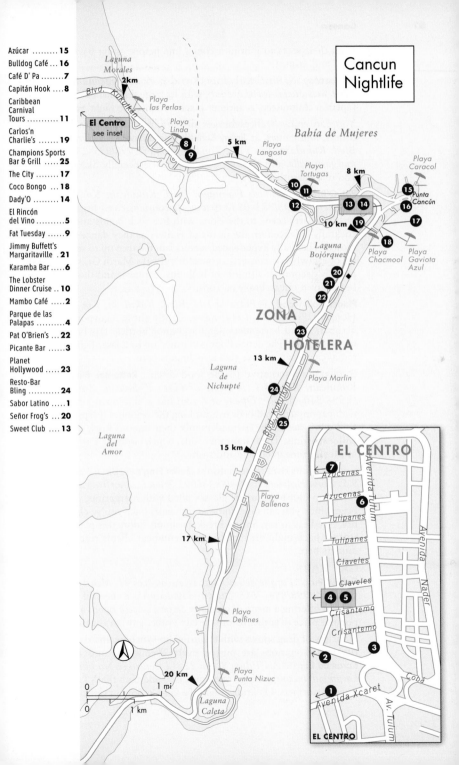

Cancun
Nightlife

El Centro
see inset

Bahía de Mujeres

*Laguna
Morales*

*Playa
las Perlas*

*Playa
Linda*

*Playa
Langosta*

*Playa
Tortugas*

*Playa
Caracol*

*Punta
Cancún*

*Laguna
Bojórquez*

*Playa
Chacmool*

*Playa
Gaviota
Azul*

ZONA

HOTELERA

*Laguna
de
Nichupté*

Playa Marlin

*Laguna
del
Amor*

*Playa
Ballenas*

*Playa
Delfines*

*Playa
Punta Nizuc*

*Laguna
Caleta*

2km

5 km

8 km

10 km

13 km

15 km

17 km

20 km

0   1 mi

0   1 km

EL CENTRO

Azucenas

Azucenas

Tutipanes

Tutipanes

Claveles

Claveles

Crisantemo

Crisantemo

Avenida Tulum

Avenida Nader

Coba

Avenida Xcaret

Av. Tulum

EL CENTRO

from their seats to join in a conga line before going back to serving food and drinks.

Fat Tuesday (✉ *Blvd. Kukulcán, Km 6.5, Zona Hotelera* ☎ 998/849–7201 ⊕ *www.fat-tuesday.com*), with its large daiquiri bar and live and piped-in club music, is another place to dance the night away.

You can enjoy a cheeseburger in paradise, along with live music, drinks, and games, at **Jimmy Buffett's Margaritaville** (✉ *Plaza Flamingo, Blvd. Kukulcán, Km 11.5, Zona Hotelera* ☎ 998/885–2375 ⊕ *www. margaritaville.com.mx*). Of course, you'll especially like this place if you're a parrothead.

Pat O'Brien's (✉ *Plaza Flamingo, Blvd. Kukulcán, Km 11.5, Zona Hotelera* ☎ 998/883–0832 ⊕ *www.patobriens.com*) brings the New Orleans party scene to the Zona with live rock bands and its famous cocktails balanced on the heads of waiters as they dance through the crowd. The really experienced servers can balance up to four margaritas or strawberry daiquiris at once! It's always Mardi Gras here, so the place is decorated with lots of balloons, banners, and those infamous beads given out to brave patrons.

Planet Hollywood (✉ *Plaza la Isla, Blvd. Kukulcán, Km 12.5, Zona Hotelera* ☎ 998/883–1944) has a nightly show incorporating aerial acrobatics and bartenders juggling liquor bottles. DJs begin playing music at 8 pm. The dance floor is warmed up by a laser light show. Avis rental car clients receive two free dinners here.

A relaxing alternative to the loud discos, **Resto-Bar Bling** (✉ *Blvd. Kukulcán, Km 13.5, in front of Plaza Kukulcán, Zona Hotelera* ☎ 998/840–6015 ⊙ *Opens at 6 pm*) has a chic open-air lounge bar with canopy-covered beds overlooking the lagoon. DJs spin house and chill-out tunes as the bartenders mix their famous kiwi, cucumber, or coffee martinis. The restaurant inside, which closes at 1 am, specializes in Mediterranean cuisine and sushi.

Known for its over-the-top drinks, **Señor Frog's** (✉ *Blvd. Kukulcán, Km 9.5, Zona Hotelera* ☎ 998/883–1092 ⊕ *www.senorfrogs.com/cancun*) serves up foot-long funnel glasses filled with margaritas, daiquiris, or beer, which you can take home as souvenirs once you've chugged them dry. Needless to say, Spring Breakers simply adore this place and often stagger back night after night. Avis rental car clients receive two free dinners here.

GAY BARS

Café D' Pa (✉ *Parque de las Palapas, Alcatraces 41, Mza 16, Sm 22, El Centro* ☎ 998/884–7615 ⊕ *www.eldpa.com*) is a cheerful bar and restaurant offering a menu of specialty crepes; since it opens at 6 pm, it's a popular place to gather before the city's other gay bars open their doors.

A variety of drag shows with the usual lip-synching and dancing celebrity impersonations are put on every Wednesday and Thursday at **Karamba Bar** (✉ *Av. Tulum 9, Sm 22, El Centro* ☎ *No phone* ⊕ *www. karambabar.com*), a large open-air disco and club that's known for its stage performers. On Friday night the Go-Go Boys of Cancún entertain,

Continued on page 90

TEQUILA AND MEZCAL—¡SALUD!

If God were Mexican, tequila and mezcal would surely be our heavenly reward, flowing in lieu of milk and honey. Before throwing back your first drink, propose a toast in true Mexican style and wave your glass accordingly— *"¡Arriba, abajo, al centro, pa' dentro!"* ("Above, below, center, inside!")

Historians maintain that, following the Spanish conquest and the introduction of the distillation process, tequila was adapted from the ancient Aztec drink *pulque*. Whatever the true origin, Mexico's national drink long predated the Spanish, and is considered North America's oldest spirit.

When you think about tequila, what might come to mind are spaghetti-Western-style bar brawls or late-night teary-eyed confessions. But tequila is more complex and worldly than many presume. By some accounts it's a digestive that reduces cho-

lesterol and stress. Shots of the finest tequilas can cost upward of $100 each, and are meant to be savored as ardently as fine cognacs or single-malt scotches.

Just one of several agave-derived drinks fermented and bottled in Mexico, tequila rose to fame during the Mexican Revolution when it became synonymous with national heritage and pride. Since the 1990s tequila has enjoyed a soaring popularity around the globe, and people the world over are starting to realize that tequila is more than a one-way ticket to (and doesn't necessitate) a hangover.

Harvesting agave in Jalisco.

TEQUILA AND MEZCAL 101

Harvesting blue agave to make tequila.

WHICH CAME FIRST, TEQUILA OR MEZCAL?

Mezcal is tequila's older cousin. Essentially, all tequila is mezcal but only some mezcal is tequila. The only difference between tequila and mezcal is that the tequila meets two requirements: 1) it's made only from blue agave (but some non-agave sugar can be added) and 2) it must be distilled in a specific region in Jalisco or certain parts of neighboring Guanajuato, Michoacán, Nayarit, and Tamaulipas. Unlike tequila, all mezcal must be made from 100 percent agave and must be bottled in Mexico.

CHOOSE YOUR LIQUOR WISELY

Your first decision with tequila is whether to have a *puro* or a *mixto*. You'll know if a bottle is *puro* because it will say so prominently on the label; if the words "100% *de agave*" don't appear, you can be sure you're getting *mixto*. Don't be fooled by bottles that say, "Made from agave azul," because all tequila is made from agave azul; that doesn't mean that cane sugar hasn't been added. Popular wisdom holds that *puro* causes less of a hangover than mixto, but we'll leave that to your own experimentation.

Even among *puros*, there's a wide range of quality and taste, and every fan has his or her favorite. For sipping straight (*derecho*), most people prefer *reposado*, *añejo*, or extra *añejo*. For mixed drinks you'll probably want either a *blanco* or a *reposado*.

Herradura

TEQUILA TIMELINE

Aztec ritual human sacrifice as portrayed on the Codex Magliabechiano.

Pre-Columbian	Aztecs brew pulque for thousands of years; both priests and the sacrificial victims consume it during religious rituals.
1600	The first commercial distillery in New Spain is founded by Pedro Sanches de Tagle, the father of tequila, on his hacienda near the village of Tequila.
1740	*Mezcal de Tequila* earns an enthusiastic following and King Philip V of Spain grants José Antonio Cuervo the first royal license for a mezcal distillery.

THE MAKING OF MEZCAL

1 To make both mezcal and tequila, the agave may be cultivated for as long as ten years, depending on growing conditions and the variety of plant.

2 When the agave is ripe, the leaves, or *pencas*, are removed and the heavy core (called a *piña*, Spanish for "pineapple," because of its resemblance to that fruit) is dug up, 3 cut into large chunks, and cooked to convert its starches into sugars.

4 The *piñas* are then crushed and their juice collected in tanks; yeast is added and the liquid ferments for several days.

After the fermentation, the resulting *mosto* generally measures between 4 and 7 percent alcohol. 5 Finally it's distilled (usually twice for tequila, once for mezcal). This process of heating and condensing serves to boost the alcohol content.

6 And finally, the alcohol is aged in barrels.

While the process is the same, there are a few critical differences between tequila and mezcal. Mezcal is made in smaller distilleries and still retains more of an artisanal quality; mezcal magueys are grown over a wider area with more diverse soil composition and microclimate, giving mezcals more individuality than tequila. Lastly, the *piñas* for mezcal are more likely to be baked in stone pits, which imparts a distinctive smoky flavor.

The World's Columbian Fair in Chicago, 1893.

1800s	As the thirst for mezcal grows, wood (used to fire the stills) becomes scarce and distilleries shift to more efficient steam ovens.
1873	Cenobio Sauza exports mezcal to the United States via a new railroad to El Paso, Texas.
1893	*Mezcal de Tequila* (now simply called "tequila") receives an award at Chicago's Columbian Exposition.

TEQUILA COCKTAILS

Margarita: The original proportions at Rancho La Gloria were reportedly 3 parts tequila, 2 parts Triple Sec, and 1 part lime juice, though today recipes vary widely. In Mexico an orange liqueur called Controy is often substituted for the Triple Sec. The best margaritas are a little tart and are made from fresh ingredients, not a mix. Besides deciding whether you want yours strained,

on the rocks, or frozen, you have dozens of variations to choose from, many incorporating fruits such as strawberry, raspberry, mango, passion fruit, and peach. To salt the rim or not to salt is yet another question.

Sangrita: The name meaning "little blood," this is a very Mexican accompaniment, a spicy mixture of tomato and orange juice that's sipped between swallows of straight tequila (or mezcal).

Tequila refresca: Also very popular in Mexico, this is tequila mixed with citris soft drinks like Fresca, or Squirt. Generally served in a tall glass over ice.

Tequila Sunrise: Invented in the 1950s, this is a distant runner-up to the margarita, concocted from tequila, orange juice, and grenadine syrup. The grenadine sinks to the bottom, and after a few refills you might agree that the resulting layers resemble a Mexican sky at dawn.

Bloody Maria: One to try with brunch, this is a bloody Mary with you-know-what instead of vodka.

DID YOU KNOW?

Aging mezcal and Tequila imparts a smoothness and an oaky flavor, but over-aging can strip the drink of its characteristic agave taste.

TEQUILA TIMELINE

Mexican revolutionaries

1910–1920	During the Mexican Revolution, homegrown tequila becomes a source of national pride, associated with the hard-riding, hard-drinking rebels.
1930s	Federal land reforms break up the great haciendas and Mexico's agave production slumps by two thirds. To make up for the shortfall, the government allows distillers to begin mixing non-agave sugars into their tequila. This blander drink, called mixto, is better suited to American tastes and sales surge.

TEQUILA AND MEZCAL VOCABULARY

pulque: an alcoholic drink made by the Aztecs

mexcalmetl: Nahuatl word for agave

mixto: a type of tequila that is mixed with non-agave sugars

puro: tequila made with no non-agave sugars

reposado: aged between two months and a year

añejo: aged between one and three years

extra añejo: aged longer than three years

blanco: tequila that is aged less than two months

joven: young tequila, usually a mixto with colorings and flavors

caballito: tall shot glass

pechuga: mezcal flavored with raw chicken breast

cremas: flavored mezcal

aguamiel: agave juice

piña: the agave core

salmiana: a type of agave

pencas: agave leaves

mosto: fermented agave before it is distilled

gusano: the larva found in mescal bottles

WHAT'S WITH THE WORM

Some mezcals (never tequila) are bottled with a worm (*gusano*), the larva of one of the moths that live on agave plants. Rumor has it that the worm was introduced to ensure a high alcohol content (because the alcohol preserves the creature), but the truth is that the practice started in the 1940s as a marketing gimmick. The worm is ugly but harmless and the best mezcals are not bottled *con gusano*.

Early 1940s — The history of mixology was forever altered when Carlos Herrera invented the margarita for American starlet Marjorie King.

2004 — The agave fields around Tequila become a UNESCO World Heritage Site.

Agave fields

CHOOSING A BOTTLE

Reposado (rested)   Silver   Añejo (mature)

Corralejo

BUYING TEQUILA

There are hundreds of brands of tequila, but here are a baker's half dozen of quality *puros* to get you started; generally these distillers offer blanco, reposado, añejo, and extra añejo.

Corralejo—An award winner from the state of Guanajuato, made on the historic hacienda once owned by Pedro Sanchez de Tagle, "the father of tequila" and birthplace of Miguel Hidalgo, the father of Mexican independence.

Corzo—Triple distilled, these tequilas are notably smooth and elegant.

Don Julio—This award-winning tequila, one of the most popular in Mexico, is known for its rich, smooth flavor; the *blanco* is especially esteemed.

Espolón—A relative newcomer founded only in 1998, this distiller has already won several international awards.

Herradura—This is a venerable, popular brand known for its smoky, full body.

Patrón—Founded in 1989, this distiller produces award-winning tequilas. The *añejo* is especially noteworthy for its complex earthiness.

Siete Leguas—Taking their name ("Seven Leagues") from the horse of Pancho Villa, a general in the Mexican Revolution, these quality tequilas are known for their big, full flavor.

TYPES OF TEQUILA AND MEZCAL

Three basic types of tequila and mezcal are determined by how long they've been aged in oak barrels.

Blanco (white) is also known as *plata* or silver. It's been aged for less than two months.

Reposado ("rested") is aged between two months and a year.

añejo ("mature") is kept in barrels for at least a year and perhaps as long as three. Some producers also offer an extra *añejo* that is aged even longer.

Herradura

Don Julio

Gusano Rojo

BUYING MEZCAL

As for enjoying mezcal, it can be substituted in any recipe calling for tequila. But more often it's drunk neat, to savor its unique flavor. Like tequila, straight mezcal is generally served at room temperature in a tall shot glass called a *caballito*.

Some producers now add flavorings to their mezcals. Perhaps the most famous is *pechuga*, which has a raw chicken breast added to the still, supposedly imparting a smoothness and subtle flavor. (Don't worry, the heat and alcohol kill everything.) Citrus is also a popular add-in, and *cremas* contain flavorings such as peaches, mint, raisins, or guava, along with a sweetener such as honey or *aguamiel* (the juice of the agave).

Part of the fun of mezcal is stumbling on smaller, less commercial brands, but here are a few recognized, quality producers. Most make *blancos, reposados,* and *añejos,* and some offer extra *añejos,* flavored mezcals, and *cremas* as well.

El Señorio—Produced in Oaxaca the traditional way, with stone ovens and a stone wheel to crush the *piñas*.

El Zacatecano—Founded in 1910 in the northern state of Zacatecas; in a recent competitive tasting, their añejo was judged the best in its category.

Gusano Rojo—This venerable Oaxaca distillery makes the number-one-selling mezcal in Mexico. Yes, there's a worm in the bottle.

Jaral de Berrio—From Guanajuato, this distiller uses the *salmiana* agave. Their *blanco* recently garnered a silver medal.

Real de Magueyes—From the state of San Luis Potosí, these fine mezcals are also made from the local *salmiana* agave. Try the flavorful añejo.

Scorpion—More award-winning mezcals from Oaxaca. Instead of a worm, there's a scorpion in the bottle.

and strip shows are on weekends. The bar opens at 10:30 pm and the party goes on until dawn. There's no cover charge.

The oldest gay bar in Cancún, **Picante Bar** (✉ *Plaza Galerias, Av. Tulum 20, Sm 5, El Centro* 🕾 *No phone*) has been operating for over 15 years. The drag shows here tend to reflect local culture; for instance, during Carnival there's a special holiday beauty pageant followed by the crowning of "the Queen." The owner, "Mother Picante," emcees the floor show that includes Las Vegas–type dance revues, singers, and strippers. Doors open at 9 pm and close at 5 am, and there's no cover.

SPORTS BARS

Champions Sports Bar & Grill (✉ *CasaMagna Marriott Cancún Resort, Blvd. Kukulcán, Km 14.5, Zona Hotelera* 🕾 *998/881–2000 Ext. 6341*) has a giant TV screen and 26 smaller monitors on which to watch all kinds of sporting events. You can also play pool here and dig in to American-style bar grub.

WINE BARS

El Rincón del Vino (✉ *Alcatraces 29, Mza 10, Sm 22, in front of Parque de las Palapas, next to Los Huaraches de Alcatraces. El Centro* 🕾 *998/898–3187*) is a popular wine and tapas bar where you can enjoy the sounds of live *trova*, rumba, flamenco, and jazz music. The bar has 250 varieties of *vino* hailing from the world's top wine-making regions, and tapas like *tortilla española* (a potato omelet) and *chistorra* (a Spanish sausage). It's open from 6 pm to midnight Tuesday through Saturday.

DANCE CLUBS

Cancún wouldn't be Cancún without its glittering discos, which generally start jumping around 10:30 pm (though some open at around 9) and often carry on until 6 am. As the hours roll on, clothes are peeled off and frenzied dancing seems to quake the building around and the floor beneath. Most clubs offer open bar tickets ($35 to $40) that cover admission and unlimited drinks until 3 am; this is the way to go if you plan on having more than a couple of drinks. If you stay past 3, however, you'll have to pay by the drink. You can also pay a lower cover charge of $10 to $20 and buy drinks separately. Typical prices range from $3 for a shot to $8 for a cocktail. Although every spot seems to be pumping by midnight (especially during March and April), the most popular clubs include Coco Bongo, Dady'O, The City, and Sweet Club.

Azúcar (✉ *Dreams Cancún Resort & Spa, Blvd. Kukulcán, Km 9.5, Zona Hotelera* 🕾 *998/848–7000* 💲*$10*) showcases the very best Latin American bands. Go just to watch the locals dance (the beautiful people tend to turn up here really late). Proper dress is required—no jeans or sneakers.

The City (✉ *Blvd. Kukulcán, Km 9.5, Zona Hotelera* 🕾 *998/848–8380* ⊕ *www.thecitycancun.com*) is a giant party complex with a daytime water park; at night there's a cavernous dance floor with stadium seating and several large bars selling overpriced drinks. Dancing and live shows are the main draw, as well as a Tuesday-night beach party and bikini contest. This is by far the loudest club in the Zona Hotelera, so

Cancún meets Vegas at the Coca Bongo.

don't be surprised if you go home with a ringing in your ears. Doors open at 10 pm.

The wild, wild **Coco Bongo** (✉ *Blvd. Kukulcán, Km 9.5, across street from Dady'O, Zona Hotelera* ☎ *998/883–5061* ⊕ *www.cocobongo. com.mx* ✉ *$20, $60 for open bar*) has no chairs, but there are plenty of tables that everyone dances on and capacity for 1,800 people. There's also a popular show billed as "Las Vegas meets Hollywood," featuring celebrity impersonators and an amazing gravity-defying acrobatic show with an accompanying 12-piece orchestra. After the shows, the techno gets turned up to full volume and everyone gets up to get down.

Dady'O (✉ *Blvd. Kukulcán, Km 9.5, Zona Hotelera* ☎ *998/883–3333* ⊕ *www.dadyo.com.mx* ✉ *$20, $45 for open bar*) has been around for a while, but it's still very "in" with the younger set. A giant screen projects music videos above the always-packed dance floor, while laser lights whirl across the crowd. During Spring Break the place gets even livelier for the Hawaiian Bikini contests. No cover charge for women on Wednesday.

Mambo Café (✉ *Plaza Las Avenidas, Sm 35, Mza 2, Lote 3, corner of Avs. Cobá and Yaxchilan, El Centro* ☎ *998/887–8761* ⊕ *www.mambocafe. com.mx* ✉ *$10, $30 for open bar*) features some of the city's hottest live bands and DJs playing tropical music, making it the ideal disco in which to practice your salsa and merengue steps.

Sweet Club (✉ *Blvd. Kukulcán, Km 9.5, Zona Hotelera* ☎ *998/883–3333 Ext. 138* ⊕ *www.sweetnightclub.com* ✉ *$20, $45 for open bar*) draws a high-energy crowd that likes entertainment along with their drinks. Live bands usually start off the action, followed by DJs spinning dance tracks

Getting down at Dady'O

into the wee hours of the morning. Girls drink free on Wednesday, wet body contests are on Thursday, and hot male contests on Sunday. Winners take home $2,000 in cash and prizes. It's open daily from 8 pm on.

DINNER CRUISES

Sunset boat cruises that include dinner, drinks, music, and sometimes dancing are popular in Cancún—especially among couples looking for a romantic evening and visitors who'd rather avoid the carnival atmosphere of the clubs and discos.

On the **Capitán Hook** (✉ *El Embarcadero, Blvd. Kukulcán, Km 4.5, Zona Hotelera* ☎ *998/849–4451* ✉ *$82–$92* ☾ *Daily 7:30–10:30 pm*), watch a private show aboard a replica of an 18th-century Spanish galleon, then enjoy a lobster dinner and drinks as the ship cruises around at sunset. Beware of pirate attacks!

Caribbean Carnival Tours (✉ *Playa Tortugas, next to Dos Playas Hotel, Blvd. Kukulcán, Km 6.5, Zona Hotelera* ☎ *998/884–3760* ⊕ *www.cancunfuntours.com* ✉ *$65* ☾ *Daily 6–11 pm*) start off on a large two-level catamaran at sunset. There's an open bar for the sail across to Isla Mujeres; once you reach shore, you'll join in a moonlight calypso cookout and a full dinner buffet, followed by a Caribbean carnival show and dancing.

The Lobster Dinner Cruise (✉ *Agua Tours Marina, Blvd. Kukulcán, Km 6.5, in front of Playa Tortugas, Zona Hotelera* ☎ *998/849–4748* ⊕ *www.thelobsterdinner.com* ✉ *$89* ☾ *Daily 5 pm and 8 pm*) offers tranquil, couples-only cruises on a 62-foot galleon. A fresh lobster dinner is served while the sun sets over Laguna Nichupté; afterward, the boat continues to cruise so you can stargaze. No children under 14.

LIVE MUSIC

Bulldog Cafe (⊠ *Krystal Cancún hotel, Blvd. Kukulcán, Km 9, Zona Hotelera* ☎ *998/848–9850* ⊕ *www.bulldogcafe.com* ✉ *$40*) has an all-you-can-drink bar, live rock groups, the latest dance music, and an impressive laser light show. The stage here is large, and some very well-known bands have played on it, including Guns n' Roses and Radiohead. Another, somewhat bawdier draw is the private hot tub, where you can have "the Jacuzzi bikini girls" scrub your back. Naturally, this place is popular with Spring Breakers.

To mingle with locals and hear great music for free, head to the **Parque de las Palapas** (⊠ *Bordered by Avs. Tulum, Yaxchilán, Uxmal, and Cobá, Sm 22, El Centro*). Every Friday night at 7:30 there's live music that ranges from jazz to salsa to Caribbean; lots of locals show up to dance. On Sunday afternoon the Cancún Municipal Orchestra plays.

Sabor Latino (⊠ *Plaza Hong Kong, Loc 31, Sm 20, El Centro* ☎ *998/898–4006* ☉ *Opens at 10 pm, Wed.–Sun.*) has live salsa bands and lots of locals to show you new dance moves. If you want something more structured, you can take dance lessons here.

SHOPPING

The *centros comerciales* (malls) in Cancún are fully air-conditioned and as well kept as similar establishments in the United States or Canada. Like their northerly counterparts, they also sell just about everything: designer clothing, beachwear (including tons of raunchy T-shirts aimed at the Spring Break crowd), sportswear, jewelry, music, video games, household items, shoes, and books. Some even have the same terrible mall food that is standard north of the border. Prices are fixed in shops. They're also generally—but not always—higher than in the markets, where bargaining for better prices is a possibility. Perfumes in Cancún are considerably less expensive than you might find at home, and you'll even beat the duty-free price you would pay at the airport. Of course tequila is a bargain here as well, but make sure you buy at the supermarket rather than at a souvenir shop.

There are many duty-free stores that sell designer goods at reduced prices—sometimes as much as 30% or 40% below retail. Although prices for handicrafts are higher here than in other cities and the selection is limited, you can find handwoven textiles, leather goods, and handcrafted silver jewelry.

Shopping hours are generally weekdays 10 to 1 and 4 to 7, although more stores are staying open throughout the day rather than closing for siesta. Many shops keep Saturday morning hours, and some are now open on Sunday until 1. Centros comerciales tend to be open daily at 9 am or 10 am to 8 pm or 9 pm.

GALLERIES

Serious collectors visit **Casa de Cultura** (⊠ *Prolongación Av. Yaxchilán, Sm 25* ☎ *998/884–8364*) for regular art shows featuring Mexican artists.

Dorfman's Art Gallery (⊠ *Inside the Royal Caribbean hotel, Blvd. Kukulcán, Km 17, Zona Hotelera* ☎ *998/881–0100 Ext. 63610*) features Mayan-inspired and environmentally themed sculptures and paintings by local artists and brothers Renato and Adán Dorfman.

El Pabilo (⊠ *Av. Yaxchilán 3, Sm 7* ☎ *998/892–4553*) is a downtown café that showcases Mexican painters and photographers on a rotating basis.

AVOID TORTOISESHELL

Refrain from buying anything made from tortoiseshell. The *carey,* or hawksbill turtles from which most of it comes, is an endangered species, and it's illegal to bring tortoiseshell products into the United States and several other countries. Also be aware that there are some restrictions regarding black coral. You must purchase it from a recognized dealer.

GROCERY STORES

Chedraui (⊠ *Av. Tulum 57, at Av. Cobá, El Centro* ☎ *998/884–1024* ⊠ *Plaza las Americas, Av. Tulum 260, Sm 7* ☎ *998/887–2111*) is a popular superstore with six locations.

If you're a member in the States, you can visit **Costco** (⊠ *Avs. Kabah and Yaxchilán, Sm 21* ☎ *998/881–0250*).

Mega Comercial Mexicana (⊠ *Avs. Tulum and Uxmal, Sm 2* ☎ *998/884–3330* ⊠ *Avs. Kabah and Mayapan, Sm 21* ☎ *998/880–9164*) is one of the major Mexican grocery-store chains, with three locations. The most convenient is at Avenidas Tulum and Uxmal, across from the bus station; its largest store is farther north on Avenida Kabah, which is open 24 hours.

Sam's Club (⊠ *Av. Cobá, Lote 2, Sm 21* ☎ *998/881–0200*) has plenty of bargains on groceries and souvenirs.

Super Aki (⊠ *Av. Xel-Há, Lote 1, next to Mercado Veintiocho, Sm 28* ☎ *998/884–2812*) is a smaller grocery store downtown.

Wal-Mart (⊠ *Av. Cobá, Lote 2, Sm 21* ☎ *998/884–1383*) is a popular shopping spot where you can find beach supplies, snacks, and necessities you forgot to pack.

■TIP→ The few grocery stores in the Zona Hotelera tend to be expensive. It's better to shop for groceries downtown.

MARKETS AND MALLS

ZONA HOTELERA

Coral Negro (⊠ *Blvd. Kukulcán, Km 9, Zona Hotelera*), next to the convention center, is an open-air market that has about 50 stalls selling crafts and souvenirs. It's open daily until late evening. Everything here is overpriced, but bargaining does work. Stalls deeper in the market tend to have better deals than those around the market's periphery.

Forum-by-the-Sea (⊠ *Blvd. Kukulcán, Km 9.5, Zona Hotelera* ☏ *998/ 883–4428*) is a three-level entertainment and shopping plaza in the Zona. This open-air mall features brand-name restaurants, upscale clothing boutiques, a food court, and chain stores, all in a circuslike atmosphere. For Spring Breakers, the main draws are the nightclubs, Coco Bongo and Hard Rock Cafe, which are identified by the massive guitar at the mall entrance. The bungee trampolines set up here during high season are especially popular with children.

★ The glittering, ultratrendy, and ultraexpensive **Isla Shopping Village** (⊠ *Blvd. Kukulcán, Km 12.5, Zona Hotelera* ☏ *998/883–5025*) is on the Laguna Nichupté under chic, white canopies. A series of canals and small bridges is designed to give the place a Venetian look. In addition to more than 200 shops, the mall has a marina, a disco, restaurants, and movie theaters. There's also an interactive aquarium where you can swim with the dolphins and feed the sharks.

North of the convention center, the two-story **Plaza Caracol** (⊠ *Blvd. Kukulcán, Km 8.5, Zona Hotelera* ☏ *998/883–4760*) houses chain stores like Sunglass Island, Benetton, and Ultrafemme, along with souvenir and jewelry shops and pharmacies. Making up this contemporary mall are 150 shops, as well as a small food court, an enormous Starbucks, and the fine Italian restaurant Casa Rolandi. The Plaza is closed on weekends.

In from the convention center, **Plaza la Fiesta** (⊠ *Blvd. Kukulcán, Km 9, Zona Hotelera* ☏ *998/883–2116*) has 20,000 square feet of showroom space and more than 100,000 different products for sale. Probably the widest selection of Mexican goods in the Hotel Zone, it includes leather goods, silver and gold jewelry, handicrafts, souvenirs, and swimwear. There are some good bargains here.

Plaza Flamingo (⊠ *Blvd. Kukulcán, Km 11.5, across from Hotel Flamingo Resort & Plaza, Zona Hotelera* ☏ *998/883–2855*) is a small mall that houses around 80 different shops that sell mainly clothing, jewelry, and souvenirs. The main attractions here are the chain restaurants Jimmy Buffet's, Margaritaville, Outback Steakhouse, Bubba Gump, and Pat O'Brien's, which fill up with partiers during Spring Break.

★ **Plaza Kukulcán** (⊠ *Blvd. Kukulcán, Km 13, Zona Hotelera* ☏ *998/193– 0161*) is a large, upscale mall with around 100 shops and six restaurants. Some highlights include a bar with a bowling alley and the Luxury Avenue section of the mall, which offers brand names from Cartier, Fendi, and Burberry to Coach. While parents shop, kids can enjoy the game arcade, a play area, and Chocolate City, a theme restaurant with table games, live music, and a weekly circus show. The mall hosts art exhibits and other cultural events. If you stop in any night at 8 pm, you can watch the 10-minute, English-language light show under the Mayan stained-glass dome. If you fell in love with the European clothing chain Mango on your last trip to Paris, swing by the branch here.

Plaza El Zócalo (⊠ *Blvd. Kuckulcán, Km 9, Zona Hotelera* ☏ *998/883– 3698*) may look small from the entrance, but it has about 60 stalls where you can find traditional Mexican handicrafts, silver jewelry, and handmade sandals. El Zócalo also houses four restaurants—including Mextreme, which still sports a banner announcing its claim to fame as a set in the 1980s movie *Cocktail*.

EL CENTRO

There are lots of interesting shops downtown along Avenida Tulum (between Avenidas Cobá and Uxmal). The oldest and largest of Cancún's crafts markets is **Ki Huic** (⊠ *Av. Tulum 17, between Bancomer and Bital banks, Sm 3* ☎ *998/884–3347*). It's open daily 9 am to 10 pm and houses about 100 vendors. **Mercado Veintiocho** *(Market 28)*, just off Avenidas Yaxchilán and Sunyaxchén, is the largest open-air market in Cancún. In addition to a few small restaurants, here you'll find around 100 stalls selling many of the same items found in the Zona Hotelera but at half the price. **Ultrafemme** (⊠ *Av. Tulum 111, at Calle Claveles, Sm 21* ☎ *998/884–1402*) is a popular downtown store that carries duty-free perfume, cosmetics, and jewelry. It also has branches in the Zona Hotelera at Plaza Caracol, Plaza las Américas, Plaza Kukulcán, and La Isla Shopping Village. The downtown store is open daily 9:30 am to 9 pm.

Cancún Gran Plaza (⊠ *Av. Nichupté, Mza 18, Lote 1, Loc 24, 30 and 62A, Sm 51, El Centro* ☉ *Daily 9–9*) offers jewelry shops, fashion boutiques, and major department stores such as Sanborns and Wal-Mart. There are also cinemas, cafés, and restaurants in the shopping mall, which is mainly frequented by El Centro residents.

Parque Lumpkul (⊠ *Between Av. Margaritas and Calle Azucenas, Sm 22, El Centro*) is a small park with a hippy vibe. Vendors sell their wares here Wednesday through Sunday, but Friday and Saturday are the best nights to go. There are only about 20 tables, but you can find bargains on beautiful handmade jewelry with unusual stones, as well as hand-painted clothes. There are sometimes music and artistic performances on market days.

Paseo Cancún (⊠ *Av. Andrés, Sm 39, El Centro* ☎ *998/872–3735*) was developed by the same company that owns La Isla in the Zona Hotelera, so it has the same open-air design with modern white canopies throughout. Here you'll find a small ice-skating rink, a movie theater, a bowling alley, a pet store, a food court, several cafés, and around 60 stores.

Plaza Las Américas (⊠ *Av. Tulum, Sm 4 and Sm 9* ☎ *998/887–3863*) is the largest shopping center in downtown Cancún. Its 50-plus stores, three restaurants, two movie theaters, video arcade, fast-food outlets, and several large department stores will—for better or worse—make you feel right at home. This mall is intolerably crowded on weekends.

Plaza Las Avenidas (⊠ *Av. Yaxchilán, Sm 35, N.C-2, El Centro* ☎ *998/ 887–7552*) has gift shops, fast-food restaurants, cafés, nightclubs, and a karaoke bar. There are also a drugstore and a bakery on the premises. Far from the Hotel Zone, this shopping area is most convenient for those staying in El Centro.

Plaza Bonita (⊠ *Av. Xel-Há 1 and 2, Sm 28* ☎ *998/884–6812*) is a small outdoor plaza attached to Mercado Veintiocho (Market 28). It has many wonderful specialty shops carrying Mexican goods and crafts.

Plaza Chinatown (✉ *Sm 35, Mza 2, Lote 6, between Labná and Av. Xcaret, El Centro* ☎ *998/887–6315*) commonly referred to as Plaza Hong Kong, seems strikingly out of place with it massive pagoda structure. Here you'll find Mexican handicrafts, souvenir shops, and a restaurant appropriately named Hong Kong. There is also a babysitting service available in the mall.

Plaza Hollywood (✉ *Av. Xcaret at Rubi Cancún, El Centro* ☎ *998/887–3187*) is one of the newest strip malls to join El Centro. Here you'll find several small boutiques and restaurants as well as a bank, post office, and Starbucks. For the wine connoisseur, there is La Europe Wine Market, which carries a wide selection of imported cheeses and meats, as well as Mexican reds.

SPORTS AND THE OUTDOORS

BOATING AND SAILING

There are lots of ways to get your adrenaline going on the waters of Cancún. You can arrange to go parasailing (about $50 for 10 minutes), waterskiing ($70 per hour), or Jet Skiing ($70 per hour, or $80 for Wave Runners). Paddleboats, kayaks, catamarans, and banana boats are readily available, too. Jungle boat tours, which usually last from 2 to 2½ hours, are also popular. They cost around $60 per person.

AquaWorld (✉ *Blvd. Kukulcán, Km 15.2, Zona Hotelera* ☎ *998/848–8300* ⊕ *www.aquaworld.com.mx*) rents boats and water toys like Aqua Twister, a high-speed boat that fishtails 270 degrees. They also offer parasailing and submarine tours.

Delta Tours (✉ *Playa Tortugas, Blvd. Kukulcán, Km 6.5, Zona Hotelera* ☎ *998/849–4995*) has banana boats, snorkeling gear, Wave Runners, and parasails. Willing to match competitive prices, they also offer night cruises, paddleboats, catamarans, and all-inclusive tours to Isla Mujeres.

El Embarcadero (✉ *Blvd. Kukulcán, Km 4, Zona Hotelera* ☎ *998/849–7343*), the marina complex at Playa Linda, is the departure point for ferries to Isla Mujeres and several tour boats.

Marina Barracuda (✉ *Blvd. Kukulcán, Km 14, in front of Ritz-Carlton, Zona Hotelera* ☎ *998/885–3444*) rents out Wave Runners and offers daily jungle tours.

Marina Punta del Este (✉ *Blvd. Kukulcán, Km 10.3, Zona Hotelera* ☎ *998/883–1210*) has Wave Runners and offers jungle tours that leave every hour from 9 am to 3 pm.

Marina del Rey (✉ *Blvd. Kukulcán, Km 15.6, in front of Grand Oasis Cancún, Zona Hotelera* ☎ *998/885–0363*) rents out Wave Runners and offers jungle tours that leave several times a day.

CLOSE UP

Wet, Wild Water Sports

Cancún is one of the water-sports capitals of the world, and, with the Caribbean on one side of the island and the still waters of Laguna Nichupté on the other, it's no wonder. The most popular water activities are snorkeling and diving along the coral reef just off the coast.

Due to northeasterly winds, sports such as kiteboarding and windsurfing have become increasingly popular. Although waves are not as constant as those on the Pacific side, it's possible to find some decent surf in and around Cancún. During December and January, waves peak at about 6 feet, but it usually takes a windstorm or winter swell to make the choppy paddle worthwhile. During hurricane season, from May through November, the surf can be borderline epic on a good day. For the avid beach-break surfer, the sandbars are best at Playa Delfines, Chamol, and City Beach. Thirty-two kilometers (20 mi) south of Cancún are several point breaks off the coast of Puerto Morelos and Punta Brava.

If you want to view the mysterious underwater world but don't want to get your feet wet, a glass-bottom boat or "submarine" is the ticket. You can also fish, sail, Jet Ski, or parasail.

Since the beaches along the Zona Hotelera can have a strong undertow, you should always respect the flags posted in the area. A black flag means you cannot swim at all. A red flag means you can swim but only with extreme caution. Yellow means approach with caution, while green means water conditions are safe. You'll seldom see the green flag—even when the water is calm—so swim cautiously, and don't assume you're immune to riptides because you're on vacation. At least one tourist drowns per season after ignoring the flags.

Unfortunately, Laguna Nichupté has become polluted from illegal dumping of sewage and at times can have a strong smell. In 1993 the city began conducting a cleanup campaign that included handing out fines to offenders, so the quality of the water is slowly improving. There's very little wildlife to see in the lagoon, so most advertised jungle tours are glorified Jet Ski romps where you drive around fast, make a lot of noise, and don't see many animals. American crocodiles still reside in these waters though, so do not stand or swim in the lagoon.

Although the coral reef in this area is not as spectacular as farther south, there's still plenty to see, with more than 500 species of sea life in the waters. It's actually quite common to see angelfish, parrotfish, blue tang, and the occasional moray eel. But the corals in this area are extremely fragile and currently endangered. To be a good world citizen, follow the six golden rules for snorkeling or scuba diving:

1. Don't throw any garbage into the sea, as the marine life will assume it's food, an often lethal mistake.

2. Never stand on the coral.

3. Secure all cameras and gear onto your body so you don't drop anything onto the fragile reef.

4. Never take anything from the sea.

5. Don't feed any of the marine animals.

6. Avoid sunblock or tanning lotion just before you visit the reef.

FISHING

Some 500 species—including sailfish, wahoo, bluefin, marlin, barracuda, and red snapper—live in the waters off Cancún. You can charter deep-sea fishing boats starting at about $380 for four hours, $470 for six hours, and $550 for eight hours. Rates generally include a captain and first mate, gear, bait, and beverages.

Asterix Tours (⊠ *Blvd. Kukulcán, Km 5.5, Zona Hotelera* ☎ *998/886–4847* ⊕ *www.contoytours.com*) offers nighttime "party fishing" trips that cost $78 per person and include dinner and drinks. With an emphasis on nature conservation, Asterix is the only tour company permitted to visit Isla Contoy and the underwater gardens of Isla Mujeres. Tours to Isla Contoy ($90 per person) depart at 9 am and return at 5:30 pm on Tuesday, Thursday, and Saturday.

FISHING AND DIVING COMBOS

Mundo Marino (⊠ *Blvd. Kukulcán, Km 5.5, Zona Hotelera* ☎ *998/849–7257 or 998/849–7339*) is the marina closest to downtown, and specializes in diving and fishing, including deep-sea fishing expeditions. Prices range from $380 to $940, depending on the size of the boat and the length of the trip. They also offer small game-fishing trips that cost $250 for four hours or $350 for six hours.

Scuba Cancún (⊠ *Blvd. Kukulcán, Km 5, Zona Hotelera* ☎ *998/849–7508, 998/849–4736, or 998/849–5225* ⊕ *www.scubacancun.com.mx*) also offers deep-sea fishing and diving. Prices are $550 for a four-hour fishing trip, $650 for six hours, and $800 for an eight-hour expedition.

GO-CARTS

ᕙ About 10 minutes south of Cancún, speed demons can get their fix at **Go Karts Cancún**. There's a racetrack where Honda-engine go-carts reach speeds of up to 80 kph or 50 mph (there are also slower carts for children). Your choice of cart determines the price, but standard go-carts begin at $13 per 10-minute race session. For the experienced driver, motorcycles and V8 Nascars are also available by the hour. If you don't have a vehicle to get here, a taxi ride should run $10 to $15 from downtown (and considerably more from the Zona Hotelera). Buses leave every 20 minutes from the downtown terminal and cost about $1.20. Check to make sure your bus is not a direct route and will let you off. ⊠ *Carretera Cancún–Aeropuerto, Km 7.5, Residencial Campestre* ☎ *998/882–1275 or 998/882–1246* ⊕ *www. autodromocancun.com.mx* ☉ *Tues.–Sun. 10–6.*

GOLF

Many hotels offer golf packages that can considerably reduce your greens fees at Cancún golf courses. Cancún's main golf course is at **Cancún Golf Club at Pok-Ta-Pok** (⊠ *Blvd. Kukulcán, Km 7.5, Zona Hotelera* ☎ *998/883–1230* ⊕ *www.cancungolfclub.com*). The club has fine views of both sea and lagoon; its 18 holes were designed by Robert Trent Jones Jr. It also has two practice greens, three tennis courts, a pro shop,

Cancún has quite a few enviable courses.

and a restaurant. The greens fees go from $145 to $175, and include your cart, food, and beverages; club rentals are $40, shoes $18.

The 9-hole executive course, **Gran Sol Meliá** (✉ *Gran Melia Cancún Resort, Blvd. Kukulcán, Km 16.5, Zona Hotelera* ☎ *998/881–1100* ⊕ *www.solmelia.com*) forms a semicircle around the property and looks out onto the lagoon. The greens fee is $35, but the course is for the exclusive use of hotel guests.

There's an 18-hole championship golf course at the **Hilton** (✉ *Hilton Cancún Golf & Spa Resort, Blvd. Kukulcán, Km 17, Zona Hotelera* ☎ *998/881–8016* ⊕ *www.hiltoncancun.com/golf.htm*). Lying along the Nichupté Lagoon, the course has a practice facility with driving range and putting green. The 16th hole overlooks the Mayan Ruinas del Rey. Greens fees are $199 ($159 for hotel guests), carts included.

The newest course in Cancún is the **Playa Mujeres Golf Club** (✉ *Playa Mujeres Beach Resort, Prolongación Bonampak, Punta Sam* ☎ *998/887–7322 or 998/892–0874* ⊕ *www.playamujeresgolf.com.mx*). Designed by Greg Norman, this 18-hole, par-72 course is within the 930-acre Playa Mujeres Resort in Punta Sam. Practice facilities include a driving range, two putting greens, and a short game area. You can also arrange for individual and group instruction. Greens fees run from $230 to $260.

Puerto Cancún Golf (✉ *Blvd. Kukulcán, Km 1.5, Zona Hotelera* ☎ *998/898–3306* ⊕ *www.puertocancun.com*) designed by Tom Weiskopf, is an 18 hole, championship golf course in Puerto Cancún that stretches out over 185 acres and has ocean views and two holes that play on the marina.

Moon Spa & Golf Club (✉ *Carretera Cancún-Chetumal, Km 340, Sm 40 about 15 mins from airport* ☎ *998/881–6000* ⊕ *www.palaceresorts. com*) has three 9-hole courses. The 18-hole greens fee, which includes a cart, food, and drink service, is $260. If you're staying at the Moon Palace, inquire about the hotel's all-inclusive golf package.

Riviera Cancún Golf (✉ *Blvd. Kukulcán, Km 25, Zona Hotelera* ☎ *998/193–2010 Ext. 8760* ⊕ *www.palaceresorts.com*) designed by Jack Nicklaus, is an 18-hole golf course with ocean views and a Mexican-style clubhouse surrounded by mangroves. A 30% discount is available for guests of all Palace Resorts. All others pay $200 greens fees.

SNORKELING AND SCUBA DIVING

The snorkeling is best at Punta Nizuc, Punta Cancún, and Playa Tortugas, although you should be careful of the strong currents at Tortugas. You can rent gear for about $10 per day from many of the scuba-diving places as well as at many hotels.

Scuba diving is popular in Cancún, though it's not as spectacular as in Cozumel. Look for a scuba company that will give you lots of personal attention: smaller companies are often better at this than larger ones. Regardless, ask to meet the dive master, and check the equipment and certifications thoroughly. ■ TIP➡ A few words of caution about one-hour courses that many resorts offer for free: such courses *do not* prepare you to dive in the open ocean—only in shallow water where you can easily surface without danger. If you've caught the scuba bug and want to take deep or boat dives, prepare yourself properly by investing in a full certification course.

Aqua Fun (✉ *Blvd. Kukulcán, Km 16.5, Zona Hotelera* ☎ *998/885–0195 or 998/885–1682* ⊕ *aquafun.com.mx*) offers a two-hour tour of the mangroves that costs $66 per person and includes snorkeling at the Punta Nizuc reef.

AquaWorld (✉ *Blvd. Kukulcán, Km 15.2, Zona Hotelera* ☎ *998/848–8300* ⊕ *www.aquaworld.com.mx*) has a day-trip snorkeling excursion to Isla Mujeres that costs $77 per person. This operation also offers diving; a one-tank dive costs $72 and two-tank dives start at $77. Dive explorations of boat wrecks cost $85, and three-day dive packages cost $266.

Marina Barracuda (✉ *Blvd. Kukulcán, Km 14, Zona Hotelera* ☎ *998/885–2444* ⊕ *www.marinabarracuda.com*) has a two-hour jungle boat tour through the mangroves, which ends with snorkeling at the Punta Nizuc coral reef. The fee (starting at $66) includes snorkeling equipment, life jackets, and refreshments.

Marina Punta del Este (✉ *Blvd. Kukulcán, Km 10.3, Zona Hotelera* ☎ *998/883–1210*) is right in front of the Cancún Caribe Park Royal Grand. They have dives that last from 3½ to 4 hours and cost $72 if you are certified or $88 if you need a lesson. Daily lessons begin at 8 am and 1 pm.

Mundo Marino (✉ *Blvd. Kukulcán, Km 5.5, Zona Hotelera* ☎ *998/849–7257 or 998/849–7258*) has a 2½-hour snorkeling excursion that costs

$28 per person. They also offer a single-tank dive ($55), two-tank dive ($70), night dive ($70), and diving instruction course ($90).

Scuba Cancún (⊠ *Blvd. Kukulcán, Km 5, Zona Hotelera* ☎ *998/849-7508* ⊕ *www.scubacancun.com.mx*) specializes in diving trips and offers NAUI, CMAS, and PADI instruction. It's operated by Tomás Hurtado, who has more than 56 years of experience. A two-tank dive starts at $68.

Solo Buceo (⊠ *Blvd. Kukulcán, Km 9.5, Zona Hotelera* ☎ *998/883-3979* ⊕ *www.solobuceo.com*) charges $55 for one-tank dives, $70 for two-tank dives, and $90 for twilight diving every Tuesday and Thursday. They also have NAUI, FMAS, CMAS, and PADI instruction (lesson prices range from $90 to $240).

The Caribbean Coast

WORD OF MOUTH

"You have lots of options between Puerto Morelos and Tulum. Tulum is known for small cabaña-type accommodations along the beach and Akumal is a quiet enclave of condos and hotels. Puerto Morelos is the most 'Mexican' feeling town, just thirty minutes south of Cancun."

— zootsi

WELCOME TO
THE CARIBBEAN COAST

TOP REASONS TO GO

★ **Visiting the only Mayan site that overlooks the Caribbean:** The ruins at Tulum, only an hour south of Playa del Carmen, are a dramatic remnant of a sophisticated pre-Columbian people.

★ **Casting for bonefish:** These elusive shallows-dwellers, off the Chinchorro Reef near the Reserva de la Biosfera Sian Ka'an, can match wits with even the most seasoned fly-fisher.

★ **Indulging in a decadent massage or body treatment:** The Riviera Maya is flush with luxurious spa resorts that will make you ooh and aah.

★ **Diving or snorkeling with parrot fish and spotted eagle rays:** The Puerto Morelos Maritime National Park, a marine preserve, is just off the Yucatán's east coast, so you get that classic Caribbean aquamarine water with a bevy of sea creatures.

★ **Exploring the inland jungle:** South of Rio Bec, the forests grow thick, and you might glimpse howler monkeys, coatimundi, and Yucatán parrots.

1 The Riviera Maya. The coastal communities along the Caribbean vary widely: some are sleepy fishing villages, others are filled with glitzy resorts, and one—Tulum—is an ancient Mayan port city. The pyramids at Cobá are surrounded by jungle, where birds and monkeys call overhead. The beaches along this stretch are stunning, and are heralded by scuba divers, snorkelers, anglers, bird-watchers, and beachcombers.

2 Reserva de la Biosfera Sian Ka'an. The 1.6 million acres of this reserve—now more than 20 years old—protect thousands of wildlife species. Its mass is split between the Riviera Maya and the Costa Maya, and encompasses cenotes (sinkholes), coastal mangrove forests, and dense inland vegetation, resplendent with monkeys, coatimundis, and jaguars.

3 The Costa Maya. Once a no-man's-land stretching south of Felipe Carrillo Puerto to Chetumal, the Costa Maya is now being eyed by developers. Although the newly built port of Puerto Costa Maya attracts droves of cruise-ship passengers, it's still possible to enjoy a sleepy, sunbaked, and inexpensive Mexican vacation here.

CAMPECHE

Caobas

Rio Bec

Kohun

18

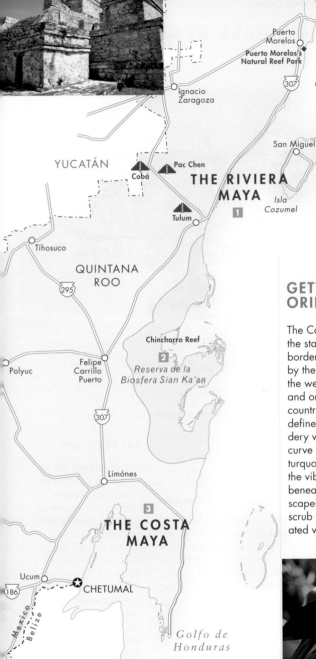

3

Puerto
Morelos

Puerto Morelos's
Natural Reef Park

307

Ignacio
Zaragoza

San Miguel

YUCATÁN

Pac Chen

Cobá

**THE RIVIERA
MAYA**

*Isla
Cozumel*

1

Tulum

Tihosuco

QUINTANA
ROO

295

Chinchorro Reef

2

*Reserva de la
Biosfera Sian Ka'an*

Polyuc

Felipe
Carrillo
Puerto

307

Limónes

3

**THE COSTA
MAYA**

Ucum

186

⭐ CHETUMAL

Mexico
Belize

*Golfo de
Honduras*

GETTING
ORIENTED

The Caribbean Coast is in
the state of Quintana Roo,
bordered on the northwest
by the state of Yucatán, on
the west by Campeche, and
on the south by the
country of Belize. Beaches
define this region—pow-
dery white sands that
curve to embrace clear
turquoise lagoons, and
the vibrant marine life
beneath. Inland land-
scapes, which range from
scrub to jungle, are punctuated with Mayan ruins.

CARIBBEAN'S BEST BEACHES

Turquoise waters, sugary sand, arching palms — this postcard perfection is about as ideal as it gets, and it aptly describes the stretch from Cancún to Tulum. The fact that there's no ocean view from the highway or a coastal road along the Caribbean make that first step onto the powdery sand that much more breathtaking.

(Above) The famous ruins of Tulum. (Oppostie top) Deck chairs and deserted beaches. (Opposite bottom) the emerald waters of Playa del Secreto.

Beaches along the Riviera Maya are regularly groomed by adjacent resorts. Unfortunately many beaches are inaccessible from Carretera 307, as security gates block such properties. The best way to reach the water is by taking one of the public roads that run between resorts, or by purchasing a drink in a hotel lobby before hitting the beach.

If you're looking for lively (but populated) beaches, head to one of the beach clubs that parallel Playa del Carmen's Fifth Avenue. Although Playa's beaches (as well as those in Tulum) lack protective outer reefs, the strong wind and waves make these areas great for water sports.

SAFETY FIRST

Empty coastlines can be susceptible to car break-ins and theft. Beware: even the calmest-looking waters can have currents and riptides. If visiting isolated beaches, bring sunscreen and drinking water to avoid overexposure and dehydration. Take note that waves are most powerful during December, and that hurricane season lasts from June through November.

BEST BEACHES

Playa del Secreto (North of Punta Maroma)

The turquoise and emerald waters of Punta Maroma are as beautiful as it gets. Like fine powdered crystals, the soft white sand sparkles under the sun and the beaches are kept spotless by neighboring resorts that groom them daily. The warm water is outstanding, and there are no sudden drop-offs or rocks in sight; although not completely calm, it's never too rough to keep you from swimming. Farther north of here is a stretch of coastline where clothing is optional.

Playa X'cacel (X'cacel)

The deep sand, outer reef, and isolated beaches make this a haven for sea turtles that nest here between May and November. If you plan on visiting during turtle season, don't disturb the raised mounds of sand and avoid any turtles you see on shore. What makes this beach so appealing is the natural setting, completely devoid of resorts and amenities. Snorkeling is best toward the north end of the beach, and since the waters are protected by the outer reef, wind and waves are seldom a problem here. To reach Playa X'cacel, turn onto the dirt road between Chemuyil Xel-Há off Carretera 307. There's usually a guard who charges $2 to enter. Since this beach is desolate, make sure you don't leave any valuables in your car.

Tankah Bay (Tankah)

Overshadowed by the southern beaches of Tulum, this wide, protected beach has an outer reef that blocks the wind and waves. The bay itself offers excellent snorkeling and kayaking, but you'll want to avoid swimming, since a few rocks line the shore. Throw down a towel and sink into the sugary-white sand or head to the neighboring Manatee Cenote for an underwater adventure. Surrounded by mangroves, this freshwater pool is rich with abundant sea life, and spills directly into the bay. Although there are no amenities directly on the beach, you'll find wonderful restaurants nearby at Blue Sky Hotel and Casa Cenote.

Tulum Beach (Tulum)

The biggest draw to Tulum's beaches, are the fact that they're surrounded by ancient Mayan ruins. Here you'll find some of the softest sand on the coast, with water that illuminates four shades of turquoise. The small cove at the base of the ruins is accessible by way of a long wooden staircase. You'll have to pay the park entrance fee to get to the sand. This is by far the most picturesque of Tulum's beaches, but not the biggest. Head farther south, along the road to Boca Paila, for endless beach options.

TOP RESORTS

Champagne greetings, private butlers, beach-front massages—the services provided by Riviera Maya's resorts are endless. Recently, luxury has been taken even further with everything from in-room chefs to personal Range Rovers.

(Above) The Tides. (Opposite top) Mandarin Oriental. (Opposite bottom) Rosewood Mayakoba.

Although not as prevalent as in Cancún, all-inclusive beachfront resorts still define the Riviera Maya. Popular with families, the majority have plenty of activities, entertainment, food options, and of course, swimming pools for the kids.

Whether you choose to relax poolside or on the beach in a sun bed (some have built-in mist-sprayers), chances are you'll spend a good part of your trip admiring the ocean view. In fact, it's rare to find a resort that is not perched on the white sands of the Caribbean. Nearly all resorts (and public beaches) along the Riviera Maya are only accessible through a security gate off Carretera 307.

DEATH OF THE ALL-INCLUSIVE?

A crop of new resorts along the Riviera Maya takes pampering to a higher level. By eliminating the all-inclusive option, they can provide every luxury imaginable. The price for a room at these resorts is exorbitant and you'll be charged for every single indulgence you consume. But in the end, you'll get exactly what you pay for, rather than paying for something you don't want.

BANYAN TREE

Named for the Banyan tree that centers the property, the focus of this Asian-style resort is the award-winning spa. The service here is unparalleled, and the location is downright surreal. Designed to blend with their natural surroundings, some villas are built on stilts over the water, while others rest on the white sandy beaches of the Caribbean. For the ultimate in relaxation, every villa has a private pool, sundeck, and pavilion.

MANDARIN ORIENTAL

At the Mandarin Oriental Spa, you can meet with a lifestyle guru who determines what herbs would be most beneficial to your body. Once these herbs are selected from the on-site garden, they are infused into everything from your massage oils to your bathwater. Each of the villas (either lagoon or ocean view) has its own plunge pool, onyx sinks, hardwood floors, and, of course, a private butler. The use of indigenous materials such as limestone, wood, and coconut skillfully blends the natural environment with each villa's modern design. Many rooms are structured around a series of "art patios," and 99% of the property remains a conservation area. The resort also has a private marina, three pools, and a trendy beach club where sushi is served. Diving courses are also an option.

ROSEWOOD MAYAKOBA

Pushing the boundaries of luxury, this exquisite resort spills across 20 acres of crystal-clear lagoons. Nestled under a canopy of mangroves, rooms are spacious (some 3,200 square feet) and include outdoor showers, plunge pools, garden baths, rooftop sundecks, and private docks from which guests are transported throughout the property by boat. Reminiscent of Venice, roads are replaced by water canals that wind from the limestone lobby to the pristine beaches. The 17,000-square-foot spa is on its own private island.

THE TIDES RIVIERA MAYA

Tucked in the forest of Riviera Maya, this luxury refuge embraces nature in every sense of the word. Thirty air-conditioned bungalows are surrounded by waterfalls and jungle. On arrival, guests are greeted with a coconut-lemongrass cocktail and then escorted to their suites by private butlers. Sprinkled rose petals create a natural path, leading from your private plunge pool into the *palapa* (thatch roofs) suite, with its garden terrace, crocheted hammock, and outdoor shower. Those who want to explore the area can use one of the hotel's Range Rovers, reserved exclusively for guests. Unlike many properties in the area, the Tides introduces guests to the environment and traditions of Mexico with tequila tastings, diving courses, and Mayan rituals.

Updated by
Marlise Kast

Mexico's Caribbean coastline is divided into two major areas. The stretch from Punta Tanchacté to Punta Allen—the Riviera Maya—has the most sights and accommodations, and includes some of the Yucatán's most beautiful ruins and cenotes. The more southern stretch, from Punta Allen to Chetumal, has been dubbed the "Costa Maya." This is where civilization thins out. Here you'll find the most alluring landscapes, including the pristine jungle wilderness of the Reserva de la Biosfera Sian Ka'an.

Wildlife has been affected by the development of coastal resorts. Thanks to the federal government's foresight, however, 1.6 million acres of coastline and jungle have been set aside for protection as the Reserva de la Biosfera Sian Ka'an. Whatever may happen elsewhere along the coast, this preserve is a haven for the wildlife and the travelers who seek the Yucatán of old.

PLANNING

WHEN TO GO

From November to April, the coastal weather is heavenly, with temperatures hovering around 80°F and near-constant ocean breezes. In July and August, however, the breezes disappear and humidity soars, especially inland where temperatures often reach the mid-90s. September and October bring the worst weather, with frequent rain, mosquitoes, and the risk of hurricanes.

Hotel rates can drop on the Caribbean Coast by as much as 50% in the low season (September to approximately mid-December). In high season, however, it's virtually impossible to find low rates, especially in Playa del Carmen. During Christmas week, prices can rise as much as $100 a night—so if you're planning a Christmas vacation, you'd do well to book six months in advance.

Keep in mind that visiting during a traditional festival such as the Day of the Dead (which culminates on November 2 after three nights of candlelit ceremonies) can be more expensive—but it can also be unforgettable.

TIMING

Five days will give you enough time to enjoy the beach, and explore many of the best parts of the Caribbean Coast. If you use Playa del Carmen as a base, you can easily take day trips to Xcaret eco-park or visit cliff-side ruins of Tulum. Don't miss swimming at Xel-Há or one of the numerous cenotes along Carretera 307. The beaches at Paamul and Xpu-Há are also within driving distance, as is the Mayan village of Pac Chen, the ruins at Cobá, and the Reserva de la Biosfera Sian Ka'an.

MONEY MATTERS

Foreigners may not exchange more than $1,500 U.S. dollars (cash) per person, per month into Mexican Pesos. Mexican travelers are also limited to $1,500 U.S.D. cash per person, per month, with the added restriction of no more than $300 U.S.D. cash per day. Most banks along Carretera 307 have ATMs where you can withdraw local currency, or you can pay for services with a debit or credit card without restrictions. There's no limit to the number of purchases or the amount of each individual transaction. We recommend having Mexican pesos on hand, especially if you intend to use public transportation, leave tips, or pay cash during your trip.

HOTELS

Many resorts are in remote areas; if you haven't rented a car and want to visit local sights or restaurants, you may find yourself at the mercy of the hotel shuttle service (if there's one) or waiting for long stretches of time for the bus. Although pricey, taxis run up and down Carretera 307 between Tulum and Playa del Carmen looking for passengers. You can usually find taxis parked outside major resorts. Smaller hotels and inns are often family-run; a stay in one of them will give you the chance to mix with the locals.

RESTAURANTS

Restaurants here vary from quirky beachside affairs with outdoor tables and palapas to more-elaborate and sophisticated establishments. Dress is casual at most places, so leave your tie and jacket at home. Smaller cafés and fish eateries may not accept credit cards or traveler's checks, especially in remote beach villages. Bigger establishments and those in hotels normally accept plastic. Unlike restaurants in Playa del Carmen, those in Puerto Morelos do not factor *propinas* (tips) into the bill. Depending on the service, a 10% to 15% gratuity is usually standard. It's best to order fresh local fish—grouper, dorado, red snapper, and sea bass—rather than shellfish like shrimp, lobster, and oysters, since the latter are often flown in frozen from the Gulf. The largest selection of restaurants can be found in Playa del Carmen.

Continued on page 119

CANCUN AND RIVIERA SPAS

by Marlise Kast

This area offers plenty of pampering, be it footbaths or facials, manicures or massages. Whether in a spa pavilion, on a soft white beach, or in a palapa nestled in the jungle, you'll experience the ultimate in relaxation of body, mind, and spirit.

Most spas in the region also have heated pools, steam rooms, beachside massages, and fitness facilities. Some even offer beauty salons, personal consultants, organic cafés, and natural cenotes.

A visit to the region is not complete without participating in a temazcal ritual based on traditional Mayan healing methods. Temazcal is a type of sweat lodge that's used to purify the body and cleanse the mind and spirit. You can also indulge in one of the other Mayan-inspired spa remedies like chaya detoxification, chocolate body wraps, or ground corn and honey exfoliation. Additonally most resorts offer treatments from around the globe. Japanese shiatsu, Swedish massage, and deep-tissue Thai massage are just a few of the ways to rejuvenate your body.

There's a package for just about everyone: for men, for golfers, for expectant mothers. Send the kids to the teen spa for a Peppermint Patty foot massage or an ice cream pedicure. Newlyweds can indulge in candlelit massages for two or aroma baths brimming with floating petals.

Most spas are open to the public, but appointments are mandatory since walk-ins aren't the norm. Be sure to set aside extra time before or after your treatment to take advantage of all the facility has to offer.

Resort/Spa name	Body Treatments	Facials	Outdoor Treatments	Couples Treatments	Fitness Day Pass	Sauna	Steam Room
Rosewood	$85–$195	$165–$255	Lagoon	yes	Free	yes	yes
Mandarin Oriental	$145–$205	$205	Garden	yes	Free	yes	yes
JW Marriott	$60–$270	$75–$155	Pool	yes	no	yes	yes
Banyan Tree	$90–$210	$180–$190	Lagoon	yes	no	yes	yes
The Tides	$70–$240	$85–$180	Jungle or Ocean	yes	no	yes	yes
Fairmont	$129–$499	$129–$229	Jungle	yes	$25	yes	yes
Azulik	$73–$165	$66–$90	Ocean	no	no	no	no
Maroma	$125–$215	$125–$210	Garden	yes	Free	yes	yes
Zoëtry Paraiso	$129–$220	$129–$250	Ocean	yes	Resort guests only	yes	yes
Hilton	$109–$199	$119–$179	Ocean	yes	Resort guests only	yes	no

The Banyan Tree uses customized lotions and oils.

TOP SPOTS

Banyan Tree Spa

Rosewood Mayakoba

BANYAN TREE SPA, MAYAKOBA

Built over freshwater lagoons, the Banyan Tree Spa draws on centuries old Asian traditions. The therapists (80% of whom are from Thailand) begin with a heavenly footbath, followed by your choice of healing treatments. Unique to Banyan Tree is its signature Rainmist Steam Bath and the 12-step Rainforest Experience that combines hydrotherapy with infrared light to release tension and revitalize the body.

BODY TREATMENTS. Massage: Sukhothai, Balinese, Swedish, Thai, Chinese footwork, lomi lomi, Indian head massage. **Wraps/Baths:** Tumeric and lemongrass scrub, green tea scrub, lulur scrub, yogurt splash, fresh milk bath, sandalwood and ginger scrub, marigold and honey scrub, footbath. **Other:** Rainmist Steam Bath, detox mud wrap, rain shower, 12-step Rainforest, Thai herbal compress, yoga lessons, men's treatments

BEAUTY TREATMENTS. Facials, hair/scalp conditioning, manicures, pedicures, waxing, makeovers

PRICES. Body Treatments: $90–$210. Facials: $180–$190. Hair: $50–$90. Manicure/Pedicure: $70–$90.

Banyan Tree Spa. ⊠ *Carretera 307, Km 298. Mayakoba.* ☎ *984/877–3688* ⊕ *www. banyantree.com/mayakoba. Parking: Valet* ☐ *AE, MC, V*

SENSE, ROSEWOOD MAYAKOBA

Rosewood's 17,000-sq-ft spa is in a jungle on its very own island. Wooden walkways lead to a swimming pool and limestone cenote, which is fed by subterranean springs. Many treatments, such as the temazcal ritual and the Mayakoba ancient massage, incorporate the Mayan tradition of aligning the energies of the body in rhythmic harmony. Leave time to enjoy the spa facilities, including the gym, sauna, Jacuzzi, plunge pool and eucalyptus steam room.

BODY TREATMENTS. Massage: Swedish, deep tissue, hot stone, aromatherapy, reflexology, Asian. **Wraps/Baths:** Hydrating, chocolate, detox, revitalization, toning. **Other:** Natural cenote, temazcal ritual, 12 lagoonside treatment rooms, 8 spa suites, Itzamná café, private yoga lessons, treatments for pregnant women.

BEAUTY TREATMENTS. Facials, hair cuts/style, manicures, pedicures, waxing, makeovers

PRICES. Body Treatments: $85–$195. Facials: $165–$255. Hair: $65–$85. Manicure/Pedicure: $75–$85.

Sense, Rosewood Spas. ⊠ *Carretera 307, Km 298. Mayakoba* ☎ *984/875–8000* ⊕ *www.rosewoodmayakoba.com. Parking: Valet* ☐ *AE, MC, V*

The Tides

Mandarin Oriental

THE TIDES, PUNTA BETE

Although not as grandiose as most spas in the area, the Tides is unique in its use of indigenous materials and local ingredients, such as chocolate, seaweed, aloe vera, and heated lava shells. It also offers a series of unusual treatments, like the Hammock Massage that allows the therapist to knead you through a hammock. Another massage uses a *manteada* (blanket stretch) to adjust posture and elongate muscles. The Sweet Honey and Rain Massage combine herbal bouquets, wild honey, and drops of water.

BODY TREATMENTS. Massage: Deep tissue, Thai, jantzu water massage, hot stone, reflexology, lunar, hammock. **Wraps/Baths:** Red seaweed wrap, aloe vera bath, mud wrap, Mayan bath. **Other:** Oceanfront yoga and Pilates, aromatherapy, fertility ceremony, temazcal ritual, men's treatments.

BEAUTY TREATMENTS. Facials, manicures, pedicures, waxing

PRICES. Body Treatments: $70–$240. Facials: $85–$180. Manicure/Pedicure: $85–$95.

The Tides. ✉ *Playa Xcalacoco Frac 7, Punta Bete* ☎ *984/877–3000* ⊕ *www. tidesrivieramaya.com. Parking: Valet* 🖃 *AE, MC, V*

MANDARIN ORIENTAL

Both the design and philosophy of the spa are inspired by the Mayan healing elements of water, air, fire, and earth. Signature treatments include Oriental Harmony (four-hands massage), temazcal ceremony (guided by a Mayan shaman), and the Mayan Na Lu'Um massage (which opens blocked energy paths). For travelers who have spent too many days basking in the sun, the soothing Kinich Ahau program includes a sunburn remedy wrap, hair treatment, and hydrating facial.

BODY TREATMENTS. Massage: Shiatsu, hot stone, Thai, Oriental foot therapy, Swedish, deep tissue. **Wraps/Baths:** Yucatan mud wrap, Oriental salt scrub, herbal wrap, watsu pool, chocolate body treatment. **Other:** Aromatherapy, Kinesis fitness studio, yoga/pilates/meditation classes, temazcal, ice fountains.

BEAUTY TREATMENTS. Facials, manicures, pedicures

PRICES. Body Treatments: $145–$315. Facials: $205. Hair: $65–$85. Manicure/Pedicure: $80–$95.

The Spa at Mandarin Oriental. ✉ *Carretera 307, Km 298.8* ☎ *984/877–3888* ⊕ *www. mandarinoriental.com/rivieramaya Parking: Valet* 🖃 *AE, MC, V*

HONORABLE MENTIONS

Fairmont Mayakoba

ZOËTRY PARAISO DE LA BONITA, PUNTA TANCHACTE

It's the only certified Thalassotherapy Spa and Anti-Aging Center in Riviera Maya, meaning many of it's treatments incorporate seawater. The extensive menu features body wraps, holistic treatments, saltwater hydrotherapy, and temazcal rituals. Although most treatments involve getting wet, you'll also find healing dry remedies like wraps, facials, massages, and acupuncture. To eliminate toxins, spa products are infused with sea kelp and marine mud.

Within the 22,000 sq-ft spa are facilities for yoga, Tai-Chi, acupuncture and Chinese medicine.

BODY TREATMENTS. Massage: Mayan, reflexology, pressotheraphy, Swedish, Thai, hot stone, therapeutic, regenerative, marine affusion shower massage, janzu massage. Wraps/Baths: Seaweed wrap, mud wrap, balneotheraphy. Other: Temazcal, hydrotheraphy, private yoga, Tai Chi, acupuncture, Kinesiology, saltwater pool, fitness center, men's treatments.

BEAUTY TREATMENTS. Facials, manicures, pedicures, waxing, hair cut/style

PRICES. Body Treatments: $129–$220. Facials: $129–$250. Manicure/Pedicure: $55–$110.

Zoëtry Paraiso de la Bonia. ✉ Carretera 307, Km 328 ☎ 984/872–8300 ⊕ www.zoetryparaisodelabonita.com/Paraiso. Parking: Valet ▭ AE, MC, V

WILLOW STREAM, FAIRMONT MAYAKOBA

It's easy to loose yourself (literally) within the enormous 37,000 sq-ft spa. Favorite treatments are the Mexican stone massage, the Cha Chac Rain Ritual (a massage that takes place on a seven-jet Vichy table), and Honey in the Heart (honey body mask and massage). Weary travelers will want to try the Jet Lag Recovery, an aromatherapy bath and massage that reverses the negative effects of flying and time zone changes. After a gym workout, ease your muscles in the rooftop vitality pool.

BODY TREATMENTS. Massage: hot stone, reflexology, aromatheraphy, deep tissue. Wraps/Baths: Seaweed bath, thermal mineral bath, chocolate wrap, rose bath, Mayan bath, clay purification. Other: Vichy shower, saltwater pool, fitness center, specialized wedding menu, men's treatments.

BEAUTY TREATMENTS. Facials, manicures, pedicures, waxing, hair cut/color/style, make-up application

PRICES. Body Treatments: $129–$499. Facials: $129–$229. Manicure/Pedicure: $59–$89.

Willow Stream at Fairmont Mayakoba. ✉ Carretera 307, Km 298 ☎ 984/206–3039 ⊕ www.willowstream.com. Parking: Valet ▭ AE, MC, V

JW Marriott   Aventura Spa Palace

JW MARRIOTT, CANCUN

Located in Cancun proper, this 35,000 sq-ft spa should be included as one of the area's best. Choose from one of 13 invigorating facials including the pumpkin enzyme treatment or the cucumber green-tea facial. Women will enjoy Precious Stones and Flowers which begins with a detoxifying marine mask followed by flower petals and crystals placed over energy points to bring balance and harmony to the body. The JW Spa even offers specialized treatments for men, golfers, couples, and teens. For the ultimate Caribbean experience, take a dip in the ocean followed by a beachside massage.

BODY TREATMENTS. Massage: Swedish, Oriental, lomi lomi, deep tissue, shiatsu, hot stone. **Wraps/Baths:** Mayan herbal bath, chocolate body scrub. **Other:** Vichy shower, indoor/outdoor pool, fitness center, temezcal, teen spa menu (ages 6–17), men's treatments.

BEAUTY TREATMENTS. Facials, manicures, pedicures, waxing, hair cut/color/style, make-up application

PRICES. Body Treatments: $60–$270. Facials: $75–$155. Manicure/Pedicure: $10–$70.

JW Marriott Cancun Resort & Spa. ⊠ *Blvd Kukulcan Km 14.5, Zona Hotelera, Cancun* 🖨 *998/848-9700 Parking: Valet* ⊟ *AE, MC, V*

ALSO WORTH NOTING

Several other Riviera Maya spas are also worth mentioning. The **Kinan Spa at Maroma Resort** (⊠ *Carretera 307, Km 51* 🕾 *998/872-8200* ⊕ *www.maromahotel. com*), has treatments based on ancient Mayan healing. **Aventura Spa Palace** (⊠ *Carretera 307, Km 72, Puerto Aventuras* 🕾 *984/875-1100* ⊕ *www.palaceresorts. com*) is known for its excellent hydrotherapy facilities. For treatments with a view, head to **Azulik Eco-Resort** in Tulum (⊠ *Carretera Tulum Ruinas Km 5* 🕾 *800/123-3278* ⊕ *www.azulik.com*).

Located in Cancun's Zona Hotelera, this impressive spa at **The Hilton** (⊠ *Blvd. Kukulcan, Km 17, Zona Hotelera, Cancun* 🕾 *998/881-8000* ⊕ *www.hiltoncancun. com*) has a Zen garden, relaxation lounge and treatments on the beach for men and women.

Also located in Cancun is the **Kayantá Spa at The Ritz Carlton** (⊠ *Blvd. Kukulcan, Km 14, Zona Hotelera, Cancun* 🕾 *998/881-0808* ⊕ *www.ritzcarlton.com*) where you can experience the "Deep Blue Peel." This massage and body-scrub combo consists of marine extracts, seaweed, bergamot and jojoba oil. The avocado and yogurt wrap will leave your skin feeling silky smooth.

At the **Ceiba del Mar Spa** (⊠ *Costera Norte, Puerto Morelos* 🕾 *998/872-8063* ⊕ *www. ceibadelmar.com*) you can begin with a biotensor rod for testing vital energy. Based on the findings, specific treatments are then selected to help restore energy levels.

GLOSSARY

acupuncture. Painless Chinese procedure in which needles are inserted into key spots on the body to restore the flow of qi and allow the body to heal itself.

aromatherapy. Massage and other treatments using plant-derived essential oils intended to relax the skin's connective tissues and stimulate the flow of lymph fluid.

balneotherapy. Theraputic hot baths and natural vapor baths.

body brushing. Drybrushing of the skin to remove dead cells and stimulate circulation. Also called body scrub; see also salt glow.

body polish. Use of scrubs, loofahs, and other exfoliants to remove dead skin cells.

janzu. An aquatic therapeutic technique that unblocks physical, emotional and mental energy by movement in the water.

hot-stone massage. Massage using smooth stones heated in water and applied to the skin with pressure or strokes or simply rested on the body.

hydrotherapy. Underwater massage, alternating hot and cold showers, and other water-oriented treatments.

lomi lomi. A type of massage that imposes a rhythmic, rocking sensation, while stimulating the circulatory system.

pressotheraphy. compression technique to help improve circulation and tone the circulatory system.

Reiki. A Japanese healing method involving universal life energy, the laying on of hands, and mental and spiritual balancing. It's intended to relieve acute emotional and physical conditions. Also called adiance technique.

salt glow. Rubbing the body with coarse salt to remove dead skin.

shiatsu. Japanese massage that uses pressure applied with fingers, hands, elbows, and feet.

shirodhara. Ayurvedic massage in which warm herbalized oil is trickled onto the center of the forehead, then gently rubbed into the hair and scalp.

Swiss shower. A multi-jet bath that alternates hot and cold water, often used after mud wraps and other body treatments.

temazcal. Mayan meditation in a sauna heated with volcanic rocks.

Thai massage. Deep-tissue massage and passive stretching to ease stiff, tense, or short muscles.

thalassotherapy. Water-based treatments that incorporate seawater, seaweed, and algae.

Vichy shower. Treatment in which a person lies on a cushioned, waterproof mat and is showered by overhead water jets.

Watsu. A blend of shiatsu and deep-tissue massage with gentle stretches—all conducted in a warm pool.

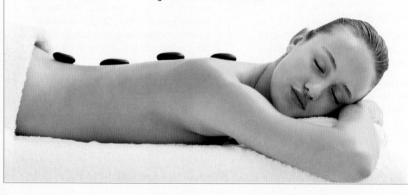

DINING AND LODGING PRICES

	WHAT IT COSTS IN DOLLARS				
	¢	$	$$	$$$	$$$$
Restaurants	under $5	$5–$10	$10–$15	$15–$25	over $25
Hotels	under $50	$50–$75	$75–$150	$150–$250	over $250

Restaurant prices are per person, for a main course at dinner, excluding tax and tip. Hotel prices are for a standard double room in high season.

3

SAFETY

With its massive resorts and beachside accommodations, the Caribbean Coast is free of most dangers found in big cities. Playa del Carmen is a big tourist area and extremely safe. In general, resorts are the best bet for a worry-free vacation, since they have 24-hour security and in-room safes. Water is usually purified at hotels, but it's always smart to drink bottled water just to be safe.

The greatest dangers here are caused on the road. Make sure you obey speed limits: Speed bumps, police radars, and sudden decreases in speed limits are easy traps for travelers. When renting a car, ask the agency for a "Tourist Traffic Card." This voucher allows you to pay a ticket at the car rental agency when you return the car, rather than having to spend several hours at the police station. It also helps eliminate corruption. Avis offers drivers a card that actually serves as "payment" for two minor traffic violations. By presenting the card to authorities, the fine will be paid by Avis when you return the vehicle.

⇨ *Check out our Travel Smart chapter for rules of the road if you plan on driving.*

Before your trip, be sure to purchase travel insurance, monitor the weather, and notify your embassy and credit card company of your whereabouts. It's also a good idea to make a copy of your passport, and leave your travel itinerary with a friend or family member. To avoid unwanted situations, steer clear of remote locations, travel with a partner, and refrain from driving long distances at night.

TOURS

Alltournative (⊠ *Carretera Chetumal-Puerto Juárez, Km 287, Lote 13 Sur, in front of Playacar development* ☎ *984/803–9999 or 800/507–1092* ⊕ *www.alltournative.com*) offers eco-friendly adventures for travelers of all ages and fitness levels.

Hilario Hiller (⊠ *La Jolla, Casa Nai Na, 3rd fl.* ☎ *984/875–9066*) customizes tours of Mayan villages, ruins, and the jungle.

Maya Sites Travel Services (☎ *505/255–2279 or 877/620–8715* ⊕ *www. mayasites.com*) uses archaeologists and other experts to lead inexpensive tours of ruins.

VISITOR INFORMATION
For additional information on the Caribbean Coast, check out any of the following Web sites: ⊕ *www.locogringo.com,* ⊕ *www.yucatantoday. com,* ⊕ *www.sac-be.com,* ⊕ *www.playamayanews.com*

THE RIVIERA MAYA

It takes patience to discover the treasures along this part of the coast. Beaches and towns aren't easily visible from the main highway—the road from Cancún to Tulum is 1 to 2 km (½ to 1 mi) from the coast. Thus there's little to see but dense vegetation, lots of billboards, many roadside markets, and signs marking entrances to various hotels and attractions.

Still, the treasures—which include spectacular white-sand beaches and some of the peninsula's most beautiful Mayan ruins—are here, and they haven't been lost on resort developers. In fact, the Riviera Maya, which stretches from Punta Tanchacté in the north down to Punta Allen in the south, currently has about 23,512 hotel rooms. This frenzy of building has affected many beachside Mayan communities, which have had to relocate to the inland jungle. The residents of these settlements, who mainly work in the hotels, have managed to keep Yucatecan traditions alive including food, music, and holiday celebrations.

PLAYA DEL CARMEN

68 km (42 mi) south of Cancún.

Playa has become one of Latin America's fastest-growing communities, with a population of more than 135,000 and a pace almost as hectic as that of Cancún. Hotels, restaurants, and shops multiply here faster than you can say "Kukulcán." Some are branches of Cancún eateries whose owners have taken up permanent residence in Playa, while others are owned by American and European expats (predominately Italians) who came here years ago. It makes for a varied, international community.

Considered the South Beach of Mexico, the club scene (raging night and day) is one of the main draws here. In fact, you may have trouble sleeping if you're staying in the heart of downtown. By day, Playa's lively beach clubs are packed with travelers lounging in the sun or dancing to the sounds of a live DJ. By night, the action moves to Calle 12, where a cluster of nightclubs line the street.

Unfortunately, it's not that easy to get off the beaten path. Most of the area is developed, and only a few patches of property farther north remain barren, though building height restrictions have helped to keep Playa from turning into the next Cancún. In recent years, all-inclusive resorts have made their way to the outskirts of town.

GETTING HERE AND AROUND

Almost everyone who arrives in this region by air flies into Cancún's *Aeropuerto Internacional.* Buses traveling south from Cancún stop at Playa del Carmen's bus terminal at Avenida 20 and Calle 12. Buses headed to Cancún from Playa del Carmen use the main bus terminal

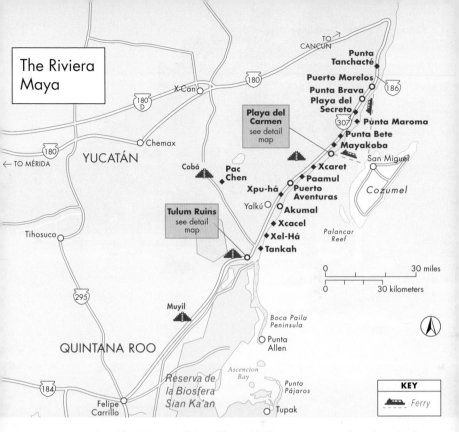

The Riviera Maya

TO CANCÚN

Punta Tanchacté
Puerto Morelos
Punta Brava
Playa del Secreto
Punta Maroma
Punta Bete
Mayakoba
San Miguel
Cozumel
Xcaret
Paamul
Puerto Aventuras
Akumal
Palancar Reef
Xcacel
Xel-Há
Tankah

X-Can
Playa del Carmen
see detail map
Chemax
YUCATÁN
TO MÉRIDA
Cobá
Pac Chen
Xpu-há
Yalkú
Tulum Ruins
see detail map
Tihosuco

Muyil

QUINTANA ROO

Boca Paila Peninsula
Punta Allen

Reserva de la Biosfera Sian Ka'an
Ascencion Bay
Punta Pájaros
Tupak

Felipe Carrillo

| 0 | | | 30 miles |
| 0 | | | 30 kilometers |

KEY
🚢 Ferry

at Avenida Juárez and Avenida 5. ADO runs express, first-class, and second-class buses to major destinations. You can hire taxis in Cancún to go as far as Playa del Carmen, but the price is steep—about $55 for the one-hour drive. Shared vans from Cancún airport generally cost $80 for a six-person van, or $120 for a 10-person van; if you're traveling with a group or even find some other Playa-bound travelers at the airport, a van can be a good way to go.

⚠ In Playa del Carmen, parking is prohibited at yellow curbs. If you're ticketed, your license plate will be taken to a nearby police station and only returned after the fine has been paid.

ESSENTIALS

Bus Contacts ADO (☎ 983/832–5110 ⊕ www.ado.com.mx).

Car Rental Avis ✉ Carretera 307, Lote 4, Mza 73, next to fire station, Playa del Carmen ☎ 984/873–3843 ⊕ www.avis.com).

Currency Exchange Banamex (✉ Av. Juárez between Avs. 20 and 25 ☎ 984/873–0825 ✉ Av. 10 at Av. 12 ☎ 984/873–2947). **Bancomer** (✉ Av. Juárez between Calles 25 and 30 ☎ 984/873–0356).

Police Police Department (✉ *Playa del Carmen* ☎ *984/877–3340*). **Federal Police** (✉ *Playa del Carmen* ☎ *998/884–1107*).

Medical Assistance Centro de Salud (✉ *Av. Juárez and Av. 15* ☎ *984/873–1230 Ext. 147*) **Clinica Medica del Carmen** ✉ *Av 25 between Calle 2 and Juarez, Playa del Carmen* ☎ *984/873–0885*).

Visitor and Tour Info Playa del Carmen tourist information booth (✉ *Av. Juárez by police station, between Calles 15 and 20* ☎ *984/873–2804 in Playa del Carmen, 888/955–7155 in U.S., 604/990–6506 in Canada*). **Tierra Maya Tours** (✉ *Av. 5 and Calle 6* ☎ *984/873–1385*).

EXPLORING

La Casa del Arte Popular Mexicano. This entrancing folk-art museum is a must for anyone interested in Mexican culture and handicrafts. It's brimming with original works by the country's finest artisans, which are arranged in fascinating tableaux. The collection represents different regions of Mexico—from nativity scenes sculpted out of Oaxaca's clays to the intricate *arbol de la vida* (tree of life) sculptures crafted in Metepec. Children will love the toy room, which includes an impressive display of *alebrijes* (dreamworld animals). In addition to the handicrafts, there are scenes set up throughout the museum to give visitors an idea of traditional Mexican life. The mannequins used in these re-creations, which include a church and a market setting, were actually modeled on real people that the museum director met during her trips through Mexico. ✉ *Carretera 307, Km 282, 10 km (6 mi) south of Playa del Carmen* ☎ *984/871–5200 Ext. 399* ⊕ *www.xcaret.com* ✂ *Free (museum only)* ☉ *Weekdays 8:30 am–10 pm.*

The excellent 32-acre **Xaman Ha Aviary** (✉ *Paseo Xaman-Ha, Mza 13-A Lote 1, Playacar* ☎ *984/873–0330* ⊕ *www.aviarioxamanha.com*), in the middle of the Playacar development, is home to more than 30 species of native birds. Bring insect repellent. It's open daily 9 to 5, and admission is $22.

BEACHES

Playa del Carmen is as famous for its pristine beaches as it is for its thriving nightlife. This charming coastal city has managed to blend the two into one with its trendy beach clubs, offering everything from cabanas and cocktails to dancing and DJs. Although the beaches themselves are pleasant, the focus is more on what the clubs have to offer than what's happening on the water. The music, combined with cocktails and bikinis, makes these open-air bars extremely popular with young singles. They're also the only places (other than resorts) where you'll find beach amenities.

Most beach clubs are located between Calles 26 and 30, with crowds gathering along the stretch from the ferry dock all the way to Coco Beach. This northern area, where Avenida 46 meets the ocean, is popular with snorkelers who are drawn to the outer Chunzubul Reef. The southern beaches of Playacar have suffered erosion, but the government is taking measures to slowly restore them to their original condition. For deserted beaches, head farther north, where the waves are small and the water is shallow. All of Playa's beaches are open to the public, with various access points staggered between the hotels on La Quinta Avenida. If you are set on snorkeling in Playa's waters, you'll most likely see nothing but sand. For a real underwater adventure, organize a tour with one of the local dive companies that will take you to outer reefs and cenotes.

Main Beach. Stretching from the ferry docks to Calle 14, Main Beach is the most central beach in Playa del Carmen. You'll find clean white sand, but it's not as powdery as the coastline farther north. Within walking distance are countless bars and restaurants lining Fifth Avenue, and it's easy to find a dive shop ready to take you out to sea. The closer you get to the ferry docks, the more people you'll find. If you're looking for seclusion, head farther north outside Playa del Carmen. **Best For:** swimming, sunbathing. **Amenities:** none. ⊠ *Calle 14 and the beach, Playa del Carmen.*

BEACH CLUBS

Canibal Royal. With 1950s Brazilian-inspired architecture, this funky beach club has incredible food (braised octopus, tarte flambé, fish ceviche), breathtaking views, and a wide selection of genre-crossing eclectic music. The beach area is equipped with plenty of lounge chairs and there's a rooftop bar with a plunge pool and sundeck. There's also a juice bar and full cocktail menu featuring their signature rosemary *caipiroska* (vodka with lime and sugar). **Best For:** restaurant, singles scene, amenities, music. **Amenities:** chaise lounges, toilets, restaurant. ⊠ *Calle 48 and the beach; in front of Elements Condominiums and next to Grand Coco Bay, Playa del Carmen* ☎ *984/859–1443* ⊙ *Daily 10–10.*

Indigo Beach. Cure your morning hangover with free yoga and a breakfast buffet ($11) at this beach club located beside El Taj Condo Hotel. The restaurant serves fresh fusion cuisine that blends Italian, Asian, and Mexican dishes. Lounge chairs and beach beds are plentiful and there are changing rooms, outdoor showers, and oversize towels for your convenience. **Best For:** restaurant, morning yoga, amenities. **Amenities:** restaurant, toilets, umbrellas, chaise lounges. ⊠ *Calle 14 and the beach* ☎ *984/138–7783* ⊕ *www.indigobeach.com.mx* ⊙ *Daily 8–5:30.*

Kool Beach. Formerly Tukan Beach Club, this coastal paradise offers private cabanas, water sports, gourmet cuisine, and exotic drinks. Guests can relax in the VIP area while a DJ spins tunes beside the freshwater pool. Kool Beach also hosts private weddings and events. This premier lounge spot is next to Mamitas, where Calle 28 meets the beach. **Best For:** singles scene, live music, sunbathing. **Amenities:** restaurant, toilets, umbrellas, chaise lounges, sun beds. ⊠ *Calle 28 and the beach/Zona Federal Maritima, Playa del Carmen* ☎ *984/803–1961* ⊠ *$7 chairs, $12 beds* ⊙ *Daily 8–6.*

Mamitas. Accessible by way of Calle 28, this is Playa's hottest spot to catch some rays. For $2 you can rent an umbrella or chair, and $10 will get you a suspended bed that sways above the sand. Facilities include a dive shop, swimming pool, lounge bar, and dressing room. Guests can also enjoy beach volleyball, and chilled-out music provided by a live DJ. **Best For:** singles scene, amenities, beach volleyball. **Amenities:** umbrellas, chaise lounges, toilets, dive shop, restaurant. ⊠ *Calle 28 and the* *beach, Playa del Carmen* ☎ *984/803–2867* ⊕ *www.mamitasbeachclub. com* ☞ *$2 chairs, $10 bed* ⊗ *Daily 9–6.*

Zenzi. This beach club and restaurant is one of the few spots open every day until late. Take a dip in the ocean and then catch some rays on one of the sun beds or chaise lounges. When the sun goes down, they offer live music and movies on the beach. The fish tacos and daily happy-hour specials make it difficult to ever leave. **Best For:** singles scene, amenities, live music, nightly entertainment. **Amenities:** umbrellas, chaise lounges, toilets, restaurant. ⊠ *Calle 10 and the beach, Playa del Carmen* ☎ *984/876–2191 or 984/125–3074* ⊕ *www.zenzi-playa. com* ⊗ *Daily 7:30 am–2 am.*

WORD OF MOUTH

If you happen to be visiting the last week of November, be sure to check out the Riviera Maya Jazz Festival held each year in Playa del Carmen. ⊕ *www.rivieramayajazzfestival.com*

WHERE TO EAT

$ ╳ **Los Aguachiles.** Launched by the same creative team who brought

MEXICAN Santanera, Diablita, and Canibal Royal to Playa del Carmen, this "secret" Mexican restaurant was opened exclusively for locals seeking an alternative culinary scene. Beloved favorites include shrimp tacos with "black gold" (beans) and fish ceviche with green salsa. Fish tacos come wrapped in your choice of corn or flour tortillas, or on huge leaves of Bibb lettuce. Everything is sautéed in olive oil and flavored with lime juice, rather than the traditional deep-frying method. Healthy toppings like cucumber, cilantro, and cabbage are dribbled with unique salsas including chipotle, *tamarindo*, and strawberry-habanero. The best part of this laid-back restaurant is the positive vibe that makes everyone feel welcome. ⊠ *Calles 34 and 25* ☎ *984/142–7380* ▭ *No credit cards* ⊗ *Daily noon–7.* ✛ *A6*

$$ ╳ **Babe's Noodles & Bar.** Photos and paintings of old Hollywood pinup

THAI models decorate the walls and are even laminated onto the bar of this

★ Swedish-owned Thai restaurant, known for its fresh and interesting fare. Everything is cooked to order—no prefab dishes here. Try the spring rolls with peanut sauce, or the sesame noodles, made with chicken or pork, veggies, lime, green curry, and ginger. In the Buddha Garden you can sip a mojito or sit at the bar and watch the crowds on nearby Fifth Avenue. The lemonade, blended with ice and mint, is incredibly refreshing. If the place is crowded, head to their second location on Avenida 5 between Calles 28 and 30. ⊠ *Calle 10 between Avs. 5 and 10* ☎ *984/120–2592* ⊕ *www.babesnoodlesandbar.com* ⊠ *Av. 5 between Calles 28 and 30* ☎ *984/803–0056* ✛ *C4, C6.*

$$$–$$$$ ╳ **Blue Lobster.** You can choose your dinner live from a tank here, and

SEAFOOD if it's grilled, you pay by the weight—a small lobster costs $20, while a monster will set you back $100. At night, the candlelit dining room draws a good crowd. People come not only for the lobster but also for the ceviche, mussels, and jumbo shrimp. Ask for a table on the terrace overlooking the street. ⊠ *Calle 12 and Av. 5* ☎ *984/873–1360* ✛ *C4.*

¢–$ ╳ **Café Sasta.** This sweet little café serves fantastic coffee drinks (cap-

CAFÉ puccino, espresso, mocha blends), teas, bagel sandwiches, and baked goods. The flan is sinfully delicious, and the staff is very pleasant. ✉ *Av. 5 between Calles 8 and 10* ☎ *984/125–3516* ▭ *No credit cards* ✛ *C3.*

$$$$
SEAFOOD

✕ **La Casa del Agua.** This eatery features four separate levels, each with its own atmosphere. From the street-level bistro, a dramatic staircase leads to a small cocktail bar where candelabras drip onto the stone floors. A stone waterfall is the focal point in the dining rooms illuminated by wrought-iron chandeliers. The open layout provides nearly every table with an ocean breeze. Among the menu favorites are grilled grouper with goat cheese, blue-fin tuna with portobello mushrooms, and seafood risotto. Remarkably flavorful are the short ribs, which are cooked for eight hours in black beer, Dijon mustard, red wine, and honey. ✉ *Av. 5 and Calle 2* ☎ *984/803–0232* ⊕ *www.lacasadelagua. com* ✛ *C2.*

$–$$
VEGETARIAN

✕ **Casa Tucan.** The refined Italian, Swiss, and Greek dishes at this sidewalk restaurant are top-notch. Everything on the menu is fresh; even the herbs are homegrown. The spanakopita and lasagna are especially good. There's additional seating on the rooftop terrace. ✉ *Calle 4 between Avs. 10 and 15* ☎ *984/873–0283* ✛ *B2.*

$
CAFÉ
Fodor'sChoice
★

✕ **Chez Celine.** Take one bite of Celine's chocolate croissants and you'll think you've died and gone to Paris. Fresh baked breads and pastries rival anything in France, especially the exquisite desserts like the lemon tart. The menu also features healthy-fare options like quiche, sandwiches, fruit, and yogurt. There are street side tables where you can enjoy a cappuccino and watch pedestrians stroll by. ✉ *5th Av. and Calle 34* ☎ *984/308–3480* ⊕ *www.chezceline.com.mx* ☾ *No dinner.*

$$$$
MEDITERRANEAN
Fodor'sChoice
★

✕ **Di Vino.** Centrally located in the heart of Fifth Avenue, this Italian restaurant serves food inspired by the regional cuisines of Naples, Rome, Milan, and Venice. The gelato lends an authentic touch, as do the rough brick walls, wooden floors, and chalkboard inscribed with the daily specials. All breads and pastas, which include potato ravioli and spaghetti with mussels and clams, are made from scratch. The panfried scallops and grilled octopus are delicious, as is the Chilean sea bass served with grape and ginger reduction. The desserts here are said to be the best in Playa, especially the bitter chocolate cake with homemade ice cream. Large groups can reserve the Imperial Table for 18; the street-level patio is the best place to sit if you want to people-watch. The bar is open until 2 am. ✉ *Av. 5 and Calle 12* ☎ *984/803–1270* ⊕ *www.divino. com.mx* ✛ *C3.*

¢–$
CAFÉ

✕ **Hot.** This café is a great place to get an early start before a full day of sightseeing, shopping, or even sunbathing. It opens at 7 am and whips up great egg dishes (the chile-and-cheese omelet is particularly good), baked goods, and hot coffee. Everything, including delicious bagels and bread, is made on the premises. Salads and sandwiches are available at lunch. ✉ *Calle 14 Norte, between Avs. 5 and 10* ☎ *984/879–4520* ⊕ *www.hotbakingcompany.com* ▭ *No credit cards* ✛ *C4.*

$$$
ECLECTIC
Fodor'sChoice
★

✕ **John Gray's Place.** This sophisticated and inviting bistro is tucked away at the end of Calle Corazon near Fifth Avenue. Large picture windows offer a glimpse into the bustling kitchen, where Chef John Gray prepares such dishes as pork loin with Roquefort crust and salmon fillet wrapped in crispy potatoes. Offering a gourmet touch to ordinary food, the menu

Don't miss the daily specials at John Gray's Place.

features macaroni and cheese with grilled shrimp and black truffle oil. The duck pâté with purple onion marmalade is uniquely wonderful. After dinner, you can head across the way to The Den at John Gray's Place. This quaint bar serves cocktails, appetizers, and wines, including John Gray's private barrel selection, El Corazón. John Gray's Place makes everything from scratch including the sausages, ketchup, and fruit jams and also serves breakfast. The menu is constantly changing, so ask about the daily specials. ☒ *Calle Corazón just off Av. 5, between Calles 12 and 14* ☎ *984/803–3689* ⊕ *www.johngrayrestaurantgroup. com* ☉ *Closed Sun.* ✛ *C4.*

$$$$ ✕ **Mosquito Blue Restaurant.** For those who like to see and be seen, this
ITALIAN   trendy new restaurant is centrally located in the heart of the action. The wall-less dining area allows every table to have a view of bustling Fifth Avenue where mariachi bands and florists stroll past tables. A modern theme is evident in everything from the long-handled cutlery to the tasting menu delivered on a three-tiered glass tower. Top selections include linguine with truffle oil and duck, fig-crusted rack of lamb, and the citrus shrimp with lemongrass, avocado mousse, and serrano. To complete your Italian meal, request the mouthwatering tiramisu. Arrive with an empty stomach and a full wallet since portions are large and prices are high. ☒ *Av. 5 between Calles 12 and 14,* ☎ *984/803–3172* ⊕ *www.mosquitoblue.com* ☉ *Closed lunch.* ✛ *C4,*

$$$ ✕ **La Parrilla.** Reliably tasty Mexican fare is the draw at this boister-
MEXICAN   ous, touristy restaurant. The smell of sizzling *parrilla mixta* (a grilled, marinated mixture of lobster, shrimp, chicken, and steak) can make it difficult to resist grabbing one of the few available tables. The margaritas here are strong, and there's often live music. ☒ *Av. 5 and*

Calle 8 ☎ *984/873–0687* ⊕ *www. laparrilla.com.mx* ✛ *C3.*

$$$–$$$$ × **Playasia.** With something to
ASIAN appeal to all five senses, Playasia's
jungle setting offers a waterfall for
sight, a DJ for sound, bamboo for
touch, flowers for smell, and sushi
for taste. The focus of the open-
air courtyard is an illuminated koi
pond around which stand six tree
houses hung with strands of fairy
lights. Asian specialties are served
with a tropical twist, such as bat-
tered shrimp rolled in coconut. A
local favorite is the tuna trilogy of
tartar, carpaccio, and steak. From
the top-level palapa bar, sushi fans

can try one of the 10 signature rolls. Be sure to leave room for the
tempura cheesecake dribbled with chocolate and mango puree. ⊠ *Av.
5 between Calles 10 and 12* ☎ *984/206–3350* ⊕ *www.blueparrot.com/
playasia-restaurant* ⊘ *No lunch* ✛ *D4.*

$$$ × **Ristorante da Bruno.** Since 1997, this restaurant has been serving a
ITALIAN little slice of Italy on every plate. The kitchen creates traditional Emilia
Romagna dishes like homemade ravioli with mascarpone and fresh
gnocchi with eggplant and ricotta cheese. For a signature entrée, try the
beef *tagliata* with arugula, Parmesan, and balsamic vinegar. The cheeses
and olive oils are imported from Italy, as are the 55 varieties of wine.
Of course the menu also has thin-crust pizzas and traditional Italian
desserts like tiramisu and *panna cotta.* Request one of the romantic
tables that spill onto Fifth Avenue. This isn't, however, a place to simply order an appetizer and spend the afternoon; the restaurant has a
strict policy of "one entrée per person minimum." ⊠ *Av. 5 and Calle
12* ☎ *984/873–0553* ⊕ *www.dabrunoplaya.com.* ✛ *C4,*

$–$$ × **Super Carnes HC de Monterrey.** Follow your nose to this Mexican grill
MEXICAN house, where locals gather for some of the best-tasting steak in town.
Far from romantic, the open-air restaurant is filled with the sounds of
mariachi music blaring from the radio; bright piñatas and a mounted
bull's head hang above the plastic tables and chairs. The main draws
are the huge cuts of beef, pork, and chicken served with baskets of corn
tortillas, baked potatoes, and ripe avocados. Be sure to try their refreshing *horchata* (a beverage made with rice and cinnamon). The restaurant
is also a butcher shop, and many of Playa's restaurants buy their meat
here. There are three locations in Playa del Carmen. ⊠ *Calle 1 between
Avs. 20 and 25* ☎ *984/803–4727*⊠ *Av. 10 between Calles 10 and 12*
⊠ *Constituyentes between Avs. 25 and 30 (across from Mega Grocery
Store)* ☎ *984/803–0488* ⊟ *No credit cards* ✛ *A1.*

$$$$ × **Sur.** This two-story enclave of food from the Pampas region of Argen-
ARGENTINE tina is a trendy spot. Dine outside on the garden terrace or in the intimate upstairs dining room. Entrées come with four sauces, dominant
among them is *chimichurri,* made with oil, vinegar, and finely chopped

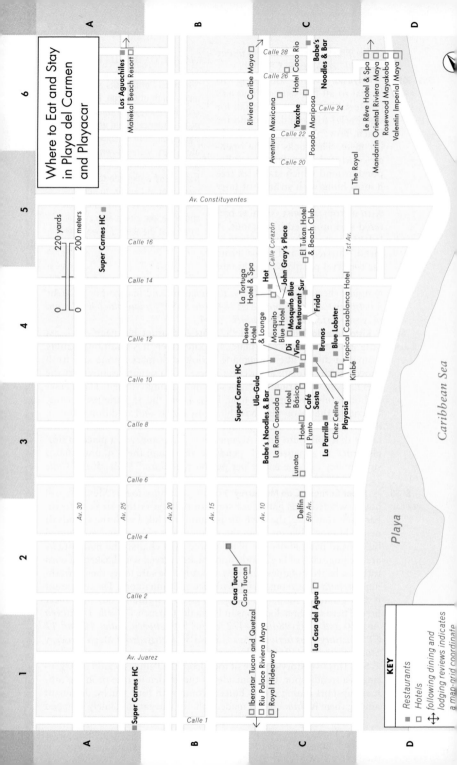

Where to Eat and Stay in Playa del Carmen and Playacar

Restaurants ■
Hotels □
following dining and lodging reviews indicates a map-grid coordinate ⊕

KEY

Caribbean Sea

Playa

Map Labels

Los Aguachiles ■
Mahekal Beach Resort □

Super Carnes HC ■

220 yards
200 meters
0

Calle 16
Calle 14
Calle 12
Calle 10
Calle 8
Calle 6
Calle 4
Calle 2

Av. 30
Av. 25
Av. 20
Av. 15
Av. 10
5th Av.

Av. Juarez
Av. Constituyentes

Calle 1

Super Carnes HC ■

Casa Tucan ■
Casa Tucan

La Casa del Agua □

Iberostar Tucan and Quetzal □
Riu Palace Riviera Maya □
Royal Hideaway □

Delfin □

Lunata □
La Rana Cansada □
Hotel El Punto □

Super Carnes HC ■

Babe's Noodles & Bar ■
Ula-Gula ■

Hotel Básico □

Café Sasta ■
La Parrilla ■
Chez Celine ■
Playasia ■

Di Vino ■

Deseo Hotel & Lounge □
Mosquito Blue Hotel □

Brunos ■
Blue Lobster ■

Mosquito Blue ■
Restaurant Sur ■
Frida ■

Tropical Casablanca Hotel □
Kinbé □

La Tortuga Hotel & Spa □
Hot ■
John Gray's Place ■
Calle Corazón

El Tukan Hotel & Beach Club □
1st Av.

Riviera Caribe Maya □

Calle 28
Calle 26

Hotel Coco Rio □
Babe's Noodles & Bar ■

Aventura Mexicana □
Yaxche ■
Calle 24

Posada Mariposa □
Calle 22
Calle 20

The Royal □

Le Rêve Hotel & Spa □
Mandarin Oriental Riviera Maya □
Rosewood Mayakoba □
Valentin Imperial Maya □

herbs. You can start off with meat or spinach empanadas or Argentine sausage, followed by a sizzling half-pound vacio (flank steak), and finish your meal with hot soufflé with ice cream. ⊠ *Av. 5 between Calles 12 and 14* ☎ *984/803–2995* ✛ *C4.*

$$$–$$$$
ECLECTIC
✕ **Ula-Gula.** As original as its name, this rooftop restaurant boldly experiments with a variety of textures, colors, and flavors. Sushi, tapas, and spring rolls make the perfect martini companions, with portions large enough to satisfy without leaving you stuffed. Unusual combinations in the list of entrées include lamb burger with fries, and mascarpone ravioli with mushroom sauce. For dessert, don't miss the liquid chocolate cake served with vanilla ice cream and peach marmalade—a truly exceptional dish. More lively than the secluded restaurant is the street-level bar of the same name. ⊠ *Av. 5 and Calle 10* ☎ *984/879–3727* ⊕ *www.ula-gula.com* ☾ *No lunch* ✛ *C4.*

$$–$$$
MEXICAN
✕ **Yaxche.** One of Playa's best restaurants has reproductions of stelae (stone slabs with carved inscriptions) from famous ruins, and murals of Mayan gods and kings. Mayan dishes such as *cochinita pibil* (roasted pork wrapped in a banana leaf) are superb, and you can finish your meal with a Café Maya (made from Kahlúa, brandy, vanilla, and Xtabentun, the local liqueur flavored with anise and honey). Watching the waiter pour and light Café Maya from its silver demitasse is almost as seductive as the drink itself. For a romantic setting, request a table on the garden terrace. ⊠ *Av. 5 and Calle 22* ☎ *984/873–3011* ⊕ *www.mayacuisine.com* ✛ *C6.*

WHERE TO STAY

For expanded hotel reviews, visit Fodors.com.

PLAYA DEL CARMEN

$$
🏨 **Aventura Mexicana.** This small inn, three blocks from the beach, is a work of art, with burnt-orange and ocher color schemes, batik wall hangings, and rustic wood-frame beds. **Pros:** spotless; friendly staff; spacious rooms. **Cons:** uncomfortable beds; unimaginative breakfasts. **TripAdvisor:** "very clean and well maintained," "best location," "quiet, clean and beautiful grounds." ⊠ *Calle 24 between Avs. 5 and 10* ☎ *984/873–1876* ⊕ *www.aventuramexicana.com* ⇆ *49 rooms* ᗩ *In-room: kitchen (some). In-hotel: restaurant, bar, pools, spa, parking* ❙◯❙ *Breakfast* ✛ *C6.*

¢–$
🏨 **Casa Tucan.** For the price, it's hard to beat this warm, eclectic hotel a few blocks from the beach. **Pros:** multilingual staff; on-site car-rental agency; exceptional restaurant. **Cons:** some rooms lack air-conditioning. **TripAdvisor:** "noise from surrounding clubs is loud," "cozy hotel in downtown playa," "newly renovated pool." ⊠ *Calle 4 between Avs. 10 and 15* ☎ *984/873–0283* ⊕ *www.casatucan.de* ⇆ *24 rooms, 4 apartments, 10 cabanas* ᗩ *In-room: no safe, no a/c (some), no TV. In-hotel: restaurant, bar, pool, water sports, parking* ❙◯❙ *No meals* ✛ *B2.*

$–$$
🏨 **Delfín.** The Delfín is covered with ivy and looks fresh and smart. **Pros:** quiet setting; central location. **Cons:** no common areas; no restaurant or bar; lots of steps to climb (and no elevator). **TripAdvisor:** "great location and nice accommodations," "a lot of stairs," "clean, comfortable, and affordable." ⊠ *Av. 5 and Calle 6* ☎ *984/873–0176* ⊕ *www.hoteldelfin.com* ⇆ *12 rooms* ❙◯❙ *No meals* ✛ *C3.*

Deseo Hotel & Lounge

La Tortuga Hotel & Spa

$$$$
Fodor'sChoice
★
📷 **Deseo Hotel & Lounge.** This adults-only hotel is known for its cutting-edge design. **Pros:** contemporary decor; friendly staff; comfortable beds; films shown nightly. **Cons:** small pool; no kids under 15 allowed. **TripAdvisor:** "no room service," "design is clean and minimalist with interesting touches," "a party atmosphere." ⊠ *Av. 5 and Calle 12* ☎ *984/879–3620* ⊕ *www.hoteldeseo.com* 🛏 *12 rooms, 3 suites* ⚘ *In-room: Wi-Fi. In-hotel: bar, pool, some age restrictions* ⊙ *Breakfast* ⊹ *C4.*

$$$$
📷 **Hotel Básico.** This ultrahip hotel has won awards for its innovative design. **Pros:** innovative and eco-friendly design; great rooftop lounge; showers have strong water pressure; huge beds. **Cons:** limited storage space in rooms; not family-friendly; late-night noise. **TripAdvisor:** "a joy to look at and stay at," "rooms were just a little too basic," "staff was brilliant." ⊠ *Av. 5 at Calle 10 Norte* ☎ *984/879–4448* ⊕ *www.hotelbasico.com* ⚘ *In-room: no safe. In-hotel: restaurant, bar* ⊙ *Breakfast* ⊹ *C3.*

$–$$
📷 **Hotel Coco Rio.** A tropical garden beckons near the entry to this small hotel on a tree-lined street in Playa's north end. **Pros:** pleasant staff; charming setting. **Cons:** some rooms better than others; weak water pressure. **TripAdvisor:** "quiet part of town and close to the best beach," "great restaurants nearby," "really felt like coming home." ⊠ *Calle 26 between Avs. 5 and 10* ☎ *984/879–3361* ⊕ *www.hotelcocorio.com* 🛏 *12 rooms, 5 suites* ⚘ *In-room: Wi-Fi. In-hotel: parking* ⊙ *No meals* ⊹ *C6.*

$$
📷 **Hotel el Punto.** As one of the newest properties to join Fifth Avenue, this boutique hotel is as chic as it gets. **Pros:** contemporary decor; great lounge bar. **Cons:** small pool; not all rooms have ocean view; no kids under 18. **TripAdvisor:** "great free breakfast," "well appointed and well situated," "excellent service, price, and quality." ⊠ *Av. 5 and Calle 8* ☎ *984/803–0288* ⊕ *www.hotelelpunto.com* 🛏 *16 rooms* ⚘ *In-room: Wi-Fi. In-hotel: restaurant, bar, pool, some age restrictions* ⊙ *Breakfast.* ⊹ *C3,*

$$
Fodor'sChoice
★
📷 **Kinbé.** This boutique hotel, whose decor is an interesting fusion of Mayan and contemporary styles, is set in a tropical garden steps from the beach. **Pros:** great value; discounted rates at nearby Indigo Beach Club. **Cons:** small rooms; rustic decor is not family-friendly; strict cancellation policy. **TripAdvisor:** "a great rooftop seating area," "great ambiance, location, and staff," "charming garden courtyard and chic pool." ⊠ *Calle 10 Norte between Avs. 1 and 5* ☎ *984/873–0441 or 984/873–0443* ⊕ *www.kinbe.com* 🛏 *19 rooms, 10 suites* ⚘ *In-room: Wi-Fi. In-hotel: pool* ⊙ *Breakfast* ⊹ *C4.*

$$–$$$
📷 **Lunata.** An elegant entrance, Spanish-tile floors, and hand-tooled furniture from Guadalajara greet you at this classy inn. **Pros:** prime location; impeccable rooms; intimate setting. **Cons:** street facing rooms tend to be noisy; mediocre breakfast; mosquitoes in common areas. **TripAdvisor:** "location in Playa can't be beat," "beautiful manicured grounds," "quiet, beautiful and extremely peaceful." ⊠ *Av. 5 between Calles 6 and 8* ☎ *984/873–0884* ⊕ *www.lunata.com* 🛏 *10 rooms* ⊙ *Breakfast* ⊹ *C3.*

$$$$
📷 **Mahekal Beach Resort.** Although this resort's location used to be considered the outskirts of Playa, it's now simply the northern end

of the downtown area. **Pros:** private patios with hammocks; excellent service; outstanding breakfast. **Cons:** no evening entertainment; long walk to center. **TripAdvisor:** "resort is right on the beach," "gorgeous location and real hospitality," "food was amazing." ⊠ *Calle 38 between Av. 5 and Zona Playa* ☎ *984/873–0611 or 877/235–4452* ⊕ *www.mahekalplaya.com* ⌨ *121 cabanas* ⌂ *In-hotel: restaurants, pools, spa, beach, water sports* ❘❍❘ *Multiple meal plans* ⊹ *A6.*

$$$–$$$$ ▦ **Mosquito Blue Hotel.** Modern, exotic, and elegant, this hotel has Indonesian decor, mahogany furniture, and soft lighting. **Pros:** access to Mosquito Beach Hotel; billiards; spotless rooms; access to nearby fitness center. **Cons:** area tends to get loud at night; kids not allowed. **TripAdvisor:** "pool area is really lovely," "nice bathroom with a rain-type shower," "next to the night club Coco Bongo." ⊠ *Calle 12 between Avs. 5 and 10* ☎ *984/873–1245* ⊕ *www.mosquitoblue.com* ⌨ *44 rooms, 1 suite* ⌂ *In-room: Internet, Wi-Fi. In-hotel: restaurant, bar, pools, spa, some pets allowed, some age restrictions* ❘❍❘ *Breakfast* ⊹ *C4.*

$–$$
Fodor's Choice
★   ▦ **Posada Mariposa.** Not only is this Italian-style property in the quieter north end of town impeccable and comfortable, it's also a great value. **Pros:** cozy setting; good shuttle service; rustic decor. **Cons:** hard beds; no pool; ocean view blocked by new hotels. **TripAdvisor:** "great atmosphere and service," "loved everything about this place," "hotel is charming, quiet, and calm." ⊠ *Av. 5 No. 314, between Calles 24 and 26* ☎ *984/873–3886* ⊕ *www.posada-mariposa.com* ⌨ *18 rooms, 4 suites* ⌂ *In-room: Wi-Fi* ❘❍❘ *Breakfast* ⊹ *C6.*

$$ ▦ **La Rana Cansada.** Close to the downtown action yet far enough away to have a peaceful feel, this little hotel has all the creature comforts. **Pros:** great bar; free purified drinking water; clean rooms. **Cons:** hard beds; east rooms sometimes lack hot water; poor ventilation. **TripAdvisor:** "knowledgeable and friendly staff," "great place to stay," "quaint and charming hotel." ⊠ *Calle 10 between Avs. 5 and 10* ☎ *984/873–0389* ⊕ *www.ranacansada.com* ⌨ *14 rooms, 1 suite* ⌂ *In-room: no safe, kitchen (some), no TV (some). In-hotel: bar* ❘❍❘ *No meals* ⊹ *C3.*

$$ ▦ **Riviera Caribe Maya.** It may not have the bells and whistles of other hotels, but this small property is very pleasant. **Pros:** breezy rooms; outstanding pool area. **Cons:** hard mattresses. **TripAdvisor:** "rooms and lobby are impeccably clean," "free internet access in the lobby," "very convenient location." ⊠ *Av. 10 and Calle 30* ☎ *984/873–1193* ⊕ *www.hotelrivieramaya.com* ⌨ *21 rooms, 4 suites* ⌂ *In-hotel: restaurant, pool, water sports* ❘❍❘ *Breakfast* ⊹ *B6.*

$$$$ ▦ **The Royal.** One block from Fifth Avenue, this is the only all-inclusive resort in downtown Playa del Carmen. **Pros:** live entertainment; on-site

Playa del Carmen remains less developed and more pedestrian friendly than Cancún.

dive school, ATM, car rental, travel agent, and doctor. **Cons:** Playa del Carmen's largest property; $25 charge to use the spa; most rooms face the garden rather than the ocean; no kids under 17. **TripAdvisor:** "food and food service was exceptional," "rooms are beautiful," "attention to detail is fantastic." ⊠ *Av. Constituyentes, No 2* ☎ *984/877–2900* ⊕ *www.realresorts.com/the_royal_playa_carmen* ⟋ *507 rooms* ⟋ *Inroom: Wi-Fi. In-hotel: restaurants, bars, pools, tennis courts, gym, spa, beach, water sports, business center, parking, some age restrictions* ⟋○⟋ *All-inclusive.*

$$–$$$
Fodor's Choice
★

La Tortuga Hotel & Spa. European couples often choose this inn, which is on a quiet side street. **Pros:** some rooms have rooftop terraces; gorgeous grounds; outstanding breakfast. **Cons:** late-night street noise; flat pillows; kids not allowed. **Trip-Advisor:** "quaint, beautiful, peaceful hotel," "quality of service was unbelievable," "oasis in the center of Playa." ⊠ *Calle 14 and Av. 10* ☎ *984/873–1484 or 800/822–3274* ⊕ *www.hotellatortuga.com* ⟋ *45 rooms, 6 junior suites* ⟋ *In-hotel: restaurant, pool, spa, some age restrictions* ⟋○⟋ *Breakfast* ⊹ *C4.*

> **WORD OF MOUTH**
>
> "We stayed at La Tortuga a couple of years ago.. just plain dreamy! A little slice of heaven smack dab in the middle of it all." — chrism125

$$

Tropical Casablanca Hotel. Branded as "The Feel Good Hotel" of Playa del Carmen, this charming property embraces nature in every sense of the word. **Pros:** on-site dive center; great martini bar; airport transportation. **Cons:** only showers in the bathrooms; street noise; no ocean views. **TripAdvisor:** "amenities are really nice," "great for those interested in experiencing local culture," "noise at night is beyond imaginable." ⊠ *Av. 1 between Calles 12 and 10* ☎ *984/873–0057* ⊕ *www. tropicalcasablanca.com* ⇆ *20 rooms, 1 villa* ⚄ *In-room: kitchen (some), no safe, no TV, Wi-Fi (some). In-hotel: bar, pool, water sports* ⦾ *No meals.* ✛ *C4.*

$$ – $$$ ⊡ **El Tukan Hotel & Beach Club.** The immense jungle garden at the entrance to this hotel leads to a lobby and sitting area, and separates it from the hustle and bustle of La Quinta Avenida. **Pros:** ideal location; casual atmosphere; free parking. **Cons:** must reserve breakfast in advance; cold-water Jacuzzi; 10-minute walk to beach club. **TripAdvisor:** "garden atmosphere was really nice," "can be loud during the night," "no frills, budget hotel." ⊠ *Av. 5 between Calles 14 and 16* ☎ *984/873–1255* ⊕ *www.tukanhotels.com* ⇆ *133 rooms* ⚄ *In-hotel: restaurant, bar, pool, parking* ⦾ *Multiple meal plans* ✛ *C5.*

PLAYACAR

$$$$ ⊡ **Iberostar Tucan and Quetzal.** This unique all-inclusive resort has preserved its natural surroundings—among the resident animals are flamingos, turtles, toucans, peacocks, and monkeys. **Pros:** oceanfront rooms; tropical setting; bicycles for guests; separate areas for families and singles. **Cons:** food lacks variety; small beach; water at swim-up bar can be chilly; Wi-Fi costs extra. **TripAdvisor:** "beach was great, as was the pool," "rooms are spacious, colorful and clean," "no internet in the rooms." ⊠ *Fracc. Playacar* ☎ *984/877–2000* ⊕ *www.iberostar. com* ⇆ *700 rooms* ⚄. *In-hotel: restaurants, bars, pools, tennis courts, room service, gym, spa, beach, water sports, children's programs, parking* ⦾ *All-inclusive* ✛ *C1.*

$$$$ ⊡ **Riu Palace Riviera Maya.** This enormous all-inclusive takes luxury seriously: room service is available 24 hours a day. **Pros:** sports bar open nonstop; friendly staff; lots of scheduled activities. **Cons:** need to make dinner reservations in advance at certain restaurants; no poolside service; hallways echo at night. **TripAdvisor:** "lines for restaurants were long," "within walking distance to Playa," "pool and beach were breathtaking." ⊠ *Av. Xaman-Ha, Lote 1* ☎ *984/877–2280* ⊕ *www.riu. com* ⇆ *460 rooms* ⚄ *In-hotel: restaurants, bars, pools, tennis court, gym, spa, beach, children's programs, parking* ⦾ *All-inclusive* ✛ *C1.*

$$$$ ⊡ **Royal Hideaway.** Located on a stretch of beach, this 13-acre resort has exceptional amenities and superior service. **Pros:** romantic setting; attentive service; the ultimate in pampering. **Cons:** no children under 13; cold pool; roaming beach vendors can be bothersome. **TripAdvisor:** "food's excellent with plenty of choices," "massages are to die for," "well served in all areas." ⊠ *Fracc. Playacar, Lote 6* ☎ *984/873–4500 or 800/858–2258* ⊕ *www.royalhideaway.com* ⇆ *194 rooms, 6 suites* ⚄ *In-room: Wi-Fi. In-hotel: restaurants, bars, pools, tennis courts, spa, beach, water sports, parking, some age restrictions* ⦾ *All-inclusive* ✛ *C1.*

NIGHTLIFE

Inside a cavern, **Alux** (⊠ *Av. Juárez, Mza 217, Lote 2, Colonial Eijidal, Playa del Carmen* ☎ *984/803–2936*) has a bar, disco, and restaurant. Live DJs spin everything from smooth jazz to electronica until 2 am.

Bar Ranita (✉ *Calle 10 between Avs. 5 and 10* ☎ *984/873–0389*), a cozy alcove, is run by a Swedish couple who really know how to party. The prices are unbeatable, and the margaritas pack a powerful punch.

La Bodeguita del Medio (✉ *Av. 5 and Calle 34* ☎ *984/803–3950* ⊕ *www. labodeguitadelmedio.com.mx*) is a Cuban bar featuring live music every night. They claim to have the "world's best mojitos."

Following the success of its sister property in Cancún, **CoCo Bongo** (✉ *Av. 10 Norte* ☎ *984/803–3232* ⊕ *www.cocobongo.com.mx* ⬛ *$50* ☾ *Closed Sun.*) has flying acrobats, bar-top conga lines, live bands, and DJs mixing everything from rock to hip-hop. The $50 cover charge includes unlimited drinks.

Classic films are projected on the wall as DJs spin chill-out music nightly at the **Deseo Lounge** (✉ *Av. 5 at Calle 12, Playa del Carmen* ☎ *984/879– 3620* ⊕ *www.hoteldeseo.com*), a rooftop bar and local hot spot that pours amazing cucumber martinis.

Diablito Cha Cha Cha (✉ *Calle 12 between Avs. 5 and 1, Playa del Carmen* ☎ *984/803–3695* ⊕ *www.diablitochachacha.com*) is a popular palapa bar. The open-air setting is the perfect place to grab sushi, a cocktail, and people-watch while a DJ spins until 2 am.

Kartabar (✉ *Calle 12 at Av. 1, Playa del Carmen* ☎ *984/873–2228*) has a laid-back vibe. The sweet scent of strawberry, mint, apple, and rose waft from the hookah pipes as belly dancers weave between the tables. The house martini is sinfully divine.

At **Mambo Cafe** (✉ *Calle 6 between Avs. 5 and 10, Playa del Carmen* ☎ *984/879–2304*) a dance review begins at 9:30 every night, followed by live salsa music. A younger crowd of locals and tourists typically fills the dance floor.

Mandala (✉ *Calle 12 between Avs. 1 and 5, Playa del Carmen* ☎ *984/803– 0183*) is the area's newest party spot. This trendy venue is divided into a street-level bar, a rooftop terrace, and a dance club. Each section has its own DJ spinning everything from house and hip-hop to disco and techno. The patent-leather sofas are great places to chill out.

★ **La Santanera** (✉ *Calle 12 between Avs. 5 and 10, Playa del Carmen* ☎ *984/ 803–4506* ⊕ *www.lasantanera.com* ⬛ *$8* ☾ *Closed Sun. and Mon.*) In Studio 54–like fashion, this "clubsito" has patent-leather sofas and a distinctive retro-tropical Mexican essence. To escape the dance floor, head upstairs to the rooftop lounge, where a DJ spins chill-out music.

SHOPPING

Avenida 5 between Calles 4 and 10 is the best place to shop along the coast. Boutiques sell folk art and textiles from around Mexico, and clothing stores carry lots of sarongs and beachwear made from Indonesian batiks. A shopping area called Calle Corazon, between Calles 12 and 14, has a pedestrian street, art galleries, restaurants, and boutiques.

BOOKS

★ **Mundo Librería–Bookstore** (✉ *Calle 1 Sur No. 189, between Avs. 20 and 25* ☎ *984/879–3004, 984/109–1566 at Plaza las Américas in Playa del Carmen*) has an extensive selection of books on Mayan culture, along with used English-language books. Profits from all English-language books here are donated to Mexican schools to buy textbooks.

CLOTHING

The retro '70s-style fashions at **Blue Planet** (⊠ *Av. 5 between Calles 10 and 12* ☎ *984/803–1504*) are great for a day at the beach.

Crunch (⊠ *Av. 5 between Calles 6 and 8* ☎ *984/873–1240*) sells high-style evening gowns, swimsuits, and sportswear for women. **Xbaal** (⊠ *Av. 5 and Calle 14* ☎ *984/803–4107*) is filled with attractive men's and women's cotton shirts, woven skirts, and stylish sundresses.

CRAFTS

La Calaca (⊠ *Av. 5 between Calles 12 and 14* ☎ *984/873–0174*) has an eclectic selection of wooden masks, whimsically carved angels and devils, and other crafts.

★ **Hacienda Tequila** (⊠ *Av. 5 and Calle 14, Playa del Carmen* ☎ *984/803–0821*) sells traditional Mexican crafts and clothing as well as 480 different types of tequila. Free tastings are available, and there's a small museum displaying the various stages of tequila production.

At **La Hierbabuena Artesanía** (⊠ *Av. 5 between Calles 8 and 10* ☎ *984/873–1741*), owner Melinda Burns offers a collection of fine Mexican clothing and crafts.

Maya Arts Gallery (⊠ *Av. 5 between Calles 6 and 8* ☎ *984/879–3389*) has an extensive collection of *huipiles*, the embroidered cotton dresses worn by Maya women in Mexico and Guatemala.

JEWELRY

Ambar Mexicano (⊠ *Av. 5 between Calles 4 and 6* ☎ *984/873–2357*) has amber jewelry crafted by a local designer who imports the amber from Chiapas. The **Opal Mine** (⊠ *Av. 5 between Calles 4 and 6* ☎ *984/879–5041* ⊠ *Av. 5 and Calle 12* ☎ *984/803–3658*) has fire, white, pink, and orange opals from Jalisco State. You can buy loose stones or commission pieces of custom jewelry. **Santa Prisca** (⊠ *Av. 5 between Calles 2 and 4* ☎ *984/873–0960*) has silver jewelry, flatware, trays, and decorative items from the town of Taxco. Some pieces are set with semiprecious stones.

MALLS

Centro Maya (⊠ *Carretera Federal 2100* ☎ *984/803–9057*) has Soriana, Mexico's large retail outlet, and more than 50 other stores. **Paseo del Carmen** (⊠ *Av. 10 and Calle 1* ☎ *984/803–3789*) is an open-air shopping mall with a number of boutiques, including Diesel, Ultrafemme, and American Apparel. Caffeine junkies can get their fix at the Starbucks that dominates the center of the mall. A cobblestone path makes this mall one of the area's most popular and pleasant shopping destinations. **Plaza Las Américas** (⊠ *Carretera Federal* ☎ *984/109–2161*) is a family-friendly mall featuring restaurants, shops, and cinemas.

SPORTS AND THE OUTDOORS

ADVENTURE TOURS

Alltournative (⊠ *Carretera Federal 307, Km 287, in front of Playacar development, Playa del Carmen* ☎ *984/803–9999* ⊕ *www.alltournative.com*) will have you feeling like Indiana Jones in no time. Trips, which range in price from $82 to $125, focus on ecological preservation and

Mexican culture. You can kayak through a lagoon, snorkel in a cenote, or zip-line above a lush jungle. The company also organizes trips to Mayan communities.

South of Playa del Carmen, **Punta Venado** (⊠ *Carretera Federal 307, Km 278, Calica* ☎ *998/887–1191 or 800/503–0046* ⊕ *www.puntavenado. com*) offers adventure tours in all-terrain vehicles, on mountain bikes, or in jeeps. The 4 km (2½ mi) of isolated coastline are perfect for horse-back riding, snorkeling, and kayaking. Packages range from $48 to $90.

Yucatán Sky Explorer (⊠ *Playa del Carmen Airport, Playa del Carmen* ☎ *984/873–1626* ⊕ *www.playatoursdirect.com*) will take you on an exhilarating aerial tour above the Caribbean's turquoise waters. The ultralight airplane comfortably seats one person plus the licensed pilot. The 25-minute trips cost $99 per person.

GOLF

Playa del Carmen's golf course is an 18-hole, par-72 championship course designed by Robert von Hagge. The greens fee is $180; there's also a special twilight fee of $120. Information is available from the **Casa Club de Golf** (☎ *984/873–0624 or 998/881–6088*). The **Golf Club at Playacar** (⊠ *Paseo Xaman-Ha and Mza 26, Playacar* ☎ *984/873–4990* ⊕ *www.palaceresorts.com*) has an 18-hole course; the greens fee is $190 and the twilight fee $130.

HORSEBACK RIDING

Two-hour horseback rides along beaches and jungle trails are run by **Rancho Loma Bonita** (⊠ *Carretera Federal 307, between Km 317 and Km 316* ☎ *998/887–5465*). The $84 fee includes transportation, insurance, guides, lunch, drinks, and the use of the property's swimming pool and playground. Children under five are free.

SCUBA DIVING

The PADI and SSI-affiliated **Abyss** (⊠ *Av. 1 between Calles 10 and 12* ☎ *984/873–2164* ⊕ *www.abyssdiveshop.com*) offers introductory courses and dive trips ($50 for one tank, $70 for two tanks). The friendly staff at **Diversity Diving** (⊠ *Calle 24 between Avs. 5 and 10, Playa del Carmen* ☎ *984/803–1042* ⊕ *www.diversitydiving.com*) takes you snorkeling at three different locations: open ocean, cenote, and lagoon. The trips cost $85 per person and include lunch, beverages, snorkeling gear, park entrance fees, and a guide.

Mexico Blue Dream (⊠ *Between Av. 1 and Mamitas Beach, Playa del Carmen* ☎ *984/803–0660* ⊕ *www.mexicobluedream.com*) provides custom tours to Cozumel, Yal-Ku, Akumal, and nearby cenotes. Four-tank dives start at $136; boats depart five times daily. The oldest shop in town, **Tank-Ha Dive Center** (⊠ *Calle 10 between Avs. 5 and 10, Playa del Carmen* ☎ *984/873–0302* ⊕ *www.tankha.com*) has PADI-certified teachers and runs diving and snorkeling trips to the reefs and caverns. A one-tank dive costs $45; for a two-tank trip it's $75. Dive packages are also available, as well as trips to Cozumel.

★ **Yucatek Divers** (⊠ *Av. 15 Norte between Calles 2 and 4, Playa del Carmen* ☎ *984/803–2836* ⊕ *www.yucatek-divers.com*), which is affiliated with PADI, specializes in cenote dives, dive packages, and dives for those with disabilities. Introductory courses start at $95 for a one-tank dive and go as high as $390 for a four-day beginner course in open water.

SKYDIVING

Thrill seekers can take the plunge high above Playa in a tandem sky dive (where you're hooked up to the instructor the whole time). **Sky-Dive** (⊠ *Plaza Marina 32, Playa del Carmen* ☎ *984/873–0192* ⊕ *www.skydive.com.mx*) even videotapes your trip so you have proof that you did it. Jumps take place every hour, and cost $230. Reserve at least one day in advance.

MAYAKOBA

6 km (4 mi) north of Playa del Carmen; 70 km (44 mi) south of Cancún.

Considered the "Venice" of the Caribbean, Mayakoba (meaning "village of water") is home to four of the world's most exclusive resorts. The 1,600-acre enclave supports mangrove forest, freshwater lagoons, beach dunes, and sunken cenotes. It's also home to a variety of wildlife, including monkeys, turtles, crocodiles, manatees, and flamingos. A network of canals connects one property to the other. Here spas are perched amid jungle treetops and boats drift between limestone waterways. This is a car-free zone, and transportation is limited to golf carts, bicycles, and thatch-roof boats.

GETTING HERE AND AROUND

The only way to reach this resort-community is by car. If you're heading south from Cancún, take Carretera 307 to the east turnoff at Km 298. The entrance is marked by a large platinum gate and silver lettering reading "Mayakoba." Security guards will direct you to the property of your choice.

WHERE TO STAY

For expanded hotel reviews, visit Fodors.com.

$$$$
Fodor's Choice
★

Banyan Tree. As Mexico's first resort to offer plunge pools for each room, this stunning property welcomes guests with true Asian hospitality and tradition. **Pros:** incredible spa; excellent food; remarkable service. **Cons:** no sign of Mexico; not very child-friendly; fee to use bicycles on property. **TripAdvisor:** "rooms were well appointed," "each suite has a private pool and jacuzzi," "breakfast buffet is the best." ⊠ *Carretera Federal, Km 298* ☎ *984/877–3688* ⊕ *www.banyantree.com* ⟳ *132 rooms* ⌂ *In-room: kitchen (some), Wi-Fi. In-hotel: restaurants, bars, golf course, pools, tennis court, gym, spa, beach, water sports, children's programs, parking* ⍰ *No meals.*

$$$$

Fairmont. Set under a mangrove canopy, this luxury resort has three types of accommodations—guest rooms in the main building, oceanfront suites, and casitas with lagoon or mangrove views. **Pros:** free shuttle to neighboring properties; excellent spa; stunning grounds. **Cons:** Internet costs $20 per day; some rooms lack water views; 20-minute walk from the lobby to the ocean; no Jacuzzi at pool area. **TripAdvisor:** "simply heaven," "property and facilities were beautiful," "very long walk to the beach." ⊠ *Carretera Federal, Km 298* ☎ *984/206–3000* ⊕ *www.fairmont.com/mayakoba* ⟳ *367 rooms, 34 suites* ⌂ *In-room:*

Banyan Tree

Rosewood Mayakoba

*kitchen (some), Internet. In-hotel: restaurants, bars, golf course, pools,
tennis courts, gym, spa, beach, water sports, children's programs, park-
ing, some pets allowed* |○| *No meals.*

$$$$ ⊡ **Rosewood Mayakoba.** From the moment your private butler greets
Fodor'sChoice   you with a *chaya mojito*, you know you're in the lap of luxury. **Pros:**
★   free kids' club; complimentary bottle of tequila in rooms; extraordinary
spa. **Cons:** narrow beach; limited food options; 10-night minimum stay
during holidays. **TripAdvisor:** "contemporary property with a Mexican flair," "golf course is well maintained," "the most relaxing and
beautiful weekend." ⊠ *Carretera Federal, Km 298* ☎ *984/875–8000*
⊕ *www.rosewoodmayakoba.com* ⇔ *128 suites* △ *In-room: Wi-Fi. In-
hotel: restaurants, bar, golf course, pools, gym, spa, beach, water sports,
children's programs, some pets allowed* |○| *No meals* ⊕ *D6.*

PUNTA BETE (XCALACOCO)

*10 km (6 mi) north of Playa del Carmen; 55 km (34 mi) south of
Cancún.*

Dividing Punta Maroma from Punta Bete (also known as Xcalacoco)
is a river that spills into the sea. South of the split, Punta Bete consists of a 7-km-long (5½-mi-long) beach dotted with bungalow hotels
and thatch-roof restaurants, isolated because it backs into dense forest. From Carretera 307, there are two access points to reach this little
paradise. If you're coming from Cancún, look for the newer road at
Km 296 at the Princess Resort. Completed in 2011, this paved route
makes for a smooth ride but lacks the adventure of the original road
just south. For a more scenic ride, take the 2-km (1-mi) pitted path dotted with potholes the size of swimming pools. From Playa del Carmen
(northbound), the dirt road is located at Km 42. Lining both sides of this
gutted trek is a jungle that provides refuge to green parrots and squirrel
monkeys. Just as you begin to smell the ocean, the road forks—the left
leading to more-affordable accommodations and the right to luxury
hotels. Since Punta Bete is simply a beach area dotted with hotels, there
are no shops, bars, or restaurants other than what are available in the
hotels themselves. For those who don't mind getting sand in their suitcase, there's a beachfront campsite where you can hang your hammock
for less than $5 a night.

GETTING HERE AND AROUND

There's no public transportation in Punte Bete, and taxis seldom pass.
The best way to reach this beautiful beach area is by car. If you're
heading south from Cancún, take Carretera 307 to the east turnoff at
Km 296. You can either take the paved road at Princess Resort or the
original road marked by a large "Azul Fives Condominiums" sign and
the Coca Cola Cristal Building. Both entrance points have signs for all
beachfront properties. Continue 3 km (2 mi) along a jungle road until
the road splits, running parallel to the beach. The north (left) fork leads
to a string of hotels and resorts, while the south (right) fork will eventually meet with Le Rêve Hotel & Spa. From here, you can walk along
the beach to Playa del Carmen in just under 1½ hours.

BEACHES

If long walks on the beach are your thing, you'll love the 10-km (6-mi) stretch from Playa Xcalacoco to Playa del Carmen. Chances are, you'll only be stirred by the swaying of palms and the gentle lapping of waves. Although desolate, the beach itself is not overly appealing; the sand is somewhat coarse and often draped in sea grass. The snorkeling however, is decent, and the isolation is unbeatable.

WHERE TO STAY

For expanded hotel reviews, visit Fodors.com.

$ ⊡ **Cocos Cabanas.** Tranquillity and seclusion are the name of the game in these cozy bungalows a stone's throw from the beach. **Pros:** the ultimate in relaxation; friendly staff; gorgeous beach. **Cons:** rough journey to get here; a bit of a drive from Playa del Carmen. **TripAdvisor:** "service is top-notch and very personalized," "off the beaten path," "menu is so diverse." ⊠ *Playa Xcalacoco, Carretera 307, Km 42 (turn east at Coca Cola Factory) or take the paved road just south at Princess Resort.* ☎ *998/874–7056* ⊕ *www.cocoscabanas.com* ⟿ *5 bungalows, 2 rooms* ⚏ *In-room: no a/c (some), no safe, no TV. In-hotel: restaurant, pool, beach* ⊟ *No credit cards* ⦿ *No meals.*

$$$–$$$$ ⊡ **Petit Lafitte Seaside Bungalow Resort.** This warm, family-friendly resort ☼ is named after a pirate known to have frequented local waters; small cannons on the sundeck point toward the ocean. **Pros:** peaceful atmosphere; on-site library; kids love the small zoo; on-site dive center. **Cons:** long, bumpy road to the resort; uncomfortable beds. **TripAdvisor:** "small quiet hotel on the beach," "beach is quiet and very clean," "food is good and plentiful." ⊠ *Carretera 307, Km 295* ☎ *984/877– 4000* ⊕ *www.petitlafitte.com* ⟿ *30 rooms, 17 bungalows* ⚏ *In-hotel: restaurant, bar, pool, beach, water sports* ⦿ *Some meals.*

$$$$ ⊡ **Le Rêve Hotel & Spa.** If you're seeking privacy and serenity, you'll appreciate the luxury at this beachfront boutique hotel just outside Playa. **Pros:** beautiful pool area; great restaurant. **Cons:** no children under 16; no airport shuttle. **TripAdvisor:** "nice little secluded piece of paradise," "accommodations are lovely," "staff were welcoming, friendly and helpful." ⊠ *Playa Xcalacoco Fraccion 2A, Playa del Carmen, Quintana Roo* ☎ *984/109–5660 or 5661* ⟿ *25 rooms* ⚏ *In-room: no TV. In-hotel: restaurant, bar, pool, gym, spa, beach, parking, some age restrictions* ⦿ *No meals* ⊹ *D6.*

$$$$ ⊡ **The Tides.** This romantic jungle lodge epitomizes understated luxury
Fodor's Choice and sophistication. **Pros:** private pools; on-site film and book library;
★ delicious dining options. **Cons:** hidden service charges; construction noise from neighboring projects; no children under 16; mosquitoes in jungle setting. **TripAdvisor:** "beautiful villas set in a jungle-type setting," "quality of amenities exceed expectations," "staff was second to none." ⊠ *Playa Xcalacoco, Fracc. 7* ☎ *984/877–3000 or 888/230–7330* ⊕ *www.tidesrivieramaya.com* ⟿ *29 villas, 1 suite* ⚏ *In-room: Wi-Fi. In-hotel: restaurant, bar, pool, gym, spa, beach, water sports, parking, some age restrictions* ⦿ *Breakfast.*

PUNTA MAROMA

23 km (14 mi) north of Playa del Carmen.

On a bay where the winds don't reach the waters, this gorgeous beach remains calm even on blustery days. To the north you can see the land curve out to another beach, Playa del Secreto. To the south, the curve that leads eventually to Punta Bete is visible. Guarding this tropical paradise is a security gate that leads to three beachfront resorts—Maroma Secrets, Catalonia Playa Maroma, and Maroma Resort & Spa. Although not accessible through this main entrance, Mandarin Oriental Resort is situated on the far south end of Maroma Beach between Punta Maroma and Punta Bete. Despite the string of towering resorts, the beach here is considered to be one of the best in Mexico.

GETTING HERE AND AROUND

If you're heading south from Cancún, take Carretera 307 to the east (left) turnoff at Km 306.5. If you're heading north from Playa del Carmen, turn right into the Punta Maroma gate at Km 51. Signs (and a security guard) will point you to the beach or the resort of your choice.

ESSENTIALS

Since Punta Maroma is a gated community rather than a developed town, the only available facilities are within the resorts themselves. The closest shops and restaurants are 10 minutes south in Playa del Carmen or 15 minutes north in Puerto Morelos. For shops, restaurants, banks, and emergency facilities, head to Playa del Carmen.

Medical Emergencies Mandarin Oriental has a doctor on-site. **Dr. Vlasak M.D** ⊠ *Playa del Carmen* ☎ *984/876–2758*) exclusively serves tourists in hotels. **Dr. Bernardo J. Diaz Avila** ⊠ *Calle 20 North between Avs. 1 and 5 North, Playa del Carmen* ☎ *984/745–0294*) serves the entire Riviera Maya from Cancún to Tulum. He lives in Playa del Carmen but is on call via cell and speaks excellent English.

BEACHES

Punta Maroma inarguably has one of the most beautiful beaches in the country. In fact, you may never make it to your resort swimming pool. The coastline is immaculate, with deep white sand that feels like powdered sugar between your toes. The water is crystal-clear and free of rocks, which makes this a great place to bodysurf the small waves that crash onshore. Just 10 minutes off the coast of Mandarin Oriental, you'll find incredible diving which can be arranged directly through the resort itself. If you're staying at any of the nearby resorts, you'll find plenty of lounge chairs and umbrellas, as well as excellent beach service for which this area is known. Resorts generally organize beach activities like volleyball, yoga, and remote-control boat racing.

WHERE TO STAY

For expanded hotel reviews, visit Fodors.com.

$$$$
Fodor'sChoice
★
🛏 **Mandarin Oriental Riviera Maya.** Blending Mayan and Asian traditions, this extraordinary resort is on the south end of Maroma Beach, midway between Punta Bete and Punta Maroma. **Pros:** golf carts available for exploring property; free kids' club; jogging trails; 24-hour butler service. **Cons:** organized excursions are pricey; spa treatments are overpriced. **TripAdvisor:** "unparalleled service and renowned attention to

Mandarin Oriental Riviera Maya

The Tides

detail," "food was of an extremely high standard," "rooms were fantastic." ⊠ *Carretera Federal 307, Km 298.8* ☎ *984/877–3888* ⊕ *www. mandarinoriental.com* ⤳ *128 rooms* ⚬ *In-room: Wi-Fi. In-hotel: restaurants, bar, pools, gym, spa, beach, water sports, children's programs* ⑩ *No meals* ⊹ *D6.*

$$$$ ⛼ **Maroma Resort & Spa.** At this elegant hotel, parrots and butterflies fly through the jungle and the scent of flowers fills the air. **Pros:** nearly every room has an ocean view; exceptional service; great place to escape the crowds. **Cons:** no nightlife or entertainment; difficult to find from the highway. **TripAdvisor:** "exceeded my expectations," "spa and gym are great," "food at the restaurants is excellent." ⊠ *Carretera 307, Km 306* ☎ *998/872–8200, 866/454–9351 in U.S.* ⊕ *www.maromahotel. com* ⤳ *38 rooms, 27 suites, 1 villa* ⚬ *In-room: no TV, Wi-Fi. In-hotel: restaurants, bar, pools, tennis courts, gym, spa, beach, water sports, some age restrictions* ⑩ *Breakfast.*

PLAYA DEL SECRETO

23 km (14½ mi) north of Playa del Carmen.

Until recently, Playa del Secreto was a "secret" half-mile-long stretch of white sandy beach. Now, it's slowly gaining recognition as one of the most beautiful coastal communities in Riviera Maya. Surrounded by jungle and Caribbean waters, this area is comprised of residential homes, vacation rentals, and the Valentin Imperial Maya Resort. Travelers are drawn to the protected shores that serve as a nesting ground for giant sea turtles. From May through October, 300-pound leatherbacks return to Playa del Secreto to lay their eggs in the soft sand. Early risers can see baby turtles hatch from their shells and battle their way to the ocean. The bordering jungle is home to foxes, deer, crocodiles, wild boars, and even jaguars. Bird-watching is excellent here with species ranging from wild parrots and hawks to kingfishers and black-necked stilts.

Playa del Secreto is conveniently located midway between Cancún and Playa del Carmen, meaning that nightclubs, shopping, and restaurants are less than 20 minutes away.

GETTING HERE AND AROUND

From Cancún, take Carretera 307 south. Approximately 10 km (6 mi) past Puerto Morelos, turn left at Km 312 onto the Playa del Secreto road that leads to the beach. For those staying at Valentine Resort, there's a designated entrance off Carretera 307 at Km 311. Since only private villas and a resort make up this beach community, there are no restaurants, shops, or services available. The nearest are north in Puerto Morelos.

BEACHES

With no rocks, sea grass, or drop-offs, Playa del Secreto is perfect for swimming, kayaking, or snorkeling; On windy days the waves are large enough for boogie boarding or bodysurfing. At the nearby reef, divers will discover a variety of marine life including lobster, octopus, crabs, and turtles.

WHERE TO STAY
For expanded hotel reviews, visit Fodors.com.

$$$$ 🖼 **Valentin Imperial Maya.** Nestled in the thriving mangrove forests of Playa del Secreto, this adults-only, all-inclusive resort is one of the few hotels that still embraces Mexican tradition. **Pros:** impeccable service; enormous pool; authentic Mexican coffee. **Cons:** evening entertainment disappointing; no kids under 18. **TripAdvisor:** "variety of restaurants," "food and service was fantastic," "grounds are well-maintained and beautiful." ⊠ *Carretera Federal 307, Km 311.5* ☎ *984/206–3660* ⊕ *www.valentinmaya.com* 🛏 *540 rooms* 🛇 *In-room: Internet. In-hotel: restaurants, bar, pools, tennis courts, gym, spa, beach, water sports, some age restrictions* ⏀ *All-inclusive* ✛ *D6.*

PUNTA BRAVA

24 km (15 mi) north of Playa del Carmen.

Punta Brava is also known as South Beach. It's a long, winding beach strewn with seashells. The only direct access to this beach area is through the security gate at El Dorado Royal. Past the entrance is a tropical jungle and over a mile of coastline at Punta Brava Beach. In an effort to calm the powerful waves, the resort built artificial sandbars along the shore. Not only are these burlap sacks an eyesore, but they have also eliminated one of the few spots in the area where bodysurfing was once possible.

GETTING HERE AND AROUND
If you're heading north from Playa del Carmen, turn right into El Dorado Royal gate at Km 45. Currency exchange is available within El Dorado Royal Resort. Otherwise, the nearest banks, medical facilities, and police stations are 8 km (5 mi) north in Puerto Morelos.

WHERE TO STAY
For expanded hotel reviews, visit Fodors.com.

$$$$ 🖼 **El Dorado Royale.** This beachfront resort has been overshadowed by the newer resorts, but the staff is friendly, and the location—amid 500 acres of lush jungle—is just as alluring as ever. **Pros:** on-site health bar with fruit smoothies and health foods; sprawling property; on-site ATM. **Cons:** gym crowded in the morning; slow room service; no kids under 18; rocky beach. **TripAdvisor:** "gorgeous landscape and the best cuisine," "decent pool area and towel service," "totally relaxing and luxurious in every way." ⊠ *Carretera 307, Km 45* ☎ *998/872–8030* ⊕ *www.eldorado-resort.com* 🛏 *480 rooms, 117 casitas* 🛇 *In-room: Wi-Fi. In-hotel: restaurants, bars, pools, tennis courts, spa, beach, water sports, some age restrictions* ⏀ *All-inclusive.*

PUERTO MORELOS

32 km (20 mi) north of Playa del Carmen.

The sleeping beauty is awakening. For years Puerto Morelos was known only for being the coastal town where the car ferry departed for Cozumel. Over the past decade, this cargo port has morphed into the gateway to the Riviera Maya. About halfway between Cancún and Playa del Carmen, Puerto Morelos makes a great base for exploring the region. The town itself is quaint and colorful, with a central plaza surrounded by shops and restaurants. Its trademark is a leaning lighthouse.

The pace is slow, the vibe is relaxed, and the atmosphere bohemian enough to attract a cluster of artists, painters, and poets. Many of the residents are Americans and Canadians who own local businesses or commute daily to Cancún.

Puerto Morelos's greatest appeal lies out at sea: the superb coral reef only 1,800 feet offshore is an excellent place to snorkel and scuba dive. This thriving reef and the surrounding mangrove forests are a protected national park, meaning trips can only be made with licensed guides. The park is home to 36 species of birds, making it a great place for bird-watchers. (The mangroves are also a haven for mosquitoes—bring repellant, especially after dusk.)

Environmental laws and building restrictions keep growth under tight control. This has prevented Puerto Morelos from becoming the next Cancún or Playa del Carmen—which many locals consider a blessing. Although these are not the turquoise waters of Cancún, they are calm and safe. The sand may not be as immaculate as elsewhere, but you can walk for miles and see only a few people.

LOCAL GOODNESS

The **Jungle Market & Spa** (⊠ Calle 2 ☎ 998/208–9148 ⊕ www.mayaecho.com) is a non-profit organization that generates income for Maya women and their families. The Jungle Market features traditional dances, regional foods, and handmade crafts sold by Maya women dressed in embroidered dresses. Between December and April the market takes place Sunday from 9:30 to 2. The spa offers traditional Mayan treatments such as hot-stone massages and aloe vera body wraps. It's open Wednesday and Friday from 10:30 to 4.

GETTING HERE AND AROUND

Located 36 km (22 mi) south of Cancún, Puerto Morelos is the first major town on Carretera 307. From the highway, turn left at the first traffic light and follow the road 2 km (1 mi) east to Puerto Morelos. This will take you directly to the town square and lighthouse. This "downtown" area can be explored on foot, but those staying on the outskirts of Puerto Morelos might need a car to get around. Taxis are parked around the perimeter of the square.

ESSENTIALS

Banks and Currency Exchange **HSBC** (⊠ Blvd. Jose M. Morelos, next to Super Casa Martin, Puerto Morelos).

Medical Emergencies **Dr. Bernardo J. Diaz Avila** ⊠ Calle 20 Norte between Avs. 1 and 5 Norte, Playa del Carmen ☎ 984/745–0294) serves the entire Riviera Maya from Cancún to Tulum. **Farmacia San Jose Obrero** (⊠ Av. Rojo Gomez, north side of the church, Puerto Morelos).

Taxi **Taxi Service** (☎ 998/871–0090).

EXPLORING

There are plenty of beaches in Puerto Morelos; the best is two blocks north of the square. They're rarely crowded, except on Sunday, when Cancún locals visit the area for a weekend escape.

The biologists running the **Croco-Cun** (✉ *Carretera 307, Km 31* ☎ *998/850–3719* ⊕ *www.crococunzoo.com*), an animal farm just north of Puerto Morelos, have collected specimens of many of the reptiles and some of the mammals indigenous to the area. They offer immensely informative tours—you may even get to handle a baby crocodile or feed a monkey. Be sure to wave hello to the 500-pound crocodile secure in his deep pit. The farm is open daily 9 to 5. Admission is $23.

South of Puerto Morelos, the 150-acre **Yaax Che Jardín Botánico del Dr. Alfredo Barrera Marín** (*Dr. Alfredo Barrera Marín Botanical Garden-* ✉ *Carretera 307, Km 33* ☎ *998/206–9233*) is the largest botanical garden in Mexico. Named for a local botanist, the garden exhibits the peninsula's plants and flowers, which are labeled in English, Spanish, and Latin. The park features a 130-foot suspension bridge, three observation towers, and a library equipped with reading hammocks. There's also a tree nursery, a remarkable orchid and epiphyte garden, an authentic Mayan house, and an archaeological site. A nature walk goes directly through the mangroves for some great birding. More than 220 species have been identified here (be sure to bring the bug spray, though). Spider monkeys can usually be spotted in the afternoons, and a tree-house lookout offers a spectacular view—but the climb isn't for those afraid of heights. The park is open daily 8 to 4. It's closed Sunday May through November. Admission is $10.

BEACHES

When you arrive in Puerto Morelos, don't be disappointed by the rocky beaches and blankets of seaweed that wash ashore; this place is actually better known for the remarkable snorkeling that takes place just offshore in front of La Suegra restaurant. Measuring nearly 100 feet wide, this enormous reef has underwater caves filled with abundant sea life. If you'd rather spend a day in the sun, head to the narrow stretch of beach in front of Ojo de Agua Hotel. A snack at their restaurant will give you access to their beach amenities.

WHERE TO EAT

ECLECTIC **✕ Le Café D'Amancia.** This colorful local hangout on the corner of the main plaza is the best place in town to grab a seat and a cup of coffee and a pastry to munch as you watch the world go by. The fruit smoothies are also delicious. Or take your food upstairs and use one of the café's computers for $2 per hour. ⊠ *Av. Tulum, Lote 2* ☎ *998/206–9242* ▭ *No credit cards* ⊘ *Closed Tues.*

$–$$
ASIAN

✕ **Hola Asia.** This small, open-air restaurant is a local favorite that serves generous portions of tasty Chinese, Japanese, and Thai food. Be sure to sample the most popular dish in the place, General Tso's Chicken, a sweet and sour chicken with a dash of spice. The pad thai is also very good. A rooftop bar offers minty mojitos and stunning ocean views. ⊠ *Av. Tulum 1* ☎ *998/871–0679* ⊕ *www.holaasia.com* ⊘ *Closed Tues.*

> **A SACRED JOURNEY**
>
> In ancient times Puerto Morelos was a point of departure for pregnant Maya women making pilgrimages by canoe to Cozumel, the sacred isle of the fertility goddess, Ixchel. Remnants of Mayan ruins survive along the coast here, although none of them have been restored.

$$$
INTERNATIONAL
Fodor's Choice
★

✕ **John Gray's Kitchen.** This former Ritz-Carlton chef's current restaurant, which is right next to the jungle, draws a regular crowd of Cancún and Playa locals. Using only the freshest ingredients—from local fruits and vegetables to seafood right off the pier—Gray works his magic in a comfortable and contemporary setting that feels more Manhattan than Mayan. Don't miss the delicious tender roasted duck breast with tequila, chipotle, and honey. Another great option is Coronado, a local white fish grilled to perfection and served with mango salsa. ⊠ *Av. Niños Heroes, Lote 6* ☎ *998/871–0665* ⊕ *www.johngrayrestaurantgroup.com* ⊘ *Closed Sun. No lunch.*

$$–$$$
ITALIAN

✕ **L'Oazis.** The earthy atmosphere of this Italian restaurant is balanced by the sweet spirit of its Canadian owners, Martine and Flavio. The place has a bohemian feel, with ceramic lamps, bamboo railings, and candleholders made from bits of glass. House specialties include shrimp Sambuca or the balsamic-marinated tuna, which looks like a steak but has the grilled flavor of nothing you've ever tasted. The grouper is bathed in a white-wine-and-lime sauce. All meals come with wild rice, rosemary potatoes, or grilled eggplant. Ask for an inside table, as street traffic and mosquitoes tend to be bothersome. ⊠ *Av. Tulum and Av. Javier Rojo Gómez* ☎ *998/184–0652* ▭ *No credit cards* ⊘ *Closed Mon. No lunch.*

$$$
SEAFOOD

✕ **Los Pelicanos.** Enjoy the fresh, well-prepared seafood on the shaded patio at this family-owned restaurant in the heart of town. Try the fresh fish prepared *al ajo* (in a delicious, garlicky butter sauce). The fried shrimp, served in a coconut shell, is the perfect blend of sweet and salty. The massive margaritas pack a powerful punch. On a small dock, the restaurant offers a variety of four-hour day trips that include fishing, snorkeling, and cooking at the restaurant. ⊠ *Av. Rafael E. Melgar, Lote 2, in front of beach, at Av. Tulum* ☎ *998/871–0014.*

$$$
MEXICAN

✕ **El Pirata.** A popular spot for breakfast, lunch, dinner, or just a drink from the bar, this open-air restaurant seats you at the center of the action on Puerto Morelos's town square. If you have a hankering for American food, you can get a good hamburger with fries here; there are also great daily specials. If you're lucky, they might include *pozole,* a broth made from cracked corn, chicken, chiles, and bay leaves and served with tostada shells. The tacos are delicious. ⊠ *Av. Rafael E Melgar, Lote 4* ☎ *998/251–7948.*

$$
MEXICAN
★
✕**Posada Amor**. This restaurant, the oldest in Puerto Morelos, has retained a loyal clientele for nearly four decades. In the palapa-covered dining room with its picnic-style wooden tables and benches, the gracious staff serves up terrific Mexican and seafood dishes, including a memorable whole fish dinner and a rich seafood bisque. The Sunday buffet is also delicious. Live music, including Spanish guitar, can be heard weekends at the patio bar. ⊠ *Avs. Javier Rojo Gómez and Tulum* ☎ *998/871–0033.*

$–$$
MEXICAN
✕**La Suegra**. *La suegra* means "mother-in-law," and this new restaurant is named for Mary Navarro, the mother-in-law of famed chef John Gray. An accomplished chef herself, Mary creates dishes like grilled pork chops, sautéed shrimp tacos, and ceviche, all served with steak fries and coleslaw. Early risers can start the day with the delicious *huevos rancheros* (fried eggs) piled on crispy tortillas layered with bacon, beans, and tomato sauce. There's an all-you-can-eat barbecue ($14) on Sunday from noon to 5. The palapa-covered patio overlooks one of the largest reefs in the world, making this an ideal spot to drop by for a slice of homemade cheesecake or linger over a refreshing lemonade. ⊠ *Av. Rafael Melgar No. 181, Mza 3, Lote 6; 165 feet from the lighthouse* ☎ *998/871–0774* ⊕ *www.johngrayrestaurantgroup.com* ☉ *Closed Mon.*

WHERE TO STAY

For expanded hotel reviews, visit Fodors.com.

¢
🛖**Acamaya Reef Cabanas and RV Park**. North of Puerto Morelos, this beachfront RV park and campground is sandwiched between two massive resorts. There are six cabanas here, four of which have private baths, and three of which have air-conditioning ($100 per night). There are also 10 RV sites, 50 tent sites, and a small restaurant. **Pros:** a 20-minute walk along the beach brings you right into town. **Cons:** cabanas are pricey for what you get; no pets allowed at campground due to owner's dogs. ⊠ *Carretera 307, Km 29* ☎ *998/871–0131* ⊕ *www.acamayareef.com* ↩ *50 tent sites, $15 per person, per day; 10 RV sites with full hookups, $33–$49 per day; 4 cabanas, $100 for 2 people per night (private bathroom) or $47 for 2 people (shared bathroom)* ⚒ *Flush toilets, full hookups, showers, picnic tables, food service, electricity, general store, play area, swimming, no safe* ❙◎❙ *No meals.*

$$$$
Fodor$Choice
★
🏨**Ceiba del Mar Hotel & Spa**. Rooms at this secluded beach resort north of town are in eight thatch-roof buildings, all with ocean-view terraces. **Pros:** delicious coconut ice cream; excellent service; romantic setting. **Cons:** cold pool; no children's activities. **TripAdvisor:** "welcome to paradise," "yoga in the morning outside," "grounds and pools are well maintained." ⊠ *Costera Norte* ☎ *998/872–8060 or 877/545–6221* ⊕ *www.ceibadelmar.com* ↩ *88 rooms, 7 suites* ⚒ *In-room: Wi-Fi. In-hotel: restaurants, bar, pools, tennis court, gym, spa, beach, water sports, parking* ❙◎❙ *All-inclusive.*

$$$$
☺
🏨**Dreams Riviera Cancún**. As one of the newest properties in Riviera Maya, this sprawling resort offers both mangrove and ocean views. **Pros:** family-friendly; hydrotherapy circuit at the spa garden; new

Ceiba del Mar Hotel & Spa

Zoëtry Paraíso de la Bonita

facilities. **Cons:** Internet costs extra; only 40% of rooms have ocean view. **TripAdvisor:** "great lounge with awesome nightly entertainment," "best all-inclusive we've encountered," "room was extremely comfortable." ⊠ *Calle 55, Sm 11, Mza 4, Puerto Morelos* ☎ *998/872–9200* ⊕ *www.dreamsresorts.com* ⇒ *486 rooms* ⬧ *In-room: Wi-Fi. In-hotel: restaurants, bars, pools, tennis court, gym, spa, beach, water sports, children's programs, parking* ℃ *All-inclusive.*

$$$$ ★ **Excellence Riviera Cancún.** A grand entrance leads to a Spanish marble lobby, where bellmen in pith helmets await. **Pros:** caters to honeymooners; plenty of pool lounging space; rooms have private hot tubs for two. **Cons:** 25 minutes from town; no kids allowed. **TripAdvisor:** "staff is incredible," "all of our requests were made," "the restaurants are fantastic." ⊠ *Carretera Federal 307, Mza 7, Lote 1* ☎ *998/872–8500* ⊕ *www.excellence-resorts.com* ⇒ *440 rooms* ⬧ *In-room: Wi-Fi. In-hotel: restaurants, bars, pools, tennis courts, gym, spa, beach, water sports, some age restrictions* ℃ *All-inclusive.*

$–$$ **Hotel Ojo de Agua.** This peaceful, family-run beachfront hotel is a great bargain. **Pros:** spotless rooms; spectacular ocean views. **Cons:** slow service in restaurant; poor maintenance; low water pressure. **TripAdvisor:** "short walk to the town square," "pretty good restaurant on premise," "a bit run-down." ⊠ *Av. Javier Rojo Gómez, Sm 2, Lote 16* ☎ *998/871–0027* ⊕ *www.ojo-de-agua.com* ⇒ *36 rooms* ⬧ *In-room: kitchen (some). In-hotel: restaurant, pool, beach, business center, parking* ℃ *No meals.*

$$ **Hotelito y Studios Marviya.** Close to the town center and to the beach, this hotel has a great location. **Pros:** bicycles available; multilingual staff; communal kitchen. **Cons:** three blocks to town center; no air-conditioning. **TripAdvisor:** "ocean view from the balcony is gorgeous," "beach is beautiful and groomed regularly," "breakfasts were very good." ⊠ *Avs. Javier Rojo Gómez and Ejercito Mexicano* ☎ *998/871–0049* ⊕ *www.marviya.com* ⇒ *6 rooms, 9 studios* ⬧ *In-room: no a/c, kitchen, no safe, no TV, Wi-Fi. In-hotel: water sports* ℃ *Breakfast.*

¢–$ **Posada Amor.** In the early 1970s, the founder of this small, cozy downtown hotel dedicated it to the virtues of love (*amor*). **Pros:** excellent food; friendly staff; family-run business. **Cons:** rooms can get musty and some lack air-conditioning. **TripAdvisor:** "rooms are simple and very quiet," "the ceviche is superb," "great little town off the beaten path." ⊠ *Avs. Javier Rojo Gómez and Tulum* ☎ *998/871–0033* ⇒ *13 rooms* ⬧ *In-room: no a/c (some), no safe, no TV. In-hotel: restaurant, bar* ℃ *No meals.*

SHOPPING

BOOKS

Alma Libre Bookstore (⊠ *Av. Tulum* ☎ *998/871–0713* ⊕ *www.almalibrebooks.com*) has more than 20,000 titles in stock. You can trade in your own books for 25% of their cover prices here and replenish your holiday reading list. It's open October through June, Tuesday through Saturday 10 am to 3 pm and 6 pm to 9 pm, and on Sunday 4 pm to 9 pm. Owners Robert and Joanne Birce are also great sources of information on local happenings.

CRAFTS AND FOLK ART

The **Colectivo de Artesanos de Puerto Morelos** (*Puerto Morelos Artists' Cooperative*⊠ *Avs. Javier Rojo Gómez and Isla Mujeres* ☏ *No phone*) is a series of palapa-style buildings where local artisans sell their jewelry, hand-embroidered clothes, hammocks, and other items. You can sometimes find real bargains. It's open daily from 8 am until dusk.

SPORTS AND THE OUTDOORS

ADVENTURE TOURS

Selvática (⊠ *Carretera 307, Km 321, 19 km (12 mi) from turnoff* ☏ *998/ 898–4312* ⊕ *www.selvatica.com.mx*), just outside the center of Puerto Morelos, offers tours over the jungle on more than 3 km (2 mi) of zip-lines. The entire tour will take you a little over two hours, so you'll be glad to have a snack afterward in the on-site cafeteria. Mountain-biking tours are also available. If you want a taste of all the activities, you can go on a four-hour zip-line, biking, and swimming tour for $95. Advance reservations are required.

FISHING

Pelicanos (⊠ *Av. Rafael E. Melgar, Lote 2* ☏ *998/871–0014*), a downtown restaurant, offers four-hour tours that include fishing, snorkeling, and cooking up the catch of the day. The tour cost is either $250 for a 27-foot boat or $300 for a 31-foot boat. Drinks and snacks on the boat are included.

SCUBA DIVING

Almost Heaven Adventures (⊠ *Av. Javier Rojo Gómez, Mza 2, Lote 10* ☏ *998/871–0230* ⊕ *www.almostheavenadventures.com*), the oldest dive shop in the area, is the only one owned and operated by locals. Snorkeling trips cost $55, and two-tank reef dives cost $75. Night tours are especially popular in summer, so book at least a day in advance. **Diving Dog Tours** (☏ *998/201–9805 or 998/848–8819* ⊕ *www. puertomorelosfishing.com*) runs snorkeling trips at various sites on the Great Mesoamerican Reef for $30 per person.

PUNTA TANCHACTÉ (BAHÍA PETEMPICH)

8 km (5 mi) north of Puerto Morelos.

The Riviera Maya region technically starts at Punta Tanchacté (pronounced tan-chak-*te*), also known as Bahía Petempich, with small hotels on long stretches of beach caressed by turquoise waters. Historically a fishing village, this area has recently developed into an extension of Puerto Morelos with the addition of new hotels and resorts. Just 20 minutes south of Cancún and 5 minutes north of Puerto Morelos, Punta Tanchacté is quieter than neighboring towns but still close enough to the action.

GETTING HERE AND AROUND

If you're heading north on Carretera 307, turn right at Km 328. If you are driving south on Carretera 307, turn left at Km 27.5. The entrance is marked by a large gate reading Bahía Petempich. This community of resorts does not offer any facilities other than those that are available within the hotels. The nearest shops, restaurants, banks, and clinics are in Cancún and Puerto Morelos.

WHERE TO STAY

For expanded hotel reviews, visit Fodors.com.

$$$$ 🛏 **Azul Beach Hotel**. On a beautiful beach, this all-inclusive hotel has ocean views, lush grounds, and *palapa*-covered walkways. **Pros:** intimate setting; excellent service; romantic beach dinners. **Cons:** smallish rooms; mediocre menu; crowded during spring. **TripAdvisor:** "beach beds are amazing," "lots of activities for kids," "pretty much heaven." ⊠ *Carretera 307, Km 27.5* ☎ *998/872–8080* ⊕ *www.karismahotels.com* ⇆ *97 rooms, 1 suite* ⏃ *In-room: Wi-Fi. In-hotel: restaurants, bars, pools, beach, water sports, children's programs* ❑ *All-inclusive.*

$$$$ 🛏 **Zoëtry Paraíso de la Bonita**. Eclectic is the byword at this luxurious
Fodor's Choice hotel, which is now managed by Zoëtry Wellness & Spa Resorts. **Pros:**
★ attentive staff; tasteful room design; delicious breakfast. **Cons:** no evening entertainment; no children under two; no nightlife; expensive compared to other properties. **TripAdvisor:** "rooms were lovely and spacious," "staff wait on you hand and foot," "meals were very good to excellent." ⊠ *Carretera 307, Km 328* ☎ *998/872–8300 or 998/872–8314* ⊕ *www.zoetryparaisodelabonita.com* ⇆ *90 suites* ⏃ *In-room: Wi-Fi. In-hotel: restaurants, bar, pools, tennis court, gym, spa, beach, water sports, parking, some age restrictions* ❑ *All-inclusive.*

> ### NAVIGATING THE PARK
>
> You can easily spend at least a full day at Xcaret. The park is big, so it's a good idea to check the daily activities against a map of the park to organize your time. Plan to be in the general area of an activity before it's scheduled to begin—you'll beat the crowds and avoid having to run across the park.

XCARET

11 km (6½ mi) south of Playa del Carmen.

Once a sacred Mayan city and port, Xcaret (pronounced *ish*-car-et) is now home to two theme parks on a gorgeous stretch of coastline. The 250-acre ecological theme park, simply known as "Xcaret," is the coast's most heavily advertised attraction. Billed as "nature's sacred paradise," it has a network of buses, its own published magazines, and a collection of stores. Just 2 km (1 mi) from Xcaret is the new adventure park, Xplor. This sister property is designed especially for extreme adventure seekers.

GETTING HERE AND AROUND

Xcaret and Xplor are 56 km (35 mi) south of Cancún International Airport and 6 km (4 mi) south of Playa del Carmen. The entrance for both parks and Occidental Grand Xcaret Resort is at Km 282 on Carretera 307.

There's plenty to do and see in Xcarat.

EXPLORING

Xcaret. Among the most popular attractions are the Paradise River raft tour that takes you on a winding, watery journey through the jungle; the Butterfly Pavilion, where thousands of butterflies float dreamily through a botanical garden while New Age music plays in the background; and an ocean-fed aquarium where you can see local sea life drifting through coral heads and sea fans.

The park has a Wild Bird Breeding Aviary, nurseries for both abandoned flamingo eggs and sea turtles, and a series of underwater caverns that you can explore by snorkeling or snuba (a hybrid of snorkeling and scuba). A replica Mayan village includes a colorful cemetery with catacomb-like caverns underneath; traditional music and dance ceremonies (including performances by the famed *Voladores de Papantla*—the Flying Birdmen of Papantla) are performed here at night. But the star show is the evening "Spectacular Mexico Night Show," which tells the history of Mexico through song and dance.

The list of Xcaret's attractions goes on and on: you can visit a dolphinarium, a bee farm, a manatee lagoon, a bat cave, an orchid and bromeliad greenhouse, an edible-mushroom farm, and a small zoo. You can also visit a scenic tower that takes you 240 feet up in the air for a spectacular view of the park.

■ TIP→ Although Xcaret has eight restaurants, many visitors bring their own lunches and take advantage of picnic tables scattered throughout the park. The entrance fee covers only access to the grounds and the exhibits; all other activities and equipment—from sea treks and dolphin tours to lockers and swim gear—are extra. The $99 Plus Pass includes park entrance, lockers, snorkel equipment, food, and drinks. You can buy tickets from any travel agency or major hotel along the coast. ☎ 984/871–5200, 998/883–0470 in Cancún ⊕ www.xcaret.com ✍ $69 Basic Pass; $99 Plus Pass ☉ Daily 8:30 am–10 pm.

Xplor. Designed for thrill-seekers, this 125-acre park features underground rafting in water caves and the cenotes of Riviera Maya. You can also swim in a stalactite river, ride in an amphibian vehicle, or soar across the park on the longest zip-line in Mexico. ⊠ Carretera 307, Km 282 ☎ 998/849–5275 ⊕ www.xplor.travel ✍ $99 ☉ Mon.–Sat. 8:30–5.

WHERE TO STAY

$$$$ 🏨 **Occidental Grand Xcaret**. In such an enormous all-inclusive hotel it's surprising to find the excellent, personal service that you have here. **Pros:** pleasant lagoon; good teen club; excellent buffet. **Cons:** small beach; squawking parrots in the lobby; Internet costs extra; parts of resort get crowded. **TripAdvisor:** "food was terrible," "hotel is in the jungle," "very clean and well maintained." ⊠ Carretera Federal 307, off Puerto Juárez, Km 282 ☎ 984/871–5400 ➻ 724 rooms, 45 suites ⚐ In-room: Wi-Fi. In-hotel: restaurants, pools, tennis courts, gym, spa, beach, water sports, business center, children's programs ⛱All-inclusive ✛ C1.

PUERTO AVENTURAS

26 km (16 mi) south of Playa del Carmen.

GETTING HERE AND AROUND

Puerto Aventuras is a 20-minute drive south of Playa del Carmen along Carretera 307. Taxis from Playa del Carmen cost about $15.

ESSENTIALS

Currency Exchange Asesores Turisticos Cambiarios (⊠ Carretera Chetumal-Cancún, Km 269.5 ☎ 984/873–5177). **HSBC - ATM** ⊠ Carretera 307, next to the main entrance of Puerto Aventuras, Puerto Aventuras.

Medical Emergencies First Aid Pharmacy ⊠ Marina Puerto Aventuras, Puerto Aventuras ☎ 984/873–5305, 984/801–8306 24 hr service ☉ Daily 9 am–11 pm).

Post Office The only post office in Puerto Aventuras is in a small kiosk outside of the commercial center. It's open Monday through Saturday from 11 am to 2:30 pm.

TAXIS

Taxis are stationed at the small parking area near the marina outside Omni Hotel. You can also find them parked outside all major hotels.

VISITOR INFORMATION

The main visitor center is just before the commercial center, on the main road as you enter Puerto Aventuras. A second booth is inside the marina at the Marina San Carlos Information Center.

EXPLORING

While the rest of the coast has been caught up in a development furor, the small community of Puerto Aventuras has been quietly doing its own thing. It's become a popular vacation spot, particularly for families—although it's certainly not the place to experience authentic Yucatecan

A CRESCENT-SHAPE LAGOON

Beachcombers, campers, and snorkelers are fond of **Paamul** (pronounced pah-*mool*), a crescent-shape lagoon with clear, placid waters sheltered by a coral reef that's 21 km (13 mi) south of Playa del Carmen. Shells, sand dollars, and even glass beads—some from the sunken, 18th-century pirate ship *Mantanceros*, which lies off nearby Akumal—wash onto the sandy parts of the beach. In June and July you can see one of Paamul's chief attractions: sea-turtle hatchlings. If you'd like to stay on this piece of paradise, the hotel below is a solid option. ⊡ **Cabanas Paamul**, a rustic hostelry, sits on a perfect white-sand beach. Ten bungalows have two double beds each, air-conditioning, and Wi-Fi. Farther along the beach are 12 even more private suites ($120). There's also a swimming pool, mini-mart, restaurant and dive shop. The property includes 220 RV sites ($30 a day), as well as tent sites ($13 a day). An on-site, full-service dive shop conducts PADI- and NAUI-certification courses. **Pros:** on the beach; some lovely views; nice open-air restaurant. **Cons:** need car to get around; some rooms need repainting. ⊠ *Carretera 307, Km 85* ☎ *984/875–1053* ⊕ *www.paamulcabanas.com; www.scubamex.com* ⇨ *12 suites, 10 cabanas, 220 RV sites, 30 campsites* ⚲ *In-room: no TV. In-hotel: restaurant, bar, pool, beach, water sports.*

culture. The 900-acre self-contained resort is built around a 95-ship marina. It has a beach club, golf course, tennis courts, restaurants, and a great dive center. Children may enjoy the dolphin-training center or the nautical museum.

The **Museo CEDAM** displays coins, sewing needles, nautical devices, clay dishes, and other artifacts from 18th-century sunken ships. All recoveries were made by members of the Mexican Underwater Expeditions Club, founded in 1959 by Pablo Bush Romero. ⊠ *North end of marina* ⊡ *Donation* ☉ *Daily 10–1 and 2:30–5:30.*

BEACHES

Although the marina is the main focus of Puerto Aventuras, its beaches are naturally stunning and seldom crowded. The main beach, Fatima Bay, is commonly referred to as "Omni Beach." It stretches nearly 3 km (2 mi) south between Chac Hal Al condominiums and the Grand Peninsula residence. To the north is a smaller bay known as Chan Yu Yum that services guests of Catalonia Resort. These bays are ideal for swimming and snorkeling. Excellent beaches can also be found just south of Puerto Aventuras in the community of Xpu-Há.

WHERE TO EAT

$$–$$$ ✕ **Café Olé International.** The laid-back hub of Puerto Aventuras is a
SEAFOOD   terrace café with a varied menu. The coconut shrimp is a good choice, as is the chicken with a chimichurri sauce made from red wine, garlic, onion, and fine herbs. If you're lucky, the nightly specials might include locally caught fish in garlic sauce. The homemade cheesecakes and pies are delicious. Each Sunday, Wednesday, and Friday during high season, musicians from around the world play until the wee hours. ⊠ *Across from Omni Puerto Aventuras hotel* ☎ *984/873–5125* ☉ *Closed Sept.*

Continued on page 164

ANCIENT ARCHITECTS
THE MAYA

Visiting the Yucatán Peninsula and not touring any Mayan sites is like going to Greece and not seeing the Acropolis or the Parthenon. One look at the monumental architecture of the Maya and you might feel transported to another world. The breathtaking structures are even more impressive when you consider that they were built 1,000 to 2,000 years ago or more without iron tools, wheels, pulleys, or beasts of burden—and in terrible heat and difficult terrain.

El Castillo, Tulum.

THE ARCHITECTURAL PERIODS

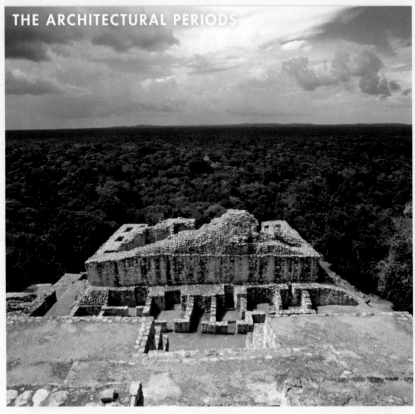

Calakmul

PRECLASSIC PERIOD: Petén

Between approximately 2000 BC and AD 100, the Maya were centered around the lowlands in the south-central region of Guatemala. Their communities were family-based, and governed by hereditary chiefs; their worship of agricultural gods (such as Chaac, the rain god), who they believed controlled the seasons, led them to chart the movement of heavenly bodies. Their religious beliefs also led them to build enormous temples and pyramids—such as El Mirador, in the Guatemalan lowlands—where sacrifices were made and ceremonies performed to please the gods.

The structures at El Mirador, as well as at the neighboring ruin site of Tikal, were built in what is known today as the Petén style; pyramids were steeply pitched, built on stepped terraces, and decorated with large stucco masks and ornamental (but sometimes "false" or unclimbable) stairways. Petén-style structures were also often roofed with corbeled archways. The Maya began to move northward into the Yucatán during the late part of this period, which is why Petén-style buildings can also be found at Calakmul, just north of the Guatemalan border.

EARLY CLASSIC PERIOD: Río Usumacinta

The Classic Period, often referred to as the "golden age," spanned from about AD 100 to AD 1000. Maya civilization expanded northward and became much more complex. A distinct ruling class emerged and hereditary kings ruled over densely populated jungle cities, filled with increasingly impressive-looking palaces and temples.

During the early part of the Classic Period, Maya architecture began to take on some distinctive characteristics. Build-ers placed their structures on hillsides or crests, and the principal buildings were covered with bas-reliefs carved in stone. The pyramid-top temples had vestibules and rooms with vaulted ceilings; many chamber walls were carved with scenes recounting important events during the reign of the ruler who built the pyramid. Some of the most stunning examples of this style are at the ruins of Palenque, near Chiapas.

Palenque

Chicanná

MID-CLASSIC PERIOD: Río Bec and Chenes

It was during the middle part of the Classic Period (roughly between AD 600 and AD 800) that the Maya presence exploded into the Yucatán Peninsula. Several Maya settlements were established in what is now Campeche state, including Chicanná and Xpujil, near the southwest corner of the state. The architecture at these sites was built in what is now known as the Río Bec style. As in the earlier Petén style, Río Bec pyramids had steeply pitched sides and ornately decorated foundations. Other Río Bec-style buildings, however, were long, one-story affairs incorporating two or sometimes three tall towers. These towers were typically capped by large roof combs that resembled mini-temples.

During the same part of the Classic Period, a different architectural style, known as Chenes, developed in some of the more northerly Maya cities, such as Hochob. While some Chenes-style structures share the same long, single-story construction as Río Bec buildings, others have strikingly different characteristics—like doorways carved in the shape of huge Chaac faces with gaping open mouths.

Chichén Itzá

The fusion of two distinct Maya groups—the Chichén Maya and the Itzás—produced another striking architectural style. This style, known as Northeast Yucatán, is exemplified by the ruins at Chichén Itzá. Here, columns and grand colonnades were introduced. Palaces with row upon row of columns carved in the shape of serpents looked over grand patios, platforms were dedicated to the planet Venus, and pyramids were raised to honor Kukulcán (the plumed serpent god borrowed from the Toltecs, who called him Quetzalcoátl). Northeast Yucatán structures also incorporated carved stone Chacmool figures—reclining statues with offering trays carved in their midsections for sacrificial offerings.

Some of the Yucatán's most spectacular Mayan architecture was built between about AD 800 and AD 1000. By this time, the Maya had spread into territory that is now Yucatán state, and established lavish cities at Labná, Kabah, Sayil, and Uxmal—all fine examples of the Puuc architectural style. Puuc buildings were beautifully proportioned, often designed in a low-slung quadrangle shape that allowed for many rooms inside. Exterior walls were kept plain to show off the friezes above—which were embellished with stone-mosaic gods, geometric designs, and serpentine motifs. Corners were edged with gargoyle-like, curved-nose Chaac figures.

Uxmal

▼
Between 2000 BC and AD 100, the Maya are based in lowlands of south-central Guatemala, and governed by hereditary chiefs.

POSTCLASSIC PERIOD: Quintana Roo Coast

Although Maya culture continued to flourish between AD 1000 and the early 1500s, signs of decline also began to take form. Wars broke out between neighboring city-states, leaving the region vulnerable when the Spaniards began invading in 1521. By 1600, the Spanish had dominated the Maya empire.

Mayan architecture enjoyed its last hurrah during this period, mostly in the region along the Yucatán's Caribbean coast. Known as Quintana Roo Coast architecture, this style can be seen today at the ruins of Tulum. Although the

structures here aren't as visually arresting as those at earlier, inland sites, Tulum's location is breathtaking: it's the only major Maya city overlooking the sea.

Tulum

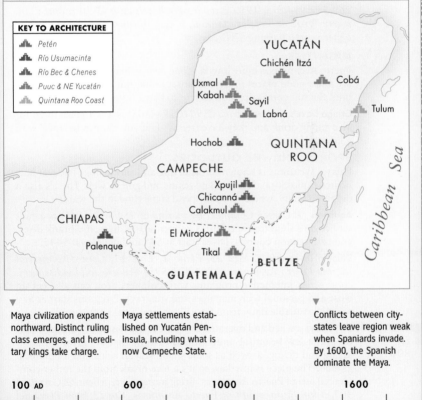

KEY TO ARCHITECTURE
- Petén
- Río Usumacinta
- Río Bec & Chenes
- Puuc & NE Yucatán
- Quintana Roo Coast

YUCATÁN
Chichén Itzá
Uxmal
Kabah
Sayil
Labná
Cobá
Tulum
Hochob
QUINTANA ROO
CAMPECHE
Xpujil
Chicanná
Calakmul
CHIAPAS
Palenque
El Mirador
Tikal
BELIZE
GUATEMALA
Caribbean Sea

Maya civilization expands northward. Distinct ruling class emerges, and hereditary kings take charge.

Maya settlements established on Yucatán Peninsula, including what is now Campeche State.

Conflicts between city-states leave region weak when Spaniards invade. By 1600, the Spanish dominate the Maya.

| 100 AD | 600 | 1000 | 1600 |

RÍO USUMACINTA | RÍO BEC | PUUC | QUINTANA ROO COAST

CLASSIC —————— POSTCLASSIC

3
IN FOCUS ANCIENT ARCHITECTS: THE MAYA

WHERE TO STAY

For expanded hotel reviews, visit Fodors.com.

$$$$ **Aventura Spa Palace**. This 85-acre all-inclusive resort is so big, and has so many activities, that you may have trouble finding a reason to leave. **Pros:** breakfast delivered to your door; access to neighboring golf course. **Cons:** lots of sales pitches for time-shares; beach is artificial. **TripAdvisor:** "restaurants are all good," "staff was attentive to our every need," "water's perfect for swimming and snorkeling." ⊠ *Km 72, Carretera Cancún-Tulum* ☎ *984/875–1100 or 800/346–8225* ⊕ *www.palaceresorts.com* ⟿ *1,213 rooms, 45 suites* ⚲ *In-room: Wi-Fi. In-hotel: restaurants, golf course, pools, tennis courts, gym, spa, water sports, some age restrictions* ⏐⊙⏐ *All-inclusive.*

$$$$ **Omni Puerto Aventuras**. Simultaneously low-key and elegant, this intimate resort is a great place for some serious pampering. **Pros:** pretty beach; sushi restaurant; nearby marina with dolphins; decent golf course. **Cons:** food choices could be better; no elevator. **TripAdvisor:** "luxury hotel at a reasonable price," "very relaxing and beautiful," "everything you need within walking distance." ⊠ *Carretera 307, Km 269.5* ☎ *984/875–1950* ⊕ *www.omnihotels.com* ⟿ *30 rooms* ⚲ *In-room: Wi-Fi. In-hotel: restaurant, bars, golf course, pool, gym, beach, water sports, parking* ⏐⊙⏐ *Breakfast.*

NIGHTLIFE

Puerto Aventuras is more low-key than nearby Playa del Carmen. There are a few good places to have a sunset drink, but if you want to dance until the sun comes up, a quick trip to Playa is your best bet.

Gringo Dave's (⊠ *On marina* ☎ *984/127–4508*) is a fun place to go for an evening drink and they have free Wi-Fi if you happen to travel with a laptop.

SPORTS AND THE OUTDOORS

Puerto Aventuras is known for its diving and snorkeling. The reef here invites exploration. You can find tennis and golf as well. There's also a dolphin facility, where you can spend some time in the water.

Aquanuts (⊠ *Center Complex, by marina* ☎ *984/873–5041*) is a full-service dive shop that specializes in open-water dives, multitank dives, and certification courses. Dives start at $45 and courses at $445.

Dolphin Discovery (⊠ *Mza 23, Plano 1, Lote 11, Centro Comercial Marina Puerto Aventuras* ☎ *984/873–5954* ⊕ *www.dolphindiscovery. com*) offers interactive programs with dolphins. You can also get up close and personal with manatees and stingrays. Programs start at $70 and are available daily from 9 to 11 am and 1 to 3 pm.

EN ROUTE   The Maya-owned and operated eco-park of **Cenotes Kantún Chi** has cenotes and a few beautiful underground caverns that are great for snorkeling and diving, as well as some small Mayan ruins and a botanical garden. The place is low-key, so it's a nice break from the rather commercial feel of Puerto Aventuras. Bring mosquito repellent. ⊠ *Carretera 307, 3 km (2 mi) south of Puerto Aventuras, Km 22 from Playa del Carmen* ☎ *984/873–0021* ⊕ *www.kantunchi.com* ⊠ *$59 for cenote and cave tour; $20 for access to cenote only* ⊙ *Daily 9–5.*

AKUMAL

37 km (23 mi) south of Playa del Carmen; 104 km (65 mi) south of Cancún.

In Mayan, Akumal (pronounced ah-koo-*maal*) means "place of the turtle," and for hundreds of years this beach has been a nesting ground for turtles. The season is June through August, and the best place to see them is on Half Moon Bay. Akumal first attracted international attention in 1926, when explorers discovered the *Mantanceros,* a Spanish galleon that sank there in 1741.

Today Akumal is probably the most Americanized community on the coast. It consists of three areas: Half Moon Bay, with its pretty beaches, terrific snorkeling, and large number of rentals; Akumal proper, a large resort with a market, grocery stores, laundry facilities, and a pharmacy; and Akumal Aventuras, to the south, with more condos and homes. The original Mayan community has been moved to a planned location across the highway.

GETTING HERE AND AROUND

Akumal is an easy drive south from Puerto Aventuras. You can hire taxis in Cancún to go as far as Akumal, but the price is steep unless you have many passengers.

ESSENTIALS

Currency Exchange TSA Akumal (✉ *Carretera 307* ☎ *984/875–9030*).

Medical Emergencies Dr. Elizabeth Mendoza ✉ *Akumal Center, on the main street at the top of the hill, Akumal* ☎ *984/108–0094*). **Dr. Nestor Gutierrez** ✉ *Next to the basketball court, Akumal* ☎ *984/875–4051*).

Taxis Travel Services Akumal ✉ *In the round "TSA" building next to Akumal Dive Shop, Akumal* ☎ *984/875–9030*).

Visitor Information Akumal's tourist office is in front of the Hekab Be library, on the main road into town.

EXPLORING

Fodor's Choice ★ **Aktun-Chen** is Mayan for "the cave with cenotes inside." These amazing underground caves, estimated to be about 5 million years old, are the area's largest. You walk through the underground passages, past stalactites and stalagmites, until you reach the cenote with its various shades of deep green. There's also a canopy tour and one cenote where you can swim. You don't want to miss this one. When you rent a car through Avis, you receive free entrance to Aktun-Chen. ✉ *Carretera 307, Km 107* ☎ *984/109–2061* ⊕ *www.aktunchen.com* 🗐 *$26 cave tour, $38 canopy tour, $21 cenote tour; children 6 and under free* ☉ *Daily 9–4.*

Brought to you by the people who manage Xcaret, **Xel-Há** (pronounced shel-*hah*) is a natural aquarium made from coves, inlets, and lagoons cut from the limestone shoreline. The name means "where the water is born," and a natural spring here flows out to meet the salt water, creating a perfect habitat for tropical marine life. There's still enough here to impress novice snorkelers, although there seem to be fewer fish each year, and the mixture of fresh and salt water can cloud visibility.

Scattered throughout the park are small Mayan ruins, including Na Balaam, known for a yellow jaguar painted on one of its walls. Low wooden bridges over the lagoons allow for leisurely walks around the park, and there are spots to rest or swim.

Xel-Há gets overwhelmingly crowded, so come early. The grounds are well equipped with bathrooms, restaurants, and a shop. At the entrance you'll receive specially prepared sunscreen that won't kill the fish; other sunscreens are prohibited. For an extra charge, you can "interact" (not swim) with dolphins. There's also an all-inclusive package with a meal, a towel, a locker, and snorkel equipment for $79. Other activities like scuba diving, and an underwater walk, are available at an additional cost and should be reserved at least a day in advance. Discounts are available when you book online. When you rent a car through Avis, you receive two free passes to Xel-Há. ☎ 984/875–6000, 998/884–7165, or 800/009–3542 ⊕ www.xelha.com ☉ Daily 8:30–6.

> ## WORD OF MOUTH
>
> "If you are traveling with a young child, you might want to look at the many options available in Riviera Maya; especially Akumal, Tulum, and Playa del Carmen. There are miles and miles of great beaches, fantastic snorkeling, kid-friendly attractions (like Xcaret) and all sorts of tours and other activities that can keep you all happy. Plus Playa del Carmen has stores where you can find all those things you forgot to bring with you." — succeed

Devoted snorkelers may want to walk the unmarked dirt road to **Yalkú**, a couple of miles north of Akumal in Half Moon Bay. A series of small lagoons that gradually reach the ocean, Yalkú is an eco-park that's home to schools of parrot fish in superbly clear water with visibility to 160 feet. The entrance fee is about $10. You can rent snorkeling equipment in the parking lot for $10, a life jacket for $6, and a locker for $2. The park is open daily 8 to 5:30.

BEACHES

This community, comprised of divers and fishermen, is a great place to get your feet wet. Beaches are safe, waters are calm, and there are roped-off swimming areas for children. To reach the shores, take the main entrance from Carretera 307 and turn right past the Akumal arches. This will drop you right at Akumal Dive Shop. Snorkeling is wonderful in this area, and you're bound to see a giant sea turtle. If you want to relax, there are plenty of palm trees for shade, as well as nearby shops and cafés to meet your every need. If you continue on the main road into Akumal, you'll eventually pass Half Moon Bay and Yalkú Lagoon, both good places for snorkeling.

South of Akumal, X'cacel Beach (also written Xca-Cel), has thick powdery sand and a nearby cenote that can be accessed through a jungle path to your right. To reach the beach from Carretera 307, turn at the dirt road that runs between Chemuyil and Xel-Há. The route is blocked by a guard who will charge you $2 to enter. Follow the dirt road that spills onto the white sandy beach. From May through November, this area is reserved for turtle nesting.

WHERE TO EAT

$$–$$$
SEAFOOD
✕**La Cueva del Pescador.** Dig your toes in the sand floor at this simple restaurant and enjoy the catch of the day. Their ceviche, a mix of shrimp, octopus, and fish "cooked" with lime juice and flavored with cilantro, is one of the best around because the ingredients are so fresh. All the servings are generous, so a soup and an entrée might be perfect for two. If you really have a big appetite, try the seafood medley of lobster, octopus, and shrimp. ⊠ *Akumal Rd. at plaza* ☎ *984/875–9002* 🖃 *No credit cards.*

$$–$$$
ITALIAN
Fodor'sChoice
★
✕**Que Onda.** A Swiss-Italian couple created this northern Italian restaurant at the end of Half Moon Bay. Dishes are served under a palapa and include great homemade pastas, shrimp flambéed in cognac with a touch of saffron, and vegetarian lasagna. The Nutella crepes are to die for. Que Onda also has a neighboring seven-room hotel that's creatively furnished with Mexican and Guatemalan handicrafts. ⊠ *Caleta Yalkú, Lotes 97–99; enter through Club Akumal Caribe, turn left, and go north to end of road at Half Moon Bay* ☎ *984/875–9101* ⊕ *www. queondaakumal.com* ⊗ *Closed Tues.*

¢–$
CAFÉ
✕**Turtle Bay Café & Bakery.** This funky café has delicious (and healthy) breakfasts, lunches, and dinners; the smoothies, homemade ice cream, and fresh baked goods are especially yummy. It has a garden where you can sit and drink coffee, and its location by the ecological center makes it the closest thing Akumal has to a downtown. ⊠ *Half Moon Bay Rd. at Plaza* ☎ *984/875–9138* ⊗ *No dinner in Sept.*

WHERE TO STAY

For expanded hotel reviews, visit Fodors.com.

$$
🏨 **Club Akumal Caribe & Villas Maya.** Back in the 1960s, Pablo Bush Romero established this resort as a place for his diving buddies to crash. **Pros:** reasonable rates; on the beach; easy snorkeling. **Cons:** basic decor; sometimes a bit noisy; no elevator. **TripAdvisor:** "reminiscent of an old time beach colony," "rooms all face the ocean and pool," "beautiful beach, great snorkeling and diving." ⊠ *Carretera 307, Km 104* ☎ *984/875–9012* ⊕ *www.hotelakumalcaribe.com* 🛏 *21 rooms, 40 bungalows, 4 villas, 1 condo* ♿ *In-room: no safe, kitchen (some), no TV (some), Internet. In-hotel: restaurants, bar, pool, spa, beach, water sports* ❙❘❙ *Breakfast.*

$$$$
🏨 **Gran Bahía Príncipe.** This all-inclusive is a mega complex consisting of three hotels (Akumal, Cobá, Tulum) with shared facilities. **Pros:** on the beach; attentive staff; good food. **Cons:** beach is rocky; no Internet in rooms. **TripAdvisor:** "golf course is a must see and do," "staff were beyond friendly," "grounds are beautiful and very clean." ⊠ *Carretera Chetumal-Akumal, Km 250* ☎ *984/875–5000, 866/282–2442 in U.S.* ⊕ *www.bahiaprincipeusa.com* 🛏 *630 rooms* ♿ *In-hotel: restaurants, bars, pools, tennis courts, gym, golf course, spa, beach, water sports, children's programs* ❙❘❙ *All-inclusive.*

$$–$$$
🏨 **Vista Del Mar.** Each small room in the main building here has an ocean view, a private terrace, and colorful Guatemalan-Mexican accents. **Pros:** on beach; great ocean views; well-kept grounds. **Cons:** beach is a little rocky; beds aren't very comfortable; Wi-Fi only available in condos. **TripAdvisor:** "free Wi-Fi worked excellently," "snorkeling and diving

are top notch," "hotel was beautifully furnished." ✉ *Carretera 307, Km 104, at south end of Half Moon Bay* ☎ *984/875–9060* 🌐 *www.akumalinfo.com* 16 *rooms, 16 condos* *In-room: kitchen (some), no safe, Wi-Fi (some). In-hotel: restaurant, pool, beach, water sports* *No meals.*

WORD OF MOUTH

"The Club Akumal Caribe is a small gem. Much of the Mayan Rivera is lined with large, all-inclusive hotels. Akumal has not been developed in the same way. Besides the Caribe, there are a few other small hotels and several condos. We loved the bungalow—private and quiet even though it was steps from the beach and restaurant." – justretired

SHOPPING

Galería Lamanai Caribbean Arts & Crafts (✉ *Carretera 307, Km 104* ☎ *984/875–9055*) is a laid-back gallery under a palapa roof. There's a real mix of folk art and fine art from Mexican and international artists.

Mexicarte (✉ *Carretera 307* ☎ *984/875–9115*) is a little shop that sells high-quality crafts from around the country.

SPORTS AND THE OUTDOORS

★ The **Akumal Dive Center** (✉ *About 10 mins north of Club Akumal Caribe* ☎ *984/875–9025* 🌐 *www.akumaldivecenter.com*) is the area's oldest and most experienced dive operation, offering reef or cenote diving, fishing, and snorkeling. Dives cost from $40 (one tank) to $130 (four tanks); a three-hour fishing trip for up to four people runs $150. Take a sharp right at the Akumal arches and you'll see the dive shop on the beach.

TSA Travel Agency and Bike Rental (✉ *Carretera 307, Km 104, next to Ecology Center* ☎ *984/875–9030* 🌐 *www.akumaltravel.com*) rents bikes for a 3½-hour jungle-biking adventure. The cost is $45 per person.

EN ROUTE

Hidden Worlds Cenotes Park. This park was made semi-famous when it was featured in a 2002 IMAX film, *Journey into Amazing Caves,* which was shown at theaters across North America. The park, which was founded by Florida native Buddy Quattlebaum in 1998, contains some of the Yucatán's most spectacular cenotes. You can explore these startlingly clear freshwater sinkholes, which are full of fantastic stalactites, stalagmites, and rock formations, on guided diving or snorkeling tours. To get to the cenotes, you ride in a jungle buggy through dense tropical forest from the main park entrance. You can also ride the skycycle, a cable bicycle that glides over the abundant Mayan rain forest. Prices start at $25 for snorkeling tours and go up to $100 for two-tank diving tours. Canopying on the 600-foot zip-line will set you back $35. Be sure to bring your bug spray. ✉ *1.5 km (0.9 mi) south of Xel-Há on Carretera 307* ☎ *984/115–4514 or 984/877–8535* 🌐 *www.hiddenworlds.com* *Mon.–Sun. 9–5; snorkeling tours at 9, 11, 1, and 3.*

TULUM

61 km (38 mi) southwest of Playa del Carmen.

Tulum, which means "wall" in Mayan, is a quickly growing town built near the spectacular ruins that draw most visitors here. But its charm extends past the famous ruins: Pristine beaches, $10 cabanas, and open-air markets explain the town's increasing popularity with travelers. The town is divided into three main sections: the archaeological site, the pueblo (town), and Zona Hotelera, the hotel area.

The Tulum site itself is the Yucatán Peninsula's most-visited Mayan ruin, attracting more than 2 million people annually. Though most of the architecture is of unremarkable postclassic (1000–1521) style, the amount of attention that Tulum receives is not entirely undeserved. Its location—on a beach known for its sugar-white sand, by the blue-green Caribbean—is breathtaking.

Carretera 307, the main thoroughfare, runs through the pueblo and is lined with dozens of food stalls, souvenir shops, budget hotels, and nightlife spots. If you stay in this part of town, you'll be close to the ruins, though you'll sacrifice a beach view. You can walk the 2 km (1 mi) to the park entrance, or catch one of the shuttles that pass every few minutes.

A mile east of Carretera 307 you'll find the more relaxed Zona Hotelera, where a string of rustic cabanas, colorful cafés, and palapa boutiques line the beach. This secluded area is growing rapidly, and now has Internet cafés, organic restaurants, luxury accommodations, holistic centers, and spas. A number of eco-resorts, which rely on wind turbines, solar renewable energy, recycled water, and generators and/or candlelight, have sprung up along Tulum's coastline. Beaches south of the hotel zone tend to be less rocky and more secluded than the northern beaches, although it's almost impossible to find a bad stretch of sand in Tulum.

Small-town facilities such as grocery stores and pharmacies are available in Tulum Pueblo, but the nearest hospital is 45 minutes north in Playa del Carmen. Buses don't serve the hotel zone, so travelers must rely on taxis, cars, or bikes to get around. Although the area is generally safe, walking around at night is not recommended because there are no street lamps in this part of town. At the time of writing, a sidewalk was being constructed. If you plan on driving, watch carefully for the large beach crabs that cross the roads after dark.

GETTING HERE AND AROUND

Tulum is a 10-minute drive from Akumal and a 45-minute drive from Playa del Carmen. You can hire taxis in Cancún to go as far as Tulum, but the price is approximately $75 unless you have many passengers.

To reach Tulum's Zona Hotelera, head south on Carretera 307 and turn left (east) at the second stoplight in Tulum. Shortly after passing a fire station, you'll come to a "T" in the road. There you'll find dozens of signs directing travelers to both north- and south-end resorts.

ESSENTIALS

Currency Exchange **Asesores Turísticos Cambiarios del Caribe** (⊠ *Av. Tulum, Pueblo Tulum* ☎ *984/871–2078).*

Bus The main **Bus Terminal** ✉ *Zona Hotelera* ☎ *800/702–8000*) for ADO, Mayab, OCC, ATS, and Oriente is in the center of town next to Charlie's Restaurant.

Taxi **Tucan Kin** ☎ *984/134–7535, 984/134–7535 from the rest of Mexico* ⊕ *www.fromcancunairport.com*)

Police There's a police station next to the HSBC on the east side of Avenida Tulum.

EXPLORING

Tulum is one of the few Mayan cities known to have been inhabited when the conquistadores arrived in 1518. In the 16th century it functioned as a safe harbor for trade goods from rival Mayan factions; it was considered neutral territory, where merchandise could be stored and traded in peace. The city reached its height when traders, made wealthy through the exchange of goods, for the first time outranked Maya priests in authority and power. When the Spaniards arrived, they forbade the Maya traders to sail the seas, and commerce among the Maya died.

Fodor's Choice
★

Tulum has long held special significance for the Maya. A key city in the League of Mayapán (AD 987–1194), it was never conquered by the Spaniards, although it was abandoned by the Maya about 75 years after the conquest of the rest of Mexico. For 300 years thereafter it symbolized the defiance of an otherwise subjugated people, and it was one of the last outposts of the Maya during their insurrection against Mexican rule in the War of the Castes, which began in 1846. Uprisings continued intermittently until 1935, when the Maya ceded Tulum to the Mexican government.

■TIP→ At the entrance to the ruins you can hire a guide for $25, but keep in mind that some of their information is more entertainment than historical accuracy. (Disregard that stuff about virgin sacrifices atop the altars.) Although you can see the ruins in two hours, you might want to allow extra time for a swim or a stroll on the beach.

The first significant structure is the two-story **Templo de los Frescos,** to the left of the entryway. The temple's vault roof and corbel arch are examples of classic Mayan architecture. Faint traces of blue-green frescoes outlined in black on the inner and outer walls refer to ancient Mayan beliefs (the clearest frescoes are now hidden from sight as entry to the temple has been restricted). Reminiscent of the Mixtec style, the frescoes depict the three worlds of the Maya and their major deities, and are decorated with stellar and serpentine patterns, rosettes, and ears of maize and other offerings to the gods. One scene portrays the rain god seated on a four-legged animal—probably a reference to the Spaniards on their horses.

The largest and most famous building, the **Castillo** (Castle), looms at the edge of a 40-foot limestone cliff just past the Temple of the Frescoes. Atop it, at the end of a broad stairway, is a temple with stucco ornamentation on the outside and traces of fine frescoes inside the two chambers. (The stairway has been roped off, so the top temple is inaccessible.) The front wall of the Castillo has faint carvings of the Descending God and columns depicting the plumed serpent god, Kukulcán, who was introduced to the Maya by the Toltecs. To the left of the Castillo is the **Templo del Díos Descendente**—so called for the carving over the doorway of a winged god plummeting to earth.

A few small altars sit atop a hill at the north side of the cove with a good view of the Castillo and the sea. ⊠ *Carretera 307, Km 133, Tulum* ☎ *983/837–2411* ✉ *$5 entrance, $3 parking, $4 video fee, $1.50 shuttle from parking to ruins* ☉ *Daily 8–5.*

BEACHES

Talk about a beach with a view! Here you'll find the Caribbean's signature white sand, turquoise waters, and (as an added bonus) the Tulum ruins as your backdrop. This small cove can get extremely crowded, especially during peak season when travelers flock to the ruins for a day of sightseeing. The south end by the rocks tends to have fewer people. Outside of the ruins, Tulum has other beautiful beaches lining the Zona Hotelera, but many of these areas have sea grass and are not very good for snorkeling.

WHERE TO EAT

$–$$
MEXICAN
✕**Charlie's.** This eatery is a happening spot where local children display their artwork. Wall murals are made from empty wine bottles, and painted chile peppers adorn the dining tables. There's a charming garden in back with a stage for live salsa and rock. The chicken tacos and black-bean soup are especially good here, and the chiles rellenos are a house favorite. Attached to the restaurant is a wonderful boutique selling jewelry, clothing, and souvenirs. ⊠ *Avs. Tulum and Jupiter, next to bus station* ☎ *984/871–2573* ☉ *Closed Mon.*

$$–$$$
ECLECTIC
Fodor's Choice
★
✕**Ginger.** With its red walls, exotic menu, martini bar, and metropolitan vibe, this chic restaurant has taken Tulum dining to a whole new level. Flavorful starters include tropical ceviche, goat-cheese tart, and spinach salad with Camembert and green apple. Select from entrées like fettuccine al pesto with grilled peppers and portobello mushrooms or grouper fillet topped with passion fruit. Fresh herbs are grown on-site and the chef purchases fish directly from the local fishermen each morning. Save room for the sweet fruit flambé and vanilla ice cream. This is a great spot to relax with a martini, listen to chill-out music, and meet some locals. ⊠ *Av. Polar Poniente between Satelite and Centauro, next to Donususa* ☎ *984/116–4033* ☉ *Closed Sun.*

$$
ARGENTINE
Fodor's Choice
★
✕**El Pequeño Buenos Aires.** Owner Sergio Patrone serves delicious *parrilladas* (a mixed grill made with marinated chicken, beef, and pork) at this Argentine-inspired restaurant. There are excellent empanadas as well as a nice selection of wines. If you have a sweet tooth, be sure to try the flan or chocolate crepes. Soft candlelight adds a romantic touch, even though you're eating under a palapa roof. A second location opened up in Tulum's Hotel Zone. ⊠ *Av. Tulum 42* ✉ *Carretera Tulum-Boca Paila, Km 4, Zona Hotelera* ☎ *984/871–2708 or 984/806–4505* ⊕ *www.pequenobuenosaires.com* ☉ *Closed Wed.*

$$$–$$$$
ITALIAN
✕**La Vita e Bella.** Italian tourists travel miles out of their way to eat at this utterly rustic, authentically Italian place, where wooden tables and chairs are set on a sandy floor. The menu offers six pasta dishes and 14 types of pizza prepared in a brick oven with toppings like squid,

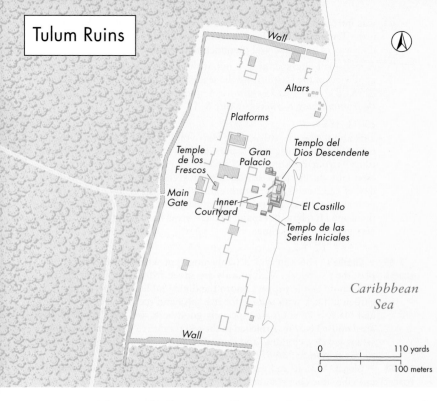

Tulum Ruins

Wall

Altars

Platforms

Temple de los Frescos

Gran Palacio

Templo del Dios Descendente

Main Gate

Inner Courtyard

El Castillo

Templo de las Series Iniciales

Caribbbean Sea

Wall

| 0 | | 110 yards |
| 0 | | 100 meters |

lobster, and Italian sausage. There are wine, beer, and margaritas to sip with your supper. Save room for the tiramisu and chocolate crepes—they're heavenly. ⊠ *Carretera Tulum Ruinas, Km 1.5, Zona Hotelera* ☎ *984/151–4723.*

WHERE TO STAY
For expanded hotel reviews, visit Fodors.com.

$$$$ 🏨 **Azulik Eco-Resort.** Billed as a high-end barefoot resort, Azulik will soothe your senses. **Pros:** spacious rooms; relaxing atmosphere. **Cons:** not family-friendly; hard beds; jungle setting attracts mosquitoes. **Trip-Advisor:** "location is spectacular," "no electricity and slightly rustic," "backpacker standards at luxury prices." ⊠ *Carretera Tulum Ruinas, Km 5, Zona Hotelera* ☎ *800/123–3278 in Mexico, 888/898–9922 in U.S.* ⊕ *www.azulik.com* 🛏 *15 villas* ⚒ *In-room: no a/c, no TV, Wi-Fi, no safe. In-hotel: spa, beach, some age restrictions* ⊙ *Breakfast.*

$$$$
Fodor's Choice
★

🏨 **Be Tulum.** Designed by owner-architect Sebastian Sas, this chic beachfront hotel is like stepping onto a beautifully executed canvas—each room is a pure work of art, with Brazilian wood floors, cowhide rugs, marble bathrooms, and outdoor showers. **Pros:** most upscale resort in Tulum; garden showers; excellent restaurant. **Cons:** pricey; usually full. **TripAdvisor:** "staff were incredibly attentive and helpful," "beautiful and chic and comfortable," "rooms are incredibly comfortable and

CLOSE UP

Caribbean Coastal History

The Mayan culture is the enduring backdrop for Mexico's Caribbean Coast. Archaeologists have divided this civilization, which lasted some 3,000 years, into three main periods: preclassic and late preclassic together (2000 BC–AD 100), classic (AD 100–1000), and postclassic (AD 1000–1521). Considered the most advanced civilization in the ancient Americas, the Maya are credited with several major breakthroughs: a highly accurate calendar based on astronomical study; the mathematical concept of zero; hieroglyphic writing; and extraordinary ceremonial architecture. Although the Maya's early days were centered around the lowlands in the south-central region of Guatemala, Mayan culture spread north to the Yucatán Peninsula sometime around AD 987. Tulum, which was built during this period, is the only ancient Mayan city constructed right on the water.

Until the 1960s, Quintana Roo (a Mexican territory, not a state) was considered the most savage coast in Central America. The Caste Wars of the Yucatán, which began in 1847 and ended with a halfhearted truce in 1935, herded hardy Maya to this remote region. With the exception of *chicleros* (men who tapped *zapote* or chicle trees for the Wrigley Chewing Gum Corporation), few non-Maya roamed here. Whites and *mestizos* were unwelcome because it was not safe.

By the 1950s the Mexican government began giving tracts of land to the *chicleros* in hopes of colonizing Quintana Roo. At that time there were no roads. A few *cocals,* or coconut plantations, were scattered throughout the peninsula, headed by a handful of Maya families.

In 1967 the Mexican government sought a location for an international tourist destination with the finest beaches, the most beautiful water, and the fewest hurricanes. A stretch of unpopulated sand at the northeast tip of the Yucatán Peninsula fit the bill. Soon after identifying Cancún as the fortunate winner, Quintana Roo became Mexico's 31st state.

The 1980s saw an initial surge in tourism with the advent of the Riviera Maya in 2000. This 96-km (60-mi) region stretching south from Puerto Morelos to Tulum developed into one of the world's most popular beach destinations, with Playa del Carmen becoming the fastest growing city in Latin America.

3

beautifully designed." ⌧ *Carretera Tulum-Boca Paila Km 10, Zona Hotelera* ☎ *984/803–2243, 877/265–4139 in U.S.* ⊕ *www.betulum. com* ⌻ *20 rooms* ☐ *In-room: a/c, no TV, Wi-Fi. In-hotel: restaurant, bar, pool, beach, parking* ❍❘ *Breakfast.*

$$–$$$ ⊡ **Cabanas Copal.** The smell of incense wafts through the grounds of this hippy-esque eco-hotel where guests can choose to rough it or stay in relative luxury. **Pros:** on the beach; eco-friendly; clothing optional. **Cons:** clothing optional; showers use salt water; some cabanas share bathrooms. ⌧ *Carretera Tulum Ruinas, Km 5, turn right at fork in highway; hotel is less than 1 km (½ mi) on right, Zona Hotelera* ☎ *984/807–9519* ⊕ *www.cabanascopal.com* ⌻ *47 rooms* ☐ *In-room: no a/c, no safe, no TV. In-hotel: restaurant, bar, beach, spa* ❍❘ *Breakfast.*

$$$
Fodor's Choice
★

Mezzanine. Music lovers will enjoy this small, hip hotel where DJs mix lounge and house music on the patio. **Pros:** incredible Thai restaurant; DVD library; two-for-one margaritas daily from 1 to 4; free morning coffee brought to your door. **Cons:** small pool area gets crowded; some rooms lack view; noisy on weekends. **TripAdvisor:** "perfect balance between luxury and laid back," "food at the restaurant was wonderful," "the view was divine from our room." ⊠ *Carretera Tulum–Boca Paila, Km 1.5, Zona Hotelera* ☎ *984/131–1596* ⊕ *www.mezzanine.com.mx* ↘ *7 rooms, 2 suites* ⌂ *In-room: no a/c, Wi-Fi. In-hotel: restaurant, bar, pool, beach, some age restrictions* ❚◯❚ *No meals.*

$$–$$$

Tierras Del Sol. Situated on a long, secluded beach, this charming resort has eight cabanas, each with a private balcony and ocean view. **ripAdvisor:** "you almost feel at home here," "best stretch of beach in Tulum," "rustic-but-upmarket feel of the place." ⊠ *Carretera Tulum–Boca Paila, Km 10, Tulum, Zona Hotelera* ☎ *984/807–9387* ⊕ *www.tierrasdelsol.com* ↘ *8 rooms* ⌂ *In-hotel: no safe, restaurant, bar, beach, water sports, parking* ▭ *No credit cards* ❚◯❚ *No meals.*

$$

La Vita e Bella Beachfront Bungalows. Perched on sand dunes above the sea, this small Italian resort has lodgings that are rustic but also very comfortable. **Pros:** beautiful beach; laid-back atmosphere; nice restaurant. **Cons:** electricity is limited; mosquitoes at dusk. **TripAdvisor:** "nice cabanas but a bit worn," "laid-back, friendly atmosphere," "every meal was a relaxing, pleasant experience." ⊠ *Carretera Tulum Ruinas, Km 1.5, Zona Hotelera* ☎ *984/151–4723* ⊕ *www.lavitaebella-tulum.com* ↘ *22 bungalows* ⌂ *In-room: no a/c, no safe. In-hotel: restaurant, bar, water sports* ❚◯❚ *No meals.*

¢

Weary Traveler Hostel, Cafe and Bar. Tulum is backpacker central, and if you're roughing it, this is one of the cheapest, most convenient spots to hang your hat. **Pros:** reasonable rates; friendly atmosphere; free drinking water. **Cons:** not on the beach; noise from bar. **TripAdvisor:** "safe and clean," "free transportation to the beach and ruins," "shared open-air kitchen." ⊠ *Av. Tulum between Avs. Jupiter and Acuario* ☎ *984/871–2390* ⊕ *www.wearytravelerhostel.com* ↘ *10 private rooms, 11 dorms* ⌂ *In-room: no a/c (some), no safe, kitchen, no TV. In-hotel: restaurant, bar, business center* ▭ *No credit cards* ❚◯❚ *Breakfast.*

$$$
Fodor's Choice
★

Zamas. On the wild, isolated Punta Piedra (Rock Point), this hotel has ocean views as far as the eye can see. **Pros:** great restaurant; unspoiled views. **Cons:** rocky beach; on noisy street. **TripAdvisor:** "a really cozy place," "food was consistently amazing," "room was spotlessly clean." ⊠ *Carretera Tulum–Boca Paila, Km 5, Zona Hotelera* ☎ *984/877–8523, 415/387–9806 in U.S.* ⊕ *www.zamas.com* ↘ *24 cabanas* ⌂ *In-room: no a/c. In-hotel: restaurant, bar, beach, water sports* ❚◯❚ *No meals.*

$$$ La Zebra. This jungle-chic hotel is as well known for its restaurant
★   as it is for its cabanas. **Pros:** authentic Mexican food; on-site tequila
bar; environmentally conscious; free salsa lessons 6 to 7 pm on Sunday.
Cons: usually booked six months in advance; no Internet in rooms;
slightly far from town. **TripAdvisor:** "food was killer, amazing break-
fasts," "beautiful property in a perfect location," "best spot in Tulum
for a family with young children." ⊠ *Carretera Tulum–Punta Allen, Km
8.2, Zona Hotelera* ☎ *984/876–2614* ⊕ *www.lazebratulum.com* �);15
rooms ⚒ *In-room: no TV. In-hotel: restaurant, bar, pool, spa, beach,
parking* ⦿ *No meals.*

SPORTS AND THE OUTDOORS
Punta Piedra Bike Rental (⊠ *Carretera Tulum–Boca Paila, Km 4, Tulum,
Zona Hotelera* ☎*984/116–4296* ⊗ *Daily 7:30–7*) is a small shack
that rents equipment by the day. Boogie boards cost $5, bikes are $8,
and snorkel gear is $5. The owner, Felix, can also organize two-hour
snorkeling tours for $25. Cash only. **Uolis-Nah Kite School** (⊠ *Carret-
era Tulum–Cobá, Km 2* ☎*984/130–1596 or 984/745–4555* ⊕*www.
extremecontrol.net*) offers three-hour kitesurfing lessons and equipment
for $150. Led by IKO instructor Marco Cristofanelli, courses take place
at Tulum's El Paraiso Beach and must be booked 24 hours in advance.
Under the same ownership is the new kite shop and info center located
at the Tulum entrance opposite the San Francisco Commercial Center.
Those who stay at Kite Hotel "Uolis Nah" receive a 10% discount on
kitesurfing courses. To get here, exit Carretera 307 at Km 2 and head
west on the road toward Cobá. Uolis-Nah is on the left just beyond the
intersection, next to Super San Francisco Market. The school's hours
literally change with the wind, so call ahead to be sure they're open.

COBÁ

50 km (31 mi) northwest of Tulum.

Fodor'sChoice Mayan for "water stirred by the wind," **Cobá** flourished from AD 800
★ to 1100, with a population of as many as 55,000. Now it stands in soli-
tude, and the jungle has overgrown many of its buildings. Cobá exudes
stillness, the silence broken only by the occasional shriek of a spider
monkey or the call of a bird. Unlike Tulum, Cobá's ruins are spread
out and best explored by bike. Most of the trails here are pleasantly
shaded by overgrown jungle. Processions of huge army ants cross the
footpaths as the sun slips through openings between the tall hardwood
trees, ferns, and giant palms.

■TIP→ Cobá is often overlooked by visitors who opt for better-known
Tulum. This site is less crowded, giving you a chance to immerse yourself
in ancient culture. If you plan on walking (rather than exploring by bike),
expect to cover anywhere between 5 and 6 km (3 and 4 mi). Cobá is open
daily from 8 to 5, and costs $4.50 to enter (use of video camera $4; taxi-bike
tours $8; bike rental $3).

Near five lakes and between coastal watchtowers and inland cities,
Cobá (pronounced ko-*bah*) exercised economic control over the region
through a network of at least 16 *sacbéob* (white-stone roads), one of

which measures 100 km (62 mi) and is the longest in the Mayan world. The city once covered 70 square km (27 square mi), making it a noteworthy sister state to Tikal in northern Guatemala, with which it had close cultural and commercial ties. It's noted for its massive temple-pyramids, one of which is 138 feet tall, the largest and highest in northern Yucatán. The main groupings of ruins are separated by several miles of dense vegetation, so the best way to get a sense of the immensity of the city is to scale one of the pyramids. Don't be tempted by the narrow paths that lead into the jungle unless you have a qualified guide with you. ■TIP→ It's easy to get lost here, so stay on the main road, wear comfortable shoes, and bring insect repellent and drinking water.

GETTING HERE AND AROUND

Cobá is a 45-minute drive northwest of the city of Tankah, where most of the accommodations are located, along a road that leads straight through the jungle. Buses depart to and from Cobá for Playa del Carmen and Tulum at least twice daily. Taxis from Tulum are about $20.

OFF THE BEATEN PATH

Pac Chen is a Maya jungle settlement of 125 people who still live in round thatch huts. There's no electricity or indoor plumbing, and the roads aren't paved. The inhabitants, who primarily make their living farming pineapple, beans, and plantains, still pray to the gods for good crops.

■TIP→ You can only visit Pac Chen (pronounced *pak-chin*) on trips organized by Alltournative, an ecotour company based in Playa del Carmen. The unusual, soft-adventure experience is definitely worth your while. Alltournative pays the villagers by the number of tourists it brings in, though no more than 80 people are allowed to visit on any given day. There's an additional $2 entrance fee per person. This money has made the village self-sustaining, and has given the people an alternative to logging and hunting, which were their main means of livelihood before.

The half-day tour starts with a trek through the jungle to a cenote where you grab onto a harness and zip-line to the other side. Next is the Jaguar cenote, set deeper in the forest, where you must rappel down the cavelike sides into a cool underground lagoon. You'll eat lunch under an open-air palapa overlooking another lagoon, where canoes await. The food includes such Mayan dishes as grilled achiote (annatto seed) chicken, fresh tortillas, beans, and watermelon.

Kukulkan Tirolesa Zipline. The best way to view Lago Cobá (and the 10-foot crocodiles below) is by soaring over the water on a 500-meter zip-line. The lookout tower is also a great place to photograph the ruins poking out of the treetops. ⊠ *At the entrance to the Cobá ruins* 🖃 *$4 lookout tower; $12 zip-line* ⊙ *Daily 10–6.*

WHERE TO EAT

¢–$
MEXICAN

✕ **El Bocadito.** This restaurant near the Cobá ruins is run by a gracious Maya family that serves simple, traditional cuisine. A three-course fixed-price lunch costs $6. Look for such classic dishes as *pollo pibil* and *cochinita pibil* (slow-roasted

The ruins of Cobá are best explored by bike.

chicken or pork). There are also a few bare-bones rooms for $20 a night for those who want to stay close to the ruins. ⊠ *On road to Cobá ruins, ½ km (½ mi) from ruin-site entrance* ☎ *984/ 876–3738* ▭ *No credit cards.*

$ ✕ **Ki-Janal.** You can't get any closer to the Cobá ruins than this two-

MEXICAN story restaurant. Adding color to the palapa setting are colorful Mexican blankets draped over wooden tables. Some of the more traditional selections include fish prepared Yucatán style, chicken in banana leaves, and cochinita pibil. You can also find soups, salads, and pastas. Plan to stay a while since the service isn't the best. ⊠ *To the right of the Cobá ruins entrance* ▭ *No credit cards.*

TANKAH

If you plan on staying in the Cobá area, nearby Tankah is your best option. In ancient times Tankah was an important Mayan trading city. Over the past few centuries it has lain mostly dormant. That's now beginning to change. A number of small, reasonably priced hotels have cropped up here over the past few years, and several expats who own villas in the area rent them out year-round.

GETTING HERE AND AROUND

To reach the coastal road in Tankah, turn east off Carretera 307 (a faded green sign marks the turning point). At the end of the long pitted road, turn left (north) where a string of villas and small hotels parallel the beach. Tankah is approximately 90 minutes south of Cancún. The closest Internet cafés, medical clinics, grocery stores, and emergency services are in Tulum.

BEACHES

Often overlooked by travelers, this spectacular stretch of coastline offers great snorkeling, diving, and best of all, isolation. Unfortunately, the closest dive shops are in Tulum, which means you'll have to organize your own equipment.

WHERE TO EAT

$$$ ✕ **Restaurante Oscar y Lalo.** A couple of miles outside Tankah, alone on
ECLECTIC Carretera 307, sits this wonderful palapa restaurant with a pebble floor and a peaceful garden. The seafood is excellent here, although a bit pricey. Lalo's Special, a dish made with local lobster, shrimp, conch, and fish, and the chicken fajitas, prepared for 2 to 10 people, are standouts. The ceviche made of fresh fish and lobster, and the *caracol* (snails) with citrus juice are also exceptional. ⊠ *Carretera 307 at Km 3 from Xel-Há (northbound) or Km 241 (southbound). Look for large billboard and Mayan sculptures* ☎ *984/804–4189.*

WHERE TO STAY

For expanded hotel reviews, visit Fodors.com.

$$$ ⛫ **Blue Sky Hotel and Restaurant.** Guest quarters here have one-of-a-kind
★ touches, such as Cuban oil paintings, handblown vases, inlaid-silver mirrors, and chairs hand-tooled from native *chichén* wood. **Pros:** on beach; excellent brick-oven pizza at restaurant. **Cons:** need car to get around. **TripAdvisor:** "small hotel in a beautiful setting," "best snorkeling experiences," "rooms were clean, well appointed, great ocean views." ⊠ *Bahía Tankah, past Casa Cenote* ☎ *306/972–4283 or 306/690–6203* ⊕ *www.blueskymexico.com* ⤴ *2 rooms, 4 suites* ⚭ *In-room: no TV, Wi-Fi, no safe. In-hotel: restaurant, pool, beach, water sports* ⏐⊙⏐ *No meals.*

$$$ ⛫ **Maya Jardin.** Available by the week, this five-bedroom villa can comfortably sleep up to 14 guests. **Pros:** on beach; clean and comfortable rooms; friendly owners. **Cons:** need car to get around; must rent minimum two rooms and stay for at least a week. ⊠ *Lote 4B, Bahía de Soliman* ☎ *509/540–4880 in U.S.* ⊕ *www.mayajardin.com* ⤴ *5 rooms* ⚭ *In-hotel: pool, beach* ⏐⊙⏐ *No meals.*

SPORTS AND THE OUTDOORS

★ The **Gorgonian Gardens** have made Tankah a particular destination for divers and snorkelers thanks to the offshore underwater environment. From southern Tankah to Bahía de Punta Soliman, the sand-free ocean floor has allowed for the proliferation of Gorgonians, or soft corals— sea fans, candelabras, and fingers that can reach 5 feet in height—as well as a variety of colorful sponges. Fish love to feed here, and so many of them swarm the gardens that some divers have compared the experience to being surrounded by clouds of butterflies. Although this underwater habitat goes on for miles, Tankah is the best place to view it.

Caste Wars

When Mexico achieved independence from Spain in 1821, the Maya didn't celebrate. The new government didn't return their lost land or treat them with respect. In 1847 a Mayan rebellion began in Valladolid. The Maya were rising up against centuries of being relegated to the status of "lower caste" people. Hence the conflict was called the Guerra de las Castas, or "War of the Castes." A year later, they had killed hundreds of Mexicans and the battle raged on.

Help for the embattled Mexicans arrived with a vengeance from Mexico City, Cuba, and the United States. By 1850 many Maya had been mercilessly slaughtered, their population plummeting from 500,000 to 300,000. Survivors fled to the jungles and held out until government troops withdrew in 1915. The Maya controlled Quintana Roo from Tulum, their headquarters, and finally accepted Mexican rule in 1935.

RESERVA DE LA BIOSFERA SIAN KA'AN

15 km (9 mi) south of Tulum to Punta Allen turnoff; 252 km (156 mi) north of Chetumal.

GETTING HERE AND AROUND

To explore on your own, follow the road past Boca Paila to the secluded 35-km (22-mi) coastal strip of land that's part of the reserve. You'll be limited to swimming, snorkeling, and camping on the beaches, as there are no trails into the surrounding jungle. The narrow, extremely rough dirt roads down the peninsula are filled with monstrous potholes, which are completely impassable after a rainfall. Don't attempt it unless you have four-wheel drive.

The archaeological site at Muyil is about 16 km (10 mi) south of Tulum (village and archaeological site) on Federal Highway 307, which passes through the site. By car it's 145 km (90 mi) south of Cancún and 212 km (132 mi) north of Chetumal.

ESSENTIALS

Visitor Information Sian Ka'an Visitor Center ☎ 998/884–3667 or 998/884–9580 ⊕ www.ecotravelmexico.com) is 18 km (11 mi) south of Tulum, on Punta Allen toward Boca Paila Village by the coastal road.

EXPLORING

The **Sian Ka'an** (translated as "where the sky is born," pronounced see-*an* caan) region was first settled by the Maya in the 5th century AD. In 1986 the Mexican government established the 1.3-million-acre Reserva de la Biosfera Sian Ka'an as a protected area. The next year it was named a UNESCO World Heritage Site. The Riviera Maya and Costa Maya split the biosphere reserve; Punta Allen and north belong to the Riviera Maya, and everything south of Punta Allen is part of the Costa Maya.

Fodor's Choice ★

The 1.3-million-acre Reserva de la Biosfera Sian Ka'an is now a UNESCO World Heritage Site.

The Sian Ka'an reserve constitutes 10% of the land in Quintana Roo, and covers 100 km (62 mi) of coastline. Hundreds of species of local and migratory birds, fish, other animals and plants, and fewer than 1,000 residents (primarily Maya) share this area of freshwater and coastal lagoons, mangrove swamps, cays, savannas, tropical forests, and a barrier reef. There are approximately 27 ruins (none excavated) linked by a unique canal system—one of the few of its kind in the Mayan world in Mexico. This is one of the last undeveloped stretches of North American coast. There's a $4 entrance charge and to visit the sites, you must take a guided tour.

Many species of the once-flourishing wildlife have fallen into the endangered category, but the waters here still teem with rooster fish, bonefish, mojarra, snapper, shad, permit, sea bass, and crocodiles. Fishing the flats for wily bonefish is popular, and the peninsula's few lodges also run deep-sea fishing trips.

Most fishing lodges along the way close for the rainy season in August and September, and accommodations are hard to come by. The road ends at Punta Allen, a fishing village whose main catch is spiny lobster, which was becoming scarce until ecologists taught the local fishing cooperative how to build and lay special traps to conserve the species. There are several small, expensive guesthouses. If you haven't booked ahead, start out early in the morning so you can get back to civilization before dark.

Several kinds of tours, including bird-watching by boat and night kayaking to observe crocodiles, are offered on-site through the **Sian Ka'an Visitor Center** (☎ 998/884–3667 or 998/884–9580 ⊕ www.ecotravelmexico.

com), which also offers five rooms with shared bath and one private suite for overnight stays. Prices range from $70 to $100, and meals are separate. For the more adventurous, there are also three- and five-day camping trips, which include kayaking, hiking, snorkeling, bicycling, and wildlife observation in the reef, wetlands, and jungle.

The visitor center's observation tower offers the best view of the Sian Ka'an Biosphere from high atop their deck and wood bridge. It's 18 km (11 mi) south of Tulum on Punta Allen toward Boca Paila Village.

This photogenic archaeological site at the northern end of the *Reserva de la Biosfera Sian Ka'an* is underrated. Once known as Chunyaxché, it's now called by its ancient name, **Muyil** (pronounced moo-*hill*). It dates from the late preclassic era, when it was connected by road to the sea and served as a port between Cobá and the Mayan centers in Belize and Guatemala. A 15-foot-wide *sacbé*, built during the postclassic period, extended from the city to the mangrove swamp and was still in use when the Spaniards arrived.

Structures were erected at 400-foot intervals along the white limestone road, almost all of them facing west, but there are only three still standing. At the beginning of the 20th century the ancient stones were used to build a chicle (gum arabic) plantation, which was managed by one of the leaders of the War of the Castes. The most notable site at Muyil today is the remains of the 56-foot **Castillo**—one of the tallest on the Quintana Roo coast—at the center of a large acropolis. During excavations of the Castillo, jade figurines representing the moon and fertility goddess Ixchel were found. Recent excavations at Muyil have uncovered some smaller structures.

The ruins stand near the edge of a deep-blue lagoon and are surrounded by almost impenetrable jungle—so be sure to bring insect repellent. You can drive down a dirt road on the side of the ruins to swim or fish in the lagoon. The bird-watching is also exceptional here. ⊕ *muyil.smv. org* 🖅 *$3* ⊙ *Daily 8–5.*

WHERE TO STAY

For expanded hotel reviews, visit Fodors.com.

$$$$ 🏨 **Boca Paila Fishing Lodge.** Home of the "grand slam" (fishing lingo for catching three different kinds of fish in one trip), this charming lodge has nine cottages, each with air-conditioning, two double beds, couches, and bathrooms, and some with screened-in sitting areas. **Pros:** on beach; attentive staff; great fishing. **Cons:** not much to do in area besides fish; drinks are not included in AI package. **TripAdvisor:** "lodge was very clean," "clean basic rooms with air conditioning," "experienced fishing guides." ⊠ *Boca Paila Peninsula* ⌂ *Reservations: Frontiers, Box 959, Wexford, PA 15090* ☎ *724/935–1577, 800/245–1950 for Frontiers* ⊕ *www.bocapailamexico.com* 🛏 *9 cottages* ⚒ *In-room: no TV. In-hotel: restaurant, bar, beach, water sports* ⦿ *All-inclusive.*

$$$$ 🏨 **Casa Blanca Lodge.** This lodge is on a rocky outcrop on remote Punta
★ Pájaros Island, which is reputed to be one of the best places in the world for light-tackle saltwater fishing. **Pros:** remote location; comfortable

rooms. **Cons:** the minimum stay; far from anywhere else; drinks are not included in AI package. ⊠ *Punta Pájaros* ⬧ *Reservations: Frontiers, Box 959, Wexford, PA 15090* ☎ *724/935–1577, 800/245–1950 for Frontiers* ⊕ *www.frontierstravel.com* ⇋ *9 rooms* ♻ *In-room: no TV. In-hotel: restaurant, bar, beach, water sports* ⑩ *All-inclusive.*

THE COSTA MAYA

The coastal area south of Punta Allen is more purely Maya than the stretch south of Cancún. Fishing collectives and close-knit communities carry on ancient traditions here, and the proximity to Belize lends a Caribbean flavor, particularly in Chetumal, where you'll hear both Spanish and a Caribbean patois. A multimillion-dollar government initiative is attempting to support ecotourism and sustainable development projects here, which might prevent resorts from taking over the landscape.

CHETUMAL

328 km (283 mi) southeast of Playa del Carmen.

At times, Chetumal feels more Caribbean than Mexican; this isn't surprising, given its proximity to Belize. A population that includes Afro-Caribbean and Middle Eastern immigrants has resulted in a mix of music (reggae, salsa, calypso) and cuisines (Yucatecan, Mexican, and Lebanese). Although Chetumal's provisions are modest, the town has a number of parks on a waterfront that's as pleasant as it is long: the Bay of Chetumal surrounds the city on three sides. Tours go to the fascinating nearby ruins of Kohunlich, Dzibanché, and Kinichná, a trio dubbed the "Valley of the Masks."

Since this is the closest major town to Bacalar, Majahual, and Xcalak, many neighboring residents come here to do banking and stock up on supplies. Traffic can get very congested. In the town of Chetumal itself, you probably won't see another tourist.

GETTING HERE AND AROUND

Chetumal's airport, Aeropuerto de Chetumal, lies on its southwestern edge. Mexicana Airlines flies from Mexico City to Chetumal five times a week. Chetumal's main bus terminal, at Avenida Salvador Novo 179, is served mainly by ADO. Caribe Express also runs buses regularly from Mexico City and other distant destinations. Omnibus Cristóbal Colón has buses that run to Palenque and San Cristóbal. If you're driving here, be sure to fill up with gas at the Pemex station in Felipe Carrillo Puerto, one of the few stations along this stretch of Carretera 307.

ESSENTIALS

Banks There's an ATM at the bus station near the San Francisco Grocery Store. On Insurrengtes Avenida, there's a bank and ATM in the center of the shopping mall. There's also a Bital Bank where Juárez Avenida crosses Obregon Avenida.

Bus Contacts ADO (☎ *983/832-5110* ⊕ *www.ado.com.mx*). **Caribe Express** (☎ *983/832-7889*). **Omnibus Cristóbal Colón** (☎ *983/832-5110*).

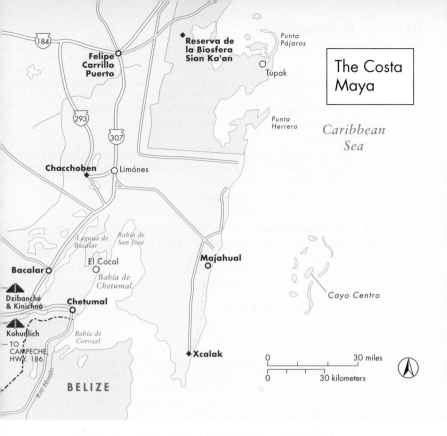

Post Office Main Post Office (✉ *Calle Plutarco E. Calles s/n*).

Medical Assistance General Hospital (✉ *Av. Andrés Quintana Roo 399, between Isla Cancún and J. Sordia* ☎ *983/832–1932*) **Hospital Morelos** (✉ *Av. Juárez between Efraín and Héroes de Chapultepec* ☎ *983/832–4598*)

Visitor and Tour Info Chetumal tourist information booths (✉ *Calles Cinco de Mayo and Carmen Ocho* ☎ *983/832–6647*✉ *Calle 22 de Enero and Av. Reforma* ☎ *983/832–6647*).

EXPLORING

☺ The **Museo de la Cultura Maya**, a sophisticated interactive museum dedicated to the complex world of the Maya, is outstanding. Displays, which have explanations in Spanish and English, trace Mayan architecture, social classes, politics, and customs. The most impressive display is the three-story Sacred Ceiba Tree. The Maya use this symbol to explain the relationship between the cosmos and the earth. The first floor represents the roots of the tree and the Mayan underworld, called Xibalba. The middle floor is the tree trunk, known as Middle World, home to humans and all their trappings. The top floor is the leaves and branches and the 13 heavens of the cosmic otherworld. ✉ *Av. Héroes and Calle Mahatma Gandhi* ☎ *983/832–6838* ⊕ *www.secqr.gob.mx* 🎫 *$5* ⊙ *Tues.–Sun. 9–7.*

Paseo Bahía, Chetumal's main thoroughfare, runs along the water for several miles. A walkway runs parallel to this road and is a popular gathering spot at night. If you follow the road it turns into the Carretera Chetumal–Calderitas, and after 16 km (11 mi) leads to the small ruins of **Oxtankah**. Archaeologists believe this city's prosperity peaked between AD 200 and 600. ⛏ $3 ⏱ *Daily 8–5.*

BEACHES

Surrounding the bay of Chetumal are several beaches including Punta Estrella and Dos Mulas. Punta Estrella offers parking, toilets, volleyball courts, and a small boat marina

WHERE TO EAT AND STAY

For expanded hotel reviews, visit Fodors.com.

¢–$

CAFÉ

✕ **Restaurant Encuentro**. At this bright café, you can enjoy fresh salads, pastas, sandwiches, and chicken dishes. Early risers can try a house omelet stuffed with *chaya* (tree spinach), tomatoes, and salsa verde. They also have 15 kinds of coffee. This is a great place to quickly escape the busy streets outside the restaurant. ⊠ *Av. Alvaro Obregón No. 193* ☎ *983/833–3013* ⏱ *Closed Sun.*

$–$$

PIZZA

★

✕ **Sergio's Restaurant & Pizzas**. Locals rave about this restaurant's grilled steaks, barbecued chicken (made with the owner's special sauce), and garlic shrimp, along with smoked-oyster and seafood pizzas. There's a huge breakfast menu and a variety of lunchtime pasta dishes. This is one of the nicest restaurants in Chetumal and the staff is gracious. When you order the delicious Caesar salad for two, a waiter prepares it at your table. You can also order takeout or delivery, or come in for a snack and use the restaurant's free Wi-Fi. ⊠ *Av. Alvaro Obregón 182, at Av. 5 de Mayo* ☎ *983/832–2991.*

$$

▦ **Los Cocos**. The rooms at this hotel are painted in subdued pastels. **Pros:** reasonable rates; friendly staff; clean rooms. **Cons:** uncomfortable beds; dated decor. **TripAdvisor:** "mini refrigerator, safe and Wi-Fi in each room," "service keeps getting better and better," "hotel and grounds are well looked after." ⊠ *Av. Héroes 134, at Calle Chapultepec* ☎ *983/835–0430* ⊕ *www.hotelloscocos.com.mx* ⮌ *171 rooms, 5 suites* ⚿ *In-room: no safe, Wi-Fi. In-hotel: restaurant, bar, pool, gym, business center* ⭘ *No meals.*

$

▦ **Hotel Marlon**. This comfortable hotel with a pastel color scheme is one of the best deals in town. **Pros:** reasonable rates; good food; kids' pool. **Cons:** uncomfortable beds; no bathtubs. ⊠ *Av. Juárez 87* ☎ *983/832–9411 or 983/832–1065* ⊕ *www.hotelesmarlon.com* ⮌ *50 rooms* ⚿ *In-room: Wi-Fi, no safe. In-hotel: restaurant, bar, pool* ⭘ *No meals.*

XCALAK

180 km (111 mi) southwest of Chetumal.

As the southernmost town in Quintana Roo, Xcalak (pronounced *ish-ka-lack*), is 11 km (7 mi) (by water) from the Belize border. It's quite a journey to get here, but well worth the effort. A charming blend of Mexico and Belize, you'll find that most people speak English, although Spanish is still the primary language. This remote area offers excellent saltwater fly-fishing for a variety of catches including tarpon, bonefish, and permit.

This national reserve is on the tip of a peninsula that divides Chetumal Bay from the Caribbean. Flowers, birds, and butterflies are abundant here, and the terrain is marked by savannas, marshes, streams, and lagoons dotted with islands. There are also fabulously deserted beaches, and a small town center comprised of bars, restaurants, and a few food shops. Although Xcalak has electricity, it's not very dependable, nor is the town ready to become "high tech." Buried along Carretera 307 (along Majahual Road) are fiber-optics that provide electricity to neighboring Xcalak.

Visitor amenities are few, and the town itself lacks a nightlife; the hotels cater mostly to rugged types who come to bird-watch on Bird Island or to dive at Banco Chinchorro, a coral atoll and national park some two hours northeast by boat. This is also a great launching point for day trips to Belize. Most hotels and businesses close down during hurricane season so check ahead to make sure your destination is open.

Although there has been minimal coastal development of private homes, all construction near Xcalak is bound by stringent environmental laws. The entire coast in this area is a designated National Marine Park, which protects the natural beauty of this frontier village.

GETTING HERE AND AROUND
The drive from Xcalak to Chetumal is about 201 km (125 mi), but most people fly in to Cancún, rent a car, and drive here. It's about a five-hour drive from Cancún, but relatively easy with straight, flat roads. Once you get out of Cancún Airport, head south on Carretera 307 past Tulum. The four-lane highway will become a two-lane traffic-less road.

Be sure to fill up with gas at the Pemex station in the city of Felipe Carillo Puerto. There's also a bank and ATM machine there. Although you can find a gas station in Majahual, you might not always find gas there since they tend to run out during high season. Continue on Carretera 307 for approximately 45 minutes until you reach the city of Limones.

Head east (left) on Carretera 10 toward the coastal town of Majahual. The paved road becomes pitted, and soon you'll reach a police checkpoint where most cars are routinely inspected for drugs and arms. After the checkpoint, turn right at the intersection 2 km (1 mi) before Majahual and continue along the road until you reach Xcalak. From the intersection to Xcalak is about 55 km (34 mi). Stay on the beach road, now heading north toward "Zona Hotelera," a 14-km (9-mi) stretch of properties lining the beach. Your hotel will probably be within this main area.

On a map, the route from Chetumal to Xcalak appears like it could be easily done by boat since it's only 55 km (34 mi) across the water. Unfortunately, shallow sections of the bay make it impassable.

For people without cars, there are two buses each day between Xcalak and Chetumal. If you arrive in Xcalak without a car, don't rely on taxi service or local transportation. Consider staying close to town or in a hotel that offers bicycles.

SAFETY AND PRECAUTIONS

Make sure you have a full tank of gas before you head south. Gas stations are few and far between, and often closed for no apparent reason.

Unlike the trafficked roads along Riviera Maya, the two-lane stretch near Belize is seldom visited by tourists. It's always best to travel with a partner and to drive during daylight hours. Drive with caution and be careful of wild animals and potholes. The road is especially bad at Km 19, 29, and 30. Once you leave the paved road and enter Xcalak, the road goes from bad to worse. Be sure to rent a car that can handle pitted dirt roads.

BEACHES

Far from the bustling beaches of Riviera Maya, Playa Xcalak is remarkably tranquil. The white-sand beach stretches for miles, and the offshore reef of nearby Banco Chinchorro is great for snorkeling, diving, and fishing. Much of the sand has been eaten away by past hurricanes, making the shores narrow and somewhat unpleasant for a stroll. The isolated location however, means you might not see another person on the beach for days. Waters are pristine and placid, making this one of the area's best spots for swimming, kayaking, or just a day in the sun.

ESSENTIALS

Banks and Currency Exchange Properties here don't accept credit cards, and there are no banks or ATMs in or near Xcalak. Bring plenty of cash for your entire stay. The closest ATMs are 64 km (40 mi) north in Majahual, though they often run out of money. Another option is to try one of the ATMs in the village of Bacalar.

Medical Emergencies Xcalak has a growing number of expats, including several nurses who are always willing to help. There's a small clinic in the center of town, however, the "medic" (not always a doctor) is seldom around. Usually, a local can point you in the right direction for rudimentary first aid until you can reach the nearest staffed clinic in Bacalar. The closest small hospital (Carranza Clinic) is in Chetumal.

Communication The phone system in Xcalak is like two tin cans strung on a wire...well, almost. Local establishments with phones (a "box," similar to the first cell phones) are subject to charges of $2.75/minute. The box is connected to local antennae that are aimed across the Bahía of Chetumal (about 100 km [60 mi]) to a receiving radio tower. Most people here use Skype, but the best form of communication in Xcalak is email. Don't be surprised if you have trouble reaching a restaurant or hotel by phone; you may have better luck sending an email through their Web site.

Taxi As an alternative to renting a car, there are buses to and from Majahual from Cancún twice daily at 7:30 am and 11:30 pm. There's a five-hour "Majahual Bus" route (first-class ADO), stopping incrementally at Puerto Morelos, Playa del Carmen, Tulum, Felipe Carrillo Puerto, Limones, and finally at Majahual. Visitors traveling to Xcalak from Majahual can get a taxi for about $50. Make note that all ADO and Caribbe buses stop in Limones, where one can easily transfer to a north–south bus running from Cancún to Chetumal all hours of the day.

WHERE TO EAT AND STAY

For expanded hotel reviews, visit Fodors.com.

$
SEAFOOD
Fodor's Choice
★

✕ **The Leaky Palapa.** Nobody expected the kind of sophisticated flavors that the Leaky Palapa brought to town. But this little 13-table palapa, commonly called by its former name, Conchita's, is done up in twinkling lights and has quickly become *the* place for both tourists and locals to meet, enjoy a beer, and sample tasty food. There are seafood options like the delicious lobster bisque or the seared shrimp on bean cakes with tamarind salsa. Homemade pastas practically melt in your mouth, especially the ravoli with corn truffle served with squash-flour bread. The menu changes weekly depending on what local fisherman bring to the dock. Canadian owners Linda and Marla believe in using local ingredients as much as possible. ✉ *Leona Vicario s/n, beside the port captain's office* ☎ *No phone* ⊕ *www.leakypalaparestaurant.com* ⊟ *No credit cards* ☻ *Closed Sept. and Oct.; Mon. Nov.–May; weekdays June–Aug.*

$$
MEXICAN

✕ **Toby's.** Near the entrance to Xcalak is this modest Mexican restaurant made up of a few plastic tables and chairs. Stop by for Toby's famous fajitas, fried fish, coconut shrimp, and chicken quesadillas. The place comes alive on Friday nights when locals gather for the daily special. This is one of the few spots in town where wireless Internet is available (free with food or $1/hour). ✉ *Leona Vicario s/n, across from parking lot and volleyball court* ☎ *983/839–9479* ⊟ *No credit cards* ☻ *Closed Sun.*

$$
Fodor's Choice
★

▦ **Casa Carolina.** This small hotel is a wonderful place to stay if you want to dive, snorkel, kayak, or just relax in one of the hammocks. **Pros:** on a nice beach; diving lessons available; kayaks and bikes available. **Cons:** no restaurant; no air-conditioning. **TripAdvisor:** "snorkeling is spectacular and convenient," "wonderful location on a beautiful beach," "rooms were great, excellent kitchen." ✉ *Carretera Majahual–Xcalak, Km 48* ☎ *610/616–3862 in U.S.* ⊕ *www.casacarolina.net* ⊠ *4 rooms* ⚐ *In-room: no a/c, kitchen. In-hotel: beach, bar* ⊟ *No credit cards* ⊚*Breakfast.*

$$
★

▦ **Sin Duda.** Situated on a lovely beach, this property has several parts: a house divided into three suites; two apartments; and one studio apartment set in the jungle. **Pros:** solar powered; very private. **Cons:** getting here isn't easy; owner's dogs may bark at night; no children under eight. **TripAdvisor:** "snorkeling was great," "everything you need for a fine vacation," "rooms overlooked the azure Caribbean sea." ✉ *Xcalak Peninsula, 60 km (33 mi) south of Majahual, 5½ km (4 mi) north of Costa de Cocos* ☎ *415/868–9925 in U.S.* ⊕ *www.sindudavillas. com* ⊠ *3 rooms, 1 studio, 2 apartments* ⚐ *In-room: no a/c, no safe, kitchen, no TV. In-hotel: beach, water sports, Wi-Fi, some age restrictions* ⊟ *PayPal only* ⊚ *Breakfast.*

SPORTS AND THE OUTDOORS

XTC Dive Center (✉ *650 feet north of the main bridge in Xcalak; Camino Costero Majahual–Xcalak, Km 54* ☎ *983/120–5804* ⊕ *www. xtcdivecenter.com*) is the only full-service dive shop in Xcalak. In addition to recreational diving, they offer NAUI, DAN, and PADI scuba diving instruction. Two tank dives cost $70, and snorkeling and boat trips to Belize can be arranged for groups of six to eight people ($280). They also have the only boat that's licensed to take passengers to Chinchorro.

BACALAR

 40 km (25 mi) northwest of Chetumal.

Founded in AD 435, Bacalar (pronounced *baa*-ka-lar) is one of Quintana Roo's oldest settlements. There's a mix of freshwater and salt water in Laguna de Bacalar because it's fed by cenotes. This mixing intensifies the color, which earned the lagoon the nickname "Lago de los Siete Colores" (Lake of the Seven Colors). Marking the entrance to Bacalar (Carretera 307 at Km 34) is Cenote Azul, a crystal clear cenote that's 300 feet deep and 600 feet in diameter. The water is clean and the diving is excellent here. Drive along the lake's southern shores to enter the affluent section of the town of Bacalar, with elegant waterfront homes.

GETTING HERE AND AROUND

Bacalar is 3½ hours south of Cancún and 30 minutes north of Chetumal. It's just off Carretera 307, south of Felipe Carrillo Puerto and Limones. If you're coming from Cancún, follow the well-marked signs toward Bacalar. Upon entering the town, you'll cross over two huge speed bumps. Pass the Catholic church on your right, take a left at the first corner, and continue straight to the town center; to your left will be the Fort of San Felipe. Northbound drivers should take Carretera 106 to 307.

ESSENTIALS

Banks and Currency Exchange Although there are no banks in Bacalar, there's an ATM in the town square. Just past Km 22, turn left at the sign "Bacalar Salida 500m." Pass the white church and turn left. Make the first left again and you'll see the town square and the ATM on your right.

Medical Emergencies Bacalar's nearest medical facilities are in the neighboring town of Chetumal (⇨ *above*). **Centro Medico Internacional** ✉ *Av. Juárez No. 168, Chetumal* ☎ *983/832–6490*). **General Hospital** (✉ *Av. Andrés Quintana Roo 399, between Isla Cancún and J. Sordia* ☎ *983/832–1932*) **Hospital Morelos** (✉ *Av. Juárez between Efraín and Héroes de Chapultepec* ☎ *983/832–4598*)

EXPLORING

Bacalar. The alliance between sister cities Dzibanché and Kinichná was thought to have made them the most powerful cities in southern Quintana Roo during the Mayan classic period (AD 100–1000). The fertile farmlands surrounding the ruins are still used today as they were hundreds of years ago, and the winding drive deep into the fields makes you feel as if you're coming upon something undiscovered.

Archaeologists have been making progress in excavating more and more ruins, albeit slowly. At **Dzibanché** ("place where they write on wood," pronounced zee-ban-*che*), several carved wooden lintels have been discovered; the most perfectly preserved sample is in a supporting arch at the **Plaza de Xibalba**. Also at the plaza is the **Templo del Búho** (Temple of the Owl), atop which a recessed tomb was found, the second discovery of its kind in Mexico (the first was at Palenque in Chiapas). In the tomb were magnificent clay vessels painted with white owls—messengers of the underworld gods. More buildings and three plazas have been restored as excavation continues. Several other plazas are surrounded by temples, palaces, and pyramids, all in the Petén style. The carved stone steps at **Edificio 13** and **Edificio 2** (Buildings 13 and

Interesting limestone formations on the shore of lake Bacalar.

2) still bear traces of stone masks. A copy of the famed lintel of **Templo IV** (Temple IV), with eight glyphs dating from AD 618, is housed in the Museo de la Cultura Maya in Chetumal. (The original was replaced in 2003 because of deterioration.) Four more tombs were discovered at **Templo I** (Temple I). ☎ *No phone* ✉ *$4* ⊙ *Daily 8–5.*

After you see Dzibanché, make your way back to the fork in the road and head to **Kinichná** (House of the Sun, pronounced kin-itch-*na*). At the fork, you'll see the restored **Complejo Lamai** (Lamai Complex), the administrative buildings of Dzibanché. Kinichná consists of a two-level pyramidal mound split into Acropolis B and Acropolis C, apparently dedicated to the sun god. Two mounds at the foot of the pyramid suggest that the temple was a ceremonial site. Here a giant Olmec-style jade figure was found. At its summit, Kinichná affords one of the finest views of any archaeological site in the area. Admission is good for both Dzibanché and Kinichná archaeological sites. ☎ *No phone* ✉ *$4* ⊙ *Daily 8–5.*

Fuerte de San Felipe Bacalar *(San Felipe Fort)* is a 17th-century stone fort built by the Spaniards using stones from the nearby Mayan pyramids. It was constructed as a haven against pirates and marauding bandits though during the War of the Castes it was a Mayan stronghold. Today the monolithic structure, which overlooks the enormous Laguna de Bacalar, houses government offices and a museum with exhibits on local history (ask for someone to bring a key if museum doors are locked). ☎ *983/832–6838* ✉ *$5* ⊙ *Tues.–Thurs. and Sun. 9–7, Fri. and Sat. 9–8.*

Kohunlich (pronounced *ko*-hoon-lich) is renowned for the giant stucco masks on its principal pyramid, the **Edificio de los Mascarones** (Mask

Building). It also has one of Quintana Roo's oldest ball courts and the remains of a great drainage system at the **Plaza de las Estelas** (Plaza of the Stelae). Masks that are about 6 feet tall are set vertically into the wide staircases at the main pyramid, called **Edificio de las Estelas** (Building of the Stelae). First thought to represent the Mayan sun god, they're now considered to be composites of the rulers and important warriors of Kohunlich. Another giant mask was discovered in 2001 in the building's upper staircase.

In 1902 loggers came upon Kohunlich, which was built and occupied during the classic period by various Mayan groups. This explains the eclectic architecture, which includes the Petén and Río Bec styles. Although there are 14 buildings to visit, it's thought that there are at least 500 mounds on the site waiting to be excavated. Digs have turned up 29 individual and multiple burial sites inside a residence building called **Temple de Los Viente-Siete Escalones** (Temple of the Twenty-Seven Steps). This site doesn't have a great deal of tourist traffic, so it's surrounded by thriving flora and fauna. ⊠ *42 km (26 mi) west of Chetumal on Carretera 186* ☎ *No phone* 🖾 *$4* ☉ *Daily 8–5.*

WHERE TO EAT

$
SEAFOOD
✕ **Chepe's Taqueria la Sabrosita.** Bacalar's mayor, José Contreras, known as Chepe, runs this little taco shop. The most famous tacos here are made with a delicious house cochinita pibil. If you're still a little sleepy when the restaurant opens at 7 am, the spicy habanero salsa should wake you right up. Get here early and grab a seat at one of the red plastic tables, because the handmade taquitos are gone before lunchtime. ⊠ *1 block south of the town church* ☎ *983/126–3732* ▭ *No credit cards.*

$$
SEAFOOD
✕ **Restaurant Cenote Azul.** Perched on the rim of the 300-foot-deep cenote, this palapa restaurant serves good chicken, pork, and fish dishes. House specialties include the seafood platter and shrimp kebab. Here you can linger over fresh fish and a beer while gazing out over the deep blue waters, or enjoy a swim off the dock. There's also a souvenir shop popular with tour groups. ⊠ *Carretera Chetumal–Cancún, Km 34* ☎ *983/834–2460* ⊕ *www.cenoteazul.com* ☉ *Daily 8–6.*

WHERE TO STAY

For expanded hotel reviews, visit Fodors.com.

$$
Fodor's Choice
★
🏨 **Las Aluxes.** Located right on the water's edge, Las Aluxes' manicured gardens lead to an enormous palapa restaurant beside a private dock and swing-set suspended over the water. **Pros:** quiet location; private dock; family friendly. **Cons:** staff doesn't speak English; not all rooms have an ocean view. ⊠ *Av. Costera Bacalar No.67* ☎ *983/834–2817* ⊕ *www.bacalarlagunazul.com* ⤷ *8 rooms* ☖ *In-room: no safe, a/c, no TV (some), Wi-Fi. In-hotel: restaurant, bar, beach, parking* |◯| *No meals.*

$$$–$$$$
Fodor's Choice
★
🏨 **Explorean Kohunlich.** At the edge of the Kohunlich ceremonial grounds, this ecological resort gives you the chance to have an adventure without giving up life's comforts. **Pros:** attentive staff; tours included in room rate. **Cons:** expensive rates; no Internet. **TripAdvisor:** "staff is absolutely delightful," "food was high above expectations," "rooms are beautiful, spacious and comfortable." ⊠ *Carretera Chetumal–Escarega, Km 6.5,*

same road as ruins ☎ *55/5201–8350 in Mexico City, 877/397–5672, 800/343–7821* ⊕ *www.theexplorean.com* ⤳ *40 suites* ⚲ *In-room: no TV, no safe. In-hotel: restaurant, bar, pool, spa* ¶◎¶ *All-inclusive.*

$ 🏨 **Hotel Laguna.** This four-story white hotel outside Bacalar is perched on a hill overlooking the water. **Pros:** wonderful water views; close to town; kayak rental and boat tours available. **Cons:** plain rooms; not all rooms have air-conditioning. **TripAdvisor:** "beautiful lakeside setting," "balconies for every room," "old but very well kept hotel." ✉ *Carretera 307, Km 40* ☎ *983/834–2205* ⊕ *www.hotellagunabacalar. com* ⤳ *3 cabins, 30 rooms* ⚲ *In-room: no safe, no a/c (some), Wi-Fi, no TV. In-hotel: restaurant, bar, pool.*

$$$ 🏨 **Rancho Encantado.** On the shores of Laguna Bacalar, 30 minutes north
★ of Chetumal, the enchanting Rancho Encantado consists of Mayan-themed casitas. **Pros:** great location on lagoon; breakfast included; friendly staff; huge Jacuzzi; Wi-Fi in restaurant. **Cons:** some traffic noise; need car to get around; low water pressure; mosquitoes. **TripAdvisor:** "excellent restaurant with great fish," "perfect place if you enjoy nature," "grounds are beautiful and the lake is incredible." ✉ *Off Carretera 307, Km 24, look for turnoff sign* ☎ *998/884–2071, 877/229–2046 in U.S.* ⊕ *www.encantado.com* ⤳ *12 casitas* ⚲ *In-room: no safe, no a/c (some), no TV. In-hotel: restaurant, bar* ¶◎¶ *Breakfast.*

MAJAHUAL

143 km (89 mi) northwest of Chetumal via Carreteras 186 and 307.

Prior to a devastating 2007 hurricane, most travelers overlooked the small fishing village of Majahual (pronounced ma-ha-*wal*). Though there are still only about 300 residents, post-hurricane renovations have put the village on the map; it now has its own pier as well as a smattering of hotels, restaurants, and shops. The new cement boardwalk along the beach has made Majahual an ideal spot for a sunset stroll. The crystal-clear waters and unspoiled beaches are delightful for snorkeling, diving, and fishing. The latest addition to the area is New Majahual. It's comprised of boutique shops, a Hard Rock Café, a Senior Frogs, and a Lapis Jewelry store. This section of town was constructed for the thousands of cruise-ship passengers that disembark here weekly, however it lacks the charm of the nearby beachfront area.

GETTING HERE AND AROUND

There's a first-class ADO bus ($23) that departs every day at 7 am from Cancún (stopping in Playa del Carmen and Tulum). Majahual isn't included on ADO's on-line reservation system so you must book a seat from either Cancún or Playa Del Carmen. There's an ADO terminal inside the Cancún airport. This direct transportation to Majahual has made the area popular with backpackers. The ADO bus from Playa del Carmen departs at 8:20 am and arrives in Majahual at 12:30 pm with brief stops in Tulum, Carrillo Puerto, and Limones.

To get here by car, take Carretera 307 to Highway 10, approximately 2½ km (1½ mi) past Limones. Continue on this road for 50 km (30 mi) until you reach the coast. Turn right at the lighthouse and follow the road into the town of Majahual where a string of hotels and restaurants line the beach.

To reach New Majahual, turn left at Km 55, just past the mayor's office.

BEACHES

Three cruise ships stop here daily, meaning that Majahual's beach is the liveliest place in town. Seaside restaurants provide enough cerveza and ceviche to keep everyone happy, and there are several vendors offering boat tours and rental equipment like glass-bottomed kayaks. The main beach in the center of town has plenty of fine sand and glassy waters for a cushy afternoon in the sun. This area is best for swimming and snorkeling.

ESSENTIALS

Banks and Currency Exchange Most properties don't accept credit cards. Six ATMs are available in town, and there's a small exchange booth (orange building) on the main beach road.

Medical Emergencies An ambulance is always on-site at the Chetumal ruins and there's a small clinic on the south end of the soccer field. Majahual's local doctor, Oscar Ramirez, provides medical service until 2 pm daily.

Police There's a police station on Calle Huachinango across from the soccer field. The emergency phone number is 066.

Taxi A taxi stand is at the corner of Avenida Majahual and Calle Rubic. A full day of transportation, with a private driver, can be arranged for around $100. Additional taxis are parked around the soccer field. Always ask to see a rate card before agreeing to a price.

Visitor Information Although there isn't a visitor center, Fernando, owner of 100% Agave in town, is a true ambassador for Majahual, and gladly offers advice on what to see and where to go.

WHERE TO EAT

★ ✕ **100% Agave.** This small restaurant-shack is a must for tequila lovers.
MEXICAN Owner Fernando serves up delicious Mexican food and is an expert on tequila and other agave liquors. His margaritas rival any cocktail in Majahual and his "Micheladas" (beer, lime, and hot sauce) are refreshingly punchy. The affordable menu features traditional Mexican, Yucatán, and Tex-Mex specialties. Tequila tasting is part of the experience so be sure to ask Fernando about his barrels of 100% agave blends. The place is easily recognizable by the big tequila bottle out front. ⊠ *Calle Huachinango, second road parallel to the Malecon* 🕾 *No phone* ⊟ *No credit cards.*

$$ ✕ **Nacional Beach Club.** Many travelers stumble on this colorful beach
★ club and end up staying past sunset. For just $10, you get a beach chair,
MEXICAN umbrella, and access to the pool, shower, and changing facilities. Margaritas can be delivered to you beachside or you can escape the heat by grabbing a bite in the enclosed patio. By day you can munch on tacos, enchiladas, and sandwiches and by night enjoy the delicious smoked fish or grilled shrimp. The $2 Coronas make this a popular spot to waste away the day. There are also three bungalows for rent if you feel like

Majahual is a lively little community with a wonderful beach.

staying the night. ⊠ *Majahual Av. s/n, Lote 4, Mza 14,* ☎ *983/110–5354* ⊕ *www.nacionalbeachclub.com* ▭ *No credit cards.*

WHERE TO STAY

For expanded hotel reviews, visit Fodors.com.

$$ **Arenas**. Given its location just across the street from the beach, the exceptional ocean views (especially from the third floor) aren't surprising. **Pros:** great location near restaurants and shops; every room has ocean view. **Cons:** no elevator. ⊠ *Av. Majahual, Lote 7, Mza 27* ☎ *983/101–8219* ⊕ *www.hotelarenasmx.com* ⤸ *8 rooms, 4 suites* ⌂ *In-room: no safe, Wi-Fi, a/c (some). In-hotel: restaurant, bar* ⦿ *No meals.*

$$ **Balamku**. While vacationing in the area, Canadian expats Carol Tumber and Alan Knight missed their turnoff to Punta Allen and ended up spending the night in Majahual. **Pros:** beachfront location; comfortable rooms; staff makes you feel at home; room price includes taxes. **Cons:** need car to get around; restaurant serves only breakfast and lunch; rooms lack air-conditioning. **TripAdvisor:** "units are beautiful and very comfortable," "eco resort right on beach," "hospitality is superb." ⊠ *Av. Majahual, Km 5.7* ☎ *983/732–1004* ⊕ *www.balamku.com* ⤸ *10 rooms* ⌂ *In-room: no safe, no a/c, no TV, Wi-Fi. In-hotel: restaurant, beach, water sports* ▭ *No credit cards* ⦿ *Breakfast.*

Fodor's Choice
★

$$ **El Caballo Blanco**. When the owner's son was a young boy, he cherished the family's *caballo blanco* (white horse) for which the hotel is named. **Pros:** great views; one wheelchair accessible room; all rooms have balconies. **Cons:** small bathrooms; back room lacks ocean view. **TripAdvisor:** "rooms were great and service is fantastic," "very clean, charming, warm and friendly," "food is excellent." ⊠ *Av. Majahual,*

Lote 1, Mza 12 ☎ *983/126–0319* ⚞ *7 rooms* ⚐ *In-room: no safe, Wi-Fi. In-hotel: restaurant, bar, pool, beach, water sports, parking* ⚑ *Breakfast.*

$–$$ ⚐ **Hotel Castillo.** On a pristine beach just in front of a coral reef, this
⚘   small hotel is a paradise for families, water-sports enthusiasts, and anyone looking to relax. **Pros:** owners catch and prepare fresh fish; family-friendly. **Cons:** no air-conditioning; 10 km (6 mi) from main village. ⚐ *From Carretera 307, turn east after Majahual and continue along coast road for 11.6 km (7 mi) toward Xcalak* ☎ *983/110–5918* ⊕ *www. hotel-castillo.com* ⚞ *7 rooms, 1 suite* ⚐ *In-room: no safe, no a/c, no TV. In-hotel: restaurant, bar, water sports* ⚌ *No credit cards* ⚑ *No meals.*

$$ ⚐ **Maya Luna.** This small lodging on the beach, far from the boardwalk, is a quiet place to relax and enjoy the sand and the sun. **Pros:** beachfront location; nice restaurant open to the public; relaxed atmosphere. **Cons:** no air-conditioning. **TripAdvisor:** "wonderful rooftop terrace," "relaxing, peaceful, romantic," "friendly and well-spirited staff." ⚐ *Av. Majahual, Km 4* ☎ *983/836–0905* ⊕ *www.hotelmayaluna.com* ⚞ *5 rooms* ⚐ *In-room: no safe, no a/c, no TV. In-hotel: restaurant, parking* ⚌ *No credit cards* ⚑ *Breakfast.*

$$ ⚐ **Mayan Beach Garden.** Nineteen kilometers (12 mi) north of Majahual,
Fodor's Choice   this charming bed-and-breakfast has two types of rooms: beachfront
★   cabanas and two-story beach-view suites. **Pros:** optional all-inclusive plan available; beautiful garden restaurant; use of bikes and snorkels. **Cons:** minimum three-night stay during high season; 50% deposit required for reservation; bumpy dirt road means 30-minute drive to town. **TripAdvisor:** "a comfortable atmosphere," "food was fantastic," "cabana was right on the beach." ⚐ *N. Carretera Costera Majahual–Punta Herrera, Km 20.5* ☎ *983/132–2603, 206/905–9665 in U.S.* ⊕ *www.mayanbeachgarden.com* ⚞ *2 cabanas, 3 rooms, 1 suite* ⚐ *In-room: no a/c (some), kitchen, Wi-Fi (some). In-hotel: restaurant, bar, beach, water sports* ⚑ *Multiple meal plans.*

$$ ⚐ **La Posada de los 40 Cañones.** This nautically themed hotel is adorned with anchors, wooden pathways, and queen-size beds that swing from ropes. **Pros:** beautifully landscaped; reasonably priced rooms. **Cons:** no pool; reservations require nonrefundable payment; not all rooms have ocean view; neighboring construction. **TripAdvisor:** "relaxing place, excellent cuisine, friendly service," "food was yummy and reasonably priced," "room was clean and pleasant." ⚐ *Calle Huachinango* ☎ *983/123–8591* ⊕ *www.40canones.com* ⚞ *12 rooms* ⚐ *In-room: no safe, a/c, no TV, Wi-Fi. In-hotel: restaurant, bar, beach, parking* ⚑ *No meals.*

$$ ⚐ **Posada Pachamama.** This simple, charming little hotel is just across the street from the beach on Majahual's main boardwalk. **Pros:** beachfront location; good rates; near restaurants and shops. **Cons:** no pool. **TripAdvisor:** "great place, great service, and excellent location," "rooms are small and trendy," "restaurant with great coffee." ⚐ *Calle Huachinango s/n* ☎ *983/134–3049* ⊕ *www.posadapachamama.net* ⚞ *6 rooms* ⚐ *In-room: no safe, no TV, Wi-Fi.*

Mayan Beach Garden Inn.

SPORTS AND THE OUTDOORS
ADVENTURE TOURS
Yolanda Ros (✉ *Hotel Mayaluna, Carretera Majahual Xcalak, Km 4* ☎ *983/103–4739* ⊕ *www.tortugazul.com*) is experienced in all kinds of outdoor adventure. She offers personalized biking, kayaking, and horseback tours in the area for groups of up to eight people. Tours range from $25 to $160.

SCUBA DIVING
Dreamtime Dive Resort (✉ *Av. Majahual s/n, Km 2.5* ☎ *983/700–5824, 904/730–4337 in U.S.* ⊕ *www.dreamtimediving.com*) offers snorkeling tours and night dives managed by some of the most experienced divers in the area. Single-tank dives cost $40; two-tank dives are $75.

FELIPE CARRILLO PUERTO

156 km (97 mi) north of Chetumal.

Formerly known as Chan Santa Cruz, Felipe Carrillo Puerto—the Costa Maya's first major town—is named for the man who became governor of Yucatán in 1920 and who was hailed as a hero after instituting a series of reforms to help the impoverished *campesinos* (peasants). Not far away is Chacchoben, a little-explored archaeological site.

GETTING HERE AND AROUND
The entire 382-km (237-mi) coast from Punta Sam near Cancún to the main border crossing to Belize at Chetumal is traversable on Carretera 307—a straight, paved highway. A few years ago only a handful of gas stations serviced the entire state of Quintana Roo, but now—with the

exception of the lonely stretch from Felipe Carrillo Puerto south to Chetumal—they are plentiful.

ESSENTIALS

Banks and Currency Exchange As you enter the town, there's a Bital Bank complete with an ATM located next to the Pemex Gas Station.

Medical Emergencies Hospital General SESA (☎ 983/834–0092). **Clínica San Rafae** (☎ 983/834–0700). **Centro Diagnóstico Jesús** (☎ 983/834–0538). Local doctors include David Chay Vivas (☎ 983/834–0071), Lidia Tún Molina (☎ 983/834–0211), and Miguel Chí Lavadores (☎ 983/809–2447).

EXPLORING

Interesting **Chacchoben** (pronounced *cha*-cho-ben) is one of the more recent archaeological sites to undergo excavation. An ancient city that was a contemporary of Kohunlich and the most important trading partner with Guatemala north of the Bacalar Lagoon area, the site contains several newly unearthed buildings that are still in good condition. The lofty **Templo Uno,** the site's main temple, was dedicated to the Mayan sun god Itzamná, and once held a royal tomb. (When archaeologists found it, though, it had already been looted.) Most buildings were constructed in the early classic period around AD 200 in the Petén style, although the city could have been inhabited as early as 200 BC. The inhabitants made a living by growing cotton and extracting chewing gum and copal resin from the trees. ⊠ *Carretera 307, turn right on Carretera 293 south of Cafetal, continue 9 km (5½ mi) passing Lázaro Cardenas town* ☎ *No phone* ⊕ *www.chacchobenruins.com* ⊠ *$3; additional $3 to use video cameras* ⊙ *Daily 8–5.*

WHERE TO STAY

For expanded hotel reviews, visit Fodors.com.

¢   **El Faisán y El Venado.** The price is right at this simple three-story hotel, where rustic rooms accommodate up to three people. **Pros:** best place to stay in town. **Cons:** simple rooms; staff speaks little English. ⊠ *Av. Benito Juárez, Lote 781* ☎ *983/834–0702* ⇒ *37 rooms* ⌂ *In-room: kitchen. In-hotel: restaurant, bar.*

Isla Mujeres

WORD OF MOUTH

"Isla is very REAL and there are places to stay that suit every budget.
The north beach is very safe—good choices in restaurants, many
quite casual."
— Fanjoy

WELCOME TO ISLA MUJERES

TOP REASONS TO GO

★ **Getting away from the crowd:** Although Isla Mujeres is just across the bay from Cancún, the peace and quiet make it seem like another universe.

★ **Exploring the southeastern coast:** Bump along in a golf cart where craggy cliffs meet the blue Caribbean.

★ **Eating freshly grilled seafood:** For some reason it always tastes best under a beachfront *palapa* (thatch roof) at lovely Playa Norte.

★ **Diving with "sleeping sharks":** They dwell in the underwater caverns off Isla.

★ **Taking a boat trip to Isla Contoy:** On this even smaller island, more than 70 species of birds make their home.

1 The Western Coast. Midway along the western coast of Isla you can glimpse the lovely Laguna Makax. At the lagoon's southeastern end are the shady stretches of Playa Tiburón and Playa Lancheros. At Isla's southernmost tip is El Garrafón National Park.

2 Playa Norte. With its waist-deep turquoise waters and wide soft sands, Playa Norte is the northernmost and most beautiful beach on Isla Mujeres. Most of the island's resorts and hotels are here; El Pueblo and historic El Cementerio are just a short walk away.

3 El Pueblo. Directly in front of the ferry piers, El Pueblo is Isla's only town. It extends the full width of the northern end and is sandwiched between sand and sea to the south, west, and northeast. The zócalo (main square) here is the hub of Isleño life.

GETTING ORIENTED

Isla Mujeres is still quiet by Riviera Maya standards. It retains the small-town feel that makes it a great escape from Cancún. (Don't mention that to locals, who will tell you that the influx of big hotels has changed it forever.) Just 8 km (5 mi) long and 1 km (½ mi) wide, its landscapes include flat sandy beaches in the north and steep rocky bluffs to the south. The liveliest activities here are swimming or snorkeling, exploring the remnants of the island's past, drinking cold beer, eating fresh seafood, and lazing under palapas.

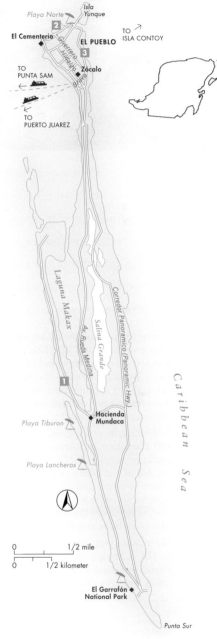

4

Updated by
Marlise Kast

Once a small fishing village, this colorful destination has become a favorite for travelers seeking natural beauty, island serenity, and a slower pace of life. Without compromising its cultural traditions, Isla Mujeres is one of the most relaxing and affordable places to vacation. Winter months offer excellent sportfishing and the calm waters are great for snorkeling and swimming year-round.

During high season, boatloads of visitors pop over from Cancún to have a taste of the island life. This midday rush is a boon for vendors and hagglers offering every kind of service from braided hair to beach massages. By late afternoon the masses disappear and return to their big-city nightlife and the comforts of the mainland. Those who stay behind discover that on Isla Mujeres concerns fade with the sinking of the sun and are washed away by the cool breezes of the Caribbean morning.

Embracing its rewards are Isla's permanent residents, including nearly 100 Canadian and American expats (most operating hotels and restaurants) and 15,000 friendly Maya, many of whom earn a living selling fish at the docks or plates of food outside their homes. There are plenty of opportunities to practice your Spanish, and you'll find that most locals beam when you try. Taxi drivers are genuinely interested in sharing details of the island's history, or telling you about their families who were born and raised on Isla Mujeres.

The minute you step off the boat, you'll get a sense of how small Isla is. The sights and properties on the island are strung along the coasts. There's not much to the interior except the two saltwater marshes, Salina Chica and Salina Grande, where the Maya harvested salt centuries ago.

PLANNING

WHEN TO GO

Isla enjoys its best weather between November and May, when temperatures usually hover around 80°F. June, July, and August are the hottest and most humid months, when temperatures routinely top 95°F. There are a few fun festivals and holidays to keep in mind while you're planning your trip: the Sol a Sol Regatta is in late April; Founder's Day is on August 17; the Day of the Dead celebrations are from October 31 to November 2; the Immaculate Conception Feast runs December 1 to 8; and the Day of the Virgin de la Caridad del Cobre, the patron saint of local fishermen, is on September 9. Be sure to book well in advance if you'll be on the island on any of these days

TIMING

Although most mainland travelers visit Isla for the day, it's definitely worth spending the night if you're looking for a mix of culture, tranquillity, good food, and island life. In a single afternoon you can visit all the best beaches and major attractions. You may even have enough time to snorkel or swim.

GETTING HERE AND AROUND

Isla ferries are actually speedboats that run between the main dock on the island and Puerto Juárez on the mainland. The *Miss Valentina,* the *Ultramar,* and the *Caribbean Lady* are small air-conditioned cruisers able to make the crossing in just under 20 minutes. A one-way ticket costs $3.50, and the boats leave daily every 30 minutes from 5:30 am to 8:30 pm, with a late ferry at 11:30 pm for those returning from partying in Cancún. You can also choose to take a slower open-air ferry; these trips take about 45 minutes, but the fare is cheap: $1.60 per person. Slow ferries run from 5 am until 6 pm.

More-expensive fast ferries to Isla's main dock also leave from El Embarcadero marina complex, and from the Xcaret office complex at Playa Caracol just across from Plaza Caracol Shopping Mall. Both are in Cancún's Zona Hotelera. The cost is between $10 and $15 round-trip, and the voyage takes about 30 minutes. Although it's not necessary to have a car on Isla, there's a car ferry that travels between the island and Punta Sam, a dock north of Puerto Juárez. The ride takes about 45 minutes, and the fare is $1.50 per person and about $18 to $26 per vehicle, depending on the size of your car.

■ TIP→ Scooters are the most popular mode of transportation on Isla. Most rental places charge $25 to $35 a day, or $8 to $11 per hour, depending on the scooter's make and age. One of the most reliable rental outfits is Rentadora Ma José; rentals start at $10 per hour or $25 per day (9 am to 5 pm) or $35 for 24 hours. You can also rent bicycles on Isla, but keep in mind that it's hot here and the roads have plenty of speed bumps. Don't ride at night, as many roads don't have streetlights. David's Bike Rental rents bikes starting at $10 per day for beaters and $18 per day for fancy three-speeds.

Golf carts are another fun way to get around the island, especially with kids. Ciro's Motorent has an excellent choice of new flatbed golf carts, which cost from $45 to $75 for 24 hours, depending on the season. Pepe's Rentadora also has a large fleet of carts (rental prices start at $55 for 24 hours) and mopeds (rental prices start at $25 per day).

MONEY MATTERS

It's best to arrive at Isla Mujeres with pesos or exchange money at the "cambio" window located at the Ultramar ferry dock in Cancún. On Isla Mujeres, ATMs are located at the San Francisco Super Express store in the town square and at the HSBC across from the ferry port. Both machines tend to run out of money on weekends and holidays.

Island banks will no longer exchange U.S. dollars to Mexican pesos. However, there are many "Casa De Cambio" (exchange houses) that will exchange dollars to pesos, making this the only option to exchange U.S. currency. Few places on Isla Mujeres, including banks, will accept traveler's checks and the minority of establishments accept credit cards, mostly MasterCard and Visa.

HOTELS

There are several Internet-based rental agencies that can help you rent a home on the island: ⊕ *www.islabeckons.com*, for example, lists fully equipped apartments and houses (and also handles reservations for hotel rooms); ⊕ *www.morningsinmexico.com* offers smaller and less expensive properties. Most rental homes have fully equipped kitchens, bathrooms, and bedrooms. You can opt for a house downtown or a more secluded one on the eastern coast.

DINING AND LODGING PRICES

WHAT IT COSTS IN DOLLARS				
	¢	$	$$	$$$	$$$$
Restaurants	under $5	$5–$10	$10–$15	$15–$25	over $25
Hotels	under $50	$50–$75	$75–$150	$150–$250	over $250

Restaurant prices are based on the median entrée price at dinner. Hotel prices are for a standard double room in high season.

SAFETY

Since Isla Mujeres is a small island there's little crime and it's considered an excellent choice for visitors traveling alone. Common sense precautions do apply: Stay clear of drugs, don't leave personal items unattended on the beach or in a golf cart, and lock your hotel room when you leave. Some of the greatest safety concerns are related to dehydration; drink plenty of bottled water and order beverages without ice unless you're dining at a restaurant that uses purified water. Also be careful when driving along the narrow roads, especially since many have gravel surfaces and potholes.

TOURS

There aren't any tours of the island itself. Most are actually trips around the island, including catamaran party boats or open-bar ferries. For an island tour, it's best to take the Ultramar ferry from Cancún to Isla Mujeres and explore at your own pace.

VISITOR INFORMATION

The **tourist office** (✉ *Av. Rueda Medina 130, across from the pier* ☎ 998/
877–0307 *or* 998/877–0767 ⊕ *www.isla-mujeres.com.mx*) is open
weekdays 8 to 8 and has lots of general information about the island.

ESSENTIALS

Currency Exchange Cunex Money Exchange (✉ *Av. Francisco Madero 12A, at
Av. Hidalgo* ☎ 998/877–0474). **HSBC** (✉ *Av. Rueda Medina Num 3, across from
ferry port, El Pueblo* ☎ 998/877–0005).

Monex Exchange (✉ *Av. Morelos 9, Lote 4* ☎ *No phone*).

Medical Assistance Centro de Salud (✉ *Av. Guerrero de Salud* ☎ 998/877–
0117). **Farmacia Isla Mujeres** (✉ *Av. Juárez 8* ☎ 998/877–0178). **Hospital de
la Armada** (✉ *Av. Rueda Medina at Ojón P. Blanco* ☎ 998/877–0001).

Red Cross Clinic (✉ *Colonia La Gloria* ☎ 998/877–0280).

Rental Cars Ciro's Motorent (✉ *Av. Guerrero Norte 1, at Av. Matamoros*
☎ 998/877–0578). **David's Bike Rental** (✉ *Across from Pemex station, Av.
Rueda Medina* ☎ *No phone*). **Gomar** (✉ *Av. Rueda Medina and Calle Nicolas
Bravo* ☎ 998/877–0541). **Pepe's Moto Rental** (✉ *Av. Hidalgo 19* ☎ 998/877–
0019). **Rentadora Ma José** (✉ *Av. Francisco Madero 25* ☎ 998/877–0130).

Visitor and Tour Info Caribbean Realty & Travel Enterprises (✉ *Calle Abasolo 6* ☎ 998/877–1371 or 998/877–1372). **La Isleña Tours** (✉ *Av. Morelos,
1 block up from ferry docks* ☎ 998/877–0578). **Viajes Prisma** (✉ *Av. Rueda
Medina 9C* ☎ 998/877–0938).

4

EXPLORING

To get your bearings, try thinking of the island as a long, narrow fish:
the head is the southeastern tip, the tail is the northwest prong. Eight
kilometers (5 mi) long and 1 km (½ mi) wide, Isla Mujeres can easily be
explored in a single day. If you take your time however, you'll discover
that the island is not a destination to be rushed. Virtually car-free, the
dirt roads of this quaint fishing village are best traveled by golf cart,
scooter, or bike.

⚠ Before leaving the rental agency, check your scooter and golf cart for
scratches and dings. You may even want to take a photo for additional proof
of the original condition. Otherwise, you'll pay dearly for any damage that
was not noted prior to your rental agreement.

If you're staying at one of the remote hotels on the southern tip, a taxi
will take you from one end of the island to the other for $6.

BY GOLF CART

Start by looping the island exterior, and stopping midway at the southernmost tip. Here you can walk down to the rocky shores where waves
crash right at your feet. The views from Punta Sur (south end) are magnificent, and the temple of Goddess Ixchel is worth a visit. Head back
north and explore the tiny streets and colorful neighborhoods, or relax
at Playa Lancheros on the island's west side. Stop by to see the area's
dolphins, turtles, or nursing sharks, and then enjoy a traditional Mayan

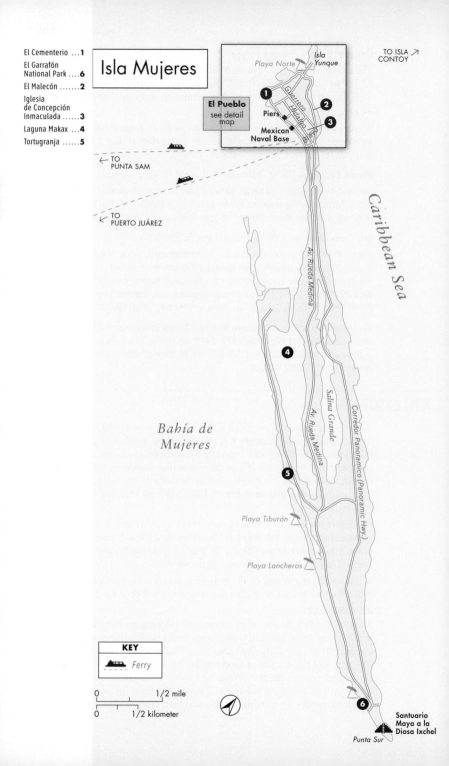

Isla Mujeres

TO ISLA
CONTOY

Playa Norte

Isla
Yunque

El Pueblo
see detail
map

Piers

Mexican
Naval Base

← TO
PUNTA SAM

← TO
PUERTO JUÁREZ

Caribbean Sea

Av. Rueda Medina

Salina Grande

Av. Rueda Medina

Corredor Panoramico (Panoramic Hwy.)

*Bahía de
Mujeres*

Playa Tiburón

Playa Lancheros

KEY

Ferry

0   1/2 mile

0   1/2 kilometer

**Santuario
Maya a la
Diosa Ixchel**

Punta Sur

lunch at Playa Tiburón. Finish your tour with a sunset cocktail at Playa Norte before heading downtown for dinner and live music.

■TIP→ To learn more about the history of Isla's famous sites, check out Hear & There, an audio tour available for checkout at Casa el Pio.

TOP ATTRACTIONS

El Garrafón National Park. Despite participation in the much-publicized "Garrafón Reef Restoration Program," much of the coral reef at this national marine park remains dead (the result of hurricanes, boat anchors, and too many careless tourists). There are still colorful fish, but many of them will only come near if bribed with food. Although there's no longer much for snorkelers, the park does have kayaks, restaurants, bathrooms, and a gift shop. Be prepared to spend $59 for the basic package called "Garrafón Discovery," which includes gear, breakfast, lunch, a bicycle tour, transportation from Cancún, and access to a climbing tower, activities, and an open bar. An additional $5 includes zip-lining. Another option is Dolphin Discovery ($69–$129), where you can use the parks amenities and swim with dolphins or bull sharks. ■TIP→ The Beach Club Garrafón de Castilla next door is a much cheaper alternative; the snorkeling is at least equal to that available in the park. The club is open to everyone, and the entrance fee is 50 pesos. You can take a taxi from town. The park is home to the **Santuario Maya a la Diosa Ixchel,** the sad vestiges of a Mayan temple once dedicated to the goddess Ixchel. A lovely walkway around the area remains, but the natural arch beneath the ruin has been blasted open and "repaired" with concrete badly disguised as rocks. The views here are spectacular, though: you can look to the open ocean where waves crash against dramatic cliffs on one side, and the Bahía de Mujeres (Bay of Women) on the other. On the way to the temple there's a cutesy Caribbean-style shopping center selling overpriced jewelry and souvenirs, as well as a park with abstract sculptures painted in bright colors. The ruins near the old lighthouse, which are open daily 9 to 5, is at the point where the road turns northeast into the Corredor Panorámico. To visit just the ruins and sculpture park, the admission is $3 or is included with El Garrafón entrance fee. Admission to the village is free. ⊠ *Carretera El Garrafón, 6 km (3¾ mi), Mza 41, Lote 12, Sm 9, Punta Sur, southeast of Playa Lancheros* ☎ *998/877–1100 or 998/193–3360* ⊕ *www.garrafon. com* ⊠ *Tours from Cancún $69; tours from Isla $59* ☉ *Daily 10–5. Closed Sat. Dec., Jan., June, and July.*

OFF THE BEATEN PATH

When exploring the southeastern tip of Isla Mujeres, be sure to visit the unique seashell-shape house located on Corredor Panorámico. Owned by artist Octavio Ocampo, the house is far from traditional, with both the interior and exterior resembling an enormous conch shell.

Iglesia de Concepción Inmaculada *(Church of the Immaculate Conception).* In 1890 local fishermen landed at a deserted colonial settlement known as Ecab, where they found three identical statues of the Virgin Mary,

Who Was Ixchel?

Ixchel (ee-*shell*) is a principal figure in the pantheon of Mayan gods. Originally married to the earth god Voltan, Ixchel fell in love with the moon god Itzamna, considered the founder of the Maya because he taught them how to read, write, and grow corn. When Ixchel became his consort, she gave birth to four powerful sons known as the Bacabs, who continue to hold up the sky in each of the four directions. Sometimes called Lady Rainbow, Ixchel is the goddess of childbirth, fertility, and healing. She controls the tides and all water on earth.

Often portrayed as a wise crone, she is seen wearing a skirt decorated with crossbones and a crown of serpents while carrying a jug of water. The crossbones are a symbol of her role as the giver of new life and keeper of dead souls. The serpents represent her wisdom and power to rejuvenate. The water jug alludes to her dual role as both a benign and destructive deity. Although she gives mankind the continual gift of water—the most essential element of life—according to Mayan myth, Ixchel also sent floods to cleanse the earth of wicked men who had stopped thanking the gods. She is said to give special protection to those making the sacred pilgrimage to her sites on Cozumel and Isla Mujeres.

each carved from wood with porcelain face and hands. No one knows for certain where the statues originated, but it's widely believed that they were gifts from the Spanish during a visit in 1770. One statue went to the city of Izamal in the Yucatán, and another was sent to Kantunikin in Quintana Roo. The third remained on the island. It was housed in a small wooden chapel while this church was being built; legend has it that the chapel burst into flames when the statue was removed. Some islanders still believe the statue walks on the water around the island from dusk until dawn, looking for her sisters. You can pay your respects daily from 10 am until 11:30 am and then from 7 pm until 9 pm. ⊠ *Avs. Morelos and Bravo, south side of the zócalo.*

NEED A BREAK? It's a small island, but there are several small shops selling gelato.

Cool Gelato (⊠ *Av. Hidalgo next to Plaza Los Almendros* ☎ *998/167–6351*) has more than a dozen flavors, and is the only island gelateria to make 100% natural ice cream.

Isla Mujeres Underwater Museum. Combining art and nature, Sculptor Jason de Caires Taylor has created "underwater museums" off the shores of Punta Cancún, Punta Nizuc, and Isla Mujeres at Manchones Reef. His main work features more than 400 lifelike statues that serve as artificial reefs to attract marine life. The displays have conveniently been placed in shallow areas for viewing by divers, snorkelers, and glass-bottom boats. Acting as a restoration project, this new artificial habitat also helps restore the natural reefs that have suffered damage over the years. ⊠ *Punta Cancún, Punta Nizuc, and Manchones Reef in Isla Mujeres Cancún and Isla Mujeres* ☎ *998/192–1189* ⊕ *www.underwatersculpture.com* ⊠ *Free.*

☺ **Tortugranja** *(Turtle Farm).* This scientific station is run by the Mexican government in partnership with private funding. Its mission is to continue conservation efforts on behalf of the endangered sea turtle. You can see rescued turtle hatchlings in three large pools or watch the larger turtles in sea pens. There's also a small museum with an excellent display about turtles and the ecosystem. From May through October you can make arrangements to join the staff in collecting and hatching eggs, and in the fall you can assist in releasing the baby turtles. ⊠ *Take Av. Rueda Medina south of town; about a block southeast of Hacienda Mundaca, take right fork (smaller road that loops back north called Sac Bajo); entrance is about ½ km (¼ mi) farther, on left* ☎ *998/888–0705* ☜ *$3* ⊘ *Daily 9–5.*

4

WORTH NOTING

El Cementerio. Isla's unnamed cemetery, with its century-old colorful gravestones, is on Avenida López Mateos, the road that runs parallel to Playa Norte. Many of the tombstones are covered with carved angels and flowers; the most elaborate and beautiful mark the graves of children. Hidden among them is the tomb of the notorious Fermín Mundaca de Marechaja. This 19th-century slave trader—who's often billed more glamorously as a pirate—carved his own skull-and-crossbones gravestone with the ominous epitaph: "As you are, I once was; as I am, so shall you be." Mundaca's grave is empty, however; his remains lie in Mérida, where he died. The monument is tough to find—ask a local to point out the unidentified marker.

Laguna Makax. Pirates are said to have anchored their ships in this lagoon while waiting to ambush hapless vessels crossing the Spanish Main (the area in which Spanish treasure ships sailed). These days the lagoon houses a local shipyard and provides a safe harbor for boats during hurricane season. It's off Avenida Rueda Medina, about 2½ km (1½ mi) south of town, about two blocks south of the naval base and some *salinas* (salt marshes).

BEACHES

Despite the fact the island is surrounded by water, there are actually only three beaches suitable for visitors—Playa Norte, Playa Lancheros, and Playa Tiburón. The crystal-clear north beaches are generally tranquil and better for swimming than eastern beaches facing the Caribbean. Susceptible to strong winds and riptides, those facing east are rough, rocky, and have very little sand. They're also barren, windswept, and not very good for swimming or sunbathing.

The south island has several secluded beaches, but they too are dangerous due to exposed reefs and strong currents. Seldom are they groomed, which means that sea grass and debris often wash ashore. Despite their inaccessibility, both east- and south-facing beaches have a wild beauty of their own.

In 2008, high winds and stormy seas stole nearly 30 yards of Isla's sandy beaches. In fact, many say the beaches never fully recovered from

A GOOD WALK

You can walk to Isla's historic **Cementerio** by going northwest from the ferry piers on Avenida López Mateos. Then head southeast (by vehicle) along Avenida Rueda Medina, to reach the Mexican naval base, where you can see flag ceremonies at sunrise and sunset. (Just don't take any pictures—it's illegal to photograph military sites.) Continue southeast to **Laguna Makax** on your right.

At the lagoon's southeast end, a dirt road on the left leads to the remains of the **Hacienda Mundaca**. About a block west, where Avenida Rueda Medina splits, is a statue of Ramón Bravo, Isla's first environmentalist. If you turn right (northwest), you'll reach Playa Tiburón and the

Tortugranja (turtle farm). If you turn left (southwest), you'll see Playa Lancheros. Both are good swimming beaches.

Continue southeast past Playa Lancheros to **El Garrafón National Park**. Slightly farther along the same road, on the windward side of the tip of Isla, is the site of the former temple dedicated to the goddess Ixchel. Although little remains, the ocean views are still worth the stop. Follow the paved eastern perimeter road northwest, past a huge seashell-shape house, back into town. Known as either the Corredor Panorámico (Panoramic Highway) or Carretera Perimetral al Garrafón (Garrafón Perimeter Highway), this is a scenic drive with a few pull-off areas.

Hurricane Wilma in 2005. The local government is slowly working to replenish sand and is taking other measures to restore the island's stunning beaches.

★ **Playa Norte (North Beach)** is easy to find: simply head north on any of the north–south streets in town until you hit this superb beach. The turquoise sea is as calm as a lake here, though developers have arrived on the scene and the area no longer has a secluded feel. The small cove between Avalon Reef Club and the Caribbean is the nicest section of Playa Norte. Although relatively shallow, the water flows directly from the open sea, making this protected area cool and clean. Play a game of beach volleyball, or enjoy a drink at one of the area's palapa bars, where wooden swings take the place of bar stools; **Buho's** is especially popular with locals and tourists who gather to chat, eat fresh seafood, drink cold beer, and watch the sunset. Lounge chairs and hammocks at **Sergio's** are free for customers, but to relax in front of **Maria del Maria** in a lounge chair will cost you $3. **Na Balam** charges a whopping $10 for one chair and umbrella. **Best For:** swimming, kayaking, relaxing, beach volleyball. **Amenities:** toilets, umbrellas, and chaise lounges available at beach bars.

There are two beaches between Laguna Makax and El Garrafón National Park.

Playa Lancheros (Boatman's Beach) is a popular spot with an open-air restaurant where locals gather to eat freshly grilled fish. The beach has grittier sand than Playa Norte, but more palm trees. The calm water makes it the perfect spot for children—although it's best if they stay close to shore, since the ocean floor drops off steeply. The souvenir stands,

CLOSE UP

Isla's History

The name Isla Mujeres means "Island of Women," although no one knows who dubbed it that. Many believe it was the ancient Maya, who were said to use the island as a religious center for worshipping Ixchel, the Mayan goddess of rainbows, the moon, and the sea, and the guardian of fertility and childbirth. Another popular legend has it that the Spanish conquistador Hernández de Córdoba named the island when he landed here in 1517 and found hundreds of female-shape clay idols dedicated to Ixchel and her daughters. Others say the name dates later, from the 17th century, when visiting pirates stashed their women on Isla before heading out to rob the high seas. (Legend has it that both Henry Morgan and Jean Lafitte buried treasure on Isla, although no one has ever found any pirate's gold.)

It wasn't until after 1821, when Mexico became independent, that people really began to settle on Isla. In 1847 refugees from the War of the Castes fled to the island and built its first official village of Dolores—which was welcomed into the newly created territory of Quintana Roo in 1850. By 1858 a slave trader–turned-pirate named Fermín Mundaca de Marechaja began building an estate on Isla, which took up 40% of the island. By the end of the century the population had risen to 651, and residents had begun to establish trade—mostly by supplying fish to the owners of chicle and coconut plantations on the mainland coast. In 1949 the Mexican navy built a base on Isla's northwestern coast; around this time, the island also caught the eye of some wealthy Mexican sportsmen, who began using it as a vacation spot.

Tourism flourished on Isla during the later half of the 20th century, partly due to the island's most famous resident, Ramón Bravo (1927–98). A diver, cinematographer, ecologist, and colleague of Jacques Cousteau, Bravo was the first underwater photographer to explore the area. He discovered the now-famous Cave of the Sleeping Sharks and produced dozens of underwater documentaries for American, European, and Mexican television. Bravo's efforts to maintain the ecology on Isla has helped keep development here to a minimum. Even today, Bravo remains a hero to many *isleños* (ees-*lay*-nyos); his statue can be found where Avenida Rueda Medina changes into the Carretera El Garrafón, and there's a museum named after him on nearby Isla Contoy.

renting kayaks, canoes, and beach toys, are fairly low-key and run by local families. Most bars and restaurants will give you access to beach chairs, umbrellas, and facilities provided you order a drink. There's a small pen with domesticated and quite harmless *tiburones gatos*—nurse sharks. (These sharks are much friendlier than the *tintoreras*, or blue sharks, which live in the open seas, have seven rows of teeth, and weigh up to 1,100 pounds.) You can swim with the nurse sharks or get your picture taken with them for $1. **Best For:** snorkeling, families with children. **Amenities:** toilets, food concessions, umbrellas, beach chairs.

Playa Tiburón (Shark Beach), like Playa Lancheros, is on the west coast facing Bahía de Mujeres, and so its waters are also exceptionally calm. It's a more developed beach, with a large, popular seafood restaurant

Relaxing under an umbrella on Playa Norte.

(through which you actually enter the beach), serving burgers, hot dogs, and fish. There are several souvenir stands selling the usual T-shirts as well as handmade seashell jewelry. On certain days there are women who will braid your hair or give you a henna tattoo. This beach also has two sea pens with the sleepy and relatively tame nurse sharks. Swim with them for $2. **Best For:** snorkeling, swimming, sunbathing. **Amenities:** food concessions, toilets at restaurants.

WHERE TO EAT

Dining on Isla is a casual affair. Restaurants tend to serve simple meals: seafood, pizza, salads, and Mexican dishes, mostly prepared by local cooks. Fresh ingredients and hospitable waiters make up for the island's lack of elaborate menus and master chefs. It's cash-only in most of the restaurants.

Though informal, most indoor restaurants do require that you wear a shirt and shoes when dining. Some outdoor terrace and palapa restaurants also request that you wear shoes and some sort of cover-up over your bathing suit.

It's customary in Mexico for the waiter not to bring you the bill until you ask for it (*"la cuenta, por favor"*). Always check your bill to make sure you didn't get charged for something you didn't order, and to make sure the addition is correct. The "tax" on the bill is often a service charge—kind of a guaranteed tip.

CLOSE UP

Islas Salt Mines

The ancient salt mines, remains of which still exist in Isla's interior, were constructed during the postclassic period of Mayan history, which lasted roughly between the years AD 1000 and 1500. Salt was an important commodity for the Maya; they used it not only for preserving and flavoring food, but for creating battle armor. Since the Maya had no metal, they soaked cotton cloth in salt until it formed a hard coating—innovative, to say the least.

Today the shallow marshes where salt was long ago harvested bear modern names: Salina Chica (small salt mine) and Salina Grande (large salt mine). Unfortunately there's little to see at the salt mines today. They're simply shallow marshes with murky water and quite a few mosquitoes at dusk. Since both of the island's main roads (Avenida Rueda Medina and the Corredor Panorámico) pass by them, however, you can have a look at them on your way to visiting other parts of Isla.

EL PUEBLO

¢ ✕**Los Aluxes Cafe**. The perfect spot for an early-morning or late-night
CAFÉ cappuccino (it opens at 7 am and closes at 10 pm), this place also has terrific desserts, smoothies, and baked goods. The New York–style cheesecake and triple-fudge brownies are especially decadent. There's also a great selection of exotic teas and locally made jewelry for sale. If you want the café's famous banana bread, get here early—the loaves usually sell out by 10 am. ⊠ *Av. Matamoros 87* ☎ *998/218–5843* ▭ *No credit cards* ⊘ *Closed Tues.* ✛ *B4.*

$$ ✕**Amigos**. This authentic isleño eatery really lives up to its name; once
ECLECTIC you've settled at one of the street-side tables, the staff treats you like an old friend. The friendly vibe makes Amigos a favorite among locals, so you can expect a taste of real island life. Though it used to be known mainly for its superb pizza, the restaurant serves excellent fish, meat, and vegetarian dishes as well. The fish baked in sea salt is a good bet, as are desserts like the rich chocolate cake or flambéed crepes. ⊠ *Av. Hidalgo 19, between Avs. Matamoros and Abasolo* ☎ *998/877–0624.* ✛ *C4.*

$$$ ✕**Angelo**. Named for Angelo Sanna, its Italian chef, this charming bis-
ITALIAN tro is done up with soft lighting and a wood-fired oven. The pizzas are decent, but the meat dishes are even tastier. Try their famous wood-oven lasagna or mussels steamed in white wine. Angelo, who has lived and worked in Isla Mujeres for more than 15 years, is also a great source of local information. ⊠ *Av. Hidalgo 14* ☎ *998/877–1273* ✛ *B4.*

$$ ✕**L'Argentina Grill**. As famous for its location as it is for its food, this
ARGENTINE boisterous restaurant offers both Mexican and Argentine dishes. There are more than 150 entrées on the menu, including ostrich, lamb, wild boar, filet mignon, and honey-glazed quail. For a sample platter, try the Argentine Grill for Two. Portions are huge and revolve around meat, so this isn't a great choice for vegetarians. Dinner comes with a free bottle of house wine. For a quiet table away from the lively streets, head indoor to the restaurant's lounge bar that's open until 2 am. ⊠ *Corner*

of *Av. Hidalgo and Matamoros, El Pueblo* ☎ *998/877–1560 or 998/100–0431* ✛ *B4.*

$$
ECLECTIC
✕ **Bamboo.** This casual restaurant, with its bamboo-covered ceilings, offers seafood, steak, and Mexican dishes The chef cooks up hearty steaks, tacos, and Asian-fusion-style lunches and dinners, including knockout shrimp tempura, vegetable stir-fry, and chicken satay in a spicy peanut sauce. Two-for-one drink specials start at 3 pm. During high season live music attracts locals who linger until around midnight. ⊠ *Plaza Los Almendros No. 4* ☎ *998/877–1355* ✛ *B4.*

$
CAFÉ
✕ **Café Cito.** This cheery, seashell-decorated café was opened in 1988 as one of Isla's first cafés—and it's still one of the best places to breakfast on the island. The breakfast menu

includes fresh waffles, fruit-filled crepes, and egg dishes, as well as great cappuccino and espresso. Every breakfast comes with complimentary coffee or tea. Lunch specials are also available daily. ⊠ *Avs. Juárez and Matamoros* ☎ *998/877–1470* ▤ *No credit cards* ☾ *No dinner* ✛ *B4.*

$$
MEXICAN
✕ **Don Chepo.** Mexican-style grilled meats (tacos, fajitas, and steaks) are the draw at this lively restaurant that resembles a small hacienda. Inside, the focal point is the large and well-stocked bar where you can chat with other visitors or enjoy the (sometimes live) mariachi music. Tables outside are perfect for watching all the downtown action on Hidalgo Street. The *arrachera*, a fine cut of beef grilled to perfection and served with rice, salad, baked potato, warm tortillas, and beans, is a reliably excellent choice as is the chile relleno. ⊠ *Avs. Hidalgo and Francisco Madero* ☎ *998/877–0165* ✛ *C4.*

$$$
MEXICAN
✕ **Fayne's.** The vibe at this brightly painted spot is hip and energetic. Best known for its terrific cocktails (don't miss the mango margaritas), this funky restaurant serves good island fare such as garlic shrimp, ceviche enchiladas, calamari stuffed with seafood and spinach, and grilled snapper. There's live music nightly starting at 10:30. ⊠ *Av. Hidalgo 12A, between Avs. Mateos and Matamoros* ☎ *998/877–0528* ✛ *B4.*

$$
MEXICAN
✕ **Fredy's Restaurant & Bar.** This family-run restaurant specializes in simple fish, seafood, and traditional Mexican dishes like fajitas and oven-baked shrimp. They also serve shish kebabs, soups, salads, and whole fried fish. There isn't much here in the way of decor—they use plastic chairs and tables—but the staff is wonderfully friendly, the food is fresh, and the beer is cold. The tasty daily specials are a bargain and attract both locals and visitors. ⊠ *Av. Hidalgo just below Av. Mateos* ☎ *998/877–1339* ⊕ *fredys.myislamujeres.com* ☾ *Closed Tues.* ✛ *B4.*

Dining on the island is a casual and friendly affair.

$$ ✕ **Jax Bar & Grill.** The downstairs of this hot spot is a lively sports bar
ECLECTIC that serves huge, thick, perfectly grilled burgers and with cold beer. If
☺ you're not in the mood for a burger, you can choose from more than
70 items on the menu, including fish tacos, corn dogs, and filet mignon.
The satellite TV is always turned to the big game, and there's a table for
those who want to shoot some pool. Upstairs is a terrace where you can
enjoy dishes like fresh grilled seafood and the house "bucket of beer"
(five Coronas for $6) while watching the sunset. The friendly staff caters
to kids, and is often able to procure their favorite dishes, even if they
aren't on the menu. ⊠ *Av. Adolfo Mateos 42* ☎ *998/887–1218* ⊕ *www.
jaxsportfishing.com* ✛ *A4.*

$ ✕ **Loncheria La Lomita.** Don't judge a restaurant by its setting. This hole
MEXICAN in the wall, with its red plastic tables and chairs, pleases everyone who
Fodor's Choice eats here. Prepare yourself for enormous portions beginning with the
★ bean soup made with onions, tomatoes, lime and *queso fresco* (fresh
cheese). If you only try one dish, make it the chile relleno. These stuffed
chiles are lightly battered and fried and served with a side of pickled
cabbage and rice. Moist and flavorful, fish fillets are cooked in a bed of
oil and herbs and wrapped in a sheet of foil. Bring an appetite and an
open mind since you'll most likely be tasting the best Mexican food of
your life. ⊠ *Av Juarez Sur No. 25-B, El Pueblo* ☎ *998/186–1813* ▬ *No
credit cards* ⊗ *Closed Sun.* ✛ *D5.*

$$–$$$ ✕ **Mama Rosa.** In the heart of downtown, this Italian restaurant is the
ITALIAN newest and most upscale eatery to join the string of island proper-
ties. Despite its catchy name, the place is run by Italian owner and
chef, Rebecca, whose menu blends Italian and Caribbean cuisine with
such dishes as the "diamante" (pizza topped with lobster, basil, and

mozzarella). The spinach-and-ricotta tortellini is a pasta favorite, but it's the meat dishes—like Angus beef and broiled lamb—that keep people coming back for more. Although the outdoor seating is limited to a few tables, the exposed dining area is extremely charming, with arched ceilings, yellow walls, and black-and-white photographs. Don't leave without sampling the homemade tiramisu. ⊠ *Av. Hidalgo at Matamoros Centro, Downtown* ☎ *998/713–1900* ⊗ *No lunch* ✛ *B4.*

$
CAFÉ
✕ **Mañana Restaurant & Bookstore.** It's hard to miss this bright fuchsia restaurant with a yellow sun stretching its rays over the front door. But you won't want to miss the great breakfasts, with excellent egg dishes, fresh baguettes, and Italian coffee. Salads, homemade burgers (meat or vegetarian), and fresh fruit shakes are served at lunch. If you're in a hurry, you can grab a quick snack like their falafel and hummus at the outdoor counter with its palapa roof, but since Cosmic Cosas bookstore is also here, you may want to lounge on the couch and read after your meal. ⊠ *Av. Guerrero 17* ☎ *998/877–0555* ▭ *No credit cards* ⊗ *Closed Sun. No dinner* ✛ *C4.*

$$
MEDITERRANEAN
Fodor'sChoice
★
✕ **Olivia.** The delightful dishes at this Mediterranean restaurant are fusions of Moroccan, Greek, and Turkish flavors based on owners Lior and Yaron Zelzer's old family recipes. Everything from the freshly baked spanakopita to the flaky baklava is made from scratch in the open-air kitchen. Start with the Greek or Moroccan tapas and move onto house favorites like the *shawarma* pita wrap filled with grilled chicken, hummus, tahini, and fried eggplant, or the *mafrum* (a blend of potatoes stuffed with ground beef in a Moroccan red sauce). The setting is casual yet romantic, with tiki torches lighting the way to a tropical garden where rustic tables sit beneath a palapa roof. A visit to Oliva's isn't complete without a bowl of homemade cherry ice cream. ⊠ *Av. Matamoros between Juárez and Medina, El Pueblo* ☎ *998/877–1765* ⊕ *www.olivia-isla-mujeres.com* ▭ *No credit cards* ⊗ *Closed Sun. and Mon. No lunch* ✛ *B4.*

$
ECLECTIC
✕ **El Patio.** With its sandy floors, rooftop terrace, and smooth jazz, this low-key eatery is a peaceful oasis in the heart of El Pueblo's action. Chit palms and ocean grape trees decorate the open-air restaurant, each branch wrapped in fairy lights and adorned with seashell lanterns. House specialties like T-bone steak and shrimp wrapped in prosciutto are smoked over a bed of coals and served with grilled vegetables and a baked potato. The menu features more than 20 vegetarian dishes including a tofu pâté, soy burgers, and a spinach salad. A complimentary glass of house wine is served with dinner; you can also go for El Patio's two-for-one margaritas. ⊠ *Av. Hidalgo 17, El Pueblo* ☎ *998/877–1457* ⊗ *Closed Sun.* ✛ *C4.*

NOT ALL BEACHES ARE FOR SWIMMING!

Although the beaches on the eastern side of the island (often referred to as the Caribe side) are quite beautiful, they're not safe for swimming because of the dangerous undertows; several drownings have occurred at these beaches. Another gorgeous but dangerous beach is found northeast, just kitty-corner to Playa Norte. **Playa Media Luna** (Half Moon beach) is very tempting, but the strong currents make it treacherous for swimmers.

$$ ✕**Picus Cocktelería**. Kick off your shoes and settle back with a cold beer
SEAFOOD at this charming beachside restaurant right near the ferry docks. You
can watch the fishing boats come and go while you wait for some of
the freshest seafood on the island. The grilled fish and grilled lobster
with garlic butter are both magnificent, as are the shrimp fajitas—but
the real showstopper is the mixed seafood ceviche, which might include
conch, shrimp, abalone, fish, or octopus. ⊠ *Av. Rueda Medina, 1 block
northwest of ferry docks* ☎ *998/274–0083* ⌖ *B5.*

$ ✕**Qubano**. One of the main draws to this delightful Cuban restaurant is
CUBAN its vivacious owner and chef, Vivian Reynaldo. Her Hungarian potatoes
Fodor'sChoice (a recipe from her mother) have been known to leave customers speech-
★ less. Many of the grilled sandwiches, like the "Toston," creatively use
fried plantain instead of bread. Try the juicy hamburger stuffed with
goat cheese and served with yucca fries. Salads are topped with the
freshest ingredients, like garbanzo beans, avocado, and jicama. There
are also several vegetarian dishes as well as fresh-squeezed juices—
the watermelon is divine. The simple setting, with four tables inside a
turquoise-color shack, is cozy, pleasant, and welcoming. ⊠ *Av. Abasolo
between Hidalgo and Vicente Guerrero* ☎ *998/214–2118* ▭ *No credit
cards* ☽ *Closed weekends. No dinner* ⌖ *C4.*

$ ✕**Sergio's Playa Sol**. Delicious chicken nachos, creamy guacamole, and
MEXICAN savory fish kebabs are on the menu at this great beach bar at Playa
Norte. You can easily spend the whole day here and stay for the sunset;
there are free hammocks, beach chairs, and umbrellas for customers.
The kitchen closes at 5 pm. ⊠ *North end of Rueda Medina on Playa
Norte* ☎ *998/130–1924* ▭ *No credit cards* ⌖ *A4.*

$$$ ✕**Sunset Grill**. The perfect place to savor the sunset, this spot has a cov-
SEAFOOD ered dining terrace with large picture windows that overlook the sea. Soft
★ music and candlelight add to the romantic ambience. Grab a table outside
and you can take a dip in the ocean between your appetizer and main
course. The dinner menu has a wide range of dishes, including favorites
like grilled tuna steak, coconut shrimp, and Parmesan-crusted fish fillet.
The kitchen offers a lunch of Mexican favorites like tacos and quesadil-
las, but also fries up a great burger. Service is very good, and there's live
music nightly. ⊠ *Av. Rueda Medina, North End, Condominios Nauti-
beach, Playa Norte* ☎ *998/877–0785* ⊕ *www.sunsetgrill.com.mx* ⌖ *A4.*

$$ ✕**Zazil Ha**. At this beachside restaurant (meaning "clear water" in
MEXICAN Mayan), you can dine downstairs under big, shady palms or upstairs
under a palapa roof. Homemade breads, yogurt, and granola make
breakfast a treat. Later in the day the kitchen serves innovative veg-
etarian fare—like salads with avocado and grapefruit, or with coconut,
mango, and mint vinaigrette—as well as traditional Mexican dishes. The
chicken with cilantro sauce is especially good. Musicians from Mexico,
Cuba, and the Caribbean often play during the weekends. ⊠ *Na Balam
Hotel, Calle Zazil-Ha 118* ☎ *998/881–4770* ⊕ *www.nabalam.com* ⌖ *B2.*

ELSEWHERE ON THE ISLAND

$ ✕**Bistro Français**. This casual café, with menu items painted on the walls in
FRENCH bright colors, serves up tasty French dishes at reasonable prices. Breakfast
is particularly nice, with tasty fruit salads and practically perfect waffles.

Later on in the day, try French dishes like chicken *cordon bleu* or coq au vin. The deck overlooks the street, so you can watch the world go by. ⊠ *Av. Matamoros 29* 🕾 *No phone* 🖃 *No credit cards*.

$$$
ECLECTIC
Fodor's Choice
★

✕ **Casa Rolandi.** This hotel restaurant is casually sophisticated, with an open-air dining room leading out to a deck that overlooks the water. Tables are set with beautiful linens, china, and cutlery. The northern Italian menu here includes the wonderful carpaccio *di tonno alla Giorgio* (thin slices of tuna with extra-virgin olive oil and lime juice), along with excellent pastas—even the simplest dishes, such as angel-hair pasta in tomato sauce, are delicious. For something different, try the saffron risotto or the *costolette d'agnello al forno* (lamb chops with a thyme infusion). The sunset views are spectacular. ⊠ *Hotel Villa Rolandi, Fracc. Laguna Mar, Sm 7, Mza 75, Lotes 15 and 16* 🕾 *998/999–2000* ✛ *C1.*

$
MEXICAN

✕ **Playa Lancheros Restaurant.** If you want to savor one of the island's most authentic meals, take a short taxi ride to this casual eatery under a big palapa roof. It's right on the beach, so it's no surprise that the kitchen takes pride in serving the freshest fish. The house specialty is the Yucatecan *tikinchic* (fish marinated in a sour-orange sauce and cooked in a banana leaf over an open flame). There are also delicious tacos, fresh guacamole, and spicy salsa. The food (served 10 am to 7 pm) may take a while to arrive, so bring your swimsuit and take a dip while you wait. On Sunday there's music, dancing, and the occasional shark wrestler. ⊠ *Playa Lancheros where Av. Rueda Medina splits into Sac Bajo and Carretera El Garrafón* 🕾 *998/274–0018.*

WHERE TO STAY

Many of the smaller hotels on the island don't accept credit cards, and some add a 10% surcharge if you use one. Isla has also been tightening up its cancellation policy, so check with your hotel about surcharges for changing reservations. ■ TIP→ Before paying, always ask to see your room to make sure everything is satisfactory—especially at the smaller hotels.

A growing number of Isla hotels are now encouraging people to make their reservations online. Some allow you to book rooms right on their Web sites, but even hotels without their own sites usually offer reservations via online booking agencies, such as ⊕ *www.docancun.com* and ⊕ *www.lostoasis.net.* ■ TIP→ Be sure to ask whether construction is taking place nearby; it's often the reason a hotel lowers its rates, but the savings may not be worth the disruption.

Booking online is certainly convenient, and can often get you a 10% to 20% discount on room rates. The bad news, though, is that there may be an occasional breakdown in communication between a booking agency and a hotel. ■ TIP→ If you do end up booking online, be sure to print out copies of all your Internet transactions, including receipts and confirmations, and bring them with you.

For expanded hotel reviews, visit Fodors.com.

EL PUEBLO

$-$$
★
Los Arcos. In the heart of downtown, this hotel is a terrific value. The comfortable suites are all cheerfully decorated with Mexican-style furnishings. Each has a small kitchenette with a microwave and fridge, a fully tiled bathroom with great water pressure, a small sitting area, and a king-size bed. The large and sunny balconies on the front have views of the street, whereas those at the back are more private. The pleasant and helpful staff is an added bonus. The hotel management encourages online booking. **Pros:** reasonable rates; spacious rooms; near restaurants and shops. **Cons:** some linens feel worn; sparse furnishings; no elevator. **TripAdvisor:** "clean cheap brilliant," "nice and close to everything," "clean and convenient." ⊠ *Av. Hidalgo 58, across from Amigos restaurant between Abasolo and Matamoros* ☎ *998/877–1343* ⊕ *www.suites-los-arcos.myislamujeres.com* ➭ *12 rooms* ⌂ *In-room: a/c, Wi-Fi, kitchen* ⊙ *No meals* ✦ *C4.*

$$-$$$
Avalon Reef Club. This all-inclusive resort sits on a tiny island at the northern tip of Isla Mujeres. **Pros:** beautiful location; calm bay; all-inclusive meal plan available. **Cons:** constant sales pitches; some rooms lack views. **TripAdvisor:** "great beach snorkeling area right on site," "perfect sunset or sunrise," "this hotel could do a whole lot better." ⊠ *Calle Zazcil-Ha s/n 7, Isla Yunque* ☎ *998/999–2050* ⊕ *www.avalonvacations.com* ➭ *74 rooms, 6 suites, 49 villas* ⌂ *In-room: a/c, kitchen (some). In-hotel: restaurants, pool, gym, spa, beach* ⊙ *Multiple meal plans* ✦ *B1.*

$
Fodor's Choice
★
Casa el Pio. Off the town square, this boutique hotel—owned by a graphic designer and hair stylist—is bursting with character, charm, and creativity. It's ideally suited for independent travelers who don't require 24-hour service, but appreciate value, comfort, and modern design. Inspired by the owners' trips to Greece, the property is stark white with hints of aqua. The sound of crashing waves can be heard from every room, each with its own reading nook, kitchenette, and lounge area with an extra daybed. There's also a small plunge pool and courtyard where guests can enjoy an evening cocktail. **Pros:** unlimited fresh drinking water; spotless property; MP3 audio tour available detailing sites of Isla Mujeres. **Cons:** no restaurant; no housekeeping on Sunday; lacks 24-hour service. **TripAdvisor:** "within walking distance of the beach and many fine restaurants," "rooms were sparse and had everything you needed," "almost like staying with your friends." ⊠ *Av. Hidalgo between Bravo and Allende* ☎ *998/229–2799* ⊕ *www.casaelpio.com* ➭ *4 rooms* ⌂ *In-room: a/c, no TV, Wi-Fi. In-hotel: pool, beach, some age restrictions* ▭ *No credit cards* ⊙ *No meals* ✦ *D4.*

$-$$
Hotel Belmar. This hacienda-style hotel has cozy rooms that are cheerfully decorated with flowers, plants, and Mexican artwork. **Pros:** clean and comfortable; near shops and restaurants. **Cons:** some street noise; no elevator. ⊠ *Av. Hidalgo Norte 110, between Avs. Madero and Abasolo* ☎ *998/877–0430* ⊕ *www.rolandi.com* ➭ *10 rooms, 1 suite* ⌂ *In-room: a/c* ⊙ *Breakfast* ✦ *C4.*

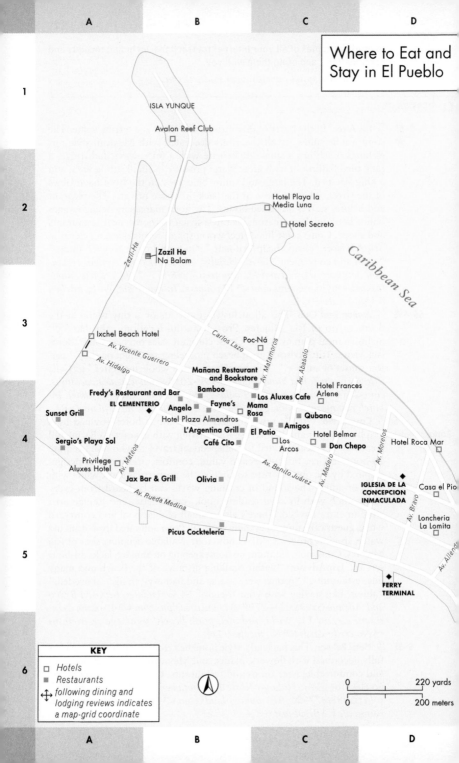

Where to Eat and Stay in El Pueblo

A   B   C   D

1

ISLA YUNQUE

Avalon Reef Club □

2

Hotel Playa la Media Luna □
□ Hotel Secreto

Caribbean Sea

Zazil Ha
Na Balam ■

3

□ Ixchel Beach Hotel
Av. Vicente Guerrero
Carlos Lazo
Poc-Ná □
Av. Matamoros
Av. Abasolo
Av. Hidalgo

Mañana Restaurant and Bookstore ■
Bamboo ■
Hotel Frances Arlene □
Fredy's Restaurant and Bar ■
EL CEMENTERIO ◆
Angelo ■   Fayne's ■   Los Aluxes Cafe ■
Mama Rosa ■
Sunset Grill ■
Hotel Plaza Almendros   Qubano ■
L'Argentina Grill ■   Amigos ■
El Patio ■
Sergio's Playa Sol ■   Café Cito ■   Los Arcos □   Hotel Belmar □
Don Chepo ■
Hotel Roca Mar □

4

Av. Mateos
Privilege Aluxes Hotel □
Jax Bar & Grill ■   Olivia ■
Av. Benito Juárez
Av. Madero
Av. Morelos
Av. Bravo
IGLESIA DE LA CONCEPCION INMACULADA ◆
Casa el Pio □
Av. Rueda Medina

Loncheria La Lomita □
Av. Allende

Picus Cocktelería ■

5

FERRY TERMINAL ◆

KEY

6

□ *Hotels*
■ *Restaurants*
✛ *following dining and lodging reviews indicates a map-grid coordinate*

0   220 yards
0   200 meters

A   B   C   D

$-$$ **Hotel Frances Arlene**. This small hotel is a perennial favorite. **Pros:** reasonable rates; friendly staff. **Cons:** some street noise; not all rooms have balconies. **TripAdvisor:** "an absolute gem," "okay but could improve," "clean hotel for the right price." ✉ *Av. Guerrero 7* ☎ *998/877–0310* ⊕ *www.francisarlene.com* ⇆ *26 rooms* ⚬ *In-room: a/c (some), kitchen (some), no safe* ⦿ *No meals* ✛ *C4.*

$$$ **Hotel Playa la Media Luna**. This breezy palapa-roofed bed-and-breakfast lies along Half Moon Beach, just south of Playa Norte. **Pros:** rooms have balconies; nearby beach is calm and shallow. **Cons:** thin towels; no bar; lost safe key costs $50 and lost towel costs $10. ✉ *Sección Rocas, Punta Norte, Lote 9/10* ☎ *998/877–0759* ⊕ *www.playamedialuna.com* ⇆ *22 rooms* ⚬ *In-room: a/c. In-hotel: pool, beach* ⦿ *Breakfast* ✛ *C2.*

$$ **Hotel Plaza Almendros**. This little hotel is right in the center of the action, close to all the restaurants and bars on Avenida Hidalgo. **Pros:** central location; family-friendly atmosphere. **Cons:** can be noisy; basic and musty rooms. **TripAdvisor:** "pleasant and welcoming hotel," "can't say enough good things," "only complaint was the shower." ✉ *Av. Hidalgo, Lote 14* ☎ *998/877–1217* ⊕ *www.hotelplazaalmendros.com* ⇆ *39 rooms* ⚬ *In-room: a/c, Wi-Fi. In-hotel: pool, business center* ⦿ *No meals* ✛ *B4.*

$$ **Hotel Roca Mar**. You can smell, hear, and see the ocean from the simply furnished, blue-and-white guest rooms at this hotel; it's right on the eastern *malecón* (boardwalk), and is one of the few hotels on the island that overlooks the Caribbean. **Pros:** rooms are steps away from the water; friendly and helpful staff. **Cons:** glass-walled bathrooms lack privacy; air-conditioning costs $10 extra; no elevator. ✉ *Calle Nicolas Bravo and Zona Maritima* ☎ *998/877–0101* ⊕ *www.rocamar-hotel.com* ⇆ *31 rooms* ⚬ *In-room: a/c (some), no safe, no TV, Wi-Fi. In-hotel: pool, spa, beach, water sports* ⦿ *No meals* ✛ *D4.*

$$$ **Hotel Secreto**. It's beautiful. **Pros:** in-room massage and facials; pool overlooks ocean; peace and quiet. **Cons:** not good for children; books up in advance; no restaurant. **TripAdvisor:** "in a secluded location with a quiet beach and pristine pool," "pleasing to all of the senses," "comfy and gorgeous." ✉ *Sección Rocas, Lote 11, Half Moon Beach* ☎ *998/877–1039* ⊕ *www.hotelsecreto.com* ⇆ *12 rooms* ⚬ *In-room: a/c, Wi-Fi. In-hotel: bar, pool, gym, water sports, beach, parking* ⦿ *Breakfast* ✛ *C2.*

Fodor's Choice ★

$$-$$$ **Ixchel Beach Hotel**. This location—on a beach with clear, calm water—is unbeatable. **Pros:** beautiful location; reasonable rates; complimentary beach chairs. **Cons:** small pool; no meals. **TripAdvisor:** "perfect location for swimming wading and simply lounging," "operates like a small polished beach hotel," "were very pleasantly surprised." ✉ *Playa Norte, Calle Guerrero, Sm 1* ☎ *998/999–2010* ⊕ *www.ixchelbeachhotel.com* ⇆ *103 rooms* ⚬ *In-room: a/c, kitchen (some), Wi-Fi. In-hotel: restaurant, bar, pool, gym, spa, beach* ⦿ *No meals* ✛ *A3.*

$$$$ ★   **Na Balam**. Elegant without being pretentious, this tranquil hotel is a true sanctuary. **Pros:** excellent restaurant; beautiful beach; 24-hour security. **Cons:** not all rooms are on the beach; mosquitoes at night. **TripAdvisor:** "simple but elegant place," "great location but service needs improvement," "in a quiet location but still close to the center." ✉ *Calle Zazil-Ha 118* ☎ *998/881–4770* ⊕ *www.nabalam.com* ⇆ *35 rooms* ⚬ *In-*

room: a/c, no TV. In-hotel: restaurant, bar, pool, spa, beach ❤❤ Multiple meal plans ✛ B3.

¢ ▦ **Poc-Ná**. This coed youth hostel is
one of El Pueblo's best deals. **Pros:**
convivial; unbeatable price. **Cons:**
party atmosphere; rooms not that
clean. **TripAdvisor:** "if you're a
backpacker this is the place to be,"
"a great hostel," "everyone was
friendly." ✉ Av. Matamoros 15
☎ 998/877–0090 ⊕ www.pocna.
com ⤴ 187 beds, 20 campsites
♿ In-room: a/c (some), no safe, no
TV (some). In-hotel: restaurant, bar, business center ❤❤ Breakfast ✛ C3.

$$ – $$$ ▦ **Privilege Aluxes**. Perched on the sugary shores of Playa Norte, this
five-story hotel is the largest, and newest, property on the island. **Pros:**
excellent location; all-inclusive meal plan available; Wi-Fi on the beach.
Cons: some rooms have cemetery views; watered-down cocktails; small
spa; standard rooms lack tubs. **TripAdvisor:** "loved this hotel in every
way," "exactly like all the pictures," "lovely place to stay with fabulous food." ✉ Av. Adolfo Lopez Mateos ☎ 998/848–8473 ⊕ www.
privilegehotels.com ⤴ 124 rooms ♿ In-room: a/c, kitchen (some),
Wi-Fi. In-hotel: restaurants, bars, pools, gym, spa, beach, water sports,
children's programs, parking ❤❤ Multiple meal plans ✛ A4.

ELSEWHERE ON THE ISLAND

$ ▦ **Hotel & Beach Club Garrafón de Castilla**. The snorkeling at this small
family-owned hotel is better than what you're likely to experience at El
Garrafón National Park next door; the reef is less crowded, and there
are more fish. Non-hotel guests can snorkel here and use the facilities
for 50 pesos. Hotel rooms have double beds and balconies overlooking the water; some have refrigerators. Decorations are minimal, but
the overall effect is bright, cheery, and comfortable. **Pros:** one of the
best locations on the island; great for snorkeling and diving. **Cons:** taxi
ride away from downtown; no Internet. ✉ Carretera Punta Sur, Km 6
☎ 998/877–0107 ⤴ 12 rooms ♿ In-room: a/c, no safe, no TV. In-hotel:
beach, water sports ▭ No credit cards ❤❤ Breakfast.

$$$$
Fodor'sChoice
★

▦ **Hotel Villa Rolandi**. A private yacht delivers you to the hotel's lagoon
dock from Cancún's Embarcadero Marina. Each elegant suite has an
ocean view, a king-size bed (pillow menu available), and a sitting area
that leads to a balcony with a heated whirlpool bath. Italian marble
floors, vaulted ceilings, and stained-glass archways create a feeling of
decadence. Showers have six adjustable heads and can be converted into
saunas. Both the restaurant and the infinity pool overlook the Bahía de
Mujeres; a path leads down to an intimate beach. For additional pampering, try thalassotherapy, an ancient form of natural healing that uses
hot seawater, at the spa. The hotel runs on-site cooking classes and can
arrange whale-shark swimming expeditions. For the best view, ask for
a second- or third-floor room. **Pros:** attentive staff; great ocean views;

Hotel Villa Rolandi

Casa el Pio

luxurious touches like fragrant towels and bathrobes. **Cons:** expensive; pool and beach can get crowded; young children not allowed. **TripAdvisor:** "everything you could ever want or need," "feels like an Italian villa," "everything was spot on." ⊠ *Fracc. Laguna Mar, Sm 7, Mza 75, Lotes 15 and 16, Carretera Sac-Bajo* ☎ *998/999–2000* ⊕ *www.villarolandi.com* ⇆ *35 suites* ⇗ *In-room: a/c. In-hotel: restaurant, room service, pool, gym, spa, beach, water sports, some age restrictions* ⏰ *Some meals.*

$$$$ ⛱ **Isla Mujeres Palace.** At this all-inclusive hotel you can forget about ever leaving the property and take advantage of the restaurants, the beach, and the pool. The modern rooms are beige and white and built around a palapa-covered lobby. Each room has its own Jacuzzi, with either an ocean or mangrove view. The service is excellent. A three night-stay includes a tour of the island, fishing, or a snorkeling trip. In the evening there are music and dance performances. **Pros:** large pool; comfortable rooms. **Cons:** far from downtown; no children under 18. **TripAdvisor:** "intimate and romantic," "on a gorgeous island next to a beautiful reef," "room was built with upper class materials." ⊠ *Carretera Garrafón, Km 4.5, Mza 62, Sm 8* ☎ *998/999–2020, 800/346–8225 in U.S.* ⊕ *www.islamujerespalace.com* ⇆ *62 rooms* ⇗ *In-room: a/c, Wi-Fi. In-hotel: restaurant, bar, pool, spa, beach, water sports, business center, parking, some age restrictions* ⏰ *All-inclusive.*

$$–$$$ ⛱ **Villa La Bella.** Located on the eastern coast, this romantic B&B is one of the most laid-back spots on the island. Rooms have funky designs, fantastic sea views, and are equipped with king-size beds, conch-head showers, ceiling fans, and refrigerators. Spa service, food delivery (from outside restaurants), and a pool mean you don't have to leave the property unless you feel like exploring the island. There's also a large living room with wireless Internet. It's a bit of a hike to downtown, but you can arrange for a taxi or a golf-cart rental. This hotel gets lots of wind. **Pros:** welcoming owners; relaxing atmosphere; tasty breakfasts. **Cons:** taxi ride from downtown; kids under 18 not allowed. **TripAdvisor:** "totally relaxing," "very much worth it," "amazing place for an island getaway." ⊠ *Carretera Perimetral al Garrafón* ☎ *998/888–0342* ⊕ *www.villalabella.com* ⇆ *6 rooms* ⇗ *In-room: a/c (some), no TV, no phone, no safe. In-hotel: bar, pool, spa, some age restrictions* ⏰ *Breakfast.*

NIGHTLIFE

Isla Mujeres has begun to develop a healthy nightlife with a variety of clubs from which to choose. Most bars close by midnight, but the party continues at Isla's nightclubs until 2 or 3 am. The majority of venues are staggered within "downtown's" four-block radius, with a few others along Playa Norte. The distance from one to the other makes bar-hopping on foot conveniently dangerous.

GET YOUR CULTURE ON

Isleños celebrate many religious holidays and festivals in El Pueblo's zócalo, usually with live entertainment. Carnival, held annually in February, is spectacular fun. Other popular events include the springtime regattas and fishing tournaments. Founder's Day, August 17, marks the island's official founding by the Mexican government. Isla's cemetery is among the best places to mark the Día de los Muertos (Day of the Dead) on November 1. Families decorate the graves of loved ones with marigolds and their favorite objects from life, then hold all-night vigils to commemorate their lost loved ones.

BARS

La Adelita (⊠ *Av. Hidalgo Norte 12A* ☎ *998/877–0528*) is a popular spot for enjoying reggae, salsa, and Caribbean music while trying out a variety of tequilas and cigars.

Buho's (⊠ *Av. Carlos Lazo 1, at Cabanas Marina del Mar on Playa Norte* ☎ *998/877–0179* ⊘ *10 am–midnight*) has three palapa beach bars with swings and hammocks where you can pass away the day with a tropical drink or ice-cold beer. From 5 to 7, take a seat at the bar and enjoy happy-hour sunset.

Designed by renowned architect Lluís Güell, **Café del Mar** (⊠ *Av. Adolfo Lopez Mateos, at Privilege Aluxes in front of Playa Norte* ☎ *998/848–8473*) is an Ibiza-inspired beach bar that plays chill-out music by day and live music by night. The fish tacos are a perfect cerveza accompaniment.

Casa de la Cultura (⊠ *Avs. Guerrero and Abasolo* ☎ *998/877–0639*) has classes in art, music, painting, and folkloric dance year-round. It's open weekdays 9 am to 4 pm.

Jax Bar & Grill (⊠ *Av. Adolfo Mateos 42, near lighthouse* ☎ *998/887–1218* ⊘ *9 am–11 pm*) has live music, cold beer, good bar food, and satellite TV that's always turned to whatever game happens to be on at the time.

Romi's (⊠ *Av. Rueda Medina at Posada del Mar* ☎ *998/877–0044*) has happy-hour specials including piña coladas, margaritas, and cold beers. The thatched roof and swings (instead of bar stools) have made this one of the island's most festive bars for more than 25 years (open 9 am to 11 pm.

DANCE CLUBS

Bar OM (⊠ *Av. Matamoros, Lote 19, Mza 15* ☎ *998/820–4876*) is an eclectic lounge bar offering wine, organic teas, and self-serve draft-beer taps at each table. Chill out to the sounds of acid jazz, bossa nova, and reggae.

La Luna (⊠ *Av. Guerreo s/n, Centro, opposite church square* ☎ *998/704–7920*), just across from the downtown main square, is the only downtown bar that overlooks the Caribbean. There's a lovely terrace bar that serves a variety of sinful cocktails and a DJ who sets the mood with techno, reggae, and dance music. Salsa Saturdays is popular with the locals. The owners recently added a courtyard restaurant to the lively scene.

You can dance the night away with the locals at **Nitrox** (⊠ *Av. Guerrero 11* ☎ *998/887–0568*). Wednesday night is ladies' night, Friday is Latin night, and the weekend is a blend of disco, techno, and house. It's open Wednesday through Sunday from 9 pm until 3 am.

SHOPPING

Aside from seashell art and jewelry, Isla produces few local crafts. The streets are filled with souvenir shops selling cheap T-shirts, garish ceramics, and seashells glued onto a variety of objects. But amid all the junk, you may find good Mexican folk art, hammocks, textiles, and silver jewelry. Most stores are small family operations that don't take credit cards, but everyone gladly accepts American dollars. Stores that do take credit cards sometimes tack on a fee to offset the commission they must pay. Hours are generally Monday through Saturday 10 to 1 and 4 to 7, although many stores stay open during siesta hours (1 to 4).

BOOKS

Cosmic Cosas (⊠ *Av. Guerrero 17* ☎ *998/877–0555*) is the island's only English-language bookstore, and is found in **Mañana Restaurant & Bookstore**. This friendly shop offers two-for-one trades (no Harlequin romances) and rents out board games. You can have something to eat and then settle in on the couch for some reading.

CRAFTS

Artesanías Arcoiris (⊠ *Avs. Hidalgo and Juárez* ☎ *No phone*) has Mexican blankets and other handicrafts. The staffers here also braid hair. Look for Mexican ceramics and onyx jewelry at **Artesanías Lupita** (⊠ *Av. Hidalgo 13* ☎ *No phone*). Many local artists display their works at the **Artesanías Market** (⊠ *Avs. Matamoros and Arq. Carlos Lazo* ☎ *No phone*), where you can find plenty of bargains. For custom-made clothing, visit **Hortensia**—the last stall on the left after you come through the market entrance. You can choose from bright Mexican fabrics and then pick a pattern for a skirt, shirt, shorts, or a dress; Hortensia will sew it up for you within a day or two. You can also buy off-the-rack designs. **Casa del Arte Mexicano** (⊠ *Av. Hidalgo 16* ☎ *No phone*) has a large selection of Mexican handicrafts, including ceramics and silver jewelry. **De Corazón** (⊠ *Av. Abasolo between Avs. Hidalgo and Guerrero* ☎ *998/877–1211*) has a wide variety of jewelry, T-shirts, and personal-care products. **Gladys Galdamez** (⊠ *Av. Hidalgo 14* ☎ *998/877–0320*) carries Isla-designed and -manufactured clothing and accessories for both men and women, as well as bags and jewelry.

DID YOU KNOW?

Many of the sland's bars and clubs are located within downtown's four-block radius, as are many of Isla's small, alfresco dining establishments. We recommend Olivia's for dinner, and for a satisfying lunch before a day of exploring, stop by Qubano.

GROCERY STORES

For fresh produce, the **Mercado Municipal** (⊠ *Av. Guerrero Norte near post office* ☎ *No phone*) is your best bet. The Municipal Market is open daily until noon. **Mirtita Grocery** (⊠ *Av. Juárez 6, at Av. Bravo* ☎ *No phone*) is a good place to find American products like Kraft Dinner, Cheerios, and Ritz Crackers. **Super Express** (⊠ *Av. Morelos 3, in plaza* ☎ *No phone*), Isla's main grocery store, is well stocked with all the basics.

JEWELRY

Jewelry on Isla ranges from tasteful creations to junk. Bargains are available, but beware of street vendors—most of their wares, especially the amber, are fake. **Galeria de Arte Mexicano** (⊠ *Av. Guerrero No. 3 [across from the hospital]* ☎ *998/877–1272* ⊕ *www.islamujeresjewelry. com*) has fine silver, Talavera, and custom-made jewelry at amazing prices. **Gold and Silver Jewelry** (⊠ *Av. Hidalgo 58* ☎ *No phone*) specializes in precious stones such as sapphires, tanzanite, and amber in a variety of settings. **Joyería Maritz** (⊠ *Av. Hidalgo between Avs. Morelos and Francisco Madero* ☎ *998/877–0526*) sells jewelry from Taxco (Mexico's silver capital) and crafts from Oaxaca, at reasonable prices.

You can also check out the **Silver Factory** (⊠ *Avs. Juárez and Morelos* ☎ *998/877–0331*), which has a variety of designer pieces at reduced prices.

SPORTS AND THE OUTDOORS

BOATING

Searious Diving (⊠ *DigaMe Internet, Av. Guerrero between Matamoros and Abasolo* ☎ *No phone* ⊕ *www.islawhalesharks.com*) will take you into the heart of whale shark territory, where you can swim with these gentle creatures. Owner Ramon Guerrero Garcia is a professional diver who has dedicated more than 20 years to researching whale sharks. Included in the boat trip are beverages, a light snack, and snorkel gear. Tours are approximately five hours long, cost $125, and must be pre-booked online. Ramon is available to answer questions nightly from 7 to 8 at DigaMe Internet or via email at ✍ *seariousdiving@yahoo.com*.

Villa Vera Puerto Isla Mujeres (⊠ *Puerto de Abrigo, Laguna Makax* ☎ *998/ 287–3340* ⊕ *www.puertoislamujeres.com*) is a full-service marina for vessels up to 175 feet. Services include a fuel station, a 150-ton lift, customs assistance, 24-hour security, and laundry and cleaning services. Docking prices depend on the size of your boat and how long you stay. If you prefer to sleep on land, the Villa Vera Puerto Isla Mujeres resort is steps away from the docks.

CLOSE UP

In Search of the Dead

El Día de los Muertos (the Day of the Dead) is often billed as "Mexican Halloween," but it's much more than that. The festival, which takes place November 1 and November 2, is a hybrid of pre-Hispanic and Christian beliefs that honors the cyclical nature of life and death. Local celebrations are as varied as they are dynamic, often laced with warm tributes and dark humor.

To honor departed loved ones at this time of year, families and friends create *ofrendas*, altars adorned with photos, flowers, candles, liquor, and other items whose colors, smells, and potent nostalgia are meant to lure spirits back for a family reunion. The favorite foods of the deceased are also included, prepared extra spicy so that the souls can absorb the essence of these offerings. Although the ofrendas and the colorful *calaveritas* (skeletons made from sugar that are a treat for Mexican children) are common everywhere, the holiday is

observed in so many ways that a definition of it depends entirely on what part of Mexico you visit.

In a sandy Isla Mujeres cemetery, Marta, a middle-aged woman wearing a tidy pantsuit and stylish sunglasses, rests on a fanciful tomb in the late-afternoon sun. "She is my sister," Marta says, motioning toward the teal-and-blue tomb. "I painted this today." She exudes no melancholy; rather she's smiling, happy to be spending the day with her sibling.

Nearby, Juan puts the final touches—vases made from shells he's collected—on his father's colorful tomb. A glass box holds a red candle and a statue of the Virgin Mary, her outstretched arms pressing against the glass as if trying to escape the flame. "This is all for him," Juan says, motioning to his masterpiece, "because he is a good man."

—David Downing

FISHING

Captain Anthony Mendillo Jr (✉ *Av. Arq. Carlos Lazo 1* ☎ 998/877–0759) provides specialized fishing trips from December to June aboard his 41-foot vessel, the *Keen M.* He charges $1,000 for a daylong trip for four people. **Jax Sport Fishing** (✉ *Av. Adolfo Mateos 42, near lighthouse* ☎ 998/877–1218, 214/295–7104 in U.S.) offers a 29-foot custom charter boat for $850 per full day. Captain Michael has more than 20 years' experience in offshore fishing. **Sea Hawk Divers** (✉ *Av. Arq. Carlos Lazo* ☎ 998/877–1233 ⊕ *www.sea-hawk-divers.myislamujeres.com*) runs fishing trips—for barracuda, snapper, and smaller fish—that start at $350 for a half day. **Sociedad Cooperativa Turística** (✉ *Av. Rueda Medina at Contoy Pier* ☎ 998/887–0800) is a fishermen's cooperative that rents boats for a maximum of four hours and six people ($150). An island tour with lunch costs $55 per person.

Some impressive catches are to be had off the coast of the island.

SNORKELING AND SCUBA DIVING

Most area dive spots are described in detail in *Dive Mexico* magazine, available in many local shops. Coral reefs at El Garrafón National Park have suffered tremendously for a variety of factors, some unavoidable (hurricanes) and some all too avoidable (boats dropping anchors onto soft coral, a practice now outlawed). Some good snorkeling can be had near Playa Norte on the north end.

Isla is a good place for learning to dive, since the snorkeling is close to shore. Offshore, there is excellent diving and snorkeling at Xlaches (pronounced *ees*-lah-chayss) reef, due north on the way to Isla Contoy. One of Contoy's most alluring dives is the **Cave of the Sleeping Sharks,** east of the northern tip. The cave was discovered by an island fisherman, Carlos Gracía Castilla, and extensively explored by Ramón Bravo, a local diver, cinematographer, and Mexico's foremost expert on sharks. The cave is a fascinating 150-foot dive for experienced divers only.

At 30 feet to 40 feet deep and 3,300 feet off the southwestern coast, the coral reef known as **Manchones** is a good dive site. During the summer of 1994 an ecological group hoping to divert divers and snorkelers from El Garrafón commissioned the creation of a 1-ton, 9¾-foot bronze cross, which was sunk here. Named the Cruz de la Bahía (Cross of the Bay), it's a tribute to everyone who has died at sea. Another option is the Barco L-55 and C-58 dive, which takes in sunken World War II boats just 20 minutes off the coast of Isla.

CLOSE UP

Shhh . . . Dont Wake the Sharks

The underwater caverns off Isla Mujeres attract a dangerous species of shark—though nobody knows exactly why. Stranger still, once the sharks swim into the caves they enter a state of relaxed nonaggression seen nowhere else. Naturalists have two explanations, both involving the composition of the water inside the caves—it contains more oxygen, more carbon dioxide, and less salt. According to the first theory, the decreased salinity causes the parasites that plague sharks to loosen their grip, allowing the remora fish (the sharks' personal vacuum cleaner) to eat the parasites more easily. Perhaps the sharks relax in order to facilitate the cleaning, or maybe their deep state of relaxation is a side effect of having been scrubbed clean.

Another theory is that the caves' combination of freshwater and saltwater may produce euphoria, similar to the effect scuba divers experience on extremely deep dives. Whatever the sharks experience while "sleeping" in the caves, they pay a heavy price for it: a swimming shark breathes automatically and without effort (water is forced through the gills as the shark swims), but a stationary shark must laboriously pump water to continue breathing. If you dive in the Cave of the Sleeping Sharks, be cautious: many are reef sharks, the species responsible for the largest number of attacks on humans. Dive with a reliable guide and be on your best diving behavior.

4

DIVE SHOPS

Most dive shops offer a variety of dive packages with rates depending on the time of day, the reef visited, and the number of tanks. A PADI-affiliated dive shop, **Aqua Adventures** (⊠ *Plaza Almendros 10* ☎ *998/877–1615* ⊕ *www.diveislamujeres.com*) offers dives to shipwrecks and sleeping-shark caves as well as whale-shark tours from June to September. A one-tank dive is $40 and a two-tank dive costs $79. **Cruise Divers** (⊠ *Avs. Rueda Medina and Matamoros* ☎ *998/877–1190*) offers two-tank reef dives starting at $49 and a resort course (a quickie learn-to-scuba course) for $69. The company also organizes nighttime dives. **Sea Hawk Divers** (⊠ *Av. Arq. Carlos Lazo* ☎ *998/877–1233* ⊕ *www.sea-hawk-divers.myislamujeres.com*) runs reef dives from $50 (for one tank) to $65 (for two tanks). Special excursions to the more-exotic shipwrecks cost $75 to $95. The PADI courses taught here are highly regarded. For non-divers there are snorkel trips that depart at 9:30 and 2:30 daily.

SIDE TRIP TO ISLA CONTOY

30 km (19 mi) north of Isla Mujeres.

A national wildlife park and bird sanctuary, Isla Contoy (Isle of Birds) is just 6 km (4 mi) long and less than 1 km (about ½ mi) wide. The island is a protected area—the number of visitors is carefully regulated in order to safeguard the flora and fauna. Isla Contoy has become a favorite among bird-watchers, snorkelers, and nature lovers who come to enjoy its unspoiled beauty.

More than 70 bird species—including gulls, pelicans, petrels, cormorants, cranes, ducks, flamingos, herons, doves, quail, spoonbills, and hawks—fly this way in late fall, some to nest and breed. Although the number of species is diminishing—partly as a result of human traffic—Isla Contoy remains a treat for bird-watchers.

The island is rich in sea life as well. Snorkelers will see brilliant coral and fish. Manta rays, which average about 5 feet across, are visible in the shallow waters. Surrounding the island are large numbers of shrimp, mackerel, barracuda, flying fish, and trumpet fish. In December, lobsters pass through in great (though diminishing) numbers, on their southerly migration route.

Sand dunes inland from the east coast rise as high as 70 feet above sea level. Black rocks and coral reefs fringe the island's east coast, which drops off abruptly 15 feet into the sea. The west coast is fringed with sand, shrubs, and coconut palms. At the north and the south ends you find nothing but trees and small pools of water.

GETTING HERE AND AROUND

The trip to Isla Contoy takes about 45 minutes to 1½ hours, depending on the weather and the boat; the cost is between $38 and $50. Everyone landing on Isla Contoy must purchase a $5 authorization ticket; the price is usually included in the cost of a guided tour. The standard tour begins with a fruit breakfast on the boat and a stopover at Xlaches reef on the way to Isla Contoy for snorkeling (gear is included in the price). As you sail, your crew trolls for the lunch it will cook on the beach—you may be in for anything from barracuda to snapper (beer and soda are also included). While the catch is being barbecued, you have time to explore the island, snorkel, check out the small museum and biological station, or just laze under a palapa.

The island is officially open to visitors daily from 9 to 5:30; overnight stays aren't allowed. Other than the birds and the dozen or so park rangers who live here, the island's only residents are iguanas, lizards, turtles, hermit crabs, and boa constrictors. You can read more about Isla Contoy by visiting a Web site devoted to the island: ⊕ *www. islacontoy.org.*

Captain Ricardo Gaitan (⊠ *Contoy Pier, Av. Rueda Medina* 🕾 *998/877–0798*), a local Isla Contoy expert, also provides an excellent tour for large groups (6 to 20 people) aboard his 36-foot boat *Estrella del Norte.*

Sociedad Cooperativa Isla Mujeres (⊠ *Contoy Pier, Av. Rueda Medina* 🕾 *998/877–0800*) offers daily boat trips from Isla Mujeres to Isla Contoy Pier at Rueda Medina. Groups are a minimum of 6 and a maximum of 12 people.

Cozumel

WORD OF MOUTH

"I'm a Cozumel gal. I spend a month there every year. . . . You can take in a local ballgame, take a cooking class, shop in the local food markets, enjoy a spa. It's all there."

—TC

WELCOME TO COZUMEL

TOP REASONS TO GO

★ **Scuba dive the Great Maya Reef:** A Technicolor profusion of fish, coral, and other underwater creatures resides in this 966-km-long (600-mi-long) reef, stretching from Cozumel to Central America.

★ **Utterly unwind:** Lounge poolside, stroll along a white-sand beach, or explore the gardens at Chankanaab. You can spend hours just sitting in the main plaza (or at a sidewalk café) watching island life pass by.

★ **Taste local flavor:** On Sunday nights at San Miguel's Plaza Central, join the families who gather for music and dancing. Visit during Carnival, the spring Fería del Cedral, or any national holiday, and you'll find parades, processions, and seasonal treats sold at food stands.

★ **Contemplate the Maya:** Explore the temples dedicated to Ixchel, the Mayan goddess of fertility and the moon, at San Gervasio, and study the exhibits on Mayan culture past and present at the Museo de Cozumel.

1 The Northwest Coast. Broad beaches and the island's first golf course lie at the northwest tip of Cozumel. The sand gives way to limestone shelves jutting over the water; hotels that don't have big beaches provide ladders down to excellent snorkeling spots, where parrot fish crunch on coral.

2 San Miguel. Cozumel's only town, where cruise ships loom from the piers and endless souvenir shops line the streets, still retains some of the flavor of a Mexican village. On weekend nights musical groups and food vendors gather in the main square, attracting a lively crowd.

3 The Southwestern Beaches. Proximity to Cozumel's best reefs makes the beaches south of San Miguel a home base for divers. A parade of hotels, beach clubs, commercial piers, and dive shops lines the shore here.

4 The Southern Nature Parks. Cozumel's natural treasures are protected both above and below the sea. At Faro Celarain Eco Park, mangrove lagoons and beaches shelter nesting sea turtles. Parque Chankanaab, one of Mexico's first marine parks, is superb for snorkeling. Parque Marino Nacional Arrecifes de Cozumel encompasses the coral reefs along the southwest edge of the island.

5 The Windward Coast. The rough surf of the Caribbean pounds against the limestone shore here, creating pocket-size beaches perfect for solitary sunbathing. The water can be rough, though, so pay attention to the tides, currents, and sudden drop-offs in the ocean floor.

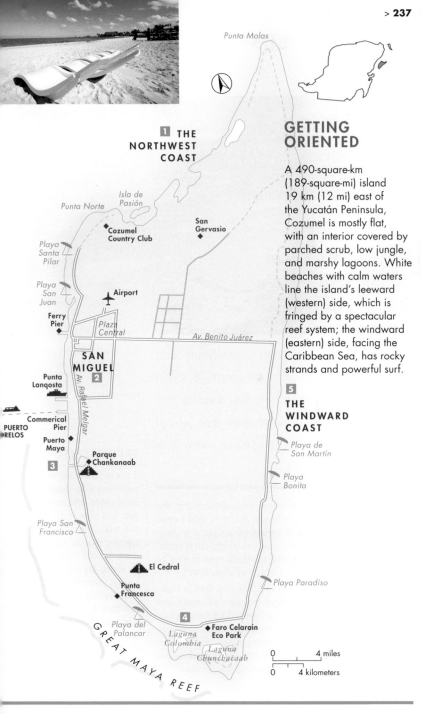

Punta Molas

1 THE NORTHWEST COAST

Isla de Pasión

Punta Norte

San Gervasio

Playa Santa Pilar

◆ Cozumel Country Club

Playa San Juan

✈ Airport

Ferry Pier ◆

Plaza Central

Av. Benito Juárez

SAN MIGUEL 2

Av. Rafael Melgar

Punta Lanqosta

Commerical Pier

PUERTO MORELOS

Puerto Maya ◆

Parque
▲ Chankanaab 3

Playa San Francisco

▲ El Cedral

Punta Francesca ◆

Playa del Palancar

Laguna Colombia

4

◆ Faro Celarain Eco Park

Laguna Chunchacaab

GREAT MAYA REEF

GETTING ORIENTED

A 490-square-km (189-square-mi) island 19 km (12 mi) east of the Yucatán Peninsula, Cozumel is mostly flat, with an interior covered by parched scrub, low jungle, and marshy lagoons. White beaches with calm waters line the island's leeward (western) side, which is fringed by a spectacular reef system; the windward (eastern) side, facing the Caribbean Sea, has rocky strands and powerful surf.

5

5 THE WINDWARD COAST

Playa de San Martín

Playa Bonita

Playa Paradíso

| 0 | 4 miles |
| 0 | 4 kilometers |

COZUMEL'S BEST BEACHES

Cozumel's aquamarine sea is irresistible and easy to access from most of the coastline. Calm water laps the soft sand beaches, tropical fish swim alongside limestone shelves that jut out over the sea, and white anemones wave with the currents in tide pools.

(Above) Punta Sur National Park, Cozumel. (Top right) The coastline around Punta Sur is rocky in spots. (Bottom right) Playa Palancar.

At some spots you can see tropical fish swimming in the crystal-clear water so close to shore that you don't even have to get a toe wet. But it would be a shame to skip seeing the endless array of tropical fish along coral reefs. Most swimmers don masks and snorkels even if they're just paddling about beside the beach at their hotel.

Cozumel lacks the long, broad beaches you find in Cancún or the Riviera Maya. Instead, pockets of sand form between sections of brittle limestone. The best sandy beaches are along the island's southern shores, where sea grass mars the underwater scenery. Gorgeous isolated beaches stretch along portions of the windward coast, where rough tides can make swimming dangerous.

SAFETY FIRST

If you're snorkeling or swimming from shore, swim shoes will protect your feet from coral and rocks. The water is typically shallow close to shore, though currents can be strong if you swim out several yards. It's best to swim against the current first then float back with it to your starting point. The sun is strong even on cloudy days. Lather on biodegradable sunscreen frequently.

BEST BEACHES

PLAYA SAN MARTIN

The water is usually calm at this windward-side beach, making it a great place to enjoy the island's wild side without worrying about rough waves. When the winds are high it's fun to sit on the beach and watch kiteboarders swoop along the water with the swells. Sea-turtle nests dot the beach in summer, and are usually marked with sticks or nets circling mounds of sand. Keep clear to avoid harming the babies hatching from their eggs. Bring your own beach blanket, towels, and drinking water, and enjoy the solitude.

ISLA PASIÓN

If your idea of paradise is a tranquil island with beaches stretching toward the horizon beside still clear waters, you'll absolutely love this patch of sand and palms off Cozumel's northwest point. Cruise-ship tours do land here, but when they're gone you'll feel delightfully isolated (with plenty of fresh water, a bountiful Mexican buffet, and cervezas close at hand). The crystal-clear water is very shallow, and the reefs are too far away for good snorkeling, but you can grab an inflatable raft and float beneath the clouds for hours. Kayaking is another good activity, especially if you're a novice. There's no need to worry about tipping over. The water's so warm you'll feel like you just slipped into the bath. There's a small golf course, children's playground, and wedding chapel—a perfect spot for a proposal.

PUNTA SUR

Faro Celarain Eco Park, at Cozumel's southern tip, claims some of the island's most gorgeous white-sand beaches. The water here is calm, and you'll find excellent snorkeling. It's worth the park's admission fee to spend hours lingering here. Be sure to climb to the top of the lighthouse for breathtaking views of the island. You can even see the Riviera Maya across the water. Lizards sun on rocks all around the park, and crocodiles hide in the mangrove lagoons. Naturalists run turtle programs in summer, taking small groups to the beach late at night to watch mother sea turtles dig deep nests in the sand and lay their eggs.

PLAYA PALANCAR

There's nothing fancy or phony about this simple beach club—just the aroma of fish grilled with garlic, the sound of the sea, and the sensation of lazily swinging in a hammock. Even the sign is simple. Look for it between Playa San Francisco and Faro Celarain Eco Park. The small dive shop on-site rents snorkeling and dive gear, and dive masters will take you to some of the best reefs along the coast.

Updated
by Steven
McCutcheon-
Rubio

It may not be Cancún, but Cozumel's days as a rustic diver's hangout are ancient history. Whether arriving by plane, or at the island's gleaming ferry terminal (it has its own baggage carousel), travelers soon let go of any lingering fears of finding themselves in a beautiful but underdeveloped backwater.

This mix of stunning natural beauty—it's all about the shimmering, clear-as-glass, aquamarine sea—and first-rate services and accommodations draws a diverse crew of visitors and devotees. Any given day you may run into packs of easygoing divers savoring a beer in between trips to the reefs, families relaxing at one of the island's many beach clubs, local couples of all ages flirting and dancing to the sound of live salsa music in the central plaza, and, without fail, thousands of cruise-ship passengers poking around the countless crafts and jewelry stores that line the downtown's seaward boulevard.

That's not to say Cozumel has nothing to offer those who prize a little peace and quiet. A rental car (or scooter) and a short drive can earn the adventurous a quiet, windswept beach all to themselves.

Just 19 km (12 mi) off the coast, Cozumel is 53 km (33 mi) long and 15 km (9 mi) wide, making it the country's third-largest island. Plaza Central, or "la plaza," the heart of San Miguel, is directly across from the docks. Residents congregate here in the evening, especially on weekends, when free concerts begin at 8. Heading inland (east) takes you away from the tourist zone and toward the residential sections. Most of the island's restaurants, hotels, stores, and dive shops are concentrated downtown, and along either of the two hotel zones that fan out along the leeward coast to the north and south of San Miguel. The heaviest commercial district is concentrated between Calle 10 Norte and Calle 11 Sur to beyond Avenida Pedro Joaquin Coldwell. There are, however, a few restaurants, and one hotel for those who prefer to explore Cozumel's solitary windward side.

PLANNING

WHEN TO GO

Weather conditions are more extreme here than you might expect on a tropical island. *Nortes*—winds from the north—blow through in December and January, churning the sea and making air and water temperatures drop. If you visit during this time, bring a shawl or jacket for the chilly 65°F evenings. Summers, on the other hand, can be beastly hot and humid. The windward side is calmer in winter than the leeward side, and the interior is warmer than the coast.

GETTING HERE AND AROUND

The Aeropuerto Internacional de Cozumel is 3 km (2 mi) north of San Miguel, and receives a few international and domestic flights. Flights to Cancún may be considerably less expensive. A small airline called Mayair is offering flights between Cancún and Cozumel, but the prices are high (about $70 each way) and passengers' luggage is limited to 25 kilos (55 pounds). A less expensive alternative is to take a bus from the Cancún airport to Playa del Carmen and then the ferry to Cozumel. The trip should cost less than $20 and take about three hours if everything runs on schedule.

At the airport, the *colectivo,* a van that seats up to eight, takes arriving passengers to their hotels; the fare is about $7 to $20 per person. Passenger-only ferries to and from Playa del Carmen leave approximately every hour on the hour from early morning until late night. The trip takes 45 minutes and costs about $14 each way. Car ferries leave from Puerto Morelos and Calica.

Bus service on Cozumel is basically limited to San Miguel, so a rental car is recommended. Though it's tempting to drive on Cozumel's dirt roads (which lead to uncrowded beaches), most car-rental companies have a policy that voids your insurance once you leave the paved roadway.

Cabs wait at all the major hotels, and you can hail them on the street. The fixed rates run about $3 within town; $8 to $20 between town and either hotel zone; $10 to $30 from most hotels to the airport; and about $20 to $40 from the northern hotels or town to Parque Chankanaab or Playa San Francisco. The cost from the Puerta Maya cruise-ship terminal by El Cid La Ceiba to San Miguel is about $10.

BY AIR

Mayair (⌂ *Cozumel Airport, Blvd. Aeropuerto at Av. 65* ☎ *998/881–9400 [Cancún]* ⊕ *www.mayair.com.mx*).

BY BOAT

Passenger-only ferry from Playa del Carmen (☎ *987/872–1578 or 987/869–2223*). **Car ferry from Puerto Morelos** (☎ *987/872–0950*). **Car ferry from Calica** (☎ *987/872–7688*).

BY CAR

Aguila Rentals (⌂ *Av. Rafael E. Melgar 685* ☎ *987/872–0729*). **CP Rentals** (⌂ *Av. 10 Norte, between Calles 2 and 4* ☎ *987/878–4055*). **Thrifty** (⌂ *Blvd. Aeropuerto at Av. 70* ☎ *987/869–2957*).

BY SCOOTER

Scooters are popular here, but also extremely dangerous because of heavy traffic, potholes, and hidden stop signs; accidents happen all too frequently. Mexican law requires all riders to wear helmets (it's a $25 fine if you don't).

If you do decide to rent a scooter, drive slowly, check for oncoming traffic, and don't ride when it's raining or if you've been drinking. Scooters rent for about $25 per day or $15 for a half day, including insurance.

Ernesto's Scooter Rental (⊠ *Carretera Costera Sur, Km 4* ☎ *987/871–1223*).

Rentadora Cozumel (⊠ *Avs. Juárez and Calle 10* ☎ *987/872–3488*).

Rentadora Marlin (⊠ *Av. 5 and Calle 1 Sur* ☎ *987/872–1586*).

HEALTH AND SAFETY

Cozumel is the type of place where people can stroll about town at any hour of the day or night without worry. Accidents, however, can happen anywhere, so take appropriate precautions if driving a car or a scooter. If you practice water sports, make sure that your insurance has a sports rider.

MONEY MATTERS

San Miguel is dotted with bank offices, and ATMs are abundant, including a few that dispense U.S. dollars. Some major hotels and resorts along the northern and southern hotel zones have ATMs on-site. Credit cards are readily accepted, as are U.S. dollars (although often at a disadvantageous exchange rate).

RESTAURANTS

At first glance, the restaurant scene seems typical of a touristy island—simple but fresh seafood dishes, hearty American fare, and as many flavored cocktails as you can imagine. A handful of creative chefs, however, have started serving up more-sophisticated dishes.

HOTELS

A growing number of Cozumel hotels encourage people to make their reservations online. Some allow you to book rooms through their own Web sites, and those without one usually offer reservations via online booking agencies, such as ⊕ *www.cozumel-hotels.net*. Since hotels customarily work with several different agencies, it's a good idea to shop around online for the best rates.

Besides being convenient, booking online can often get you a 10% to 20% discount on room rates. The downside, though, is that there are occasional breakdowns in communication. You may arrive to discover that your Spanish-speaking front desk clerk has no record of your Internet reservation or has reserved a room that's different from the one you specified. To prevent such mishaps from ruining your vacation, be sure to bring copies of all your Internet transactions, including receipts and confirmations, with you.

DINING AND LODGING PRICES

	¢	$	$$	$$$	$$$$
WHAT IT COSTS IN DOLLARS					
Restaurants	under $5	$5–$10	$10–$15	$15–$25	over $25
Hotels	under $50	$50–$75	$75–$150	$150–$250	over $250

Restaurant prices are based on the median entrée price at dinner. Hotel prices are for a standard double room in high season.

VISITOR INFORMATION

The Web site ⊕ *www.thisiscozumel.com* has up-to-date news items and info on everything you need to know for a great stay on the island. They also book tours. The site ⊕ *www.cozumelmycozumel.com*, edited by full-time residents of the island, has insider tips on activities, sights, and places to stay and eat. There's a bulletin board, too, where you can post questions.

TOURS

Tours of the island's sights, including the San Gervasio ruins, El Cedral, Parque Chankanaab, and the Museo de la Isla de Cozumel, cost about $50 a person and can be arranged through travel agencies. **Fiesta Holidays** (⊠ *Calle 11 Sur 598, between Avs. 25 and 30* ☎ *987/872–0923*), which has representatives in many hotels, sells several tours. Another option is to take a private tour of the island via taxi, which costs about $60 for a half-day tour.

ESSENTIALS

Currency Exchange American Express (⊠ *Punta Langosta, Av. Rafael E. Melgar 599* ☎ *987/869–1389*). **Promotora Cambiaria del Centro** (⊠ *Av. 5 between Calles 1 Sur and Adolfo Rosado Salas* ☎ *987/872–2165*).

Medical Assistance Air Ambulance (☎ *987/872–4070*). **Centro Médico de Cozumel** (*Cozumel Medical Center* ⊠ *Calle 1 Sur 101 and Av. 50* ☎ *987/872–9400*). **Police** (⊠ *Anexo del Palacio Municipal* ☎ *987/872–0092, 065 for emergencies*). **Red Cross** (⊠ *Calle Lourdes between Avs. 65 and 70* ☎ *987/872–1058, 065 for emergencies*).

Recompression Chambers Buceo Médico Mexicano (⊠ *Calle 5 Sur 21B* ☎ *987/872–1430 24-hr hotline*). **Cozumel Recompression Chamber** (⊠ *San Miguel Clinic, Calle 6 Norte between Avs. 5 and 10* ☎ *987/872–3070*).

Visitor and Tour Info Fideicomiso and the Cozumel Island Hotel Association (⊠ *Calle 2 Norte and Av. 15* ☎ *987/872–7585* ⊕ *www.islacozumel.com.mx*).

EXPLORING

Unless you want to stick around your hotel, or downtown San Miguel for your whole stay, renting a car or a scooter is a must. Many worthwhile sites, such the island's Mayan ruins, and pristine windward beaches are only readily accessible by motorized vehicle. Taxi fares on

Cozumel

KEY

⛴ *Cruise Ship*

🚢 *Ferry*

*Caribbean
Sea*

Punta
Molas

◆ Faro Punta
Molas

Punta Norte

◆ Cozumel
Country Club

Playa
Santa
Pilar

Playa
San
Juan

✈ Airport

Playa
Los Cocos

❷

Plaza
Central

❸

Av. Benito Juárez

◆ Punta
Este

◆ Punta
Morena

TO PLAYA
DEL CARMEN

Av. Rafael Melgar

Punta
Langosta

Puerta Maya ◆

❹

❺

Playa de
San Martín

Playa
Corona

Playa San
Clemente

◆ Punta
Chiqueros

Playa San
Francisco

Playa
Sol

R E E F S

❻

Punta
Francesca ◆

Playa
Paradiso

❼

0   3 miles

0   3 kilometers

Playa del
Palancar

Laguna
Colombia

Laguna
Chunchacaab

El Caracol

TO PUNTA
CELERAIN FARO

Caribbean Sea

❶

Cozumel is a favorite cruise-ship destination.

the island are astronomical, and after just a few trips even a slightly nicer rental car is a better deal.

TOP ATTRACTIONS

Museo de la Isla de Cozumel. Cozumel's island museum is housed on two floors of a former hotel. It has displays on natural history—with exhibits on the island's origins, endangered species, topography, and coral-reef ecology—as well as the pre-Columbian and colonial periods. The photos of the island's transformation over the 20th and 21st centuries are especially fascinating, as is the exhibit of a typical Mayan home. Guided tours are available. ⊠ *Av. Rafael E. Melgar, between Calles 4 and 6 Norte* 🕾 *987/872–1475* 💲*$3* ⊙ *Daily 9–5.*

QUICK
BITES

On the terrace off the second floor of the Museo de la Isla de Cozumel, the **Restaurante del Museo** (🕾 *987/872-0838*) serves breakfast and lunch from 7 to 2. The Mexican fare is enhanced by a great waterfront view, and the café is as popular with locals as tourists.

Parque Chankanaab. Chankanaab (which means "small sea") is a national park with a saltwater lagoon, an archaeological park, and a botanical garden. Scattered throughout are reproductions of a Mayan village, and of Olmec, Toltec, Aztec, and Mayan stone carvings. You can enjoy a cool walk along pathways leading to the sea, where parrot fish and sergeant majors swarm around snorkelers.

You can swim, scuba dive, or snorkel at the beach. There's plenty to see: underwater caverns, a sunken ship, crusty old cannons and anchors, and

a sculpture of la Virgen del Mar (Virgin of the Sea). To preserve the ecosystem, park rules forbid touching the reef or feeding the fish.

Dive shops, restaurants, gift shops, a snack stand, and dressing rooms with lockers and showers are right on the sand. A small museum has exhibits on coral, shells, and

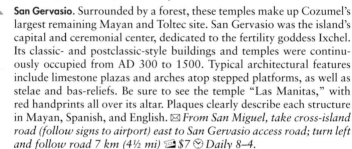

WORD OF MOUTH

"There are several small Mayan Ruins in Cozumel itself. They are small in comparison to Tulum or Coba. San Gervasio is probably your best bet." — Eschew

the park's history, as well as some sculptures. ⊠ *Carretera Sur, Km 9* ☎ *987/872–1522* 🖼 *$21* ⊙ *Daily 8–4.*

⛰ **San Gervasio.** Surrounded by a forest, these temples make up Cozumel's largest remaining Mayan and Toltec site. San Gervasio was the island's capital and ceremonial center, dedicated to the fertility goddess Ixchel. Its classic- and postclassic-style buildings and temples were continuously occupied from AD 300 to 1500. Typical architectural features include limestone plazas and arches atop stepped platforms, as well as stelae and bas-reliefs. Be sure to see the temple "Las Manitas," with red handprints all over its altar. Plaques clearly describe each structure in Mayan, Spanish, and English. ⊠ *From San Miguel, take cross-island road (follow signs to airport) east to San Gervasio access road; turn left and follow road 7 km (4½ mi)* 🖼 *$7* ⊙ *Daily 8–4.*

★ **San Miguel.** Wait until the cruise ships sail toward the horizon before visiting San Miguel, Cozumel's only town. Then stroll along the *malecón* (boardwalk) and take in the ocean breeze. The waterfront has been taken over by large shops selling jewelry, imported rugs, leather boots, and souvenirs to cruise-ship passengers. The northern end of the malecón, past Calle 10 Norte, is a pleasant area lined with sculptures of Mayan gods and goddesses that draws more locals than tourists. The town feels more traditional as you head inland to the pedestrian streets around the plaza, where family-owned restaurants and shops cater to locals and savvy travelers. The plaza and surrounding buildings are the heart of San Miguel, with plenty of benches for watching he action. The central *kiosko* (bandstand) and clock tower are local landmarks—and a good place to rendezvous with the shoppers in your group. There's live music most Sunday nights, and families gather to dance, chat, and watch the children race around after pigeons. Behind the bright yellow Plaza del Sol building facing the plaza, an artisan's market is packed with both tacky and desirable souvenirs.

WORTH NOTING

⛰ **El Cedral.** Spanish explorers discovered this site, once the hub of Mayan life on Cozumel, in 1518. Later it became the island's first official city, founded in 1847. Today it's a farming community with small well-tended houses and gardens. Conquistadores tore down much of the Mayan temple, and during World War II the U.S. Army Corps of Engineers destroyed the rest to make way for the island's first airport. All that remains of the Mayan ruins is one small structure with an arch. Nearby is a green-and-white cinder-block church, decorated inside with crosses shrouded in embroidered lace; legend has it that Mexico's first Mass was held here. Vendors display embroidered blouses, hammocks, and other souvenirs at stands around the main plaza. ⊠ *Turn at Km 17.5 off Carretera Sur or Av. Rafael E. Melgar, then drive 3 km (2 mi) inland to site* ☎ *No phone* 🎟 *Free* ⊙ *Daily dawn–dusk.*

🔄 **Discover Mexico.** This ingenious attraction allows visitors to learn about Mexico's archaeological sites, important architectural landmarks, and cultures. A gorgeous film about Mexico runs continuously, and exhibits display collector-quality textiles, pottery, and painted figurines. Outdoors are scale models of temples, pyramids, monasteries, and Mexico City's main square, the Zócalo. An outdoor café serves tasty fruit sorbets and light meals. The gift shop has the island's finest array of Mexican folk art. Expect to spend about two hours to fully experience the entire exhibit, or longer if you sign on for one of the daily tequila tastings (reserve in advance). A combo entry ticket includes admissions to Discover Mexico and Parque Chankanaab. ⊠ *Carretera Sur, Km 5.5* ☎ *987/875–2820* ⊕ *www.discovermexico.org* 🎟 *$20* ⊙ *Mon.–Sat. 8–4.*

🔄 **Faro Celarain Eco Park.** This 247-acre national preserve at Cozumel's southernmost tip is a protected habitat for numerous birds and animals, including crocodiles, flamingos, egrets, and herons. Cars aren't allowed, so you'll need to use park transportation (rented bicycles or park shuttles) to get around here. From observation towers you can spot crocodiles and birds in **Laguna Colombia** or **Laguna Chunchacaab.** Or visit the ancient Mayan lighthouse, **El Caracol,** designed to whistle when the wind blows in a certain direction. At the park's (and the island's) southernmost point is the **Faro de Celarain,** a lighthouse that's now a museum of navigation. Climb the 134 steps to the top; it's a steamy effort, but the views are incredible. Beaches here are wide and deserted, and there's great snorkeling offshore. Snorkeling equipment is available for rent, as are kayaks, and there are restrooms at the museum and by the beach. Without a rental car, expect to pay about $40 for a round-trip taxi ride from San Miguel. ⊠ *Southernmost point of Carretera Sur and coastal road* ☎ *987/872–2940 or 987/872–8462* 🎟 *$10* ⊙ *Daily 9–4.*

LEEWARD BEACHES

Wide sandy beaches washed with shallow waters are typical at the far north and south ends of Cozumel's west coast. The topography changes between the two, with small sandy coves interspersed with limestone outcroppings. ■TIP→ **Generally, the best snorkeling is wherever piers or rocky shorelines provide a haven for sergeant majors and angelfish. Shore diving and snorkeling aren't as good as they were before Hurricane Wilma, though they're improving gradually. You're best off taking a boat tour to the reefs to see swarms of fish.**

Isla de Pasión (⊠ *Off Punta Norte* ☎ *987/872–6941* ⊕ *www.isla-pasion. com*) lies a short boat ride off Punta Norte on the leeward coast and has one of Cozumel's loveliest beaches. A private company, called Isla Pasión, controls the island and keeps it clean and safe. Most guests reach the island on an organized tour (about $80 or more per person

Cozumel's History

Cozumel's name is believed to have come from the Mayan "Ah-Cuzamil-Peten" ("land of the swallows"). For the Maya, who lived here intermittently between about AD 600 and 1200, the island was not only a center for trade and navigation, but also a sacred place. Pilgrims from all over Mesoamerica came to honor Ixchel, the goddess of fertility, childbirth, the moon, and rainbows. Viewed as the mother of all other gods, Ixchel was often depicted with swallows at her feet. Maya women, who were expected to visit Ixchel's site at least once during their lives, made the dangerous journey from the mainland by canoe. Cozumel's main exports were salt and honey; at the time, both were considered more valuable than gold.

In 1518 Spanish explorer Juan de Grijalva arrived on Cozumel, looking for slaves. His tales of treasure inspired Hernán Cortés, Mexico's most famous Spanish explorer, to visit the island the following year. There he met Geronimo de Aguilar and Gonzales Guerrero, Spanish men who had been shipwrecked on Cozumel years earlier. Initially enslaved by the Maya, the two were later accepted into their community. Aguilar joined forces with Cortés, helping set up a military base on the island and using his knowledge of the Maya to defeat them. Guerrero died defending his adopted people; the Maya still consider him a hero. By 1570 most Maya islanders had been massacred by Spaniards or killed by disease. By 1600 the island was abandoned.

In the 17th and 18th centuries, pirates found Cozumel to be the perfect hideout. Two notorious buccaneers, Jean Laffite and Henry Morgan, favored the island's safe harbors and hid their treasures in the Mayan catacombs and tunnels. By 1843 Cozumel had again been abandoned. Five years later, 20 families fleeing Mexico's brutal War of the Castes resettled the island; their descendants still live on Cozumel.

By the early 20th century the island began capitalizing on its abundant supply of *zapote* (sapodilla) trees, which produce chicle, prized by the chewing-gum industry (think Chiclets). Shipping routes began to include Cozumel, whose deep harbors made it a perfect stop for large vessels. Jungle forays in search of chicle led to the discovery of ruins; soon archaeologists began visiting the island as well. Meanwhile, Cozumel's importance as a seaport diminished as air travel grew, and the demand for chicle dropped off with the invention of synthetic chewing gum.

For decades Cozumel was another backwater where locals fished, hunted alligators and iguanas, and worked on coconut plantations to produce *copra,* the dried kernels from which coconut oil is extracted. Cozumeleños subsisted largely on seafood, still a staple of the local economy. During World War II the U.S. Army built an airstrip and maintained a submarine base here, accidentally destroying some Mayan ruins. Then in the 1960s the underwater explorer Jacques Cousteau helped make Cozumel a vacation spot by featuring its incredible reefs on his television show. Today Cozumel is among the world's most popular diving locations.

5

depending on the type of tour and transportation). You can go on your own by arriving at the dock at the end of the dirt road to Punta Norte and paying $45 per person. This is an all-inclusive fee that includes the round-trip boat ride, a buffet lunch, soft drinks, some alcoholic drinks, and the use of the extensive facilities and amenities. Visitors tend to spend most of the day here, strolling the mile-long beach, floating in the shallow water, swinging in a hammock, playing volleyball, and indulging in a massage (for an extra fee). Cruise-ship tours do come here, bringing literally hundreds of tourists. But the beach is long enough that you can get away from the crowds. You can even arrange to get married at the island's chapel. **Best For:** solitude, romance, families, kayaking, sunbathing, all-inclusive food and drink. **Amenities:** lifeguard, chaise lounges, lockers, playground, showers, toilets.

Playa Santa Pilar runs along the northern hotel strip and ends at Punta Norte. Long stretches of sand and shallow water encourage leisurely swims. The privacy diminishes as you swim south past hotels and condos. Hotels along the beach have all the facilities you would need, but most are all-inclusive and don't allow nonguests on the premises. **Best For:** families with small children, easy snorkeling. **Amenities:** parking, showers (at hotels).

Playa San Juan, south of Playa Santa Pilar, has a rocky shore with no easy ocean access. You can park on the roadside just south of the fence surrounding the ruins of the Sol Cabañas del Caribe hotel, which was destroyed by Hurricane Wilma. The winds can be strong here, so it's popular with kiteboarders. **Best For:** solitude, snorkeling. **Amenities:** none.

Playa Azul (⊠ *Carretera Norte Km 4* ☎ *987/869–5160* ⊕ *www.playa-azul. com*) sits just north of the hotel of the same name and is under the same management. The beach has pockets of sand between limestone shelves; there's a pool at the hotel but it's only for hotel guests. The restaurant beneath a large A-frame *palapa* (thatch-roof hut) serves delicious ceviche and bountiful club sandwiches and fries. A salsa band plays on Sunday afternoons and draws a crowd of fun-loving dancers—older couples, parents dancing with their kids, friends of all ages boogying alone or together. **Best For:** sunbathing, swimming, snorkeling, music, sunsets. **Amenities:** food concession, lockers, parking lot, showers.

Playa Casitas (⊠ *Carretera Norte at Blvd. Aeropuerto*), a hugely popular locals' beach which was completely remodeled in 2009, now has a restaurant, several large palapas for shade, a parking area, and a long stretch of sand and calm water. It's fairly deserted on weekdays and absolutely packed on Sunday, the traditional day for family outings. **Best For:** families, sunbathing, swimming, mingling with locals. **Amenities:** food concession, lockers, toilets, parking lot, showers.

The **Money Bar Beach Club** (⊠ *Carretera Sur, Km 6* ☎ *987/869–5141* ⊕ *www.moneybarbeachclub.com*) has replaced the wildly popular Dzul Ha beach club. A water-sports center offers rental scuba and snorkeling gear, kayaks, and small sailboats as well as showers, restrooms, and lockers. You can buy one of various packages, which include meals, massage, and snorkel tours, or you can just rent a snorkel and mask and check out the angelfish gliding over Dzul Ha reef before lunching under the peaked palapas. Happy regulars and visitors come to sip frothy cocktails during the daily sunset happy hour and linger into the night. **Best For:** boating, couples, kayaking, singles, snorkeling, sunsets, sunbathing, swimming. **Amenities:** chaise lounges, food concession, lockers, parking lot, showers.

Uvas (✉ *Carretera Sur, Km 8.5* ☎ *987/103–5504*) started out with a sexy, South Beach–style attitude, but now caters to small cruise-ship groups and individual tourists. Facilities include lockers, restrooms with showers, and a dive shop. Advance reservations are required, since the club tries to keep crowds away and limits the number of guests. Make reservations by phone. Fees vary with packages that include entrance and lunch, and additional activities. The basic entrance fee—including one drink and use of beach umbrellas, lounge chairs, and other amenities—is $7. **Best For:** lounging on the beach, dining, quiet relaxation, dive shop, snorkeling, massage, handicrafts shop, pool, easy access from cruise-ship piers and hotels. **Amenities:** chaise lounges, food concession, lockers, parking lot, showers.

Playa San Francisco (✉ *Carretera Costera Sur, Km 14* was one of the first beach clubs on the coast. The inviting 5-km (3-mi) stretch of sandy beach, which extends along Carretera Sur south of Parque Chankanaab at about Km 14, is among the longest and finest on Cozumel. Encompassing beaches known as Playa Maya and Santa Rosa, it's typically packed with cruise-ship passengers in high season. On Sunday locals flock here to eat fresh fish. Amenities include two outdoor restaurants, a bar, dressing rooms, gift shops, beach chairs, restrooms, massage treatments, and water-sports equipment rentals. Divers use this beach as a jumping-off point for the San Francisco reef. The abundance of turtle grass in the water, however, makes this a less-than-ideal spot for swimming. In lieu of a fee, there's a required $10 minimum food and drinks purchase for adults. **Best For:** banana-boat rides, boat diving, families, parasailing. **Amenities:** chaise lounges, food concessions, lockers, parking lot, showers.

Carlos 'n Charlie's Beach Club (✉ *Carretera Costera Sur, Km 14* ☎ *987/564–0960* ⊕ *www.carlosandcharlies.com/cozumelclub*) abuts Playa San Francisco. It's a rowdy, bawdy affair with a restaurant and bar where waiters break into song and draw customers into line dances. The food is typical of the chain—burgers, barbecued ribs, tacos—and alcohol flows generously. The beach is shallow, and the water not always clear, and the scene best suits youthful fun seekers. **Best For:** singles scene. **Amenities:** chaise lounges, food concession, lockers, parking lot, showers.

The club at **Paradise Beach** (✉ *Carretera Sur, Km 14.5* ☎ *987/871–9010* ⊕ *www.paradise-beach-cozumel.net*) has cushy lounge chairs ($2, plus a $10 minimum food and drinks purchase for adults). The $12 Fun Pass gets you a full-day's use of kayaks, snorkel gear, a trampoline, the swimming pool, and a climbing wall that looks like an iceberg in the water. Parasailing equipment and Jet Skis are available for rent. Food at the club's three bars is expensive, but if you're lucky, Sunshine, the resident parrot, will open your beer for you with his beak. It's open daily from 9 to 5. **Best For:** families, swimming, singles scene. **Amenities:** chaise lounges, food concession, swimming pool, Wi-Fi, computer terminals, lockers, parking lot, playground, showers.

🕐 **Mr. Sancho's Beach Club** (✉ *Carretera Sur, Km 15* ☎ *987/876–1629*
★ ⊕ *www.mrsanchos.com*) always has a party going on: scores of holidaymakers come here to swim, snorkel, and drink buzz-inducing concoctions out of pineapples. Seemingly every water toy known to man is here; kids shriek happily as they hang onto banana boats dragged behind speedboats. Guides lead horseback and ATV rides into the jungle and along the beach, and the restaurant holds a lively, informative tequila seminar at lunchtime. Grab a swing seat at the beach bar and sip a mango margarita, or settle into the 30-person hot tub. Showers, lockers, and restrooms are available, and there are souvenirs aplenty for sale. **Best For:** ATV rides, banana-boat rides, families, horseback riding, shopping, swimming. **Amenities:** lifeguard, chaise lounges, food concession, lockers, parking lot, playground, showers.

★ South of the resorts lies the mostly ignored (and therefore serene) **Playa Palancar** (✉ *Carretera Sur.* The deeply rutted and potholed road to the beach is a sure sign you've left the tourist hot spots. Offshore is the famous Palancar Reef, easily accessed by the on-site dive shop. There's also a water-sports center, a bar-café, and a long beach with hammocks hanging under coconut palms. Playa del Palancar keeps prices low and rarely feels crowded. **Best For:** diving, snorkeling, sunbathing, swimming. **Amenities:** food concession, parking lot.

WINDWARD BEACHES

The east coast of Cozumel presents a splendid succession of mostly deserted rocky coves and narrow powdery beaches poised dramatically against the turquoise Caribbean. ⚠ Swimming can be treacherous here if you go out too far—in some parts a deadly undertow can sweep you out to sea in minutes. But the beaches are perfect for solitary sunbathing. Several casual restaurants dot the coastline; they all close after sunset.

Punta Chiqueros, a half-moon-shape cove sheltered by an offshore reef, is the first popular swimming area as you drive north on the coastal road (it's about 12 km [8 mi] north of Faro Celarain Eco-Park). Part of a longer beach that some locals call Playa Bonita, it has fine sand, clear water, and moderate waves. This is a great place to swim, watch the sunset, and eat fresh fish at the restaurant, also called Playa Bonita. **Best For:** families, sunbathing, swimming. **Amenities:** food concession, parking on road.

Not quite 5 km (3 mi) north of Punta Chiqueros, a long stretch of beach begins along the Chen Río Reef. Turtles come to lay their eggs on the section known as **Playa de San Martín**. During full moons in May and June the beach is sometimes blocked by soldiers or ecologists to prevent poaching of the turtle eggs. Directly in front of the reef is a small bay with clear waters and surf that's relatively mild, thanks to a protective rock formation. When the wind is blowing from the south, however, the water is best for kiteboarders. This is a particularly good spot for swimming when the water is calm. A restaurant, also called

The Quieter Cozumel

Blazing-white cruise ships parade in and out of Cozumel as if competing in a big-time regatta. Rare is the day there isn't a white behemoth looming on the horizon. Typically, hundreds of day-trippers wander along the waterfront, packing franchise jewelry and souvenir shops and drinking in tourist-trap bars. Precious few explore the beaches and streets favored by locals.

Travelers staying in Cozumel's one-of-a-kind hotels experience a totally different island. They quickly learn to stick close to the beach and pool when more than two ships are in port (some days the island gets six). If you're lucky enough to stay overnight, consider these strategies for avoiding the crowds.

1. Time your excursions. Go into San Miguel for early breakfast and errands, then stay out of town for the rest of the day. Wander back after you hear the ships blast their departure warnings (around 5 or 6 pm).

2. Dive in. Hide from the hordes by slipping underwater. But be sure to choose a small dive operation that travels to less-popular reefs.

3. Drive on the wild side. Rent a car and cruise the windward coast, still free of rampant construction. You can picnic and sunbathe on private beaches hidden by limestone outcroppings. Use caution when swimming; the surf can be rough.

4. Frequent the "other" downtown. Most of Cozumel's residents live and shop far from San Miguel's waterfront. Avenidas 15, 20, and 25 are packed with taco stands, stationery stores (or *papelerías*), farmacias, and neighborhood markets. Driving here is a nightmare. Park on a quieter side street and explore the shops and neighborhoods to glimpse a whole different side of Cozumel.

5

Chen Río, serves cold drinks and decent seafood. **Best For:** swimming, kiteboarding, solitude. **Amenities:** parking on road.

★ About 1 km (½ mi) to the **north of Playa San Martín,** the island road turns hilly, providing panoramic ocean views. **Coconuts,** a hilltop restaurant, is an additional lookout spot, and serves good food. The adjacent **Ventanas al Mar** hotel is the only hotel on the windward coast, and attracts locals and travelers who value solitude. Locals picnic on the long beach directly north of the hotel. When the water's calm there's good snorkeling around the rocks beneath the hotel, but don't go in if the water's splashing on the rocks. **Best For:** couples, romance, solitude, snorkeling. **Amenities:** food concession, parking on road.

Surfers and boogie-boarders have adopted **Punta Morena,** a short drive north of Ventanas al Mar, as their official hangout. The pounding surf creates great waves, and the local restaurant serves typical surfer food (hamburgers, hot dogs, and french fries). Vendors sell hammocks by the side of the road. The owners allow camping here. **Best For:** surfing. **Amenities:** food concession, parking on road.

The beach at **Punta Este** has been nicknamed Mezcalitos, after the much-loved restaurant here. **Mezcalito Café** serves seafood and beer and can get pretty rowdy. Punta Este is a typical windward beach—great for beach-combing but unsuitable for swimming. **Best For:** drinking and dining with a fun-loving crowd. **Amenities:** food concession, parking on road.

The sandy road beside Mezcalitos leading to the wild northeast coast is sometimes open and sometimes gated—a shame, since the beaches here are superb. At press time there were no tours to this part of the coast, and the road is too rutted for rental cars. Rumors abound as to this area's future—some say there will be a small-scale resort here someday, while others hope it will become an ecological reserve. A small navy base is the only permanent settlement on the road for now, though some of the scrub jungle is divided into housing lots.

WHERE TO EAT

Dining options on Cozumel reflect the island's nature: breezy and relaxed with few pretensions (casual dress and no reservations are the rule here). Most restaurants emphasize fresh ingredients, simple presentation, and amiable service. Nearly every menu includes seafood; for a regional touch, go for *pescado tixin-xic* (fish spiced with achiote and baked in banana leaves). Only a few tourist-area restaurants serve regional Yucatecan cuisine, though nearly all carry standard Mexican fare like tacos, enchiladas, and huevos rancheros. Budget meals are harder and harder to find, especially near the waterfront. The best dining experiences are usually in small, family-owned restaurants that seem to have been here forever. Many restaurants accept credit cards; café-type places generally don't. ■TIP→ **Don't follow cab drivers' dining suggestions; they're often paid to recommend restaurants.**

ZONA HOTELERA SUR

$$$ ✕ **Alfredo di Roma.** The opportunity to dine graciously amid crystal and
ITALIAN candlelight (and blessedly cool air-conditioning) is just one reason to book a special dinner at Alfredo's. The pastas are made fresh daily, and cheeses are flown in from Italy so the chef can prepare authentic fettuccine Alfredo table-side. The carpaccio, spaghetti with lobster, and Chilean sea bass in a white-wine-and-tomato sauce are all superb, and the wine cellar is the largest on the island. Book a table for early evening and enjoy the sunset view through wall-length windows. Diners not staying at the hotel must have advance reservations. ⊠ *Presidente InterContinental Cozumel, Carretera Chankanaab, Km 6.5* ☎ *987/872–9500* ⚑ *Reservations essential* ☉ *No lunch* ✛ *B4.*

SAN MIGUEL

$ ✕ **Casa Denis.** This little yellow house near the plaza has been satisfying
MEXICAN cravings for Yucatecan *pollo pibil* (spiced chicken baked in banana leaves)
★ and other local favorites since 1945. *Tortas* (sandwiches) and tacos are a real bargain, and you'll start to feel like a local if you spend an hour at one of the outdoor tables, watching shoppers dash about. ⊠ *Calle 1 Sur 132, between Avs. 5 and 10* ☎ *987/872–0067* ⊟ *No credit cards* ✛ *B3.*

$$ ✕ **Casa Mission.** Part private home and part restaurant, this estate evokes
MEXICAN a country hacienda in mainland Mexico. The on-site botanical garden
☺ has mango and papaya trees and a small zoo with caged birds. The set-
ting, with tables lining the veranda, outshines the food. Stalwart fans
rave about huge platters of fajitas and grilled fish. It's a few blocks from
the waterfront so you may want to take a cab. Or, visit one of their
two more-central sister restaurants, La Mission and Parilla Mission.
⊠ *Av. Juárez and Calle 55A* ☎ *987/872–1641* ⊕ *www.missioncoz.com*
☺ *No lunch* ✛ *D3.*

$ ✕ **La Choza.** Locals get together for breakfasts of *migas* (scrambled eggs
MEXICAN with bits of bacon and tortilla) and the daily lunchtime *comida cor-*
★ *rida,* a set-priced meal of the day (about $4.50 to $6) with a choice
of appetizers and entrées. Favorite dishes include *pollo con mole pob-
lano* (chicken in chocolate, cinnamon, and chiles) and chile relleno
de camarón (chile stuffed with shrimp). Leave room for the chilled
avocado pie. ⊠ *Av. 10 between Calle Adolfo Rosado Salas and Av. 3*
☎ *987/872–0958* ✛ *B3.*

$$$ ✕ **La Cocay.** This casually sophisticated dining room is one of the most
ECLECTIC exciting culinary venues on the island, thanks to the creative chef. The
Fodor's Choice menu changes frequently, but you can expect to find salad with mixed
★ baby lettuces, salmon pâté, and entrées like seared sashimi-grade tuna.
Such fare may be the norm in Los Angeles or Honolulu, but is hard to
find on Cozumel. Consider sharing several small plates, such the blue-
cheese phyllo rolls, the *empanaditas* (tiny empanadas) with goat cheese
and caramelized apple, and the figs with prosciutto. There are reasonably priced wines by the glass from Argentina, Chile, and Mexico.
⊠ *Calle 8 Norte between Avs. 10 and 15* ☎ *987/872–5533* ⊕ *www.
lacocay.com* ☺ *Closed Sun. No lunch* ✛ *C1.*

$ ✕ **El Foco.** Locals fuel up before and after partying at this traditional
MEXICAN taquería (it's open until midnight, or until the last customer leaves).
The soft tacos stuffed with pork, chorizo, cheese, or beef are cheap
and filling; the graffiti on the walls and the late-night revelers provide
the entertainment. ⊠ *Av. 5 Sur 13B, between Calles Adolfo Rosado
Salas and 3 Sur* ☎ *987/872–5980* ▭ *No credit cards* ☺ *No lunch* ✛ *B3.*

$$–$$$ ✕ **Guido's.** Chef Yvonne Villiger works wonders with fresh fish—if the
ITALIAN wahoo with capers and black olives is on the menu, don't miss it. But
★ Guido's is best known for its pizzas baked in a wood-burning oven, which
makes sections of the indoor dining room rather warm. Sit in the pleasant,
recently expanded courtyard instead, and order a pitcher of sangria to go
with the puffy garlic bread. ⊠ *Av. Rafael E. Melgar 23, between Calles 6
and 8 Norte* ☎ *987/872–0946 or 987/869–2589* ☺ *No lunch Sun.* ✛ *C1.*

$–$$ ✕ **Kinta.** Both locals and visitors rave about this little café, which is
MEXICAN owned by former Guido's chef Kris Wallenta. It's easy to overlook the
Fodor's Choice entrance (look for a bright orange facade on the west side of the street),
★ but once you've discovered the blissfully air-conditioned dining room,
romantic outdoor garden, and impressive menu, you'll likely return.
When he's not at his newest restaurant, Condesa, Wallenta rushes about
the open kitchen, whipping up sophisticated interpretations of classic
Mexican dishes. He updates the menu often, but among the favorites,
which he promises not to change, are his savory black-bean soup, a chile

5

Mopeds are the perfect way to explore the island.

relleno filled with vegetable ratatouille and Chihuahua cheese, pork in a smoky *pasilla* chile sauce, and a tender filet mignon with *huitlaoche* (a corn truffle) and cheese. Hand-crushed mojitos, fruity sangria, and virgin *limomenta* (lemonade with mint) add a refreshing lilt, and the bread pudding with Mexican chocolate and *cajeta* (caramel sauce) is a fitting end to a stellar meal. ⊠ *Av. 5 between Calles 2 and 4* ☎ *987/869–0544* ⊘ *Closed Mon.* ✛ *C2.*

$$–$$$
MEXICAN
★
⨯ **Pancho's Backyard.** Marimbas play beside the bubbling fountain in this gorgeous courtyard behind one of Cozumel's best folk-art shops. Though Pancho's is always busy, the waitstaff is amazingly patient and helpful. Cruise-ship passengers seeking a taste of Mexico pack the place at lunch; dinner is a bit more serene. The menu is definitely geared toward tourists (written in English with detailed descriptions and prices in dollars), but regional ingredients make even the standard steak stand out when it's flavored with smoky chipotle chile. Other stellar dishes include the cilantro cream soup and shrimp flambéed with tequila. ⊠ *Av. Rafael Melgar between Calles 8 and 10 Norte* ☎ *987/872–2141* ⊕ *www. panchosbackyard.com* ⊘ *No lunch Sun.* ✛ *C1.*

$$$
STEAK
⨯ **Pepe's Grill.** This nautical-themed eatery has model boats, ships' wheels, and weather vanes covering the walls—appropriate because it's popular with the cruise-ship crowds. The upstairs dining room's tall windows allow for fantastic sunset views. The chateaubriand, T-bone steaks, and prime rib please American palates, though the meat isn't up to steak-house standards. Long waits for tables aren't uncommon. ⊠ *Av. Rafael E. Melgar and Calle Adolfo Rosado Salas* ☎ *987/872–0213* ⊘ *No lunch* ✛ *B3.*

$ ✕**Plaza Leza**. The outdoor tables here are a wonderful place to linger;
MEXICAN you can watch the crowds in the square while savoring Mexican dishes
like *poc chuc* (tender pork loin in a sour-orange sauce), enchiladas, and
lime soup. Breakfast is available here as well. For more privacy, there's
also a somewhat secluded inner patio. ⊠ *Calle 1 Sur #58, south side of
Plaza Central* ☎ *987/872–1041* ✛ *B2*.

$ ✕**Rock 'n Java Caribbean Café**. The extensive breakfast menu here
CAFÉ includes whole-wheat French toast and cheese crepes. For lunch or
dinner try the vegetarian tacos or linguine with clams, or choose from
more than a dozen salads. Scrumptious pies, cakes, and pastries are
baked here daily. You can enjoy your healthy meal or sinful snack while
enjoying a sea view through the back windows. Used books are piled
on shelves along one wall, and the bulletin board by the front door is
an interesting read. ⊠ *Av. Rafael E. Melgar 602-6* ☎ *987/872–4405*
🕙 *No dinner Sat.* ✛ *A3*.

$$$ ✕**La Veranda**. Romantic and intimate, this wooden Caribbean house has
CARIBBEAN comfortable rattan furniture, soft lighting, and a terrace that's perfect
for evening cocktails (it's also a popular wedding venue). You can start
with Roquefort quesadillas, then move on to shrimp curry, jerk chicken,
or a seafood-stuffed poblano chile. ⊠ *Calle 4 Norte 140, between Avs.
5 and 10 Norte* ☎ *987/872–4132* 🕙 *Closed Sun. No lunch* ✛ *C2*.

WINDWARD COAST

$–$$ ✕**Coconuts**. The T-shirts and bikinis hanging from the palapa roof at this
MEXICAN windward-side hangout are a good indication of its party-time atmo-
★ sphere. Jimmy Buffett tunes play in the background while crowds down
cervezas. The scene is more peaceful if you choose a palapa-shaded table
on the rocks overlooking the water. The garlic shrimp are good enough
to write home about. Assign a designated driver and hit the road home
before dark (remember, there are no streetlights). ⊠ *East-coast road
near junction with Av. Benito Juárez* ☎ *No phone* ▭ *No credit cards*
🕙 *No dinner* ✛ *C4*.

$ ✕**Playa Bonita**. Locals gather on Sunday afternoons at this casual beach
MEXICAN café. The water here is usually calm, and families alternate between
swimming and lingering over long lunches of fried fish. Weekdays are
quieter; this is a good place to spend the day if you want access to food,
drinks, and showers but aren't into the rowdy beach-club scene. ⊠ *East-
coast road* ☎ *987/872–4868* ▭ *No credit cards* 🕙 *No dinner* ✛ *C4*.

WHERE TO STAY

For expanded hotel reviews, visit Fodors.com.

Small, one-of-a-kind hotels have long been the norm in Cozumel. Most
of Cozumel's hotels are on the leeward (west) and south sides of the
island; but there's one peaceful hideaway on the windward (east) side.
The larger resorts are north and south of San Miguel; the less-expensive
places are in town.

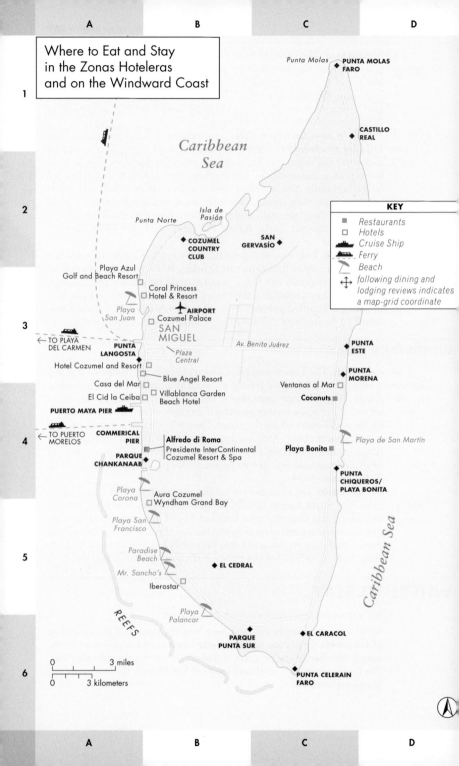

Where to Eat and Stay in the Zonas Hoteleras and on the Windward Coast

KEY
- ■ Restaurants
- □ Hotels
- Cruise Ship
- Ferry
- Beach
- following dining and lodging reviews indicates a map-grid coordinate

Caribbean Sea

Punta Molas
PUNTA MOLAS FARO

CASTILLO REAL

Punta Norte

Isla de Pasión

COZUMEL COUNTRY CLUB

SAN GERVASIO

Playa Azul Golf and Beach Resort

Coral Princess Hotel & Resort

Playa San Juan

✈ **AIRPORT**

Cozumel Palace

SAN MIGUEL

← TO PLAYA DEL CARMEN

PUNTA LANGOSTA

Plaza Central

Av. Benito Juárez

PUNTA ESTE

Hotel Cozumel and Resort

Blue Angel Resort

PUNTA MORENA

Casa del Mar

Ventanas al Mar

El Cid la Ceiba

Villablanca Garden Beach Hotel

Coconuts ■

PUERTO MAYA PIER

← TO PUERTO MORELOS

COMMERICAL PIER

Alfredo di Roma
Presidente InterContinental Cozumel Resort & Spa

Playa de San Martín

Playa Bonita ■

PARQUE CHANKANAAB

Playa Corona

Aura Cozumel
□ Wyndham Grand Bay

PUNTA CHIQUEROS/ PLAYA BONITA

Playa San Francisco

Paradise Beach

◆ EL CEDRAL

Mr. Sancho's

Iberostar

Caribbean Sea

Playa Palancar

◆ EL CARACOL

PARQUE PUNTA SUR

REEFS

0   3 miles

0   3 kilometers

PUNTA CELERAIN FARO

ZONA HOTELERA NORTE

$$ ⊞ **Coral Princess Hotel and Resort.** Good snorkeling off the rocky shore-
☺ line and a relaxed family feel makes this a north-coast favorite. **Pros:**
excellent snorkeling right off beach; decent, well-priced meals; family-
friendly. **Cons:** can be noisy; some rooms lack bathtubs. **TripAdvisor:**
"location was quiet and far away from the cruise ship crowds," "on one
of the best snorkeling reefs in Cozumel," "great value for the money."
⊠ *Carretera Costera Norte, Km 2.5* ☎ *987/872–3200 or 800/253–2702*
⊕ *www.coralprincess.com* ⤴ *109 rooms, 24 suites* ♿ *In-room: a/c, safe,*
kitchen (some). In-hotel: restaurant, bar, pools, gym, water sports, park-
ing ❡⊘ *Breakfast.* ✛ *B3.*

$$$ ⊞ **Playa Azul Golf and Beach Resort.** This romantic boutique hotel has
★ bright and airy rooms facing the ocean. **Pros:** small and intimate feel;
excellent spa; no greens fees. **Cons:** unheated pool and no hot tub; may
be too quiet for some; rocky beach. **TripAdvisor:** "great for a family,"
"attentive service charm cleanliness," "every room has a porch looking
over the ocean." ⊠ *Carretera Costera Norte, Km 4* ☎ *987/869–5160*
⊕ *www.playa-azul.com* ⤴ *36 rooms, 16 suites, 1 house* ♿ *In-room: a/c,*
safe, Wi-Fi. In-hotel: restaurants, bars, pool, spa, beach, water sports,
parking ❡⊘ *Breakfast* ✛ *A3.*

ZONA HOTELERA SUR

$$$$ ⊞ **Aura Cozumel Wyndham Grand Bay.** Opened in 2008, this elegant,
all-inclusive boutique hotel raises the standard for the southern coast's
string of all-inclusive resorts. **Pros:** high-tech; luxurious suite amenities (rare on Cozumel); intimate, sophisticated ambience. **Cons:** far
from town; offshore snorkeling not very good; no kids. **TripAdvisor:**
"lived up to everything we expected," "total relaxation in a smaller
intimate setting," "food at Aura is fantastic." ⊠ *Carretera Costera Sur,*
Km 12.9 ☎ *987/872–9320, 800/773–4349 in U.S.* ⊕ *www.auraresorts.*
com ⤴ *87 suites* ♿ *In-room: a/c, safe, Wi-Fi. In-hotel: restaurants, bars,*
pools, gym, beach, water sports, laundry, parking, some age restrictions
❡⊘ *All-inclusive* ✛ *B5.*

$$ ⊞ **Blue Angel Resort.** A complete makeover in 2009 has turned this small
★ diver-friendly hangout into a real gem. **Pros:** friendly, repeat clientele;
clean; close to town; great snorkeling. **Cons:** non-divers may feel out of
place. **TripAdvisor:** "liked the smallness of it," "scuba trips were profes-
sionally done," "the facility keeps getting better." ⊠ *Carretera Sur, Km*
2.2 ☎ *987/872–0819 or 866/779–9986* ⊕ *www.blueangelresort.com*
⤴ *22 rooms* ♿ *In-room: a/c, safe. In-hotel: restaurant, pool, beach,*
water sports ❡⊘ *Breakfast* ✛ *B3.*

$$ ⊞ **Casa del Mar.** Rooms vary considerably at this three-story hotel, which
caters mostly to divers. **Pros:** good dive shop; optional, reasonably
priced all-inclusive plan. **Cons:** air-conditioning weak in some rooms;
non-divers may feel out of place. **TripAdvisor:** "affordable accommodations with many perks," "a nice non all inclusive hotel," "good value
dive resort." ⊠ *Carretera Sur, Km 4* ☎ *987/872–1900 or 888/577–2758*
⊕ *www.casadelmarcozumel.com* ⤴ *98 rooms, 8 cabanas* ♿ *In-room:*

5

Presidente InterContinental Cozumel Resort and Spa

a/c. In-hotel: restaurant, bars, pool, water sports, tennis court, business center, parking †⦾† *No meals* ✛ *B4.*

$$$ ⊞ **El Cid la Ceiba.** A favorite among divers and frequent Cozumel visitors, this compact property was originally built in 1978 beside a shady ceiba (a tree sacred to the Maya). **Pros:** great Mexican food in restaurant and reasonably priced all-inclusive option available; good snorkeling offshore. **Cons:** massive cruise ships nearby mar sea view; pool scene can be rowdy. **TripAdvisor:** "outdoor spa near the beach," "view was spectacular," "close to downtown for shopping and dining." ✉ *Carretera Chankanaab, Km 4.5* ☎ *987/872–0844* ⊕ *www.elcid.com* ⬅ *60 rooms* ⌂ *In-room: a/c, safe, kitchen (some). In-hotel: restaurants, bars, pools, tennis court, gym, spa, beach, water sports, parking* †⦾† *Multiple meal plans* ✛ *B4.*

$$$$ ⊞ **Cozumel Palace.** This gorgeous all-inclusive hotel is part of the popular Palace Resorts chain. **Pros:** in-room hot tubs; good honeymoon hideaway. **Cons:** sales pressure; slow elevators. **TripAdvisor:** "staff at this resort was simply incredible," "loved the snorkeling right off of the deck," "simply one of the best values." ✉ *Av. Rafael E. Melgar, Km 1.5* ☎ *987/872–9430 or 800/635–1836* ⊕ *www.palaceresorts.com* ⬅ *175 rooms* ⌂ *In-room: a/c, safe, Wi-Fi. In-hotel: restaurants, bars, pools, gym, spa, water sports, children's programs, parking* †⦾† *All-inclusive* ✛ *B3.*

$$ ⊞ **Hotel Cozumel and Resort.** On sunny days in high season, families and revelers surround the enormous pool at this hotel close to town; activity directors enliven the crowd with games and loud music. **Pros:** 10-minute walk from town; near grocery stores and restaurants; recently added 10 fully handicap-accessible rooms. **Cons:** rocky beach area; poolside entertainment sometimes loud and annoying; Wi-Fi access unreliable. **TripAdvisor:** "guests have no value," "hotel in need of repair and refreshing," "decent resort but would look for other lodging." ✉ *Carretera Sur, Km 1.7* ☎ *987/872–9020* ⊕ *www.hotelcozumel.com.mx* ⬅ *181 rooms* ⌂ *In-room: a/c, safe, Wi-Fi. In-hotel: restaurants, bar, pools, gym, beach, water sports, children's programs, parking* †⦾† *Multiple meal plans* ✛ *B3.*

$$$$ ⊞ **Iberostar Cozumel.** Jungle greenery surrounds this all-inclusive resort at Cozumel's southernmost point. **Pros:** large pool area with plenty of lounge chairs. **Cons:** murky water; so-so food without much variety. **TripAdvisor:** "nice resort that is well worth the money," "very kid friendly," "expect good value but not great in every detail." ✉ *Carretera Chankanaab, Km 17, past El Cedral turnoff* ☎ *987/872–9900 or 888/923–2722* ⊕ *www.iberostar. com* ⬅ *300 rooms 6 suites* ⌂ *In-room: a/c, safe. In-hotel: restaurants, bars, pools, tennis courts, gym, spa, beach, water sports, children's programs, parking* †⦾† *All-inclusive* ✛ *B5.*

> **WORD OF MOUTH**
>
> "This may be on the higher end of reasonable, but I've gone there twice for the snorkeling—Presidente InterContinental. I've booked it through Apple or Funjet or similar and stayed in one of the less expensive room options to get the great snorkeling right from the beach, which is right out of your hotel door. The resident iguanas are photogenic, too."
> — atravelynn

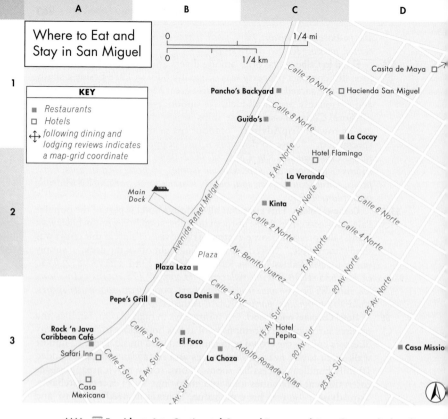

Where to Eat and
Stay in San Miguel

0   1/4 mi

0   1/4 km

KEY

■ Restaurants
□ Hotels
✥ following dining and
  lodging reviews indicates
  a map-grid coordinate

Casita de Maya □

Pancho's Backyard ■   □ Hacienda San Miguel

Guido's ■

La Cocay ■

Hotel Flamingo
□

La Veranda ■

Main
Dock

Kinta ■

Calle 10 Norte
Calle 8 Norte
5 Av. Norte
Calle 6 Norte
10 Av. Norte
Calle 4 Norte
Avenida Rafael Melgar
Calle 2 Norte
15 Av. Norte
20 Av. Norte
25 Av. Norte

Plaza

Av. Benito Juarez

Plaza Leza ■

Calle 1 Sur

Pepe's Grill ■   Casa Denis ■

Rock 'n Java
Caribbean Café ■
Safari Inn □

Calle 3 Sur

El Foco ■

La Choza ■

Adolfo Rosada Salas

Hotel
Pepita
□

15 Av. Sur
5 Av. Sur
20 Av. Sur
25 Av. Sur

Casa Missio ■

Casa
Mexicana □

$$$$ ⌂ **Presidente InterContinental Cozumel Resort and Spa**. Cozumel's loveliest
Fodor's Choice   ⏲ resort is a thoroughly modern, sophisticated property. **Pros**: secluded
★   and spacious feel; high-quality beds and linens; professional service.
Cons: may be too quiet for partyers; far from town. **TripAdvisor**: "ocean
on one side and lush jungle on the other," "ideal spot for relaxation,"
"away from the hustle and bustle." ✉ *Carretera Chankanaab, Km 6.5*
☎ *987/872–9500 or 800/327–0200* ⊕ *www.intercontinentalcozumel.
com* ⇆ *183 rooms, 37 suites* ♿ *In-room: a/c, safe, Wi-Fi. In-hotel: restaurants, bars, pools, tennis courts, gym, spa, beach, water sports, children's programs, parking* ¶⚪ *No meals* ✥ *B4.*

$$ ⌂ **Villablanca Garden Beach Hotel**. The architecture at this hotel is
unusual—several low-rise buildings framing generous lawns house the
guest rooms, the largest of which have white Moorish facades and arch-
ways separating the living and sleeping areas. **Pros**: lush gardens around
pool; good value. **Cons**: no dressers in rooms. **TripAdvisor**: "great loca-
tion for diving," "for the money this is a great place," "price is awe-
some." ✉ *Carretera Chankanaab, Km 3* ☎ *987/872–0730* ⊕ *www.
villablanca.net* ⇆ *45 rooms and suites, 1 penthouse, 3 villas* ♿ *In-room:
a/c, kitchen (some), Wi-Fi (extra charge). In-hotel: restaurant, pool,
tennis court, parking* ¶⚪ *No meals* ✥ *B4.*

SAN MIGUEL

$$$ **Casa Mexicana.** A dramatic staircase leads up to this hotel's wind-
Fodor's Choice swept lobby, and distinctive rooms are decorated in subtle blues and
★ yellows. **Pros:** great downtown location near restaurants and shops;
friendly staff (especially bartenders); substantial breakfast. **Cons:** no
beach; tiny pool; some street noise. **TripAdvisor:** "ton of bar noise,"
"elegant hotel right in the center of town," "best value around." ⊠ *Av.
Rafael E. Melgar Sur 457, between Calles 5 and 7* ☎ *987/872–9090 or
877/228–6747* ⊕ *www.casamexicanacozumel.com* ⤴ *90 rooms* △ *In-
room: a/c, safe, Internet. In-hotel: bar, pool, gym* |◯| *Breakfast* ⊹ *A3.*

$$ **Casita de Maya.** Though it's practically across the street from the airport and a 10-minute drive from the waterfront, this small inn garners
raves from return guests. **Pros:** low rates; non-touristy locale. **Cons:**
noise from other guests in the courtyard setting; distance from plaza
and beach. **TripAdvisor:** "a true gem," "close to town," "downtown is
within walking distance." ⊠ *Av. Bis 65 and Blvd. Aeropuerto No. 420*
☎ *987/869–2606* ⊕ *www.casitademaya.com* △ *In-room: a/c, Internet.
In-hotel: pool, parking* ⊹ *D1.*

$$ **Hacienda San Miguel.** At this small inn, with its two-story buildings set
around a lush courtyard, you can have continental breakfast delivered
to your room. **Pros:** quiet but central; plenty of great restaurants nearby;
courtyard gardens make it feel like a private home. **Cons:** musty smell
in some rooms; air-conditioning can be noisy; no pool. **TripAdvisor:**
"convenient to great restaurants," "beautiful courtyard," "beds were
like concrete." ⊠ *Calle 10 Norte 500, at Av. 5* ☎ *987/872–1986 or
866/712–6387* ⊕ *www.haciendasanmiguel.com* ⤴ *7 studios, 3 suites,
1 town house* △ *In-room: a/c, safe, kitchen* |◯| *Breakfast* ⊹ *C1.*

$$ **Hotel Flamingo.** You get a lot for your pesos at this budget hotel, which
includes a rooftop sundeck with a view of the water. **Pros:** close to res-
taurants and shops; staff and guests share budget travel tips; friendly
bartender. **Cons:** street and bar noise; limited street parking. **TripAdvisor:** "nice open air courtyard," "chic little boutique hotel close to
everything," "a good find." ⊠ *Calle 6 Norte 81, near Cozumel Museum*
☎ *987/872–1264 or 800/806–1601* ⊕ *www.hotelflamingo.com* ⤴ *16
rooms, 1 penthouse* △ *In-room: a/c, safe, kitchen (some). In-hotel: res-
taurant, bar* |◯| *Breakfast* ⊹ *C2.*

¢ **Hotel Pepita.** Despite being more than 50 years old, the Pepita is one
of the best budget hotels on the island. **Pros:** untouristy neighborhood;
amiable staff. **Cons:** buggy (keep doors closed); no phones in rooms;
some staff speak Spanish only. **TripAdvisor:** "best value," "nothing special but a clean place," "great deal." ⊠ *Av. 15 Sur 120* ☎ *987/872–0098*
⊕ *www.hotelpepitacozumel.com* ⤴ *27 rooms* △ *In-room: a/c, Internet*
▭ *No credit cards* |◯| *No meals* ⊹ *C3*

¢ **Safari Inn.** Above the Aqua Safari dive shop on the waterfront,
this small hotel has comfy beds, powerful hot-water showers, air-
conditioning, and the camaraderie of fellow scuba fanatics. **Pros:** above
an excellent dive shop; immaculately clean; in middle of town action.
Cons: some street noise; no in-room phones or TV. **TripAdvisor:** "great
dive package," "rooms are basic very clean," "showers were great."
⊠ *Av. Rafael E. Melgar and Calle 5 Sur* ☎ *987/872–0101* ⊕ *www.*

5

aquasafari.com ⌁ *12 rooms* ⬙ *In-room: a/c, no TV. In-hotel: water sports* ⓘ *No meals* ✛ *A3.*

WINDWARD COAST

$$ \quad $$

$$ ⊞ **Ventanas al Mar.** The lights of San Miguel are but a distant glow on the horizon when you look west from the only hotel on the windward coast. **Pros:** blissful solitude; long beach great for sunset walks. **Cons:** limited food and drink options; driving at night not advisable, as coastal road is not lighted. **TripAdvisor:** "splendid isolation but car essential," "ocean lover's delight," "isolation and security." ✉ *East-coast road north of Coconuts* ☎ *987/105–2684* ⊕ *www.ventanasalmar.com.mx* ⌁ *13 rooms, 1 suite* ⬙ *In-room: a/c, kitchen, no TV. In-hotel: beach, water sports, parking* ⊟ *No credit cards* ⓘ *Breakfast* ✛ *C4.*

NIGHTLIFE

Discos and trendy clubs are not Cozumel's scene. In fact, some visitors complain that the town seems to shut down completely by midnight. Perhaps it's the emphasis on sun and scuba diving that sends everyone to bed early. (It's hard to be a night owl when your dive boat leaves first thing in the morning.) Cruise-ship passengers mobbing the bars seem to party more than those staying on the island, so the rowdiest action sometimes takes place in the afternoon, when revelers pull out the stops before reboarding. A few excellent salsa bands have come to the island recently and play at bars and beach clubs. Their performances tend to draw more locals and foreigners living on the island than tourists.

BARS

Martinis and high-end tequilas are on order at **1.5 Tequila Lounge** (✉ *Av. Rafael Melgar at Calle 11 Sur* ☎ *987/872–4421*) on the south end of downtown. The waterfront location and classy lounge ambience set it apart from the rowdier bars, though the nighttime scene does get pretty wild here as well.

Carlos 'n Charlie's and Señor Frog's (✉ *Av. Rafael E. Melgar at Punta Langosta* ☎ *987/872–0191*) are members of the Carlos Anderson chain of rowdy restaurant-bars that attract crowds. The *Animal House* ambience includes loud rock music and a libertine, anything-goes dancing scene that seems to have special allure to the cruising set.

Nothing beats live entertainment.

For a more sophisticated scene with mojitos and great cigars, check out **DLounge** (formerly Havana Blue) (⊠ *Av. Rafael E. Melgar and Calle 10 Norte, 2nd fl.* ☎ *987/869–5300*) in the flashy Forum shopping mall.

Lively, rowdy **Fat Tuesdays** (⊠ *Av. Juárez between Av. Rafael E. Melgar and Calle 3 Sur* ☎ *987/872–5130*) draws crowds day and night for frozen daiquiris, ice-cold beers, and blaring rock.

Viva Mexico (⊠ *Av. Rafael E. Melgar* ☎ *987/872–0799*) sometimes has a DJ who spins Latin and American dance music into the wee hours. There's also an extensive snack menu. This place is wildly popular anytime of day or night. The best seats are near the second-story railing overlooking the waterfront.

DANCE CLUBS

Tiki Tok. A tiki-themed bar by day, this locale comes back to life as a dance club come nightfall. Local group Explosión Latina draws salsa aficionados of all stripes from 10:30 pm to 2 am Thursday through Saturday, while a DJ spins '70s, '80s, Latin, and reggaeton (a blend of West-Indian and Latin beats) the rest of the week. ⊠ *Av. Rafael E. Melgar between Calles 2 and 4 Norte* ☎ *987/869–8119.*

LIVE MUSIC

Sunday evenings from 8 to 10, locals head for the *zócalo* (main square) to hear mariachis and island musicians playing tropical tunes.

The band at the **Hard Rock Cafe** (✉ *Av. Rafael E. Melgar between Av. Juárez and Calle 2, 2nd fl.* ☎ *987/872–5273*) often rocks until near dawn. Air-conditioning is a major plus.

If tearing up the dance floor isn't your thing, but you still find yourself craving some live music, swing by **'Ohana** ✉ *Av. 5 between Calles 6 and 8 Norte* ☎ *987/119–0343* ⊕ *www.ohanacozumel.com*. This new café-bar for live jazz is open from 8:30 to 11 pm Thursday through Saturday.

Salsa bands play on Friday nights at **Palapito Delmedio** (✉ *Carretera Chankanaab, Km 3* ☎ *987/869–1406*). This palapa-covered club across the street from the Villablanca hotel rocks until the wee hours from Thursday through Saturday night.

The salsa band Aquino plays beneath the palapas on Sunday afternoons at **Playa Azul** (✉ *Carretera Norte Km 4*). They're onstage from 3 to 4:30 pm (though sometimes play longer).

SHOPPING

Cozumel's main souvenir-shopping area is downtown along Avenida Rafael E. Melgar and on some side streets around the plaza. There are also clusters of shops at **Plaza del Sol** (✉ *East side of main plaza*) and **Vista del Mar** (✉ *Av. Rafael E. Melgar 45, between Calles 5 and 7*). Malls at the cruise-ship piers aim to please passengers seeking jewelry, perfume, sportswear, and low-end souvenirs at high-end prices.

Most downtown shops accept U.S. dollars; many goods are priced in dollars. To get better prices, pay with cash or traveler's checks—some shops tack a hefty surcharge on credit-card purchases. Shops, restaurants, and streets are always crowded between 10 am and 2 pm, but get calmer in the evening. Traditionally, stores are open from 9 to 1 (except Sunday) and 5 to 9, but those nearest the pier tend to stay open all day, particularly during high season. Most shops are closed Sunday morning.

■TIP➜ When you shop in Cozumel, be sure you don't buy anything made with black coral. Not only is it overpriced, it's also an endangered species, and you may be barred from bringing it to the United States and other countries.

MARKETS

☾ There's a **crafts market** (✉ *Calle 1 Sur, behind Plaza del Sol building*)
★ in town that sells a respectable assortment of Mexican wares. It's the best place to practice your bartering skills while shopping for blankets, T-shirts, hammocks, and pottery.

For fresh produce, fish, chiles, and a taste of local life, try the **Mercado Municipal** (✉ *Calle Adolfo Rosado Salas between Avs. 20 and 25 Sur* ☎ *No phone*) open daily from 6:30 am to 3 pm.

SHOPPING MALLS

Forum Shops (✉ *Av. Rafael E. Melgar and Calle 10 Norte* ☎ *No phone*) is a flashy marble-and-glass mall with jewels glistening in glass cases and an overabundance of eager salesclerks. Diamonds International

and Tanzanite International have shops in the Forum and all over Avenida Rafael E. Melgar, as does Roger's Boots, a leather store. There's a Havana Blue bar upstairs, where shoppers select expensive cigars.

Puerta Maya (⊠ *Carretera Sur at southern cruise dock*) is a mall geared to cruise-ship passengers, with branches of many of downtown's most popular shops, restaurants, and bars. It's close to the ships at the end of a huge parking lot.

Punta Langosta (⊠ *Av. Rafael E. Melgar 551, at Calle 7*), a fancy multi-level shopping mall, is across the street from the cruise-ship dock. An enclosed pedestrian walkway leads over the street from the ships to the center, which houses several jewelry and sportswear stores. The center is designed to lure cruise-ship passengers into shopping in air-conditioned comfort and has reduced traffic for local businesses.

SPECIALTY STORES

CLOTHING

Several trendy sportswear stores line Avenida Rafael E. Melgar between Calles 2 and 6.

Exotica (⊠ *Av. Juárez at plaza* ☎ 987/872–5880) has high-quality sportswear and shirts with nature-themed designs.

Island Outfitters (⊠ *Av. Rafael E. Melgar at plaza* ☎ 987/872–0132) has Mexican crafts, high-quality sportswear, beach towels, and sarongs.

Mr. Buho (⊠ *Av. Rafael E. Melgar between Calles 3 and 5* ☎ 987/872–1832) specializes in white-and-black clothes and has well-made guayabera shirts and cotton dresses.

CRAFTS

At **Balam Mayan Feather** (⊠ *Av. 5 and Calle 2 Norte* ☎ 987/869–0548) artists create intricate paintings on feathers from local birds.

★   **Los Cinco Soles** (⊠ *Av. Rafael E. Melgar and Calle 8 Norte* ☎ 987/872–0132 ⊕ *www.loscincosoles.com*) is the best one-stop shop for crafts from around Mexico. Several display rooms, covering almost an entire block, are filled with clothing, furnishings, home-decor items, and jewelry. They also have a shop at the Puerta Maya cruise pier and at the Punta Langosta shopping mall.

At Cozumel's best art gallery, **Galería Azul** (⊠ *449 Av. 15 Norte between Calles 8 and 10* ☎ 987/869–0963 ⊕ *www.cozumelglassart.com*), artist Greg Deitrich displays his engraved blown glass along with paintings, jewelry, and other works by local artists. Deitrich recently moved the gallery to his home, where you can see him working with his glassware and silk paintings. It's open Monday to Friday from 11 to 7 and by appointment.

El Porton (⊠ *Av. 5 Sur and Calle 1 Sur* ☎ 987/872–5606) has a collection of masks and unusual crafts.

Antiques and high-quality silver jewelry are the draws at **Shalom** (⊠ *Av. 10, No. 25* ☎ 987/872–3783).

Viva Mexico (⊠ *Av. Rafael Melgar at Adolfo Rosado Salas* ☎ 987/872–5466) sells souvenirs and handicrafts from all over Mexico; it's a great place to find T-shirts, blankets, and trinkets. There are also branches at the Puerta Maya cruise pier, and on Avenida Rafael Melgar between Calles 4 and 6 Norte.

GROCERY STORES

The grocery store **Chedraui** (⊠ *Carretera Chankanaab, Km 1.5, and Calle 15 Sur* ☎ *987/872–5404*) is open daily from 7 am to 10 pm, and also carries clothing, kitchenware, appliances, and furniture.

The superstore **Mega** (⊠ *Av. Rafael E. Melgar at Calle 11*), operated by the giant chain Commercial Mexicana, opened its doors in 2009. It's a grocery, pharmacy, and department store all under one big roof. It has a huge enclosed parking lot and pretty much anything you would need for a short or extended stay on Cozumel. It's open daily from 8 am to 10 pm.

JEWELRY

Diamond Creations (⊠ *Av. Rafael E. Melgar Sur 131* ☎ *987/872–5330*) lets you custom-design pieces of jewelry from a collection of loose diamonds, emeralds, rubies, sapphires, or tanzanite. The shop and its affiliates, Tanzanite International and Silver International, have multiple locations along the waterfront and in the shopping malls—in fact, you can't avoid them.

Look for silver, gold, and coral jewelry—especially bracelets and earrings—at **Joyería Palancar** (⊠ *Av. Rafael E. Melgar Norte 15* ☎ *987/872–1468*).

Luxury Avenue (Ultrafemme) (⊠ *Av. Rafael E. Melgar 341* ☎ *987/872–1217*) sells high-end goods including watches and perfume.

Pama (⊠ *Av. Rafael E. Melgar Sur 9* ☎ *987/872–0090*), near the pier, carries imported jewelry, perfumes, and glassware.

One of Mexico's most famous jewelry designers, **Tanya Moss** (⊠ *Av. Rafael E. Melgar at Punta Langosta* ☎ *987/869–1612*) creates original silver and gold necklaces and earrings that have become collectibles for those in the know. There's also a shop at the Hotel Presidente InterContinental.

Innovative designs and top-quality stones are available at **Van Cleef and Arpels** (⊠ *Av. Rafael E. Melgar Norte across from ferry* ☎ *987/872–6540*).

SPORTS AND THE OUTDOORS

Most people come to Cozumel for the water sports—especially scuba diving, snorkeling, and fishing. Services and equipment rentals are available throughout the island, especially through major hotels and watersports centers at the beach clubs.

If you're curious about what's underneath Cozumel's waters but don't like getting wet, **Atlantis Submarine** (⊠ *Carretera Sur, Km 4, across from Hotel Casa del Mar* ☎ *987/872–5671 or 866/546–7820* ⊕ *www.atlantisadventures.com*) runs 1½-hour submarine rides that explore the Chankanaab Reef and surrounding area; tickets for the tours are $100. Even divers enjoy going down 100 feet below sea level. Claustrophobes may not be able to handle the sardine-can conditions.

FISHING

The waters off Cozumel swarm with more than 230 species of fish, making this one of the world's best deep-sea fishing destinations. During billfish migration season, from late April through June, blue marlin, white marlin, and sailfish are plentiful, and world-record catches aren't uncommon.

WORD OF MOUTH

My husband is a bottom fisherman and has done that many times in Cozumel. He usually goes with one of the boats from the marina. Many times the guys just go down to the Caleta (marina) and make contact with one of the local boats to go out for a day of fishing. — TC

Most sportfishing boats are located in the Puerto Abrigo marina just north of San Miguel. Fishing boats are also located at **La Caleta,** the marina on the south side, beside the Presidente InterContinental resort. At this writing, La Caleta was being refurbished. Most sportfishing companies are affiliated with dive shops and offer a full range of water activities.

CHARTERS

You can charter high-speed fishing boats for about $420 per half day or $600 per day (with a maximum of six people). Your hotel can help arrange daily charters—some offer special deals, with boats leaving from their own docks.

3 Hermanos (☎ 987/872–6417, 651/755–4897 in U.S. ⊕ www. cozumelfishing.com) specializes in deep-sea and fly-fishing trips. Their rates for a half-day deep-sea fishing trip start at $350; a full day is $450. They also offer scuba-diving trips, and their boats are available for group charters (a great way to snorkel and cruise around at your own pace) for $400 for up to six passengers.

Albatros Deep Sea Fishing (☎ 987/872–7904 or 888/333–4643 ⊕ www. albatroscharters.com) offers full-day trips that include boat and crew, tackle and bait, and lunch with beer and soda starting at $575 for up to six people.

All equipment and tackle, lunch with beer, and the boat and crew are also included in **Ocean Tours'** (☎ 987/872–9530 Ext. 8) full-day rates, which start at $650.

GOLF

The **Cozumel Country Club** (⊠ Carretera Costera Norte, Km 5.8 ☎ 987/872–9570 ⊕ www.cozumelcountryclub.com.mx) has an 18-hole championship golf course. The gorgeous fairways amid mangroves and a lagoon are the work of the Nicklaus Design Group, and have been declared an Audubon nature reserve. The greens fee is $169 before 12:30 pm and $105 after, and includes a shared golf cart. Some hotels, including Playa Azul, offer golf packages here.

HORSEBACK RIDING

Rancho Buenavista (✉ *Carretera Perimetral, Km 32.5* ☎ *987/872–1537* ⊕ *www.buenavistaranch.com*) provides four-hour rides through the jungle starting at $65 per person.

KITEBOARDING

Raul De Lille, a Cozumel native, former Olympic kiteboarding competitor, and certified instructor offers lessons and kiteboarding sessions through **Kite Cozumel** (☎ *987/103–6711* ⊕ *kitecozumel.com*). Individual and group classes cost $150 to $250 for a two- to three-hour class. Tours take kiteboarders to various parts of the island where the winds are strongest. The Downwinder tour, which includes a boat ride to the best areas, costs $300.

SNORKELING AND SCUBA DIVING

Aqua Safari (✉ *Av. Rafael E. Melgar 429, between Calles 5 and 7 Sur* ☎ *987/872–0101*) is among the island's oldest and most professional shops. Owner Bill Horn has long been involved in efforts to protect the reefs and stays on top of local environmental issues. The shop provides beginning and advanced PADI certification, and daily introductory scuba courses.

Sergio Sandoval of **Aquatic Sports and Scuba Cozumel** (✉ *Calle 21 Sur and Av. 20 Sur* ☎ *987/872–0640* ⊕ *www.scubacozumel.com*) gets rave reviews from his clients, many of them guests at the Flamingo Hotel. His boats carry only six to eight divers so the trips are extremely personalized.

Blue Angel (✉ *Carretera Sur Km 2.2* ☎ *987/872–1631 or 866/779–9986*) offers combo dive and snorkel trips so families who don't all scuba can still stick together. Along with dive trips to local reefs, they offer PADI courses.

Del Mar Aquatics (✉ *Casa Del Mar Hotel Carretera Sur, Km 4* ☎ *987/872–5949*) has been in operation since 1987 and offers dive trips, certification, and fishing trips.

Eagle Ray Divers (✉ *La Caleta Marina near the Presidente InterContinental hotel* ☎ *987/872–5735 or 866/465–1616* ⊕ *www.eagleraydivers.com*) offers snorkeling trips (the three-reef trip lets nondivers explore beyond the shore) and dive instruction. As befits their name, the company keeps track of the eagle rays that appear off Cozumel from December to February and runs trips for advanced divers to walls where the rays congregate. Beginners can also see rays around some of the reefs.

Fury Catamarans (✉ *Carretera Sur beside Casa del Mar Hotel* ☎ *987/872–5145*) runs snorkeling tours from its 45-foot catamarans. Rates begin at about $59 per day and include equipment and a guide, and soft drinks, beer, margaritas, and a beach party with lunch.

Dive magazines regularly rate **Scuba Du** (✉ *At the Presidente InterContinental hotel* ☎ *987/872–9505, 310/684–5556 from the U.S.*) among the best dive shops in the Caribbean. Along with the requisite Cozumel dives, the company offers an advanced divers trip to walls off Punta Sur.

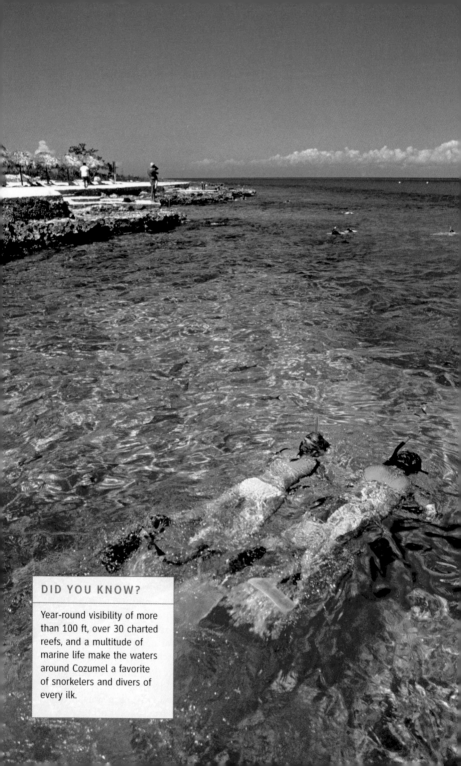

DID YOU KNOW?

Year-round visibility of more than 100 ft, over 30 charted reefs, and a multitude of marine life make the waters around Cozumel a favorite of snorkelers and divers of every ilk.

COZUMEL DIVING AND SNORKELING

First comes the giant step, a leap from a dry boat into the warm Caribbean Sea. Then the slow descent to white sand framed by rippling brain coral and waving purple sea fans. If you lean back, you can look up toward the sea's surface. The water off Cozumel is so clear you can see puffy white clouds in the sky even when you're submerged 20 feet under.

With more than 30 charted reefs whose depths average 50–80 feet and water temperatures around 24°C–27°C (75°F–80°F) during peak diving season (June–August, when hotel rates are coincidentally at their lowest), Cozumel is far and away the place to dive in Mexico. More than 60,000 divers come here each year.

Because of the diversity of coral formations and the dramatic underwater peaks and valleys, divers consider Cozumel's Palancar Reef (promoters now call it the Maya Reef) to be one of the top five in the world. Sea turtles headed to the beach to lay their eggs swim beside divers in May and June. Fifteen-pound lobsters wave their antennae from beneath coral ledges; they've been protected in Cozumel's National Marine Park for so long they've lost all fear of humans. Long, green moray eels still appear rather menacing as they bare their fangs at curious onlookers, and snaggle-toothed barracuda look ominous as they swim by. But all in all, diving off Cozumel is relaxing, rewarding, and so addictive you simply can't do it just once.

Hurricane Wilma damaged the reefs somewhat during her 2005 attack and rearranged the underwater landscape. Favorite snorkeling and diving spots close to shore were affected, and the fish may not be as abundant as they were in the past.

The reef is home to brain coral and huge sponges.

DIVE SITES

Cozumel's reefs stretch for 32 km (20 mi), beginning at the international pier and continuing to Punta Celarain at the island's southernmost tip. Following is a rundown of Cozumel's main dive destinations.

◼ **Chankanaab Reef.** This inviting reef lies south of Parque Chankanaab, about 350 yards offshore. Large underground caves are filled with striped grunt, snapper, sergeant majors, and butterfly fish. At 55 feet, there's another large coral formation that's often filled with crabs, lobster, barrel sponges, and angelfish. If you drift a bit farther south, you can see the Balones de Chankanaab, balloon-shaped coral heads at 70 feet.

◼ **Colombia Reef.** Several miles off Palancar, the reef reaches 82–98 feet and is best suited for experienced divers. Its underwater structures are as varied as those of Palancar Reef, with large canyons and ravines to explore. Clustered near the overhangs are large groupers, jacks, rays, and an occasional sea turtle.

◼ **Felipe Xicotencatl (C-53 Wreck).** Sunk in 2000 specifically for scuba divers, this 154-foot-long minesweeper is located on a sandy bottom about 80 feet deep near Tormentos and Chankanaab. Created as an artificial reef to decrease some of the traffic on the natural reefs, the ship is open so divers can explore the interior and is gradually attracting schools of fish.

◼ **Maracaibo Reef.** Considered one of the most difficult reefs, Maracaibo is a thrilling dive with strong currents and intriguing old coral formations. Although there are shallow areas, only advanced divers who can cope with the current should attempt Maracaibo.

◼ **Palancar Reef.** About 2 km (1 mi) offshore, Palancar is actually a series of varying coral formations with about 40 dive locations. It's filled with winding canyons, deep ravines, narrow crevices, archways, tunnels, and caves. Black and red coral and huge elephant-ear, and barrel sponges are among the attractions. At the section called Horseshoe, a series of coral heads form a natural horseshoe

shape. This is one of the most popular sites for dive boats and can become crowded.

◼ **Paraíso Reef.** About 330 feet offshore, running parallel to the international cruise-ship pier, this reef averages 30–50 feet. It's a perfect spot to dive before you head for deeper drop-offs. There are impressive formations of star and brain coral as well as sea fans, sponges, sea eels, and yellow rays. It's wonderful for night diving.

◼ **Paseo El Cedral.** Running parallel to Santa Rosa reef, this flat reef has gardenlike valleys full of fish, including angelfish, grunt, and snapper. At depths of 35–55 feet, you can also spot rays.

◼ **San Francisco Reef.** Considered Cozumel's shallowest wall dive (35–50 feet), this 1-km (1/2-mi) reef runs parallel to Playa San Francisco and has many varieties of reef fish. You'll need to take a dive boat to get here.

◼ **Santa Rosa Wall.** North of Palancar, Santa Rosa is renowned among experienced divers for deep dives and drift

Chankanaab Reef

Young yellow sponges, Palancar Reef.

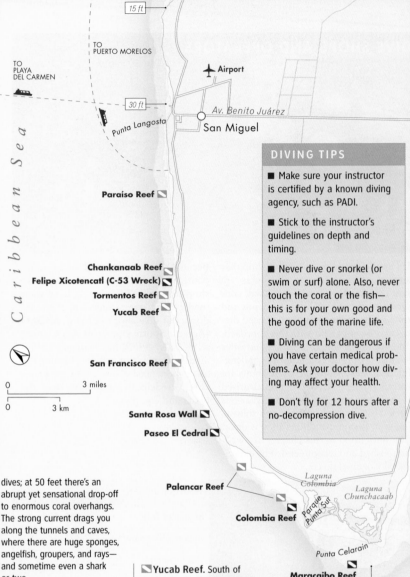

15 ft

TO
PUERTO MORELOS

✈ Airport

TO
PLAYA
DEL CARMEN

Caribbean Sea

30 ft

Av. Benito Juárez

Punta Langosta

○ San Miguel

Paraíso Reef ◳

DIVING TIPS

■ Make sure your instructor is certified by a known diving agency, such as PADI.

■ Stick to the instructor's guidelines on depth and timing.

■ Never dive or snorkel (or swim or surf) alone. Also, never touch the coral or the fish—this is for your own good and the good of the marine life.

■ Diving can be dangerous if you have certain medical problems. Ask your doctor how diving may affect your health.

■ Don't fly for 12 hours after a no-decompression dive.

5

IN FOCUS COZUMEL DIVING AND SNORKELING

Chankanaab Reef ◳
Felipe Xicotencatl (C-53 Wreck) ◲
Tormentos Reef ◳
Yucab Reef ◳

⊘

San Francisco Reef ◳

0 —————— 3 miles
0 —————— 3 km

Santa Rosa Wall ◲
Paseo El Cedral ◲

◳
Laguna
Colombia
Laguna
Chunchacaab

Palancar Reef ‹
◳
◳
Colombia Reef ◲
Parque
Punta Sur

Punta Celarain

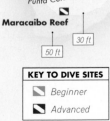

◳
Maracaibo Reef

30 ft

50 ft

KEY TO DIVE SITES

◳ *Beginner*
◲ *Advanced*

dives; at 50 feet there's an abrupt yet sensational drop-off to enormous coral overhangs. The strong current drags you along the tunnels and caves, where there are huge sponges, angelfish, groupers, and rays—and sometime even a shark or two.

◲**Tormentos Reef.** The abundance of sea fans, sponges, sea cucumbers, arrow crabs, green eels, groupers, and other marine life—against a terrifically colorful backdrop—makes this a perfect spot for underwater photography. This variegated reef has a maximum depth of around 70 feet.

◳**Yucab Reef.** South of Tormentos Reef, this relatively shallow reef is close to shore, making it an ideal spot for beginners. About 400 feet long and 55 feet deep, it's teeming with queen angelfish and sea whip swimming around the large coral heads. The one drawback is the strong current, which can reach two or three knots.

DIVE SHOPS AND OPERATORS

It's important to choose a dive shop that suits your expectations. Beginners are best off with the more established, conservative shops that limit the depth and time spent underwater. Experienced divers may be impatient with this approach, and are better suited to shops that offer smaller group dives and more challenging dive sites. More and more shops are merging these days, so don't be surprised if the outfit you dive with one year has been absorbed by another the following year. Recommending a shop is dicey. The ones listed in this chapter are well-established and recommended by experienced Cozumel divers.

Because dive shops tend to be competitive, it's well worth your while to shop around. Many hotels have their own on-site operations, and there are dozens of dive shops in town. **ANOAAT** (Aquatic Sports Operators Association; ☎ 987/872–5955) has listings of affiliated dive operations. Before signing on, ask experienced divers about the place, check credentials, and look over the boats and equipment.

(top) Felipe Xicotencatl (C-53 Wreck). (bottom) Coral, coral and more coral.

WHAT IT COSTS	
Regulator & BC	$15–$25
Underwater camera	$35–$45
Video camera	$75
Pro videos of your dive	$160
Two-tank boat trips	$60–$90
Specialty dives	$70–$100
One-tank afternoon dives	$35–$45
Night dives	$35–$45
Marine park fee	$2

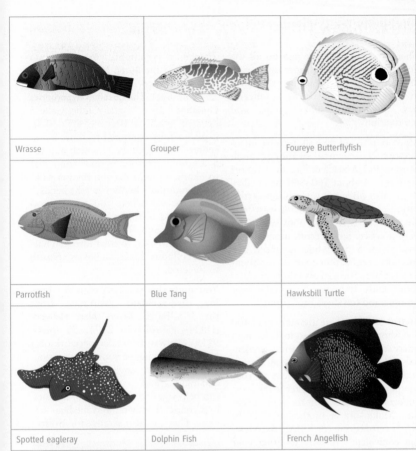

Wrasse	Grouper	Foureye Butterflyfish
Parrotfish	Blue Tang	Hawksbill Turtle
Spotted eagleray	Dolphin Fish	French Angelfish

SNORKELING TIPS

Snorkeling equipment is available at nearly all hotels and beach clubs as well as at Parque Chankanaab, Playa San Francisco, and Parque Punta Sur. Gear rents for less than $10 a day. Snorkeling tours run about $60 and take in the shallow reefs off Palancar, Chankanaab, Colombia, and Yucab.

■ Never turn your back on the ocean, especially if the waves are big.

■ Ask about rip tides before you go in.

■ Enter and exit from a sandy beach area.

■ Avoid snorkeling at dusk and never go in the water after dark.

■ Wear lots of sunscreen, especially on your back and butt cheeks.

■ Don't snorkel too close to the reef. You could get scratched if a wave pushes you.

■ Be mindful of boats.

5

IN FOCUS COZUMEL DIVING AND SNORKELING

SCUBA DIVING

There's no way anyone can do all the deep dives, drift dives, shore dives, wall dives, and night dives in one trip, never mind the theme dives focusing on ecology, archaeology, sunken ships, and photography.

Many hotels and dive shops offer introductory classes in a swimming pool. Most include a beach or boat dive. Resort courses cost about $60–$80. Many dive shops also offer full open-water certification classes, which take at least four days of intensive classroom study and pool practice. Basic certification courses cost about $350, while advanced and specialty certification courses cost about $250–$500. You can also do your classroom study at home, then make your training and test dives on Cozumel.

DIVING SAFELY There are more than 100 dive shops in Cozumel, so look for high safety standards and documented credentials. The best places offer small groups and individual attention. Next to your equipment, your dive master is the most important consideration for your adventure. Make sure he or she has PADI or NAUI certification (or FMAS, the Mexican equivalent). Be sure to bring your own certification card; all reputable shops require customers to show them before diving. If you forget, you may be able to call the agency that certified you and have the card number faxed to the shop.

Keep in mind that much of the reef off Cozumel is a protected National Marine Park. Boats aren't allowed to anchor in certain areas, and you shouldn't touch the coral or take any "souvenirs" from the reefs when you dive there. It's best to swim at least three feet above the reef— not just because coral can sting or cut you, but also because it's easily damaged and grows very slowly; it has taken 2,000 years to reach their present size.

There's a reputable recompression chamber at the **Buceo Médico Mexicano** (⊠ Calle 5 Sur 21B ☎ 987/872–1430 24-hr hotline). The **Cozumel Hyperbarics Chamber** (⊠ San Miguel Clinic, Calle 6 between Avs. 5 and 10 ☎ 987/872–3070) is also a fully equipped recompression center. These chambers, which aim for a 35-minute response time from reef to chamber, treat decompression sickness, commonly known as "the bends," which occurs when you surface too quickly and nitrogen bubbles form in the bloodstream. Recompression chambers are also used to treat nitrogen narcosis, collapsed lungs, and overexposure to the cold.

You may also want to consider buying dive-accident insurance from the U.S.-based **Divers Alert Network** (DAN) (☎ 800/446–2671, 919/684–9119 ⊕ www.diversalertnetwork.org) before embarking on your dive vacation. DAN insurance covers dive accidents and injuries, and their emergency hotline can help you find the best local doctors, hyperbaric chambers, and medical services. They can also arrange for airlifts.

Diver on the Paradise Reef.

Yucatán and Campeche States

WORD OF MOUTH

"Merida is awesome. We based ourselves there for a few days and took a private guided tour of all the ruins nearby (Uxmal and the Puuc region). We also did a day trip out to the coast to the town of Celestun to see the flocks of thousands of pink flamingos . . . it was surreal."

— CarolM

WELCOME TO YUCATÁN AND CAMPECHE STATES

TOP REASONS TO GO

★ **Visiting spectacular Mayan ruins:** Chichén Itzá and Uxmal are two of the largest, most beautiful sites in the region.

★ **Living like a wealthy hacendado:** You can stay in a restored *henequen* (sisal) plantation-turned-hotel and delight in its Old World charm.

★ **Browsing at fantastic craft markets:** This region is known for its handmade *hamacas* (hammocks), piñatas, and other local handicrafts.

★ **Swimming in the secluded, pristine freshwater cenotes:** These sinkholes, like portals to the underworld, are scattered throughout the inland landscape.

★ **The chance to taste the diverse flavors of Yucatecan food:** Mérida has 50-odd restaurants, which serve up local specialties like fish stews and Mayan-originated dishes like *pollo pibil* (chicken cooked in banana leaves).

1 Mérida. Fully urban, and bustling with foot and car traffic, Mérida was once the main stronghold of Spanish colonialism in the peninsula. Tucked among the restaurants, museums, and markets are grand, old, beautifully ornamented mansions and buildings that recall the city's heyday as the wealthiest capital in Mexico.

2 Chichén Itzá, Uxmal, and the Mayan Interior. Yucatán's spectacular Mayan ruins are famous all over the world. The best-known, Chichén Itzá, draws thousands of visitors every year. Farther south is the less-known but beautiful (and typically far less crowded) site of Uxmal. Many smaller archaeological sites—some hardly visited—lie along the Ruta Puuc south of Mérida.

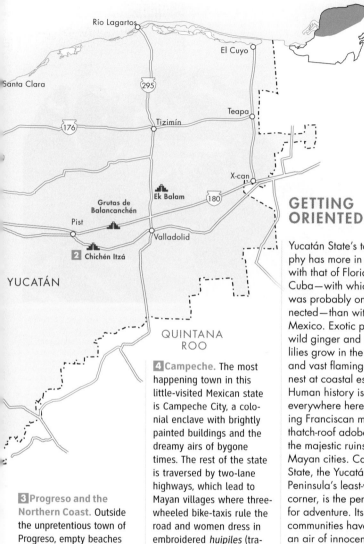

6

GETTING ORIENTED

Yucatán State's topography has more in common with that of Florida and Cuba—with which it was probably once connected—than with central Mexico. Exotic plants like wild ginger and spider lilies grow in the jungles, and vast flamingo colonies nest at coastal estuaries. Human history is evident everywhere here—in looming Franciscan missions, thatch-roof adobe huts, and the majestic ruins of ancient Mayan cities. Campeche State, the Yucatán Peninsula's least-visited corner, is the perfect place for adventure. Its colonial communities have retained an air of innocence, and its protected biospheres, farmland, and jungles are relatively unspoiled. Campeche City, the state's most accessible spot, makes a good hub for exploring other areas, many of which have only basic restaurants and primitive lodgings.

3 Progreso and the Northern Coast. Outside the unpretentious town of Progreso, empty beaches stretch for miles in either direction—punctuated only by fishing villages, estuaries, and salt flats. Bird-watchers and nature lovers gravitate to rustic Celestún and Río Lagartos, home to one of the hemisphere's largest colonies of pink flamingos.

4 Campeche. The most happening town in this little-visited Mexican state is Campeche City, a colonial enclave with brightly painted buildings and the dreamy airs of bygone times. The rest of the state is traversed by two-lane highways, which lead to Mayan villages where three-wheeled bike-taxis rule the road and women dress in embroidered *huipiles* (traditional, white embroidered dresses). Far to the south, along the Guatemalan border, the Reserva de la Biosfera Calakmul is home to thousands of birds, butterflies, and plants—but only hosts about a dozen visitors a day.

YUCATÁN CUISINE

Chefs in Mexico skillfully combine ingredients and techniques from the New World and Old, but the cuisines here vary dramatically from region to region. The flavors of Yucatán are subtle, unique, and not to be missed.

(Above and top right) Cochinita pibil's presentation can vary from restaurant to restaurant. (Bottom right) *Huevos motuleños.*

Regional culinary traditions in the country can be divided into four regions. Foods from the north have an unpretentious culinary tradition; here you'll find dishes that were originally served on ranches and haciendas. On both coasts, seafood takes center stage. The central region includes the area in and around Mexico City, where many of country's most characteristic plates were invented in convent kitchens during colonial times. Foods from the south, including the Yucatán, are singular within Mexico. This region was once a difficult area to access, so the culinary traditions that developed on the isolated peninsula were quite different from those in other areas of the country. At the same time, centuries of commercial and cultural trade with Cuba, Europe (especially France), and New Orleans have left their mark on Yucatán culinary traditions. More recent Middle Eastern influences are also visible.

AGUA

In the Yucatán's warm weather, nothing satisfies like a cool *aguas fresca* (fruit-infused water). One drink that you won't want to miss is *agua de chaya.* Chaya, sometimes called Mayan spinach, is a nutritious leafy green that's used in a wide variety of recipes, including soups, omelets, tamales, and a sweet agua fresca.

REGIONAL CUISINES

Vistors to the Yucatán often discover a wide variety of dishes they've never seen before. This is because Yucatán cuisine is not often served in Mexican restaurants north of the border, or even in other areas of the country. Here are some of the most typical dishes—all of them well worth a try!

Huevos motuleños. This is a popular breakfast dish that originated in Motul, a small town east of Mérida, where the ancient Mayan city of Zacmotul once stood. Eggs, sunny side up, are covered with black beans and cheese and served on a crispy tortilla. Other ingredients like red salsa, ham, and green peas are usually heaped on top. Fried plantains are often served on the side.

Sopa de lima. This soup is traditionally prepared with turkey, indigenous to the Yucatán, and includes pieces of tomatoes, sweet chile or green pepper, and lime juice. It's garnished with strips of lightly fried tortilla.

Queso relleno. Legend has it that in the 19th century a boat from Holland was forced to dock on the peninsula because of bad weather, and the people in Mérida were delighted with the cargo of Dutch cheese. From this trip, a typical Yucatecan dish made with Gouda or Edam cheese was born. A salty cow's-milk cheese is stuffed with spiced ground beef and served with

two sauces: a tomato-caper sauce and a milder creamy sauce.

Cochinita pibil. This is perhaps the most representative dish in the Yucatecan repertoire. The word *pibil* means "roasted in the hole," which describes just how this dish is classically prepared. The Maya used to roast venison in this way, but the Spanish-introduced pork is now the standard. The meat is first marinated in a mixture of bitter orange juice (from the Seville oranges that grow in this region), *achiote* (an intensely peppery flavored paste that some describe as having a nutmeg-like flavor, made from annatto seeds), oregano, salt, and pepper. Next, it's wrapped in banana leaves and placed in a hole lined with stones that have been heated with fire. The meat cooks slowly. These days, this dish is often made in a pot on the stove or slow-roasted in the oven. It's usually served in tacos with pickled onions called *cebolla en escabeche*.

6

In sharp contrast to the resort lifestyle of Cancún and Riviera Maya, the Yucatán and Campeche states cater to a more tranquil traveler who is looking to avoid the Spring Break atmosphere. Here you'll find innumerable natural and historic wonders, including mangrove forests, unspoiled beaches, quaint colonial villages, and more than 50% of Mexico's bird species.

Unlike Quintana Roo, Yucatán and Campeche states have few international residents, and there's much less emphasis on beachside activities. And with the largest indigenous population in the country, these states are defined by Mayan culture and traditions; the area's history, people, and food set it apart from the rest of Mexico.

One of Yucatán State's biggest draws is its capital, Mérida. As it's the hub of art and culture, locals and travelers alike gather in the town square for weekend performances. Izamal, the oldest town in the Yucatán, will take you back in time with its cobblestone streets, iron lampposts, yellow painted buildings, and horse-drawn carriages. Near the state's eastern border, the town of Valladolid offers excellent birdwatching and freshwater cenotes where you can explore underwater caves.

More than 2,000 Mayan ruins lie within these two states, but only a handful have been restored for tourism. Nestled amid rampant jungles are the magnificent archaeological sites of Uxmal, Kabah, Labna, Sayil, Dzibilchaltún, and Chichén Itzá, a UNESCO Natural World Heritage site. Roughly one hour southeast of Uxmal, the Grutas de Loltún show signs of human civilization dating as far back as 800 BC. At these natural caverns, illuminated pathways meander past stalactites, stalagmites, and limestone formations.

For nature lovers, the beach town of Celestún serves as a natural habitat for hundreds of pink flamingoes. To combine wildlife and adventure, head to Río Lagartos, where you can kayak through the mangroves. Off the coast of Isla Holbox, diving with whale sharks is possible from

June through August. This small island is one of the area's best spots to relax and enjoy beach life. The laid-back beach community of Progreso is another coastal favorite.

Campeche, the neighboring state, is more remote and less visited than Yucatán, and is known for its haciendas and colonial towns. The state's capital, by the same name, sits within a 26-foot wall that once served as a protective border against pirates in the 17th century. Today this harbor city is centered by a charming plaza where people gather to admire the cathedral, browse the market, or enjoy *pan de cazon*, traditional shredded fish with black beans. For a mellow alternative, you can explore the coastline by boat or spend a day relaxing in the small fishing village of Champotón.

WHEN TO GO

Rainfall is heaviest in the Yucatán between June and October, bringing with it an uncomfortable humidity. The coolest months are December to February, when it can get chilly in the evening, while April and May are usually the hottest. Afternoon showers are the norm June through September, and hurricane season is late September through early November.

As with many other places in Mexico, the weeks around Christmas and Easter are peak times for visiting Yucatán State. Making reservations up to a year in advance is common.

6

If you like music and dance, Mérida hosts its Otoño Cultural, or Autumn Cultural Festival, during the last week of October and first week of November. El festival de Mérida, which celebrates the founding of the city, also runs through nearly the entire month of January. Over the course of January, a thousand artists participate in nearly 200 free events (⊕ *www.merida.gob.mx/festival*). During both of these events, music concerts, dance performances, and art exhibits take place almost nightly at theaters and open-air venues around the city.

Thousands of people, from international sightseers to Mayan shamans, swarm Chichén Itzá on the vernal equinox (the first day of spring). On this particular day the sun creates a shadow that looks like a snake—meant to evoke the ancient Maya serpent god, Kukulcán—that moves slowly down the side of the main pyramid. If you're planning to witness it, make your travel arrangements many months in advance.

GETTING HERE AND AROUND

Mérida is the hub of the Yucatán Peninsula, and a good base for exploring the rest of the state. From there, highways radiate in every direction. To the east, Carreteras 180 *cuota* and 180 *libre* are, respectively, the toll and free roads to Cancún. The toll road (which costs about $30 from Cancún to Mérida, ⊕ *www.sct.gob.mx*) has exits for the famous Chichén Itzá ruins and the low-key colonial city of Valladolid; the free road passes these and many smaller towns. Heading south from Mérida on Carretera 261 (Carretera 180 until the town of Umán), you come to Uxmal and the Ruta Puuc, a series of small ruins (most have at least one outstanding building) of relatively uniform style. Carretera 261 north from Mérida takes you to the port and beach resort of Progreso. To the west, the laid-back fishing village of Celestún—which borders on protected wetland—can be accessed by a separate highway from Mérida.

■ TIP→ If you're independent and adventurous, hiring a rental car is a great way to explore. Be sure to check the lights and spare tire before taking off, carry plenty of bottled water, fill up the gas tank whenever you see a station, and try to avoid driving at night.

ABOUT THE RESTAURANTS

Expect a superb variety of cuisines—primarily Yucatecan, of course, but also Lebanese, Italian, French, Chinese, vegetarian, and Mexican—at very reasonable prices. Reservations are advised for the pricier restaurants on weekends and in high season. Beach towns, such as Progreso, Río Lagartos, and Celestún, tend to serve fresh, simply prepared seafood. The regional cuisine of Campeche is renowned throughout Mexico. Specialties include fish and shellfish stews, cream soups, shrimp cocktail, squid and octopus, and *panuchos* (chubby rounds of fried cornmeal covered with refried beans and topped with onion and shredded turkey or chicken).

Mexicans generally eat lunch in the afternoon—certainly not before 2. If you want to eat at noon, call ahead to verify hours. In Mérida the locals make a real event of late dinners, especially in summer. Casual, but neat, dress is acceptable at all restaurants. Avoid wearing shorts or casual sandals in the more expensive places, and anywhere at all—especially in the evening—if you don't want to look like a tourist.

ABOUT THE HOTELS

Yucatán State has around 8,500 hotel rooms—a little over a third of what Cancún has. Try to check out the interior before booking a room, as the public spaces in Mérida's hotels are generally better kept than the sleeping rooms. Most hotels have air-conditioning, and even many budget hotels have installed it in at least some rooms—but it's best to ask ahead.

■ TIP→ If you plan to spend most of your time enjoying downtown Mérida, stay near the main square or along Calle 60. If you're a light sleeper, however, opt for one of the high-rises along or near Paseo Montejo, about a 20-minute stroll (but an easy cab ride) from the main square.

Inland towns such as Valladolid and Ticul are good options for a look at the slow-paced countryside. There are several charming hotels near the major archaeological sites Chichén Itzá and Uxmal, and a growing number of small beachfront hotels in Progreso, which previously had only a couple of foreign-run bed-and-breakfasts. Campeche City has a few interesting lodgings converted from old homes (and in some cases mansions), as well as newer, large hotels along the *malecón* (boardwalk). These are mostly aimed at business travelers.

WHAT IT COSTS IN DOLLARS				
¢	$	$$	$$$	$$$$
Restaurants	under $5	$5–$10	$10–$15	$15–$25	over $25
Hotels	under $50	$50–$75	$75–$150	$150–$250	over $250

Restaurant prices reflect the median entrée price at dinner. Hotel prices are for a standard double room in high season.

TIMING

You should plan to spend at least five days in the Yucatán. It's best to start your trip with a few days in Mérida; the weekends, when streets are closed to traffic and there are lots of free outdoor performances, are great times to visit. You should also budget enough time to day-trip to the sites of Chichén Itzá and Uxmal; visiting Mérida without traveling to at least one of these sites is like driving to the beach and not getting out of the car.

MÉRIDA

Updated by Steven McCutcheon-Rubio

Bustling streets, lively parks, a tropical version of the Champs-Elysées, endless cultural activities, and a varied nighlife: Mérida is the beating urban heart of the Yucatán. The hubbub of the city can seem frustrating—especially if you've just spent a peaceful few days on the coast or visiting Mayan sites—but as the cultural and intellectual hub of the peninsula, Mérida is rich in art, history, and tradition.

If you need extra orientation, be sure to stop in at the tourism offices, where you'll find friendly, helpful staff. After recent scandals involving scam artists who hang official-looking "tourist guide" badges around their necks, the tourism office staff warns tourists not to trust people offering themselves as guides. A two- to three-hour group tour of the city, including museums, parks, public buildings, and monuments, costs $20 to $35 per person. Free guided tours are offered daily by the Municipal Tourism Department. These last about an hour and 45 minutes and depart from City Hall, on the main plaza, at 9:30 am Monday through Saturday. Or you can rent gear for a four-hour audio-guide tour for about $7. More information is available at ☎ *999/942–0000.*

There have also been recent reports of vendors increasing the prices of their art and crafts by the hundreds, claiming that the value of their wares is far greater than it really is. Most vendors are honest, so just be sure to shop around and acquaint yourself with the kinds of crafts, and the levels of quality, that are available. Once you have an idea of what's out there, you'll be much better able to spot fraud, and you may even have some fun bargaining.

■ TIP→ **Most streets in Mérida are numbered, not named, and most run one-way. North–south streets have even numbers, which descend from west to east, east–west streets have odd numbers, which ascend from north to south. Street addresses are confusing because they don't progress in even increments by blocks, for example, the 600s may occupy two or more blocks. A particular location is therefore usually identified by indicating the street number and the nearest cross street, as in "Calle 64 and Calle 61," or "Calle 64 between Calles 61 and 63," which is written "Calle 64 x 61 y 63."**

GETTING HERE AND AROUND

Mérida's airport, Aeropuerto Manuel Crescencio Rejón, is 7 km (4½ mi) west of the city on Avenida Itzáes. Getting there from the downtown area usually takes 20 to 30 minutes by taxi. Numerous airlines, including Aerocaribe, Aeroméxico, and Mexicana fly from Cancún, Mexico

City, Villahermosa, and other cities. Continental flies daily nonstop from Houston.

For travel outside the city, ADO and UNO have direct buses to many coastal cities and ruins. They depart from the first-class CAME bus station. Regional bus lines to intermediate or more out-of-the-way destinations leave from the second-class terminal. City buses charge about 60¢ (6 pesos); having the correct change is helpful but not required.

Regular taxis in Mérida charge beach-resort prices, and most don't use meters. Taxis that do use meters have a sign that reads "taximetro" on the roof. These are recommended, since they offer a fair price.

TOURS

Mérida has more than 50 tour operators, and it could be said that they generally take you to the same places. Since there are so many reputable and reasonably priced operators, there's no reason to opt for the less-predictable *piratas* ("pirates") who sometimes stand outside tour offices offering to sell you a cheaper trip and don't necessarily have much experience or your best interests at heart. If you enjoy walking, the Mérida English-Library *(⇨ see the Shopping section, below)* conducts home and garden tours (2½ hours costs $20) every Wednesday morning. Meet at the library at about 9:45 am. More information is available on the Mérida English Library Web site at ⊕ *www.meridaenglishlibrary.com.*

ARCHAEOLOG-
ICAL TOURS

Amigo Travel is a reliable operator offering group and private tours to the major archaeological sites and also to Celestún, the town known for the massive flamingo colonies living in its river. Amigo has transfer-accommodation packages and well-crafted tours, like their Campeche and Yucatán combo, and have adopted a pace that allows you to actually enjoy the sites you visit.

If you don't have your own wheels, but like the freedom afforded by traveling on your own, a great option for seeing the ruins of the Ruta Puuc is the unguided **ATS** tour that leaves Mérida at 8 am from the second-class bus station (Terminal 69, ATS line). The tour stops for a half hour each at the ruins of Labná, Xlapak, Sayil, and Kabah, giving you just enough time to scan the plaques, poke your nose into a crevice or two, and pose before a pyramid for your holiday card picture. You get almost two hours at Uxmal before heading back to Mérida at 2:30 pm. The trip costs $10 per person (entrance to the ruins isn't included) and is worth every penny.

EcoTurismo Yucatán has a good mix of day and overnight tours. Their Calakmul tour includes several nights camping in the biosphere reserve for nature spotting, as well as visits to Calakmul, Chicanná, and other area ruins. The one-day biking adventure packs in biking as well as brief visits to two archaeological sites, a cave, and two cenotes.

CITY TOURS
BY BUS

Within Mérida, a fun way to get around, get a feel for the city layout, and hear some of its history is to spend some time on the red, open-roof, double-decker **Turibus.** You buy your ticket ($10) onboard the bus, and you can get on and off at seven stops as you please. The complete bus route is 1 hour and 45 minutes. Buses operate from 9:05 am until 9 pm, and stop at the Holiday Inn, Fiesta Americana, and Hyatt hotels (clustered near one another on Paseo Montejo), the Museo de

Antropología e Historia, the old barrio of Izimná, the Gran Plaza mall (with its 250 stores), the Monument to the Flag, and finally the Parque de las Américas.

A second, smaller tour bus operator is the **Carnavalito**, which visits many of the same sites. The advantage to this tour is that it's given by real people (in both Spanish and English) as opposed to a recording, so you can ask questions. The disadvantage is that you can't get on and off the bus at will. The tour lasts around two hours, with a 20-minute break at a small shopping center where you can stretch your legs or buy something to drink. The colorful Carnavalito bus takes off from Parque Santa Lucia Monday through Saturday at 10 am, 1 pm, and 7 pm.

CITY TOURS
BY CARRIAGE

One of the best ways to get a feel for the city of Mérida is to hire a *calesa*—a horse-drawn carriage. You can hail one of these at the main square or, during the day, at Palacio Cantón, site of the archaeology museum on Paseo Montejo. Choose your horse and driver carefully, as some of the horses look dispirited, but others are fairly well cared for. Drivers charge about $15 for an hour-long circuit around downtown and up Paseo de Montejo, pointing out notable buildings, and providing a little historic background along the way. An extended tour costs $22.

ESSENTIALS

Bus Contacts Autobuses de Occidente (✉ *Calle 70 between 79 and 71, Centro* ☎ *999/924–8391 or 999/924–9741* ⊕ *www.ado.com.mx*). **CAME** (✉ *Calle 71 No. 555, between Calles 69 and 71, Centro* ☎ *999/924–9130*).

Currency Exchange Banamex (✉ *Calle 59 No. 485, Centro* ☎ *01800/021–2345 toll-free in Mexico* ⊕ *www.banamex.com*). **Banorte** (✉ *Prolongación Paseo de Montejo No. 497, Itzimna* ☎ *999/926–6060* ⊕ *www.banorte.com*). **HSBC** (✉ *Paseo Montejo 467ACentro* ☎ *999/942–2378* ⊕ *www.hsbc.com*).

Medical Assistance Centro Médico de las Américas (✉ *Calle 54 No. 365, between Calle 33A and Av. Pérez Ponce, Centro* ☎ *999/926–2111* ⊕ *www.centromedicodelasamericas.com.mx*). **Clínica Santa Helena** (✉ *Calle 14 No. 81, between Calles 5 and 7, Col. San Antonio Cinta* ☎ *999/943–1334 or 999/943–1335*). **Star Médica** (✉ *Calle 26 No. 199, between Avs. 15 and 16, Alta Brisa* ☎ *999/930–2800* ⊕ *www.starmedica.com*).

Rental Cars Avis (✉ *Fiesta Americana, Calle 60 No. 319-C, near Av. Colón, Centro* ☎ *999/925–2525 or 999/920–1101* ⊕ *www.avis.com*). **Budget** (✉ *Holiday Inn, Av. Colón 498, at Calle 60, Centro* ☎ *999/920–4395 or 999/925–6877 Ext. 516* ✉ *Airport* ☎ *999/946–1323* ⊕ *www.budget.com*).

Visitor and Tour Info Amigo Travel (✉ *Av. Colón 508C, Col. García Ginerés* ☎ *999/920–0104 or 999/920–0103* ⊕ *www.amigoyucatan.com*). **ATS** (✉ *Calle 69 No. 544, between Calles 68 and 70, Centro* ☎ *999/923–2287*). **Carnavalito** (☎ *999/927–6119 or 999/928–7916* ⊕ *www.citytouryucatan.com*) **EcoTurismo Yucatán** (✉ *Calle 3 No. 235, between Calles 32A and 34, Col. Pensiones* ☎ *999/920–2772* ⊕ *www.ecoyuc.com*). **Municipal Tourism Department** (✉ *Calles 61 and 60, Centro* ☎ *999/930–3101* ⊕ *www.merida.gob.mx/turismo*). **Municipal Tourist Information Center** (✉ *Calle 62, ground floor of Palacio Municipal, Centro* ☎ *999/928–2020 Ext. 133*). **Turibus** (☎ *999/946–2424; 55/5563–6693 in Mexico City* ⊕ *www.turibus.com.mx*).

EXPLORING

The *zócalo*, or main square, is in the oldest part of town—the Centro Histórico. On Saturday night and Sunday practically the entire population of the city gathers in the parks and plazas surrounding the zócalo to socialize and watch live entertainment. Cafés along this route are perfect places from which to watch the parade of people as well as folk dancers and singers. Calle 60 between Parque Santa Lucía and the main square gets especially lively. Restaurants here set out tables in the streets, which quickly fill with patrons enjoying the free hip-hop, tango, salsa, or jazz performances.

Every Sunday, from 8 am to 12:30 pm, downtown streets are closed for pedestrians and cyclists. The route begins at the Parque de la Ermita, and travels through the Plaza Grande, out on to the Paseo Montejo (⊕ *www.merida.gob.mx/biciruta*).

TOP ATTRACTIONS

Casa de Montejo. Two Franciscos de Montejo—father and son—conquered the peninsula and founded Mérida in January of 1542, and they built their stately "casa" 10 years later. In the late 1970s it was restored by banker Agustín Legorreta, converted to a branch of Banamex bank, and now sits on the south side of the plaza. It's the city's finest—and oldest—example of colonial plateresque architecture, a Spanish architectural style popular in the 16th century and typified by the kind of elaborate ornamentation you'll see here. A bas-relief on the doorway—the facade is all that remains of the original house—depicts Francisco de Montejo the younger, his wife, and daughter, as well as Spanish soldiers standing on the heads of the vanquished Maya. ⊠ *Calle 63, Centro* ⊙ *Weekdays 9–5, Sat. 9–1.*

Catedral de San Ildefonso. Begun in 1561 and completed 38 years later, St. Ildefonso is the oldest cathedral on the American continent (though an older one can be found in the Dominican Republic). It took several hundred Maya laborers, working with stones from the pyramids of the ravaged Mayan city, 36 years to complete it. Designed in the somber Renaissance style by an architect who had worked on the Escorial in Madrid, its facade is stark and unadorned, with gunnery slits instead of windows, and faintly Moorish spires. Inside, the black *Cristo de las Ampollas* (Christ of the Blisters) occupies a side chapel to the left of the main altar. At 23 feet tall, it's the tallest Christ in Mexico inside a church. The statue is a replica of the original, which was destroyed during the revolution in 1910, which is also when the gold that typically decorated Mexican cathedrals was carried off. According to one of many legends, the Christ figure burned all night yet appeared the next morning unscathed—except that it was covered with the blisters for which it's named. You can hear the pipe organ play at the 11 am Sunday Mass. ⊠ *Calles 60 and 61, Centro* ☏ *No phone* ⊙ *Daily 7–11:30 and 4:30–8.*

Mérida

Centro Cultural de Mérida Olimpo. Referred to as simply Olimpo, this is the best venue in town for free cultural events. The beautiful porticoed cultural center was built adjacent to City Hall in late 1999, occupying what used to be a parking lot. The marble interior is a showcase for top international art exhibits, classical-music concerts, conferences, and theater and dance performances. The adjoining 1950s-style movie house shows classic art films by directors like Buñuel, Fellini, and Kazan. There's also a planetarium with 90-minute shows explaining the solar system ($3, Tuesday through Saturday at 6 pm and Sunday at 11, noon, and 6; be sure to be there 15 minutes early, since nobody is allowed to sneak in once the show has begun). Next door there's a bookstore, and a wonderful cybercafé-restaurant. ✉ *Calle 62 between Calles 61 and 63, Centro* ☎ *999/942–0000* ⊕ *www.merida.gob.mx/planetario* ✉ *Free* ⊙ *Tues.–Sun. 10–8.*

Paseo Montejo. North of downtown, this 10-block-long street was *the* place to reside in the late 19th century, when wealthy plantation owners sought to outdo each other with the opulence of their elegant mansions. Mansion owners typically opted for the decorative styles popular in New Orleans, Cuba, and Paris—imported Carrara marble, European antiques—rather than any style from Mexico. The broad boulevard, lined with tamarind and laurel trees, has lost much of its former panache; some of the mansions have fallen into disrepair. Many are now used as office buildings, while others have been or are being restored as part of a citywide, privately funded beautification program. The street is a lovely place to explore on foot or in a horse-drawn carriage.

Teatro Peón Contreras. This 1908 Italianate theater was built along the same lines as grand turn-of-the-20th-century European theaters and opera houses. In the early 1980s, the marble staircase, dome, and frescoes were restored. Today, in addition to performing arts, the theater houses the **Centro de Información Turística** (Tourist Information Center), which provides maps, brochures, and details about attractions in the city and state. The theater's most popular attraction, however, is the café-bar spilling out into the street facing Parque de la Madre. It's crowded every night with people enjoying the balladeers singing romantic and politically inspired songs. ✉ *Calle 60 between Calles 57 and 59, Centro* ☎ *999/923–7354 Tourist Information Center, 999/924–9290, 999/923–7354 theater* ⊙ *Tourist Information Center daily 8 am–9 pm.*

Universidad Autónoma de Yucatán. Pop into the university's main building—which plays a major role in the city's cultural and intellectual life—to check the bulletin boards just inside the entrance for upcoming cultural events. The folkloric ballet performs on the patio of the main building most Fridays between 9 and 10 pm ($5). You'll easily find this imposing Moorish-inspired building, which dates from 1711, with its crenellated ramparts and arabesque archways. ✉ *Calle 60 between Calles 57 and 59, Centro* ☎ *999/930–0900 operator, 999/924–6429 art and culture programming* ⊕ *www.uady.mx/sitios/cultura/ballet.html.*

Zócalo. Méridians traditionally refer to this main square as the Plaza de la Independencia, or the Plaza Principal. Whichever name you prefer, it's a good spot to start a tour of the city, watch music or dance performances, or chill in the shade of a laurel tree when the day gets too hot. The plaza was laid out in 1542 on the ruins of T'hó, the Mayan city demolished to make way for Mérida, and is still the focal point around which the most important public buildings cluster. *Confidenciales* (S-shape benches) invite intimate tête-à-têtes, and lampposts keep the park beautifully illuminated at night. ⊠ *Bordered by Calles 60, 62, 61, and 63, Centro.*

WORTH NOTING

 Aké, a compact archaeological site 35 km (22 mi) southeast of Mérida, offers the unique opportunity to see architecture spanning two millennia in one sweeping vista. Standing atop a ruined Mayan temple built more than a thousand years ago, you can see the incongruous sight of workers processing sisal in a rusty-looking factory, which was built in the early 20th century. To the right of this dilapidated building are the ruins of the old Hacienda and Iglesia de San Lorenzo Aké, both constructed of stones taken from the Mayan temples.

Experts estimate that Aké was populated between around 200 BC and AD 900; today many people in the area have Aké as a surname. The city seems to have been related to the very important and powerful one at present-day Izamal; in fact, the two cities were once connected by a *sacbé* (white road) 43 feet wide and 33 km (20 mi) long. All that has been excavated so far are two pyramids, one with rows of columns (35 total) at the top, very reminiscent of the Toltec columns at Tula, north of Mexico City. ⊠ *$3.70 ⊙ Daily 9–5.*

Ermita de Santa Isabel. At the southern end of the city stands the restored and beautiful Hermitage of St. Isabel. Built circa 1748 as part of a Jesuit monastery, also known as the Hermitage of the Good Trip, it served as a resting place for colonial-era travelers heading to Campeche. It's one of the most peaceful places in the city, with an interesting, inlaid-stone facade (although the church itself is almost always closed), and is a good destination for a ride in a horse carriage. Behind the hermitage are its huge and lush tropical gardens, with a waterfall and footpaths, which are usually unlocked during daylight hours. ⊠ *Calles 66 and 77, La Ermita* ☎ *No phone* ⊠ *Free ⊙ Church open only during Mass.*

Iglesia de la Tercera Orden de Jesús. Just north of Parque Hidalgo is one of Mérida's oldest buildings and the first Jesuit church in the Yucatán. It was built in 1618 from the limestone blocks of a dismantled Mayan temple, and faint outlines of ancient carvings are still visible on the west wall. Although a favorite place for society weddings due to its antiquity, the church interior is not ornate.

The former convent rooms in the rear of the building now host the **Pinoteca Juan Gamboa Guzmán,** a small but interesting art collection. The most engaging pieces here are the striking bronze sculptures of indigenous Maya crafted by celebrated 20th-century sculptor Enrique Gottdiener Soto. On the second floor are about 20 forgettable oil paintings—mostly of past civic officials of the area. ⊠ *Calle 59 between Calles 58 and 60, Centro* ☎ *999/924–5233* ⊕ *www.inah.gob.mx* ⊠ *$3* ☉ *Tues.–Sat. 9–5, Sun. 10–5.*

Mercado de Artesanías García Rejón. Although many deal in the same wares, the shops or stalls of the García Rejón Crafts Market sell some quality items, and the shopping experience here can be less of a hassle than at the municipal market. You'll find reasonable prices on palm-fiber hats, hammocks, leather sandals, jewelry, and locally made liqueurs. Persistent but polite bargaining may get you even better deals. ⊠ *Calles 60 and 65, Centro* ☎ *No phone* ☉ *Weekdays 9–6, Sat. 9–4, Sun. 9–1.*

Mercado Municipal. Sellers of chiles, herbs, crafts, trinkets, and fruit fill this pungent and labyrinthine municipal market. In the early morning the first floor is jammed with housewives and restaurateurs shopping for the freshest seafood and produce. The stairs at Calles 56 and 57 lead to the second-floor Bazar de Artesanías Municipales, on either side, where you'll find local pottery, embroidered clothes, men's guayabera dress shirts, hammocks, and straw bags. Note that most prices are inflated, and vendors expect you'll bargain—one way to begin is to politely request a discount. ⊠ *Calles 56 and 67, Centro* ☎ *No phone* ☉ *Daily 5 am–10 pm.*

Museo de Arte Contemporáneo. Originally designed as an art school and used until 1915 as a seminary, this enormous, light-filled building now showcases the works of contemporary Yucatecan artists such as Gabriel Ramírez Aznar and Fernando García Ponce, as well as a variety of temporary exhibits. If you want to explore beyond the outside plaza, be sure to sign in first. ⊠ *Pasaje de la Revolución 1907, between Calles 58 and 60 on main square, Centro* ☎ *999/928–3236 or 999/928–3258* ⊠ *Free* ☉ *Wed.–Mon. 10–5:30.*

Museo de Arte Popular de Yucatán. Facing the Plaza Mejorada, this museum is funded by the Banamex Cultural Foundation, and offers a comprehensive introduction to different kinds of Mexican art craft including ceramics, textiles, stone work, cardboard art, woodwork, and glass. Even if you don't want to see the whole museum, take a look in the gift shop, which sells shawls, baskets, dolls, and masks. Prices are a bit high, but so is the quality of the crafts; even if you don't buy anything here, a look around will inform your purchases at area markets. ⊠ *Calle 50 No. 487, between Calles 57 and 59, Centro* ☎ *999/ 928–5263* ⊠ *Free* ☉ *Tues.–Sat. 10–7.*

Palacio Cantón. The most compelling of the mansions on **Paseo Montejo,** this stately palacio was built as the residence for a general between 1909 and 1911. Designed by Enrique Deserti, who also did the blueprints for the Teatro Peón Contreras, the building has a grandiose air that seems more characteristic of a mausoleum than a home: there's marble everywhere, as well as Doric and Ionic columns and other Italianate beaux arts flourishes. The building also houses the air-conditioned **Museo Regional de Yucatán,** which introduces visitors to ancient Mayan culture. Temporary exhibits sometimes brighten the standard collection.

✉ *Paseo Montejo 485, at Calle 43, Paseo Montejo* ☎ *999/928–6719*
⊕ *www.inah.gob.mx* ☞ *$3.50* ⊙ *Tues.–Sun. 8–5.*

Palacio del Gobierno. Visit the seat of state government to see Fernando
Castro Pacheco's murals of the bloody history of the conquest of the
Yucatán, painted in bold colors in the 1970s and influenced by the
Mexican muralists José Clemente Orozco and David Alfaro Siquieros.
On the main balcony (visible from outside on the plaza) stands a repro-
duction of the Bell of Dolores Hidalgo, on which Mexican independence
rang out on the night of September 15, 1810, in the town of Dolores
Hidalgo in Guanajuato. On the anniversary of the event, the governor
rings the bell to commemorate the occasion. ✉ *Calle 61 between Calles
60 and 62, Centro* ☎ *999/930–3101* ☞ *Free* ⊙ *Daily 8 am–9 pm.*

Palacio Municipal. The west side of the main square is occupied by City
Hall, a 17th-century building trimmed with white arcades, balustrades,
and the national coat of arms. Originally erected on the ruins of the last
surviving Mayan structure, it was rebuilt in 1735 and then completely
reconstructed along colonial lines in 1928. It remains the headquarters
of the local government, and houses the municipal tourist office, where
you can pick up free maps or rent a four-hour audio guide for about $7.
✉ *Calle 62 between Calles 61 and 63, Centro* ☎ *999/928–2020* ⊙ *Palacio daily 9–8, Tourist Information Center weekdays 8–8, Sat. 9–1.*

**NEED A
BREAK?**   The homemade ice cream and sorbet at El Colón have been keeping locals
cool since 1907. The tropical fruit flavors, like *chico zapote* (a brown fruit
native to Mexico that has a flavor a little like cinnamon and comes from
a tree that's used in chewing-gum production), served up in a pyramid-
shape scoop are particularly delicious and refreshing. The shop also sells
cookies and fresh candies—the meringues are exceptional. The Paseo
Montejo branch has the same menu with both outdoor and indoor seating.
The tables inside are under whirling fans that make it a comfortable spot
to cool off on a hot afternoon, and the Paseo Montejo location makes it a
great place to watch people walking by. ✉ *Calle 62 No. 500, at Calle 59 and
Calle 61, Centro* ☎ *999/928–1497* ▭ *No credit cards* ✉ *Paseo de Montejo
No. 474, at Calle 39 and Calle 41* ☎ *999/927–6443.*

Parque Hidalgo. A half block north of the main plaza is this small cozy
park, officially known as Plaza Cepeda Peraza. Historic mansions,
now reincarnated as hotels and sidewalk cafés, line the south side of
the park and at night the area comes alive with marimba bands and
street vendors. On Sunday the streets are closed to vehicular traffic,
and there's free live music performed throughout the day. ✉ *Calle 60
between Calles 59 and 61, Centro* ☎ *No phone.*

☺ **Parque Zoológico El Centenario.** Mérida's greatest children's attraction, this
large amusement complex features playgrounds, inexpensive rides like
motorized cars, small electric merry-go-round style rides, pony rides,
a small train ($1) that circles the park, a rollerblading rink, and cages
with more than 300 native animals as well as exotics such as lions,
tigers, and bears. At the exit, there are snack bars and vendors. It also

has picnic areas, pleasant wooded paths, and a small lake where you can rent rowboats. The French Renaissance–style arch (1921) commemorates the 100th anniversary of Mexican independence. ⊠ *Av. Itzáes between Calles 59 and 65, entrances on Calles 59 and 65, Centro* ☎ *999/928–5815 or 999/945–0733* ⊕ *www.merida.gob.mx/centenario* 🎫 *Free* ☉ *Zoo Tues.–Sun. 8–6.*

WHERE TO EAT

With more than 250 restaurants (not to mention the markets and street-food stands) there are plenty of dining options to choose from in Mérida. Regional dishes and Middle Eastern cuisine are staples, but the flavors and preparations don't stop there. You can even find places serving hamburgers and sandwiches if you're craving something familiar.

$$
MIDDLE EASTERN

✕ **Alberto's Continental Patio.** Though locals say this eatery has lost some of its star power, it's still a dependable place for shish kebab, fried *kibbe* (meatballs of ground beef, wheat germ, and spices), hummus, tabbouleh, baba ghanoush, and other Lebanese dishes. The strikingly handsome dining spot is full of character, with an eclectic collection of antiques, paintings, and sculptures. The building itself dates to 1727, and is adorned with some of the original stones from the Mayan temple it replaced, as well as mosaic floors from Cuba. Even if you choose to have lunch or dinner elsewhere, stop in for almond pie and Turkish coffee in the romantic, candlelit courtyard. ⊠ *Calle 64 No. 482, at Calle 57, Centro* ☎ *999/928–5367* ✦ *B5.*

$
MEXICAN

✕ **Los Almendros.** This classic Yucatecan eatery has been a favorite with locals since the 1960s, when the owners opened their first restaurant in nearby Ticul. The Mérida branch has been here since 1972, and many say it's still the best place to eat in town. The restaurant is actually separated in two buildings called Los Almendros and Gran Almendros. The menu and prices are the same, but the atmosphere and schedules are slightly different—Los Alemdros has a more casual feel, while the Gran Almendros's high colonial ceilings create a slightly more elegant atmosphere—so take a look around to see where you'd like to sit before settling in. The *combinado yucateco* (Yucatecan combination plate) is a great way to try different dishes: cochinita pibil, *longaniza asada* (grilled pork sausages), *escabeche de Valladolid* (turkey with chiles, onions, and seasonings in an acidic sauce), and *poc-chuc* (slices of pork marinated in sour-orange sauce and spices). In fact, they invented some dishes that have become Yucatecan classics, including the poc-chuc and the cheese soup, which is also spectacular. ⊠ *Calle 50A No. 493, between Calles 57 and 59, facing Parque La Mejorada, Col. Centro* ☎ *999/928–5459 or 999/923–8135* ✦ *C6.*

$
ECLECTIC

✕ **Amaro.** The open patio of this historic home glows with candlelight in the evening; during the day things look a lot more casual. Meat, fish, and shellfish are served here in moderation, but the emphasis is on vegetarian dishes like eggplant curry and *chaya* soup (made from a green plant similar to spinach), and healthful juices. Prices are reasonable, and the service is always excellent. If you're missing your favorite comfort foods, get your fix with a side order of mashed potatoes or french

Enjoying a meal at La Casa de Frida.

fries. Amaro stays open until 2 am from Monday to Saturday. Expect live music Monday through Saturday between 9 pm and midnight. ⊠ *Calle 59 No. 507, between Calles 60 and 62, Centro* ☎ *999/928–2451* ⊕ *www.restauranteamaro.com* ✛ *B6.*

$$ ✕ **La Bella Epoca.** The coveted, tiny private balconies at this elegantly
ECLECTIC restored mansion overlook Parque Hidalgo. You'll need to call in advance to reserve one for a 7 pm or 10 pm seating, as tables that overlook the park go especially fast. On weekends, when the street below is closed to traffic and tables are set up outside, it's pleasant to survey the park while feasting on Mayan dishes like *sikil-pak* (a dip with ground pumpkin seeds, charbroiled tomatoes, and onions) or succulent pollo pibil (chicken baked in banana leaves). ⊠ *Calle 60 No. 497, between Calles 57 and 59, Centro* ☎ *999/928–1928* ☉ *No lunch* ✛ *B6.*

$ ✕ **Café La Habana.** A gleaming wood bar, white-jacketed waiters, and
MEXICAN the scent of cigarettes contribute to the Old European feel at this overwhelmingly popular spot, a branch of a Mexico City café that has been around since the 1950s. Overhead, brass-studded ceiling fans swirl the air-conditioned air. Sixteen specialty coffees are offered (some spiked with spirits like Kahlúa or cognac), and the menu has light snacks as well as some entrées, including tamales, fajitas, and enchiladas. The waiters are friendly, and there are plenty of them, although service is not always brisk. Both the café and upstairs Internet joint are open 24 hours a day; free Wi-Fi is available downstairs for laptop-toting customers. ⊠ *Calle 59 No. 511A, at Calle 62, Centro* ☎ *999/928–6502* ✛ *B6.*

$$ ✕ **Café Lucía.** Opera music floats above black-and-white tile floors in
ITALIAN the dining room of this century-old restaurant in the Hotel Casa Lucía near the main plaza. Pizzas and calzones are the linchpins of the Italian

menu, and luscious pecan pies, cakes, and cookies beckon from behind the glass dessert case. The original art on the walls is for sale, however the paintings by the late Oaxacan artist Rodolfo Morales are not, so don't bother asking. ⊠ *Calle 60 No. 474A, Centro* ☏ *999/928–0704* ⊕ *www.casalucia.com.mx* ⊕ *B5*.

$$ ✕ **La Casa de Frida**. Chef-owner Gabriela Praget puts a healthful, cos-
MEXICAN mopolitan spin on Mexican fare at her restaurant. This is a great place
★ to sample foods from around Mexico. Praget prepares all the dishes herself, and is usually on hand to greet guests. Traditional dishes like duck in a dark, rich mole sauce (made with chocolate and chiles) share the menu with gourmet vegetarian cuisine: potato and cheese tacos, ratatouille in puff pastry, and crepes made with *cuitlachoche* (a delicious truffle-like corn fungus). The flavors here are so divine that diners have been known to hug Praget after a meal. The dining room—a casual covered patio decorated with plants, copies of Frida Kahlo self-portraits, several Frida dolls, and other art—is a comfortable place to enjoy a leisurely meal. ⊠ *Calle 61 No. 526, at Calle 66, Centro* ☏ *999/928–2311* ⊕ *www.lacasadefrida.com.mx* ⊟ No *credit cards* ⊗ No *lunch Mon.–Sat.* ⊕ *A6*.

$ ✕ **Dante's**. Couples, groups of students, and lots of families crowd this
CAFÉ bustling coffeehouse at the Centro Cultural Dante, just above one of
☺ Mérida's largest bookshops. The house specialty is crepes: there are 18 varieties with either sweet or savory fillings. Light entrées such as sandwiches, burgers, pizzas, and *molletes*—large open-face rolls smeared with beans and cheese and then broiled—are also served, along with cappuccino, specialty coffees, beer, and wine. At the time of this writing, the restaurant was preparing to redo the menu and include more-traditionally Yucatecan dishes. A small theater puts on evening comic sketches and live music from time to time, and free children's programs on Sunday mornings. ⊠ *Prolongación Paseo Montejo 138B, Paseo Montejo* ☏ *999/927–2692 or 999/927–7441* ⊕ *C1*.

$ ✕ **Eladio's**. Part bar, part restaurant,
MEXICAN and part theater, this lively, recently remodeled venue is often crammed with local families and couples. There's an ample dance floor and a free, supervised children's play area—you can also buy ceramic figures for them to paint while you dance. There's a full menu of tasty Yucatecan dishes like *papadzules* (hard-boiled eggs wrapped in warm tortillas and covered with a thick pumpkin-seed sauce) and sopa de lima. Free appetizers, which are actually just smaller portions of the dishes on the menu, come with your beer. From 2 to 6:30 pm there's live salsa, cumbia, and other Latino

6

tunes, punctuated by stage-show–style talking. At 7:30 most families disappear, and singles and couples arrive to watch whatever football or boxing match is on TV. ⊠ *Calle 24 No. 101C, at Calle 59, Col. Itzimná* ☎ *999/927–2126* ✚ *B1.*

$$
MEXICAN
Fodor'sChoice
★

✕ **Hacienda Teya.** Once a henequen-producing site, this beautiful hacienda just outside the city serves some of the best regional food around. It has attracted some big names, like Vicente Fox (back when he was president, and would order the queso relleno to go) and even Hillary Clinton. Most patrons are well-to-do Méridians enjoying a leisurely lunch, so you don't want to wear your beach clothes. In fact, men wearing tank tops will be asked to change. It's open from noon to 6 daily (though most Mexicans don't show up until after 3), and a guitarist serenades the tables between 2 and 5 on weekends. After a fabulous lunch like cochinita pibil (pork baked in banana leaves), take a stroll through the surrounding orchards and botanical gardens. If you find yourself wanting to spend the night, you can. The hacienda has six handsome suites ($$), which are often available on short notice, although they need to be reserved in advance over long weekends and holidays. ⊠ *12.5 km (8 mi) east of Mérida on Carretera 180, Kanasín* ☎ *999/988–0800* ⊕ *www.haciendateya.com* ⊘ *No dinner* ✚ *B6.*

$$$–$$$$
MEXICAN

✕ **Néctar Food & Wine.** His restaurant may be the mecca of fine dining in the Yucatán, but if you ask him, Chef Roberto Solis will admit that when he started over 10 years ago, he was a pretty bad cook. So he dragged himself to Europe and New York and worked at some of the world's best restaurants, such as the Fat Duck, Noma, and Per Se, befriending and learning from the greats. Today, Néctar's mix of haute technique and Yucatecan recipes and ingredients is that standard by which all other fine-dining establishments in the area are measured. The real star here is the six-course tasting menu, which could feature such dishes as lamb in a Yucatecan *recado negro* sauce or venison *dzic* (cold meat salad) on fried plantain chips. The menu costs about $75, and reservations must be made at least a day in advance. ⊠ *Av. 1 No 402 between Calles 6A and 8, Col. Díaz Ordáz* ☎ *999/938–0838* ⌂ *Reservations essential* ⊘ *Closed Mon.* ✚ *B1.*

$$–$$$
MEXICAN

✕ **Pancho's.** In the evening this patio restaurant (which frames a small, popular bar) is bathed in candlelight and the glow from tiny white lights decorating the tropical shrubs. Much of the menu, as well as the decor, is geared toward foreigners, and you can even buy a Pancho's T-shirt on your way out. Tasty tacos, fajitas, and other dishes will be pleasantly recognizable to those familiar with Mexican food served north of the border. Waiters—dressed in white muslin shirts and pants of the Revolution era—recommend the shrimp flambéed in tequila, and the tequila in general. Happy hour is 6 pm to 8 pm. There's also live music on the tiny dance floor Wednesday through Saturday. ⊠ *Calle 59 No. 509, between Calles 60 and 62, Centro* ☎ *999/923–0942* ⊕ *www.panchosmerida.com* ⊘ *No lunch* ✚ *B6.*

$
ITALIAN

✕ **Ristorante & Pizzería Bologna.** You can dine alfresco or inside at this beautifully restored old mansion, a few blocks off Paseo Montejo. Tables have fresh flowers and cloth napkins, walls are adorned with pictures of Italy, and there are plants everywhere. Most menu items are ordered à la carte; among the favorites are the shrimp pizza and pizza *diabola,* topped with salami, tomato, and chiles. The beef fillet—served solo or covered in cheese or mushrooms—is served with a baked potato and a medley of mixed sautéed vegetables. ⊠ *Calle 21 No. 117A, between Calle 24 and 28, Col. Izimná* ☎ *999/926–2505* ✛ *C1.*

$ ✕ **La Tradición.** This family restaurant is popular among locals—in fact, many say it's their favorite restaurant in town. It's also one of the most
MEXICAN
formal places that serves the region's cuisine, but you'll still fit right in if you're wearing jeans. Proprietor Albino Medina is a third-generation chef and restaurant owner in his family. Dishes are prepared with a charcoal stove, like your grandma might have used, if you were from around here. The kitchen standards of cleanliness are so strict that the restaurant has received recognition from the Secretary of Tourism. Just about everything you'll try is tasty, but you might not want to pass up the cream of chaya soup, since you won't find it in many other restaurants. ⊠ *Calle 60 No. 293, at Calle 25, Col. Alcalá Martin* ☎ *999/925–2526* ⊕ *www.latradicionmerida.com* ✛ *B1.*

$ ✕ **La Vía Olimpo.** Lingering over coffee and a book is a pleasure at this smart Internet café, and the outdoor tables are a great place to watch
CAFÉ
the nonstop parade—or the free Sunday performances—on the main square. In the air-conditioned dining room you can feast on turkey sandwiches, burgers and fries, or poc-chuc. Crepes are also popular, and there are lots of salads and juices if you're in the mood for something light. Crowds keep this place hopping from 7 am to 11 pm daily. Spirits are served, and you'll get an appetizer, like a basket of chips with freshly made guacamole, with most drink orders. ⊠ *Calle 62 No. 502, between Calles 63 and 61, Centro* ☎ *999/923–5843* ✛ *B6.*

WHERE TO STAY

Mérida has a wide range of lodging choices, from old haciendas and privately owned, converted colonial homes to big corporate hotels. Generally, you'll find smaller hotels in the downtown area, within walking distance of most sights; nights are inevitably a little louder here, especially if your room faces the street. A few larger chain hotels around the Paseo de Montejo offer quiet rooms, and are still near major streets, and only a short ride from downtown.

For expanded hotel reviews, visit Fodors.com.

$$ ⊞ **Casa del Balam.** This pleasant hotel has an excellent location two
★ blocks from the zócalo in downtown's best shopping area. **Pros:** easy walk to many sights; spacious rooms; tasty food; great restaurant service (particularly at breakfast). **Cons:** slow elevator; street noise can be a problem. **TripAdvisor:** "a beautiful old hacienda," "free Wi-Fi and internet use," "an oasis of rest after a hot day." ⊠ *Calle 60 No. 488, Centro* ☎ *999/924–8844 or 800/624–8451* ⊕ *www.casadelbalam.com* ⟿ *44 rooms, 7 suites* ⌂ *In-room: a/c. In-hotel: restaurant, bar, pool, parking* ⎮⊙⎮ *Breakfast* ✛ *B6.*

$ ⊞ **Casa Mexilio.** This small, homey hotel is four blocks from the main square. **Pros:** pleasant courtyard; easy walk to downtown attractions; excellent room prices; nice breakfasts; free international calls.

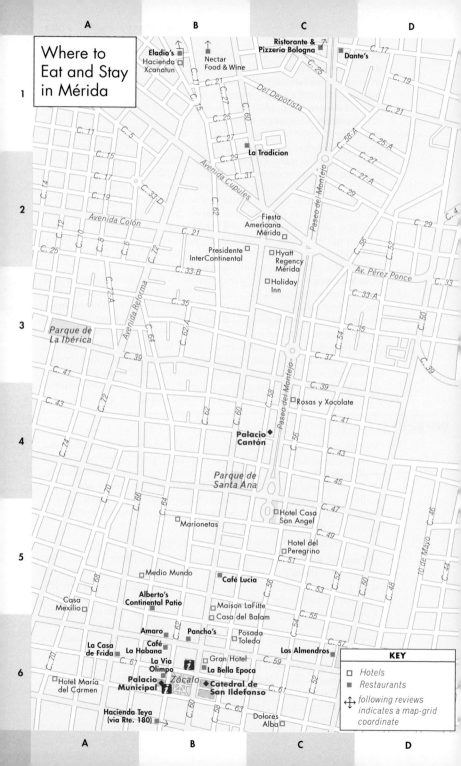

Where to Eat and Stay in Mérida

KEY

□ Hotels
■ Restaurants
✦ following reviews indicates a map-grid coordinate

Eladio's
Hacienda Xcanatun
Nectar Food & Wine
Ristorante & Pizzería Bologna
Dante's

C. 77
C. 79
C. 25
C. 21
C. 27
C. 15
C. 60
C. 25
C. 27
C. 29
La Tradicion
C. 31
Del Depotista
C. 25-A
C. 58-A
C. 27
C. 27-A
C. 29
C. 29
C. 4

Avenida Cupules

C. 11
C. 5
C. 15
C. 17
C. 33-D
C. 19
Avenida Colón
C. 14
C. 12
C. 10
C. 8
C. 6
C. 72
C. 72-A
C. 25
C. 62
C. 21
Paseo de Montejo

Fiesta Americana Mérida

Presidente InterContinental
C. 33-B
Hyatt Regency Mérida
Holiday Inn
Av. Pérez Ponce
C. 33

Avenida Reforma
C. 64
C. 62-A
C. 35
C. 33-A
C. 58
C. 52
C. 50

Parque de La Ibérica
C. 39
C. 37
C. 54
C. 35
C. 39

C. 41
C. 43
C. 72
C. 62
C. 60
C. 39
Rosas y Xocolate
C. 41

Palacio Cantón ✦
Paseo del Montejo
C. 56
C. 43

C. 74
Parque de Santa Ana
C. 45

C. 70
C. 66
C. 64
Hotel Casa San Angel
C. 47

Marionetas
C. 49
Hotel del Peregrino
C. 51
C. 46

Medio Mundo
Café Lucia
C. 56
C. 53
C. 52
C. 50
C. 48
C. 44

Casa Mexilio
Alberto's Continental Patio
Maison LaFitte
Casa del Balam
C. 55
C. 54
10 de Mayo

C. 68
C. 62
Amaro
Pancho's
Posada Toledo
C. 57
Los Almendros

La Casa de Frida
Café La Habana
La Via Olimpo
Gran Hotel
La Bella Epoca
C. 59
C. 52

C. 70
C. 67
Palacio Municipal
Zócalo
Catedral de San Ildefonso
C. 61
C. 63
C. 60
C. 58

Hotel María del Carmen
Hacienda Teya (via Rte. 180)
Dolores Alba

Cons: small bathrooms; rooms on upper floors can be a bit of hike to reach. **TripAdvisor:** "wonderful, unique house in quiet setting," "breakfasts are fabulous," "rooms are attractive and comfortable." ⊠ *Calle 68 No. 495, between Calles 57 and 59, Centro* ☎ *999/928–2505* ☎ *888/819–0024* ⊕ *www.casamexilio.com* ⌐*11 rooms* ⌂ *In-room: a/c, no TV, Wi-Fi. In-hotel: restaurant, bar, pool, some age restrictions* |◎| *Breakfast* ✛ *A5.*

> **MARKET SNACKS**
>
> The simple market in **Parque Santa Ana** (⊠ *Calle 60 between Calles 45 and 47, Centro* ☎ *No phone*) is a popular breakfast spot where you'll find locals happily starting their day with regional dishes and fresh juices at plastic tables. The tamales are good and the *tortas de cochinita*, pork sandwiches flavored with a few drops of sour-orange chile sauce, are heavenly. Most vendors here close around 1:30 in the afternoon, but some reopen to sell snacks between 7 pm and midnight.

$ ★ **Dolores Alba.** The newer wing of this comfortable, cheerful hotel has spiffy rooms with quietly powerful air-conditioning, comfortable beds, and amenities like large TVs, balconies, and telephones. **Pros:** great room prices; nice pool (if a little on the small side); clean rooms; short walk to the zócalo. **Cons:** mediocre breakfast; no Internet access from rooms. **TripAdvisor:** "located right in town," "fully fanned and air conditioned," "private parking within the hotel." ⊠ *Calle 63 No. 464, between Calles 52 and 54, Centro* ☎ *999/928–5650* ⊕ *www.doloresalba.com* ⌐*100 rooms* ⌂ *In-room: a/c. In-hotel: restaurant, bar, pool, laundry facilities, business center, parking* |◎| *Breakfast* ✛ *C6.*

$$$ **Fiesta Americana Mérida.** The facade of this posh hotel echoes the grandeur of the mansions on Paseo Montejo. **Pros:** comfortable beds; exceptionally varied and tasty breakfast buffet; shopping area just down the stairs; powerful air-conditioning. **Cons:** a taxi ride away from downtown; very small bathtubs. **TripAdvisor:** "rooms are comfortable," "great location; breakfast was amazing," "a little too far from downtown." ⊠ *Av. Colón 451, Paseo Montejo* ☎ *999/942–1111 or 800/343–7821* ⊕ *www.fiestaamericana.com* ⌐*323 rooms, 27 suites* ⌂ *In-room: Internet. In-hotel: restaurant, bar, pool, tennis court, gym, spa, parking* |◎| *Multiple meal plans* ✛ *C2.*

$$ **Gran Hotel.** Cozily situated on Parque Hidalgo, this legendary 1901 hotel does look its age, with extremely high ceilings, wrought-iron balcony and stair rails, and ornately patterned tile floors. **Pros:** beautiful antique decorations (especially in public areas); in the middle of downtown bustle, sights, and shops. **Cons:** downtown noise; no elevator makes upstairs rooms quite a hike; not easy to park in front, and parking is sometimes unavailable (check ahead if you are driving). **TripAdvisor:** "quiet and the price is okay," "bathrooms are large and clean," "location couldn't be better." ⊠ *Calle 60 No. 496, Centro* ☎ *999/923–6963* ⊕ *www.granhoteldemerida.com.mx* ⌐*25 rooms, 7 suites* ⌂ *In-room: a/c, Wi-Fi. In-hotel: parking* |◎| *No meals* ✛ *B6.*

$$$$ ★ **Hacienda Xcanatun.** The furnishings at this beautifully restored 18th-century henequen hacienda include African and Indonesian antiques, locally made lamps, and comfortable, oversize couches and chairs

6

from Puebla. **Pros:** good restaurant; expansive gardens; poolside bar service; two wheelchair-accessible rooms. **Cons:** a drive from the city; pricey. **TripAdvisor:** "service was attentive, friendly and very professional," "gourmet cuisine," "very comfortable and handsome rooms." ✉ *Carretera 261, Km 12, 13 km (8 mi) north of Mérida* ☎ *999/941–0213 or 888/883–3633* ⊕ *www.xcanatun.com* ⤳ *5 rooms 13 suites* ⚇ *In-room: a/c, no TV. In-hotel: restaurant, bars, pools, spa, parking* �’❘ *Breakfast* ⊕ *B1.*

$$ 🖭 **Holiday Inn.** The most light-filled hotel in Mérida, the Holiday Inn has floor-to-ceiling windows throughout the colorful lobby and tiled dining room. **Pros:** spacious rooms; nice breakfast buffet. **Cons:** about a mile from downtown; pool too small for serious swimming; gym is not well equipped. **TripAdvisor:** "free parking and free Wi-Fi and pool," "central to shopping, restaurants, and historical sites," "dependable service and quality rooms." ✉ *Av. Colón 468, at Calle 60, Paseo Montejo* ☎ *999/942–8800 or 800/465–4329* ⊕ *www.ichotelsgroup.com* ⤳ *197 rooms, 15 suites* ⚇ *In-room: a/c, Wi-Fi. In-hotel: restaurant, bar, pool, gym, parking* ❘❘ *No meals* ⊕ *C3.*

$$$ 🖭 **Hotel Casa San Angel.** The comfortable lobby of this small hotel has an open-air central courtyard with a fountain surrounded by plants and brightly painted walls of a tropical motif by local artist "Calocho" Millet. **Pros:** unique setting; comfortable rooms with spacious bathrooms; fantastic service. **Cons:** small pool. **TripAdvisor:** "large quiet comfortable room with comfy bed," "home-like hotel is a great experience," "restaurant has outstanding food." ✉ *Paseo de Montejo 1, Centro* ☎ *999/928–0800 or 999/928–1155* ⊕ *www.hotelcasasanangel. com* ⤳ *14 rooms, 1 suite* ⚇ *In-room: a/c, Wi-Fi. In-hotel: restaurant, some age restrictions* ❘❘ *No meals* ⊕ *C5.*

$ 🖭 **Hotel del Peregrino.** This recently restored old home is now a comfortable and inexpensive hotel. **Pros:** inexpensive; easy walk downtown; staff can arrange tours and Spanish tutoring. **Cons:** spacious but basic rooms; kitchen and lounge areas can get noisy. **TripAdvisor:** "people are very friendly and helpful," "charm and elegance of a Mexican hotel," "easy-going breakfast, very helpful staff, and attractive decor." ✉ *Calle 51 No. 488, between Calles 54 and 56, Centro* ☎ *999/924–5491* ⊕ *www.hoteldelperegrino.com* ⤳ *13 rooms* ⚇ *In-room: a/c, Wi-Fi. In-hotel: bar* ❘❘ *Breakfast* ⊕ *C5.*

$ 🖭 **Hotel María del Carmen.** This rather bland hotel caters to business travelers, tour groups, and those who desire secure parking and an innocuous environment. **Pros:** great downtown location; spacious rooms; big pool; good restaurant with reasonable prices. **Cons:** slow service; rooms facing street are noisy. **TripAdvisor:** "clean, well-managed, well-located hotel," "internet in the room was fast and free," "restaurant offered many choices." ✉ *Calle 63 No. 550, between Calles 68 and 70, Centro* ☎ *999/930–0390 or 800/712–0015* ⊕ *www.hotelmariadelcarmen.com. mx* ⤳ *83 rooms, 11 suites* ⚇ *In-room: a/c, Wi-Fi. In-hotel: restaurant, bar, pool, parking* ❘❘ *No meals* ⊕ *A6.*

$$ 🖭 **Hyatt Regency Mérida.** The city's first deluxe hotel is still among its
★   most elegant. **Pros:** attentive service; reasonably priced compared to neighboring hotels; popular Peregrina bistro. **Cons:** just off the Paseo

Montejo but far from downtown; Internet access costs around $13 per day. **TripAdvisor:** "central position on Paseo Montejo," "breakfast buffet was divine," "good value." ⊠ *Calle 60 No. 344, at Av. Colón, Paseo Montejo* ☎ *999/942–0202, 999/942–1234, or 800/233–1234* ⊕ *merida. regency.hyatt.com.mx* ⇴ *285 rooms, 4 suites* ⚮ *In-room: a/c, Internet, Wi-Fi. In-hotel: restaurants, bars, pool, tennis courts, gym, laundry, parking* ◉ *Multiple meal plans* ✛ *C2.*

$$ ⊞ **Maison LaFitte.** Jazz and tropical music float quietly above this hotel's two charming patios, where you can sip a drink near the fountain or swim in the small pool. **Pros:** pretty patio areas; parking makes staying downtown much easier; attentive staff. **Cons:** street noise almost as loud as courtyard fountain; small rooms; no elevator. **TripAdvisor:** "in the heart of the colonial quarter of Merida," "water pressure is excellent," "computers with internet access available." ⊠ *Calle 60 No. 472, between Calles 53 and 55, Centro* ☎ *999/923–9159* ☎ *800/538–6802 in U.S. and Canada* ⊕ *www.maisonlafitte.com.mx* ⇴ *38 rooms* ⚮ *In-room: a/c, Wi-Fi. In-hotel: restaurant, bar, pool, business center, parking* ◉ *Breakfast* ✛ *B5.*

$$ ⊞ **Marionetas.** Attentive proprietors Daniel and Sofija Bosco, who are
★ originally from Argentina and Macedonia, have created this lovely B&B on a quiet street seven blocks from the main plaza. **Pros:** intimate feel; personal attention from proprietors and staff; courtyard and pool area are a calm escape from the bustling Mérida streets. **Cons:** reservations can be hard to come by in high season; restaurant only serves breakfast. **TripAdvisor:** "breakfast served poolside was delicious," "centrally located and close to most sights," "book your tours through the hotel." ⊠ *Calle 49 No. 516, between Calles 62 and 64, Centro* ☎ *999/928–3377 or 999/923–2790* ⊕ *www.hotelmarionetas.com* ⇴ *8 rooms, 1 suite* ⚮ *In-room: a/c. In-hotel: pool, Wi-Fi* ◉ *Breakfast* ✛ *B5.*

$$ ⊞ **Medio Mundo.** A Lebanese-Uruguayan couple runs this hotel in a residential area downtown. **Pros:** great location; friendly staff; reasonable rates. **Cons:** breakfast costs extra and no other meals are served; guests' comings and goings can be noisy at night. **TripAdvisor:** "aesthetics of Medio Mundo are exquisite," "cool, tastefully simple room," "a real gem." ⊠ *Calle 55 No. 533, between Calles 64 and 66, Centro* ☎ *999/924–5472* ⊕ *www.hotelmediomundo.com* ⇴ *12 rooms* ⚮ *In-room: a/c (some), no TV. In-hotel: pool, parking, some age restrictions* ◉ *No meals* ✛ *B5.*

$ ⊞ **Posada Toledo.** This beautiful centuries-old house has retained its elegance with high ceilings, floors of patterned tile, and carved, colonial-style furniture. **Pros:** inexpensive; friendly staff. **Cons:** room quality varies; sound from courtyard audible from nearby rooms; small bathrooms. ⊠ *Calle 58 No. 487, at Calle 57, Centro* ☎ *999/923–1690* ⇴ *21 rooms, 2 suites* ⚮ *In room: a/c. In-hotel: restaurant, parking* ◉ *No meals* ✛ *B6.*

$$ ⊞ **Presidente InterContinental.** A salmon-color replica of a 19th-century French-colonial mansion, the Presidente is a bit of a hike from the main plaza, but sits right next to the Santiago church and public square, where a big, live band attracts whirling couples on Tuesday at 9 pm. **Pros:** spacious rooms; comfortable beds; good value. **Cons:** far from main plaza.

TripAdvisor: "bathroom large and well stocked with supplies," "try to arrange for a pool view," "excellent service." ⊠ *Calle 59 No. 589, at Calle 76, Barrio Santiago* ☏ *999/924–3899 or 999/924–3099* ⊕ *www.hotelresidencial.com.mx* ⇨ *64 rooms, 2 suites* ⚹ *In-room: a/c, Wi-Fi. In-hotel: restaurant, bar, pool, parking* ⎮⊙⎮ *No meals* ⊹ *B2.*

$$$ ▦ **Rosas & Xocolate.** This is one of the newest boutique hotels in Mérida and it's been designed with romance and opulence in mind. **Pros:** beautiful architecture; location along main street with easy access to shopping and restaurants. **Cons:** pool is beautiful but small and in a very public area; with no elevator, some upstairs rooms feel like quite a hike. **TripAdvisor:** "beautifully created from two original mansions," "delightful setting, excellent food and quite reasonably priced," "bed, bedding and pillows were cozy comfortable." ⊠ *Paseo de Montejo 480, at Calle 41, Centro* ☏ *999/924–4304* ⊕ *www.rosasandxocolate.com* ⇨ *14 rooms, 3 suites* ⚹ *In-room: a/c, Wi-Fi. In-hotel: restaurant, bars, gym, spa, some pets allowed* ⎮⊙⎮ *No meals* ⊹ *C4.*

> **MAKING YOURSELF AT HOME**
>
> There are a few Internet agencies that can help you rent a home if you plan on staying in the area for a while. At ⊕ *www.bestofyucatan. com*, you can find some stunningly remodeled old Mérida homes, and haciendas remodeled by artists John Powell and Josh Ramos.

NIGHTLIFE

Mérida has an active and diverse cultural life, which features free government-sponsored music and dance performances many evenings, as well as sidewalk art shows in local parks. On Thursday at 9 pm Méridians enjoy an evening of outdoor entertainment at the **Serenata Yucateca.** At **Parque Santa Lucía** (Calles 60 and 55) you'll see trios, the local orchestra, and soloists performing compositions by Yucatecan composers. On Saturday evenings after 7 pm the **Noche Mexicana** (corner of Paseo Montejo and Calle 47) hosts different musical and cultural events. More free music, dance, comedy, and regional handicrafts can be found at the **Corazón de Mérida,** on Calle 60 between the main plaza and Calle 55. Between 8 pm and 1 am, multiple bandstands throughout this area (which is closed to traffic) entertain locals and visitors with an ever-changing playbill, from grunge to classical.

On Sunday, six blocks around the zócalo are closed off to traffic, and you can see performances—often mariachi and marimba bands or folkloric dancers—at Plaza Santa Lucía, Parque Hidalgo, and the main plaza. For a schedule of current performances, consult the tourist offices, the local newspapers, or the billboards and posters at the Teatro Peón Contreras or the Centro Cultural Olimpo.

BARS AND DANCE CLUBS

Mérida has always been a great city to walk in by day and dance in by night. Méridians love music, and they love to dance, but since they also have to work, many discos are open only on weekend nights, or Thursday through Sunday. ■ TIP→ Be aware that it's becoming more and more common for discos and restaurants with live music and "comedy" acts (geared toward young people), to invite customers onstage for some rather shocking "audience participation" acts. Since these are otherwise fine establishments, we can only suggest that you let your sense of outrage be your guide. Locals don't seem to mind.

★ Popular with the local *niños fresa* (which translates as "strawberry children," meaning upper-class youth) as well as some middle-age professionals, indoor-outdoor lounge **El Cielo** (⊠ *Prolongación Paseo Montejo between Calles 15 and 17, Col. México* ☎ *999/944–5127* ⊕ *www. elcielobar.com*) is one of the latest minimalist hot spots where you can drink and dance to party or lounge-music videos. It's open Wednesday through Saturday nights from 10 pm till 4 am. Thursday and Saturday there's a $12 cover charge for men ($4 for women), as well as an open bar until 11 pm.

El Nuevo Tucho (⊠ *Calle 60 No. 482, between Calles 55 and 57, Centro* ☎ *999/924–2323*) has cheesy cabaret-style entertainment beginning at 4 pm, with no drink minimum and no cover. In fact, despite the music and comedy, this is not just a place for young people or for dancing. Families dine here as well. There's music for dancing in this cavernous—sometimes full, sometimes empty—venue. Drinks come with free appetizers.

Pancho's (⊠ *Calle 59 No. 509, between Calles 60 and 62, Centro* ☎ *999/ 923–0942* ⊕ *www.panchosmerida.com*), open daily 6 pm–2:30 am, has a lively bar and a restaurant. It also has a small dance floor that attracts locals and visitors for a mix of live salsa and English-language pop music.

If dancing to the likes of Los Panchos and other romantic trios of the 1940s is more your style, don't miss this Tuesday-night ritual at **Parque de Santiago** (⊠ *Calles 59 and 72, Centro* ☎ *No phone*), where older folks and the occasional young lovers gather for dancing under the stars at 8:30 pm.

Fodor'sChoice
★ Enormously popular and rightly so, the red-walled **Slavia** (⊠ *Calle 29 No. 490, at Calle 58* ☎ *999/926–6587*) is an exotic Orientalist beauty. There are all sorts of nooks where you can be alone yet together with upscale Méridians. Lounge and ambient music in the background, low lighting, beaded curtains, embroidered tablecloths, mirrors, and sumptuous pillows and settees surrounding low tables produce a fabulous vibe you won't find anywhere else in Mérida. It's open daily from 7 pm to 2 am. If smoking hookah under Buddha's watchful eyes isn't your thing, check out the two other concepts the owner has opened on the same block—Cubaroo, a Latin-themed fusion restaurant and bar whose roof deck has spectacular views of the Monument to the Flag, and Tobago, a cozy replica of a Parisian café.

Tequila Rock (⊠ *Prolongación Paseo Montejo at Av. Campestre* ☎ *999/ 944–1828*) is a disco where salsa and Mexican and American pop are played Wednesday through Saturday. It's popular mainly with young people between 18 and 25.

Catedral de San Ildefonso.

FOLKLORIC SHOWS

Paseo Montejo hotels such as the Fiesta Americana, Hyatt Regency, and Holiday Inn stage dinner shows with folkloric dances. Check with concierges for schedules.

★ The **Ballet Folklórico de Yucatán** (✉ *Calles 57 and 60, Centro* ☎ *999/923–1198*) presents a combination of music, dance, and theater every Friday at 9 pm at the university; tickets are $5. (Performances are every other Friday in the off-season, and there are no shows from August 1 to September 22 and during the last two weeks of December.)

SHOPPING

Mérida has something for everyone when it comes to shopping, from the souvenir junkies to the most discriminating of market trollers. Crafts at very reasonable prices can be found in the markets, parks, and plazas, and local art can be picked up at one of the many galleries, for the art scene here is burgeoning. If you're looking for a more standard shopping experience, or need to stock up on goods like new tennis shoes or a pair of jeans, there are also a few shopping malls in town.

MALLS

Mérida has several shopping malls, but the largest and nicest, **Gran Plaza** (✉ *Calle 50 Diagonal 460, Fracc. Gonzalo Guerrero* ☎ *999/944–7657* ⊕ *www.granplaza.com.mx*), has more than 200 shops and a multiplex theater. It's just outside town, on the highway to Progreso (called Carretera a Progreso beyond the Mérida city limits). Tiny **Pasaje Picheta** is on the north side of the town square on Calle 61. It has a bus-ticket information booth and an upstairs art gallery, as well as souvenir shops and a food court. It's open 9 am to 11 pm daily. **Plaza Américas** (⊠ *Calle 21 No. 331, Col. Miguel Hidalgo* ☎ *No phone*) is a pleasant mall where you'll find the Cineopolis movie theater complex.

MARKETS

Sunday brings an array of wares into Mérida. Starting at 9 am, the Handicrafts Bazaar, or **Bazar de Artesanías** (⊠ *At main square, Centro*), sells lots of huipiles as well as hats and costume jewelry. As its name implies, popular art, or handicrafts, are sold at the **Bazar de Artes Populares** (⊠ *Parque Santa Lucía, at Calles 60 and 55, Centro*) beginning at 9 am on Sunday. If you're interested in handicrafts, **Bazar García Rejón** (⊠ *Calles 65 and 62, Centro*) has rows of indoor stalls that sell items like leather goods, palm hats, and handmade guitars.

The **Mercado Municipal** (⊠ *Calles 56 and 67, Centro*) has lots of things you won't need, but which are fascinating to look at: songbirds in cane cages, mountains of mysterious fruits and vegetables, ladles made of hollow gourds (the same way they've been made here for a thousand years). There are also lots of crafts for sale, including hammocks, sturdy leather huaraches, and piñatas in every imaginable shape and color. ■ TIP→ Guides often approach tourists near this market. They expect a tip and won't necessarily bring you to the best deals. You're better off visiting some specialty stores first to learn about the quality and types of hammocks, hats, and other crafts. Then you'll have an idea of what you're buying—and what it's worth—if you want to bargain in the market. Also be wary of pickpockets within the markets.

SPECIALTY STORES
BOOKS
Amate Books (⊠ *Calles 60 and 51* ☎ *999/924–2222* ⊕ *www.amatebooks. com* ☉ *Closed Sun.*), a new branch of an old Oaxacan bookstore, stocks books on all kinds of Mexican themes—from art and cooking to archaeology and language—in English. This cool building with high ceilings and old ceramic-tile floors is a beautiful setting in which to browse, meet people, and ask questions about local goings-on. There are plans for a café in the bookshop patio in the works.

CLOTHING
You might not wear a guayabera to a business meeting as some men in Mexico do, but the shirts are cool, comfortable, and attractive. For a good selection, try **Camisería Canul** (⊠ *Calle 62 No. 484, between Calles 57 and 59, Centro* ☎ *999/923–0158* ⊕ *www.camiseriacanul.com.mx*). Custom shirts take a week to construct, in sizes 4 to 52.

Guayaberas Jack (⊠ *Calle 59 No. 507A, between Calles 60 and 62, Centro* ☎ *99/928–6002*) has an excellent selection of guayaberas (18 delicious colors to choose from!) and typical women's cotton *filipinas* (house dresses), blouses, dresses, classy straw handbags, and lovely rayon *rebozos* (shawls) from San Luis Potosí. Guayaberas can be made to order, allegedly in less than a day, to fit anyone from a year-old baby to a 240-pound man, and anything in the shop can be altered or custom made. Everything here is of fine quality, and is often quite different from the clothes sold in neighboring shops—the prices reflect this superior quality.

BROWSING FOR BOOKS

Librería Dante has a great selection of colorful books on Mayan culture, although only a few are in English. There are many locations throughout town, including most of the malls, and there's also a large, happening shop-café-performance venue on Paseo Montejo. The Mérida English Library has novels and nonfiction in English. You can read in the library for five days without having to pay the $18 annual membership fee, and they host a gathering every Monday evening where you can meet people and practice Spanish. The giveaway "Yucatán Today," in English and Spanish, has good maps of the state and city and lots of useful information for travelers.

Librería Dante (⊠ *Calle 62 No. 502, at Calle 61 on main plaza, Centro* ☎ *999/928–2611* ⊠ *Calle 17 No. 138B, at Prolongación Paseo Montejo, Centro* ☎ *999/927–7676*). **Mérida English Library** (⊠ *Calle 53 No. 524, between Calles 66 and 68, Centro* ☎ *999/924–8401* ⊕ *www. meridaenglishlibrary.com*).

The store has a small branch near the Fiesta Americana Mérida, but it doesn't have as much variety as the downtown location. You can browse and make purchases on their Web site as well. **Mexicanísimo** (⊠ *Calle 60 No. 496, at Parque Hidalgo, Centro* ☎ *999/923–8132*) sells sleek, clean-lined clothing made from natural fibers for both women and men.

JEWELRY

Shop for malachite, turquoise, and other semiprecious stones set in silver at **Joyería Kema** (⊠ *Calle 60 No. 502-B, between Calles 61 and 63, at main plaza, Centro* ☎ *999/923–5838*). Beaders and other creative types flock to **Papagayo's Paradise** (⊠ *Calle 62 No. 488, between Calles 57 and 59, Centro* ☎ *999/993–0383*), where you'll find loose beads and semiprecious stones, lovely necklaces and earrings, and Brussels-lace-trimmed, hand-embroidered, tatted, and crocheted blouses. This small but exceptional store also sells men's handkerchiefs and place mats. **Tane** (⊠ *Centro Comercial Galerias, Carretera Mérida-Progreso, Km 5, Local 6, Paseo Montejo* ☎ *999/941–5862* ⊕ *www.tane.com.mx*) is an outlet for exquisite (and expensive) silver earrings, necklaces, and bracelets, some incorporating ancient Mayan designs.

LOCAL GOODS AND CRAFTS

A great place to purchase hammocks is **El Aguacate** (⊠ *Calle 58 No. 604, at Calle 73, Centro* ☎ *999/928–6265* ⊕ *www.hamacaselaguacate. com.mx*), a family-run outfit with many sizes and designs. It's closed Sunday. **La Casa de las Artesanías** (⊠ *Calle 63 between Calles 64 and 66, Centro* ☎ *999/928–6676* ⊙ *Mon.–Sat. 9 am–8 pm, Sun 9 am–2 pm*) is a government-run craft store offering all kinds of local crafts at fair prices. The tourism offices sometimes give out coupons for a 10% discount. There's a smaller branch in front of the Museo de Antropología e Historia on the Paseo de Montejo, but this main branch offers the best selection. Visit the government-run **Casa de las Artesanías Ki-Huic** (⊠ *Calle 63 No. 503A, between Calles 64 and 66, Centro* ☎ *999/928–6676*) for folk art from throughout Yucatán. There's a showcase of hard-to-find traditional filigree jewelry in silver, gold, and gold-dipped versions.

CLOSE UP

Hamacas: A Primer

Yucatecan artisans are known for creating some of the finest *hamacas*, or hammocks, in the country. For the most part, the shops of Mérida are the best places in Yucatán to buy these beautiful, practical items—although if you travel to some of the outlying small towns, like Tixkokob, Izamal, and Ek Balam, you may find cheaper prices—and enjoy the experience as well.

One of the first decisions you'll have to make when buying a hamaca is whether to choose one made from cotton or nylon: nylon dries more quickly and is therefore well suited to humid climates, but cotton is softer and more comfortable (though its colors tend to fade faster). You'll also see that hamacas come in both double-threaded and single-threaded weaves; the double-threaded ones are sturdiest because they're more densely woven.

Hamacas come in a variety of sizes, too. A *sencillo* (cen-*see*-oh) hammock is meant for just one person (although most people find it's a rather tight fit), a *doble* (*doh*-blay), on the other hand, is very comfortable for one but crowded for two. *Matrimonial* or king-size hammocks accommodate two, and *familiares* or *matrimoniales especiales* can theoretically sleep an entire family. (Yucatecans tend to be smaller than Anglos are, and also lie diagonally in hammocks rather than end-to-end.)

For a good-quality king-size nylon or cotton hamaca, expect to pay about $35, sencillos go for about $22. Unless you're an expert, it's best to buy a hammock at a specialty shop, where you can climb in to try the size. The proprietors will also give you tips on washing, storing, and hanging your hammock. There are lots of hammock stores near Mérida's municipal market on Calle 58, between Calles 69 and 73.

Casa de los Artesanos (⊠ *Calle 62 No. 492, between Calles 59 and 61, Centro*), half a block from the main plaza, sells mainly small ceramic pieces, including more modern, stylized takes on traditional designs. The **Casa de Cera** (⊠ *Calle 74A No. 430E, between Calles 41 and 43, Centro* ☎ *999/920–0219*) is a small shop selling signed collectible indigenous beeswax figurines. It's closed afternoons after 5 pm. **El Hamaquero** (⊠ *Calle 58 No. 572, between Calles 69 and 71, Centro* ☎ *999/923–2117*) has knowledgeable personnel who let you try out the hammocks before you buy. It's closed Sunday. **El Mayab** (⊠ *Calle 58 No. 553-A, at Calle 71, Centro* ☎ *999/924–0853*) has a multitude of hammocks and is open on Sunday until 2 pm. **Miniaturas** (⊠ *Calle 59 No. 507A, between Calles 60 and 62, Centro* ☎ *999/928–6503*) sells a delightful and diverse assortment of different crafts, but specializes in miniatures.

Tequilería Ajua (⊠ *Calle 59 No. 506, at Calle 62, Centro* ☎ *999/924–1453*) sells tequila, brandy, and mezcal as well as *Xtabentún*—a locally made liqueur flavored with anise and honey, which some claim is a aphrodisiac—and thick liqueurs made of local fruit, It's open from 10 am to 10 pm Monday through Saturday.

You can buy hammocks made to order—choose from standard nylon and cotton, super-soft processed sisal, Brazilian-style (six-stringed), or crocheted—at **El Xiric** (⊠ *Calle 57-A No. 15 and 16, Pasaje Congreso, Centro* ☎ *999/924–9906*). You can also get Xtabentún, as well as jewelry, black pottery, woven goods from Oaxaca, T-shirts, and souvenirs.

SPORTS AND THE OUTDOORS

It's possible to either watch or participate in sports, from baseball to tennis, while you're in town.

BASEBALL

Baseball is played with enthusiasm between February and July at the **Centro Deportivo Kukulcán** (⊠ *Calle 6 No. 315, Circuito Colonias, Col. Unidad Morelos ✛ Across street from Pemex gas station and next to Santa Clara Brewery* ☎ *999/940–0676 or 999/940–4261*). There are also tennis courts, soccer courts, and an Olympic pool. It's most common to buy your ticket at the on-site ticket booth the day of the game. A-league volleyball and basketball games and tennis tournaments are also held here.

GOLF

The 18-hole championship golf course at **Club de Golf de Yucatán** (⊠ *Carretera Mérida–Progreso, Km 14.5* ☎ *999/922–0053* ⊕ *www.golfyucatan.com*) is open to the public. It's about 16 km (10 mi) north of Mérida on the road to Progreso; greens fees are about $100, carts are an additional $35, and clubs can be rented. The pro shop is closed Monday, but the golf course is open seven days a week.

TENNIS

There are two cement public courts at **Estadio Salvador Alvarado** (⊠ *Calle 11 between Calles 62 and 60, Paseo Montejo* ☎ *999/925–4856*). The cost is $2 per hour during the day and $2.50 at night, after 6, when the courts are lighted. At the **Fiesta Americana Mérida** (⊠ *Av. Colón 451, Paseo Montejo* ☎ *999/942–1111*) guests have access to one lighted cement court. The **Hyatt Regency Mérida** (⊠ *Calle 60 No. 344, Colón* ☎ *999/942–0202*) has two lighted cement outdoor courts.

SIDE TRIP TO IZAMAL

68 km (42 mi) east of Mérida.

In the beautiful town of Izamal you may not find too many sights, but you'll almost certainly be taken by the town's color and carefully cared for colonial architecture. Although unsophisticated, Izamal is a charming and neighborly alternative to the sometimes frenetic tourism of Mérida. Hotels are humble, and the few restaurants offer basic fare. For those who enjoy a quieter, slower-pace vacation, Izamal is worth considering as a base. The city has recently been refurbished, and the downtown area shines with remodeled buildings, new roads, and bright yellow paint that contrasts strikingly with the blue sky. Some of these efforts have been part of the city's current efforts to be named an UNESCO World Heritage Site.

San Antonio de Padua.

One of the best examples of a Spanish colonial town in the Yucatán, Izamal is nicknamed "Ciudad Amarilla" (Yellow City), because its most important buildings are painted a golden ocher. It's also sometimes called "the City of Three Cultures," because of its combined pre-Hispanic, colonial, and contemporary influences.

GETTING HERE AND AROUND

The drive to Izamal from Mérida takes less than an hour. Take Highway 180 and follow the signs. Calesas are stationed at the town's large main square, fronting the lovely cathedral, day and night. The drivers charge about $5 an hour for sightseeing, and many will also take you on a shopping tour for whichever items you're interested in buying (for instance, hammocks or jewelry). Pick up a brochure at the visitor center for details.

ESSENTIALS

Currency Exchange Banorte (✉ *Calle 28 No. 300B, at Calle 31* ☎ *988/954–0425* ⊕ *www.banorte.com*).

Visitor and Tour Info Izamal Tourism Department (✉ *Calle 30 No. 323, between Calles 31 and 31-A, Centro* ☎ *988/954–1096*).

EXPLORING

★ **Ex-Convento y Iglesia de San Antonio de Padua.** Facing the main plaza, this enormous 16th-century former monastery and church of St. Anthony of Padua is perched on—and built from—the remains of a Mayan pyramid devoted to Itzámná, god of the heavens. The monastery's ocher-painted church, where Pope John Paul II led prayers in 1993, has a gigantic atrium (supposedly second in size only to the Vatican's) facing a colonnaded facade and rows of 75 white-trimmed arches. The Virgin of the Immaculate Conception, to whom the church is dedicated, is the patron saint of the Yucatán. A statue of Nuestra Señora de Izamal, or Our Lady of Izamal, was brought here from Guatemala in 1562 by Bishop Diego de Landa. Miracles are ascribed to her, and a yearly pilgrimage takes place in her honor. Frescoes of saints at the front of the church, once plastered over, were rediscovered and refurbished in 1996.

The monastery and church are now illuminated in a light-and-sound show of the type usually shown at the archaeological sites. You can catch a Spanish-only narration and the play of lights on the nearly 500-year-old structure at 8:30 pm Tuesday, Thursday, Friday, and Saturday—buy tickets ($4.50) on-site at 8.

Diagonally across from the massive cathedral, the small **municipal market** is worth a wander. It's a lot less frenetic than markets at major cities like Mérida, and the kind of place where if you stop to watch how the merchants prepare their food, they may spend the time to let you in on their cooking secrets.

On the other side of the square, **Hecho a Mano** (⊠ *Calle 31 No. 308, Centro* ☎ *988/954–0344*) is the only place in town to buy folk art from all over Mexico. There's something in every price category, including a growing collection of textiles.

Centro Cultural y Artesanal Izamal. Banamex has set up this small, well-organized popular art museum right on the main plaza. There are all kinds of high-quality crafts on display, from textiles and ceramics to papier-mâché and woodwork. You can also take home a souvenir from the gift shop. The center also has small café, a mini-spa that offers massages, and a pleasant patio at the foot of the Kabul pyramid. ⊠ *Calle 31 s/n, Centro* ☎ *988/954–1012* ⊕ *www.centroculturalizamal.org.mx* ⊠ *$1.50* ⊗ *Mon.–Sat. 10–8, Sun. 10–5.*

The **Kinich Kakmó** pyramid is the largest pre-Hispanic building in the Yucatán, and it's all that remains of the royal Mayan city that flourished here between AD 250 and 600. Dedicated to Zamná, Mayan god of the dew, the enormous structure is the largest of its kind in the state, covering about 10 acres. More remarkable for its size than for any remaining decoration, it's nonetheless an impressive monument, and you can scale it from the stairs on the south face for a view of the cathedral and the surrounding countryside. Entrance is $2.

WHERE TO EAT AND STAY

$ ✕ **Los Mestizos.** This humble restaurant has brightly painted walls; even MEXICAN the ceiling fans are painted bright orange. The "Combinado los Mestizos" on the dinner menu offers a taste of several regional specialties including *salbutes* and *panuchos*—both typical appetizers of fried cornmeal, the latter stuffed with beans—as well as chicken and turkey dishes. A far less common dish called *dzotobichay* is a tamale made with chaya leaves. There's a bit of a view of the church beyond the marketplace from the outdoor terrace. This is a great place to get an early start or wind up a long day of sightseeing. They're open daily from around 7 in the morning until 11 at night. ⊠ *Calle 33 301, behind market, Centro* ☎ *988/954–0289* ⊟ *No credit cards.*

$ ✕ **Restaurante Kinich**. This is the most comfortable place to eat in town.
MEXICAN   The entrance has a small shop featuring a carefully selected and cleverly
displayed collection of local folk art for sale. Beyond this, you enter a
dining area with white tablecloths under a wide *palapa* (thatched roof),
which is surrounded by plants and a burbling fountain, with a small
hut in back, where women make tortillas the old-fashioned way—by
hand. This is a great place to try local dishes as well—including locally
made *longaniza*, a tasty grilled pork sausage. The sopa de lima is also
excellent. The restaurant is open daily from 10 in the morning until
around 7 at night, but on Tuesday, Thursday, Friday, and Saturday,
when there's a light-and-sound show downtown, the restaurant stays
open late. ⊠ *Calle 27 No. 299, between Calles 28 and 30* ☎ *988/954–
0489* ⊕ *www.sabordeizamal.com.*

$$ 🏨 **Hotel Santo Domingo**. This new hotel has freestanding rooms sep-
arated by carefully tended gardens, all inspired by the old hacienda
style. **Pros:** freestanding rooms provide some privacy. **Cons:** no credit
cards accepted. **TripAdvisor:** "comfortable and welcoming," "magical
place in a magical city," "bedding comfortable, good air condition-
ing." ⊠ *Calle 18 between Calles 33 and 35* ☎ *988/967–6136* ⊕ *www.
izamalhotel.com* ⤳ *10 rooms* ⌂ *In-room: a/c (some), kitchen (some),
no TV (some). In-hotel: restaurant, pool, parking* ⊟ *No credit cards*
❄️ *Breakfast.*

$ 🏨 **Macanché**. Each freestanding guest room here has its own theme
decor: the Asian room has a Chinese checkers board and origami deco-
rations; the Safari room has artifacts from Mexico and Africa. **Pros:**
good restaurant; full breakfast included; nice limestone pool surrounded
by plants; great room price; private yoga classes available. **Cons:** sev-
eral blocks from central plaza. **TripAdvisor:** "setting is like a tropical
garden," "warm, relaxing, wonderful place to be," "water coolers in
the rooms." ⊠ *Calle 22 No. 305, between Calles 33 and 35* ☎ *988/954–
0287* ⊕ *www.macanche.com* ⤳ *15 bungalows, 2 houses* ⌂ *In-room: a/c
(some), no TV (some). In-hotel: restaurant, bar, pool, parking* ⊟ *No
credit cards* ❄️ *Breakfast.*

UXMAL AND THE RUTA PUUC

Ruta Puuc, or hilly route, is one of the highlights of any visit to Yucatán.
The series of secondary roads that wind through one of the state's least
populated areas not only leads you from one fantastic Mayan ruin to
another, but to an impressive cave system, various restored haciendas,
and numerous villages where you can stop for a bite to eat and feel the
unique rhythm of the Yucatecan countryside. The route deserves at least
two days. Most of the archaeological sites are open from 8 to 5 only,
so to devote any less time means either skipping deserving locales, or
rushing through the sites. Uxmal itself is worth at least a half day. The
roads are well marked and easy to navigate, since sites lines up one right
after another. ■TIP→ It's important to fill up on gas and visit an ATM before
entering the area, since both gas stations and ATMs are hard to come by.

Uxmal, meaning thrice built city, is the largest site along the Ruta Puuc.
Several smaller satellite sites—including Kabah, Sayil, and Labná—are

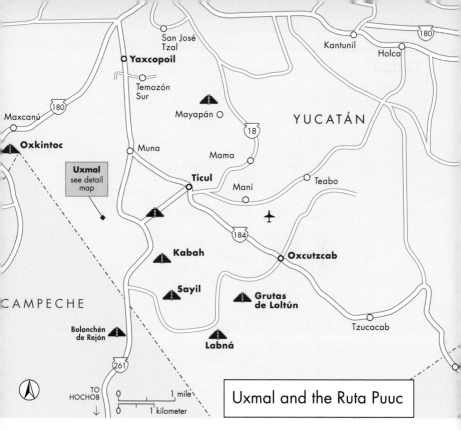

all well worth a visit. Another memorable Ruta Puuc site is the Grutas de Loltún, Yucatán's most mysterious and extensive cave system. Here you can still see evidence of ancient Mayan rituals. If you plan on exploring the cave, take along sturdy shoes and a flashlight.

If you want to use your video camera at any of the sites, expect a $3 charge.

TIMING

It's possible to visit the sites on the Ruta Puuc in one long day or over the course of two days. To do Uxmal justice, you'll want to spend anywhere from three to five hours exploring the ruins. Smaller area sites like Labná, Xlapak, Sayil, and Kabah can easily be explored in 20 to 30 minutes. Plan on spending a couple of hours at the Grutas de Loltún; be aware that guided tours through the cave are mandatory.

Uxmal is a good place to grab lunch. Snacks are sold on-site and hotel restaurants are within walking distance; food is a little harder to come by at the other sites. We also recommend the hotels around Uxmal since it's easy to catch the nightly light-and-sound show.

GETTING HERE AND AROUND

There's daily transportation on the ATS bus line to Uxmal, Labná, Xlapak, Sayil, and Kabah. A $10 ticket buys you a ride to each of these places with 20 to 30 minutes to explore the lesser sites and nearly two

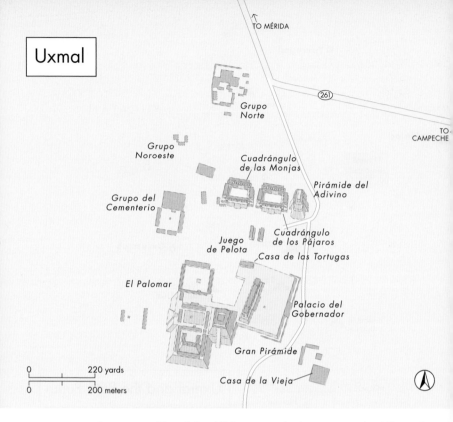

TO MÉRIDA

Grupo Norte

261

TO CAMPECHE

Grupo Noroeste

Cuadrángulo de las Monjas

Pirámide del Adivino

Grupo del Cementerio

Cuadrángulo de los Pájaros

Juego de Pelota

Casa de las Tortugas

El Palomar

Palacio del Gobernador

Gran Pirámide

Casa de la Vieja

0   220 yards
0   200 meters

hours to see Uxmal. In addition to standard tours, Mayaland Tours also offers "self-guided tours," which means that you set out on your own, but they provide a road map, itinerary, rental car, and arrange lodgings at the archaeological sites. When you consider the price of lodgings and a rental car, this is not a bad deal.

If you plan on spending the night in Uxmal, you may want to start the trip off at Grutas de Loltún and work your way toward Uxmal. To get to Grutas de Loltún from Mérida, take Highway 261 to Muná. Turn left on Highway 184. From there, it's about 65 km (40 mi) to Oxkutzcab. Once in Oxkutzcab, simply follow the signs to the Grutas de Loltún.

ESSENTIALS

Tours and Visitor Information Mayaland Tours (✉ *Calle Robalo 30, Sm 3, Cancún* ☎ *998/887–2495 in Cancún, 01800/719–5465 toll-free from elsewhere in Mexico, 800/235–4079 in U.S.* 🌐 *www.mayaland.com*).

UXMAL

78 km (48 mi) south of Mérida on Carretera 261.

If Chichén Itzá is the most expansive Mayan ruin in Yucatán, Uxmal is arguably the most elegant. The architecture here reflects the late classical renaissance of the 7th to 9th century, and is contemporary with

Uxmal is an example of the Puuc architectural style.

that of Palenque and Tikal, among other great Mayan cities of the southern highlands.

The site is considered the finest and most extensively excavated example of Puuc architecture, which embraces such details as ornate stone mosaics and friezes on the upper walls, intricate cornices, rows of columns, and soaring vaulted arches.

You could easily spend a couple of days exploring the ruins, though keep in mind that the only entertainment offered outside the ruins is provided by hotels and the odd restaurant.

GETTING HERE AND AROUND
If you plan to drive yourself, take Highway 180 south out of Mérida, and then get on Highway 261 in Umán. This will take you south all the way to Uxmal.

EXPLORING

Fodor'sChoice
★

Uxmal. Although much of Uxmal hasn't been restored, the following buildings in particular merit attention:

At 125 feet high, the **Pirámide del Adivino** is the tallest and most prominent structure at the site. Unlike most other Mayan pyramids, which are stepped and angular, the Temple of the Magician has a softer and more-refined round-corner design. This structure was rebuilt five times over hundreds of years, each time on the same foundation, so artifacts found here represent several different kingdoms. The pyramid has a stairway on its western side that leads through a giant open-mouthed mask to two temples at the summit. During restoration work in 2002 the grave of a high-ranking Maya official, a ceramic mask, and a jade

necklace were discovered within the pyramid. Continuing excavations have revealed exciting new finds that are still being studied.

West of the pyramid lies the **Cuadrángulo de las Monjas**, considered by some to be the finest part of Uxmal. The name was given to it by the conquistadores, because it reminded them of a convent building in Old Spain (*monjas* means nuns). You may enter the four buildings, each comprising of a series of low, gracefully repetitive chambers that look onto a central patio. Elaborate and symbolic decorations—masks, geometric patterns, coiling snakes, and some phallic figures—blanket the upper facades.

Heading south, you'll pass a small ball court before reaching the **Palacio del Gobernador**, which archaeologist Victor von Hagen considered the most magnificent building ever erected in the Americas. Interestingly, the palace faces east, while the rest of Uxmal faces west. Archaeologists believe this is because the palace was built to allow observation of the planet Venus. Covering 5 acres and rising over an immense acropolis, it lies at the heart of what may have been Uxmal's administrative center.

Apparently the house of an important person, the recently excavated **Cuadrángalo de los Pájaros** (Quadrangle of the Birds), located between the above-mentioned buildings, is composed of a series of small chambers. In one of these chambers, archaeologists found a statue of the royal, by the name of Chac (as opposed to Chaac, the rain god), who apparently dwelt there. The building was named for the repeated pattern of birds, which decorates the upper part of the building's frieze.

Today you can watch a sound-and-light show at the site that recounts Mayan legends. The colored light brings out details of carvings and mosaics that are easy to miss when the sun is shining. The show is performed nightly in Spanish, but earphones ($2.50) provide an English translation. ■TIP→ In the summer months, tarantulas are a common sight at the ruins and around the hotels that surround the ruins. ✉ *Site, museum, and sound-and-light show $19.50; show only $3; parking $1; use of video camera $2 (keep this receipt if visiting other archaeological sites along the Ruta Puuc on the same day); official English-language tour guide $55* ☉ *Daily 8–5; sound-and-light show 7 pm in winter, 8 pm in summer.*

WHERE TO EAT

$ ✕ **Cana Nah.** Although this large, recently remodeled roadside spot
MEXICAN mainly caters to the groups visiting Uxmal, locals recommend it as the most formally established and hygienic eatery in the area, and the friendly owners are happy to serve small parties. The basic menu includes local dishes like lime soup and pollo pibil, and such universals as fried chicken and vegetable soup. Approach the salsa on the table with a bit of caution: it's made almost purely of habanero chiles. After your meal you can dive into the property's large rectangular swimming pool. There's a small shop as well, selling pieces of popular art including figurines of *los aluxes,* the mischievous "lords of the jungle" that Mayan legend says protect farmers' fields. ✉ *Carretera Muna–Uxmal, 4 km (2½ mi) north of Uxmal* ☎ *997/113–8019 or 999/109–7513* ▭ *No credit cards.*

WHERE TO STAY

For expanded hotel reviews, visit Fodors.com.

$$$ 🏨 **Hacienda Uxmal.** The first hotel built in Uxmal, this pleasant colonial-style building was looking positively haggard before a recent face-lift, when sheets, towels, and furnishings were replaced. **Pros:** good service; good restaurant; pretty gardens; interesting on-site activities. **Cons:** fairly close (five-minute walk) to Uxmal ruins, but you could be closer. **TripAdvisor:** "room was lovely, large and comfortable," "clean, quiet, nice pool, great price," "easy driving distance of everything." ⊠ *Carretera 261, Km 78* ☎ *997/976–2012 or 800/235–4079* ⊕ *www.mayaland. com* ⤳ *54 rooms, 8 suites* ♿ *In-room: a/c. In-hotel: restaurant, bar, pools, Wi-Fi, parking.*

$$$ 🏨 **Lodge at Uxmal.** The outwardly rustic, thatch-roof buildings here have red-tile floors, doors and rocking chairs carved from polished hardwood, and local weavings. **Pros:** directly across from Uxmal entrance; simple, beautiful rooms; big pools. **Cons:** no room phones; mediocre restaurant; expensive. **TripAdvisor:** "large, open air restaurant," "across the street from the Uxmal ruin," "feels like a safari or archeological expedition." ⊠ *Carretera Uxmal, Km 78* ☎ *997/976–2031 or 800/235–4079* ⊕ *www.mayaland.com* ⤳ *40 suites* ♿ *In-hotel: restaurants, bar, pools, parking.*

$$ 🏨 **Villas Arqueológicas Uxmal.** Rooms at this pretty two-story former
Fodor's Choice Club Med property are small, like hobbit holes, but bright and func-
★ tional, with wooden furniture and cozy twin beds that fit nicely into alcoves. **Pros:** upgraded beds and other improvements; walking distance to ruins; nice pool. **Cons:** rooms could be more spacious; restaurant food is just OK. **TripAdvisor:** "prime location to the ruins," "rooms are small but attractive," "staff efficient but unfriendly." ⊠ *Carretera 261, Km 76* ☎ *997/974–6020 or 800/258–2633* ⊕ *www.villasarqueologicas. com.mx* ⤳ *40 rooms, 3 suites* ♿ *In-room: a/c. In-hotel: restaurant, bar, pool, spa, tennis court, parking.*

6

KABAH

23 km (14 mi) south of Uxmal on Carretera 261.

🏛 **Kabah.** The most important buildings at Kabah, which means "lord of the powerful hand" in Mayan, were built between AD 600 and 900, during the later part of the classic era. A ceremonial center of almost Grecian beauty, it was once linked to Uxmal by a sacbé, at the end of which looms a great independent arch—now across the highway from the main ruins. The 151-foot-long **Palacio de los Mascarones,** or Palace of the Masks, boasts a three-dimensional mosaic of 250 masks of inlaid stones. On the central plaza, you can see ground-level wells called *chultunes,* which were used to store precious rainwater. The site officially opens at 8 am, but the staff doesn't usually show up until 9. 🎫 *$3.50* ⏱ *Daily 8–5.*

SAYIL

9 km (5½ mi) south of Kabah on Carretera 31 E.

Sayil. Experts believe that Sayil, or "place of the red ants," flourished between AD 800 and 1000. It's renowned primarily for its majestic **Gran Palacio.** Built on a hill, the three-story structure is adorned with decorations of animals and other figures, and contains more than 80 rooms. The structure recalls Palenque in its use of multiple planes, columned porticoes, and sober cornices. Also on the grounds is a stela in the shape of a phallus—an obvious symbol of fertility. $3.50 ⊘ *Daily 8–5.*

LABNÁ

9 km (5½ mi) south of Sayil on Carretera 31 E.

Labná. The striking monumental structure at Labná (which means "old house" or "abandoned house") is a fanciful corbelled arch (also called the Mayan arch, or false arch), with elaborate latticework and a small chamber on each side. One theory says the arch was the entrance to an area where religious ceremonies were staged. The site was used mainly by the military elite and royalty. $3.50 ⊘ *Daily 8–5.*

GRUTAS DE LOLTÚN

19 km (12 mi) northeast of Labná, down an unmarked road toward Oxkutzcab.

Grutas de Loltún. The Loltún ("stone flower" in Mayan) is one of the largest and most fascinating cave systems on the Yucatán Peninsula. Long ago, Mayan ceremonies were routinely held inside these mysterious caves, and artifacts found inside date as far back as 800 BC. The topography of the caves themselves is fascinating: there are stalactites, stalagmites, and limestone formations known by such names as Ear of Corn and Cathedral. Illuminated pathways meander a little over a kilometer through the caverns, most of which are quite spacious and well ventilated (claustrophobics needn't worry). Nine different openings allow air and some (but not much) light to filter in. ■TIP→ You can enter only with a guide. Although these guides were once paid a small salary, they're now forced to work for tips only—so be generous. Scheduled tours are at 9:30, 12:30, 3, and 4 (in Spanish), and 11 and 2 (in English). $6.70, parking $1 ⊘ *Daily 9–5.*

TICUL

27 km (17½ mi) northwest of the Loltún Caves, 28 km (17 mi) east of Uxmal, 100 km (62 mi) south of Mérida.

One of the larger cities in the Yucatán (with a population of around 20,000), and a busy market town, Ticul is a good base for exploring the Puuc region—if you don't mind rudimentary hotels and a limited choice of simple restaurants. Many descendants of the Xiu Dynasty, which ruled Uxmal until the conquest, still live here. Industries include

Grutas de Loltún.

fabrication of huipiles and shoes, as well as much of the pottery you see around the Yucatán. It also has a handsome 17th-century church.

GETTING HERE AND AROUND
Ticul is an easy drive south of Mérida, along the Ruta Puuc. Follow México 180 from Mérida to Umán, where you'll get on the México 261 to Muná. From Muná, simply follow the signs to Ticul, by way of the México 184.

ESSENTIALS
Currency Exchange Banamex (⊠ *Calle 26 No. 199D* ☎ *01800/226–2639 toll-free in Mexico* ⊕ *www.banamex.com*).

EXPLORING

★ **Arte Maya** (⊠ *Calle 23 No. 301 [Carretera Tikul Muna at the very entrance to town, next to the cemetary]* ☎ *997/972–1669* ⊕ *www. artemaya.com.mx*) is a ceramics workshop that produces museum-quality replicas of archaeological pieces found throughout Mexico. The workshop also creates souvenir-quality pieces that are more affordable and more easily transported.

Iglesia de San Antonio de Padua. This pretty, faded, red colonial church is typical of the Yucatán colonial churches. It has been weathered and ransacked on more than one occasion, but the Black Christ altarpiece is original. The best view might be from the outside, where you can take in the facade, including its three towers, and the slow pace of the town as families ride by in carts attached to bicycles and locals mill around in traditional Mayan dress. ⊠ *On the zócalo, Centro.*

Yucatán's History

Francisco de Montejo's conquest of Yucatán took three gruesome wars over a total of 24 years. "Nowhere in all America was resistance to Spanish conquest more obstinate or more nearly successful," wrote the historian Henry Parkes. In fact, the resolute Maya, their ancestors long incorrectly portrayed by archaeologists as docile and peace-loving, provided the Spaniards and the mainland Mexicans with one of their greatest challenges. Rebellious pockets of Mayan communities held out against the *dzulo'obs* (dzoo-loh-obs)—the upper class, or outsiders—as late as the 1920s and '30s.

If Yucatecans are proud of their heritage and culture, it's with good reason. Although in a state of decline when the conquistadores clanked into their world with iron swords and fire-belching cannons, the Maya were one of the world's greatest ancient cultures. As mathematicians and astronomers they were perhaps without equal among their contemporaries, and their architecture in places like Uxmal was as graceful as that of the ancient Greeks.

To "facilitate" Catholic conversion among the conquered, the Spaniards superimposed Christian rituals on existing beliefs whenever possible, creating the ethnic Catholicism that's alive and well today. (Those defiant Maya who resisted the new ideology were burned at the stake, drowned, and hanged.) Having procured a huge workforce of free indigenous labor, Spanish agricultural estates prospered like mad. Mérida soon became a thriving administrative and military center, and the gateway to Cuba and to Spain. By the 18th century, huge maize and cattle plantations were making the *hacendados* incredibly rich.

Insurrection came during the War of the Castes in the mid-1800s, when the enslaved indigenous people rose up with long-repressed furor and massacred thousands of non-Indians. The United States, Cuba, and Mexico City finally came to the aid of the ruling elite, and between 1846 and 1850 the Indian population of Yucatán was effectively halved. Those Maya who didn't escape into the remote jungles of neighboring Quintana Roo or Chiapas, or get sold into slavery in Cuba, found themselves, if possible, worse off than before under the dictatorship of Porfirio Díaz.

The hopeless status of the indigenous people—both Yucatán natives and those kidnapped and lured with the promise of work elsewhere in Mexico—changed little as the economic base segued from one industry to the next. After the thin limestone soil failed to produce fat cattle or impressive corn, entrepreneurs turned to dyewood and then to henequen, a natural fiber used to make rope. After the widespread acceptance of synthetic fibers, the entrepreneurs used the sweat of local labor to convert gum arabic from the peninsula's prevalent *zapote* tree into European vacations and Miami bank accounts. The fruits of their labor can be seen today in the imposing French-style mansions that stretch along Mérida's Paseo Montejo.

Mayapán. Those who are enamored with Yucatán and the ancient Maya may want to take a 42-km (26-mi) detour east of Ticul (or 43 km [27 mi] from Mérida) to Mayapán, the last of the major city-states on the peninsula that flourished during the postclassic era. It was demolished in 1450, presumably by war. It's thought that the city, with an architectural style reminiscent of Uxmal, was as big as Chichén Itzá, and there are more than 4,000 mounds, which might lend truth to this. At its height, the population could have been well more than 12,000. A half dozen mounds have been excavated, including the palaces of Mayan royalty and the temple of the benign god Kukulcán, where stucco sculptures and murals in vivid reds and oranges have been uncovered. ⊠ *Off road to left before Telchaquillo, follow signs* 🖼 *$4* ☼ *Daily 8–5.*

WHERE TO EAT AND STAY

$ ✕ **Los Almendros**. One of the few places in town open from 9 am until 9 pm, "the Almonds" is a good place to sample tasty, well-prepared regional fare, served with handmade tortillas. The restaurant has been so successful that there are now branches in Mérida and Cancún, but this is the original. The *combinado yucateco* gives you a chance to try poc-chuc and cochinita pibil (two pork dishes) as well as *pavo relleno* (stuffed turkey) and sausage. The owners claim to have invented poc-chuc right here. The newish building at the edge of town is often full of tour groups—or completely empty. There's a pool out back where you can swim—but do as mama says and wait at least a half hour after eating—especially if you order a big plate like the *combinado*. ⊠ *Calle 22 s/n, at Carretera Ticul–Chetumal* ☎ *997/972–0021* ▭ *No credit cards.*

MEXICAN

$ ✕ **El Príncipe Tutul-Xiu**. About 15 km (9 mi) from Ticul in the little town of Maní, this large open restaurant under a giant palapa roof is a great place for lunch or an early dinner (it closes at 7 pm). Though you'll find the same Yucatecan dishes here as elsewhere—pollo pibil, lime soup—the preparation is excellent and portions are generous. Best of all is the poc-chuc—little bites of pork marinated in sour orange, garlic, and chiles and grilled over charcoal. ⊠ *Calle 26 No. 210, between Calles 25 and 27* ☎ *997/978–4086.*

MEXICAN
★

¢ ▦ **Plaza**. While they get no points for creativity as far as their name is concerned, the Plaza does have a convenient location about a block from the main plaza. **Pros:** downtown location; clean rooms. **Cons:** no frills; church bells might keep you up late or wake you early; 6% surcharge for paying with credit card. ⊠ *Calle 23 No. 202, between Calles 26 and 26A* ☎ *997/972–0484* ⊕ *www.hotelplazayucatan.com* ⤴ *30 rooms* ⚭ *In-room: a/c, Wi-Fi. In-hotel: restaurant, parking.*

THE MAYAN INTERIOR

120 km (74 mi) east of Mérida.

Although hordes of buses arrive daily at Chichén Itzá, dropping off groups of tourists only to whisk them away a few hours later, visiting the area this way is almost criminal. The area around the ruins is dotted with stunning cenotes, numerous smaller archaeological sites, and sleepy towns, which make you may feel like you've stepped back in time. The picturesque town of Valladolid, the second-largest city in

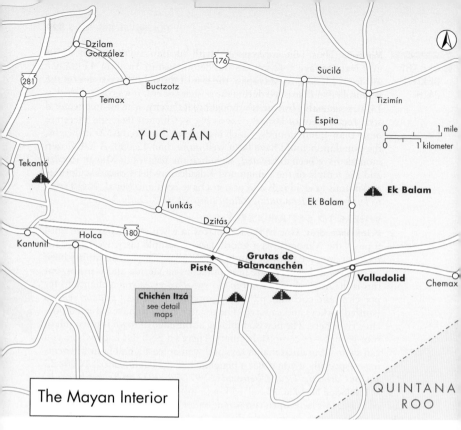

The Mayan Interior

the state, is notable for its cenote and a beautiful 16th-century church. Here, perhaps while enjoying a traditional ice cream in the central plaza, you notice that things seem to move at a slower pace. The small town of Pisté is little more than an outpost—it's a place where visitors to Chichén Itzá can rest at small hotels.

GETTING HERE AND AROUND
Although you can get to Chichén Itzá along the shorter Carretera 180, there's a more scenic and interesting alternative. Head east on Carretera 281 through Tixkokob, a Maya community famous for its hammock weavers, and continue through Citilcúm and Izamal. From there, continue on through the small, untouristy towns of Dzudzal and Xanaba en route to Kantunil. There you can hop on the toll road or continue on the free road that parallels it through Holca and Libre Unión, both of which have very swimmable cenotes.

VALLADOLID

161 km (100 mi) from Mérida, 44½ km (28 mi) east of Chichén Itzá.

The second-largest city in Yucatán State, Valladolid (vay-ah-do-*lid*), is a picturesque provincial town that's been growing popular among travelers en route to or from Chichén Itzá (or Río Lagartos, to the north).

Francisco de Montejo founded Valladolid in 1543 on the site of the Mayan town of Sisal. The city suffered during the War of the Castes—when the Maya in revolt killed nearly all Spanish residents—and again during the Mexican Revolution.

Despite its turbulent history, Valladolid's downtown has many colonial and 19th-century structures. On Sunday evenings at 8 pm the city's orchestra plays elegant, stylized *danzón*—waltzlike dance music to which unsmiling couples (think tango: no smiling allowed) swirl around the bandstand of the main square. Valladolid is renowned for its *longaniza en escabeche*—a sausage dish made with pork, beef, or venison, served in many of the restaurants facing the square. In the shops and market you can also find good buys on sandals, baskets, and Xtabentún liqueur.

GETTING HERE AND AROUND

The drive from Mérida to Valladolid via the toll road (the tolls come to about $11) takes about two hours. The free road (México 295) cuts through several small towns where speed bumps, street repairs, and traffic can increase the travel time significantly. ADO and UNO have direct buses from Mérida to Valladolid, and other Mexican cities. They depart from the first-class CAME bus station. Most buses that come into Valladolid actually stop just outside of town, where you have to get on a second bus, a city bus. This is included in the price of your ticket.

ESSENTIALS

Bus Contacts Autobuses de Occidente (☎ 999/924–8391 or 999/924–9741 ⊕ www.ado.com.mx).

Currency Exchange Banamex (✉ Calle 41 No. 206 ☎ 01800/226–2639 toll-free in Mexico ⊕ www.banamex.com).

Medical Assistance Clínica San Juan (✉ Calle 40 No. 238 ☎ 985/856–2174).

Post Office Correo (✉ Calle 40 No. 194, between Calles 39 and 41 ☎ 985/856–2623)

Visitor and Tour Info Municipal Tourist Information Center (✉ Palacio Municipal ☎ No phone ⊙ Mon.–Sat. 9–8, Sun. 9–1).

EXPLORING

The large, round, and beautiful sinkhole at the edge of town, **Cenote Zací** (✉ Calles 36 and 37 ☎ 985/856–2107), is sometimes crowded with tourists and local boys clowning it up; at other times, it's deserted. Leaves from the tall old trees surrounding the sinkhole float on the surface, but the water itself is quite clean. If you're not up for a dip, visit the adjacent handicraft shop or have a bite or a drink at the popular, thatch-roof restaurant overlooking the water.

Five kilometers (3 mi) west of the main square and on the old highway to Chichén Itzá, you can swim with the catfish in lovely, mysterious **Cenote X-Keken** *(Cenote Dzitnup)*, which is in a cave lighted by a small natural skylight. Admission is about $4, and guides offer tours for tips.

★ Five long blocks away from the main plaza is the 16th-century, terra-cotta **Ex-Convento y Iglesia San Bernadino**, a Franciscan church and former monastery. ■TIP→ If the priest is around, ask him to show you the

Continued on page 340

The towering **El Castillo** pyramid, nearly 80 feet high, is the most striking structure at Chichén Itzá. Each side of the pyramid has 91 steps, which, with the addition of the topmost platform, equal 365, one for each day of the calendar year. At the vernal and autumnal equinoxes, thousands of people gather to watch as the shadow of the serpent god Kukulcán seems to slither down the side of the pyramid.

CHICHÉN ITZÁ

One of the most beautiful of the ancient Maya cities, Chichén Itzá draws some 3,000 visitors a day from all over the world. Since the remains of this once-thriving kingdom were discovered by Europeans in the mid 1800s, many of the travelers who make the pilgrimage here have been archaeologists and scholars who study the structures and glyphs and try to piece together the mysteries surrounding them. While the artifacts here give fascinating insight into the Maya civilization, they also raise many, many unanswered questions.

The name of this ancient city, which means "the mouth of the well of the Itzás," is a mystery in and of itself. Although it likely refers to the valuable water sources at the site (there are several sinkholes here), experts have little information about who might have actually founded the city—some structures, likely built in the 5th century, pre-date the arrival of the Itzás who occupied the city starting around the late 8th and early 9th centuries. The reason why the Itzás abandoned the city, around 1224, is also unknown.

Scholars and archaeologists aside, most of the visitors that converge on Chichén Itzá come to marvel at its beauty, not ponder its significance. This ancient metropolis, which encompasses 6 square km (2½ square mi), is known around the world as one of the most stunning and well-preserved Maya sites in existence.

(opposite) The main pyramid El Castillo is also called Temple of Kukulcán, (top) Carvings of ball players adorn the walls of the *juego de pelota*, (bottom) Maya statue.

MAJOR SITES AND ATTRACTIONS

Rows of freestanding columns where the roof has long since disintegrated

The sight of the immense **❶ El Castillo** pyramid, rising imposingly yet gracefully from the surrounding plain, has been known to produce goose pimples on sight. El Castillo (The Castle) dominates the site both in size and in the symmetry of its perfect proportions. Open-jawed serpent statues adorn the corners of each of the pyramid's four stairways, honoring the legendary priest-king Kukulcán (also known as Quetzalcóatl), an incarnation of the feathered serpent god. More serpents appear at the top of the building as sculpted columns. At the spring and fall equinoxes, the afternoon light strikes the trapezoidal structure so that the shadow of the snake-god appears to undulate down the side of the pyramid to bless the fertile earth. Thousands of people travel to the site each year to see this phenomenon.

At the base of the temple on the north side, an interior staircase leads to two marvelous statues deep within: a stone jaguar, and the intermediate god Chacmool. As usual, Chacmool is in a reclining position, with a flat spot on the belly for receiving sacrifices. On the **❷ Anexo del Templo de los Jaguares** (Annex to the Temple of the Jaguars), just west of El Castillo, bas-relief carvings represent more important deities. On the bottom of the columns is the rain god Tlaloc. It's no surprise that his tears represent rain—but why is the Toltec god Tlaloc honored here, instead of the Maya rain god, Chaac?

That's one of many questions that archaeologists and epigraphers have been trying to answer, ever since John Lloyd Stephens and Frederick Catherwood, the first English-speaking explorers to discover the site, first hacked their way through the surrounding forest in 1840. Scholars once thought that the symbols of foreign gods and differing architectural styles at Chichén Itzá proved it was conquered by the Toltecs of central Mexico. (As well as representations of Tlaloc, the site also has a tzompantli—a stone platform decorated with row upon row of sculpted human skulls, which is a distinctively Toltec-style structure.) Most experts now agree, however, that Chichén Itzá was only influenced—not conquered—by Toltec trading partners from the north.

The flat part of a reclining Chacmool statue is where sacrificial offerings were laid.

It's believed that Mayan ball players had to pass some sort of ball through high stone loops.

Games may have ended with beheadings.

Just west of the Anexo del Templo de los Jaguares is another puzzle: the auditory marvel of Chichén Itzá's main ball court. At 490 feet, this **❸ Juego de Pelota** is the largest in Mesoamerica. Yet if you stand at one end of the playing field and whisper something to a friend at the other end, incredibly, you will be heard. The game played on this ball court was apparently something like soccer (no hands were used), but it likely had some sort of ritualistic significance. Carvings on the low walls surrounding the field show a decapitation, blood spurting from the victim's neck to fertilize the earth. Whether this is a historical depiction (perhaps the losers or winners of the game were sacrificed?) or a symbolic scene, we can only guess.

On the other side of El Castillo, just before a small temple dedicated to the planet Venus, a ruined sacbé, or white road leads to the **❹ Cenote Sagrado** (Holy Well, or Sinkhole), which was also probably used for ritualistic purposes. Jacques Cousteau and his companions recovered about 80 skeletons from this deep, straight-sided, subsurface pond, as well as thousands of pieces of jewelry and figures of jade, obsidian, wood, bone, and turquoise. In direct alignment with this cloudy green cenote, on the other side of El Castillo, the **❺ Xtaloc sinkhole** was kept pristine, undoubtedly for bathing and drinking. Adjacent to this water source is a steam

TIPS

To get more in-depth information about the ruins, hire a multilingual guide at the ticket booth. Guides charge about $35 for a group of up to 7 people. Tours generally last about two hours. ➤ $9.80 ⊙ Ruins daily 8–5.

TO
MÉRIDA

If you stand at one end of the juego de pelota and whisper something to a friend at the opposite end, incredibly, you will be heard.

Juego de Pelota 3

Anexo del Templo 2
de los Jaguares

Parking

Tourist
Module

Templo del
Osario
6

0   1/8 mi
0   1/8 km

The spiral staircased El Caracol was used as an astronomical observatory.

Casa Roja 7   8
Casa del
Venado

Structures at the Grupo de las Monjas have some of the site's most exquisite carvings and masks.

El Caracol 9

Templo de los
Panales 13
Cuadrados

Akab
Dzib 1

Anexo de las Monjas 11   10
Grupo de
las Monjas

4 Cenote Sagrado

↑ ✈ Airport

The Tzompantli is where the bodies of sacrificial victims were displayed.

Tzompantli

Plataforma de Venus

Plataforma de Jaguares y Aguilas

Main Plaza

1 El Castillo

Templo de los Guerreros

16

Juego de Pelota

The roof once covering the Plaza de Mil Columnas disintegrated long ago.

Plaza de Mil Columnas

15

Juego de Pelota

Juego de Pelota

14

El Mercado

Temazcal

5 Xtaloc Sinkhole

Cenote Xtaloc

THE CULT OF KUKULCÁN

Although the Maya worshipped many of their own gods, Kukulcán was a deity introduced to them by the Toltecs—who referred to him as Quetzacóatl, or the plumed serpent. The pyramid of El Castillo, along with many other structures at Chichén Itzá, was built in honor of Kukulcán.

↓ TO OLD CHICHÉN ITZÁ

bath, its interior lined with benches along the wall like those you'd see in any steam room today. Outside, a tiny pool was used for cooling down during the ritual.

The older Mayan structures at Chichén Itzá are south and west of Cenote Xtaloc. Archaeologists have been restoring several buildings in this area, including the ❻ **Templo del Osario** (Ossuary Temple), which, as its name implies, concealed several tombs with skeletons and offerings. Behind the smaller ❼ **Casa Roja** (Red House) and ❽ **Casa del Venado** (House of the Deer) are the site's oldest structures, including ❾ **El Caracol** (The Snail), one of the few round buildings built by the Maya, with a spiral staircase within. Clearly built as a celestial observatory, it has eight tiny windows precisely aligned with the points of the compass rose. Scholars now know that Maya priests studied the planets and the stars; in fact, they were able to accurately predict the orbits of Venus and the moon, and the appearance of comets and eclipses. To modern astronomers, this is nothing short of amazing.

The Maya of Chichén Itzá were not just scholars, however. They were skilled artisans and architects as well. South of El Caracol, the ❿ **Grupo de las Monjas** (The Nunnery complex) has some of the site's most exquisite façades. A combination of Puuc and Chenes styles dominates here, with playful latticework, masks, and gargoyle-like serpents. On the east side of the ⓫ **Anexo de las Monjas** (Nunnery Annex), the Chenes facade celebrates the rain god Chaac. In typical style, the doorway represents an entrance into the underworld; figures of Chaac decorate the ornate façade above.

South of the Nunnery Complex is an area where field archaeologists are still excavating (fewer than a quarter of the structures at Chichén Itzá have been fully restored). If you have more than a superficial interest in the site—and can convince the authorities ahead of time of your importance, or at least your interest in archaeology—you can explore this area, which is generally not open to the public. Otherwise, head back toward El Castillo past the ruins of a housing compound called ⓬ **Akab Dzib**

The doorway of the Anexo de las Monjas represents an entrance to the underworld.

The Templo de los Guerreros shows the influence of Toltec architecture.

and the ⓭ **Templo de los Panales Cuadrados** (Temple of the Square Panels). The latter of these buildings shows more evidence of Toltec influence: instead of weight-bearing Mayan arches—or "false arches"—that traditionally supported stone roofs, this structure has stone columns but no roof. This means that the building was once roofed, Toltec-style, with perishable materials (most likely palm thatch or wood) that have long since disintegrated.

Beyond El Caracol, Casa Roja, and El Osario, the right-hand path follows an ancient sacbé, now collapsed. A mud-and-straw hut, which the Maya called a na, has been reproduced here to show the simple implements used before and after the Spanish conquest. On one side of the room are a typical pre-Hispanic table, seat, fire pit, and reed baskets; on the other, the Christian cross and colonial-style table of the post-conquest Maya.

Behind the tiny oval house, several unexcavated mounds still guard their secrets. The path meanders through a small grove of oak and slender bean

trees to the building known today as ⓮ **El Mercado.** This market was likely one end of a huge outdoor market whose counterpart structure, on the other side of the grove, is the ⓯ **Plaza de Mil Columnas** (Plaza of the Thousand Columns). In typical Toltec-Maya style, the roof once covering the parallel rows of round stone columns in this long arcade has disappeared, giving the place a strangely Greek—and distinctly non-Maya—look. But the curvy-nosed Chaacs on the corners of the adjacent ⓰ **Templo de los Guerreros** are pure Maya. Why their noses are pointing down, like an upside-down "U," instead of up, as usual, is just another mystery to be solved.

Columns at Templo de los Guerreros.

Sacred Cenotes

To the ancient (and tradition-bound modern) Maya, holes in the ground—be they sinkholes, cenotes, or caves—are considered conduits to the world of the spirits. As sources of water in a land of no surface rivers, sinkholes are of special importance. Cenotes like Balancanchén, near Chichén Itzá, were used as prayer sites and shrines. Sacred objects and sacrificial victims were thrown in the sacred cenote at Chichén Itzá, and in others near large ceremonial centers in ancient times.

There are at least 2,800 known cenotes in the Yucatán. Rainwater sinks through the peninsula's thin soil and porous limestone to create underground rivers, while leaving the dry surface river-free.

Some pondlike sinkholes are found near ground level, most require a bit more effort to access, however. Near downtown Valladolid, Cenote Zací is

named for the Mayan town conquered by the Spanish. It's a relatively simple saunter down a series of cement steps to reach the cool green water.

Lesser-known sinkholes are yours to discover, especially in the area labeled "zona de cenotes." To explore this area southeast of Mérida, you can hire a guide through the tourism office. Another option is to head directly for the ex-hacienda of Chunkanan, outside the village of the same name, about 30 minutes southeast of Mérida. Here former henequen workers will hitch their horses to tiny open railway carts to take you along the unused train tracks. The reward for this bumpy, sometimes dusty ride is a swim in several incredible cenotes.

Almost every local has a "secret" cenote; ask around, and perhaps you'll find a favorite of your own.

16th-century frescoes, protected behind curtains near the altarpiece. The lack of proportion in the human figures shows the initial clumsiness of indigenous artisans in reproducing the Christian saints.

On the west side of the city's main plaza is the large **Iglesia de San Servacio,** which was pillaged during the War of the Castes.

WHERE TO STAY

For expanded hotel reviews, visit Fodors.com.

$$ **Ecotel Quinta Regia.** This salmon-color hotel is a mix of colonial and modern Mexico. **Pros:** short (15-minute) walk to central plaza; Wi-Fi. **Cons:** not as central as some hotels; unexciting restaurant. **TripAdvisor:** "secure and nicely located," "very family friendly hotel," "far from town center." ⊠ *Calle 40 No. 160A, at Calle 27* ☎ *985/856–3476* ⊕ *www.ecotelquintaregia.com.mx* ⟿ *106 rooms, 8 suites* ⚸ *In-room: a/c, Wi-Fi. In-hotel: restaurant, bar, pool, tennis court, parking.*

¢   **María de la Luz.** A worn but still nice budget hotel, Mary of the Light is on the main plaza. **Pros:** the price; on the zócalo; big pool; tasty restaurant food. **Cons:** sparse rooms; air-conditioning units can be noisy. **TripAdvisor:** "Wi-Fi works great in the room," "food was tasty and included both Mexican and western fare," "location cannot be beat." ⊠ *Calle 42 No. 193C* ☎ *985/856–2071 or 985/856–1181*

Swimming in Cenote X-Keken.

⊕ *www.mariadelaluzhotel.com* 🔁 *67 rooms, 2 suites* ⌂ *In-room: a/c, Wi-Fi. In-hotel: restaurant, bar, pool, parking.*

$$ 🏨 **El Mesón del Marqués.** On the north side of the main square, this well-preserved, old hacienda house was built around a lovely, colonnaded, open patio. **Pros:** great downtown location (just north of the main plaza); nice outdoor areas. **Cons:** food could be better. **TripAdvisor:** "great location and a beautiful building," "nice, clean safe place," "rooms have loads of character." ⊠ *Calle 39 No. 203, between Calles 40 and 42* ☎ *985/856–2073 or 985/856–3042* ⊕ *www.mesondelmarques. com* 🔁 *87 rooms, 3 suites* ⌂ *In-room: a/c, Wi-Fi. In-hotel: restaurant, bar, pool, parking* 🍴| *No meals.*

VILLAGES AROUND CHICHÉN ITZÁ

EK BALAM
30 km (18 mi) north of Valladolid, off Carretera 295.

🔺 **Ek Balam.** What's most stunning about the large Ek Balam ("black
★ jaguar") site are the elaborately carved and amazingly well-preserved stucco panels of one of the temples, the **Templo de los Frisos.** A giant mask crowns its summit, and its friezes contain wonderful carvings of figures often referred to as "angels" (because they have wings)—but which more likely represented nobles in ceremonial dress.

As is common with ancient Mayan structures, this temple, styled like those in the region of Chenes in the northwest, is superimposed upon earlier ones. The temple was a mausoleum for ruler Ukit Kan Lek Tok, who was buried with priceless funerary objects, including pearls, perforated seashells, jade, mother-of-pearl pendants, and small bone masks with movable jaws. At the bases at either end of the temple, the name of the leader is inscribed on the forked tongue of a carved serpent, which obviously didn't have the negative biblical connotation ascribed to the snake in Western culture today. A contemporary of Uxmal and Cobá, the city may have been a satellite city to Chichén Itzá, which rose to power as Ek Balam waned.

Another unusual feature of Ek Balam are the two concentric walls—a rare configuration in Mayan sites—that surround the 45 structures in the main part of the site. They may have provided defense, or perhaps they symbolized (more than provided safety for) the ruling elite that lived within.

Ek Balam also has a ball court and quite a few frewestanding stelae (stone pillars carved with glyphs or images for commemorative purposes). New Age groups sometimes converge on the site for prayers and seminars, but it's usually quite sparsely visited, which adds to the mystery and allure. ⌦ $5 ☉ Daily 8–4:30.

WHERE TO STAY

For expanded hotel reviews, visit Fodors.com.

¢ ⌂ **Genesis Retreat.** Close to the Ek Balam site, this simple retreat is modeled on the local dwellings of the region. **Pros:** well kept; intimate atmosphere; cultural programs; close to the Ek Balam ruins. **Cons:** most cabins have shared bathrooms; sometimes difficult to make reservations by phone, but Internet responses are always prompt. **TripAdvisor:** "outdoor showers were blessedly hot, draped by bougainvillea," "great location for visiting the central Yucatan sites," "ecologically-minded, low-impact tourism." ✉ *Domicilio Conocido* ☎ *985/100–4805 or 985/101–0277* ⊕ *www.genesisretreat.com* ⟿ *7 cabins* ⚬ *In-room: no a/c, no TV. In-hotel: restaurant* ▭ *No credit cards* ⦷ *No meals.*

¢ ⌂ **U-Najil Ek Balam.** Wooden, thatch-roof guesthouses at this eco-hotel look like the traditional homes in the area (although, with private bathrooms, they're a step above the average rural house). **Pros:** clean and comfortable cabins; very close to the ruins. **Cons:** basic rooms; uncomfortable beds; two cabins not equipped with private bathrooms. ✉ *U-Najil, Hacienda Ek Balam* ☎ *999/994–7488* ⟿ *12 cabins, 10 with bath* ⚬ *In-room: no a/c, no TV. In-hotel: restaurant, pool* ▭ *No credit cards* ⦷ *Multiple meal plans.*

PISTÉ

46 km (29 mi) west of Valladolid, 116 km (72 mi) east of Mérida, 2 km (1½ mi) west of Chichén Itzá.

The town of Pisté serves primarily as a base camp for travelers to Chichén Itzá. Hotels, campgrounds, restaurants, and handicrafts shops tend to be less expensive here than those at the ruins.

EXPLORING

Across from the Dolores Alba hotel is the **Parque Ik Kil** *("place of the winds").* A $6 entrance fee is required if you want to swim in the lovely cenote here, open daily between 8 am and 6 pm. If you're going to eat in the adjacent restaurant, or sleep overnight, you don't need to pay the entrance fee. ⊠ *Carretera Mérida–Puerto Juárez, Km 122* ☎ *985/858–1525* ▭ *No credit cards.*

WHERE TO STAY

For expanded hotel reviews, visit Fodors.com.

$ ★ ⬚ **Dolores Alba.** The best low-budget choice near the ruins is this family-run hotel with a small motel feel, a longtime favorite of international travelers. **Pros:** close to ruins; transport to ruins (though not back from them) is included. **Cons:** restaurant leaves much to be desired; small rooms; furniture and linens look a little past their prime. **TripAdvisor:** "little way out of town, but worth it," "food was pretty darn good," "the kids loved [the swimming pool]." ⊠ *Carretera 180, Km 122, 3 km (2 mi) east of Chichén Itzá* ☎ *985/858–1555* ⊕ *www.doloresalba. com* ↪ *40 rooms* ◔ *In-room: a/c. In-hotel: restaurant, pools, parking* ⍾⊙⍾ *Multiple meal plans.*

$$ ★ ⬚ **Hacienda Chichén Resort.** This refurbished hacienda with a butter-yellow exterior, has beautiful gardens, simple, but spacious rooms, and an inviting pool surrounded by palm trees. **Pros:** short walk from ruins; beautiful gardens. **Cons:** pricier than other area hotels; restaurant food just OK. **TripAdvisor:** "good location for the archeological site," "private chalets set in a semi-jungle," "felt a bit sanitized." ⊠ *Carretera Mérida–Puerto Júarez, Km 120, Zona Hotelera de Chichén Itzá cerca del Pueblo Pisté* ☎ *999/920–8407, 877/631–4005 in U.S.* ⊕ *www.haciendachichen.com* ↪ *29 rooms* ◔ *In-room: a/c, no TV. In-hotel: restaurant, pool, spa, parking.*

$$ ⬚ **Hotel Chichén Itzá.** Just over 1½ km (1 mi) from the ruins in the town of Pisté, this two-story hotel surrounding a pool feels like a motel in a very unlikely setting: a large grassy area edged with banana and other tropical trees and flowers. **Pros:** minutes from ruins; big pool. **Cons:** mediocre food; rooms' amenities vary (check out a few if possible). ⊠ *Calle 15 No. 45* ☎ *985/851–0022 or 800/235–4079* ⊕ *www.mayaland.com* ↪ *44 rooms* ◔ *In room: a/c. In-hotel: restaurant, bar, pool, parking.*

GRUTAS DE BALANCANCHÉN

38 km (24 mi) west of Valladolid, 6 km (4 mi) east of Chichén Itzá, 117 km (72 mi) east of Mérida.

☾ ⚠ **Grutas de Balancanchén.** How often do you get the chance to wander below the earth? The caves, translated as both "throne of the jaguar caves" and "caves of the hidden throne," are dank and sometimes slippery slopes to an amazing rocky underworld. The caverns are lighted to best show off their lumpy limestone stalactites and niche-like side caves. It's a privilege also to view in situ vases, jars, and incense burners once used in sacred rituals. These were discovered in the 1950s, and left right as they were. An arrangement of tiny *metates* (stone mortars for grinding corn) is particularly moving. At the end of the line is the underground cenote where Maya priests worshipped Chaac, the god of rain and water. Wear comfortable, nonslip walking shoes. The site has a sound-and-light show that recounts Mayan history. The caves are 6 km (4 mi) from Chichén Itzá, and you can catch a bus or taxi or arrange a tour at the Mayaland hotel. Although there's a six-person

6

minimum, the ticket vendor will often allow even a pair of visitors to tour. ⊠ *$8.50, including tour and sound-and-light show* ⊙ *Daily 9–5, tours leave daily at 9:30, 11, 12:30, 2, 3, and 4 (English); 9, noon, 2, and 4 (Spanish); and 10 (French).*

PROGRESO AND THE NORTH COAST

Various routes lead from Mérida to towns along the coast, which are spread across a distance of 380 km (236 mi). Separate roads connect Mérida with the laid-back fishing village of Celestún, the gateway to an ecological marine reserve that extends south to just beyond the Campeche border. Carretera 261 leads due north from Mérida to the relatively modern but humble shipping port of Progreso, where Méridians spend hot summer days and holiday weekends. To get to some of the small beach towns east of Progreso, head east on Carretera 176 out of Mérida and then cut north on one of the many access roads. Wide, white, and generally shadeless beaches here are peppered with bathers from Mérida during Holy Week and in summer—but are nearly vacant the rest of the year.

The terrain in this part of the peninsula is absolutely flat. Tall trees are scarce, because the region was almost entirely cleared for coconut palms in the early 19th century and again for henequen in the early 20th century. Local people still tend some of the old fields of henequen, even though there's little profit to be made from the rope fiber it produces. Other former plantation fields are wildly overgrown with scrub, and are only identifiable by the low, white stone walls that used to mark their boundaries. Many bird species make their home in this area, and butterflies swarm in profusion throughout the dry season.

CELESTÚN

90 km (56 mi) west of Mérida.

This tranquil and humble fishing village sits at the end of a spit of land separating the Celestún estuary from the Gulf of Mexico.

GETTING HERE AND AROUND

Celestún is easily accessible by car, tour group, or bus. To go by bus, take one of the hourly second-class buses that depart from the Noroeste Terminal in Mérida (Calle 67 at Calle 50). The first bus departs at 6:15 am, and the last returning bus leaves Celestún at 8 pm. The fare costs about $6.50 round-trip. In the town of Celestún, your best bet is moto-taxi. These charge about 80¢ around town, and $1.20 to go out to the boats from the central plaza. Make sure you establish what the fare is before you get on, as sometimes drivers will try to charge foreign tourists significantly higher rates.

Celestún is the point of entry to the **Reserva de la Biósfera Ría Celestún**, a 200,000-acre wildlife reserve with extensive mangrove forests and one of the largest colonies of flamingos in North America. Clouds of the pink birds soar above the estuary all year, but the best months for seeing them in abundance are April through July. This is also the fourth-largest

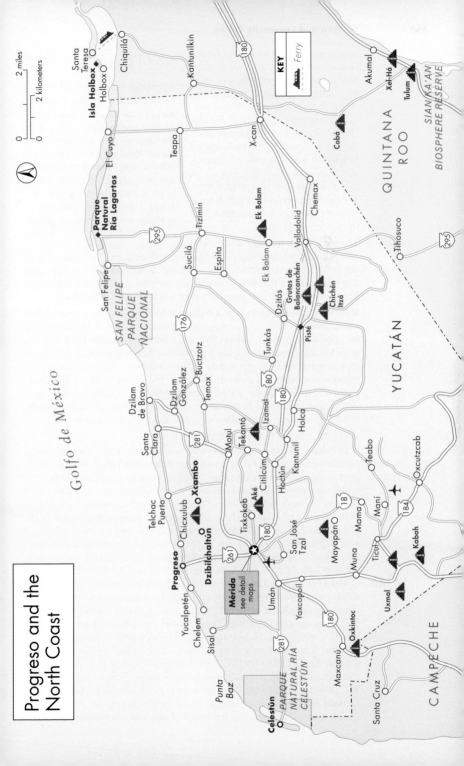

Progreso and the North Coast

KEY
--- Ferry

Golfo de México

SAN FELIPE PARQUE NACIONAL

PARQUE NATURAL RÍA CELESTÚN

QUINTANA ROO

SIAN KA'AN BIOSPHERE RESERVE

YUCATÁN

CAMPECHE

Parque Natural Ría Lagartos

2 miles
2 kilometers

Santa Teresa
Chiquilá
Santa Teresa
Isla Holbox
Holbox
El Cuyo
Kantunilkin
Teapa
X-can
Akumal
Xel-Há
Tulum
Cobá
Chemax
Ek Balam
Ek Balam
Valladolid
Tihosuco
Tizimín
San Felipe
Sucilá
Espita
Dzitás
Grutas de Balancanchén
Chichén Itzá
Pisté
Tunkás
Buctzotz
Temax
Izamal
Holca
Dzilam González
Dzilam de Bravo
Santa Clara
Motul
Tekantó
Kantunil
Teabo
Oxcutzcab
Telchac Puerto
Chicxulub
Xcambo
Aké
Citilcúm
Hoctún
Maní
Mama
Dzibilchaltún
Tixkokob
San José Tzal
Mayapán
Muna
Ticul
Kabah
Progreso
Mérida
see detail maps
Umán
Yaxcopoil
Uxmal
Yucalpetén
Chelem
Sisal
Oxkintoc
Punta Baz
Maxcanú
Celestún
Santa Cruz

wintering ground for ducks of the Gulf-coast region, and more than 300 other species of birds, as well as a large sea-turtle population, make their home here. Conservation programs sponsored by the United States and Mexico protect the birds, as well as the endangered hawksbill and loggerhead marine tortoises, and other species such as the blue crab and crocodile. Other endangered species that inhabit the area are the ocelot, the jaguar, and the spider monkey.

The park is set among rocks, islets, and white-sand beaches. There's good fishing here, too, and several cenotes that are wonderful for swimming. Most Mérida travel agencies run boat tours of the *ría* (estuary) in the early morning or late afternoon, but it's not usually necessary to make a reservation in advance.

WORD OF MOUTH

"We rented a car and drove to Celestún, just for the day. It was easy to hook up with a boat/driver in town and zip out to see the flamingos (this was early March). There were lots of other birds as well. We went to Uxmal and really enjoyed it too. We had lunch at a lovely hacienda and toured it. The weekend festivities in Mérida are fun to see." — glover

■TIP→ To see the birds, hire a fishing boat at the entrance to town (the boats hang out under the bridge leading into Celestún). A 75-minute tour for up to six people costs about $50; a two-hour tour, around $100. Popular with Mexican vacationers, the park's sandy beach is pleasant during the morning but tends to get windy in the afternoon. And, unfortunately, mosquitoes gather in great numbers on the beach at dawn and dusk, particularly during the winter months, making a walk on the beach uncomfortable. Most hotels offer mosquito netting around the beds, but bring along a good cream or spray to keep the bugs away.

WHERE TO EAT AND STAY

$$ SEAFOOD **La Palapa.** Celestún's most popular seafood place under an enormous palapa roof is known for its *camarones a la palapa* (fried shrimp smothered in a garlic-and-cream sauce) and fresh seafood cocktails. Unless it's windy or rainy, most guests dine on the beachfront terrace. The menu has lots of fresh fish (including sea bass and red snapper), as well as crab, squid, and lobster. There are a few beef plates if you're not in the mood for seafood. There are showers and dressing rooms available, if you're tempted to take a dip in the ocean. Although the restaurant's hours are 11 am to 6 pm, it sometimes closes early during the low season. ✉ *Calle 12 No. 105, between Calles 11 and 13* ☎ *988/916–2163.*

$$$$ **Hotel Eco Paraíso Xixim.** On an old coconut plantation outside town, this hotel offers classy comfort in thatch-roof bungalows along a shell-strewn beach. **Pros:** on beach; good service. **Cons:** a drive from main plaza; no air-conditioning. **TripAdvisor:** "excellent blend of nature, beach, ecology, sea, fitness and spa," "hidden gem in paradise," "traditional Yucatan meals were delicious and fresh." ✉ *Camino Viejo a Sisal, Km 10* ☎ *988/916–2100, 800/400–3333 in U.S. and Canada* 🌐 *www.ecoparaiso.com* *24 cabanas 8 suites* *In-room: no a/c, no TV. In-hotel: restaurant, bars, gym, spa, pools, beach* *Some meals.*

$$ **Hotel Manglares.** Every single room at this hotel, the most luxurious in town, has a view of the beach. **Pros:** spacious rooms; powerful

air-conditioning; on beach. **Cons:** lobby is still in planning stages; mediocre food. **TripAdvisor:** "lacks charm," "lovely setting, lovely hotel rooms," "only affordable hotel in Celestun." ⊠ *Calle 12 No. 63* ☎ *988/916–2561* ⊕ *www.hotelmanglares.com.mx* ⇌ *20 rooms, 3 cabanas* ⚿ *In-room: a/c, Wi-Fi. In-hotel: pool, bar, restaurant, beach* ▯⦶ *No meals.*

DZIBILCHALTÚN

16 km (10 mi) north of Mérida.

EXPLORING

Dzibilchaltún. Dzibilchaltún (dzi-bil-chal-*tun*), which means "the place with writing on flat stones," is not a place you'd travel miles out of your way to see. But since it's not far off the road, about halfway between Progreso and Mérida, it's convenient and, in its own small way, interesting. Although more than 16 square km (6 square mi) of land here is cluttered with mounds, platforms, piles of rubble, plazas, and stelae, only a few buildings have been excavated. According to archaeologists, the area may have been settled as early as 500 BC, and was inhabited until the time of the conquest. At its height, there were around 40,000 people living at the site.

Scientists find Dzibilchaltún fascinating because of the sculpture and ceramics from all periods of Mayan civilization that have been unearthed. Save what's in the museum, though (which at the time of this writing was closed for renovations), all you'll see is the tiny **Templo de las Siete Muñecas** ("temple of the seven dolls," circa AD 500), one of a half dozen structures excavated to date. It's a long stroll down a flat dirt track lined with flowering bushes and trees to get to the low, trapezoidal temple exemplifying the late pre-classic style. During the spring and fall equinoxes, sunbeams fall at the exact center of two windows opposite each other inside one of the temple rooms, which is an example of the highly precise mathematical calculations for which the Maya are known. Studies have found that a similar phenomenon occurs at the full moon between March 20 and April 20.

Dzibilchaltún's other main attraction is the ruined open chapel built by the Spaniards for the Indians. Actually, to be accurate, the Spanish forced Indian laborers to build it as a place of worship for themselves: a sort of pre-Hispanic "separate but equal" scenario.

One of the best reasons to visit Dzibilchaltún is **Xlacah Cenote**, the site's sinkhole, whose crystalline water is the color of smoked green glass and is ideal for cooling off in after walking around the ruins.

Another reason to visit is the **Museo Pueblo Maya**: small, yet both attractive and impressive. The museum (closed Monday) holds the seven crude dolls that gave the Temple of the Seven Dolls its name, and outside in the garden rest several huge sculptures found on the site. Museo Pueblo Maya also traces the area's Hispanic history, and highlights contemporary crafts from the region.

The easiest way to get to Dzibilchaltún is to get a *colectivo* (taxi-van) from Mérida's **Parque San Juan** (⊠ *Calles 69 and 62, a few blocks south* *of Plaza Principal*). The taxis depart whenever they fill up with passengers. Returns are a bit trickier. If a colectivo doesn't show up, you can take a regular taxi back to Mérida (it will cost you about $12 to $15). You can also ask the taxi driver to drop you at the Mérida–Progreso highway, where you can catch a Mérida-bound bus for less than $4.

🎫 *$7, including museum; parking $1.20* ☉ *Daily 8–5.*

PROGRESO

16 km (10 mi) north of Dzibilchaltún, 32 km (20 mi) north of Mérida.

The waterfront town closest to Mérida, Progreso is not particularly historic. It's also not terribly picturesque; still, it provokes a certain sentimental fondness for those who know it well. On weekdays during most of the year the beaches are deserted, but when school is out (Easter week, July, and August) and on summer weekends it's bustling with families from Mérida, and new businesses are popping up to cater to them. Low prices are luring more retired Canadians, many of whom rent apartments here between December and April. It's also started attracting cruise ships, and twice-weekly arrivals bring tourist traffic to town.

Progreso's charm—or lack thereof—seems to hinge on the weather. When the sun is shining, the water appears a translucent green and feels bathtub-warm, and the fine sand makes for lovely long walks. When the wind blows during one of Yucatán's winter *nortes,* the water churns with whitecaps and looks gray and unappealing, and the sand blows in your face. Whether the weather is good or bad, however, everyone ends up eventually at one of the restaurants lining the main street, Calle 19, across from the oceanfront malecón. These all serve up cold beer, seafood cocktails, and freshly grilled fish. There's also a small downtown area, between Calle 80 and Calle 31, with small restaurants that serve simpler fare (like tortas and tacos), shops, banks, and supermarkets.

Although Progreso is close enough to Mérida to make it an easy day trip, several B&Bs that have cropped up over the past few years make this a pleasant place to stay, and a great base for exploring the untouristy coast. Just west of Progreso, the fishing villages of Chelem and Chuburna are beginning to offer walking, kayaking, and cycling tours ending with a boat trip through the mangroves and a freshly prepared ceviche and beer or soft drink for about $33. This is ecotourism in its infancy, and it's best to set this up ahead of time through the Progreso tourism office. Experienced divers can explore sunken ships at the Alacranes Reef, about 120 km (74 mi) offshore, although infrastructure is limited. Pérez Island, part of the reef, supports a large population of sea turtles and seabirds. Arrangements for the boat trip can be made through individuals at the private marina at neighboring Yucaltepén, which is 6 km (4 mi) from Progreso.

GETTING HERE AND AROUND

Progreso is 32 km (20 mi) north of Mérida via México 261. To drive from Mérida, head north from the Paseo de Montejo and keep going north as you head out of town. It's a straight drive to the beach. Buses for Progreso also leave Mérida from Calle 62 No. 524, between Calles 65 and 67.

Pick up a shark jaw in Progreso.

ESSENTIALS

Visitor and Tour Info Progreso Municipal Tourism Office (✉ *Casa de la Cultura, Calles 80 and 25, Centro* ☎ *969/935–0104* ⊕ *www. ayuntamientodeprogreso.gob.mx*).

WHERE TO EAT AND STAY

$ ✕ **Eladio's.** This bar and restaurant is a new branch of a classic and popu-
MEXICAN lar Mérida joint. Under a tall palapa on the beach you can enjoy the view and the breeze through tall windows facing the water. Live music in the afternoons adds to the partylike atmosphere. Tasty appetizers are free with your drinks, and there are plenty to choose from. This is a good place to try different Yucatecan dishes such as longaniza asada and pollo pibil. Fresh seafood dishes are also on the menu, but these don't come with the drinks. ✉ *Av. Malecón s/n, at Calle 80, Centro* ☎ *969/935–5670* ⊕ *www.eladios.com.mx.*

$–$$ ✕ **Flamingos.** This restaurant facing Progreso's long cement promenade
SEAFOOD is a cut above its neighbors. Service is professional and attentive, and soon after arriving you'll get at least one free appetizer—maybe black beans with corn tortillas, or a plate of shredded shark meat stewed with tomatoes. The creamy cilantro soup is a little too cheesy (literally, not figuratively), but the large fish fillets are perfectly breaded and lightly fried. Breakfast is served after 7 am. There's a full bar, and although there's no air-conditioning, large, glassless windows let in the ocean breeze. ✉ *Calle 19 No. 144-D, at Calle 72* ☎ *969/935–2122.*

$–$$ ✕ **La Lagunita.** A casual family-owned restaurant, La Lagunita is a great
SEAFOOD reason to make a detour to the small fisherman's town of Santa Clara. The great seafood here manages to attract big crowds, seemingly from

out of nowhere. You'll know you've arrived when you see small ponds, which are just out front. Appetizers, such as potato salad and beets, are included with every alcoholic drink you order. The lobster dish *langosta a la mantequilla* has a delicious cheesy and buttery flavor. The fresh local fishes, including merlot, are also exquisitely prepared. Santa Clara is 50 km (31 mi) west of Progreso. ⊠ *Calle 18 No. 78-A, Puerto de Santa Clara* ☎ *991/102–2009* ▭ *No credit cards.*

$–$$
SEAFOOD
✕ **Le Saint Bonnet.** This thatch-roof restaurant and bar on the malecón is *the* place for locals. It gets its name from a French partner who has given all the dishes Gallic monikers. The shrimp St. Bonnet—jumbo shrimp stuffed with cheese, wrapped with bacon, breaded, fried, and served with crab sauce—is a perennial favorite. European and Chilean wines complement the meals, and the caramel crepes or chocolate mousse are perfect for dessert. A live band plays tropical music daily (except Monday) from 2:30 to 6:30 pm. ⊠ *Av. Malecón (Calle 19) 150D, at Calle 28* ☎ *969/935–2299.*

¢
◨ **Casa Isidora.** A couple of Canadian English teachers have restored this grand, 100-year-old house a few blocks from the beach. **Pros:** close to beach; cozy, congenial atmosphere. **Cons:** a bit of a hike from the center of town; no breakfast. ⊠ *Calle 21 No. 116* ☎ *969/935–4595* ⊕ *www.casaisidora.com* ↪ *7 rooms* ⌂ *In-room: a/c. In-hotel: business center, pool* ¶◉¶ *No meals.*

$
◨ **Condhotel Progreso.** The advantage that this small hotel offers is its location, right across from the water and close to all of the restaurants along the malecón. **Pros:** inexpensive rooms; swimming pool. **Cons:** very sparse rooms; no hotel restaurant, just a small breakfast area that offers continental breakfast (for a fee) and snacks later in the day. ⊠ *Calle 21 No.150, between Calles 66 and 68* ☎ *969/935–5079* ⊕ *www.condhotel.com* ↪ *51 rooms* ⌂ *In-room: a/c, kitchen (some). In-hotel: beach* ¶◉¶ *No meals.*

XCAMBO

32 km (20 mi) west of Progreso.

◢◣ **Xcambo.** Surrounded by a plantation where disease-resistant coconut trees are being developed, the Xcambo (*ish*-cam-bo) site is a couple of miles inland following the turnoff for Xtampu. It's also in the hometown of former governor Victor Cervera Pacheco, who, it's rumored, gave priority to its excavation. Salt, a much-sought-after item of trade in the ancient Mayan world, was produced in this area and made it prosperous. Indeed, the bones of 600 former residents discovered in burial plots showed they had been healthier than the average Maya. Two plazas have been restored so far, surrounded by rather plain structures. The tallest temple is the Xcambo, also known as the Pyramid of the Cross. On a clear day you can see the coast, about a mile away, from the summit. Ceramics found at the site indicate that the city traded with other Mayan groups as far afield as Guatemala, Teotihuácan, and Belize. The Catholic church on the site was built by dismantling some of the ancient structures, and until recently locals hauled off the cut stones to build fences and foundations. ⊠ *Turn off Progreso–Dzilam de Bravo Hwy. at Xtampu* 🖃 *Donation* ⊗ *Daily 8–5.*

PARQUE NATURAL RÍA LAGARTOS

115 km (71 mi) north of Valladolid.

🌣 **Parque Natural Ría Lagartos.** This park, which encompasses a long estu-
★ ary, was developed with ecotourism in mind—although most of the alligators for which it and the village were named have long since been hunted into extinction. The real spectacle these days is the birds. More than 350 species nest and feed in the area, including flocks of flamin-gos, snowy and red egrets, white ibis, great white herons, cormorants, pelicans, and peregrine falcons. Fishing is good, too, and the protected hawksbill and green turtles lay their eggs on the beach at night.

You can make the 90-km (56-mi) trip from Valladolid (1½ hours by car or 2 hours by bus) as a day trip (add another hour if you're coming from Mérida, or 3 hours from Cancún). There's a small information center at the entrance to town where Carretera 295 joins the coast road to San Felipe. Unless you're interested exclusively in the birds, it's nice to spend the night in Río Lagartos (the town is called *Río* Lagartos, the park *Ría* Lagartos) or nearby San Felipe. There's little to do except take a walk through town or on the beach, and grab a meal. Buses leave Mérida and Valladolid regularly from the second-class terminals to either Río Lagartos or, 10 km (6 mi) west of the park, San Felipe.

The easiest way to book a trip is through the Isla Contoy restaurant (ask for Ismael Navarro or Gabriel "El Chinomosca" Pacheco), where you can also eat a delicious dinner of fresh seafood. Call ahead to reserve an English- or Italian-speaking guide through their organiza-tion, **Ría Lagartos Expeditions** (☎ 986/862–0000 ⊕ *flyfishingyucatan. com*). This boat trip will take you through the mangrove forests to the flamingo feeding grounds (where, as an added bonus, you can paint your face or body with supposedly therapeutic white clay). A 2½-hour tour, which accommodates five or six people, costs $70. The 3½-hour tour costs $75 (both per boat, not per person). You can take a shorter boat trip for slightly less money, or a 2-hour, guided walking-and-boat tour ($50 for one to six passengers), or a night tour in search of crocs (2½ hours, one to four passengers, $70). You can also hire a boat ($20 for 1 to 10 passengers) to take you to an area beach and pick you up at a designated time.

Be aware that mosquitoes are known to gather at dusk in unpleasantly large groups in May, June, and July. So bringing along some spray to fend them off might be a good idea.

WHERE TO EAT AND STAY

$ ✕ **Isla Contoy Restaurante.** Run by the amicable family that guides lagoon
SEAFOOD tours, this open-sided seafood shanty at the dock serves generous help-
★ ings of fish soup, fried fish fillets, shrimp, squid, and crab. If you come with a group, order the combo for four (it can easily feed six, espe-cially if you order a huge ceviche or other appetizer). The delicious platter comes with four shrimp crepes, fish stuffed with seafood, a

6

CLOSE UP

Bird-Watching in Yucatán

Rise before the sun and head for shallow water to see flamingos engrossed in an intricate mating dance. From late winter into spring, thousands of bright pink, black-tipped flamingos crowd the estuaries of Ría Lagartos, coming from their "summer homes" in nearby Celestún as well as from northern latitudes to mate and raise their chicks. The largest flocks of both flamingos and bird-watching enthusiasts can be found during these months, when thousands of the birds—90% of the entire flamingo population of the western hemisphere—come to Ría Lagartos to nest.

Although the long-legged creatures are the most famous winged beasts found in these two nature reserves, red, white, black, and buttonwood mangrove swamps are home to hundreds of other species. Of Ría Lagartos's estimated 350 different species, one-third are winter-only residents—the avian counterparts of Canadian and northern-U.S. "snowbirds." Twelve of the region's resident species are endemic, found nowhere else on earth. Ría Lagartos Expeditions now leads walks through the low deciduous tropical forest in addition to boat trips through the mangroves.

More than 400 bird species have been sighted in the Yucatán, inland as well as on the coast. Bird-watching expeditions can be organized in Mérida as well as Ría Lagartos and Celestún. November brings hundreds of professional ornithologists and bird-watching aficionados to the Yucatán for a week-long conference and symposium with films, lectures, and field trips.

---

seafood skewer, and one each of grilled, breaded, garlic-chile, and battered fish fillets (usually grouper or sea trout, whatever is freshest). There are also a few regional specialties and red-meat dishes. It's open for breakfast, too, and breakfast is included if you stay in one of their four simple rooms (¢) on the beach. ⊠ *Calle 19 No. 134, at Calle 14* ☎ *986/862–0000.*

$ 🏨 **Hotel San Felipe.** This three-story white hotel in the beach town of San Felipe, 10 km (6 mi) west of Parque Natural Ría Lagartos, is basic, but adequate. **Pros:** there are oceanside rooms; some rooms have a private balcony. **Cons:** a bit of a drive from Río Lagartos; reservations are necessary in high season. ⊠ *Calle 9 No. 13, between Calles 14 and 16, San Felipe* ☎ *986/862–2027* ✉ *sanfelipehotel@hotmail.com* ⤶ *30 rooms* � *In-room: a/c, no TV (some). In-hotel: restaurant, parking* ▭ *No credit cards.*

$ 🏨 **Hotel Tabasco Río.** Located right on the plaza, this is one of the newest hotels in town. **Pros:** new linens; well-appointed rooms. **Cons:** not on water. **TripAdvisor:** "best option in Rio Lagartos," "welcome was friendly, staff great, rooms clean and comfy," "perfect location for nice romantic walks." ⊠ *Calle 12, No 15, Río Lagartos* ☎ *986/862–0508* ⊕ *www.hotelriolagartos.com* ⤶ *19 rooms* � *In-room: a/c, no safe, kitchen (some), Wi-Fi* ❍ *Breakfast.*

¢   🏨 **Punta Ponto Hotel.** The main draw here is the friendly, personal attention the owner's lavish on their guests. **Pros:** waterfront location; friendly staff. **Cons:** spartan accommodations; awkward staircase to rooms. ⊠ *Calle 9 Diagonal #140, Río Lagartos* ☎ *986/862–0509 or 999/945–2114* ↩ *9 rooms, 1 suite* ♿ *In-room: a/c, no phone, Wi-Fi. In-hotel: parking* ⊟ *No credit cards* ⦿ *Breakfast.*

ISLA HOLBOX

141 km (87 mi) northeast of Valladolid.

Tiny Isla Holbox (25 km [16 mi] long) sits at the eastern end of the Ría Lagartos estuary and just across the Quintana Roo state line. A fishing fan's heaven because of the hordes of pampano, bass, barracuda, and sharks just offshore, the island also pleases bird-watchers and seekers of tranquillity. Birds fill the mangrove estuaries on the island's leeward side, whale sharks cruise offshore April through September, and sandy beaches are strewn with seashells. Although the water is often murky— the Gulf of Mexico and the Caribbean come together here—it's shallow and warm, and there are some nice places to swim. Sandy streets lead to simple seafood restaurants where the fish fillets, conch, octopus, and other delicacies are always fresh.

Isla's lucky population numbers some 1,500 souls, and in summer it seems there are that many biting bugs per person. Bring plenty of mosquito repellent. The Internet has arrived, and there's now an ATM on the island, but most—if not all—businesses accept cash only, so visit an ATM to stock up before you get here, just in case.

There are less-expensive lodgings for those who eschew conventional beds in favor of fresh air and a hammock. Since it's a small island, it's easy to check several lodgings and make your choice. Hotel owners can help you set up bird-watching, fishing, and whale shark–viewing expeditions.

GETTING HERE AND AROUND

To get to Isla Holbox from Río Lagartos, take Carretera 176 to Kantunilkin and then head north on the unnumbered road for 44 km (27 mi) to Chiquilá. Continue by ferry to the island. Schedules vary, but there are normally five crossings a day from around 5 am to 6 pm. The fare is $5 and the trip takes about 35 minutes. A car ferry makes the trip at 11 am daily, returning at 5 pm. (You can also pay to leave your car in a lot in Chiquilá, in Quintana Roo.) Golf-cart taxis ply the island for about $15 an hour or you can rent your own for $10 an hour. You may be able to negotiate a better price if you're renting for several hours or traveling in low season.

WHERE TO EAT

$$$ ✕ **Restaurante Casa Lupita**. Formerly known as Cine Lupita, this is one MEXICAN of the more-formal dining options (i.e. the tables are not plastic) on the island, but you'll still feel right at home in jeans. The Spanish owners have decorated the walls with old, and sometimes rare, pictures of Isla Holbox in the 1940s. This is one of the few places in town where you can get Mexican dishes like *quesadillas de huitlacoche* (corn truffle), as well as some Spanish-inspired plates. They also serve one of the most reasonably priced lobsters (around $20) in the area. The owners recently opened a hotel ($) adjacent to the restaurant with clean, colorful rooms.

⊠ Calle Palomino s/n, at the Parque Central ☎ *984/875–2015* 🖃 *No credit cards.*

$ ✕ **Zarabanda Restaurante.** Not far
MEXICAN   from the main square, this unpretentious family-run restaurant is one of the oldest eateries on the island, and it's still considered one of the best places to try island-style food. There are quite a few tasty seafood dishes, including a huge *mariscada* (seafood stew) for two that includes a fish fillet, a whole fish, a lobster, and octopus. The delicious seafood soup includes the freshest seasonal seafood and is an island classic. Meat eaters can indulge in the Plato Mexicano (grilled chicken, pork, and steak dished up with several salsas and tortillas). *⊠ Calle Palomino s/n* ☎ *984/875–2094* 🖃 *No credit cards.*

WHERE TO STAY

For expanded hotel reviews, visit Fodors.com.

$$ 🏨 **Los Mapaches.** A coconut's throw from the beach, this small enclave includes several thatch-roof bungalows and a second-floor, two-bedroom apartment. **Pros:** quick walk to downtown; lovely gardens. **Cons:** fills up quickly, so reservations are often necessary. **TripAdvisor:** "amazing, friendly feel," "great location, great cabana, great beach," "tranquil garden inspires calm and well being." *⊠ Av. Pedro Joaquin Coldwell s/n* ☎ *984/875–2090* ⊕ *www.losmapaches.com* ⤳ *4 bungalows, 2 suites, 1 duplex* ⚏ *In-room: kitchen, no TV. In-hotel: restaurant, beach, some pets allowed.*

$$ 🏨 **Posada Mawimbi.** You won't find a better deal, or a more relaxed stay than at this small hotel made up of bright orange beachside bungalows. **Pros:** inexpensive rooms; beachside location. **Cons:** entryway rooms lack privacy; no room phones; no televisions. **TripAdvisor:** "beach here is the cleanest and nicest," "lovely room, beds, view, balcony," "very clean and nicely decorated." *⊠ Calle Igualdad s/n* ☎ *984/875–2003* ⊕ *www.mawimbi.net* ⤳ *11 rooms* ⚏ *In-room: a/c, kitchen (some), no TV, Wi-Fi (some). In-hotel: restaurant, beach* ❧*Breakfast.*

$$–$$$ 🏨 **Villas Delfines.** This fishermen's lodge consists of pleasant cabins on the beach. **Pros:** spacious rooms; beautiful beach setting; nice Saturday grill. **Cons:** long walk into town (you may need transport). **TripAdvisor:** "food at the restaurant absolutely great," "come armed with bug spray," "a lovely and relaxing environment." *⊠ Domicilio Conocido* ☎ *984/875–2196* ⊕ *www.villasdelfines.com* ⤳ *20 cabins* ⚏ *In-room: a/c (some), no TV. In-hotel: restaurant, bar, beach, Wi-Fi* ❧*Multiple meal plans.*

$$ 🏨 **Villas HM Paraíso del Mar.** This is one of the largest hotels on the island, with a comfortable marble-floor lobby with cushy seating There are well-tended gardens and sand pathways between the independently standing bungalow style rooms, as well as a large pool and a buffet-style restaurant—all right on the beach. **Pros:** computers for guests to use;

Isla Holbox.

nice breakfast buffet. **Cons:** some rooms lack ocean views. **TripAdvisor:** "room was large and pleasantly furnished," "great for relaxation and rest," "breakfasts were great in a beautiful dining room." ✉ *Av. Plutarco Elias s/n* ☎ *984/875–2062 or 984/875–2077* ⊕ *www.holbox-island.com* ⇦ *52 rooms, 6 suites* ⚒ *In-room: a/c. In-hotel: restaurant, bars, pool, beach, water sports* ❚❍❚ *All-inclusive.*

$$–$$$ ⌂ **Xaloc.** Each of these rustic (but comfortable) bungalows has a tall, pointy thatch roof, cool ceramic-tile floors, and shuttered windows. **Pros:** right on beach; comfortable palapa-covered rooms; lovely pools. **Cons:** relatively high prices; some rooms are for adults only, so families with children must book well in advance. **TripAdvisor:** "extremely clean, with a touch of natural materials," "terrific value for money," "hotel architecture is nice." ✉ *Calle Chacchi s/n, at Calle Playa Norte* ☎ *984/875–2160, 800/728–9098 in U.S. and Canada* ⊕ *www.holbox-xalocresort.com* ⇦ *18 bungalows, 11 suites* ⚒ *In-room: a/c, no TV. In-hotel: restaurant, pools, spa, beach, water sports* ❚❍❚ *Multiple meal plans.*

SHOPPING

Sandra Thomson, a New York native who has lived on the island for years, runs **Artesanías Las Chicas** (✉ *Domicilio conocido* ☎ *984/807–9406 or 998/875–2430*), a small shop with a delightful collection of art crafts. She carries everything from rings and mirrors to sophisticated hammocks and purses from all over Mexico.

CAMPECHE

Campeche City has to be one of the best kept secrets in the Yucatán. Its beautifully preserved colonial district is brimming with historic sites, museums, cafés, and restaurants—all within easy walking distance of each other. Yet the city is far smaller and more easygoing than its Yucatecan cousin, Mérida. Its unique history—it was once a favorite target of seafaring pirates—has left its mark. Many of the protective walls that were built to safeguard the city's inhabitants are still standing, and the colorful colonial buildings were constructed with safety in mind; they're markedly less ornate than their counterparts elsewhere on the peninsula, with well barred windows and impressively heavy-looking doors. The 18th century fort at the south of town lets you reimagine Campeche's dangerous past, and is home to a fascinating collection of Mayan artifacts taken from many archaeological sites, the highlights being the relics of the ancient Maya ruler Gran Garra de Jaguar (Great Jaguar Claw), who presided over the city of Calakmul's rise and decline.

The city is the state's most accessible spot, and makes a good hub for exploring other areas, many of which have only basic restaurants and primitive lodgings. The Edzná archaeological site is a short detour south of Carreteras 180 and 188.

■TIP➔ You'll need at least rudimentary Spanish—few people outside the capital speak English. If you plan to venture off the beaten path, pack a Spanish-English dictionary.

CAMPECHE CITY

174 km (108 mi) southeast of Mérida via Mexico 180.

Campeche is a tranquil, picturesque town, where block upon block of buildings with lovely facades, all painted in bright colors that appear to have come from the mind of an artist, meet the sea. Tiny balconies overlook clean, geometrically paved streets, and charming old street lamps illuminate the scene at night.

In colonial days the city center was completely enclosed within a 10-foot-thick wall. Two stone archways (originally there were four)—one facing the sea, the other the land—provided the only access. The defensive walls also served as a de facto class demarcation. Within them lived the ruling elite. Outside were the barrios, with blacks and mulattoes brought as slaves from Cuba, and everyone else.

On strategic corners, seven *baluartes,* or bastions, gave militiamen a platform from which to fight off pirates and the other ruffians that continually plagued this beautiful city on the bay. But it wasn't until 1771, when the Fuerte de San Miguel was built on a hilltop outside town, that pirates finally stopped attacking the city.

■TIP➔ Campeche's historic center is easily navigable—in fact, it's a walker's paradise. Narrow roads and lack of parking spaces can make driving a bit frustrating, although drivers here are polite and mellow. Streets running roughly north–south are even-numbered, and those running east–west are odd-numbered.

GETTING HERE AND AROUND

Aeroméxico flies several times daily from Mexico City to Campeche City. Campeche's Aeropuerto Internacional Alberto Acuña Ongay is 16 km (10 mi) north of downtown. Taxis are the only means of transportation to and from the airport. The fare to downtown Campeche is about $7.

Within Campeche City, the route of interest to most visitors is along Avenida Ruíz Cortínez. The ride on a bus costs the equivalent of about 30¢. There are also fairly frequent buses to points all over the Yucatán Peninsula.

■ TIP→ For trips between major destinations within the Yucatán Peninsula, purchase tickets with a credit card by phone through Ticketbus. Make sure to ask from which station the bus departs.

Campeche City is about 2 to 2½ hours from Mérida along the 180-km (99-mi) *via corta* (short way) on Carretera 180. The alternative route, the 250-km (155-mi) *via ruinas* (ruins route), on Carretera 261, takes three to four hours, but passes some major Mayan ruins.

You can hail taxis on the street in Campeche City, and there are also stands by the bus stations, the main plaza, and the municipal market. The minimum fare is $2; it's $2.50 from the center to the bus station and $4 to the airport (it's cheaper to go to the airport than from it). After 11 pm, prices may be slightly higher. There's a small fee, less than 50¢, to call for a cab through Radio Taxis, and you can also call Taxis Plus any time, day or night.

ESSENTIALS

Bus Contacts ADO (✉ Av. Patricio Trueba at Casa de Justicia 237 ☎ 981/811–9910 Ext. 2402 ⊕ www.ado.com.mx). **Ticketbus** (☎ 01800/702–8000 toll-free in Mexico ⊕ www.ticketbus.com.mx).

Currency Exchange Bancomer (✉ Av. 16 de Septiembre 120 ☎ 981/816–6622 ✉ Calle 8 No. 268 ☎ 981/816–1330 ⊕ www.bancomer.com). **Banorte** (✉ Calle 8 No. 237, between Calles 53 and 55 ☎ 981/811–4250 ⊕ www.banorte.com).

Medical Assistance Clínica Campeche (✉ Av. Central No. 65, Col. Santa Ana ☎ 981/816–5612 ⊕ www.clinicacampeche.com). **General emergencies** (☎ 060). **Hospital Manuel Campos** (✉ Av. Boulevard s/n, Centro ☎ 981/811–1709 Ext. 138 for pharmacy, 981/816–0957).

Rental Cars Europcar (✉ Av. López Portillo at Carretera Campeche-Chino, Col. Aeropuerto ☎ 981/823–4083 ⊕ www.europcar.com.mx).

Visitor and Tour Info Municipal Tourist Office (✉ Calle 55 No. 3, between Calles 8 and 10 ☎ 981/811–3989 or 981/811–3990). **State Tourism Office** (✉ Av. Ruíz Cortínez s/n, Plaza Moch Couoh, across from Gobierno, Centro ☎ 981/811–9229 ⊕ www.campeche.travel).

EXPLORING

TOP ATTRACTIONS

Baluarte de San Carlos. Named for Charles II, King of Spain, this bastion, where Calle 8 curves around and becomes Circuito Baluartes, houses the **Museo de la Ciudad.** The free museum contains a small collection of historical artifacts, including several Spanish suits of armor and a

A STREETCAR NAMED EL GUAPO

Guided trolley tours of historic Campeche City leave from Calle 10 on the Plaza Principal on the hour from 9 to noon and 5 to 8. You can buy tickets ahead of time at the adjacent kiosk or once aboard the trolley. Be prepared to wait around, since the buses only take off when a minimum of eight people have bought their tickets. (Trips run less frequently in the off-season, and it's always best to double-check schedules at the kiosk.) The one-hour tour costs $8, and if English speakers request it, guides will do their best to speak the language. For the same price, the green "Guapo" ("handsome") trolley makes unguided trips to Reducto de San José at 9 am and 5 pm (also at 10, 11, and noon during vacation periods such as Christmas and Easter). You'll only have about 10 minutes to admire the view, though.

El Guapo and Super Guapo trams (☎ *No phone*).

beautifully inscribed silver scepter. Captured pirates were once jailed in the stifling basement dungeon. The unshaded rooftop provides an ocean view that's lovely at sunset. ⊠ *Calle 8 between Calles 65 and 63, Circuito Baluartes, Centro* ☎ *No phone* ⊠ *$2.50* ⊙ *Tues.–Fri. 8–8, Sat. 8–2 and 4–8, Sun. 9–1.*

Baluarte de la Soledad. This is the largest of the bastions, originally built to protect the **Puerta de Mar,** a sea gate that was one of four original entrances to the city. Because it uses no supporting walls, it resembles a Roman triumphal arch. It has comparatively complete parapets and embrasures that offer views of the cathedral, municipal buildings, and old houses along Calle 8. Inside is the **Museo de Arqueología Maya,** with artifacts that include a well-preserved sculpture of a man wearing an owl mask, columns from Edzná and Isla de Jaina, and at least a dozen well-proportioned Mayan stelae from ruins throughout Campeche. ⊠ *Calle 8 between Calles 55 and 57, Centro* ☎ *No phone* ⊠ *$3* ⊙ *Tues.–Sun. 8–7:30.*

Calle 59. Some of Campeche's finest homes were built on this city street between Calles 8 and 18. Most were two stories high, the ground floors serving as warehouses and the upper floors as residences. These days, behind the delicate grillwork and lace curtains you can glimpse genteel scenes of Campeche life. The best-preserved houses are those between Calles 14 and 18, and many closer to the sea have been remodeled or destroyed by fire. Campeche's INAH (Instituto Nacional de Antropología e Historia) office, between Calles 16 and 14, is an excellent example of one of Campeche City's fine old homes. Each month INAH displays a different archaeological artifact in its courtyard. Look for the names of the apostles carved into the lintels of houses between Calles 16 and 18.

Casa Seis. One of the first colonial homes in Campeche is now a cultural center. It has been fully restored—rooms are furnished with original antiques and a few reproductions. Original frescoes at the tops of the walls remain, and you can see patches of the painted "wallpaper"

Campeche City

that once covered the walls, serving to simulate European trends in
an environment where wallpaper wouldn't stick due to the humidity.
The Moorish courtyard is occasionally used as a space for exhibits and
lectures. ⊠ *Calle 57 between Calles 10 and 8, Plaza Principal, Centro*
☎ *981/816–1782* ⌷ *$1* ☉ *Daily 9–9.*

Catedral de la Inmaculada Concepción. It took two centuries (from 1650
to 1850) to finish the Cathedral of the Immaculate Conception, and
as a result, it incorporates both neoclassical and Renaissance elements.
On the simple exterior, sculptures of saints in niches are covered in
black netting to discourage pigeons from unintentional desecration. The
church's neoclassical interior is also somewhat plain and sparse. The
high point of its collection, now housed in the side chapel museum, is
a magnificent Holy Sepulchre carved from ebony and decorated with
stamped silver angels, flowers, and decorative curlicues. Each angel
holds a symbol of the Stations of the Cross. ⊠ *Calle 55 between Calles
8 and 10, Plaza Principal, Centro* ☎ *No phone* ☉ *Daily 6 am–9 pm.*

☾ **Fuerte de San Miguel.** Near the city's southwest end, Avenida Ruíz Cor-
★ tínez winds its way to this hilltop fort with its breathtaking view of the
Bay of Campeche. Built between 1779 and 1801 and dedicated to the
archangel Michael, the fort was positioned to blast enemy ships with
its long-range cannons. As soon as it was completed, pirates stopped

CLOSE UP

Campeche's History

Campeche City's gulf location played a pivotal role in its history. Ah-Kim-Pech (Mayan for "lord of the serpent tick," from which the name Campeche is derived) was the capital of an Indian chieftainship here, long before the Spaniards arrived in 1517. In 1540 the conquerors—led by Francisco de Montejo and later by his son—established a real foothold at Campeche (originally called San Francisco de Campeche), using it as a base for the conquest of the peninsula.

At the time, Campeche City was the Gulf's only port and shipyard. So Spanish ships, loaded with cargoes of treasure plundered from Mayan, Aztec, and other indigenous civilizations, dropped anchor here en route from Veracruz to Cuba, New Orleans, and Spain. As news of the riches spread, Campeche's shores were soon overrun with pirates. From the mid-1500s to the early 1700s, such notorious corsairs as Diego the Mulatto, Lorenzillo, Peg Leg, Henry Morgan, and Barbillas swooped in repeatedly from Tris—or Isla de Términos, as Isla del Carmen was then known—pillaging and burning the city and massacring its people.

Finally, after years of appeals to the Spanish crown, Campeche received funds to build a protective wall, with four gates and eight bastions, around the town center. For a while afterward, the city thrived on its exports, especially *palo de tinte*—a valuable

dyewood more precious than gold due to the nascent European textile industry's demand for it—but also hardwoods, chicle, salt, and henequen (sisal hemp). But when the port of Sisal opened on the northern Yucatán coast in 1811, Campeche's monopoly on gulf traffic ended, and its economy quickly declined. During the 19th and 20th centuries, Campeche, like most of the Yucatán Peninsula, had little to do with the rest of Mexico. Left to their own devices, Campechanos lived in relative isolation until the petroleum boom of the 1970s brought businessmen from Mexico City, Europe, and the United States to its provincial doorstep.

Campeche City's history still shapes the community today. Remnants of its gates and bastions split the city into two main districts: the historical center (where relatively few people live) and the newer residential areas. Because the city was long preoccupied with defense, the colonial architecture is less flamboyant here than elsewhere in Mexico. The narrow flagstone streets reflect the confines of the city's walls, and homes here emphasize the practical over the decorative. Still, government decrees, and an on-and-off beautification program, have helped keep the city's colonial structures in good condition despite the damaging effects of humidity and salt air. An air of antiquity remains.

6

attacking the city. In fact, the cannons were fired only once, in 1842, when General Santa Anna used Fuerte de San Miguel to put down a revolt by Yucatecan separatists seeking independence from Mexico. The fort houses the **Museo de la Arquelogía Maya,** whose exhibits include the skeletons of long-ago Maya royals, complete with jewelry and pottery, which are arranged just as they were found in Calakmul tombs. Other archaeological treasures are funeral vessels, masks, many wonderfully expressive figurines and whistles from Isla de Jaina, stelae

Campeche's historic center is easy to explore on foot.

and stucco masks from the Mayan ruins, and an excellent pottery collection. Although it's a shame that most information is in Spanish only, many of the pieces speak for themselves. The gift shop sells replicas of artifacts. ⊠ *Av. Francisco Morazán s/n, west of town center, Cerro de Buenavista* ☎ *No phone* ✉ *$3* ☉ *Tues.–Sun. 8:30–5:30.*

★ **Malecón.** A broad sidewalk, more than 4 km (2½ mi) long, runs the length of Campeche's waterfront boulevard, from northeast of the Debliz hotel to the Justo Sierra Méndez monument at the southwest edge of downtown. With its landscaping, sculptures, rest areas, and fountains lighted up at night in neon colors, the promenade attracts joggers, strollers, and families. (Note the separate paths for walking, jogging, and biking.) On weekend nights, students turn the malecón into a party zone, and families with young children fill the parks on both sides of the promenade after 7 or 8 in the evening, and stay out surprisingly late to enjoy the cool of the evening.

Parque Principal. Also known as the Plaza de la Independencia, this central park is small by Mexican standards, though picturesque. In its center is an old-fashioned kiosk with a pleasing café-bar where you can sit and watch city residents out for an evening stroll and listen to the itinerant musicians that often show up to play traditional ballads in the evenings. ⊠ *Bounded by Calles 10, 8, 55, and 57, Centro.*

☺ **Puerta de Tierra.** The Land Gate, where Old Campeche ends, is the only one of the four city gates with its basic structure intact. The stone arch interrupts a stretch of the partially crenellated wall, 26 feet high and 10 feet thick, that once encircled the city. Walk the wall's full length to the **Baluarte San Juan** for excellent views of both the old and new cities. The staircase leads down to an old well, underground storage area, and dungeon. Audioguides are available for $5 in Spanish and $8 in English, French, Italian, or German. There's a two-hour light show accompanied by music and dance at Puerta de Tierra. Shows are on Tuesday, Friday, and Saturday at 8 pm, and daily in spring, summer, and Christmas vacation periods. ⊠ *Calles 18 and 59, Centro* ⊙ *Daily 8 am–9 pm.*

WORTH NOTING

Baluarte de San Pedro. Built in 1686 to protect the city from pirate attacks, this bastion flanked by watchtowers now houses one of the city's few worthwhile handicraft shops. The collection is small but of high quality, and prices are reasonable. On the roof are well-preserved corner watchtowers. You can also check out (but not use) the original 17th-century potty. ⊠ *Calles 18 and 51, Circuito Baluartes, Centro* ☎ *No phone* ☒ *Free* ⊙ *Daily 9–9.*

Baluarte de Santiago. The last of the bastions to be built (1704) has been transformed into the **X'much Haltún Botanical Gardens.** It houses more than 200 plant species, including the enormous ceiba tree, which had spiritual importance to the Maya, symbolizing a link between heaven, earth, and the underworld. The original bastion was demolished at the turn of the 20th century, and then rebuilt in the 1950s. ⊠ *Calles 8 and 49, Circuito Baluartes, Centro* ☎ *No phone* ☒ *Free* ⊙ *Tues.–Fri. 8–2 and 5–8, weekends 8–2.*

Ex-Templo de San José. The Jesuits built this fine baroque church in honor of Saint Joseph just before they were booted out of the New World. Its block-long facade and portal are covered with blue-and-yellow Talavera tiles and crowned with seven narrow stone finials—resembling both the roof combs on many Mayan temples and the combs Spanish women once wore in their elaborate hairdos. Next door is the **Instituto Campechano,** used for cultural events and art exhibitions. These events and exhibits are regularly held here Tuesday evening at 7 pm. At other times you can ask the guard (who should be somewhere on the grounds) to let you in. From the outside you can admire Campeche's first lighthouse, built in 1864, and perched atop the right-hand tower. ⊠ *Calles 10 and 65, Centro* ☎ *No phone.*

Iglesia de San Francisco. With its flat, boldly painted facade and bells ensconced under small arches instead of in bell towers, the Church of Saint Francis looks more like a Mexican city hall than a Catholic church. Outside the city center in a residential neighborhood, the beautifully restored temple is Campeche's oldest. It marks the spot where some say the first Mass on the North American continent was held in 1517—though the same claim has been made for Veracruz and Cozumel. One of Cortés's grandsons was baptized here, and the baptismal font still stands. ⊠ *Avs. Miguel Alemán and Mariano Escobedo, San Francisco* ⊙ *Daily 8–noon and 5–7.*

Iglesia de San Román. Like most Franciscan churches, this one is sober and plain, and its single bell tower is the only ornamentation. The equally sparse interior is brightened a bit by some colorful stained-glass windows, and the carved and inlaid altarpiece serves as a beautiful

TAKE A TOUR

You can take Xtampak Tours from Campeche to nearby ruins like Edzná, Calakmul, Balamku, and Uxmal. Prices for shared tours range from $15 per person (for a four-hour tour) to $65 per person (for a 12-hour tour). Some tours include guides and entry fees at the ruins, whereas others only include transport, so ask ahead about what's included in the package. Make your reservations a day in advance.

Expediciones Ecoturísticos de Campeche offers rappelling, mountain biking, and local jungle tours.

For transport to the nearby Isla de Jaina—where archaeologists are working and where you'll need to acquire permission to visit—contact Héctor Solis of Espacios Náuticos. If you like, you can augment the island tour with breakfast, lunch, or swimming at the beach. Espacios Náuticos also offers waterskiing, bay tours, snorkeling, and sportfishing. Espacios Náuticos also offers hour-long tours of the bay on a Spanish galleon ($10).

Tarpon Town offers the city's only fully licensed fishing tours, and they're experts in tailoring fishing trips to individual needs.

Espacios Náuticos (⊠ *Av. Resurgimiento 120* ☎ *981/100–5721* ⌨ *barcopiratalorencillo@hotmail. com*).

Expediciones Ecoturísticos de Campeche (⊠ *Calle 12 No. 168A, Centro* ☎ *981/111–8698 or 981/816–1310* ⌨ *junglaexpediciones@hotmail.com*).

Tarpon Town (⊠ *Marina Bahía Azul s/n* ☎ *981/133–2135* ⊕ *www. tarpontown.com*).

Xtampak Tours (⊠ *Calle 57 No. 14, Centro* ☎ *981/811–6473 or 981/812–8655*).

backdrop for an ebony image of Jesus, the "Black Christ," brought from Italy in about 1575. Although understandably skeptical of Christianity, the Indians, whom the Spaniards forced into perpetual servitude, eventually came to associate this black Christ figure with miracles. As legend has it, a ship that refused to carry the holy statue was lost at sea, while the ship that accepted him reached Campeche in record time. To this day, the Feast of San Román—when worshippers carry a blackwood Christ and silver filigree cross through the streets—remains a solemn but colorful affair. ⊠ *Calles 10 and Bravo, San Román* ☉ *Daily 7–1 and 3–7.*

Iglesia y Ex-Convento de San Roque. The elaborately carved main altarpiece and matching side altars here were restored inch by inch in 2005, and this long, narrow church now adds more than ever to historic Calle 59's old-fashioned beauty. Built in 1565, it was originally called Iglesia de San Francisco for Saint Francis. In addition to a statue of Francis, humbler-looking saints peer out from smaller niches. ⊠ *Calles 12 and 59, Centro* ☉ *Daily 8:30–noon and 5–7.*

Mansión Carvajal. Built in the early 20th century by one of the Yucatán's wealthiest plantation owners, Fernando Carvajal Estrada, this eclectic mansion is a reminder of the city's heyday, when Campeche was the peninsula's only port. Local legend insists that the art-nouveau staircase with Carrara marble steps and iron balustrade, built and delivered in one piece from Italy, was too big and had to be shipped back and redone. These days the mansion is filled with government offices—you'll have to stretch your imagination a bit to picture how it once was. ⊠ *Calle 10 No. 584, between Calles 51 and 53, Centro* ☎ *981/816–7419* ⊠ *Free* ☺ *Weekdays 8:30–2:30.*

> ## MEN IN THE MARKET
>
> According to local lore, pirate attacks in Campeche were once so surprising and frequent that, in order to protect women from the dangers of the streets, men went to the market instead of the women. It's said that men going to market is a tradition that's still alive today.

Mercado Municipal. The city's heart is this municipal market, where locals shop for seafood, produce, and housewares in a newly refurbished setting. The clothing section has some nice, inexpensive embroidered and beaded pieces among the jeans and T-shirts. Next to the market is a small yellow bridge aptly named **Puente de los Perros**—where four white plaster dogs guard the area. ⊠ *Av. Baluartes Este and Calle 53, Centro* ☺ *Daily dawn–dusk.*

6

♺ **Reducto de San José el Alto.** This lofty redoubt, or stronghold, at the northwest end of town, is home to the **Museo de Armas y Barcos.** Displays in former soldiers' and watchmen's rooms focus on 18th-century weapons of siege and defense. You'll also see manuscripts, religious art, and ships in bottles. The view is terrific from the top of the ramparts, which were once used to spot invading ships. The "Guapo" tram ($7) makes the trip here daily at 9 am and 5 pm, departing from the east side of the main plaza. Visitors get about 10 minutes to admire the view before returning to the main plaza. ⊠ *Av. Escénica s/n, north of downtown, Cerro de Bellavista* ☎ *No phone* ⊠ *$2.20* ☺ *Tues.–Sun. 8–8.*

WHERE TO EAT

$
ECLECTIC
★
✕ Casa Vieja. Whether you're having a meal or an evening cocktail, try to snag a table on this eatery's outdoor balcony for a fabulous view over Campeche's main plaza. You wouldn't know it from the tiny entrance on the main plaza, but the interior is large and inviting, and the brightly painted walls are crammed with art. There's sometimes live Cuban music in the evening, and yes, that's your waiter dancing with the singer. (Service is not a strength.) The menu displays a rich mix of international dishes, including some from the owners' native lands: Cuba and Campeche. In addition to pastas, salads, and regional food, you'll find a good selection of aperitifs and digestifs. To get here, look for the stairway on the plaza's east side. They're open from 8:30 am until midnight. ⊠ *Calle 10 No. 319 Altos, between Calles 57 and 55, Centro* ☎ *981/811–8016* ⊟ *No credit cards.*

$
MEXICAN
★
✕ Cenaduría los Portales. Campechano families come here to enjoy a light supper, perhaps a delicious sandwich *claveteado* of honey-and-clove-spiked ham, along with a typical drink such as the delicious *agua de chaya*, a mixture of pineapple water and chaya (a leafy vegetable similar to spinach). On weekends, try the *tamal torteado*, a tamale with beans, tomato sauce, turkey, and pork, wrapped in banana leaves—it's not listed on the menu but is available if you ask. Although the place

opens at 6 pm, most people come between 8 and midnight. Mark your choices on the paper menu: for tacos, "m" means *maíz*, or corn; for tortillas, "h" stands for *harina*, or flour. The dining area is a wide colonial veranda with marble flooring and tables decked out in plastic tablecloths. There's no booze, but a couple of doors down there's a beer stall called Cervefrío that's open until around 9 pm. Thursday through Saturday, there's folk dancing and live music in the evenings. ⊠ *Calle 10 No. 86, at Portales San Francisco, 8 blocks northeast of Plaza Principal, San Francisco* ☎ *981/811–1491* ⊘ *No lunch.*

$ ✕ **El Faro del Morro.** This restaurant on a pirate ship only serves food
SEAFOOD   when it set sails, and the ocean views and the bay tours are as much a draw as the excellent food. Seafood is the specialty of the house, but meat eaters have a few chicken options. A recommended dish is the seafood cocktails with onion and cilantro on the side so that you can mix it to your own taste. Try their thick tortilla, split in half, and filled with cheese, green pepper, and shrimp, and served with toasted garlic on top. The restaurant is open from 8:30 in the morning until 7 at night. The Spanish galleon sails daily at noon and 5 or 6 in the evening, depending on the season. They also only depart with a minimum of 15 people. ⊠ *Av. Resurgimiento No. 120, Marina Yacht Club* ☎ *981/816–1990.*

$$ ✕ **Marganzo.** This is a local favorite and a great place to stop in for a
MEXICAN   breakfast if you want to get an early start sightseeing (they open at 7 am). They serve everything from cereal and pancakes to traditional Yucatecan dishes like *panuchos* (fried masa cakes stuffed with beans and piled high with shredded meat, lettuce, sour onions, and other toppings). The waitresses, dressed in colorful skirts from the region, are very kind about explaining regional dishes to visitors. Note that you can try plain agua de chaya here—in other restaurants the chaya-flavored water is often sweetened with pineapple. The lunch and dinner menus also offer good seafood options. ⊠ *Calle 8, No. 267, Col. Centro* ☎ *981/811–3898.*

$–$$ ✕ **La Pigua.** This is the town's hands-down lunch favorite. The seafood
SEAFOOD   is delicious and the setting is unusual: glass walls replicate an oblong
Fodor'sChoice   Mayan house, incorporating the profusion of plants outside as a design
★   element. A truly ambitious meal might start with a plate of stone-crab claws, or *camarones al coco* (coconut-encrusted shrimp), followed by a fresh local fish, pompano, prepared in one of many ways. For dessert, the classic choice is *ate,* slabs of super-condensed mango, sweet potato, or other fruit or vegetable jelly served with tangy Gouda cheese. ⊠ *Av. Miguel Alemán 179A, Col. San Martin* ☎ *981/811–3365* ⊕ *www. lapigua.com.mx* ⊘ *Daily 4 pm–10 pm.*

WHERE TO STAY
For expanded hotel reviews, visit Fodors.com.

$$ ⊡ **Best Western Hotel del Mar.** The hotels along the malecón tend to cater to business travelers, but this one is close enough to the downtown area to make it interesting, and the outdoor pool makes it a good option for families. **Pros:** a large pool and small children's pool; close to downtown. **Cons:** drab decoration; some rooms have noisy air-conditioning. **TripAdvisor:** "hotel completely fulfilled our expectations," "perfect to use as a base to visit Campeche," "Wi-Fi and computers available in business center." ⊠ *Av. Ruiz Cortines No. 51, Col. Centro* ☎ *981/811–9191* ⊕ *www.delmarhotel.com.mx* ↪ *128 rooms, 18 suites* ♿ *In-room: a/c, Wi-Fi. In-hotel: restaurant, pools, gym, business center, parking* ¶○¶ *No meals.*

$$ ⊟ **Francis Drake.** This small, spiffy hotel sits right in the center of town. **Pros:** helpful staff. **Cons:** windows in some rooms open above garage, and exhaust enters the room; small bathrooms; traffic noise can be a problem at night; no elevator. **TripAdvisor:** "a gem in the middle of Campeche," "room was very spacious and light," "a/c worked well without being noisy or intrusive." ⊠ *Calle 12 No. 207, between Calles 63 and 65, Centro* ☎ *981/811–5626 or 981/811–5627* ⊕ *www.hotelfrancisdrake.com* ↪ *13 rooms, 12 suites* ♿ *In-room: a/c, Internet (some), Wi-Fi. In-hotel: restaurant, business center, parking.*

$$$$ ⊟ **Hacienda Puerta Campeche.** Finally, Campeche has a hotel worth fawn-
★ ing over. **Pros:** stunning surroundings; calm atmosphere; excellent res-
taurant. **Cons:** expensive; not central. **TripAdvisor:** "well located in the historical city center," "stylish suites, aristocratic breakfasts, historic property," "service was discreet and attentive." ⊠ *Calle 59 No. 71, Centro* ☎ *981/816–7508, 888/625–5144 in U.S. and Canada* ⊕ *www.starwoodhotels.com* ↪ *15 rooms, 6 suites* ♿ *In-room: a/c, Wi-Fi. In-hotel: restaurant, bar, pool, parking.*

$$ ⊟ **Holiday Inn Campeche.** This new and modern hotel was built with business travelers in mind. **ripAdvisor:** "small pool but good enough for kids," "walking distance to Malecon," "room service prompt and nice." ⊠ *Av. Resurgimiento s/n, Col. Prado* ☎ *981/127–3700* ⊕ *www.ichotelsgroup.com* ↪ *91 rooms* ♿ *In-room: a/c, Wi-Fi. In-hotel: restaurant, bar, pool, gym, business center, parking.*

$$ ⊟ **Hotel Castelmar.** This recently renovated hotel in the heart of the downtown area is an elegant and comfortable place to relax and enjoy Campeche. **Pros:** great downtown location; pretty building and rooms; pool. **Cons:** street noise at night can be a problem; rooms vary. **TripAdvisor:** "lovely Spanish colonial ambience," "pool area was pleasant," "plants and flowers everywhere." ⊠ *Calle 61 between Calles 8 and 10, Centro* ☎ *981/811–1204* ⊕ *www.castelmarhotel.com* ↪ *22 rooms, 3 suites* ♿ *In-room: a/c, Wi-Fi (some). In-hotel: pool* ¶○¶ *Breakfast.*

NIGHTLIFE

Each Saturday between 3 and 10 pm, the streets around the main square are closed to traffic and filled with folk and popular dance perfor-mances, singers, comics, handicrafts, and food and drink stands. If you're in town on a Saturday, don't miss these weekly festivities, part of a program called Un Centro Histórico para Disfrutar (A Historic Downtown to Enjoy). The entertainment is often first-rate and always free. In December, concerts and other cultural events take place as part of the Festival del Centro Histórico.

On Friday and Saturday nights there's lounge music at the Hacienda Puerta Campeche, and it's one of the nicest places in town to have a drink.

There are a few restaurant bars along the malecón. Locals like to show up around 10 pm to enjoy the cool evening air. **Mediterräneo** (⊠ *Calle 10 No. 422, Col. San Román* ☎ *981/828–0123*) is a great place to grab a late-night drink or a Middle Eastern–inspired snack. They're open Monday through Saturday until 2 am. Their sesame dip with eggplant served with fresh bread is particularly tasty. **Sole** (✉ *Malecón s/n, Centro* ☎ *981/811–5357*) is a comfortable restaurant with an open-air patio where you can enjoy food and drinks until late into the night (they're open daily until 2 am). Pasta dishes, like spaghetti with shrimp in a lime sauce, are the house specialty.

SHOPPING

Bazar Artesanal (✉ *Plaza Ah Kim Pech, Col. Centro*). This government-run bazaar offers a wide range of local crafts, including some items that are hard to come by, like bull horns carved into the shape of mirror frames, necklaces, and earrings, employing a dying artistic technique that only a small number of families in Campeche State still know. All the prices are fixed, so there's no need to bargain.

SPORTS AND THE OUTDOORS

Fishing and bird-watching are popular throughout the state of Campeche. Contact **Fernando Sansores** (✉ *Calle 30 No. 1, CentroChampotón* ☎ *982/828–0018*) at the Snook Inn to arrange area sportfishing or wildlife photo excursions.

EDZNÁ

61 km (37 mi) southeast of Campeche City.

GETTING HERE AND AROUND

From Campeche, take Carretera 261 heading east toward Holpechén. The turnoff for Edzná is clearly marked about 55 km (34 mi) southeast of Campeche.

EXPLORING

Fodor's Choice ★

Edzná. A leaf-strewn nature trail winds slowly toward the ancient heart of Edzná. Although only 55 km (34 mi)—less than an hour's drive—southeast of Campeche City, the site sees few tour groups. The scarcity of camera-carrying humans intensifies the feeling of communion with nature, and with the Maya who built this once-flourishing commercial and ceremonial city.

Despite being refreshingly underappreciated by 21st-century travelers, Edzná is considered by archaeologists to be one of the peninsula's most important ruins. A major metropolis in its day, it was situated at a crossroads of sorts between cities in modern-day Guatemala, and Chiapas and Yucatán states, and this "out-of-state" influence can be appreciated in its mélange of architectural elements. Roof combs and corbeled arches are reminiscent of those at Yaxchilán and Palenque, in Chiapas; giant stone masks are characteristic of the Petén-style architecture of southern Campeche and northern Guatemala.

Edzná began as a humble agricultural settlement around 300 BC, reaching its pinnacle in the late classic period, between AD 600 and 900, and gradually waning in importance until being all but abandoned in the early 15th century. Today soft breezes blow through groves of slender trees where brilliant orange and black birds spring from branch to

branch, gathering seeds. Clouds scuttle across a blue backdrop, perfectly framing the mossy, multistepped remains of once-great structures.

A guide can point out features often missed by the untrained eye, like the remains of arrow-straight sacbés. These raised roads in their day connected one important ceremonial building within the city to the next, and also connected Edzná to trading partners throughout the peninsula.

Edzná is one of the area's most important ruins. Here you'll see a smorgasbord of Mayan architectural styles. Roof combs and corbeled arches remind one of the early classical period and the giant stone masks are taken straight out of textbooks from the pre-classical period.

The best place to survey the site is from 102-foot tall **Pirámide de los Cinco Pisos,** built on the raised platform of the **Gran Acrópolis** (Great Acropolis). This five-story pyramid consists of five levels, terminating in a tiny temple crowned by a roof comb. Hieroglyphs were carved into the vertical faces of the 15 steps between each level, and some were re-cemented in place by archaeologists, although not necessarily in the correct order. On these stones, as well as on stelae throughout the site, you can see faint depictions of the opulent attire once worn by the Maya ruling class—quetzal feathers, jade pectorals, and jaguar-skin skirts.

In 1992 Campeche archaeologist Florentino García Cruz discovered that the Pirámide de los Cinco Pisos was constructed so that on certain dates the setting sun would illuminate the mask of the creator-god, Itzámná, inside one of the pyramid's rooms. This happens annually on May 1, 2, and 3, the beginning of the planting season for the Maya—then and now. It also occurs on August 7, 8, and 9, the days of harvesting and giving thanks. On the pyramid's fifth level, the last to be built, are the ruins of three temples and a ritual steam bath.

West of the Great Acropolis, the Puuc-style **Plataforma de los Cuchillos** (Platform of the Knives) was so named by a 1970 archaeological exploration that found a number of flint knives inside. To the south, four buildings surround a smaller structure called the **Pequeña Acrópolis.** Twin sun-god masks with huge protruding eyes, sharply filed teeth, and oversize tongues flank the **Templo de los Mascarones** (Temple of the Masks, or Building 414), adjacent to the Small Acropolis. The mask at bottom left (east) represents the rising sun, whereas the one on the right represents the setting sun.

If you're not driving, consider taking one of the inexpensive day trips offered by tour operators in Campeche. This is far easier than trying to get to Edzná by municipal buses. ⊠ *Carretera 261 east from Campeche City for 44 km (27 mi) to Cayal, then Carretera 188 southeast for 18 km (11 mi)* 🕾 *No phone* 🎫 *$3.30* ⊘ *Daily 8–5.*

WHERE TO STAY

For expanded hotel reviews, visit Fodors.com.

$$$$
Fodor's Choice
★

🍴 **Hacienda Uayamón.** Abandoned in 1913, this former hacienda was resurrected nearly a century later and transformed into a luxury hotel with an elegant restaurant. **Pros:** stunning grounds; beautiful, spacious rooms; fantastic restaurant. **Cons:** expensive; can be difficult to find. **TripAdvisor:** "authentic and luxurious jungle experiences," "once in a lifetime experience," "shamanic massage was a life changing experience." ✉ *20 km (12½ mi) northwest of Edzná, on Carretera Campeche-ZA Edzná, turn off onto unmarked road towards Seybaplaya* ☏ *981/813–0530, 888/625–5144 in U.S. and Canada* ⊕ *www. starwood.com* ⌕ *10 suites, 2 deluxe suites* ⌂ *In-room: a/c, Wi-Fi. In-hotel: restaurant, bar, pool, spa, parking.*

SANTA ROSA XTAMPAK

107 km (64 mi) from Campeche City, entrance at Carretera 261, Km 79. Travel 30 km (19 mi) down signed side road.

🔺 **Santa Rosa Xtampak.** A fabulous example of the zoomorphic architectural element of Chenes architecture, Xtampak's **Casa de la Boca del Serpiente** (House of the Serpent's Mouth) has a perfectly preserved and integrated zoomorphic entrance. Here the mouth of the creator-god Itzámná stretches wide to reveal a perfectly proportioned inner chamber. The importance of this city during the classic period is shown by the large number of public buildings and ceremonial plazas here. Archaeologists believe there are around 100 structures, although only 12 have been cleared. The most exciting find was the colossal **Palacio** in the western plaza. Inside, two inner staircases run the length of the structure, leading to different levels and ending in subterranean chambers. This combination is extremely rare in Mayan temples. ✉ *East of Hopelchén on Dzibilchaltún–Chencho Rd., watch for sign* ☏ *No phone* 🎟 *$2.50* 🕐 *Daily 8–5.*

HOCHOB

109 km (68 km) southwest of Campeche City, 55 km (34 mi) south of Hopelchén, 15 km (9 mi) west of Dzibilnocac.

EXPLORING

🔺 **Hochob.** The small Mayan ruin of Hochob is an excellent example of the Chenes architectural style, which flowered from about AD 100 to 1000. Most ruins in this area (central and southeastern Campeche) were built on the highest possible elevation to prevent flooding during the rainy season, and Hochob is no exception. It rests high on a hill overlooking the surrounding valleys. Another indication that these are Chenes ruins is the number of *chultunes,* or cisterns, in the area.

Since work began at Hochob in the early 1980s, four temples and palaces have been excavated at the site, including two that have been fully restored. Intricate and perfectly preserved geometric designs cover the temple known as **Estructura II**, which are typical of the Chenes style.

The doorway represents the open mouth of Itzámná, the creator god, and above it the eyes bulge and fangs are bared on either side of the base. It takes a bit of imagination to see the structure as a mask, as color no doubt originally enhanced the effect. Squinting helps a bit: the figure's "eyes" are said to be squinting as well. But anyone can appreciate the intense geometric relief carvings decorating the facades, including long cascades of Chaac rain-god masks along the sides. Evidence of roof combs can be seen at the top of the building. Ask the guard to show you the series of natural and man-made chultunes that extend back into the forest. ⊠ *Southwest of Hopelchén on Dzibalchén–Chencho Rd.* ☎ *No phone* ☞ *Free* ☉ *Daily 8–5.*

CARRETERA 186 INTO CAMPECHE

Xpujil, Chicanná, Calakmul . . . exotic, far-flung-sounding names dot the map along this stretch of jungly territory. These are places where the creatures of the forest outnumber the tourists: in Calakmul, four- and five-story ceiba trees sway as families of spider monkeys swing through the canopy; in Xpujil, brilliant blue motmots fly from tree to tree in long, swoopy arcs.

The vestiges of at least 10 little-known Mayan cities lie hidden off Carretera 186 between Escárcega and Chetumal. You can see Xpujil, Becán, Hormiguero, and Chicanná in one rather rushed day by starting out early from Chetumal, Quintana Roo, and spending the night in Xpujil. If you plan to visit Calakmul, spend the first night at Xpujil, arriving at Calakmul as soon as the site opens the next day. That provides the best chance to see armadillos, wild turkeys, families of howler and spider monkeys, and other wildlife.

GETTING HERE AND AROUND

From Chetumal on the coast of Quintana Roo, it's about 140 km (87 mi) to Xpujil. Carretera 186 is a two-lane highway in reasonably good condition. ■TIP→ Most hotels in the Xpujil area close around 11 pm. So, regardless of whether you have a reservation, you may find yourself locked out of all but the seediest lodgings if you show up late.

EXPLORING

There aren't many good tour guides in the region. Some of the most experienced and enthusiastic are part of a community organization called **Servidores Turísticos Calakmul**. There are bicycle tours, horseback tours, and tours where spotting plants and animals is the main focus. All tours can be customized to meet your interests, including trips that span across several days with overnight stays in the jungle. If your Spanish is shaky, ask for Leticia, who speaks basic English and has years of experience as a guide. ⊠ *Av. Calakmul between Okolwitz and Payan* ☎ *983/871–6064* ⊕ *www.ecoturismocalakmul.com.*

Hotel owners Rick Bertram and Diane Lalonde, and the knowlegable archaeologist Dan Griffin, offer tours through their hotel **Río Bec Dreams** (⇨ *see Where to Stay below*). They're native English speakers and enthusiastic guides, and will give you a comprehensive trip around the local archaeological sites. They charge between $45 and $150, depending on the site. Be sure to book ahead since they juggle duties at their hotel with their tour schedules. ⊠ *Carretera 186, Escarcega-Chetumal, Km 142* ☎ *983/124–0501* ⊕ *www.riobecdreams.com.*

XPUJIL

Carretera 186, Km 150, 300 km (186 mi) southeast of Campeche, 130 km (81 mi) south of Dzibilnocac, 125 km (78 mi) west of Chetumal.

EXPLORING

Xpujil (meaning "cat's tail," and pronounced ish-*poo*-hil) gets its name from the reedy plant that grows in the area. Elaborately carved facades and doorways in the shape of monsters' mouths reflect the Chenes style, while adjacent pyramid towers connected by a long platform show the influence of Río Bec architects.

Some of the buildings have lost a lot of their stones, making them resemble "day after" sand castles. In **Edificio I,** three towers— believed to have been used by priests and royalty—were once crowned by false temples, and at the front of each are the remains of four vaulted rooms, each oriented toward one of the compass points. On the back side of the central tower is a huge mask of the rain god Chaac. Quite a few other building groups amid the forests of gum trees and *palo mulato* (so called for its bark with both dark and light patches) have yet to be excavated. 🎫 *$3* 🕙 *Daily 8–5.*

WHERE TO STAY

For expanded hotel reviews, visit Fodors.com.

$$ ⭐ 🏨 **Chicanná Ecovillage Resort.** Rooms in this comfortable jungle lodge are in two-story stucco duplexes with thatch roofs. **Pros:** convenient to several ruins in the Río Bec region; spacious rooms. **Cons:** restaurant food is just OK. **TripAdvisor:** "located in the midst of the biosphere," "warm water the whole time," "great proximity to amazing ruins." ✉ *Carretera 186, Km 144, 9 km (5½ mi) west of village of Xpujil* ☎ *01800/560–8612, 981/811–9191 for reservations* ✉ reserves@chicannaecovillageresort.com 🛏 *42 rooms* ♿ *In-room: no a/c, no TV. In-hotel: restaurant, bar, pool, parking.*

$ ⭐ 🏨 **Río Bec Dreams.** From the moment you arrive at this hotel in the middle of the jungle, owners Rick Bertram and Diane Lalonde will make you feel at home. **Pros:** bar is great place to meet people; wonderful restaurant; owners are friendly, attentive, and excellent guides. **Cons:** some rooms lack private bathrooms; a few dogs live here. **TripAdvisor:** "gourmet meals," "friendly, knowledgeable and enthusiastic about the area," "enjoyed dining with the other guests." ✉ *Carretera 186, Escarcega-Chetumal, Km 142* ☎ *983/124–0501* ⊕ *www.riobecdreams.com* 🛏 *5 shared jungalows, 4 private cabanas* ♿ *In-room: no a/c, no TV. In-hotel: restaurant, bar* 🚫 *No credit cards* 🍴 *No meals.*

BECÁN

Carretera 186, Km 145, 264 km (164 mi) southwest of Campeche City, 7 km (4½ mi) west of Xpujil.

⭐ **Becán.** An interesting feature of this once-important city is its defensive moat—unusual among ancient Mayan cities—though barely evident today. The seven ruined gateways, which once permitted the only entrances to the guarded city, may have clued archaeologists to its presence. Becán (usually translated as "canyon of water," referring to the moat) is thought to have been an important city within the Río Bec group, which once encompassed Xpujil, Chicanná, and Río Bec. Most of the site's many buildings date from between about AD 600 and 1000, but since there are no traditionally inscribed stelae listing details of royal births, deaths, battles, and ascendancies to the throne, archaeologists have had to do a lot of guessing about what transpired here.

You can climb several of the structures to get a view of the area, and even spot some of Xpuhil's towers above the treetops. Duck into **Estructura VIII,** where underground passages lead to small subterranean rooms and to a concealed staircase that reaches the top of the temple. One of several buildings surrounding a central plaza, Estructura VIII has lateral towers and a giant zoomorphic mask on its central facade. The building was used for religious rituals, including bloodletting rites during which the elite pierced earlobes and genitals, among other sensitive body parts, in order to present their blood to the gods. ☉ *Daily 8–5.*

CHICANNÁ

Carretera 186, Km 141, 274 km (174 mi) southwest of Campeche City, 3 km (2 mi) east of Becán.

🔺 **Chicanná.** Thought to have been a satellite community of the larger, more commercial city of Becán, Chicanná ("house of the serpent's mouth") was also in its prime during the late classic period. Of the four buildings surrounding the main plaza, **Estructura II,** on the east side, is the most impressive. On its intricate facade are well-preserved sculpted reliefs and faces with long twisted noses—symbols of Chaac. In typical Chenes style, the doorway represents the mouth of the creator-god Itzámná. Surrounding the opening are large crossed eyes, fierce fangs, and earrings to complete the stone mask, which still bears traces of blue and red pigments. 🖼 *$3* ☉ *Daily 8–5.*

HORMIGUERO

272 km (169 mi) southwest of Campeche City, 14 km (9 mi) southeast of Xpujil.

🔺 **Hormiguero.** Bumping down the badly potholed, 8-km (5-mi) road leading to this site may give you an appreciation for the explorers who first found and excavated it in 1933. Hidden throughout the forest are at least five magnificent temples, two of which have been excavated to reveal ornate facades covered with zoomorphic figures whose mouths are the doorways. The buildings here were constructed roughly between 400 BC and AD 1100 in the Río Bec style, with rounded lateral towers and ornamental stairways, the latter built to give an illusion of height, which they do wonderfully. The facade of **Estructura II,** the largest structure on the site, is intricately carved and well preserved. **Estructura V** has some admirable Chaac masks arranged in a cascade atop a pyramid. Nearby is a perfectly round *chultun* (water-storage tank), and seemingly emerging from the earth, the eerily etched designs of a still-unexcavated structure.

Hormiguero is Spanish for "anthill," referring both to the looters' tunnels that honeycombed the ruins when archaeologists discovered them and to the number of large anthills in the area. Among the other fauna sharing the jungle here are several species of poisonous snakes. Although these mainly come out at night, you should always be careful of where you walk and, when climbing, where you put your hands. ▨ *$3 ☉ Daily 8–5.*

RESERVA DE LA BIOSFERA CALAKMUL

Entrance at Carretera 186, Km 65, 365 km (227 mi) southwest of Campeche City, 107 km (66 mi) southwest of Xpujil.

Fodor'sChoice
★

Reserva de la Biosfera Calakmul. Vast, lovely, green, and mysterious Calakmul may not stay a secret for much longer. You won't see any tour buses in the parking lot, and on an average day site employees and laborers still outnumber the visitors traipsing along the moss-tinged dirt paths that snake through the jungle. But things are changing. The nearest town, Xpujil, already has Internet service. And the proposed building of a water-retention aqueduct in the same area will, if it becomes a reality, almost surely bring increased tourism—maybe even chain hotels—to the area. So if you're looking for untrammeled Mexican wilderness, don't put it off any longer: the time to visit Calakmul is now.

Calakmul encompasses some 1.8 million acres of land along the Guatemalan border. It was declared a protected biosphere reserve in 1989, and is the second-largest reserve of its kind in Mexico after Sian Ka'an in Quintana Roo. All kinds of flora and fauna thrive here, including wildcats, spider and howler monkeys, hundreds of exotic birds, orchid varieties, butterflies, and reptiles. (There's no shortage of insects, either, so don't forget the bug repellent.)

The centerpiece of the reserve, however, is the ruined Mayan city that shares the name Calakmul (which translates as "two adjacent towers"). Although Carretera 186 runs right through the reserve, you'll need to drive about 1½ hours from the highway along a 60-km (37-mi) authorized entry road to get to the site. Although structures here are still being excavated, the dense surrounding jungle is being left in its natural state: as you walk among the ruined palaces and tumbled stelae, you'll hear the guttural calls of howler monkeys, and see massive strangler figs enveloping equally massive trees.

This magnificent city, now in ruins, wasn't always so lonely. Anthropologists estimate that in its heyday (between AD 542 and 695) the region was inhabited by more than 50,000 Maya. Archaeologists have mapped more than 6,250 structures and found 180 stelae. Perhaps the most monumental discovery thus far has been that of the remains of royal ruler Gran Garra de Jaguar (Great Jaguar Claw). His body was wrapped (but not embalmed) in a shroud of palm leaf, lime, and fine cloth, and locked away in a royal tomb in about AD 700. In an adjacent crypt, a young woman wearing fine jewelry and an elaborately painted wood-and-stucco headdress was entombed together with a child. Their identity remains a mystery. The artifacts and skeletal remains have been moved to the Museo de la Arqueología Maya in Campeche City.

Unlike those at Chichén Itzá (which also peaked in importance during the classic era) the pyramids and palaces throughout Calakmul can be climbed to achieve soaring vistas. You can choose to explore the site along a short, medium, or long path, but all three eventually lead to magnificent **Templo II** and **Templo VII**—twin pyramids separated by an immense plaza. Templo II, at 175 feet, is the peninsula's tallest Mayan building. Scientists are studying a huge, intact stucco frieze deep within this structure, so it's not currently open to visitors.

Arrangements for an English-speaking Calakmul tour guide should be made beforehand with Servidores Turísticos Calakmul, Río Bec Dreams, or through Chicanná Ecovillage near Xpujil. Camping is permitted with the Servidores Turistícos Calakmul, and be sure to tip the caretakers at the entrance gate. You can set up camp near the second checkpoint. Even if day-tripping, though, you'll need to bring your own food and water, as the only place to buy a meal is near the entrance and the walk to the ruins is long. ⊠ *97 km (60 mi) east of Escárcega to turnoff at Cohuás, then 60 km (37 mi) south to Calakmul* ☎ *No phone* 💰 *$5 per car, more for larger vehicles, plus $3 per person* ⊙ *Daily 8–5.*

SPANISH VOCABULARY

	ENGLISH	SPANISH	PRONUNCIATION
BASICS			
	Yes/no	Sí/no	see/no
	Please	Por favor	pore fah-**vore**
	May I?	¿Me permite?	may pair-**mee**-tay
	Thank you (very much)	(Muchas) gracias	(**moo**-chas) **grah**-see-as
	You're welcome	De nada	day **nah**-dah
	Excuse me	Con permiso	con pair-**mee**-so
	Pardon me	¿Perdón?	pair-**dohn**
	Could you tell me?	¿Podría decirme?	po-dree-ah deh-**seer**-meh
	I'm sorry	Lo siento	lo see-**en**-toh
	Good morning!	¡Buenos días!	**bway**-nohs **dee**-ahs
	Good afternoon!	¡Buenas tardes!	**bway**-nahs **tar**-dess
	Good evening!	¡Buenas noches!	**bway**-nahs **no**-chess
	Good-bye!	¡Adiós!/¡Hasta luego!	ah-dee-**ohss/ah** -stah **lwe**-go
	Mr./Mrs.	Señor/Señora	sen-**yor**/sen-**yohr**-ah
	Miss	Señorita	sen-yo-**ree**-tah
	Pleased to meet you	Mucho gusto	**moo**-cho **goose**-toh
	How are you?	¿Cómo está usted?	**ko**-mo es-**tah** oo-**sted**
	Very well, thank you.	Muy bien, gracias.	**moo**-ee bee-**en**, **grah**-see-as
	And you?	¿Y usted?	ee oos-**ted**
	Hello (on the telephone)	Diga	**dee**-gah
NUMBERS			
	1	un, uno	oon, **oo**-no
	2	dos	dos
	3	tres	tress
	4	cuatro	**kwah**-tro
	5	cinco	**sink**-oh
	6	seis	saice

ENGLISH	SPANISH	PRONUNCIATION
7	siete	see-**et**-eh
8	ocho	**o**-cho
9	nueve	new-**eh**-vey
10	diez	dee-**es**
11	once	**ohn**-seh
12	doce	**doh**-seh
13	trece	**treh**-seh
14	catorce	ka-**tohr**-seh
15	quince	**keen**-seh
16	dieciséis	dee-**es**-ee-**saice**
17	diecisiete	dee-**es**-ee-see-**et**-eh
18	dieciocho	dee-**es**-ee-**o**-cho
19	diecinueve	**dee-es**-ee-new-**ev**-eh
20	veinte	**vain**-teh
21	veinte y uno/veintiuno	**vain**-te-**oo**-noh
30	treinta	**train**-tah
32	treinta y dos	train-tay-**dohs**
40	cuarenta	kwah-**ren**-tah
43	cuarenta y tres	kwah-**ren**-tay-**tress**
50	cincuenta	seen-**kwen**-tah
54	cincuenta y cuatro	seen-**kwen**-tay **kwah**-tro
60	sesenta	sess-**en**-tah
65	sesenta y cinco	sess-**en**-tay **seen**-ko
70	setenta	set-**en**-tah
76	setenta y seis	set-en-tay **saice**
80	ochenta	oh-**chen**-tah
87	ochenta y siete	oh-**chen**-tay see-**yet**-eh
90	noventa	no-**ven**-tah
98	noventa y ocho	no-**ven**-tah-**o**-choh
100	cien	see-**en**

ENGLISH	SPANISH	PRONUNCIATION
101	ciento uno	see-**en**-toh **oo**-noh
200	doscientos	doh-see-**en**-tohss
500	quinientos	keen-**yen**-tohss
700	setecientos	set-eh-see-**en**-tohss
900	novecientos	no-veh-see-**en**-tohss
1,000	mil	meel
2,000	dos mil	dohs meel
1,000,000	un millón	oon meel-**yohn**

COLORS

black	negro	**neh**-groh
blue	azul	ah-**sool**
brown	café	kah-**feh**
green	verde	**ver**-deh
orange	naranja	na-**rahn**-hah
pink	rosa	**ro**-sah
purple	morado	mo-**rah**-doh
red	rojo	**roh**-hoh
white	blanco	**blahn**-koh
yellow	amarillo	ah-mah-**ree**-yoh

DAYS OF THE WEEK

Sunday	domingo	doe-**meen**-goh
Monday	lunes	**loo**-ness
Tuesday	martes	**mahr**-tess
Wednesday	miércoles	me-**air**-koh-less
Thursday	jueves	hoo-**ev**-ess
Friday	viernes	vee-**air**-ness
Saturday	sábado	**sah**-bah-doh

MONTHS

January	enero	eh-**neh**-roh
February	febrero	feh-**breh**-roh

ENGLISH	SPANISH	PRONUNCIATION
March	marzo	**mahr**-soh
April	abril	ah-**breel**
May	mayo	**my**-oh
June	junio	**hoo**-nee-oh
July	julio	**hoo**-lee-yoh
August	agosto	ah-**ghost**-toh
September	septiembre	sep-tee-**em**-breh
October	octubre	oak-**too**-breh
November	noviembre	no-vee-**em**-breh
December	diciembre	dee-see-**em**-breh

USEFUL PHRASES

Do you speak English?	¿Habla usted inglés?	**ah**-blah oos-**ted** in-**glehs**
I don't speak Spanish	No hablo español	no **ah**-bloh es-pahn-**yol**
I don't understand (you)	No entiendo	no en-tee-**en**-doh
I understand (you)	Entiendo	en-tee-**en**-doh
I don't know	No sé	no seh
I am American/ British	Soy americano (americana)/inglés(a)	soy ah-meh-ree- **kah**-no (ah-meh-ree- **kah**-nah)/ in-**glehs(ah)**
What's your name?	¿Cómo se llama usted?	koh-mo seh **yah**-mah oos-**ted**
My name is . . .	Me llamo . . .	may **yah**-moh
What time is it?	¿Qué hora es?	keh **o**-rah es
It is one, two, three . . . o'clock.	Es la una./Son las dos, tres . . .	es la **oo**-nah/sohnahs dohs, tress
Yes, please/ No, thank you	Sí, por favor/No, gracias	**see** pohr fah-**vor**/no **grah**-see-us
How?	¿Cómo?	**koh**-mo
When?	¿Cuándo?	**kwahn**-doh
This/Next week	Esta semana/ la semana que entra	**es**-teh seh-**mah**- nah/ lah seh-**mah**-nah keh **en**-trah

ENGLISH	SPANISH	PRONUNCIATION
This/Next month	Este mes/el próximo mes	**es**-teh mehs/el **proke**-see-mo mehs
This/Next year	Este año/el año que viene	**es**-teh **ahn**-yo/el **ahn**-yo keh vee-**yen**-ay
Yesterday/today/tomorrow	Ayer/hoy/mañana	ah-**yehr**/oy/ mahn-**yah**-nah
This morning/afternoon	Esta mañana/ tarde	**es**-tah mahn-**yah**- nah/ **tar**-deh
Tonight	Esta noche	**es**-tah **no**-cheh
What?	¿Qué?	keh
What is it?	¿Qué es esto?	keh es **es**-toh
Why?	¿Por qué?	pore **keh**
Who?	¿Quién?	kee-**yen**
Where is . . . ?	¿Dónde está . . . ?	**dohn**-deh es-**tah**
the train station?	la estación del tren?	la es-tah-see-on del trehn
the subway station?	la estación del tren subterráneo?	la es-ta-see-**on** del trehn la es-ta-see-**on** soob-teh-**rrahn**-eh-oh
the bus stop?	la parada del autobus?	la pah-**rah**-dah del ow-toh-**boos**
the post office?	la oficina de correos?	la oh-fee-**see**- nah deh koh-**rreh**-os
the bank?	el banco?	el **bahn**-koh
the hotel?	el hotel?	el oh-**tel**
the store?	la tienda?	la tee-**en**-dah
the cashier?	la caja?	la **kah**-hah
the museum?	el museo?	el moo-**seh**-oh
the hospital?	el hospital?	el ohss-pee-**tal**
the elevator?	el ascensor?	el ah-**sen**-sohr
the bathroom?	el baño?	el **bahn**-yoh
Here/there	Aquí/allá	ah-**key**/ah-**yah**
Open/closed	Abierto/cerrado	ah-bee-**er**-toh/ ser-**ah**-doh

ENGLISH	SPANISH	PRONUNCIATION
Left/right	Izquierda/derecha	iss-key-**er**-dah/ dare-**eh**-chah
Straight ahead	Derecho	dare-**eh**-choh
Is it near/far?	¿Está cerca/lejos?	es-**tah sehr**-kah/ **leh**-hoss
I'd like . . .	Quisiera . . .	kee-see-ehr-ah
a room	un cuarto/una habitación	oon **kwahr**-toh/ **oo**-nah ah-bee- tah-see-**on**
the key	la llave	lah **yah**-veh
a newspaper	un periódico	oon pehr-ee-**oh**-dee-koh
a stamp	un sello de correo	oon **seh**-yo deh korr-ee-oh
I'd like to buy . . .	Quisiera comprar . . .	kee-see-**ehr**-ah kohm-**prahr**
cigarettes	cigarrillos	ce-ga-**ree**-yohs
matches	cerillos	ser-**ee**-ohs
a dictionary	un diccionario	oon deek-see-oh-**nah**-ree-oh
soap	jabón	hah-**bohn**
sunglasses	gafas de sol	**ga**-fahs deh sohl
suntan lotion	loción bronceadora	loh-see-**ohn** brohn- seh-ah-**do**-rah
a map	un mapa	oon **mah**-pah
a magazine	una revista	**oon**-ah reh-**veess**-tah
paper	papel	pah-**pel**
envelopes	sobres	**so**-brehs
a postcard	una tarjeta postal	**oon**-ah tar-**het**-ah post-**ahl**
How much is it?	¿Cuánto cuesta?	**kwahn**-toh **kwes**-tah
It's expensive/	Está caro/barato	es-**tah kah**-roh/
cheap		bah-**rah**-toh
A little/a lot	Un poquito/ mucho	oon poh-**kee**-toh/ **moo**-choh
More/less	Más/menos	mahss/**men**-ohss

ENGLISH	SPANISH	PRONUNCIATION
Enough/too much/too little	Suficiente/ demasiado/ muy poco	soo-fee-see-**en**-teh/ deh-mah-see-**ah**- doh/ **moo**-ee **poh**-koh
Telephone	Teléfono	tel-**ef**-oh-no
Telegram	Telegrama	teh-leh-**grah**-mah
I am ill	Estoy enfermo(a)	es-**toy** en-**fehr**- moh(mah)
Please call a	Por favor llame a	pohr fah-**vor ya**-meh
doctor	un medico	ah oon **med**-ee-koh

ON THE ROAD

Avenue	Avenida	ah-ven-**ee**-dah
Broad, tree-lined boulevard	Bulevar	boo-leh-**var**
Fertile plain	Vega	**veh**-gah
Highway	Carretera	car-reh-**ter**-ah
Mountain pass	Puerto	poo-**ehr**-toh
Street	Calle	**cah**-yeh
Waterfront promenade	Rambla	**rahm**-blah
Wharf	Embarcadero	em-bar-cah-**deh**-ro

IN TOWN

Cathedral	Catedral	cah-teh-**dral**
Church	Templo/Iglesia	**tem**-plo/ee-**glehs**- see-ah
City hall	Casa de gobierno	kah-sah deh go-bee-**ehr**-no
Door, gate	Puerta portón	poo-**ehr**-tah por-**ton**
Entrance/exit	Entrada/salida	en-**trah**-dah/ sah-**lee**- dah
Inn, rustic bar, or restaurant	Taverna	tah-**vehr**-nah
Main square	Plaza principal	plah-thah prin- see-**pahl**

ENGLISH	SPANISH	PRONUNCIATION

DINING OUT

ENGLISH	SPANISH	PRONUNCIATION
Can you recommend a good restaurant?	¿Puede recomendarme un buen restaurante?	**pweh**-deh rreh-koh-mehn-**dahr**-me oon bwehn rrehs-tow- **rahn**-teh?
Where is it located?	¿Dónde está situado?	**dohn**-deh ehs-**tah** see-**twah**-doh?
Do I need reservations?	¿Se necesita una reservación?	seh neh-seh-**see**-tah **oo**-nah rreh-sehr- bah-**syohn**?
I'd like to reserve a table . . .	Quisiera reservar una mesa . . .	kee-**syeh**-rah rreh-sehr-**bahr oo**-nah **meh**-sah . . .
for two people.	para dos personas.	**pah**-rah dohs pehr- **soh**-nahs
for this evening.	para esta noche.	**pah**-rah **ehs**-tah **noh**-cheh
for 8 pm	para las ocho de la noche.	**pah**-rah lahs **oh**-choh deh lah **noh**-cheh
A bottle of . . .	Una botella de . . .	**oo**-nah bo-**teh**- yah deh
A cup of . . .	Una taza de . . .	**oo**-nah **tah**-thah deh
A glass of . . .	Un vaso de . . .	oon **vah**-so deh
Ashtray	Un cenicero	oon sen-ee-**seh**-roh
Bill/check	La cuenta	lah **kwen**-tah
Bread	El pan	el pahn
Breakfast	El desayuno	el deh-sah-**yoon**-oh
Butter	La mantequilla	lah man-teh-**key**-yah
Cheers!	¡Salud!	sah-**lood**
Cocktail	Un aperitivo	oon ah-pehr-ee-**tee**-voh
Dinner	La cena	lah **seh**-nah
Dish	Un plato	oon **plah**-toh
Menu of the day	Menú del día	meh-**noo** del **dee**-ah
Enjoy!	¡Buen provecho!	bwehn pro-**veh**-cho

ENGLISH	SPANISH	PRONUNCIATION
Fixed-price menu	Menú fijo o turistico	meh-**noo fee**-hoh oh too-**ree**-stee-coh
Fork	El tenedor	el ten-eh-**dor**
Is the tip included?	¿Está incluida la propina?	es-**tah** in-cloo-**ee**-dah lah pro-**pee**-nah
Knife	El cuchillo	el koo-**chee**-yo
Large portion of savory snacks	Raciónes	rah-see-**oh**-nehs
Lunch	La comida	lah koh-**mee**-dah
Menu	La carta, el menú	lah **cart**-ah, el meh-**noo**
Napkin	La servilleta	lah sehr-vee-**yet**-ah
Pepper	La pimienta	lah pee-me-**en**-tah
Please give me	Por favor déme	pore fah-**vor deh**-meh
Salt	La sal	lah sahl
Savory snacks	Tapas	**tah**-pahs
Spoon	Una cuchara	**oo**-nah koo-**chah**-rah
Sugar	El azúcar	el ah-**thu**-kar
Waiter!/Waitress!	¡Por favor Señor/ Señorita!	pohr fah-**vor** sen- **yor**/ sen-yor-**ee**-tah

Travel Smart

GETTING HERE AND AROUND

■ AIR TRAVEL

Cancún is 4½ hours from New York and Chicago, 2½ hours from Miami, 4 hours from Los Angeles, 3 hours from Dallas, 11¾ hours from London, and 18 hours from Sydney. Add another 1 to 4 hours if you change planes at one of the hub airports. Flights to Cozumel and Mérida are comparable in length, but are more likely to have a change along the way.

There are direct flights to Cancún from hub airports such as New York, Boston, Washington, D.C., Houston, Dallas, Miami, Chicago, Los Angeles, Orlando, Ft. Lauderdale, Charlotte, and Atlanta. From other cities, you must generally change planes. Some flights go to Mexico City, where you must pass through customs before transferring to a domestic flight to Cancún. This applies to air travel from the United States, Canada, the United Kingdom, Australia, and New Zealand. Be sure to have all your documents in order for entry back into the United States, otherwise you may be turned back.

Charter flights, especially those leaving from Cancún, are notorious for last-minute changes. Be sure to ask for an updated telephone number from your charter company before you leave, so you can call to check for any changes in flight departures. Most recommend that you call within 48 hours of departure. This check-in also applies to commercial airlines, although their departure times are more regular. Their changes are usually due to weather conditions rather than to seat sales.

Airline-Security Issues Transportation Security Administration (☎ 866/289–9673 ⊕ www.tsa.gov) has answers for almost every question that might arise.

AIRPORTS

Cancún Aeropuerto Internacional (CUN) is the area's major gateway, though some people now choose to fly directly to Cozumel (CZM). The inland Hector José Vavarrette Muñoz Airport (MID), in Mérida, is smaller but closer to the major Mayan ruins. Campeche and Chetumal have even smaller airports served primarily by domestic carriers. The ruins at Palenque and Chichén Itzá also have airstrips that handle small planes; there's an airport at Chichén (CZA), handling smaller craft as well as 747s via Azteca, Mexicana, and other major airlines.

In peak season, passenger waiting lines can be long and slow-moving; plan accordingly.

It's 20 to 30 minutes from the Hotel Zone to Cancún International or from downtown Mérida or Campeche to their airports. Allow 1½ hours from Playa del Carmen to the Cancún airport. The Cozumel airport is less than 10 minutes from downtown Cozumel.

Airport Information Contacts Cancún Aeropuerto Internacional (☎ 998/848–7200 ⊕ www.cancun-airport.com). **Cozumel Aeropuerto Internacional** (☎ 987/872–2081 ⊕ www.asur.com.mx). **Aeropuerto Internacional de Mérida** (☎ 999/946–1530 ⊕ www.asur.com.mx).

GROUND TRANSPORTATION

As you exit the Cancún airport, transportation operators can be overwhelming as they eagerly wave signs and yell names to arriving passengers. If you're taking the bus, walk past the bar and toward the right where tickets are available from a small booth. There is a bus leaving every hour from Cancún Airport to downtown Cancún.

It's not uncommon to be told that you just missed the last bus, taxi, or van to your destination. This is actually a ploy to get you to use the transportation company that is "assisting" you. Ask around if you're not entirely sure. Always arrive with small bills for taxi or bus fare, otherwise you're liable to get ripped off. Always check the identification of transportation operators and don't allow anyone to "help" you with your luggage. Many people like this work on commission for specific transportation companies. Worse yet, they might end up disappearing into the crowd with your baggage.

Some of the major hotels send shuttles to pick up arriving guests; it's worth checking into before you arrive. Private taxis from the airport charge reasonable rates within Cancún, but will charge up to $60 or more to destinations along the Riviera Maya. Airport shuttle vans, which charge set rates based on your destination, sometimes take forever before filling up and getting under way. There are taxi and shuttle desks in the baggage-claim area; go to the ones with posted prices.

From the Riviera Maya to and from the airport, it's worth looking for a shuttle service, as a private taxi can be prohibitively expensive. Some of the shuttle services can be arranged beforehand via phone or the Internet. Cancún Valet rents per van, rather than per person, for up to 10 passengers, making it a good value for couples, families, and groups. Prices from the airport to the Hotel Zone, Playa del Carmen, and Tulum, as well as intermittent points are reasonable: $35 to Cancún ($65 round-trip) or $65 to Playa del Carmen ($125 round-trip), for example. Cancún Airport Transportation charges $35 per couple or individual, one-way, to the Hotel Zone ($60 to Playa). Cancún Valet also rents cell phones for use in Mexico.

Contacts Cancún Airport Transportation (☎ 998/210–3317 ⊕ www.cancuntransfers. com). **Cancún Valet** (☎ 888/479–9095 ⊕ www.cancunvalet.com).

FLIGHTS

You can reach the Yucatán by U.S., Mexican, or regional carriers. The most convenient flight from the United States is a nonstop on either a domestic or Mexican airline. Flying within the Yucatán is neither cost-effective nor convenient. Given the additional time needed for check-in,

you might as well drive or take a bus to your destination, unless you're continuing on by plane.

The Yucatán Peninsula has international airports in Cancún, Mérida, and Cozumel. Campeche and Chetumal have international airports as well, but they don't service flights from the United States, Canada, or Europe. Domestic airports are in Playa del Carmen, Chichén Itzá, Isla Holbox, Isla Mujeres, and Majahual.

Select your hub city for exploring before making your reservation from abroad. There are more flights to business-oriented Ciudad del Carmen, in Campeche state, for example, than to the tiny airport in the more touristic capital, Campeche City.

Since all the major airlines listed here fly to Cancún, and often have the cheapest and most frequent flights there, it's worthwhile to consider it as a jumping-off point even if you don't plan on visiting the city. There are currently 190 flights that land daily at Cancún International Airport (CUN). Aeroméxico, American, Continental, and Mexicana also fly to Cozumel. Aeroméxico, American, Continental, Delta, and Mexicana fly to Mérida.

■TIP→ When you arrive at the airport, hang onto your FM-T form (tourist card) since you'll need it again upon departure.

Airline Contacts Aeroméxico (☎ 800/237–6639 in U.S. and Canada, 800/021–1400 or 55/5133–4000 in Mexico ⊕ www.aeromexico. com). **American Airlines** (☎ 800/433–7300 ⊕ www.aa.com). **Continental Airlines** (☎ 800/523–3273 for U.S. and Mexico reservations, 800/231–0856 for international reservations ⊕ www.continental.com). **Delta Airlines** (☎ 800/221–1212 for U.S. reservations, 800/241–4141 for international reservations ⊕ www.delta.com). **Mexicana** (☎ 888/882–9994 or 877/801–2010 in U.S. or Canada, 01800/837–6150 in Mexico ⊕ www. mexicana.com).

■ BUS TRAVEL

The Mexican bus network is extensive and a great means of getting around. Service is frequent, and tickets can be purchased on the spot (except during holidays and on long weekends, when advance purchase is crucial). Bring something to eat on long trips in case you don't like the restaurant or market where the bus stops; bring toilet tissue; and wear a sweater, as the air-conditioning is often set on high. Most buses play videos or television until midnight, so bring earplugs if you're bothered by noise. Smoking is prohibited on Mexican buses.

Mexican bus companies offer several classes of service: first-class (*primera clase*) and deluxe or executive-class (*de lujo* or *ejecutivo*) Mexican buses are generally punctual and comfortable air-conditioned coaches with bathrooms, movies, reclining seats with seat belts, and refreshments. They take the fastest route (usually on safer, well-paved toll roads) and make few stops between points. Less desirable, second-class vehicles (*segunda clase*) connect smaller, secondary routes; they also run along some long-distance routes, often taking slower, local roads. They're tolerable, but are usually cramped and make many stops. The class of travel will be listed on your printed ticket—if you see *económico* printed next to *servicio,* you've been booked on a second-class bus. At many bus stations, one counter will represent several lines and classes of service, and mistakes do happen. ADO (Autobuses del Oriente) is the Yucatán's principal first-class bus company. Most bus tickets, including first-class or executive- and second-class, can be reserved in advance in person at ticket offices. ADO allows you to reserve tickets online 48 hours in advance. ADO and ADO GL (deluxe service) travel between the Yucatán and Mexico City as well as other destinations in southern Mexico, especially Oaxaca, Veracruz, and Puebla.

ADO, along with other luxury liners like Omnibus de Mexico and Primera Plus travel the Yucatán loop of Cancún—Playa del Carmen—Chetumal—Campeche—Mérida—Cancún. If you're staying in Riviera Maya, *colectivos* (mini-buses) run along Carretera 307 from Cancún to Tulum. Although affordable, traveling by bus means you'll have to either walk or organize additional transportation from the bus stop.

Bus Contacts ADO (☎ 998/884–4352, 01800/702–8000 toll-free in Mexico, 800/900–0287 in U.S. ⊕ www.ado.com.mx). **Omnibus de Mexico** (☎ 01800/765–6636 ⊕ www.odm.com.mx) **Primera Plus** (☎ 01800/375–7587 ⊕ www.primeraplus.com.mx)

■ CAR TRAVEL

Renting a car is generally expensive in and around Cancún; if you're not traveling far afield, don't bother to rent, as you'll be able to arrange taxi service to nearby sights through your hotel.

However, taxis for longer trips—to Playa del Carmen, for instance—can get expensive, so renting a car for a day or two of exploring may be more economical. As a rule, avoid local agencies; stick with the major companies, because they tend to be more reliable. You can get the same kind of midsize and luxury cars in Mexico that you can rent in the United States. Economy usually refers to a small car barely fitting four passengers, which may or may not come with air-conditioning. Pancake-flat Yucatán makes for fairly easy driving, although side roads may be unsigned; four-wheel drive vehicles aren't necessary unless you plan on traveling to sites far off-the-beaten path in rainy season. Ask for a child's car seat when booking. You won't need a car on Isla Mujeres or Isla Holbox, which are too small to make driving practical. Again, a rental isn't necessary in Playa del Carmen because the downtown area is quite small and the main street is blocked off to vehicles, so you'll likely spend a great deal of time on foot anyway. Cars can actually feel like a burden in Mérida and Campeche City, because of the narrow cobbled streets and the lack of parking spaces. You'll need a car in Cozumel only if you wish to explore the eastern side of the island.

Although consolidators like Travelocity. com may offer great deals, it's a good idea to book directly through a major rental company's Web site, as consolidator sites will sometimes allow you to make a booking even when no cars are available.

Car-rental agencies in Mexico require you to purchase CDW, or Collision Damage Waiver, coverage (starts at $12 per day), regardless of any coverage afforded by your credit-card company (insurance fees are often included in quoted rates). Additional theft protection and personal injury policies are optional.

When renting a car, ask the agency for a "Tourist Traffic Card," which can be handed to police upon receiving a traffic violation. This voucher allows you to pay the ticket at the car-rental agency when you return the car, rather than having to spend several hours at the police station. It also helps eliminate corruption. Avis's Tourist Card actually serves as "payment" for two minor traffic violations. By presenting the card to authorities, the fine will be paid by Avis when you return the vehicle.

Be sure that you've been provided with proof of such insurance; if you drive without it, you're not only liable for damages, but you're also breaking the law. If you're in a car accident and you don't have insurance, you may be placed in jail until you're proven innocent. If anyone is injured you'll remain in jail until you make retribution to all injured parties and their families—which will likely cost you thousands of dollars. Mexican laws seem to favor nationals.

Even if you're absolutely certain you're fully covered by your credit-card company, we wouldn't recommend relying on it. Getting into a car accident in Mexico would be harrowing enough without having to navigate the bureaucracy of your credit-card company to clear things up with Mexican authorities. Make sure that your insurance coverage covers the cost for an attorney and claims adjusters who will come to the scene of an accident. Buying insurance makes renting a car in Mexico one of the most expensive parts of the trip, but in this case it's better to be safe than frugal.

Before setting out on any car trip, check your vehicle's fuel, oil, fluids, tires, windshield wipers, and lights. Gas stations and mechanics can be hard to find, especially in more-remote areas. Consult a map and have your route in mind as you drive. Be aware that Mexican drivers often think nothing of tailgating, speeding, and weaving in and out of traffic. Drive defensively and keep your cool. When stopping for traffic or at a red light, always leave sufficient room between your car and the one ahead so you can maneuver to safety if necessary. On the highway, a left turn signal in Mexico means the driver is signaling those behind that it's safe to pass. In Mexico the minimum driving age is 18, but most rental-car agencies have a minimum age requirement between 21 and 25; some have a surcharge for drivers under 25. Your own driver's license is acceptable; there's no reason to get an international driver's license.

GASOLINE

Pemex, Mexico's government-owned petroleum monopoly, franchises all gas stations, so prices throughout the Yucatán—and the country—are the same. Gas is always sold in liters. Some stations accept credit cards and a few have ATMs, but don't count on it—make sure you have pesos handy. Overall, prices run slightly cheaper (around 30% less) than in the United States (at this writing, about 8 pesos a liter or $2.40 a gallon).

Ask for a *recibo* if you want a receipt. Premium unleaded gas (called *premium*), the red pump, and regular unleaded gas (*magna*), the green pump, are available nationwide. Fuel quality is generally lower than that in the United States and Europe, but it has improved enough so that your car will run acceptably.

There are no self-service stations in Mexico. Ask the attendant to fill your tank—*lleno* (YAY-noh), *por favor*—or ask for a specific amount in pesos to avoid being overcharged. Check to make sure that the attendant has set the meter back to zero and that the price is shown. Watch the attendant check the oil as well—to make sure you actually need it—and watch while he pours it into your car. Never pay before the gas is pumped, even if the attendant asks you to. Always tip your attendant a few pesos. Finally, keep your gas tank full, because gas stations are not plentiful in this area. If you run out of gas in a small village and there's no gas station for miles, ask if there's a store that sells gas from containers.

PARKING

A circle with a diagonal line superimposed on the letter *E* (for *estacionamiento*) means "no parking." A red curb means parking is restricted at all times, and a white curb is designated for loading and unloading only. A blue curb is for handicap parking, a green curb allows parking during specific hours, and a yellow curb means that the parking space is private. ■ TIP→ If you're ticketed, your license plate will be taken to a nearby police station and will only be returned upon payment of the infraction. When in doubt, park your car in a parking lot instead of on the street; your car will probably be safer there anyway. Tip the parking attendant or security guard and ask him to look after your car. Never park your car overnight on the street. Never leave anything of value in an unattended car. Parking lots are plentiful, although not always clearly marked, and fees are reasonable—as little as $1 for a half day or up to $1 or more an hour. Sometimes you park your own car; more often, though, you hand the keys over to an attendant. There are a few (extremely few) parking meters in larger cities; the cost is usually about 10¢ per 15 minutes.

ROAD CONDITIONS

The road system in the Yucatán Peninsula is extensive and generally in good repair. Carretera 307 parallels most of the Caribbean Coast from Punta Sam, north of Cancún, to Tulum; here it turns inward for a stretch before returning to the coast at Chetumal and the Belize border. Carretera 180 runs west from Cancún to Valladolid, Chichén Itzá, and Mérida, then turns southwest to Campeche, Ciudad del Carmen, and on to Villahermosa. From Mérida, the winding, more scenic Carretera 261 also leads to some of the more off-the-beaten-track archaeological sites on the way south to Campeche and Escárcega, where it joins Carretera 186 going east to Chetumal. These highways are two-lane roads. Carretera 295 (from the north coast to Valladolid and Felipe Carrillo Puerto) is also a good two-lane road.

The *autopista,* or *carretera de cuota,* a four-lane toll highway between Cancún and Mérida, was completed in 1993. It runs roughly parallel to Carretera 180 and cuts driving time between Cancún and Mérida—otherwise about 4½ hours—by about 1 hour. Tolls between Mérida and Cancún total about $35, and the stretches between highway exits are long. Be careful when driving on this road, as it retains the heat from the sun and can make your tires blow if they have low pressure or worn threads.

Many secondary roads are in bad condition—unpaved, unmarked, and full of potholes. If you must take one of these roads, the best course is to allow plenty of daylight hours and never travel at night. Slow down when approaching towns and villages—which you're forced to do by the *topes* (speed bumps)—and because of the added presence of children and animals, as well as adults. People selling oranges, candy, or other food will almost certainly approach your car.

MEXICAN DRIVERS

Mexicans are generally skilled drivers, but they do drive quite fast, even on twisting or extraordinarily dark roads. That said, Mexicans are in some ways more courteous than U.S. drivers—it's customary, for example, for drivers to put on their hazard lights to warn the cars behind them of poor road conditions, slow-downs, or upcoming speed bumps; oncoming cars may flash their lights at you for the same reasons.

ROADSIDE EMERGENCIES

The Mexican Tourism Ministry operates a fleet of some 1,800 pickup trucks, known as Angeles Verdes, or the Green Angels, a 40-year-old organization that assists motorists on major highways. Dial 078 from any cell phone or Telmex phone booth and your call will be routed to the Green Angels' dispatch office. The bilingual drivers provide mechanical help, first aid, radio-telephone communication, basic supplies and small parts, towing, and tourist information. Services are free, and spare parts, fuel, and lubricants are provided at cost. Tips are always appreciated, and are sometimes openly solicited.

The Green Angels patrol fixed sections of the major highways twice daily 8 am to dusk, later on holiday weekends. If your car breaks down, pull as far as possible off the road, lift the hood, hail a passing vehicle, and ask the driver to notify the patrol. Most bus and truck drivers will be quite helpful. Don't accept rides from strangers. If you witness an accident, don't stop to help since witnesses are often detained for questioning for long periods of time. Instead find the nearest official.

Emergency Service Contacts Angeles Verdes (☏ *078 nationwide 3-digit Angeles Verdes and tourist emergency line, 55/3002-6300 Ministry of Tourism hotline*).

RULES OF THE ROAD

There are two absolutely essential points to remember about driving in Mexico. First and foremost is to carry Mexican auto insurance. If you injure anyone in an accident, you could well be jailed—whether it was your fault or not—unless you have insurance. Second, if you enter Mexico with a car, you must leave with it. In recent years the high rate of U.S. vehicles being sold illegally in Mexico has caused the Mexican government to enact stringent regulations for bringing a car into the country. You must be in your foreign vehicle at all times when it's driven. You cannot lend it to another person. Do not, under any circumstances, let a national drive your car. It's illegal for Mexicans to drive foreign cars; if a national is caught driving your car, the car will be impounded by customs and you will receive a stiff fine. Newer models of vans, SUVs, and pickup trucks can be impossible to get back once impounded.

You must cross the border with the following documents: title or registration for your vehicle; a birth certificate or passport; a credit card (AE, DC, MC, or V); and a valid driver's license with a photo. You'll also need a temporary car-importation permit and a FM-T form (Tourist Card). The title-holder, driver, and credit-card owner must be one and the same—that is, if your spouse's name is on the title of the car and yours isn't, you cannot be the one to bring the car into the country. For financed, leased, rental, or company cars, you must bring a notarized letter of permission from the bank, lien holder, rental agency, or company. When you submit your paperwork at the border and pay the approximate $27 charge on your credit card, you'll receive a car permit and a sticker to put on your vehicle. The permit is valid for the same amount of time as your tourist visa, which is up to 180 days. You may go back and forth across the border during this six-month period, as long as you check with immigration and bring all your permit paperwork with you. If you're planning to stay and keep your car in Mexico for longer than six months, however, you'll have to get a new permit before the original one expires.

One way to minimize hassle when you cross the border with a car is to have your paperwork done in advance at a branch of Sanborn's Mexico Auto Insurance; visit ⊕ *www.sanbornsinsurance.com* to find an office in almost every town on the U.S.–Mexico border. Average daily insurance rates are around $35. The fact that you drove in with a car is stamped on your tourist card, which you must give to immigration authorities at departure. If an emergency arises and you must fly home, there are complicated customs procedures to face.

When you sign up for Mexican car insurance, you should receive a booklet on Mexican rules of the road. It really is a good idea to read it to avoid breaking laws that differ from those of your country. If an oncoming vehicle flicks its lights at you in daytime, slow down: it could mean trouble ahead. When approaching a narrow bridge, the first vehicle to flash its lights has right of way. One-way streets are common. One-way traffic is indicated by an arrow; two-way, by a double-pointed arrow. Other road signs follow the widespread system of international symbols.

Mileage and speed limits are given in kilometers: 100 kph and 80 kph (62 mph and 50 mph, respectively) are the most common maximums. A few of the toll roads allow 110 mph (68 mph). In cities and small towns, observe the posted speed limits, which can be as low as 20 MPH (12 mph). Seat belts are required by law throughout Mexico.

Drunk-driving laws are fairly harsh in Mexico, and if you're caught you'll go to jail immediately. It's hard to know what the country's blood-alcohol limit really is. Everyone seems to have a different idea about it; this means it's probably being handled in a discretionary way, which is nerve-racking, to say the least. The best way to avoid any problems is simply to not drink and drive. Right turns on red are not allowed. Foreigners must pay speeding penalties on the spot, which can be steep.

Minor traffic violations can be dismissed until you return your rental car by simply showing your "Tourist Traffic Card" available from most car-rental agencies.

If you encounter a police checkpoint, stay calm. These are simply routine checks for weapons and drugs; customarily they'll check out the car's registration, look in the backseat, the trunk, and at the undercarriage with a mirror. Basic Spanish does help during these stops, though a smile and polite demeanor will go a long way.

Contact Sanborn's Mexican Auto Insurance (☎ 800/222–0158 ⊕ www.sanbornsinsurance. com).

SAFETY ON THE ROAD

Never drive at night in remote and rural areas. Although there are few *banditos* on the roads here, more common problems are large potholes, free-roaming animals, cars with no working lights, and road-hogging trucks. Getting assistance is difficult. If you must travel at night, use the toll roads whenever possible; although costly, they're much safer.

Some of the biggest hassles on the road might be from police who pull you over for supposedly breaking the law, or for being a good prospect for a scam. Remember to be polite—displays of anger will only make matters worse—and be aware that a police officer might be pulling you over for something you didn't do. Although efforts are being made to fight corruption, it's still a fact of life in Mexico, and the $5 (and up) it costs to get your license back is definitely supplementary income for the officer who pulled you over with no intention of taking you down to police headquarters.

▌ TAXI TRAVEL

Taxis are ubiquitous in both big cities and midsize towns. The standard taxi is a midsize, four-door sedan. Drivers generally speak English, either enough to negotiate the fare or, in some cases, excellent enough for a lively discussion of national politics.

In addition to private taxis, many cities have bargain-price collective taxi services using minibuses and sedans. The service is called *colectivo* or *pesero*. Such vehicles run along fixed routes, and you hail them on the street and tell the driver where you're going, he charges you based on how far you're going. Note that drivers often run out of change, so having change handy, and being able to pay the exact amount, can help make your ride smoother.

AIRPORT TAXIS

For safety, you should only take the authorized taxi service from most airports. Whenever possible, purchase the taxi vouchers sold at stands inside or just outside the terminal, which ensure that your fare is established beforehand. Check the taxi-zone map (it should be posted on or by the ticket stand) before you purchase your ticket and make sure your ticket is properly zoned. Tucan Kin offers private transportation between Cancún and Tulum for $24 per person.

FARES

A metered taxi has a taximetro, and if a cab has one, ask the driver what the rates are. Most taxis, particularly those in resort areas, are unmetered. Always confirm the fare before setting out. Major hotels post rate sheets, or you can ask a concierge or front-desk person what the rates should be. Note that even the posted rates are inflated, so always try to negotiate a slightly better price. Clearly, if any cabbie asks for more than the posted fare you're being grossly overcharged.

A surcharge of 20% to 40% may be added at night, usually after 11 pm.

If a driver doesn't know the address you give him, he'll radio either a dispatcher or other cabbie to get the info, or drive to the neighborhood and ask around. When you've negotiated the fare before starting, you needn't pay extra if the cabbie has to drive around a bit to find the address.

Tipping isn't customary, unless the driver helps you with you bags.

Tucan Kin. ☎ 984/134–7535 *from Tulum or Akumal, 984/134–7535 from the rest of Mexico* ⊕ *www.fromcancunairport.com).*

▌ CRUISE SHIP TRAVEL

Cozumel and Playa del Carmen have become increasingly popular ports for Caribbean cruises. The last few years have seen many changes in the cruise business. Several companies have merged and several more are suffering financial difficulties. Due to heavy traffic, Cozumel and Playa del Carmen have limited the number of ships coming into their ports. Carnival and Cunard leave from Galveston, New Orleans, and Miami, whereas Norwegian departs from Houston, New Orleans, Miami, and Charleston. Holland America, Cunard, Carnival, Princess, Royal Caribbean, and Celebrity Cruises dock at Cozumel. Princess and Carnival lines, among others, call at the Puerto Costa Maya in Majahual, an increasingly popular destination on the southern Yucatán Peninsula.

Cruise Line Contacts Carnival Cruise Line (☎ 305/406–4779 *or* 877/885–48652 ⊕ *www.carnival.com).* **Cunard Line** (☎ 661/753–1000 *or* 800/728–6273 ⊕ *www.cunard.com).* **Norwegian Cruise Line** (☎ 866/234–7350 ⊕ *www.ncl.com).* **Princess Cruises** (☎ 661/753–0000 *or* 800/774–6237 ⊕ *www.princess.com).* **Royal Caribbean International** (☎ 316/526–9723 *or* 866/562–7625 ⊕ *www. royalcaribbean.com).*

ESSENTIALS

■ ACCOMMODATIONS

The price and quality of accommodations in the Yucatán Peninsula vary from luxury resorts and coastal villas to seedy hostels and eco-friendly cabanas. You may find bargains while you're on the road, but if your comfort threshold is high, look for an English-speaking staff, guaranteed dollar rates, and toll-free reservation numbers. Mexico doesn't have an official star-rating system, but the usual number of stars (five being the ultimate) denotes the most luxury and amenities, while a two-star hotel might have a ceiling fan and TV with local channels only. "Gran turismo" is a special category of hotel that may or may not have all the accoutrements of a five-star hotel (such as minibars) but is nonetheless at the top of the heap, both in price and level of service and sophistication. All-inclusive hotels are a good option for families since the price of the room usually includes children's activities and meals.

APARTMENT AND HOUSE RENTALS

Local rental agencies can be found in Isla Mujeres, Cozumel, and Playa del Carmen. They specialize in renting out apartments, condos, villas, and private homes.

Rental Agency Contacts Akumal Villas (☎ 866/535–1324 ⊕ www.akumal-villas.com). **Caribbean Realty** (☎ 910/543–0019 in U.S ⊕ www.puertoaventurasrentals.com). **Cozumel Villas** (☎ 866/564–4427 or 406/686–9169 ⊕ www.cozumelvillas.com). **Lost Oasis Property Rentals** (☎ 998/887–0951, 831/274–6277 in U.S. ⊕ www.lostoasis.net). **Real Estate Yucatán** (☎ 999/944–1315 ⊕ www.realestateyucatan.com. **Turquoise Waters** (☎ 877/254–9791 ⊕ www.turquoisewater.com). **Villas & Apartments Abroad** (☎ 212/213–6435 ⊕ www.vaanyc.com). **Villas International** (☎ 415/499–9490 or 800/221–2260 ⊕ www.villasintl.com). **Villas of Distinction**

(☎ 800/289–0900 ⊕ www.villasofdistinction.com).

HOTELS

Hotel rates are subject to the 10% to 15% value-added tax, in addition to a 2% to 3% hotel tax. Service charges and meals generally aren't included in the hotel rates. Make sure to ask if tax is included in quoted rates and take this into account when comparing properties.

High- versus low-season rates can vary significantly. In the off-season, Cancún hotels can cost one-third to one-half what they cost during peak season. Keep in mind, however, that this is also the time that many hotels undergo necessary repairs or renovations.

Hotels in this guide have private bathrooms with showers, unless stated otherwise; bathtubs aren't common in inexpensive hotels and properties in smaller towns.

Reservations are easy to make over the Internet. If you call hotels in the larger urban areas, there will be someone who speaks English. In more remote regions you'll have to make your reservations in Spanish. Be sure to book online hotel reservations at least two days in advance of your stay, and always print out your confirmation. Although major resorts are generally efficient at keeping up with online bookings, there's often a lag, and the reservation desks that handle such things may be closed on weekends. In more remote areas like Xcalak, you'll have to make reservations by email since most properties don't have telephones.

It's essential to reserve in advance if you're traveling to the resort areas during high season (mid-December through Easter) or holiday periods, and it's recommended, though not always necessary, to do so elsewhere during high season. Resorts popular with college students tend to fill up in the summer months and during Spring Break season (generally March through April). Overbooking is a common practice in some parts, especially in Cancún. To protect yourself, get a written confirmation, via fax or email.

General Hotel Contacts Cancún Hotel Association (✉ Av. García de la Torre 6, Sm 15 ☎ 998/881–8730 ⊕ www.ahqr.com. mx). **Cozumel Island Hotel Association** (✉ Calle 2 Norte 299 ☎ 987/872–7585 ⊕ www.islacozumel.com.mx). **Hotels Tulum** (✉ Cozumel 22, Mza 3, Sm11, Cancún 77500 ☎ 998/865–422 ⊕ www.hotelstulum.com). **HolboxIsland.com** (⊕ www.holboxisland.com).

■ COMMUNICATIONS

INTERNET

If you're traveling with your laptop, watch it carefully. The biggest danger, aside from theft, is the constantly fluctuating electricity, which may eventually damage your hard drive. Invest in a Mexican surge protector (available at most electronics stores for about $50) that can handle the frequent brownouts and fluctuations in voltage. The surge protectors you use at home probably won't give you much protection. If possible, leave repairs until you're back home. Although there are many competent techies here as elsewhere, language may be a barrier.

In Cancún free Wi-Fi is available in most large hotels, at least in public areas. Cost for an in-room connection starts at $25 per day. Yes, it's shocking, especially when in other parts of the country Wi-Fi is a free perk offered by many hotels. The cost for public Internet is as much as 10 pesos a minute (for those with super-fast connection). For slower connections, the charge is usually more like 10 pesos for 10 minutes.

Internet Café Contacts Cybercafes (⊕ www. cybercafes.com) lists about 170 Internet cafés in Mexico.

PHONES

The good news is that you can now make a direct-dial call from virtually any point on earth. The bad news? You can't always do so cheaply. Calling from a hotel is almost always the most expensive option; hotels usually add huge surcharges to all calls, particularly international ones. Calling cards usually keep costs to a minimum. Use your international calling card or purchase a Ladatel card to use at a pay phone—although hearing above ambient noise can be a problem. And then there are cell phones (⇨ below), which are sometimes more prevalent—particularly in the developing world—than landlines. As expensive as mobile-phone calls can be, they're still usually a much cheaper option than calling from your hotel room. If you want to call a restaurant or local business, you can save money by simply walking to the concierge and asking the representative to make the call on your behalf.

The country code for Mexico is 52. When calling a Mexico number from abroad, dial the country code and then all of the numbers listed for the entry.

CALLING WITHIN MEXICO

Towns and cities throughout Mexico now have standardized three-digit area codes (LADAs) and seven-digit phone numbers. (In Mexico City, Monterrey, and Guadalajara the area code is two digits followed by an eight-digit local number.) While increasingly rare, numbers in brochures and other literature—even business cards—are sometimes written in the old style, with five or six digits. To call national long-distance, dial 01, the area code, and the seven-digit number.

Directory assistance is 040 for telephone lines run by Telmex, the former government-owned telephone monopoly that still holds near-monopoly status in Mexico. While you can reach 040 from other phone lines, operators generally don't give you any information, except, perhaps, the directory-assistance line for the provider you're using. For international assistance, dial 00 first for an international operator and most likely you'll get one who speaks English; tell the operator in what city, state, and country you require directory assistance, and he or she will connect you.

CALLING OUTSIDE MEXICO

To make an international call, dial 00 before the country code, area code, and number. The country code for the United States and Canada is 1, the United Kingdom 44, Australia 61, New Zealand 64, and South Africa 27.

The cheapest method for making local or long-distance calls is to buy a prepaid phone card and dial direct (⇨ see *Calling Cards*). Another option is to find a *caseta de larga distancia*, a telephone service usually operated out of a store such as a *papelería* (stationary store), pharmacy, restaurant, or other small business; look for the phone symbol on the door. These are few and far between in Cancún, however. Casetas may cost more to use than pay phones, but you have a better chance of immediate success. To make a direct long-distance call, tell the person on duty the number you'd like to call, and she or he will give you a rate and dial for you. Rates seem to vary widely.

Sometimes you can make collect calls from casetas, and sometimes you can't, depending on the individual operator and possibly your degree of visible desperation. Casetas will generally charge 50¢ to $1.50 to place a collect call (some charge by the minute); it's usually better to call *por cobrar* (collect) from a pay phone—but be sure to avoid phones near tourist areas that advertise, in English, "Call the U.S. or Canada here!" These charge an outrageous fee per minute. If in doubt, dial the operator and ask for rates.

Access Code Contacts AT&T Direct (☎ 01800/288–2872 or 001800/462–4240 toll-free in Mexico). **MCI World-Phone** (☎ 01800/674–7000 toll-free in Mexico). **Sprint International Access** (☎ 001800/877–8000 toll-free in Mexico).

CALLING CARDS

In most parts of the country, pay phones (predominantly operated by Telmex) accept only prepaid cards (*tarjetas Lada*), sold in 30-, 50-, or 100-peso denominations at newsstands, pharmacies, minimarkets, or grocery stores. Coin-only pay phones are few and far between. There are pay phones are all over the place—on street corners, in bus stations, and so on. They usually have two unmarked slots, one for a Ladatel (a Spanish acronym for "long-distance direct dialing") card and the other for a credit card. These are primarily for Mexican bank cards, but some accept Visa or MasterCard, though *not* U.S. phone credit cards.

To use a Ladatel card, simply insert it in the appropriate slot, dial 001 (for calls to the States) or 01 (for long-distance calls within Mexico) and the area code and number you're trying to reach. Local calls may also be placed with the card. Credit is deleted from the card as you use it, and your balance is displayed on a small screen on the phone.

MOBILE PHONES

If you have a multiband phone (some countries use frequencies different from those used in the United States) and your service provider uses the world-standard GSM network (as do T-Mobile, AT&T, and Verizon), you can probably use your phone abroad. Roaming fees can be steep, however: 99¢ a minute is considered reasonable. And you normally pay the toll charges for incoming calls. It's almost always cheaper to send a text message than to make a call, since text messages have a very low set fee (often less than 5¢).

If you just want to make local calls, consider buying a new SIM card (note that your provider may have to unlock your phone for you to use a different SIM card) and a prepaid service plan in the destination. You'll then have a local number and can make local calls at local rates. If your trip is extensive, you could also simply buy a new cell phone in your destination, as the initial cost will be offset over time.

■TIP➜ If you travel internationally frequently, save one of your old mobile phones or buy a cheap one on the Internet; ask your cell-phone company to unlock it for you, and take it with you as a travel phone, buying a new SIM card with pay-as-you-go service in each destination.

Mobile Phone Contacts Cancún Valet (☎ 888/479–9095 ⊕ www.cancunvalet.com) rents cell phones with rates at 69¢ per minute to/from the United States, Canada, and Europe. **Daystar** (☎ 877/820–7397 ⊕ www.daystarwireless.com) rents cell phones at about $3.95 per day, with incoming calls at approximately 22¢ a minute and outgoing at $1.19.

TOLL-FREE NUMBERS

Toll-free numbers in Mexico start with an 800 prefix. To reach them, you need to dial 01 before the number. In this guide, Mexico-only toll-free numbers appear as follows: 01800/123–4567. Some toll-free numbers use 95 instead of 01 to connect. Some hotels will charge for 800 numbers made from guest rooms. The 800 numbers listed simply 800/123–4567 are U.S. numbers and generally work north of the border only. Those that do work to access a U.S. company from Mexico may or may not be free; those that aren't should give you the chance to hang up before being charged. Directory assistance is 040.

■ CUSTOMS AND DUTIES

Upon entering Mexico, you'll be given a baggage-declaration form—you can fill out one per family. You'll also be given a FMT form (tourist card), to be stamped at immigration. Keep this card for the duration of your trip since you'll need to present it upon departure. Minors traveling without an adult must carry notarized written permission from a parent or guardian. Most airports have a random bag-inspection scheme in place. When you pick up your bags you'll approach something that looks like a stoplight; hand your form to the attendant, press the button, and if you get a green light you (and the rest of your family) may proceed. If you get a red light, you may be subject to further questioning or inspection. You're allowed to bring in 3 liters of spirits or wine for personal use; 400 cigarettes, 50 cigars, or 250 grams of tobacco; a reasonable amount of perfume for personal use; one movie camera and one regular camera; and gift items not to exceed a total of $300. If driving across the U.S. border, gift items must not exceed $50. You aren't allowed to bring firearms or ammunition, meat, vegetables, plants, fruit, or flowers into Mexico. You can bring in one of each of the following items without paying taxes: a cell phone, an iPod, a musical instrument, a laptop, an iPad, a Kindle, and a portable copier or printer. Compact discs are limited to 20 and DVDs to five.

Mexico also allows you to bring one cat, one dog, or up to four canaries into the country if you have these two things: (1) a pet health certificate signed by a registered veterinarian in the United States and issued not more than 72 hours before the animal enters Mexico; and (2) a pet-vaccination certificate showing that the animal has been treated for rabies, hepatitis, pip, and leptospirosis.

For more information or details on bringing other animals or more than one type of animal, contact a Mexican consulate. Aduana Mexico (Mexican Customs) has an informative Web site, though everything is in Spanish. You can also get customs information from a Mexican consulate; many major American cities have them as well as border towns. To find the consulate nearest you, check the Ministry of Foreign Affairs Web site, select Consular Services from the menu on the left, and scroll down.

Consulate Contacts Aduana Mexico (☎ 01800/463–6728 ⊕ www.aduanas.gob.mx). **Ministry of Foreign Affairs** (☎ 202/728–1600 ⊕ portal.sre.gob.mx/usa). **U.S. Customs and Border Protection** (☎ 703/526–4200 ⊕ www. cbp.gov).

▌ EATING OUT

The restaurants we list are the cream of the crop in each price category.

⇨ *For information on food-related health issues, see Health below.*

MEALS AND MEALTIMES

Desayuno can be either a breakfast sweet roll and coffee or milk or a full breakfast of an egg dish such as *huevos a la mexicana* (scrambled eggs with chopped tomato, onion, and chiles), *huevos rancheros* (fried eggs on a tortilla covered with salsa), or *huevos con jamón* (scrambled eggs with ham), plus juice and toast or tortillas. Some cafés don't open until 8 or 8:30, in which case hotel restaurants are the best bets for early risers. *Panaderías* (bakeries) open early and provide the cheapest breakfast you'll find—a bag of assorted rolls and pastries will likely cost less than $1.

Traditionally, lunch is called *comida* or *almuerzo* and is the biggest meal of the day. Most restaurants start serving lunch no earlier than 1 pm and traditional businesses close between 2 pm and 4 pm for this meal. It usually includes soup, a main dish, and dessert. Regional specialties include *pan de cazón* (baby shark shredded and layered with tortillas, black beans, and tomato sauce) in Campeche; *pollo pibil* (chicken baked in banana leaves) in Mérida; and *tikinchic* (fish in a sour-orange sauce), on the coast. Restaurants in tourist areas also serve American-style food such as hamburgers, pizza, and pasta. The evening meal is called *cena*, which is sometimes replaced by *merienda* (a lighter meal between lunch and dinner).

Most restaurants are open daily for lunch and dinner during high season (December through April), but hours may be reduced during the rest of the year. It's always a good idea to phone ahead.

Unless otherwise noted, the restaurants listed in this guide are open daily for lunch and dinner.

PAYING

Most small restaurants do not accept credit cards. Larger restaurants and those catering to tourists take credit cards.

⇨ *For guidelines on tipping, see Tipping below.*

RESERVATIONS AND DRESS

Regardless of where you are, it's a good idea to make a reservation if you can. In Cancún, for example, reservations are expected at the nicer restaurants. We only mention them specifically when reservations are essential (there's no other way you'll ever get a table) or when they're not accepted. Large parties should always call ahead to check the reservations policy. We mention dress only when men are required to wear a jacket or a tie.

Some restaurants accept online reservations, although it's always wise to confirm by phone.

WINES, BEER, AND SPIRITS

Almost all restaurants in the region serve beer and some Mexican label spirits. Larger restaurants have beer, wine, and spirits. The Mexican wine industry is relatively small, but notable producers include L.A. Cetto, Bodegas de Santo Tomás, Pedro Domecq, and Monte Xanic. As well as offering Mexican vintages, restaurants may offer Chilean, Spanish, Italian, and French wines at reasonable prices. You pay more for imported liquor such as vodka, brandy, and whiskey; some brands of tequila and rum are less expensive. Take the opportunity to try some of the higher-end, small-batch tequila—it's a completely different experience from what you might be used to. Some small lunch places called *loncherias* don't sell alcohol. Almost all corner stores sell beer, brandy, cheap wine, and tequila. Grocery stores carry all brands of beer, wine, and spirits. Liquor stores are rare and usually carry specialty items. You must be 18 to buy liquor, but this rule is often overlooked.

ELECTRICITY

Electrical converters are not necessary, because Mexico operates on the 60-cycle, 120-volt system. However, many outlets have not been updated to accommodate three-prong and polarized plugs (those with one larger prong), so bring an adapter. Some older hotels have outlets for round pin attachment plugs instead of modern flat ones, although most have been upgraded. If your room has one of these ancient plugs, ask at the front desk for an adapter.

Contacts Steve Kropla's Help for World Travelers (⊕ www.kropla.com) has information on electrical and telephone plugs around the world.

EMERGENCIES

It's helpful, albeit daunting, to know ahead of time that you're not protected by the laws of your native land once you're on Mexican soil. However, if you get into a scrape with the law, you can call the Citizens' Emergency Center in the United States. In Mexico, you can also call INFOTUR, the 24-hour English-speaking hotline of the Mexico Ministry of Tourism (Sectur). The hotline can provide immediate assistance as well as general, non-emergency guidance. In Mérida and environs, contact the tourist police (☎ 999/930–3200 Ext. 40031), although getting an English speaker is hit or miss. In an emergency, call ☎ 060 from any phone.

Consulates and Embassies U.S. Consulate (✉ Calle 60 No. 338, Col. Alcala Martin, Centro, Mérida ☎ 999/942–5700). **U.S. Consular Agency Cancún** (✉ Blvd. Kukulcán Km 13, Zona Hotelera, Cancún ☎ 998/883–0272). **U.S. Embassy** (✉ Paseo de la Reforma 305, Col.

Cuauhtémoc, Mexico City ☎ 55/5080–2000 ⊕ mexico.usembassy.gov/eng).

General Emergency Contacts Air Ambulance Network (☎ 800/327–1966 or 01800/010–0027 ⊕ www.airambulancenetwork.com). **Angeles Verdes** (Emergency roadside assistance in Mexico City ☎ 078). **Citizens' Emergency Center** (☎ 202/647–5225 weekdays 8:15 am–10 pm EST and Sat. 9 am–3 pm, 202/647–4000 after hrs and Sun. ⊕ www.travel.state.gov). **Global Life Flight** (☎ 01800/305–9400 or 01800/361–1600 toll-free in Mexico, 800/831–9307 in U.S. and Canada ⊕ www.globallifeflight.com). **INFOTUR** (☎ 01800/903–9200 toll-free in Mexico ⊕ www.sectur.gob.mx).

HEALTH

According to the U.S. government's National Centers for Disease Control and Prevention (CDC) there's a limited risk of malaria in certain rural areas of the Yucatán Peninsula, especially the states of Campeche and Quintana Roo. Dengue fever is also a limited risk along the Caribbean Coast. Travelers in mostly urban areas need not worry, nor do travelers who rarely leave artificial resort environs.

To safeguard yourself against mosquito-borne diseases like malaria and dengue, use mosquito nets, wear clothing that covers the body, apply repellent containing DEET, and use spray for flying insects in living and sleeping areas. You might consider taking anti-malarial pills, but the side effects are quite strong, and the current strain of Mexican malaria can be cured with the right medication. There's no vaccine to combat dengue.

Health Warnings National Centers for Disease Control & Prevention (CDC ☎ 800/232–4636 international travelers' health line ⊕ www.cdc.gov/travel). **World Health Organization** (WHO ☎ 4122/791–2111 ⊕ www.who.int).

FOOD AND DRINK

Despite concerns raised by the H1N1 influenza outbreak of early 2009, in Mexico the biggest health risk is traveler's diarrhea caused by consuming contaminated fruit, vegetables, or water. The usual suspects are ice, uncooked food, and unpasteurized milk and milk products.

Drink only bottled water or water that has been boiled for at least 10 minutes, even when you're brushing your teeth. At restaurants off the beaten path, be sure to ask for *agua mineral* (mineral water) or *agua purificada* (purified water). When ordering cold drinks at questionable establishments, skip the ice: *sin hielo*. (You can usually identify ice made commercially from purified water by its uniform shape and the hole in the center.) Hotels with water-purification systems will post signs to that effect in the rooms; even then, be wary. Although salads in tourist-oriented areas have usually been hygienically prepared, when in doubt don't eat any raw vegetables that haven't been, or can't be, peeled (e.g., lettuce and tomatoes).

REMEDIES

Mild cases of diarrhea may respond to Imodium (known generically as Loperamide or Lomotil) or Pepto-Bismol (not as strong), both of which you can buy over the counter. Keep in mind, though, that these drugs can complicate more serious illnesses. Drink plenty of bottled water or tea. Chamomile tea (*té de manzanilla*) is a good remedy, and it's readily available in restaurants throughout Mexico.

In severe cases, hydrate with Gatorade or a salt-sugar solution (½ teaspoon salt and 4 tablespoons sugar per quart of water). If your fever and diarrhea last more than three days, see a doctor—you may have picked up a parasite that requires prescription medication.

PESTS

It's best to be cautious and go indoors at dusk (called the "mosquito hour" by locals). An excellent brand of *repelente de insectos* (insect repellent) called Autan

is readily available; don't use it on children under age two. If you want to bring a mosquito repellent from home, make sure it has at least 10% DEET or it won't be effective. If you're hiking in the jungle or near standing water, wear repellent and/or long pants and sleeves; if you're camping in the jungle, use a mosquito net and invest in a package of mosquito coils (sold in most stores).

Another local flying pest is the *tabaño*, a type of deer fly, which resembles a common household fly with yellow stripes. Some people swell up after being bitten, but taking an antihistamine can help. Watch out for the small red ants as their bites can be quite irritating.

Scorpions also live in the region; their sting is similar to a bee sting. They're rarely fatal, but can cause strong reactions in small children and the elderly. Clean all cuts carefully (especially those produced by coral), as the rate of infection is much higher here.

The Yucatán has many poisonous snakes. The coral snake, easily identified by its black and red markings, should be avoided at all costs since its bite is fatal. If you're planning any jungle hikes, be sure to wear hard-sole shoes and stay on the path. For more remote areas, hire a guide and make sure there's an anti-venom kit accompanying you on the trip.

SUNBURN

More common hazards to travelers in the Yucatán are sunburn and heat exhaustion. The sun is strong here; it takes fewer than 20 minutes to get a serious sunburn. When practical, avoid the sun between 11 am and 3 pm. Wear a hat and use sunscreen, preferably something with zinc oxide. You should drink more fluid than you do at home—Mexico is probably hotter than what you're used to and you'll perspire more. Rest in the afternoon and stay out of the sun to avoid heat exhaustion. The first signs of dehydration and heat exhaustion are dizziness, extreme irritability, and fatigue.

TRIP INSURANCE

Consider buying trip insurance with medical-only coverage. Neither Medicare nor some private insurers cover medical expenses anywhere outside the United States. Medical-only policies typically reimburse you for medical care (excluding that related to preexisting conditions), hospitalization abroad, and provide for evacuation. You still have to pay the bills and await reimbursement from the insurer, though.

Another option is to sign up with a medical-evacuation assistance company. A membership in one of these companies gets you doctor referrals, emergency evacuation or repatriation, 24-hour hotlines for medical consultation, and other assistance. International SOS Assistance Emergency and AirMed International provide evacuation services and medical referrals. MedjetAssist offers medical evacuation.

Medical Assistance Companies AirMed International (⊕ www.airmed.com). **International SOS Assistance Emergency** (⊕ www.internationalsos.com). **MedjetAssist** (⊕ www.medjetassist.com).

Medical-Only Insurers International Medical Group (⊕ www.imglobal.com). **International SOS** (⊕ www.internationalsos.com). **Wallach & Company** (⊕ www.wallach.com). **STA** (⊕ www.statravel.com).

▌HOURS OF OPERATION

In well-traveled places such as Cancún, Isla Mujeres, Playa del Carmen, Mérida, and Cozumel, businesses generally are open during posted hours. In more off-the-beaten-path areas, neighbors can tell you when the owner will return.

Most banks are open weekdays 9 to 5, but some will exchange money only until early afternoon. Many are open Saturday until noon or 1 pm. Most businesses are open weekdays 9 to 2 and 4 to 7.

Some gas stations are open 24 hours, although those off main highways usually close from midnight until 6 am, or even close earlier.

Most museums throughout Mexico are closed on Monday and open 8 to 5 the rest of the week. But it's best to call ahead or ask at your hotel. Hours of sights and attractions in this book are denoted by a clock icon ☉.

The larger pharmacies in Cancún and Cozumel are usually open daily 8 am to 10 pm, and those in Cancún, Campeche, and Mérida have at least one 24-hour pharmacy. Smaller pharmacies are often closed on Sunday.

Tourist-oriented stores in Cancún, Mérida, Playa del Carmen, and Cozumel are usually open 10 to 9 Monday through Saturday and on Sunday afternoon. Shops in more traditional areas may close weekdays between 1 pm and 4 pm, opening again in the evening. They're generally closed Sunday.

▌MAIL

Mail can be sent from your hotel or the *oficina de correos* (post office). Be forewarned, however, that mail service to, within, and from Mexico is notoriously slow and can take anywhere from 10 days to, well, never. Don't send anything of value to or from Mexico via mail, including cash, checks, or credit-card numbers.

It costs 9.50 pesos to send a postcard or letter weighing under 20 grams to the

United States; it's 10.50 to Canada, 13 to Europe, and 14.50 to Australia.

To receive mail in Mexico, you can have it sent to your hotel or use *poste restante* at the post office. In the latter case, the address must include the words "a/c Lista de Correos" (general delivery), followed by the city, state, postal code, and country. To use this service, you must first register with the post office at which you wish to receive your mail. Mail is held for 10 days, and a list of recipients is posted daily. Postal codes for the main Yucatán destinations are as follows: Cancún, 77500; Isla Mujeres, 77400; Playa del Carmen, 77710; Cozumel, 77600; Campeche, 24000; Mérida, 97000. Keep in mind that the postal service in Mexico is very slow; it can take up to 12 weeks for mail to arrive.

Holders of American Express cards or traveler's checks can have mail sent to them in care of the local American Express office. For a list of offices worldwide, write for the *Traveler's Companion* from American Express.

SHIPPING PACKAGES

Hotel concierges can recommend international carriers, such as DHL, Estafeta, or Federal Express, which give your package a tracking number and ensure its arrival back home.

Despite the promises, *overnight* courier service is rare in Mexico. It's not the fault of the courier service, which may indeed have the package there overnight. Delays occur at customs. Depending on the time of year, all courier packages are opened and inspected. This can slow everything down. You can expect one- to three-day service in Cancún and two- to four-day service elsewhere. Never send cash through the courier services. MexPost is the Mexican postal system's version of courier service, and is found at the larger post offices. Although cheaper than FedEx and DHL, it's also slightly less reliable.

Express Services Correos de México (☎ 55/5340–3300 ⊕ www.correosdemexico.

gob.mx). **DHL** (☎ 01800/765–6345 or 55/5345–7000 ⊕ www.dhl.com). **Estafeta** (☎ 01800/378–23382 ⊕ www.estafeta.com). **Federal Express** (☎ 01800/900–1100 or 55/5228–9904 ⊕ www.fedex.com).

▌ MONEY

Because the value of the currency fluctuates, and since many businesses quote prices in U.S. dollars, most prices in this book are in dollars.

U.S. dollar bills (but not coins) are widely accepted in many parts of the Yucatán, particularly in Cancún and Cozumel, where you'll often find prices in shops quoted in dollars. However, you may get your change back in pesos. Many tourist shops and market vendors, as well as virtually all hotel service personnel, also accept dollars. Wherever you are, though, watch out for bad exchange rates—you'll generally do better paying in pesos. Hotels, restaurants, buses, and market vendors readily accept dollars but usually do not offer a good exchange rate. Many smaller businesses and most highway toll booths do not accept dollars. If you run out of pesos, then by all means use U.S. dollars, pay with a credit card, or make a withdrawal from an ATM.

ATMS AND BANKS

In 2010, Mexican authorities passed a law stating that foreign travelers may not exchange more than $1,500 U.S. dollars (cash) per person, per month into Mexican pesos. Mexican travelers are also limited to $1,500 U.S.D. cash per person, per month, with the added restriction of no more than $300 U.S.D. cash per day. Other methods of payment including credit cards, traveler's checks, and non-American foreign currencies are not affected by this new law.

When exchanging foreign currency at banks and hotels in Mexico, you must show your passport. Your own bank will probably charge a fee for using ATMs abroad; the foreign bank you use may also charge a fee. Nevertheless, you'll usually get a better rate of exchange at an ATM than you will at a currency-exchange office or even when changing money in a bank. Extracting funds as you need them is a safer option than carrying around a large amount of cash, but keep in mind that remote areas such as Xcalak near Belize don't have ATMs or banks nor do businesses there accept credit cards.

■ TIP➔ PIN numbers with more than four digits are not recognized at ATMs in many countries. If your PIN has five or more numbers, remember to change it before you leave.

ATMs (*cajeros automáticos*) are now commonplace. Cirrus and Plus are the most frequently found networks. Rural towns, however, often lack banking facilities. Unless you're in a major city or resort area, treat ATMs as you would gas stations—don't assume you'll be able to find one in a pinch. In smaller towns, even when they're present, machines are often out of order or out of cash. Many, but not all, gas stations have ATMs. All airports have ATMs but many bus stations do not.

Before you leave home, ask what the transaction fee will be for withdrawing money in Mexico (it can be up to $5 a pop). Ask your bank if it has an agreement with a Mexican bank to waive or charge lower fees for cash withdrawals. For example, Bank of America account holders can withdraw money from Santander-Serfin ATMs free of charge.

Be sure to also alert your bank's customer-protection division to let them know you will be using your card in Mexico—otherwise they may assume that the card's been stolen and put a hold on your account.

CREDIT CARDS

Throughout this guide, it's safe to assume that businesses accept major credit cards unless the service information reads ▬ *No credit cards.*

It's a good idea to inform your credit-card company before you travel to Mexico, especially if you don't travel internationally very often. Otherwise, the credit-card company might put a hold on your card owing to unusual activity—not a good thing halfway through your trip. Record all your credit-card numbers—as well as the phone numbers to call if your cards are lost or stolen—in a safe place, so you're prepared should something go wrong. Both MasterCard and Visa have general numbers you can call (collect if you're abroad) if your card is lost or stolen, but you're better off calling the number of your issuing bank, since MasterCard and Visa usually just transfer you to your bank. Your bank's number is usually printed on the back of your card.

If you plan to use your credit card for cash advances, you'll need to apply for a PIN at least two weeks before your trip. Although it's usually cheaper (and safer) to use a credit card abroad for large purchases (so you can cancel payments or be reimbursed if there's a problem), not all companies offer this service on foreign transactions. Note that some credit-card companies *and* the banks that issue them add substantial percentages to all foreign transactions. Check on these fees before leaving home, so there won't be any surprises when you get the bill.

Credit cards are accepted in most tourist areas. Smaller, less expensive restaurants and shops, however, tend to take only cash. In general, credit cards aren't accepted in small towns and villages. The most widely accepted cards are Master-Card and Visa. When shopping, you can usually get better prices if you pay with cash.

In Mexico the decision to pay cash or use a credit card might depend on whether the establishment in which you're making a purchase finds bargaining for prices acceptable. To avoid fraud, it's wise to make sure that "pesos" or the initials M.N., *moneda nacional* (national currency) is clearly marked on all credit-card receipts, unless the charge was made in U.S. dollars.

Before you leave for Mexico, be sure to find out the lost-card telephone numbers of your credit-card issuer's banks that work in Mexico. (Foreign toll-free numbers often don't work in Mexico. U.S. and Canada toll-free numbers are normally reached by dialing 001–880 instead of 1–800 before the seven-digit number.) Carry these numbers separately from your wallet, so you'll have them if you need to report lost or stolen cards.

Reporting Lost Cards American Express
(☎ 800/528–4800 in U.S., 800/268–9824 from abroad ⊕ www.americanexpress.com). **Diners Club** (☎ 800/234–6377 in U.S., 303/799–1504 collect from abroad ⊕ www.dinersclub.com). **Discover** (☎ 800/347–2683 in U.S., 801/902–3100 collect from abroad ⊕ www.discovercard.com). **MasterCard** (☎ 800/622–7747 in U.S., 636/722–7111 collect from abroad, 55/5480–8000 Mexico City ⊕ www.mastercard.com). **Visa** (☎ 800/847–2911 in U.S., 410/581–9994 collect from abroad ⊕ www.visa.com).

CURRENCY AND EXCHANGE

The approximate exchange rate at this writing was 12.04 pesos to U.S.$1. Check with your bank, the financial pages of your local newspaper, or ⊕ *www.xe.com* for current exchange rates.

Mexican currency comes in denominations of 10-, 20-, 50-, 100-, 200-, 500-, and 1,000-peso bills. The latter are not very common, and many establishments refuse to accept them due to a lack of change. Coins come in denominations of 1, 2, 5, 10, 20, and 100 pesos. Many of the coins are very similar, so check carefully. Of the older coins you may occasionally see a 10 or 20 or more often a 50 *centavo* (cent) piece.

Most banks only change money on weekdays until noon (though they stay open until 5), whereas *casas de cambio* (private exchange offices) generally stay open until 6 or 9 and often operate on weekends. Bring your photo ID or passport when you exchange money. Bank rates are regulated by the federal government, but vary slightly from bank to bank, while casas de cambio have slightly more variable rates. Exchange houses in the airports and in areas with heavy tourist traffic tend to have the worst rates, although unless you're changing large sums of money, convenience may heavily outweigh this difference. Some hotels also exchange U.S. dollars and traveler's checks, but for providing you with this convenience they give a poorer exchange rate than banks.

■TIP➔ Many shop and restaurant owners are unable to make change for large bills. Enough of these encounters may compel you to request billetes chicos (small bills) when you exchange money.

Currency Conversion Contacts Google
(⊕ www.google.com). **Oanda.com** (⊕ www.oanda.com). **XE.com** (⊕ www.xe.com).

▮ PACKING

Pack lightly, because you may want to save space in your suitcase for purchases. The Yucatán is filled with bargains on clothing, leather goods, jewelry, and other crafts. If you purchase pottery or ceramics, make sure they're carefully wrapped in your check-in luggage since TSA regulations prohibit these items from being in your carry-on.

Bring lightweight clothes, sundresses, bathing suits, sun hats or visors, and cover-ups for the Caribbean beach towns, but also pack a light jacket or sweater to wear in the chilly, air-conditioned restaurants, or to tide you over during a rainstorm or an unusual cool spell. For trips to rural areas or Mérida, where dress is typically more conservative and shorts are considered inappropriate, make sure you have at least one pair of slacks. Comfortable walking shoes with rubber soles are a good idea, both for climbing ruins and for walking around cities. Lightweight rain gear and an umbrella are a good idea during the rainy season. Cancún is the dressiest spot on the peninsula, but even fancy restaurants don't require men to wear jackets.

Pack sunscreen and sunglasses for the Yucatán's strong sun. Other handy items—especially if you're using budget hotels and restaurants or going off the beaten path—include toilet paper, facial tissues, a plastic water bottle, and a flashlight (for occasional power outages or use at camp-sites). Snorkelers should consider bringing their own equipment unless traveling light is a priority; reef shoes with rubber soles for rocky underwater surfaces are also advised. To avoid problems at customs, bring your prescription drugs in the origi-nal, current pill bottle or with a current prescription. Don't count on purchasing necessary OTC or prescription meds (such as sleeping pills); the same brands are not always available in Mexico.

▌ PASSPORTS AND VISAS

A tourist visa is required for all visitors to Mexico. If you're arriving by plane, the standard tourist visa forms will be given to you on the plane. They're also available through travel agents and Mexican consulates and at the border if you're entering by land. In addition to having your visa form, you must prove your citizenship.

▌TIP→ You're given a portion of the tourist card form upon entering Mexico. Keep track of this document throughout your trip: you will need it when you depart. You'll be asked to submit it, along with your ticket and pass-port, to airline representatives at the gate when boarding for departure. If you lose your tourist card, plan to spend some time (and about $60) sorting it out with Mexican officials at the airport before your flight home.

U.S. Homeland Security regulations require U.S. citizens of all ages returning by air to have a valid U.S. passport. Those returning by land or sea are required to present either a government-issued photo ID and a certified copy of your birth cer-tificate or a U.S. Passport Card.

Minors traveling with only one parent need notarized permission from the absent parent. You're allowed to stay 180 days as a tourist; frequently, though, immigration officials will give you less time. Be sure to ask for as much time as you think you'll need up to 180 days. Going to a Mexican immigration office to extend a visa can easily take a whole day; plus, you'll have to pay an extension fee.

U.S. Passport Information U.S. Department of State (☎ 877/487–2778 ⊕ travel.state.gov/passport).

U.S. Passport and Visa Expediters A. Briggs Passport & Visa Expediters (☎ 800/806–0581 or 202/338–0111 ⊕ www.abriggs.com). **American Passport Express** (☎ 800/455–5166 or 800/841–6778 ⊕ www.americanpassport.com). **Passport Express** (☎ 800/362–8196 ⊕ www.passportexpress.com). **Travel Document Systems** (☎ 800/874–5100 or 202/638–3800 ⊕ www.traveldocs.com). **Travel the World Visas** (☎ 866/886–8472 ⊕ www.world-visa.com).

▌ RESTROOMS

Expect to find reasonably clean flushing toilets and running water at public rest-rooms in the major tourist destinations and at tourist attractions. Toilet tissue and soap are usually, but not always, on hand. Although many markets, bus and train stations, and the like have public facilities, you usually have to pay about 5 pesos for the privilege of using them. Remember that unless otherwise indicated you should put your used toilet paper in the wastebasket next to the toilet. Many plumbing systems in Mexico still can't handle accumulations of toilet paper.

The Bathroom Diaries (⊕ www.thebathroomdiaries.com) offers info on rest-rooms the world over—each one located, reviewed, and rated.

▌ SAFETY

Unfortunately Mexico has seen a dramatic increase in violence—much of which is drug-related—over the past few years, but most of this has been concentrated in the capital, along border zones, and in less-touristed areas. The Yucatán remains one of the safest areas in Mexico.

Even in resort areas like Cancún and Cozumel you should use common sense. Make use of hotel safes when available, and carry your own baggage whenever possible unless you're checking into a hotel. Leave expensive jewelry at home, since it often entices thieves and will mark you as a *turista* who can afford to be robbed.

When traveling with all your money, be sure to keep an eye on your belongings at all times and distribute your cash and any valuables between different bags and items of clothing. Do not reach for your money stash in public. If you carry a purse, choose one with a zipper and a thick strap that you can drape across your body; adjust the length so that the purse sits in front of you at or above hip level.

There have been reports of travelers being victimized after imbibing drinks that have been drugged in Cancún nightclubs. Never drink alone with strangers, watch your drink being poured, and keep your eye on it at all times. Avoid driving on desolate streets, don't travel at night, and never pick up hitchhikers or hitchhike yourself.

Use ATMs during the day and in big commercial areas. Avoid the glass-enclosed street variety of banks where you may be more vulnerable to thieves who force you to withdraw money for them.

Bear in mind that reporting a crime to the police is often a frustrating experience unless you speak excellent Spanish and have a great deal of patience. If you're victimized, contact your local consular agent or the consular section of your country's embassy in Mexico City.

A woman traveling alone will be the subject of much curiosity, since traditional Mexican women do not generally choose to travel unaccompanied. Don't walk on deserted beaches alone, and make sure your hotel room is securely locked when you retire.

Part of the machismo culture is being flirtatious and showing off in front of *compadres,* and lone women are likely to be subjected to catcalls, although this is less true in the Yucatán than in other parts of Mexico. Although annoying, it's essentially harmless. The best way to get rid of unwanted attention is to simply ignore the advances. It's best not to enter into a discussion with harassers, even if you speak Spanish. When the suitor is persistent say "no" to whatever is said, walk briskly, and leave immediately for a safe place, such as a nearby store. Dressing conservatively may help—clothing such as brief tops or shorts may be inappropriate in more conservative rural areas. Never go topless on the beach unless it's a recognized nude beach with lots of other people. Mexicans, in general, don't sunbathe nude, and men may misinterpret your doing so as an invitation.

■ TIP → **Distribute your cash, credit cards, IDs, and other valuables between a deep front pocket, an inside jacket or vest pocket, and a hidden money pouch. Don't reach for the money pouch once you're in public.**

BEACHES

Empty coastlines can be susceptible to car break-ins and theft. Most resorts notify beachgoers of coastal conditions by displayed colored flags. **Don't swim when the red or black danger flags fly; yellow flags indicate that you should proceed with caution, and green or blue flags mean the waters are calm.** Beware: even the calmest-looking waters can have currents and riptides. If visiting isolated beaches, bring sunscreen and drinking water to avoid overexposure and dehydration. Take note that waves are most powerful during December, and that hurricane season lasts from June through November.

Contact **Transportation Security Adminis-tration** (*TSA* ⊕ *www.tsa.gov*).

▌TAXES

An air-departure tax of around $48, or the peso equivalent, must be paid at the airport for international flights from Mexico. This charge is almost always prepaid as part of your ticket; if for some reason, it's not included or only partially included, you must pay the remainder in cash at the airport. Check with your airline if you're not sure they included the tax in the ticket price.

Hotels in the state of Quintana Roo charge a 12% tax, which is a combined 10% Value Added Tax with the 2% hotel tax; in Yucatán and Campeche, expect a 17% tax, since the V.A.T. is 15% in these states.

Mexico has a value-added tax (V.A.T.), or IVA (*impuesto de valor agregado*), of 15% (10% along the Cancún–Chetumal corridor). Many establishments already include the IVA in the quoted price. When comparing hotel prices, it's important to know whether yours includes IVA and any service charge. Occasionally (and illegally) it may be waived for cash purchases; this is nothing for you to worry about.

Those who travel to Mexico by air or cruise ship are eligible to be reimbursed for the value-added tax they were charged on purchases made at stores throughout the country. There are, of course, some restrictions. You must have paid by credit card (from outside of Mexico), or cash, and your purchases must have totaled $115 (1,200 pesos). While purchasing, you must show your passport and get a receipt and a refund form. Then you visit a kiosk at the Cancún airport to receive half of your refund in the form of a credit in pesos (to a max of 10,000 pesos) that can be applied to more shopping (no meals or hotel stays); and the remainder will be credited to your credit card or bank account.

▌TIME

Mexico has three time zones. Baja California (*norte*) is on Pacific Standard Time. Baja California Sur and the northwest states are on Mountain Time. The rest of the country is on Central Standard Time, which is two hours ahead of Pacific Time. Cancún and all of the areas covered in this book are on Central Standard Time.

Time Zones Timeanddate.com (⊕ *www. timeanddate.com/worldclock*).

▌TIPPING

When tipping in Mexico, remember that the minimum wage is just a bit more than $5 a day and that many in the tourism industry don't earn much more. There are also Mexicans who think in dollars and know, for example, that in the United States porters are tipped $1 to $2 a bag. Many of them expect the peso equivalent from foreigners. Though dollars are widely accepted in Cancún and Cozumel, you should always tip using local currency whenever possible, so that service personnel aren't stuck going to the bank to exchange dollars for pesos.

What follows are some guidelines. Naturally, larger tips are always welcome: porters and bellhops, 10 pesos per bag at airports and moderate and inexpensive hotels and 20 pesos per person per bag at expensive hotels; maids, 10 pesos per night (all hotels); waiters, 10% to 15% of the bill, depending on service, and less in simpler restaurants (anywhere you are, make sure a service charge hasn't already been added, a practice that's particularly common in resorts); bartenders, 10% to 15% of the bill, depending on service (and, perhaps, on how many drinks you've had); taxi drivers, 5 to 10 pesos only if the driver helps you with your bags. Tipping cabbies isn't usual, and they often overcharge tourists when possible. Tip tour guides 50 pesos per half day, 100 for a full day; drivers about half as much. Gas-station attendants expect 3 to 5 pesos unless they check the oil, tires, and so on, in which case tip more; parking attendants, 5 to 10 pesos, even if it's for valet parking at a theater or restaurant that charges for the service.

■ TOURS

Mayaland Tours leads custom tours as well as guided eight-day trips that hit the highlights of archaeology (Chichén Itzá, Uxmal, and the Ruta Puuc sites) with forays into Campeche and Río Lagartos. California Native includes guide service, accommodations, breakfast, and most lunches in its seven-day trip with stops at Mérida, Izamal, Chichén Itzá, Ek Balam, Uxmal, and Edzná. Originally organized by birders and naturalists, Ecoturismo Yucatán, based in Mérida, now leads a large variety of guided tours hitting peninsula highlights of archaeology and culture as well as specialized tours. EcoColors and Alltournative are recommended for sustainable adventure tours on the coast, offering archaeological and nature tours.

Recommended Companies Alltournative (⊠ *Calle 5 between Calles 12 and 14, and Calle 5 between Calles 2 and 4, Playa del Carmen* ☎ *984/803-9999, 800/507-1092 from U.S. and Canada* ⊕ *www.alltournative.com).* **California Native** (⊠ *6701 W. 87th Pl., Los Angeles, CA* ☎ *800/926-1140 or 310/642-1140* ⊕ *www.calnative.com).* **Ecotour** (⊠ *Calle Camaron 32, SMNZ 32, Cancún* ☎ *866/376-5056* ⊕ *www.ecotravelmexico.com).* **Ecoturismo Yucatán** (⊠ *Calle 3 No. 235 between 32A and 34, Col. Pensiones* ☎ *999/920-2772* ⊕ *www.ecoyuc.com.mx).* **Mayaland** (☎ *998/887-2495 Cancún, 800/235-4079 in U.S.* ⊕ *www.mayaland.com).*

SPECIAL-INTEREST TOURS
ADVENTURE
Contacts Green Tortoise Adventure Travel (⊠ *494 Broadway, San Francisco, CA* ☎ *800/867-8647 or 415/956-7500* ⊕ *www.greentortoise.com).* **TrekAmerica** (⊡ *Box 189, Rockaway, NJ07866* ☎ *800/873-5872* ⊕ *www.trekamerica.com).*

ART AND ARCHAEOLOGY
Contacts Far Horizons Archaeological & Cultural Trips (⊡ *Box 2546, San Anselmo, CA94979* ☎ *800/552-4575 or 415/482-8400* ⊕ *www.farhorizons.com).* **The Mayan Traveler** (☎ *800/451-8017 or 281/367-3386* ⊕ *www.themayantraveler.com).*

BIKING
■ TIP→ Most airlines accommodate bikes as luggage, provided they're dismantled and boxed.

Contacts Backroads (⊠ *801 Cedar St., Berkeley, CA* ☎ *800/462-2848* ⊕ *www.backroads.com).*

BIRD-WATCHING
Contacts Ecoturismo Yucatán (⊠ *Calle 3 Nos. 235 between 32A and 34, Col. Pensiones* ☎ *999/920-2772* ⊕ *www.ecoyuc.com.mx).*

DIVING
Contacts Aqua Dreams Travel (⊠ *4708 S.E. 8th Ct., #3, Cape Coral, FL* ☎ *888/322-3483 toll-free, 239/540-4512* ⊕ *www.aquadreams.com).*

ECOTOURS
Contacts Alltournative (⊠ *Calle 5 between Calles 12 and 14, Playa del Carmen* ☎ *994/803-9999, 800/507-1092 from U.S. and Canada* ⊕ *www.alltournative.com).* **Ecoturismo Yucatán** (⊠ *Calle 3 No. 235, between Calles 32A and 34, Col. Pensiones, Mérida* ☎ *999/920-2772 or 999/925-2187* ⊕ *www.ecoyuc.com).* **Emerald Planet** (⊠ *1706 Constitution Ct., Fort Collins, CO* ☎ *970/372-5922).*

FISHING
Contacts Costa de Cocos (⊠ *2 km [1 mi] outside Xcalak, Quintana Roo* ⊕ *www.costadecocos.com).* **Fishing International** (⊠ *5510 Skylane Blvd., Suite 200, Santa Rosa, CA* ☎ *800/950-4242 or 707/542-4242* ⊕ *www.fishinginternational.com).* **Ecocolors** (⊠ *Calle Camaron 32, Sm. 27, Cancún* ☎ *988/884-9580* ⊕ *www.ecotravelmexico.com).*

LANGUAGE PROGRAMS
Contacts Institute of Modern Spanish (⊠ *Calle 15 Nos. 500B between 16A and 18 Col. Maya, Mérida, Yucatán* ☎ *877/463-7432 in U.S.* ⊕ *www.modernspanish.com).* **Spanish**

Institute of Mérida (✉ *Calle 60 No. 358, Col. Centro, Mérida, Yucatán* ☎ *999/925-4475 or 800/539-9710 in U.S.* ⊕ *www.simerida.com*).

▌ VISITOR INFO

ONLINE TRAVEL TOOLS

The official Web site for Mexico tourism has information on tourist attractions and activities, and an overview of Mexican history and culture. Yucatán Today and Loco Gringo have comprehensive information on nightlife, hotel listings, archaeological sites, area history, and other useful information for travelers.

Tourist Board Offices **Mexico Tourism Board** (☎ *800/446-3942 in U.S. or Canada* ⊕ *www.visitmexico.com*).

All About Cancún, Cozumel, and the Yucatán Peninsula ⊕ *www.yucatantoday.com*; ⊕ *www.locogringo.com*. Also try ⊕ *www.cozumelmycozumel.com*, ⊕ *www.islamujeres.info*, ⊕ *www.cancun.bz*, and ⊕ *www.travelyucatan.com*.

INDEX

PHOTO CREDITS

1, Kreder Katja/age fotostock. 2, Stuart Pearce/age fotostock. 5, cancuncd.com. Chapter 1: Experience Cancun: 8-9, ESCUDERO Patrick / age fotostock. 10, Mike Liu/Shutterstock. 11 (left), LipBomb/Flickr. 11 (right), GUILLERMO ALDANA/Mexico Tourism Board. 14, Cancun CVB. 15 (left), cancuncd.com. 15 (right), BRUCE HERMAN/Mexico Tourism Board. 16 (left), Curtis Kautzer/Shutterstock. 16 (top center), urosr/Shutterstock. 16 (top right), Agnes Csondor/iStockphoto. 16 (bottom right), SEUX Paule / age fotostock. 17 (top left), Drimi/Shutterstock. 17 (bottom left), Alicia Navarrete Alonso/wikipedia. org. 17 (top center), travelpixpro/iStockphoto. 17 (right), Scott Prokop/Shutterstock. 18 and 19 (left), Cancun CVB. 19 (right), BRUCE HERMAN/Mexico Tourism Board. 21 (left), idreamphoto/Shutterstock. 21 (right), Alfredo Schaufelberger/Shutterstock. 22, aceshot1/Shutterstock. 23, Yarek Gora/ iStockphoto. 24, Byron W.Moore/Shutterstock. 26, Chris Cheadle / age fotostock. Chapter 2: Cancun: 27, Victor Elias / age fotostock. 28 (top), Keith Pomakis/wikipedia.org. 28 (bottom), Joao Virissimo/ Shutterstock. 29, David Davis/Shutterstock. 30, Witold Skrypczak / age fotostock. 31 (top), Witold Skrypczak / age fotostock. 31 (bottom), Agathe B/Flickr. 32, Cancun CVB. 33 (top), Thelmadatter/ wikipedia.org. 33 (bottom), malias/Flickr. 34, aceshot1/Shutterstock. 45, JTB Photo / age fotostock. 49, The Leading Hotels of the World. 52, Ben Fink. 55, Hilton Cancun Golf and Spa Resort. 75 (top), Marriott International. 75 (bottom), The Ritz-Carlton Cancun Beach. 83, csp/Shutterstock. 84 (top left), Alfredo Schaufelberger/Shutterstock. 84 (bottom left), wikipedia.org. 84 (right), Casa Herradura/ Brown-Forman. 85 (top left), csp/Shutterstock. 85 (bottom left), Alfredo Schaufelberger/Shutterstock. 85 (top center), Jesus Cervantes/Shutterstock. 85 (bottom center), Blaine Harrington / age fotostock. 85 (top right), Jesus Cervantes/Shutterstock. 85 (bottom right), Jesus Cervantes/Shutterstock. 85 (bottom), Smithsonian Institution Archives. 86 (top left), Eduard Stelmakh/Shutterstock. 86 (center left), svry/ Shutterstock. 86 (bottom left), National Archives and Records Administration. 86 (top right), Andrew Penner/iStockphoto. 86 (bottom right), BlueOrange Studio/Shutterstock. 87 (top right), Patricia Hofmeester/Shutterstock. 87 (top left), Keith Dannemiller / Alamy. 87 (bottom left), csp/Shutterstock. 88 (left), The Patrón Spirits Company. 88 (right), rick/Flickr. 89 (top left), Casa Herradura/Brown-Forman. 89 (bottom left), shrk/Flickr. 89 (right), Neil Setchfield / Alamy. 91, Hugo Cadavez/Flickr. 92, Jan Greune / age fotostock. 100, Cancun CVB. Chapter 3: The Caribbean Coast: 103, Stuart Pearce / age fotostock. 104 (left and right), Bruce Herman/Mexico Tourism Board. 105 (top), Philip Coblentz/Brand X Pictures. 105 (bottom), Stefano Marini/Cancun Convention and Visitors Bureau. 106, Alaskan Dude/ Flickr. 107 (top) idreamphoto/Shutterstock. 107 (bottom), lecates/Flickr. 108, Viceroy Hotel Group. 109 (top), George Apostolidis. 109 (bottom), Rosewood Hotels & Resorts. 110, Markus Sevcik/Shutterstock. 112 and 114 (left), Banyan Tree Hotels & Resorts. 114 (right), Rosewood Hotels & Resorts. 115 (left), Viceroy Hotel Group. 115 (right), George Apostolidis. 116, Fairmont Hotels & Resorts. 117 (left), Marriott International. 117 (right), Palace Resorts. 118, George Doyle/iStockphoto. 122-23, Ken Welsh / age fotostock. 128, John Gray Restaurant Group. 132 (top), Jaime Navarro/Deseo. 132 (bottom), La Tortuga Hotel & Spa. 135, Corbis. 141 (top), Banyan Tree Hotels & Resorts. 141 (bottom), Rosewood Hotels & Resorts. 145 (top), George Apostolidis. 145 (bottom), Viceroy Hotel Group. 152 (top), Ceiba del Mar. 152 (bottom), amResorts. 156, SEUX Paule / age fotostock. 159, Doug Plummer/age fotostock. 160, Jose Enrique Molino/age fotostock. 161 (left), Ales Liska/Shutterstock. 161 (right), Stefano Paterna/age fotostock. 162 (top), Ken Welsh/age fotostock. 162 (bottom), Qing Ding/ Shutterstock. 163, Philip Coblentz/Brand X Pictures. 166, Cancun CVB. 171, Matty Symons/Shutterstock. 179, Nataliya Hora/iStockphoto. 182, david sanger photography / Alamy. 191, urosr/Shutterstock. 195, Stuart Pearce / age fotostock. 197, Linda Vermeulen/http://www.mermaidskissgallery.com/. Chapter 4: Isla Mujeres: 199, Cancun CVB. 200 (left), Chie Ushio. 200 (top right), Bruce Herman/ Mexico Tourism Board. 200 (bottom right), Stefano Morini/Cancun Convention and Visitors Bureau. 201, Nanako Inoue. 202, rj lerich/Shutterstock. 208-09, Alex Bramwell/iStockphoto. 214, Michael DeFreitas Central America / Alamy. 217, Chie Ushio. 225 (top), Small Luxury Hotels of the World. 225 (bottom), Casa El Pio. 229, WaterFrame / Alamy. 232, Chris Cheadle / age fotostock. Chapter 5: Cozumel: 235, B&Y Photography Inc. / age fotostock. 236 (top), Bruce Herman/Mexico Tourism Board. 236 (bottom), George Kirkaldie/Flickr. 237, eschipul/Flickr. 238, SuperStock/age fotostock. 239 (top), JesusAbizanda/Flickr. 239 (bottom), Rob Inh00d/Flickr. 240, cancuncd.com. 245, Ron Buskirk / age fotostock. 246, Mark Newman / age fotostock. 250-51, SuperStock/age fotostock. 258, Alvaro Leiva / age fotostock. 263 (top and bottom), The Leading Hotels of the World. 267, Danita Delimont / Alamy. 269, SuperStock/age fotostock. 274, John Anderson / age fotostock. 275, cancuncd.com. 276 (top left), tslane888/Flickr. 276 (bottom left), pato_garza/Flickr. 276 (top right), tslane888/Flickr. 276 (bottom right), Mike Bauer/Shutterstock. 278 (top), sethbienek/Flickr. 278 (bottom), tubuceo/Shutterstock. 279 (bottom), Julie de Leseleuc/iStockphoto. 280, Jerry McElroy/iStockphoto. Chapter 6: Yucatán and Campeche States: 281, SEUX Paule / age fotostock. 282, GUILLERMO ALDANA/Mexico

ABOUT OUR WRITERS

Steven McCutcheon-Rubio is a Mexico City–based food and travel writer. He has written for seriouseats.com, the Mexican editions of *Elle, Travel + Leisure* and *Endless Vacation*, as well as *Chilango* and CNNMéxico. For this edition, Steven updated the Cozumel and Yucatán and Campeche States chapters.

As a freelance journalist and author, **Marlise Elizabeth Kast** has contributed to more than 50 publications including *Forbes, Surfer, San Diego Magazine*, and *New York Post*. Her passion for traveling has taken her to 65 countries and led her to establish short-term residency in Switzerland, Dominican Republic, Spain, and Costa Rica. Following the release of her memoir *Tabloid Prodigy,* Marlise co-authored Fodor's Guides to Mexico (2009, 2010, 2011, 2012), San Diego (2009, 2010), Panama (2nd edition), Puerto Rico (6th edition), Peru (2012), and Corsica & Sardinia (2010). She served as a photojournalist for *Surf Guide to Costa Rica* and has written *Day & Overnight Hikes on California's Pacific Crest Trail*. Marlise recently completed a 13-month surfing-and-snowboarding expedition through 28 countries. Now based in San Diego, she is currently working on her next full-length manuscript.